Bayou Battles for Vicksburg

MODERN WAR STUDIES

William Thomas Allison
General Editor

Raymond Callahan
Allan R. Millett
Carol Reardon
David R. Stone
Heather Marie Stur
Samuel J. Watson
Jacqueline E. Whitt
James H. Willbanks
Series Editors

Theodore A. Wilson
Founding Editor

BAYOU BATTLES FOR VICKSBURG

*The Swamp and River Expeditions,
January 1–April 30, 1863*

Timothy B. Smith

University Press of Kansas

© 2023 by the University Press of Kansas
All rights reserved

Published by the University Press of Kansas (Lawrence, Kansas 66045), which was organized by the Kansas Board of Regents and is operated and funded by Emporia State University, Fort Hays State University, Kansas State University, Pittsburg State University, the University of Kansas, and Wichita State University

Library of Congress Cataloging-in-Publication Data

Names: Smith, Timothy B., 1974– author.
Title: Bayou battles for Vicksburg : the swamp and river expeditions, January 1–April 30, 1863 / Timothy B. Smith.
Other titles: Modern war studies.
Description: Lawrence, Kansas : University Press of Kansas, 2024. | Series: Modern war studies | Includes bibliographical references and index.
Identifiers: LCCN 2023000411 (print) | LCCN 2023000412 (ebook)
ISBN 9780700635665 (cloth ; alkaline paper)
ISBN 9780700635672 (ebook)
Subjects: LCSH: Grant, Ulysses S. (Ulysses Simpson), 1822–1885—Military leadership. | Strategy—Tropical conditions—History—19th century. | Vicksburg (Miss.)—History—Civil War, 1861–1865. | United States—History—Civil War, 1861–1865—Campaigns. | Vicksburg (Miss.)—History—Siege, 1863.
Classification: LCC E475.2 .S64 2024 (print) | LCC E475.2 (ebook) | DDC 973.7/344--dc23/eng/20230126
LC record available at https://lccn.loc.gov/2023000411.
LC ebook record available at https://lccn.loc.gov/2023000412.

British Library Cataloguing-in-Publication Data is available.

Printed in the United States of America

10 9 8 7 6 5 4 3 2 1

The paper used in this publication is acid free and meets the minimum requirements of the American National Standard for Permanence of Paper for Printed Library Materials Z39.48-1992.

In memory of
Barbara Castleman

CONTENTS

List of Maps   ix

List of Illustrations   xi

Preface   xiii

Prologue: Vicksburg *Not* by the Book   xix

1. "We Were Out-Generaled Some Way"   1
2. "Can the Enemy Intend Another Attempt to Approach Vicksburg?"   25
3. "We Have Disposed of This Tough Little Nut"   49
4. "The Work of Changing the Channel of the Mississippi"   83
5. "But Grant Is on Two Other Projects"   113
6. "The Prospect of Opening the Pass Is Encouraging"   145
7. "The Yankee Boats Are Here"   171
8. "The Enemy Press Me on All Sides"   214
9. "We Intend to Take the Boats"   236
10. "This Is the Only Move I Now See as Practicable"   266
11. "They Are About to Execute Some Plan"   300
12. "Attracting Attention from Grant"   336
13. "We Land the Army in the Morning"   364

Epilogue: "But I Was on Dry Ground"   389

Appendix A: Union Order of Battle for Arkansas Post,
January 11, 1863   395

Appendix B: Confederate Order of Battle for Arkansas Post,
January 11, 1863   399

Notes   401

Bibliography   475

Index   509

MAPS

Mississippi River Alluvial Plain   6
Early Union Advances   10
Grant's Attempts   18
To Arkansas Post   45
Arkansas Post   55
Vicksburg Canal   105
Bayou Routes   122
Yazoo Pass   130
Mississippi Delta   147
Fort Pemberton   184
Steele's Bayou   224
Steele's Bayou   246
Union March   277
Steele's Expedition   289
Vicksburg Batteries   302
Grierson's Raid   316
Grierson's Raid   339
Union March   352
Grand Gulf   359
Union Crossing   374

ILLUSTRATIONS

Gallery follows page 202.
Ulysses S. Grant
John A. McClernand
Peter J. Osterhaus
William T. Sherman
Frederick Steele
Frank P. Blair, Jr.
James B. McPherson
David D. Porter
Benjamin H. Grierson
James H. Wilson
John C. Pemberton
Carter S. Stevenson
William W. Loring
Dabney H. Maury
John H. Forney
Martin L. Smith
John S. Bowen
James L. Alcorn
Vicksburg Canal
USS *Louisville*
Passing of Vicksburg by James E. Taylor
Drawing of Smith Coffee Daniell II mansion near Bruinsburg

PREFACE

Historian J. F. C. Fuller cogently captured the problems facing Ulysses S. Grant as he embarked upon the first four months of campaigning near Vicksburg in 1863. It was the dead of winter as the year changed, and with it came torrential downpours, at times even storms with heavy winds and damaging lightning and hail; and all of it fell on an area that was mostly lowland alluvial river valley. As a result, it was a campaign canvass nearly covered with water. Out of the flood stood Vicksburg itself on high ground, the goal of Grant and his Army of the Tennessee, but it was isolated and defensible. Fuller lamented Grant's stake: "Whilst Grant prayed for fine weather, . . . like Noah, [he] looked out upon the waters waiting for them to subside."[1]

Weather has always been a major factor in military operations, as has the environment, and historians are beginning to catch up to that realization with books dedicated solely to those subjects. Certainly weather played a significant role in Robert E. Lee's western Virginia campaign or Ambrose Burnside's "Mud March," but there was no more of a weather-, geography-, or environment-influenced campaign than Grant's four months of misery in early 1863. Wet, muddy, and nasty, especially in this particular environment mainly in the Delta of Mississippi and Louisiana, Grant could do little to reach the high ground east of Vicksburg as long as he was so befuddled with high water and mud. Yet he tried.[2]

The context of these attempts is critically important, as Grant was between two fine periods of campaigning weather, the dry late fall of 1862 and the spring of 1863. But these three or four months in between were anything but dry and campaign-worthy in the accepted sense. The resulting problems were therefore not necessarily so much Grant's fault as they were more attributable to the stout defense put up by the Confederates and the perhaps even stouter geography Grant had to conquer. In fact, Grant had earlier started well when the ground was dry and passable, but he had been defeated twice in the attempt, both along the Mississippi Central Railroad and at Chickasaw Bayou, operations that spilled over into the harsh winter weather that he would see much more of in early 1863. Now like Noah, for the next four months he awaited the floods to part, as he could not hibernate this close to Vicksburg; he had to keep working if for nothing else to keep the enemy on the alert and his own men busy. The result was five more major attempts, and a few smaller ones, to get to Vicksburg.

Most historians combine the four waterborne efforts of this period with the first two in late 1862 to emphasize six failed attempts to reach Vicksburg before the seventh and final successful one. More often than not, that seventh one, when Grant crossed the river south of Vicksburg and started northward to encapsulate the city, is lumped in with the May inland campaign that saw Grant march all the way to Vicksburg in a mere seventeen days and successfully fight five battles in the process. To most historians, the seventh attempt goes with the inland campaign, and oftentimes firm dates are associated with it, being listed as March 29 to May 17, 1863. For many, the break between the doomed and successful attempts comes on March 29, when Grant started seriously engaging in the seventh attempt as opposed to the earlier six failures.

In a minor revision, this book will present a different calendar. The two late 1862 efforts along the Mississippi Central and at Chickasaw Bayou were so distinct from what came later as to require their own volume, which became the first of these five books covering the campaign, *Early Struggles for Vicksburg: The Mississippi Central Campaign and Chickasaw Bayou, October 25–December 31, 1862*. If the next volume (this one) ascribed to the traditional calendar, it would cover the period from January 1 to March 28 and encompass the next four major failed attempts: Grant's Canal, Lake Providence, Yazoo Pass, and Steele's Bayou. But rather than make the cutoff at March 29, it is much more contextual to include the seventh operation south of Vicksburg in the overall series of attempts to reach high ground east of the Mississippi River, because that is exactly what it was until it proved successful on April 30. Only then, once Grant finally reached the high, dry ground on the east side of the Mississippi River, did the next phase begin: the inland overland campaign for the next seventeen days. As a result, the cutoff should properly be seen as April 30, when the seventh attempt finally succeeded, thereby ushering in a new phase not of attempts but of actual campaigning. That subsequent phase will be the subject of the third volume.[3]

Consequently, this second volume covers attempts three through seven from January 1 to April 30, 1863. Some, in particular historian Fuller, have called these bayou operations "quite desperate and all of it heroic, . . . a gigantic bluff to deceive the enemy, to deceive the politicians, and to deceive his own troops, so that when he moved the enemy might be surprised." There is certainly an element of truth in that, but it gives too much credit to Grant's planning. In reality, each of the attempts, despite what Grant later said in his memoirs, was expected to be the one that succeeded, but only the seventh finally did. Grant did not plan busywork all winter to deceive almost everyone until he unleashed his brilliant seventh attempt when the water finally receded. He planned all along to succeed with plans three through six and certainly would have welcomed the success had they worked. All the while, he kept the option to move south of Vicksburg in mind, to be used if still needed once the weather began cooperating later in the spring.[4]

Rather, these different attempts came about haphazardly and experimentally. And in that sense it was totally new, as few had operated in such miry, waterlogged environments before, certainly not on such a scale in American history. As a result, Grant figuratively threw away the accepted guidance—the playbook, if you will—and worked out his own new way of doing things required by this new environment. Certainly, the chief thinkers of the day such as Jomini and Clausewitz had little to say about changing vast river courses, cutting levies and flooding whole sections of watersheds, or bypassing strongholds by digging canals far around them. While all of it entailed some type of maneuver that the theorists would have been more or less comfortable with, the means by which to do so were entirely new. And certainly, as happened in the seventh attempt, the choice of purposefully choosing an insecure supply line was foreign to the by-the-book theories, particularly of Jomini and the Union general in chief, Major General Henry W. Halleck.

But in the largest context, while new and theoretically dangerous, it was all fairly safe; none of these activities prior to the seventh attempt put much of Grant's army in danger at any one time. But the effect was that none of the attempts came close to securing Vicksburg or even getting the Union army on the high ground east of the city, which was the immediate goal after all. In large part because of the terrible weather and flooded waterways, Grant basically bided his time in low-risk/high-reward efforts that allowed him to keep his troops occupied while outlasting the winter. But if any one of these efforts had succeeded, Grant was certainly ready to pounce and take advantage of it.

Another stellar aspect of this period and also somewhat new, although not so much for Grant himself, was the naval factor. While gunboats had been key components of Grant's river activities before, the close connection and cooperation seen in these last five attempts truly showed the effect of and need for combined operations. Certainly, because most of the activities were conducted on water rather than dry land, that cooperation became even more acute and the Army–Navy relationship clearly provided large dividends for the United States. It is also critical contextually speaking that these combined operations were the first major efforts (Chickasaw Bayou notwithstanding) after the ironclads of the Mississippi Squadron had been severed from army control and passed to an independent naval command in the fall of 1862. Cooperation had to be utilized.

As important as these four months were to the Vicksburg Campaign, there have been few dedicated works to explain them. Obviously, it is easier to deal with them in a larger campaign history, so they have received little academic or even popular attention aside from larger works or isolated and uneven smaller treatments. That said, some detailed volumes have been produced on certain aspects of this portion of the campaign, including my own. For instance, *The Real Horse Soldiers* delves into detail on Grierson's Raid, as does *The Decision Was All My Own*, looking into Grant himself during the Vicksburg Campaign. These two books give specific detail to specific topics, as does *Champion Hill* on a later battle. Similar to the scant academic coverage, the fabric on which these operations played out has received little commemoration aside from a few Mississippi state historical markers that dot the area. Grand Gulf has a small state park, but it is so far off the beaten path that distance hampers visitation and attention. Fort Pemberton has a small marker, but the rest, although remarkably intact as in the cases of Yazoo Pass or Steele's Bayou, are little marked and even less visited by Vicksburg tourists. Even the wonderful ruins of Windsor Mansion, which are definitely worth the trip, are not often visited except by the stalwart because of distances from civilization. But visiting such sites, from Yazoo Pass to Windsor, only emphasizes the breadth and width of Grant's campaign for Vicksburg, especially in the messy winter months when he had little to show for the effort. But Grant never gave up, and the elusive success eventually came on that seventh try, when he finally reached that high ground he had been seeking all along.[5]

Many people have aided me in the preparation of this manuscript. I am especially thankful for the many archivists and librarians who make the treasure hunt of research easy and enjoyable. Publishing with the University Press of Kansas is a continual joy. Joyce Harrison, Kelly Chrisman Jacques, Derek Helms, and the many other staff made the process smooth and easy. Jon Howard is a wonderful copy editor and once again made this book stronger and more polished.

In addition to the peer review process, several historian-friends continually provide encouragement and support. Dr. John Marszalek, my mentor and friend, is always helpful, and Terry Winschel once again provided a solid reading. It is extremely important to have expert eyes like his on a manuscript this detailed, and I appreciate his hours and hours of work on my behalf.

As always, Kelly, Mary Kate, and Leah Grace are my most cherished earthly possessions, just as the salvation God provides is the most important spiritually. I am extremely thankful for both.

I have dedicated this volume to the memory of my wonderful mother-in-law, Barbara Castleman. Her sudden passing left a void in all our lives, but the work she did while on this earth continues to bear fruit even while she enjoys her heavenly reward.

Prologue
Vicksburg *Not* by the Book

If the Mississippi Central and Chickasaw Bayou operations, normally described as the first two of six failed Union attempts to reach Vicksburg, were pure by-the-book operations, what came afterward was anything but that. Those late 1862 efforts, along with many others such as the Tennessee River Campaign (specifically the advance on Corinth), the Peninsula Campaign, and untold others, were all straight out of the vein of Jominian Napoleonic theory. Baron Henri Jomini was one of the classic military thinkers of the nineteenth century and probably had more influence, although indirectly, on American military operations during the Civil War than anyone else. Jomini's theories of concentration of troops, supporting columns, decisive points, secure supply lines, and interior lines of communication had been hallmarks of Napoleonic warfare and became accepted military theory among European nations after his many writings, chiefly *Summary of the Art of War*, appeared in the decades after the Napoleonic Wars ended in 1815.[1]

While Jomini's work, the most famous published in 1838, appeared before the Civil War in America, few in the United States read the original in French or studied the maxims in detail. Ulysses S. Grant himself admitted "I have never read it carefully." But the teachers of those Civil War officers had studied Jomini; educators such as Sylvanus Thayer and Denis Hart Mahan influenced countless cadets at West Point who were destined to wage war later in the 1860s. Jomini's influence on Thayer and Mahan, and by extension the many Civil War generals they taught, was enormous even if not direct: a recent military history has surmised that "West Point followed the French example.... Thayer sought to transplant French professional standards to the banks of the Hudson, using Mahan as his conveyor."[2]

The reason so many Civil War campaigns took the form they did and looked strikingly similar was because of this Jominian backdrop. Many commanders in the Vicksburg Campaign certainly knew this influence, if not specifically named. Grant wrote that "up to this time, it had been regarded as an axiom in war that large bodies of troops must operate from a base of supplies which they always covered and guarded in all forward movements." William T. Sherman even used the name itself, writing in the summer of 1862 that "all officers of this command must now study their books; ignorance of duty must no longer be pleaded. The commanding general has the power at any time to order a board to examine the acquirements and capacity of any officer, and he will not fail to exercise it. Should any officer, high or low, after the opportunity and experience we have had, be ignorant of his tactics, regulations, or even of the principles of the Art of War (Mahan and Jomini), it would be a lasting disgrace." Certainly the study of warfare was on many officers' minds from evaluation boards to self-study, one Federal even mentioning in the midst of the Vicksburg campaign how "the officers have established a school for com[issioned]-officers for the discussion of military matters[.] They are just beginning to see the necessity of understanding small matters."[3]

Both sides in the early Vicksburg Campaign heavily utilized the Jominian principles of decisive points, secure supply lines, raids on enemy supply routes, supporting columns, and other facets of the Jominian's argument to wage the sharply by-the-book operations in the fall and winter of 1862. And given the equal theory waged by near equal sides, it seemed that geography and terrain made the difference as the side on the defensive, the Confederates, came out on top. Grant's supporting columns (Sherman at Chickasaw Bayou while he remained in northern Mississippi), the various raids into the enemy's rear by both sides (Nathan Bedford Forrest and Earl Van Dorn for the Confederates and Cadwallader Washburn for the Federals), decisive points (Grenada, Vicksburg, Memphis, and Holly Springs), and hopefully secure supply lines (the Mississippi Central Railroad for both) were all tenets of this Jominian playbook for the fall and winter campaigns.[4]

With the Union failure by such means, however, an alternative had to be at least considered. But Confederate commander Lieutenant General John C. Pemberton never did so. Why would he when what he was doing seemed to be working? Likely it would have continued to work had not the enemy changed theorists. While Pemberton remained in his Jominian style of defense, his counterpart Ulysses S. Grant figuratively threw away the book and started to think more outside the box. The commonly accepted alternative to Jomini was Prussian theorist Carl von Clausewitz, and many of his theories would indeed begin to invade the Union high command's thought processes during the rest of this campaign. But while Grant's continuing campaign looked less and less like Jominian operations, they did not significantly change overnight to Clausewitzian notions. In fact, Grant would grow into more and more of a Clausewitzian type of general for the rest of the war, and the American military would do the same for the rest of its history to the present, but the change was not automatic and completed at once. In fact, the change that occurred in the next stages of the Vicksburg Campaign were more non-Jominian that pro-Clausewitzian. Still, some type of change was needed, and while the leap all the way to Clausewitzian thought did not occur for Grant until later in the war and for the nation's military for another century, a change did in fact take place. Historian Bruce Catton summed up the contemporary thinking: "It was time, therefore, to go beyond military logic."[5]

For the first four months in 1863, consequently, Grant began operations that, while they did not necessarily resemble Clausewitzian theory in full, nevertheless were a sure move away from Jominian thought. Discussion of efforts to dig canals to change the course of a continent's major river would not be found in Clausewitz any more than it would in Jomini, but Grant did not start from Clausewitzian principles. He did start from Jominian theory, however, and therein was a clear break from what had come before. Similarly, there was little to be said in either Jomini or Clausewitz about the idea of utilizing flooded creeks, rivers, and bayous in a subtropical swamp environment to outmaneuver the enemy, although maneuver itself was important to both theorists; only the means of doing so were new. Perhaps most significant, Jomini would have fumed at the idea of risking a secure and vital supply line to move an army on the other side of the decisive point, thereby making the line of communication unsafe. In that regard, Clausewitz was more supportive of living off the land, but Grant was clearly going against the accepted Jominian mentality at the time, basically the only one contemporarily known. Clausewitz would not be translated into English until 1873, but Grant began to distill some of his ideas by common sense even in 1863.[6]

There was pushback of course from the old stalwarts of Jominian thought. The chief Jominian strategist in America, Henry Halleck, was nervous in Washington and sought to direct Grant into Jominian line every chance he could. Some of Grant's own officers were likewise convinced the old way of by-the-book operations was the way to go, especially after Grant announced his intention to go south of Vicksburg and leave the issue of supplies in question. Sherman in particular railed against the idea, arguing that the way to proceed would be to go back to Memphis, start over, and do it by the book along a secure railroad line of advance. Grant later explained that Sherman had argued "I was putting myself in a position voluntarily which an enemy would be glad to maneuver a year—or a long time—to get me in." As it turned out, others thought the same thing, including Rear Admiral David D. Porter and even at one point Major General John A. McClernand, who quickly turned to Grant's point of view when the prospect of doing anything surfaced. It was the old versus the new, and Grant was thinking outside the box, which made Sherman and many others very nervous.[7]

But Grant had significant reasons for doing so, he thought. And after all, he was in command. "The strategic way according to the rule ... would have been to go back to Memphis; establish that as a base of supplies; fortify it so that the storehouses could be held by a small garrison, and move from there along the line of railroad, repairing as we advanced, to the Yallabusha, or to Jackson, Mississippi," he later admitted. But he added, "It was my judgment at the time that to make a backward movement as long as that from Vicksburg to Memphis, would be interpreted, by many of those yet full of hope for the preservation of the Union, as a defeat, and that the draft would be resisted, desertions ensue and the power to capture and punish deserters lost. There was nothing left to be done but to go forward to a decisive victory." In these rearward considerations, Grant was very much in Clausewitzian territory regarding the influence of politics on military matters. "The problem then became," Grant wrote, "how to secure a landing on high ground east of the Mississippi without an apparent retreat."[8]

Causing a greater degree of difficulty than anyone could have imagined was the geography of the field of operations as well as the heavily flooded nature of the chessboard of war at the time. Unable to utilize the standard ways of army operations, Grant devised nonstandard ways just as he was utilizing nonstandard theory. His soldiers picked up on the change quickly, one writing that Grant was beginning a new way of warfare using an "audacious strategy." Another admitted the change, writing that "our work now is to be of a different kind from what it was when we was here before," and another even mentioned "a 'new plan' is 'settled upon for the campaign.'" One even used big words to describe the change: "Our Generals here are trying stratagem to take Vicksburg." But they were confident in the end result even while comparing their new operations to the old ways of doing things. One wrote that "we are going to take Vicksburg by the slow but shure way this time," and another admitted that "we have tried them once and got whipt badly but this time they must succumb I think."[9]

In the end, the goal was the same: "To redeem this lovely valley of the Mississippi from fiends and traitors who are desecrating it," as one Federal surmised. But for Grant there was no use in trying the same old failed policies of Jominian-style warfare, especially in an environment that was not conducive to that type of struggle. And the political environment, always a factor to an increasingly Clausewitzian-leaning general, had to be taken into consideration in how the operations developed. It was a chance to be sure, a great gamble with Grant's army and perhaps even with his own life. But "it was the only move which could from the nature of the position possibly prove a success," Grant argued.[10]

Once decided upon, it was freeing to Grant even if his old Jominian generals were astonished. Grant seemed to take a new breath of life as he settled on the final gamble that could lose everything, but just the decision itself gave relief. One of Grant's brigade commanders, Colonel John B. Sanborn, described the difference, writing that before the gamble he was lethargic and unanimated, but in the midst of the new Vicksburg operations "his genius and his energies seemed to burst forth with new life," even to the point of quickly walking or galloping literally everywhere he went: "He seemed wrought up to the last pitch of determination and energy."[11]

And so as the armies ushered in a new year and began to grapple with one another over the large canvas of war that covered numerous states, there was a new way of doing things for the Federals. Confident in the old way that was admittedly working up to now, Pemberton and his Confederates were content with staying the course. The result was the confrontation of old and new styles of warfare, not so much Jominian verses Clausewitzian at this point yet, but more Jominian verses non-Jominian. Adaptation was the key, and the one who did it better and faster would prove to gain the upper hand.

Bayou Battles for Vicksburg

1

"We Were Out-Generaled Some Way"

To January 1

Its importance was obvious. Numerous American statesmen through the ages testified to the Mississippi Valley's value, no less an authority than Thomas Jefferson himself prophesying that "from its fertility it will ere long yield more than half of our whole produce and contain more than half our inhabitants." Further declaring the river's importance, Jefferson foresaw that the port that gave it access to the entire world would be key in allowing the Union to win the war: "There is on the globe one single spot, the possessor of which is our natural and habitual enemy. It is New Orleans, through which the produce of three-eighths of our territory must pass to market."[1]

Jefferson told of the importance of the river and its great port, but his actions spoke louder. Both administrations prior to his presidency, and numerous statesmen before that, had negotiated, dealt, and sometimes even begged for access to the river and port while European officials who owned the opposite shore and at times the port city itself dangled full access just out of reach of the Americans and their new nation. Certainly, George Washington and John Adams kept a wary eye toward the great western expanse and the river it drained, working through treaty after treaty to achieve ultimate access and respect from the older European nations that now owned this piece of extremely valuable real estate in the new world. But Jefferson produced a near miracle in 1803 when he purchased not only New Orleans but also the vast majority of the land the river drained on the opposite bank. This became known to history as the Louisiana Purchase, but it contained far more than just Louisiana, effectively doubling the nation all the way to the Rocky Mountains and gaining most of the tributaries flowing into the Mississippi River. The effect was instantaneous and heartily approved by most; Andrew Jackson, no stranger to the river's history himself, wrote Jefferson that "all the Western Hemisphere rejoices at the Joyfull news of the cession of Louisiana, an event which places the peace happiness and liberty of our country on a lasting basis, an event which generations yet unborn on each revolving year, will hail the day, and with it the causes that give it birth."[2]

Jackson had his own day with regard to the river and New Orleans, when he defended it against British invasion and became a national hero in the process. He likewise talked of the importance of the river, writing of New Orleans as "the great emporium of the west" and declaring that "the god of the universe had intended this great valley to belong to one nation." Like Jefferson, his actions spoke louder, and his defense of the city of New Orleans on January 8, 1815, spoke the loudest. It propelled him to the presidency.[3]

Unfortunately, while no one forgot Jackson's actions, they disregarded his warning that the river should be always and forever under the rule of one nation. As Jackson and his generation, people who had compromised their way out of civil war for thirty years, passed from the scene, a new generation much less willing to comprise took the reins of government. What many founding fathers and early statesmen would have declared as the worst possible development soon occurred: the nation split and the Mississippi River once again became the property of two different entities. Worse, the United States, following the secession of the Southern states, now lost access to not only the lower river but also the great port at New Orleans. Intracontinental trade could still flourish on the upper river system, but access to worldwide markets ceased to exist by river when Louisiana and Mississippi left the Union in early January 1861. And that sparked a fight, William T. Sherman himself boasting that "to secure the safety of the navigation of the Mississippi River I would slay millions. On that point I am not only insane, but mad. Fortunately, the great West is with me there."[4]

Despite promises that "the people of Mississippi recognize the right of the free navigation of the Mississippi River, for commercial purposes, in time of peace, by all States occupying its banks, and that they are willing to enter into proper stipulations to secure the enjoyment of that right," Northern states were not convinced. Numerous legislatures passed memorials decrying the actions of the Southern states. Minnesota's legislature, for example, declared that it "hereby pledges and tenders to the General Government all its military power and industrial resources" and that "concessions and compromise are not to be entertained or offered to traitors." That a motley band of militia fired on a Mississippi River steamer at Vicksburg just a few days after

Mississippi's secession only helped convince Northern states that the river was no longer open and accessible.⁵

Not only was the river closed to Northern commerce, but all realized it would soon become the seat of war. Rivers quickly attract attention during wartime, much like during the War of 1812, because of their defensibility on one side and their aid in moving supplies on the other. The Mississippi River was no different. Immediately, the commanding general of the United States Army, Lieutenant General Winfield Scott, saw the river's importance and assigned to it one of the three major tasks in his famed Anaconda Plan. While almost everyone scoffed at his ideas and the time it would take to implement them, it was in reality very similar to the winning formula that the North ultimately took to win the war, the scoffs at the time necessarily turning to unbelief as the war dragged on for four long years. And just as Scott understood, the Mississippi River and its valley, piercing the Confederacy two-thirds of the way across its landscape, became a central theater of war.⁶

But there was more to the Mississippi River that influenced the course of the war in the valley than just the waterway itself. The river would never become that defense that many rivers running perpendicular to the axis of an enemy's advance became despite Grant writing that "the river meanders in the most torturous way, varying in direction to all points of the compass." Running as it did generally parallel with the Union advance into the Confederacy, the river itself provided Northern commanders with a broad, unstoppable course straight into the heart of the Confederacy and, significantly, to New Orleans. While aiding some early wartime intracontinental movement of men and supplies within the Confederacy, the river itself was all but useless as a defense and instead provided the Confederacy's enemies, much like the British in the War of 1812, a convenient route of advance that quickly became a problem for defense.⁷

Two basic ways of defending against enemy travel by river existed, one of which was competing naval craft. The way to combat naval movements throughout history had always been with a navy of one's own. But the Confederacy had no navy at all at the outbreak of the war and was woefully lacking in resources to produce one either on the high seas or inland waters, as in the case of the Mississippi River defense. Certainly, matching the production and utilization of the major river ironclads rapidly produced by the North in the first year of the war was impossible.⁸

As a result, the Confederacy largely depended on the second manner of river defense, and that meant constructing land fortifications along the rivers to stop all enemy traffic. Heavy guns mounted on the banks of rivers protected by primarily earthen but sometimes masonry fortifications could stop traffic if concentrated enough, especially when the enemy vessels moved upstream against the current. Similarly, barriers across the rivers in the form of chains, rafts, or any other blocking material, most of the time tied to the banks but sometimes consisting of sunken barges filled with rocks or other items in shallow places, could also inhibit travel along rivers. Combining the two gave that much more of a chance of stopping an enemy, although the Mississippi River, especially the farther south it meandered, was far too wide and swift for any such type of bank-to-bank defense. The best option, then, became land fortifications housing large guns that could forcefully stop river traffic. But these land defenses were not totally secure either, largely because of land operations that could turn or outflank any stationary land defense. An enemy could easily land troops up- or downriver from a fortified point and capture it from the rear. As a result, river fortifications often had landward defenses as well, and these by definition could also be beaten by land assaults or be bottled up in a siege that left the defenders to wither because of a lack of supplies.[9]

But complicating Northern military movements along the Mississippi River, the watershed included more than just the waterway. In fact, several additional geographic features attendant to the river initially aided in the defense of the Confederacy. While the South had little defense that would last against travel on the river itself, whether in terms of a navy or land fortifications that could not be turned, the geography of the Mississippi Valley did aid the Confederacy somewhat. If the defense had to rest on fixed fortifications to stop river travel, and it did because of a lack of a functioning and comparable navy, then these land fortifications had to be defended from the land side against enemy armies. But not all locations on the river were defensible or even capable of having land defenses to stop river travel. Still, there were certain places where the bluffs along the wide alluvial plains butted up against the river itself and were high enough to provide good areas for situating cannon to stop river traffic. The high bluffs around Columbus, Kentucky, far to the north was one such area, as were the Chickasaw Bluffs along the Tennessee stretches of the river, mainly at Memphis. Farther below, the bluffs on the Mississippi shore running from the Walnut Hills at Vicksburg southward into Louisiana and touching the river at Grand Gulf, Rodney, and Natchez, Mississippi and Port Hudson and Baton Rouge, Louisiana, were also perfect for such river blockage. But still, each of these bluff areas could be easily turned by an enemy army landing up- or downriver and marching into their rear. Therefore, the surrounding landscape became of supreme importance.[10]

In addition to these tall bluffs at certain places along the river, there was also one other geographical feature that was a two-sided coin in terms of benefit or hinderance to Confederate defense of the river. Attendant to the river for long stretches on either side in northern Mississippi and Louisiana and southern Arkansas, but more so on the western bank, were long stretches of flat bottomland, alluvial plains that were popularly termed "the Delta." One Confederate stationed at Snyder's Bluff north of Vicksburg explained in his diary that this was "romantic country. High precipitous ledge of hills . . . , endless expanse spreading out westward." On the one hand, these vast areas of flat lowlands did not allow for fixed earthen fortifications, they being basically on the bank of the river almost at water level and very much susceptible to the river's overflows throughout each year. A fortification that could be inhabited only at certain times when the river was low was no fortification worth having, as Fort Henry attested earlier in the war. On the other hand, these alluvial plains on each side of the river were so miry, swampy, and wet that regular military operations were not possible during many times of the year, thereby constricting and limiting the areas where enemy operations could be performed. These vast alluvial deltas, not to be mixed up with the formal term "delta" that defined where a river entered a sea or ocean, determined where military operations could proceed and where they could not. Moreover, the combination of tall bluffs for fortifications surrounded on some sides with low and swampy alluvial plains that restricted movement toward them actually developed into the most promising formula for success the Confederates had. And at no place did the intersection of these high bluffs and low deltas occur better than at Vicksburg, Mississippi, where one Confederate described the view: "As far as the eye can reach—[it] looks as level over the tops of the trees as it is possible to be."[11]

The entire alluvial basin along the river extended for some four hundred and thirty straight-line miles, from just south of Cape Girardeau, Missouri, across the river from Illinois itself and Union territory, southward to past Natchez, Mississippi, where it technically entered more alluvial plains that led to the Gulf of Mexico. The vast majority of the lowlands were on the west side of the river despite those east of the river becoming more famous. The widest extent of the delta lowlands from west of the river to east of the channel was over a hundred and ten miles. At its widest point west of the river, the flatlands stretched some ninety miles from the river at Memphis westward, while the narrowest width was only about twenty miles from the river westward around Greenville, Mississippi.[12]

The more important delta region, at least for military operations eventually against "the much coveted city of Vicksburg," was on the east side of the Mississippi River, which after all was where the defensive bastion of Vicksburg

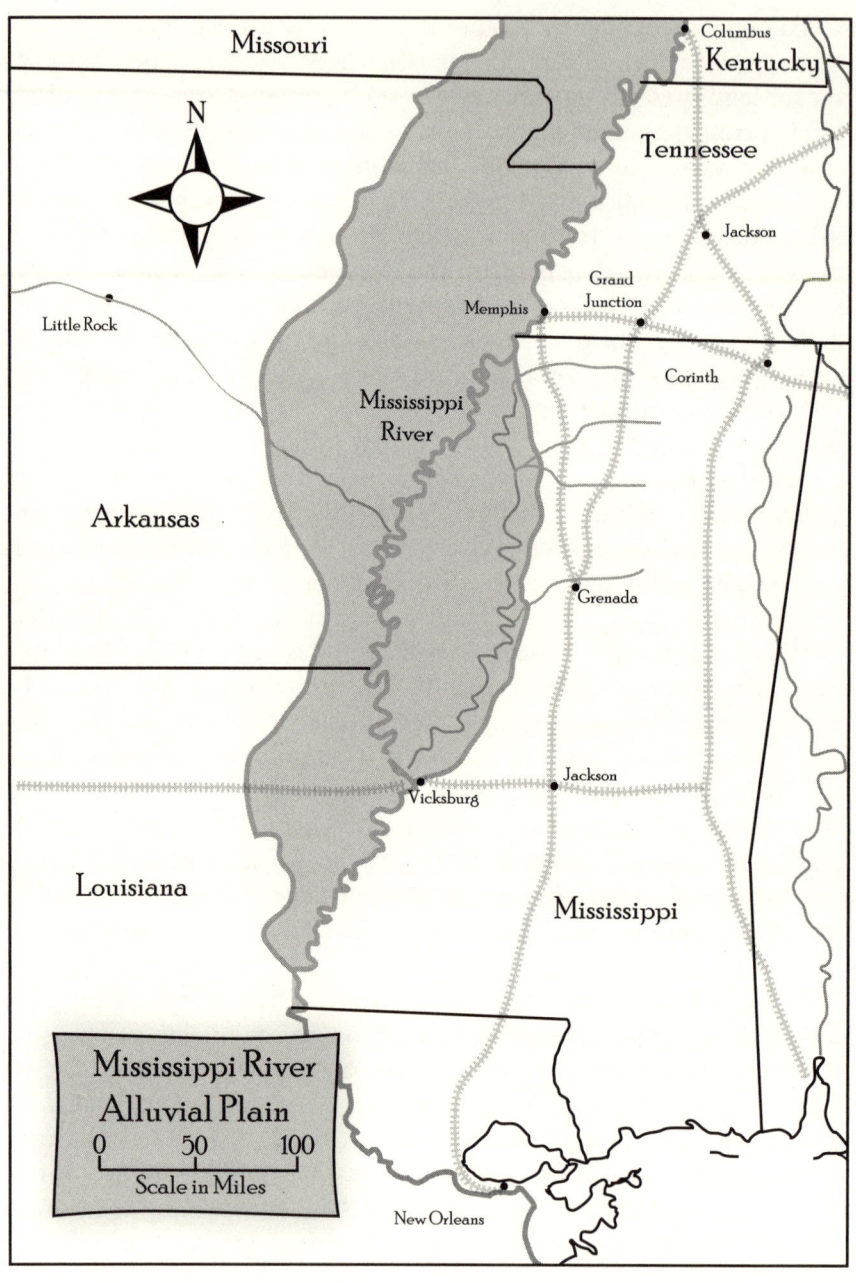

sat. Here it began only south of the high Chickasaw Bluffs at Memphis and curved in an elongated half-oval southward until it met the Walnut Hills just north of Vicksburg. At their widest point east of the river the delta lands covered some seventy miles while extending nearly two hundred miles in height between Memphis and Vicksburg.[13]

These delta regions on both sides of the river were mostly flat, swampy, and sparsely inhabited. They were filled with rivers such as the Yazoo system in Mississippi and the Ouachita, White, Arkansas, and St. Francis river systems west of the main river. In addition, the lowlands were also filled with smaller but connecting feeder rivers, creeks, bayous, and old channels, the latter of which were now filled with backwater and became lakes when river currents deposited sand and silt along its new banks to cut off the old channels. Because of the lowlands and little ability for runoff, the entire area was boggy, wet, and treacherous year-round, and because so few inhabitants lived in the water and disease-infested regions, the area teemed with all sorts of wild animals from nonthreatening vermin to bears, alligators, and all manner of poisonous snakes. Sherman actually described the Mississippi Delta as a "black vegetable mold, full of streams and bayous, and exceedingly impracticable in wet and wintry weather." It really was a wilderness, but even more complicated than the normal definition because of the lowlands and water involved. It was a gigantic, almost uninhabitable swamp.[14]

But that isolation was what the Confederacy needed, because troop movements would be extremely difficult through these delta regions. As a result, where the lower regions met and provided at least partial shields for the higher bluffs nearby, a defense could possibly be made. However, that was all but impossible on the west side of the river, where for more than four hundred miles the western bank was pretty much, with the exception of Helena, Arkansas, this alluvial lowland where no defense could be established. The southernmost point of this delta region west of the river blended right into more coastal lowlands and provided no defense possibilities, while the upper reaches in Missouri where there were highlands that could be defended were actually farther north than some sections of Illinois across the river. A defense that far north was impossible.[15]

Consequently, any Confederate defense of the Mississippi River would have to be on the east side, and fortifications soon went up all along the high bluffs in Tennessee and eventually northward all the way to Columbus in Kentucky. But they stopped at Memphis, where the Mississippi portion of the Delta began, and resumed only where it ended east of the river at the Walnut Hills and its chief city, Vicksburg. An early wartime Confederate commander described his "understanding that there are no points sufficiently high on the river between Memphis and Vicksburg which could be fortified for the defense of the Mississippi." From Vicksburg southward into Louisiana there were additional imposing bluffs capable of being fortified as well, but those did not border the vast lowlands of the Mississippi Delta that could aid in a landward defense. One Federal adequately wrote of Vicksburg's defensibility that, "surrounded by swamps and slough in the rear and flank, unapproachable by water, and accessible only by narrow roads over dykes and steep ridges, well fortified and defended, it seems indeed impregnable."[16]

As fate would have it, Vicksburg would become the last best hope for Confederate defense of "this majestic stream," mainly because of its positioning not only on the east side of the river itself but also at the intersection of the Walnut Hills and the vast Delta to the north. One soldier described it as "the city of an hundred hills." In such a position, Vicksburg was shielded from enemy advances on the river by the big guns ultimately erected there, aided by the big hairpin curve in the river right at Vicksburg that caused swift and uncontrollable currents and eddies, as well as from land advances by the alluvial plains that sat east and north of the river and the high bluffs on which the city sat.[17]

Accordingly, any enemy advance to Vicksburg was problematic. That was especially so from the west, Grant later writing that "a front attack was therefore impossible, and was never contemplated; certainly not by me." Similarly, the Delta on the Mississippi side of the river shielded Vicksburg from any major advance from the north, a Union soldier admitting that "it seems to be a pretty well established fact that Vicksburg is not to be, and cannot be, taken by a direct [northern] attack; their works are very strong and almost unapproachable on account of the *bayous* and swamps." That left only the south and east as possible easy avenues of approach to Vicksburg, and most Confederate planners viewed the biggest enemy threat as coming southward from the United States itself, that is, from the Illinois, Iowa, and Missouri areas; Confederate general Braxton Bragg in fact complained early in the war that "Mobile and New Orleans are being fortified at great expense, when they should be defended in Kentucky and Missouri." General Albert Sidney Johnston himself contended that "New Orleans is to be defended from above by defeating the enemy at Columbus." Little thought was thus given to an enemy approach from the south because any Northern armies emanating from the United States itself would have to somehow go past Vicksburg to advance from the south, which was seemingly unimaginable as well.[18]

Accordingly, the only major threat to Vicksburg seemed to be from the east, but that also provided problems for any invading Federals, as they would have to make a wide sweep eastward to circumvent the Mississippi portion of the Delta. Thus, the heartland of Mississippi seemed to be the major area for defense, and a Confederate army could more easily defend this one approach route instead of from all compass points. And better yet, the central hills area of Mississippi east of the Delta region, which was the only conceivable area for major military operations, was amply covered by some of those perpendicular rivers instead of ones parallel to the assumed Union advance. The result was at the least a semblance of a Confederate chance at defending Vicksburg from the land side, which was needed to undergird the river batteries that would block river traffic itself at Vicksburg. Thus it was in the understanding of the quirky Mississippi River valley geography that the seed of a Confederate defense of Vicksburg began to sprout.[19]

Oddly enough, the vast Mississippi Delta on either side of the river was not a major factor in wartime operations for the first year and a half of the conflict. But the river was. Confederate planners stressing the need to defend the new nation from invasion fretted over the Mississippi River, a dagger pointing directly into the heart of the Confederacy. Union planners such as Winfield Scott quickly recognized as much. But it was worse in that the river's tributaries, and their tributaries in turn such as the Tennessee and Cumberland Rivers just east of the main river, also offered easy waterborne access into the Confederacy. While there has been ample emphasis on the role of railroads in the Civil War, it is significant that three of the four major transportation artery access points to the western Confederacy at the beginning of the war were by river, not rail.[20]

Confederate president Jefferson Davis sent who he considered his best general, Albert Sidney Johnston, to solve the defense problem in the West, particularly the issue of the Mississippi River providing easy access into the Confederacy. But Johnston was at a loss with so few resources as he had, compounded by extremely questionable decisions his predecessors had made before his arrival, namely the invasion of Kentucky. Major General Leonidas Polk's entrance into neutral Kentucky in early September 1861 garnered for the Confederacy the bastion of Columbus, Kentucky, high on the bluffs overlooking the river, but it also ended Kentucky's neutrality. The gain of a soon-to-be heavily fortified Columbus that indeed stopped all traffic on the Mississippi River was significantly overshadowed by the loss of the buffer that was a neutral Kentucky, which now opened the entire northern border of Tennessee and the Confederacy to Union invasion.[21]

Johnston tried to cover all access points such as at Columbus, at the twin rivers at Forts Henry and Donelson, astride the one railroad that led to the

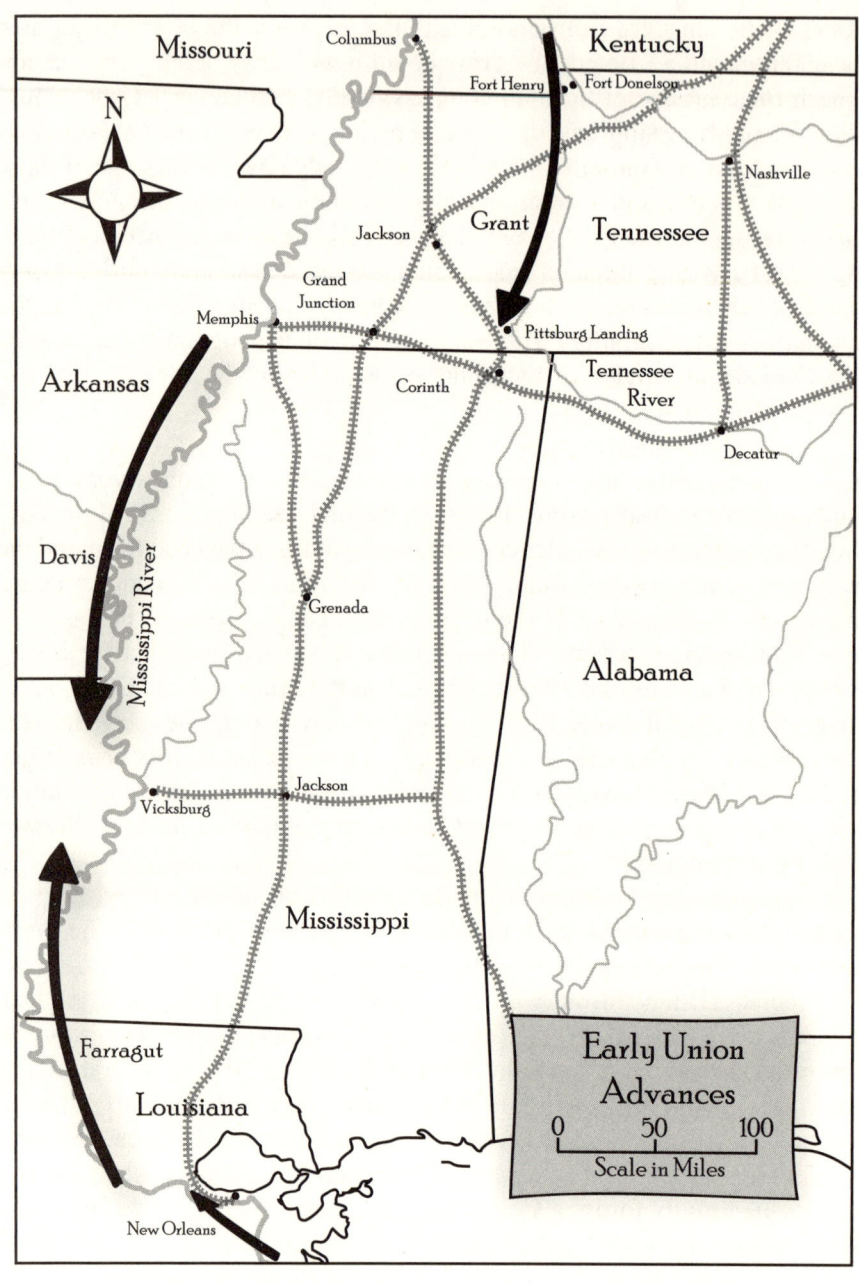

Confederacy—the Louisville and Nashville, and at the Cumberland Gap, but he could not adequately cover all approaches. Worse, the enemy could concentrate on just one and overpower it before help could arrive from the others. And that is exactly what happened. Realizing that Columbus was nearly impregnable, the aggressive tandem of Brigadier General Ulysses S. Grant and Flag Officer Andrew H. Foote decided to sidestep, or turn/outflank, Columbus by a convenient alternate route some one hundred miles to the east, the parallel-flowing Tennessee River. They mounted an advance against Fort Henry on the Tennessee River and won one of the most important victories of the war in early February 1862. The seizure of the fort and, more important, the railroad bridge over the river just to its south broke open the Confederate defense of the West at its most northern defensive line, split the Confederate defense into two unsupportable halves on each side of the Tennessee River, and caused a major rethinking of western strategy that led to a concentration of almost all Confederate forces in the West at the next tier of transportation routes in northern Mississippi and Alabama. In the process, Johnston lost much of Kentucky, most of Tennessee, Nashville, and an entire army of some fourteen thousand men at Fort Donelson while trying to cover one wing of his army's withdrawal south of the Cumberland River. Also lost was the bastion at Columbus, opening the Mississippi River to Union forces far southward. It was an unmitigated disaster.[22]

It grew even worse when the Federals under Grant and others continued on up (southward) the Tennessee River to within twenty or so miles of that next tier of Confederate transportation—namely, Corinth, Mississippi—where two major trunkline Confederate railroads crossed. Johnston made his stand there and even struck back at Shiloh in April, where he tried to defeat Grant before reinforcements arrived. "I would fight them if they were a million," he declared, but Johnston perished instead of conquered as he had famously acknowledged were his choices. The resulting Union advance on Corinth under the Federal western departmental commander himself, Major General Henry W. Halleck, took another couple months, one Confederate general declaring them "those tedious days of Halleck's approach to Corinth." But the operation ended in only a fizzle in late May as the new Confederate western commander, General P. G. T. Beauregard, who had replaced Johnston at Shiloh, withdrew without a fight. Beauregard and the Confederates retreated even farther southward into Mississippi, but the fall of Corinth had huge effects elsewhere as well. Largely outflanked by Corinth's fall, Memphis on the Mississippi River fell to a naval flotilla in early June. The Mississippi River was now open all the way to Memphis and the beginning of the vast Delta on both sides, which without Confederate defenses in the Delta itself meant the river was open all the way to the next tier of Confederate transportation and the next high ground along its course. "Vicksburg was important to the enemy because it occupied the first high ground coming close to the river below Memphis," Grant later explained. It was just as obvious to the authorities in Washington. Secretary of War Edwin M. Stanton told Halleck bluntly: "I suppose you contemplate the occupation of Vicksburg and clearing out the Mississippi to New Orleans."[23]

Worse for the Confederate river defense, there was also at the same time a Union advance surprisingly moving northward up the river. Most Confederates had envisioned the major threat coming southward out of the actual United States, but Flag Officer David G. Farragut led some of his oceangoing vessels up the Mississippi River, confronting the fixed Confederate defenses at Forts Jackson and St. Philip in April. These land fortifications provided little defense, and by late April Farragut was at New Orleans, which surrendered on April 25. Thereafter, Farragut continued on northward all the way to Vicksburg, where reeling Confederates had thrown together a hasty defense: "We might make a fair stand on a line running from Vicksburg through Jackson and Meridian," one rattled Confederate commander confirmed. Farragut bombarded the city and passed the defending Confederate batteries easily, they being nowhere near as strong then as they would be in the future. He then met up with the northern naval flotilla of ironclads that had won the fight at Memphis and continued unopposed down the river the length of the Mississippi Delta to just north of Vicksburg. There in mid-July occurred the famous events attendant to the emergence of the CSS *Arkansas*, which led to what one Tennessean described as "one of the grandest land and naval fights that ever occurred." Still, Farragut had too few resources to capture the city itself and satisfied himself with an attempt by Brigadier General Thomas Williams to dig a canal across the hairpin turn in the river opposite Vicksburg that, if it shifted the course of the river—which was entirely possible given the many oxbow lakes along its banks—could isolate Vicksburg and allow clear and unfettered passage. The Confederates stood tall throughout, however, one Mississippian deflecting the call to surrender with a boast: "Mississippians don't know, and refuse to learn, how to surrender to an enemy. If Commodore [David] Farragut or Brigadier General [Benjamin] Butler can teach them, let them come and try."[24]

The swift and impressive Union advance on Vicksburg, characterized as a siege by many inside the city and termed the "darkest hours" as yet to face the defenders, nevertheless came to a quick halt in June and July. Department of the Mississippi commander Henry W. Halleck had overseen the Forts Henry and Donelson operations as well as the advance up the Tennessee

River before arriving in person and leading the cautious advance to Corinth. But there he stopped. All the components of a continued advance were in place, including naval forces from the south under Farragut that controlled the river below Vicksburg and naval forces now under Flag Officer Charles Davis down from the north, controlling the river above the city. All that was needed was a hefty land force to take Vicksburg itself, and that was where Halleck balked not only because of the weather but also because of his own military philosophy. Indeed, the weather was getting hot and miry down in the subtropical climate, one Confederate at Vicksburg talking about the bad water: "[M[ostly from ponds that [had] a green scum over them and often we drank or sucked out water through a cloth to keep from swallowing the filth." But Halleck also stopped to consolidate what he had acquired rather than push on to gain more in his Jominian thinking of taking decisive points, securing supply lines, and moving with coordinated and supporting forces. Without the support of the army, which could conceivably and easily have moved back to the Mississippi River line of operations and steamed swiftly and unopposed down the river to the Vicksburg vicinity, as later events bore out, both Farragut and Davis were at a loss to do anything more. Farragut, in fact, moved back southward to New Orleans, giving a large stretch of the river once more to the Confederates, who had learned their lesson and fortified points farther south to resist advances from that direction, namely at Port Hudson, Louisiana. Flag Officer Davis was unable to do any more than sit tight just north of Vicksburg, awaiting in vain any Union land advance from the north. It was a critical decision by Halleck that ended the North's initiative and offensive in the West.[25]

Confederate commanders were not long in taking back that initiative for themselves. Command changes galore resulted in the summer and fall of 1862 as the war shifted into a Confederate offensive across the board. With the Federals on their heels certainly in the West but elsewhere as well, General Robert E. Lee invaded Maryland in September while a new Confederate commander in Mississippi (Jefferson Davis shelved the hated Beauregard), General Braxton Bragg, moved the bulk of his army to Chattanooga and then set off on an invasion of Kentucky. In Mississippi, an invasion of the North was also planned under the new Confederate commander in the region, Major General Earl Van Dorn, who had brought his trans-Mississippi army east of the Mississippi River during the spring concentration at Corinth. Van Dorn moved northward as well, intending to reach western Kentucky.[26]

None of the invasions worked, as Lee met defeat at Antietam, Bragg at Perryville, and Van Dorn at Corinth. All three fell back to their respective areas of defense, Lee in northern Virginia, Bragg in Middle Tennessee, and Van

Dorn in northern Mississippi. But the tide had again turned as the Federals responded with offensives of their own across the board. These would result in huge casualty-producing battles in Virginia and Tennessee, and Mississippi would see the beginnings of the campaign against Vicksburg. But the Mississippi Delta loomed large just south of the Memphis-to-Corinth line the Federals maintained throughout the summer and fall of 1862, and Union commanders there would be hard-pressed to figure out exactly how to deal with this geographical anomaly.[27]

The delay of five months for the Union advance to rekindle, from June to October 1862, lay on the shoulders of one man who made two fateful decisions: Henry Halleck. One of the decisions was the stoppage of movement southward in June after the capture of Corinth. But then Halleck compounded the problem in July when President Abraham Lincoln called him eastward to take command of the entire Union war effort. Normally a good judge of people, Lincoln at this point misconstrued the success from Forts Henry and Donelson to Corinth as being Halleck's brainchild when in fact Halleck had done about all he could to hold back the real architect of the success, Ulysses S. Grant. Lincoln found out as much when Halleck fizzled as the top Union commander, the president later referring to him as "little more than a first-rate clerk." Meanwhile, Grant languished in the West.[28]

Halleck moved to Washington in July, but when he did he did not fill his vacated position, which was a normal procedure. The top-ranking general would have been Grant, but Halleck chose to simply delete the overall western commander position and instead leave the various subcommanders in their current roles, he thinking he could still oversee them all from Washington. Grant thus kept his basic command but now under a superior hundreds of miles away rather than close by. He gained some freedom but no autonomy to make his own decisions and plan his own efforts. The result was the lack of offensive effort through October, Grant and company merely maintaining their position and wishing to be turned loose. Grant described the interim as "two and a half months of continued defense over a large district of country, and where nearly every citizen was an enemy ready to give information of our every move."[29]

A major shift in the Union high command occurred in late October, however, when Halleck, worn out from overseeing the defense against the three major Confederate advances of the fall, nearly had a breakdown, and even he realized he had to give up some of his authority. He consequently issued orders for Grant to take a higher position, the Department of the Tennessee command, on October 16. Along with it came near-autonomous authority to make his own plans and campaigns, and Grant was quick to do so after taking formal command on October 25. In fact, he began working on an advance toward Vicksburg the very next day, prodded by his friend Sherman, who continually chirped "now is the time to strike at the Yazoo and Mississippi Central roads."[30]

But how to do it was the problem. Grant could read a map as well as anyone and better than most, and all could see that the vast Mississippi Delta was a major stumbling block. The idea of moving overland toward Vicksburg from the west side of the river was equally out of the question; it was an even larger swamp than east of the river, and Vicksburg of course sat on the east side. Plus, he had no authority on that side of the river at the time. A movement down the river itself was probably the best and easiest bet, and it could be easily done, as the Union navy had proven already. And Grant was thoroughly familiar with this type of warfare, having made his name by moving in this fashion up the Tennessee and Cumberland Rivers. Yet it would take a gargantuan logistical effort to get the army down to Vicksburg; the size of the chessboard on which the coming campaign would play out was significantly larger than that of the Tennessee River operations in early 1862 and certainly dwarfed anything in the eastern theater. And just getting to the vicinity of Vicksburg was an altogether different proposition than actually getting into a position east of the city to take it. The presence of the alluvial mire west and north of the city and the high bluffs on which it sat both added additional degrees of difficulty that Grant had not faced earlier in the war. Significantly, if moving by river, Grant would have to land his army somewhere in the lowlands and then begin operations to get to the high ground east of Vicksburg so he could attack the city. Still, it was a safe if methodical play in the best Jominian mind-set, using a river as a supply and communication link to the rear.[31]

But there was another option that interested Grant more. It involved a land offensive down through the heart of Mississippi toward the state capital at Jackson, which was that very ground he sought east of Vicksburg. Moreover, placing his army there would set it astride the all-important Southern Railroad of Mississippi, the one and only lifeline into Vicksburg ever since river traffic was cut off to the north and south. Any army bent on taking Vicksburg first had to get to this high ground east of the city, and moving southward through Mississippi would do just that. "I think I would be able to move down the Mississippi Central road and cause the evacuation of Vicksburg," Grant declared.[32]

Better yet, there was an acceptable route southward from Grant's Memphis-to-Corinth line. Obviously, moving through the Delta itself in large numbers was out of the question, and the off-limits Delta thus hung right in the middle of active operations, much like a Switzerland in European warfare or Kentucky earlier in this war. But there was a path to the east, as railroad builders realized in the 1850s when the railroad boom hit the South. Engineers knew they could not build a line through the Delta and opted to lay out the path in the hills just to the east. The result was the Mississippi Central Railroad running southward from Grand Junction in Tennessee to a connection with the New Orleans, Jackson, and Great Northern line at Canton, which ran on to the state capital and New Orleans. There was also a spur line that ran from Memphis to Grenada on the Mississippi Central, the shorter Mississippi and Tennessee Railroad. Another line also appeared farther east, the Mobile and Ohio, but that was a little too far east for operations against Vicksburg.[33]

The Mississippi Central offered a perfect supply and communication route for any Jominian operation that focused on decisive points and secure supply routes; the Mississippi and Tennessee line even afforded the possibility of supporting columns as well. And Grant was very much at this point interested in the Jominian way of doing things, that being the favored approach of Halleck, who had just given Grant his big break and left it to him to plan operations. Grant obviously wanted to do things Halleck's way, to do it by the book in this his first solo operation without Halleck at least looking over his shoulder nearby. "I knew Halleck," Grant later admitted. The Jominian book said to move carefully and ploddingly down a secure supply route with supporting columns, being careful to maintain and rebuild if necessary the supply route as each incremental leap was made to another decisive point. The Mississippi Central provided just such a supply line, and Halleck could not have been happier when he heard Grant's approach. "I approve of your plan of advancing upon the enemy," Halleck wrote.[34]

The movement got under way in early November, when Grant brought three divisions westward from Corinth under Major General Charles S. Hamilton and combined them with two divisions that moved southward from Bolivar, Tennessee, under Brigadier General James B. McPherson. "I think we are started to Vicksburg," an observant Iowan wrote home. The divisions met up at Grand Junction and La Grange, Tennessee, on November 5, which put them astride the Mississippi Central. "I have commenced a movement on Grand Junction with three divisions from Corinth and two from Bolivar. Will leave here to-morrow evening and take command in person. If found practicable, I will go on to Holly Springs, and maybe Grenada, completing railroad and telegraph as I go," Grant informed Washington.[35]

Grant then probed ahead, looking for enemy resistance along the first line of Confederate defense, the Coldwater River. A series of stronger and stronger probes went forward until midmonth, when Union cavalry took Holly Springs south of the Coldwater River, but a prompt follow-up did not occur because the railroad was not yet serviceable all the way to Holly Springs. This allowed the Confederates to destroy the Coldwater River railroad bridge, and it was not until the end of the month that trains started moving south of Davis' Mill and Grant felt comfortable moving on. "I am exceedingly anxious to do something before the roads get bad and before the enemy can intrench and re-enforce," he admitted.[36]

By that time, the Confederates had taken position south of the next river in line, the Tallahatchie River just north of Oxford. "I deemed it advisable to withdraw from the indefensible position at Holly Springs and take a strong one behind Tallahatchie, and am fortifying," Pemberton informed Richmond. Also by that time the winter weather began to set in, and Grant made his next big move amid a deluge of several days' duration in early December. "The darkies say there is a great deal of this kind of weather here during the month of December and January," an Illinoisan dolefully wrote home. "The rainy season may be expected to set in by the middle of next month [December]," an Indianan similarly wrote, "and from that time to the 1st of March at least the roads are impassable to infantry and artillery." Grant and his five divisions nevertheless bore down on the Tallahatchie River line from Holly Springs while Sherman advanced from Memphis southeastward toward the same river near Wyatt's Ferry, true supporting columns of Jominian theory. All expected a battle at the Tallahatchie, one Ohioan reporting "no heavy fighting yet, but we expect a big fight at the river." But Pemberton and his Confederates again withdrew, leaving the river defense untested but again destroying the Tallahatchie River railroad bridge in turn. The main impetus for the Confederate withdrawal was a flanking movement, another Jominian attribute, across the Delta from Helena, Arkansas, in rear of the Confederate Tallahatchie line. The significant force under Brigadier General Alvin P. Hovey held a position where the Tallahatchie and Coldwater rivers joined in the Delta while cavalry under Brigadier General Cadwallader C. Washburn moved eastward and struck the two railroads north of Grenada but behind Confederate lines on the Tallahatchie River. Little damage was done outright by the cavalry raid, but its presence alone caused Pemberton to withdraw. Washburn wrote that "my main object, which was to stampede the rebel army, could not have been more effectually accomplished." Sherman simply wrote that "the enemy is shaken by their being outwitted at the Tallahatchie."[37]

Pemberton fell back through Oxford and across the third river system perpendicular to the enemy's advance, the Yocona River. "I am compelled to fall back for the defense of Vicksburg," he informed Richmond. But Pemberton

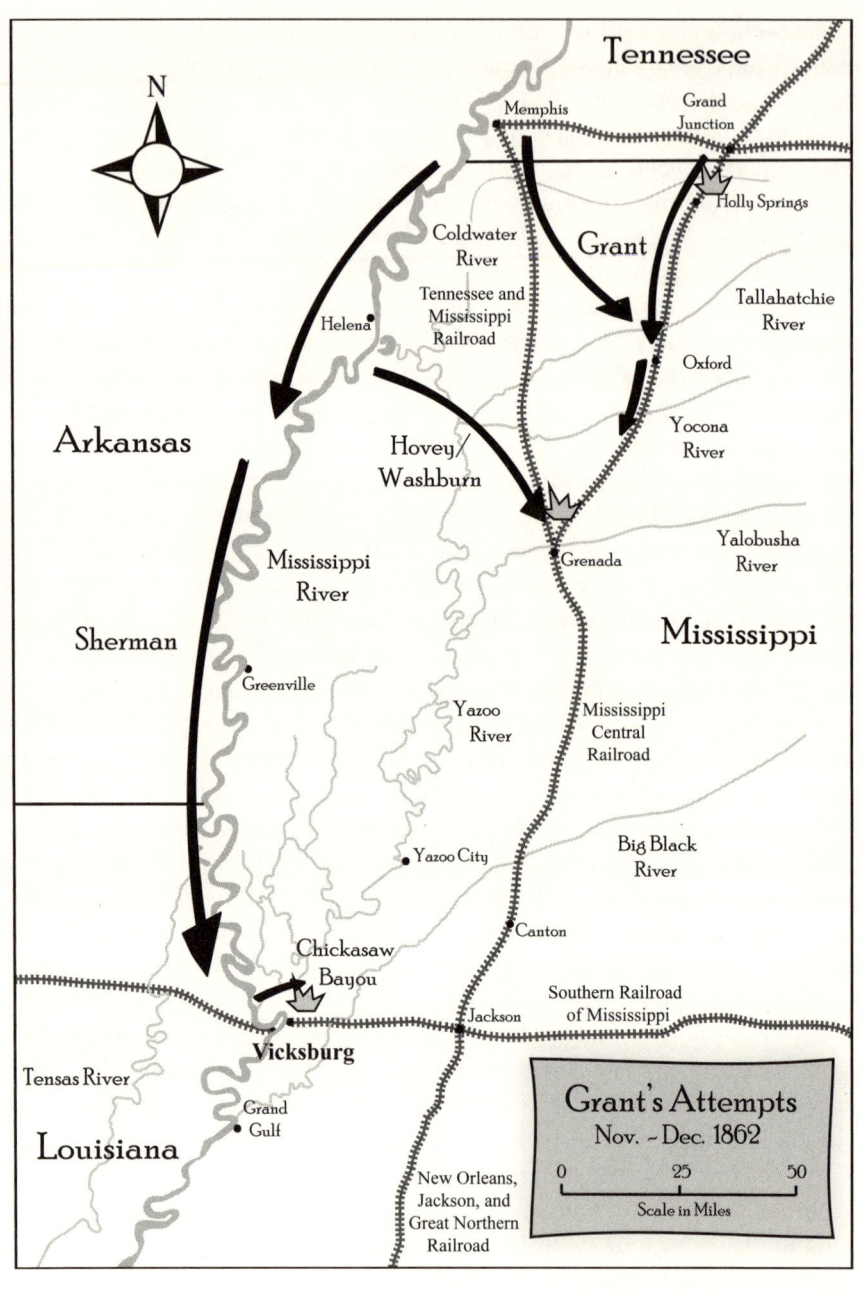

did not make a stand there and, because of such a quick follow-up by Federal cavalry, did not even have time to destroy the railroad bridge over the Yocona. But that bridge did little good because others in the rear were still not rebuilt. It was only early December when trains started rolling across the Coldwater River into Holly Springs, and it was midmonth when the Tallahatchie River bridge was repaired, allowing traffic all the way to Oxford. In the meantime, Grant stopped his advance so he would not be too far out in front of this supply and communication lifeline; wagons simply could not keep the army fed miles and miles in front of the rail terminus, especially in winter when any day could bring back the torrential rains that could all but close down travel. The first few days of December had proven as much, although the rest of December was amazingly warm and dry. But the winter rains could come at any time, and Grant just could not take a chance. "Owing to the bad conditions of the roads do not move [John] McArthur's division any farther from their supplies," one of Grant's cautioning messages ran.[38]

Accordingly, Grant went into camping mode south of Oxford while the Confederates settled into a defensive line along the fourth parallel river system, the Yalobusha River. A lull consequently came in mid-December: "We will not advance much further until the rail road bridge across the Tallahatchie River is completed," one Indiana officer wrote home, "so that we can have subsistence by way of the railroad."[39]

Yet by the second week in December Grant was beginning to figure out that this by-the-book campaign was not all it was cut out to be. He found that the farther southward he went the more and more troops he had to leave along the route behind him to protect it from raiding Confederates. One Confederate recognized that Grant "seemed to have no rear, for strong detachments were posted all along the railroad, as far as our scouts had gone, and were known to extend as far north as Holly Springs." Actually, Grant's garrisons extended all the way back to Columbus, Kentucky. Yet even then the supply route was still terribly vulnerable. Grant saw this same old pattern playing out the entire distance to Jackson and Vicksburg, still a hundred and fifty miles south of Oxford. Worse, Grant still had the Yocona, Yalobusha, and Big Black Rivers to cross until he reached the state capital, although he could conceivably stop short of Jackson and turn southwestward and wind his way down the corridor of land between the Yazoo and Big Black Rivers, the same high ground on which Vicksburg sat. But such a move still necessitated marching a long distance across several more rivers, all while Pemberton's forces would be gaining rather than losing strength due to his falling back on his base.[40]

Grant consequently began to have different ideas, although still firmly within Jominian theory. "Would it not be well to hold the enemy south of the Yalabusha and move a force from Memphis and Helena on Vicksburg?" he queried Halleck. "If the Helena troops were at my command I think it practicable to send Sherman to take them and Memphis troops south of the mouth of Black [Yazoo] River and thus secure Vicksburg and State of Mississippi." If he sent a portion of his force back to Memphis under Sherman, who would combine this force with recent arrivals as well as part of the garrison at Helena, Arkansas, he could perhaps move southward along the Mississippi River, which was not nearly as susceptible to raids as the railroad and thus did not need guarding to any great degree; the navy could do about all the guarding necessary. Plus, the river was not susceptible to the winter rains whenever they came. It was probably the smarter move to begin with, but Grant decided to put his emphasis on this river-borne effort, while still trudging southward himself, to provide that quintessential supporting column. Hopefully, the Confederates could not defend both. Sherman himself was all in: "With the Yazoo open to us," he wrote, "our land forces could disembark on its east bank on high, fine ground, the same ridge which forms the bluff of Walnut Hills at Vicksburg."[41]

There was another factor in prompting Grant to send Sherman back and make a Mississippi River move as well. President Lincoln had given Major General John A. McClernand, an Illinois politician-general Grant had a hard time liking, charge of a secret mission to raise forces in the North and then lead them down the river to take Vicksburg. It was a major tampering with the current military organization, historian T. Harry Williams labeling it "a wretched mistake and a prize example of poor military planning." McClernand took the assignment and ran with it, raising a force before starting to move southward to Vicksburg. Grant wanted no part of McClernand going rogue in his rightful department, so he sent Sherman to Memphis to gather many of the troops McClernand was sending down. Hurry was on everyone's minds if not on their lips because of the need to get away before McClernand arrived. It was a fast one that Grant and Sherman, and Halleck to a certain degree, was pulling over on McClernand, but then nothing said Grant could not take Vicksburg before McClernand did, thereby resolving the whole problem. Sherman set out on December 20, headed southward eventually with over thirty thousand troops, intent on landing in the very southern portions of the Delta south of the Yazoo River. Then he would advance up the Walnut Hills to get to the coveted high ground east of Vicksburg.[42]

Sherman got away well before McClernand arrived, and Grant planned to continue methodically southward as the railroad became more and more operational, if for nothing else than to be that Jominian supporting column for Sherman. "I am pushing down on them slowly, but so as to keep up the impression of a continuous move," he wrote. Sherman was jubilant: "You may calculate on our being at Vicksburg by Christmas," adding that "there will be no difficulty in effecting a landing up Yazoo within 12 miles of Vicksburg." But then disaster struck in two ways for Grant. First, in mid-December a cavalry raid under Brigadier General Nathan Bedford Forrest struck out from Bragg's army in Middle Tennessee across the Tennessee River and got loose amid the railroads of West Tennessee. It was "a diversion in favor of our army in Mississippi, then heavily pressed by General Grant," Bragg reported. Grant was so concerned about his supply and communication lines that he called a halt to his planned advance until Forrest could be brought to a standstill. Then, worse, another cavalry raid under Major General Earl Van Dorn struck Grant's huge supply center at Holly Springs at dawn on December 20; the attack "came like a thunderbolt from a clear sky," one of Van Dorn's Mississippians related. Van Dorn thoroughly destroyed the logistical hub, which took ready rations from Grant's army. Knowing the blow that it was, Grant ordered a turnaround even that day.[43]

The news only got worse. Van Dorn fled northward but eventually escaped back to Grenada, but Forrest remained on the hunt in West Tennessee, eventually significantly breaking the Mobile and Ohio Railroad where it crossed the Obion River bottoms in northwestern Tennessee. Forrest reported the "destruction of the bridges over the North and South [Main] Fork of Obion River, with nearly four miles of tresling in the bottom between them." The damage was extensive and Forrest escaped even though caught and mauled at Parker's Crossroads. Grant knew now that, with his supply depot gone, any chance of reestablishing it was also ended. The game was up, and Grant ordered his divisions back northward to positions above the Tallahatchie River. "We were much surprised this morning by orders to return.... We felt like we were defeated without a battle—that we were out-generaled some way," an Illinoisan admitted. Grant's part of the campaign was done, and his hopes now hinged on Sherman at Vicksburg.[44]

Those hopes were soon shattered as well as Sherman dawdled in his prong of the attack. First, one of the major ironclads, the *Cairo*, sank to the bottom of the Yazoo River on December 12 as the navy prepared the way for the army's arrival; Confederates would soon locate her grave and seek to "determine whether or not it will be desirable to try to raise the guns." Then, in the Vicksburg area by Christmas Day, which broke up the famous Confederate Christmas Eve ball at the Balfour mansion in Vicksburg, Sherman himself faced daunting problems. He wasted a day damaging a railroad in Louisiana west of the Mississippi River, then landed up the Yazoo River north of Vicksburg on

December 26. But then he wasted two more days in probing forward weakly, making his main attack only on December 29. Brigadier General Stephen D. Lee later remarked that "had Sherman moved a little faster after landing, . . . he could have gone into the city." One of Sherman's own soldiers even admitted that "the same cause that defeated the French army at Waterloo defeated ours at Chickasaw Bayou. Had Napoleon moved his army to battle early in the morning he would have whipped Wellington hours before Blucher arrived; had Sherman immediately upon landing his troops moved upon the enemy's works he could have captured them hours before Pemberton's army arrived to strengthen them." By December 29, when the main assault came, Pemberton had been able to shift troops rapidly from Grenada, where Grant was no longer threatening, to Vicksburg to meet Sherman. The use of interior lines, another Jominian policy, had allowed Pemberton to move troops from the Yalobusha River line to Vicksburg in three days while it took Sherman three weeks to do so. The result was a significantly strengthened Confederate position when Sherman finally got around to attacking.[45]

Yet another factor aided the Confederates, however, and that was the geography. One arriving Confederate marveled at the site, writing that "Vicsburg is the largest sity I ever saw." Plus, on the extreme southern tip of the Delta, the lowlands south of the Yazoo River were inundated and crisscrossed with bayous, creeks, and old channels of the Yazoo River. Sherman found himself in a maze of swamp: "The Yazoo in old times," he wrote, "evidently clung to these hills, and has left old channels or bayous of deep, stagnant water and mud, and the whole triangle is cut up in every conceivable form by these bayous." Watermarks as much as thirty feet above the ground on trees did not help the feeling of isolation. Confusion was rampant, one engineer force even laying a pontoon bridge across the wrong bayou, thinking it was the main one leading to the Confederate position.[46]

The Confederates smartly covered all approachable axes of advance, but there were few. Sherman could land only within the first twelve or so miles on the Yazoo River because of Confederate heavy artillery positioned at Snyder's and Haynes' Bluffs, where the Walnut Hills butted up against the Yazoo River for the first time along its course. Much of the twelve-mile expanse was underwater as well, leaving only a few roadways usable in the center, northeast of Vicksburg. There, on the Blake, Lake, and Johnson Plantations, Sherman disembarked his troops to take Vicksburg. It was, according to Confederate Vicksburg commander Major General Martin L. Smith, "a triangular-shaped area of bottom land, densely wooded, with the exception of one or two plantations on it, and intersected with bayous and low, swampy ground."[47]

Obviously, Sherman had to mount the high Walnut Hills to gain that coveted high ground east of Vicksburg, but the Confederate defense under Brigadier General Stephen D. Lee covered all approaches well, even leaving avenues open for a Union advance just where he wanted them to attack. "All this time we were exposed to a raking crossfire from at least a dozen concealed batteries that they had kept concealed," an attacking Ohioan wrote, adding that "in fact they had us just where they wanted us, and there was a continual buzzing of grape and canister, and shell and musket balls around our ears, and [they] plowed up the ground at our feet." Sherman consequently reaped the worst defeat of his career. In the main attack across Chickasaw Bayou itself on the Lake Plantation Road, the Confederates mowed down assaulting Federals in an extremely lopsided defeat, Sherman suffering 1,776 casualties to only 187 Confederate. "We had tried to take it," a Federal wrote in his diary, "but failed—ingloriously failed." The "white faces" of the dead that shone in the next few days told all that needed to be said. A Confederate put it more bluntly: "Wee have had a battel hear and whipt the Yankees."[48]

At a loss for what to do, Sherman sat tight and pondered his next move; "still the siege of Vicksburg continues," wrote one tired Iowan. Sherman went aboard Flag Officer David Dixon Porter's flagship to talk over their next moves, Porter humorously writing that Sherman "looked as if he had been grappling with the mud, and got the worst of it." He could not attack again, and efforts to find another area of advance were fruitless. So he sat, hoping in vain to hear something of Grant, who himself was in withdrawal mode and nowhere near Sherman. It was a dismal end to the year 1862 that saw the most well-laid plans come to naught. And worse for Grant, McClernand was on the way.[49]

Consequently, the end of the year saw Grant's first two attempts to reach Vicksburg repelled. His own force was huddled with half-rations or less north of the Tallahatchie River, wondering when or if the railroads to their rear would ever be repaired. Sherman sat miserable and cold in the swamps of the Delta, similarly pondering his next move. Only in Vicksburg and Grenada was the near miracle of pulling victory out of the jaws of certain defeat beginning to be realized. Pemberton had somehow managed to repel both major threats, although he had done it with a lot of help from his subordinates. Still, he had been able to parry Grant's first advances with much the same playbook as Grant used—the old Jominian theories of decisive points, interior lines, maneuvering raids, and secure supply lines.[50]

Thus far Pemberton had matched Grant step for step in by-the-book warfare. In fact, one Federal admitted that "we have been beat at our own game this time and no mistake." But the struggle for Vicksburg was not over by any means as long as the aggressive and determined Grant had anything to say about it, and the victory would no doubt go to the one who adapted first and best. And a miserable Grant, sulking in Holly Springs as the year ended, was already beginning to think of throwing out the book or at least modifying its rules to a large degree. This Jominian book of warfare just did not seem well adapted to this particular chessboard of war, complete with a huge alluvial plain sitting directly in the midst of the operations area. It was perhaps time to start thinking outside the book.[51]

2

"CAN THE ENEMY INTEND ANOTHER ATTEMPT TO APPROACH VICKSBURG?"

January 1–10

"I do order and declare that all persons held as slaves within said designated states, and parts of States, are, and henceforward shall be free." With the stroke of a pen on that document known to history as the Emancipation Proclamation, President Abraham Lincoln altered the Civil War forever, ushering in the year 1863 in bold fashion. He had conducted his usual New Year's Day reception, shaking hundreds and perhaps thousands of hands, before going upstairs in the Executive Mansion in Washington, DC, to sign the document. His hand trembled not from fear of the momentous effect of the signature but from the rote action of shaking so many hands. He took a moment to compose himself and his shaking fingers, knowing the eyes of history were on him.[1]

The mood was quite different in Richmond, the Confederate president himself being absent, still on his western trip that saw him tour the very Vicksburg defenses that were about to become so important. Jefferson Davis had traveled to the western theater to boost morale in that quarter, touring the defenses at Vicksburg and Grenada for several days and speaking to the Mississippi legislature in Jackson on December 26 even as Sherman's troops began their disembarkation at Chickasaw Bayou a mere forty miles away. It was certainly different in Richmond this New Year's Day without the president, one War Department clerk, John B. Jones, remarking that "this first day of the year dawned in gloom, but the sun, like the sun of Austerlitz, soon beamed forth in great splendor."[2]

Outside the capitals, military affairs took precedence, although a lot of attention still swirled for months around the proclamation, made known since September but now official, and particularly the idea of black soldiers; one opposed German Federal wrote that it "fell like a thunderbolt among the troops," and another declared the boys were "down on the Proclamation of the President." The former added, "I am sorry the old man forgot himself and took such bad advice." Just as many supported the move, and the topic naturally morphed into discussions of Copperheads and support for the war itself, which many soldiers commented on throughout the first months of 1863. One Federal spoke for many when he explained that "we respect the meanest gray back in the south that has the boldness to come out like men and meet us in open field where we can have a chance to change shots with him." That was in comparison to what he called "the low dastardly cowardly sneaking copper head in the rear and hasen't the face to come out like men but stay home and aid the enemy by incouraging and herbering deserters we scorn all such with utter contempt." The debate became so heated that one Ohioan explained, "I look for an *order* to be issued prohibiting the discussing of politics among the soldiers." While the Federals debated policy, many Confederates were just worried about survival, one Louisianan writing "the New Year is upon us and still I see no immediate prospect of a termination of our troubles. Is it possible that this horrid war must continue through the tedious months of another year, counting its victims by the hundreds of thousands."[3]

Nevertheless, the huge armies in Virginia still watched one another across the Rappahannock River near Fredericksburg, while in Middle Tennessee a lull between two harsh days of battle at Stones River allowed everyone to catch their breaths, though it was a cold and miserable existence amid snow and ice. In northern Mississippi, Grant's half-starved army huddled in cold camps north of the Tallahatchie River, aware that they had been beaten if not on the field of battle then on the great chessboard of war. To their north, Nathan Bedford Forrest was still on the rampage, although he was brought to battle the day before and nearly captured, he escaping only by the slimmest of margins; still, he was headed for an escape this day back across the Tennessee River. Farther south on the banks of Chickasaw Bayou, Sherman's troops prepared for their withdrawal, likewise well aware that they had been beaten, this time on the battlefield. Pemberton's troops still sat high and dry in Vicksburg, he having parried every threat and his troops having gained some confidence in this Northerner now in command of them.[4]

On this day seen as a certain rite of passage, many looked back over the last year with all its harshness and bloodshed from Shiloh to Antietam. Others looked forward, not knowing what would come. It was perhaps merciful no one at that point knew of the carnage the Gettysburgs and Chickamaugas would entail in the coming year, starting even the next day with the resumption of the fighting at Stones River. Still, there was a clear indication this day that something was about to happen in the Mississippi Valley, mainly because on the way southward even now was a new factor in the command structure of the Federal forces. Major General John A. McClernand had managed to pry orders for his movement to Memphis from a delaying Halleck and, amid taking time to marry his deceased wife's younger sister (he was fifty, she twenty-six), moved southward with his new bride for a honeymoon with the army, certainly every young new bride's wish. Nevertheless McClernand had an army to command and, after arriving at Memphis and waving his papers from Stanton and Lincoln in everyone's face, continued on southward aboard a chartered vessel to take command of his army from Sherman. Despite the seething disgust within the army toward Sherman, one of the soldiers below was not excited the first time he saw McClernand either, writing in his diary, "I saw Gel McClernand today for the first time: was not much impressed." Yet McClernand's movement was both an indication of coming action as well as command turmoil. "Two commanders on the same field are always one too many," Grant observed, "and in this case I did not think the general selected had either the experience or the qualifications to fit him for so important a position."[5]

Matters were not likely to stall in the Mississippi Valley just because a new year had dawned. Nor were they to slow because the last two efforts to reach Vicksburg had failed miserably, nor that winter had set in with all its wetness and fury. The ever-aggressive McClernand, whether in love, war, or politics, would no doubt shake things up around Vicksburg once more.

John C. Pemberton started off the new year on a high note. "The Yankees have all left the swamp," one Confederate explained, while another added "the Yankees have left us again, but how long they will stay away is to be seen." Pemberton had come west in early October with a lot of baggage but was quickly gaining ground with his troops. He was a Pennsylvanian to start with, and unlike many others he had not come south years before and made his home here. He married a Virginia girl but had relatively little connection with the Confederacy besides a wife adamant that he join the South; in fact, he had family members in the Union army, including brothers. His dedication would always be in question, although it was solid. Far worse, Pemberton had little to no experience commanding troops in active campaigning or certainly in battle. He came from a South Carolina administrative command, and once in Mississippi, that seemed to be where he felt most comfortable.[6]

The new commander of the Department of Mississippi and East Louisiana ran into trouble immediately. As he surveyed his department from his

Jackson headquarters, which one Confederate explained was "quite a poore place—the city is very much scattered, & most of the houses quite shabby," he dealt with problems innumerable. As a major general, he had been tasked with commanding in Mississippi once Van Dorn and Major General Sterling Price invaded Tennessee and Kentucky, where Van Dorn would command a new department while Pemberton oversaw the one in Mississippi. But Van Dorn got no farther than Corinth and by mid-October was back in Mississippi. That put the departmental commander junior to the field army commander, and Pemberton quickly complained that "the circumstances under which I was ordered to the command of this department have been so much changed by movements of the enemy in the State of Mississippi that it is now impossible to carry out instructions given me." Jefferson Davis fixed that quickly by fast-tracking Pemberton's promotion to lieutenant general through the Confederate Senate.[7]

But the first impressions for Pemberton were not good, many of his officers casting wondering glances at him. "I am afraid Pemberton won't do," one of his top generals wrote; "his ideas are too scattering—this 'Entre nous.'" Another hit him with "Pemberton is nothing" and labeled other officers as "a very poor set." He concluded that "there is no man here equal to the requirement of our case; which is a pretty bad case.... I am sick of this Army." Even some in Richmond were shaken, the continual rumors that Vicksburg had fallen appearing in the Northern papers with regularity. War Department clerk John B. Jones took exception to Pemberton's Northern birth, writing that "Northern man that he is, if Pemberton suffers disaster by any default, he will certainly incur the President's eternal displeasure." He later confided in his diary that "well, Mississippi is the President's State, and if he is satisfied with Northern generals to defend it, he is as likely to be benefited as any one else."[8]

The common soldiers gave Pemberton the benefit of the doubt. "He seemed to be about forty-five, or perhaps a little older," one Missourian related, "scarcely six feet in height, and of rather slender proportions, with dark eyes and hair—a high forehead, thin visage and regular features; he wore a heavy moustache, and whiskers closely trimmed; his face was considerably furrowed with lines, either of care or age: he appeared well on horseback, and seemed perfectly at ease in the saddle." Others remarked on his obvious administrative ability, a newspaper reporting that "no officer ever devoted himself with greater assiduity to his duties. Late and early he is at his office, laboring incessantly." Yet once the fall campaign started and Pemberton began to fall back through Holly Springs, Oxford, and to Grenada, people began to wonder, especially about his almost obsessive desire to remain in Jackson at departmental headquarters rather than with the army during the crises. Van

Dorn bluntly told him "it is advisable that you should come here as soon as possible. Events are gathering near. You cannot be here too soon to prepare for action under whatever policy you may see fit to adopt." Later, he wrote, "not being in command and having to refer to Jackson[,] you should be here to assume control. Don't you think so?" Obviously, at a desk is where Pemberton felt most comfortable.[9]

Staying in Jackson of course brought Van Dorn back into the picture, and the Mississippian was one of several subordinates Pemberton soon had trouble with. Van Dorn was rightly chagrined at losing his command: "I shall act for the best, but I am now an isolated body in the field in Mississippi, relieved of command of my department." But his reputation preceded him, one Mississippi senator assuring the president that rumors of his "negligence, whoring, and drunkenness" were true and that "an acquittal by a court-martial of angels would not relieve him of the charge." The other commanders were not a stellar bunch, either. Sterling Price and his trans-Mississippians continually begged to be sent home, although one realistic Missourian admitted "we have given up all hope of getting back to Missouri this Year. I expect to spend the winter in Dixie." Major General Mansfield Lovell, despite assurances that "I have no reason to be dissatisfied with the part that my troops took in this battle [Corinth], and think that the official reports will do me full justice," was so under scrutiny for his role at Corinth and even in abandoning New Orleans earlier that he was soon relieved of command.[10]

And the command problems did not just go down the chain to Pemberton's subordinates. He was also having major trouble with his departmental commander, General Joseph E. Johnston, with whom he seemed to have opposing views of warfare. President Davis had brought Johnston with him from Middle Tennessee in late December to tour Vicksburg and the other defenses, and Johnston remained in Mississippi much to the chagrin of Pemberton, who no doubt wished Johnston would return to Middle Tennessee. Pemberton and Johnston never could, and never would, seem to get on the same page in terms of command. The two could hardly even communicate, Johnston haranguing Pemberton that "you have been three times asked . . . ," to which Pemberton testily replied "I considered it necessary to understand your telegram in cipher before answering it." It was not a good working relationship from the beginning.[11]

The Pemberton–Johnston disconnect would of course grow to momentous proportions as the campaign unfolded, but at this point Johnston proved the more unreasonable commander. "I respectfully request you to communicate to me the substance of all the orders you may give for movement of troops, and as much as practicable to confer with me before giving them." Pemberton probably wondered why he was even there if Johnston was to make the decisions. Yet Johnston was no bold commander, he already this early in the campaign displaying his lack of interest and wish not to even be here. "Your position at Vicksburg is most important, however it interferes with the supervision of other parts of the department," Johnston lectured. "You are aware, I believe, that I was brought here by the President to assist you. My great object is to do so." But it was clear Johnston had little interest in Mississippi, as he was already displaying his defeatist attitude that would appear more and more often in the coming months. In fact, he wrote Richmond of the developments immediately after the first of the year and added directly to the president, "should the enemy's forces be respectably handled the task you have set me will be above my ability. But the hand of Almighty God has delivered us in times of as great danger. Believing that He is with us I will not lose hope." But it sure sounded as though he had. He added a few days later that "the impossibility of my knowing condition of things in Tennessee shows that I cannot direct both parts of my command at once."[12]

Still, Pemberton had somehow managed to thwart the fall/winter Union advances, on two fronts no less. He was of course in command in the department, and many relieved Confederates began to have a little different opinion of their new general. But in truth, a lot of the success had stemmed from his subordinates, whether it was Forrest or Van Dorn and their raids or even those who conceived of the plans to begin with, which Pemberton did not in either case. Likewise, it was Stephen D. Lee who fought and won the fight at Chickasaw Bayou. In addition, the scope and size of the chessboard on which Pemberton and Grant were struggling benefited the inexperienced and indecisive Pemberton in that it took a long time, sometimes weeks, for plans to develop and operations to ensue, which gave the slow and methodical Pemberton time to react. A smaller area of operations and a faster timeline might have proven more than he could handle. Nevertheless, Pemberton had overseen the whole and started the new year in much better standing than when he had entered the department back in October. His departmental commander Johnston, in fact, wrote in a seldom word of praise, "Lieutenant-General Pemberton deserves high credit." Pemberton himself deflected the congratulations to his soldiers: "All praise is due them, not alone for so bravely repulsing the renewed assaults of the enemy vastly superior in numbers, but equally for the cheerful and patient endurance with which they have submitted to the hardships and exposure."[13]

But the crisis was not over by any means, Jefferson Davis himself now back in Richmond writing, "I can hardly suppose the campaign abandoned, but of this you can best judge." The smoke from the Federal flotilla that could still be plainly seen in the river north of the city was ample testimony. Johnston similarly queried Pemberton, "Can the enemy intend another attempt to approach Vicksburg?" Pemberton and his commanders thus watched and waited in the early days of 1863 over a wide front with numerous exposed points. The most obvious crisis point was still at Chickasaw Bayou, where Sherman's force remained on land throughout this New Year's Day and evidently had a large operation planned for that very morning at Snyder's Bluff, although it did not develop. No one in the Confederate force knew Sherman was even then planning a withdrawal, which he accomplished that night, so nervous glances were frequent toward the Union lines as the first day of 1863 wore on. "All quiet in front," Major General Carter Stevenson, now commanding out at the battlefield, informed his superiors. "The enemy are engaged in constructing rifle-pits near the lake in front of Barton's brigade."[14]

Still thinking the major crisis point was at Chickasaw Bayou and Snyder's Bluff, Pemberton ordered even more troops to the Vicksburg area from Grenada, mainly the Texas cavalry brigade. But this order only prompted another round of miscommunication with Johnston. The departmental commander desired infantry to move, but Pemberton, severely lacking cavalry, wished for more mounted troops and thus desired the Texans. "Direct all of the Texas regiments of cavalry to march at once to Snyder's Mill, on the Yazoo River," he ordered on January 1. "Let the movement be as rapid as possible."[15]

But then came good news the very next day, January 2. Not only did Major General William W. Loring commanding at Grenada send word that Grant was rapidly falling back across the Tallahatchie River in northern Mississippi; word also arrived of Sherman's withdrawal, which allowed the Confederate defenders to exit their wet and muddy trenches and return to more comfortable camp life. Stevenson and Lee followed up all the way to the Yazoo River banks and skirmishing ensued, but it was clear the Federals were clearing out. "Information just received indicates re-embarkation of the enemy from my front," Pemberton notified Johnston. Pemberton accordingly countermanded the order for more troops at Vicksburg. In fact, new word arrived of some type of operation up around Moon Lake in the Delta, and Pemberton then ordered the Texans to ride in that direction, to "move to the rear of the enemy, drive him from his position, capture his artillery, and do him all the damage otherwise in your power." Obviously, Pemberton realized the capability of a cavalry raid in the rear of the enemy, and he continued to utilize this Jominian concept in his defense. At odds once more, however, Johnston desired Van Dorn to return from his leave with his family in Alabama to lead the raid, Brigadier General William H. Jackson commanding the cavalry in his absence. "It will be necessary to make another cavalry dash," Johnston wrote Van Dorn at Mobile; "come in time to overtake him." Johnston confided to President Davis that "my hope of keeping him [Grant] back is in Van Dorn, under whom I propose to unite all the available cavalry." Apparently, Johnston had little hope in Pemberton, but nothing ever came of the cavalry dash either.[16]

Most important for the troops who had defended Vicksburg at Chickasaw Bayou, the influx of fresh regiments allowed the worn-out defenders to have a break. William Pitt Chambers of the 46th Mississippi related the joy he had when ordered to camp. The regiment moved along an intolerably muddy road, but many were the jests. Invariably, someone would "amuse . . . themselves, near the *real* slippery places, by calling to some imaginary person *up a tree* and seeing some fellow lose his footing, as he looked upward while walking along." But the lack of Federals in sight did not foster a feeling of permanent safety, one Alabaman writing home that there was "no enemy in sight, but still we are not idle, for it seems that we are doomed to have a tremendous fight at this place yet."[17]

But while Pemberton looked to his most assailable front, he also kept close watch on the rest of his department. "I want to re-enforce Port Hudson," he explained to Johnston, and did so once Sherman's withdrawal was confirmed and he could spare some of the troops. Brigadier General John Gregg's brigade soon shipped out southward. He also looked to his neighboring departments for aid, sending "forthwith a reliable person across the river to communicate with our army in Arkansas, to ascertain whether there be any movements of our army there connected with ours on this side." A curt message arrived from Arkansas that "no troops will be sent," and Johnston complained directly to Richmond that "I think that we are to get no help from that side of the Mississippi." Johnston even queried, "Will the great victory at Fredericksburg enable General Lee to spare a part of his force?"[18]

Foremost in Pemberton's mind was his defense of his crown jewel, Vicksburg. He knew that, even as Grant operated on the periphery, eventually the fighting would come down to the city itself and he wanted plenty of stores gathered inside the citadel for that very instance. Johnston was already sounding off about the lack of stores and Pemberton's underestimation of what was needed. Pemberton set his goal as "stores required for 10,000 men for five months," and his commissary officer, Major T. B. Reed, was making good progress on many items but was still in need of bacon, salt, rice, coffee, and flour, among other articles such as candles and soap. As a good indication of his already-developing determination to hold Vicksburg as opposed to anything else, Pemberton had all the commissary stores moved from departmental headquarters at Jackson into Vicksburg itself. Carter Stevenson, now the ranking general below Pemberton and in charge of the Vicksburg area, got in on the stockpiling, intending to gather as much as he could "if it is intended to hold Vicksburg to the last extremity." Now in command at Vicksburg itself, he also sounded the alarm on the left, south of Vicksburg, "should they land below." It was a significant warning that obviously went unheeded.[19]

For the common Confederate soldier, however, the quieting of the armies could not alleviate a morale blow, especially in the muddy winter weather. One wrote home that "the opinion is that they have gone to some other point." One Mississippian wrote home of his gloom: "I am sure while the rainy and gloomy weather lasted that more than half our soldiers thought the Southern Confederacy was not worth fighting for." He went on to elaborate:

> We are still lying here wholly inactive, the roads are impassable, and Big Black is in a condition not to be forded at least. The Yankees are entirely quiet, indeed everything is distressingly quiet, we look anxiously for the papers, daily hoping something will turn up some where, but nothing stirs, save the cavalry, they seem to be doing some thing occasionally. All we do here is to sit around our fires and ask each other, where and when the campaign will open, the ground is too wet and muddy to drill and we are all getting too lazy to even have a Dress Parade.[20]

But Pemberton and many of his troops were still somewhat upbeat in their assessment of his departmental command in the first few days of January; one Mississippian wrote that "this place is strongly fortified and [has] the biggest hills that I ever saw." Pemberton related to Secretary of War James A. Seddon that "Vicksburg is daily growing stronger. We intend to hold it." And with word that Sherman was gone back to the Mississippi River and Grant was continually falling back even to the Memphis and Charleston Railroad, matters looked much better. Pemberton still had a good layer of defense, some fifteen thousand troops present for duty at Grenada under Loring and another twenty thousand or so around Vicksburg, with others doled out in other areas of the department such as Port Hudson.[21]

Yet there was also an ominous air about headquarters, all knowing that Grant would not give up so easily. "To hold the Mississippi is vital," Jefferson Davis himself counseled. How long this lull between advances on Vicksburg would last was not known, and Confederate officers required troops on guard at the city's waterfront at all times. One Mississippian explained that "we were required to repair to the city at 2 o'clock every third or fourth morning. This was soon changed to every alternate morning. The object we were told was to guard against any surprise the enemy might attempt." Anyone who knew the real Grant probably knew he would not be long in returning. In fact, it seemed to be already starting as the second week of January came; Pemberton received a January 10 dispatch from Loring at Grenada with threatening possibilities: "Scouts report that ninety boats have passed the mouth of White River going up the Mississippi, on the 6th and 7th." At first indication it seemed like a major withdrawal, but the underlying overtones were anything but that.[22]

No such joy accompanied Sherman's beaten Federal army as it withdrew out of the swamps of the Yazoo River in early January, although one Union soldier admitted, "right glad were we to get back on our own boat." Another simply scribbled in his diary "we have been beat at our own game this time and no mistake" before adding "[but] should like to know what we are going to do." Others felt the same tension. "I have passed through some trying times," one Federal wrote his wife. "I would much rather be at home than here but duty says here is my place and I will try and do my duty." But it hurt. He added that "we have gained nothing and lost a great deal many valuable lives."[23]

But a new effort was under way, one that inspired some confidence in the beaten Federals. "We pulled out and left them, but we are going back later and there will be a different story to tell next time," one Illinoisan explained. Yet the irony was that this newly detected Federal operation was not Grant's doing at all. The first week of January saw a befuddled Grant falling back from his positions in northern Mississippi, plagued by short rations, broken supply lines, and rumors of invasion and raids all over the map. His soldiers were no more enlightened, they wondering at the sudden reverse but knowing full well it was all because of Van Dorn and the disaster at Holly Springs. Few knew anything about the additional destruction farther north, but Grant was well aware of it and pondered his bleak situation. In all the chaos, it was a given that the advance along the Mississippi Central was at an end. These by-the-book operations just did not seem to work in this particular environment.[24]

Perhaps the worst parts of the chaos were the rumors that continually floated around, certainly of additional cavalry north of Grant's newly established lines along the Memphis and Charleston Railroad. "There were indications of a rebel force a few miles north of this place last night," Brigadier General Charles Hamilton informed Grant from La Grange on New Year's Day, "and confirmed this morning." Who it was no one knew, as Van Dorn and Forrest were both accounted for, although rumors of their future activity surged as well.[25]

Equally concerning was the ration situation. "Been on one half rations for ten days," one Illinoisan wrote forebodingly in his diary, adding that he was "not near so fat as I was during the summer." With the Mobile and Ohio broken in northwestern Tennessee and the ready foodstuffs at Holly Springs destroyed, Grant's troops were on half-rations or worse and the prospects of getting much of anything other than by foraging were not that promising. Hamilton added that same day that he was sending a party toward Somerville to "see if Somerville bacon is good." His mention of burning mills in the area to deprive whatever Confederates were nearby brought a quick correction from Grant: "I would forage off the neighborhood of Somerville, but destroy nothing, not even the mills. We can use all they have." An Illinoisan soon mentioned four mills at work "rigged to run by horse power."[26]

Then there was the larger context of departmental operations Grant had to worry about in addition to his own miserable situation in northern Mississippi. Fallout from the expulsion of the Jews back in December was still occurring, even with Congress getting involved. Yet highest on his list of concerns was Sherman at Vicksburg. Rumor after rumor floated in, first that Sherman had actually taken Vicksburg, but then worse news began to emerge, it growing worse the more that arrived. "Vicksburg is not taken," Grant informed Hamilton on January 1, but there was still indications of some progress. Word had come from Brigadier General Willis A. Gorman at Helena that Sherman had had some success: "Captured their main fort on Walnut Hills at point of bayonet," which was of course untrue, but also that he had suffered heavy casualties, as many as three thousand. While the damage assessment would not be quite that high, although high enough, the success was also overblown, and it was soon realized Sherman had achieved no progress whatsoever. Grant admitted in all the confusion, "Vicksburg is ours or Sherman is whipped before this." The latter proved to be the case.[27]

While he did not have a good assessment of anything outside his own force because of cut communication lines everywhere, Grant knew what had to be done with his own force. Little was likewise known of the Confederate intentions at Grenada, McPherson complaining that scouts were not very responsive and "the citizens generally don't know anything, and when they do are not to be trusted, unless corroborated from other sources." McPherson was especially worried about his lone brigade still south of the Tallahatchie River under Colonel Mortimer D. Leggett, he arguing that "there is nothing left at Abbeville, and the rebel fortifications on the south side have been leveled down by the contrabands." That the river was rising was another concern for the brigade's safety, as it might not be able to get across in the near future. But Grant cautioned McPherson not to destroy the newly rebuilt railroad bridge: "We may want it; at least we will keep up the appearance of wanting it." At the least, contrabands tore down the Confederate fortifications on the south side of the river and built newer and better ones on the north side for the Union defense.[28]

But it was not a crisis per se militarily, as the best indications Grant could get was that the Confederates at Grenada had mainly "gone south" and "those remaining are still fortifying." It did not look like a major operation by the Confederate army at Grenada was in the future, but rumors continued to plague Grant that small numbers of Confederates, most likely partisans or guerrilla bands, were to his north. But guerrillas could break railroads just as good as regulars, and Grant ordered additional stockades built at "every military post or station." He also began a retribution campaign: "I am taking measures to clean out the country from here to Memphis of all guerillas," he wrote Major General Stephen A. Hurlbut from Holly Springs on January 2; "if it cannot be done in any other way I will be compelled to take and destroy the last bushel of grain between the Hatchie and the Tallahatchie, and all the stock. I will make it the interest of the citizens to leave our lines of communication unmolested." Grant meant business, ordering Brigadier General Isaac Quinby, the division commander between him and Memphis, to "give notice to the citizens on the road to Memphis that if necessary to secure the railroad every family and every vestige of property, except land itself, between the Hatchie and the Coldwater will be removed out of these limits or confiscated." To Hurlbut, his commander in Memphis, Grant added:

> I will also move south every family in Memphis of doubtful loyalty, whether they have taken the oath of allegiance or not, if it is necessary for our security, and you can so notify them. For every raid or attempted raid by guerillas upon the road I want ten families of the most noted secessionists sent south. If the enemy, with his regularly-organized forces, attack us I do not propose to punish non-combatant citizens for it; but these guerillas receive support and countenance from this class of citizens, and by their acts will bring punishment upon them.[29]

Then over the course of the next few days, an even more major threat developed as rumors of another huge cavalry raid from Pontotoc under Van Dorn emerged. Van Dorn of course was on leave, and when he returned it was not for the purpose of raiding but moving the majority of the cavalry in Mississippi eastward into Tennessee. But the perceived threat was there anyway, and Grant had learned exactly what Van Dorn could do and wanted no part of a second raid. Forrest was also poised to recross the Tennessee River and make another raid, or so Grant thought. Fears of another attack on Corinth also emerged, with wild rumors that even part of Braxton Bragg's "whipped" army was retreating west of the Tennessee River. Grant asked his commanders to scout and make sure "flat-boats and other craft for crossing the Tennessee River hid away at the mouths of streams emptying into the Tennessee" were located and destroyed.[30]

Eventually, the ration situation eased somewhat, but Grant was still at a standstill as the first couple weeks of January came and went. Halleck wanted to know more detail about the valley operations, which Grant could not always provide. "Give us the earliest possible information of affairs at Vicksburg," Halleck wrote, "as movement of troops here depends upon the capture of that place." He added later that newspapers from Richmond reported as early as January 5 and 6 that "Sherman has been defeated and repulsed from Vicksburg." He finished with the admonition "we must not fail in this if within human power to accomplish it."[31]

Grant certainly did not squelch any human aid for Sherman at Vicksburg. He knew little of McClernand's plan, even sending all the ammunition he had southward to Sherman, some 230,000 rounds. Grant also planned to send reinforcements without delay, as many as fifteen thousand of them, he gathering vessels and forwarding on down the river a newly arrived brigade from the East under Brigadier General Hugh Ewing, Sherman's brother-in-law; the Easterners were out of place, obviously, but reveled in the beauty of the Mississippi River and its valley.[32]

But worse news continued to arrive from his south, and Sherman's operations were soon taken over by McClernand. As a result, Grant began to realize that the two-pronged advance, with two commanders (one of which was the newly arrived McClernand), was a formula for disaster, and there was enough of that to go around already. He thus began to make the movement singularly along the river, starting his own troops in a slow shift westward toward Memphis. He also ordered Holly Springs abandoned as early as January 8, contingent on the removal of "all public stores, sick, &c.," or all that was left after the Van Dorn raid. But most important, Grant himself (along with McPherson's XVII Corps) moved west to Memphis to "regulate matters. I am told that things are going at loose ends there." Grant had gotten word that Sherman was returning upriver at least to Napoleon, Arkansas, which was a bad sign. It would only be taken as a significant reverse among the newspapers and politicians. He had to do something to stop the bleeding.[33]

And the bad turns needed to be stopped, as they just kept on developing. Worse than anything else, firm news also arrived that McClernand had taken command at Vicksburg. Grant wrote McClernand on January 10 from Memphis that "since General Sherman left here I have been unable to learn anything official from the expedition which you now command. Your wants and requirements all have to be guessed at." He informed McClernand that he was sending a brigade from Ohio (Ewing's), a brigade from Helena, and an entire division from his own army, with possibly another if needed. He also ordered McClernand to ask Flag Officer Porter to send gunboats to ferry them southward. Grant ended with the admonition that "this expedition must not fail. If there is force enough within the limits of my control to secure a certain victory at Vicksburg they will be sent there. But I want to be advised of what has been done, what there is to contend against, and an estimate of what is required."[34]

Grant was obviously not comfortable with the situation, but he saw little else that could be done right now other than to head directly to Memphis "to attend to all wants of the expedition." He assured Halleck that he was still focused on the main goal: "I will start for Memphis immediately, and will do everything possible for the capture of Vicksburg." That was a strong face he was showing, but he privately wrote Admiral Porter the next day, January 10: "I have not had one word officially from the expedition which left Helena on the 22d December since that time, and am consequently very much at a loss to know how to proceed."[35]

Grant would have been even more perplexed had he actually known what was going on down south with Sherman and McClernand. The very same day he was writing about not knowing what to do except reinforce McClernand for operations against Vicksburg, McClernand was actually far up into Arkansas of all places about to attack a Confederate fort in preparation to advance on Little Rock, the state capital. McClernand was going the exact opposite way from Vicksburg. "It is hoped we will have better luck than we had at Vicksburg," an unconvinced Federal wrote his wife. Another was less concerned: "We are now making our way up the River somewhere I cannot tell where as yet, nor I don't care much."[36]

McClernand had arrived in Memphis a week or so late to command the original expedition against Vicksburg, just a day in fact before Sherman assaulted at Chickasaw Bayou. He nevertheless staked his territorial claim to command, sending staff officers cross-country to Grant at Holly Springs to verify his authority (showing his original orders endorsed by Lincoln himself), but more so subtly warning Grant not to interfere with him. After a couple of days at Memphis, McClernand chartered a vessel and sped on downriver to take his command. Ironically, the boat he acquired was none other than the *Tigress*, Grant's old headquarters boat during the Shiloh Campaign. Whether McClernand thought he was figuratively replacing Grant is not known.[37]

Arriving at the mouth of the Yazoo River on January 2, McClernand immediately let it be known that he was in control. He looked over the situation for a couple days, sizing up everyone and everything, and took formal command only on January 4. By that time, he had made both friends and enemies. Admiral Porter, it seemed, would not be a fan, while Sherman, chagrined to say the least at being replaced, nevertheless cooperated in an effort to get along. Sherman had earlier hedged his bets in the Grant–Halleck turmoil, staying friendly with both to see who would come out on top, and he did the same thing here, although he was firmly in Grant's corner. Still, he needed to work with McClernand cordially for the good of the country as well as his own fortune. For their part, much of the army was glad of the change. "Although I know but little of the new Commander of this Army, General McClernand," one lieutenant colonel wrote home, "I have nevertheless most implicit confidence in him, while for our old Commander [Sherman] I had nothing but contempt and detestation and looked upon him as utterly unfit to lead an Army."[38]

Much of the angst against Sherman obviously came from the Chickasaw Bayou debacle, but the army was finally out from the dingy morass, having evacuated during the night on January 1. Orders had gone out to "at once stop fortifying and intrenching of your present positions, and without noise have everything pertaining to your brigade loaded, packed, and moved back to the boats." The army thus quietly slipped away, although some minor skirmishing erupted soon after daylight as the Confederates followed up; they actually fired into some of the Union boats as they departed. The transports and gunboats made their way out to the wider expanses of the Mississippi River, where everyone could figuratively breathe a little better, Lieutenant Colonel Marcus Spiegel admitting that "the only successful part of the operation was *the evacuation*." But there Sherman, Porter, and everyone else met McClernand, and Sherman realized the game they had been playing was up. There is no doubt that Grant and Sherman, as well as Halleck, desired to delay McClernand long enough and to rush Sherman enough to grab Vicksburg without McClernand being involved. McClernand informed Secretary of War Edwin M. Stanton, in fact, that "either through the intention of the General-in-Chief or a strange occurrence of accidents, the authority of the President and yourself, as evidenced by your acts, has been set at naught, and I have been deprived of the command that had been committed to me."[39]

McClernand was an astute politician, however, and did not get to his current position for no reason. He knew he had to be careful and accordingly tried to befriend Porter and Sherman as best he could. It did not work well with Porter, who refused to be coddled, but Sherman, who knew McClernand from Shiloh and Corinth, was more cordial. In fact, McClernand began the survey of his new army and reported to Washington on January 3 that the defeat at Vicksburg was not necessarily Sherman's fault. He laid the blame on several issues, such as the delay once landed and the disorganization of the army that did land, which were indeed Sherman's fault, but he also included Grant's failure to perform his part of the plan as well as even those Federals in Louisiana and elsewhere. Still, McClernand went to great lengths to mention that placing blame solely on Sherman "would do injustice to General Sherman, whom I deem, indeed know, to be a brave and meritorious officer. He has probably done all in the present case that any one could have done, and I would not detract anything from him, but give him all credit for good purposes, which unfortunately failed in execution." In his haste to exonerate Sherman, McClernand overlooked many problems Sherman himself had caused.[40]

McClernand had no intention of dwelling on the past, however, and instead looked to new operations that had already congealed in his mind. As he wrote from the *Tigress* during a heavy rainfall on January 3 at Milliken's Bend, he already had in motion his first move as army commander while at the same time trying to deflect any more competition. He added to his long missive to Stanton that "if I am asked for a plan by which Vicksburg might yet be taken I would suggest that General Grant immediately make Memphis his base of operations, put the Mississippi and Tennessee Railroad from Memphis toward Grenada in running order, and push forward his column to the latter place and to Jackson, marching upon the rear of Vicksburg, while the forces here and those below Port Hudson co-operate by such demonstrations as may be found practicable." It was a logical military plan based firmly on the Jominian theories of war, and Sherman himself would advocate for such a plan for months. But it also had the advantage of keeping Grant busy far away from Vicksburg, effectively out of McClernand's way while he sought to capture the city himself.[41]

Such a plan, if it ever really came to it, would take time of course, and McClernand had more intermediate goals in the meantime. Taking command of the forces on January 4, after he had "verified the condition of the army," McClernand started his offensive. He did so by issuing his orders taking command, he writing Sherman that the orders from Grant back in December "requires me to take command of all the land forces of every kind forming the Mississippi River Expedition," which they did not. Supposedly acting according to Grant's order, McClernand divided the army, which he named the "Army of the Mississippi," into two corps, the First Corps commanded by himself and the Second Corps under Sherman (the army-wide numbering of corps had not been implemented yet, at which time McClernand's would become the XIII Corps and Sherman's the XV Corps). The naming of the army differentiated it from Grant's Army of the Tennessee, and more underhanded chaos emerged when McClernand declared that, because he would command the whole ("desiring to give my undivided attention to matters affecting the general command"), the First Corps would go to the senior division commander, Brigadier General George W. Morgan. Of course, it was Morgan whom Sherman was already blaming for the defeat at Chickasaw Bayou, so having a near enemy who was also his junior in command of the corps above him was a backhanded slap in the face for Sherman to be sure. Nevertheless, Morgan took control of his own division, now under just-arrived Brigadier General Peter J. Osterhaus, who was the only general in the division, as well as Brigadier General A. J. Smith's while Sherman's corps consisted of Brigadier General Frederick Steele's and Brigadier General David Stuart's, which was Brigadier General Morgan L. Smith's until his wound at Chickasaw Bayou. One of Osterhaus's officers simply noted, "I hope he is as good a man as Morgan."[42]

Sherman's reaction was muted publicly but visceral privately, he writing his senator brother, "Mr. Lincoln intended to insult me and the military profession by putting McClernand over me." In fact, he added, "I have never dreamed of so severe a test of my patriotism as being superseded by McClernand." Publicly, Sherman simply issued orders that he would now command the new corps, calling on his troops to respect the decisions made about command. Yet even in these orders there was a tinge of animosity, Sherman writing that "a new commander is now here to lead you. He is chosen by the President of the United States, who is charged by our Constitution to maintain and defend it, and he has the undoubted right to select his own agents. I know that all good officers and soldiers will give him the same hearty support and cheerful obedience they have hitherto given me." Sherman also took the opportunity to explain away some of the defeat, writing that "we failed in accomplishing one great purpose of our movement—the capture of Vicksburg, but we were but a part of a whole. Ours was but one part of a combined movement, in which others were to assist. We were on time; unforeseen contingencies must have delayed the others." He added "we have destroyed the Shreveport [rail]road; we have attacked the defenses of Vicksburg, and pushed the attack as far as prudence would justify; and having found it too strong for our single column, we have drawn off in good order and in good spirits, ready for any new move."[43]

That new move was already in the works. The flotilla moved northward and stopped at Milliken's Bend, one soldier writing home, "I doant know what the Motive is for stoping at this place." But there was no disembarkation. "The troops will not disembark at Milliken's Bend," McClernand wrote in his new orders, "but will proceed on another important military expedition." Carrying some of the dead from Chickasaw Bayou and a few contrabands, some of whom suffocated in the engine rooms of the steamboats and were simply dumped overboard, many thought they were heading back to Memphis. One Federal wrote on January 9 that "we have been one week today on the retreat from Vicksburg" and later mentioned the "retreat which we accomplished *so well*." One Illinoisan even believed they were heading back to Quincy to recruit. But the army would instead move northward on the river to the White/Arkansas Rivers, rendezvousing at Gaines' Landing, and then move up the Arkansas River to attack Arkansas Post. It was clearly the opposite direction from Vicksburg, which McClernand's orders he was so proud of stated was his goal, but he had clearly been thinking of this move for a while now. On his way down to Milliken's Bend, in fact, McClernand stopped at Helena and met, and acquired a promise of support from, General Gorman there for the operation. When Sherman put the same idea forward, it was a done deal. In fact, Sherman had already planned just such a move: Porter later wrote Sherman that "you proposed it to me on the night you embarked the troops [at Chickasaw Bayou]."[44]

Sherman had in fact gone to McClernand's headquarters boat *Tigress* and "asked leave" to attack the Confederate garrison at Arkansas Post. He had with him an escapee from the ammunition and supply steamboat *Blue Wing* that had recently been captured by the Confederates based there, one Federal describing them as "rascally pirates." Sherman related that McClernand "made various objections," but they may have been made for show because McClernand was already thinking in those terms. Both generals then went to get Porter's permission to have gunboats attend them and found Porter "in *deshabille*." Porter was extremely "curt" to McClernand, prompting Sherman to take him to the side, where the admiral admitted "he did not like him." But Porter acquiesced, adding "suppose I go along myself."[45]

McClernand had to be careful, knowing he was going against the grain, one Federal even blaming him for the retreat from Vicksburg. He informed Sherman, Porter, and Grant all about his plans, mentioning only Arkansas Post and couching it in terms of protecting the supply line that was the Mississippi River. As the *Blue Wing* had in fact been attacked on the river near the mouths of the two tributary rivers, it allowed McClernand to use that as justification. He also mentioned other issues, such as keeping his army busy while Grant retooled for future operations to the north.[46]

But it is clear that McClernand had ulterior motives, not the least of which was to win a victory of his own without Grant to show Grant and the world, but mainly Washington, that he could indeed command the army and win victories. He smartly started with low-hanging fruit such as Arkansas Post. Yet there was more to the plan that McClernand did not divulge to the Grant camp, namely continuing on up the Arkansas River after the capture of the fort and taking Little Rock itself, the Arkansas state capital. That had been in the works under trans-Mississippi commander Major General Samuel Curtis, but Federal forces there had been unable to do so. McClernand could provide a real coup if he could do it, feathering his own cap in the process. He accordingly informed Curtis of his plans, writing on January 8 that "whether I will advance beyond the Post to Brownsville and Little Rock, or to either, will depend upon circumstances yet undeveloped." But Gorman at Helena wrote Curtis only two days later that "General McClernand designs to go entirely up to Little Rock."[47]

For now, all McClernand let on about was the simple capture of the fortification to alleviate threats to the Mississippi River transportation artery. And it was admittedly a thrown-together operation, McClernand writing to Sherman that "this information has been hastily obtained, and in some instances from sources not authentic." That was not a resounding beginning, but McClernand went on with the plan: Sherman's corps would lead the way up the Arkansas, Morgan following, while Porter's gunboats, which he requested to be towed up the Mississippi against the current for faster movement and to save coal, covered the operation. Once the two corps disembarked downstream from the fortifications, they would march into position surrounding the fort and cause it to surrender. To block any possible escape, a brigade of Morgan's corps and artillery was also to cross the river and take positions opposite from the Confederate fort.[48]

McClernand and company set off immediately, some of the grizzled veterans of Chickasaw Bayou convincing themselves they were in for a break: "Fair prospect of getting to Helena before we stop," one Iowan wrote in his diary. But the effects of Chickasaw Bayou still lingered, not only in sickness among the troops but also in one Illinoisan describing "ball extracted from Gen. M. L. Smith's wound at dusk." Another more sardonically explained that "to all appearances we were now in full retreat towards Helena." McClernand had bigger prey on his mind, of course, but he waited until January 8 to inform Grant of his plans. Perhaps in no mood to ask permission or forgiveness, McClernand simply told Grant what he was doing, enumerating the reasons. These included the failure of Sherman's effort and Grant's support and the "counteraction of the moral effect of the failure of the attack near Vicksburg and the reinspiration of the forces repulsed." He also spoke of the "importance, nay duty, of actively and usefully employing our arms" as well as alleviating the danger to Mississippi River traffic and making a diversion for the Federal forces operating in Arkansas. McClernand said nothing about going on to Little Rock but did mention future plans such as taking Monroe on the Louisiana railroad and perhaps positions below Vicksburg, even on the Red River. McClernand had grand plans for his independent command.[49]

Given the distances involved and the lack of communication any faster than a steamer going upriver against the current, McClernand had plenty of time to get his quick victory before any countering word from Grant arrived and certainly before Grant could reorganize; in fact, that was part of McClernand's logic: "My forces must have continued comparatively idle at Milliken's Bend until you should have altered your plan for the reduction of Vicksburg or recalled them." McClernand thus put his forces in motion, stopping periodically to refuel from wood cut on the banks of the river and from gathering fence rails, often skirmishing with small squads of Confederates while onshore plundering the defenseless plantations. One surgeon noted "it was laughable to see them getting the mules off the quartermaster's steam boat for the purpose of hauling wood. Several of them fell into the river but soon swam ashore." Grumbling often ensued, one Federal explaining that "persuasion[,] a little swearing[,] and a few arrests of the worst grumblers, together with the apparent necessity of the case, and the wish to get on board again had the desired effect." The column also stopped at night at times because "our Arkansas pilot says it is not at all safe to run in the Arkansas at night." Still, few knew where they were going, one writing that "some expedition is on foot, but we cannot tell exactly what."[50]

McClernand's force reached the mouth of the White River, by January 8 in fact, anniversary of the famed Battle of New Orleans in 1815. One Federal saw no bright future as had been the case then: "The darkest hour is just before the dawn & may be 'tis so with us." Guided by charts sent over from Porter, McClernand moved on into the White River, then the cutoff between it and the Arkansas, and then up the Arkansas River, where one Federal explained "we received . . . friendly demonstrations from Arkansan Gals and Women . . . waving their Red and White Hankerchiefs and screaming 'hurrah for the Yankees.'" The force moved ultimately to within three miles of the Confederate fort, where McClernand began disembarking at Frederick Notrebe's (Notrib's in all the official reports) farm around 5:00 p.m. on January 9. Because of the lateness of the hour and dark, as well as a heavy rainstorm that night, the unloading was not fully begun until the next morning,

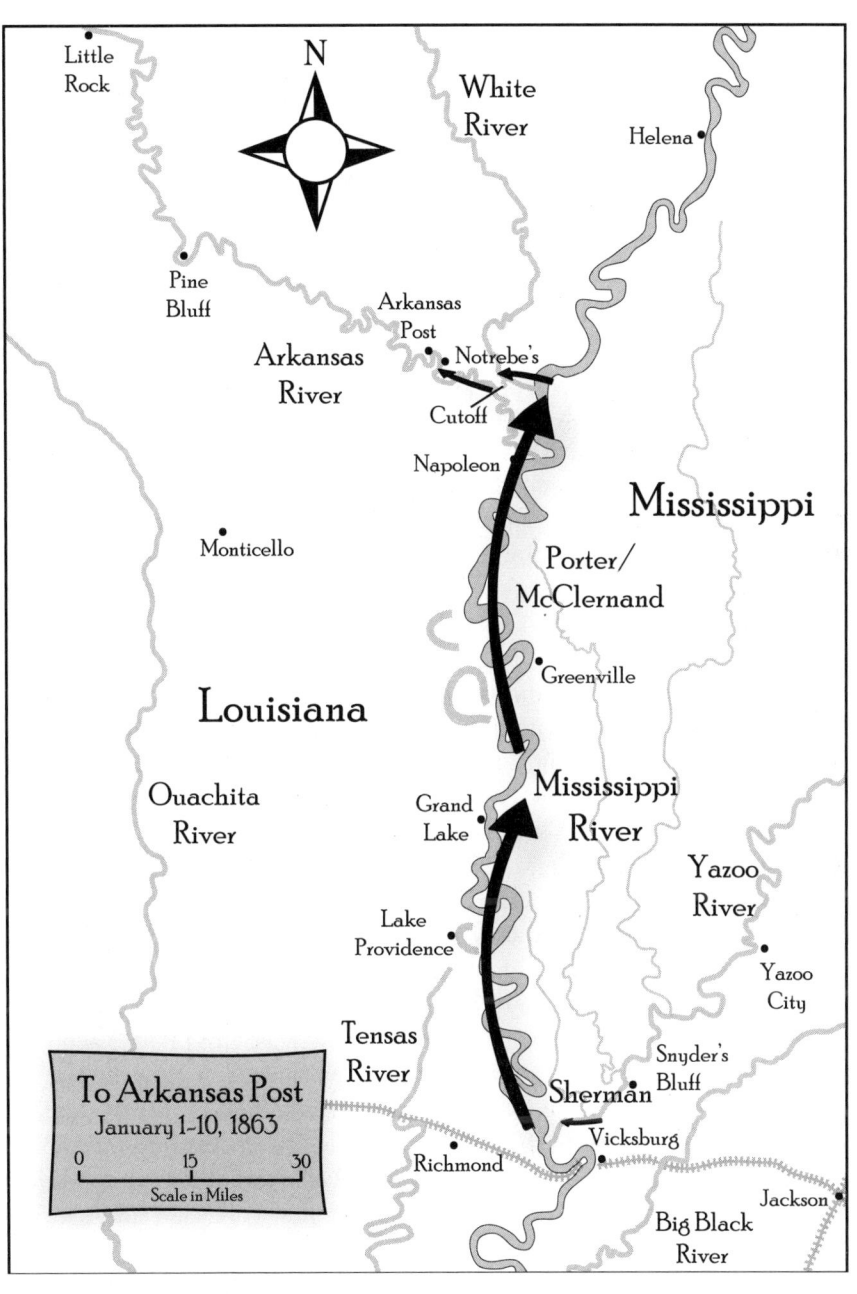

and it took until noon the next day. Others disembarked at the same time at Fletcher's Landing just downriver and on the opposite side of the river, to take the ground within the horseshoe curve of the waterway opposite the Confederate fort. This move would command the river upstream from the fort so that no Confederate reinforcements could reach them from that quarter. Informed of the lay of the land by a slave, one brigade of Morgan's corps and artillery indeed moved across the bend of the river and took possession of the river upstream of the fort at Smith's Landing. All across the board where the Federals landed, astonished Confederate scouts flooded back to the defenses with the shouts of "Yankees! Yankees!"[51]

With McClernand was a significant portion of Porter's flotilla. All were towed up the Mississippi River by transports because of the need for speed as well as to save coal, which was at a premium: "Save all the coal you can while being towed," Porter ordered his commanders. Fortunately, the *Conestoga* moved ahead of the flotilla, up the Arkansas, through the cutoff, and back down the White River, reporting "great abundance of wood on the edge of the banks all the way up." Some of the vessels coaled as they moved along, Porter writing that "I do not want to detain the Army if I can help it." Once in the Arkansas River, three of the big (and slow) ironclads, the *Louisville*, *Baron de Kalb*, and *Cincinnati*, along with Porter's flagship *Black Hawk*, moved forward slowly with the smaller *Marmora*, *Rattler*, *Forest Rose*, *Romeo*, and *Juliet* ahead making soundings for water depth. "Our progress is very slow," one Federal admitted, "as the Gunboats leading the advance draw almost all the water in the River." The *Signal* moved amid the transports and the *Lexington* of Shiloh fame brought up the rear, with the *Red Rover* and *Torrence* remaining on station at the mouth of the White River to guard it and the coal barges. Porter cautioned all to watch for torpedoes and assured them "not [to] wait for orders to fire when they see the enemy's troops or when fired upon." He warned later to "keep a sharp lookout, and do not be taken unawares."[52]

McClernand also gained some firsthand knowledge from Porter, who captured "a refugee picked up in a boat on the river in a starving condition." The man reported eleven regiments at Arkansas Post, not too far off the mark, as well as some cavalry and artillery. He gave details on the guns commanding the river, the entrenchments at the fort itself, and the road conditions. Particularly interesting to Porter was his report of a "barricade above the fort consisting of rows of piles driven in triangles and secured with hog chains." These extended outward into the river from the middle of the bend near the fort, hopefully forcing all river traffic, including gunboats, closer to the fort and destruction.[53]

Bright and early on January 10, McClernand scouted ahead with his staff and found a road that likely led around the fort; he also had small companies of cavalry out ahead as well. He ordered Sherman to advance Steele's division in that direction and reach the Arkansas River above Arkansas Post, but the division, led by contrabands and local farmers, soon encountered a swamp "as only Dixie can boast of" and a bayou that was almost impenetrable; Sherman termed it "a deep ugly swamp." Several soldiers mired down in the "bottomless" quagmire, jokes coming thick and fast at their expense by those who managed to get through; the same occurred as several officers while at rest "amuse[d] themselves by endeavoring to capture a lot of small porkers that are scampering through the woods but in the laughable undertaking they are not very successful." Moving on would obviously take the division out of the fight, or "virtually to retire it from the pending fight," as McClernand termed it, so he sent Sherman's other division under David Stuart northward on the near side of the bayou. Stuart found much better ground here despite fire from the fort itself, and upon personal inspection both Sherman and McClernand agreed that Steele's troops should be withdrawn and sent to follow Stuart. They were, watched closely by Confederate cavalry, who knew more than the poor soldiers in the column, one of whom explained "for some reason we could not go that way." The divisions of George Morgan's corps under Smith and Osterhaus also began their movement on the near side of the bayou, all moving over a Confederate position held for a time until driven away by the approaching Federals. In the slow advance across more swamps, one "fully as bad as the one we had passed," one of Sherman's soldiers explained, the 60th Indiana actually captured about sixty Confederates out in front of their lines.[54]

A slight demonstration by the navy, including the *Rattler* getting behind the Confederate position, also took place that afternoon. By late that evening all had advanced to the point that Sherman found cabins for winter quarters but, more important, the Confederate line of rifle pits that extended from the fort itself to a bayou to the north. Sherman went into position on the right in front of the works while Morgan went into line to his left, all covered by the navy's bombardment for an hour or so before dark. "The admiral advanced his boats and opened a terrific cannonade upon the fort, which was continued an hour or more and until after night-fall," the *Louisville*, *Baron de Kalb*, and *Cincinnati* taking the fort under fire and the smaller gunboats following "to make a show." The ironclads moved to within four hundred yards of the fort and pounded it, with the *Rattler* again getting by the Confederate position and enfilading it, although at a cost to the little boat that took some heavy damage and ultimately "became entangled amongst the snags placed in the river to impede our progress." The night was "bitter cold," Sherman related, an Iowan admitting that "right here I think I passed one of the most tiresome, and disagreeable nights that I experienced in helping put down the rebellion." And McClernand allowed no fires or tents. Worse was what all knew was coming in the morning. Sherman "crept up to a stump so close that I could hear the enemy hard at work." Soon, a Confederate bugler way too close for comfort "sounded as pretty a revile as I ever listened to."[55]

The Federals were ready to pounce, put in place, one admiring Union soldier wrote, "through the engineering of a good general." Ready to attack, McClernand simply informed Grant on January 10 that "I am landed within 3 miles of the Post of Arkansas." He planned to assault the very next day, gaining what he hoped would be the first of many victories leading ultimately to the capture of Vicksburg. And better yet, the only man who ranked him in the West, Grant, was well out of his way in West Tennessee. It was McClernand's show. "I hope we will be more successful this time," one of his officers candidly wrote home.[56]

3

"We Have Disposed of This Tough Little Nut"

January 11–13

What became known as Fort Hindman at the Post of Arkansas, or Arkansas Post, was the seventh iteration of the river port on the lower Arkansas River. Caught up in the European power struggle of domination of the new world in the seventeenth century, the interior of North America and especially the Mississippi Valley represented a prize to be had. The Mississippi River's major tributaries such as the Ohio, Missouri, Red, and Arkansas spread out like giant tenacles, draining two-thirds of the continent and offering access and thus riches to anyone brave enough to persist in this wilderness. The Arkansas River, for example, with its headwaters high in the Rocky Mountains west of Denver, flowed a lengthy thousand straight-line miles (many more by crooked river miles) to its confluence with the Mississippi River.[1]

Frenchmen Jacques Marquette and Luis Joliet first explored the Arkansas River mouth area, the inhabiting Quapaw Indians welcoming the newcomers as they did later explorers and traders, most famously Robert Cavalier Sieur de La Salle. Though some of his own men murdered La Salle, his partner Henri de Tonti established the trading post near the mouth of the Arkansas River in 1686, although over the years it came and went, apparently being unsettled for a time in the early 1700s and moving on occasion to higher ground amid the yearly floods of the Mississippi Valley. One of the approaching Federals simply explained it as being "renowned as one of the oldest Indian trading Posts in the Union."[2]

Ultimately, despite claims to the area from both England and Spain, France colonized the trans-Mississippi, naming it "Louisiana" after King Louis XIV. Interest in the post on the lower Arkansas River reemerged when an official colony took form in the early 1700s, the initial developers bringing in French colonists and troops to protect them. The post developed slowly and was abandoned at times for the next few years, although the permanent colony emerged in 1731 and was named the "Post de Arkansea." Over the course of the next few decades, the post grew little amid Indian wars, namely with the British-dominated and -aroused Chickasaw from east of the Mississippi River, including a failed Chickasaw attack against the post itself in 1749. Because of the threat of attack as well as continual flooding on the lower river, the French moved the site of the post again and again, always upriver. But by 1763, the end of the French and Indian War, major changes came as France lost much of its North American empire and Spain took control of the vast area of Louisiana west of the Mississippi River.[3]

The American Revolution upended peace in the new world once more, and Arkansas Post, isolated as it was, was not immune; a major raid in 1783 saw much destruction, but the paltry fortifications manned by the Spanish garrison managed to deflect the attackers, though the neighboring village saw a lot of destruction. Threats of fighting continued through the 1790s as Spain and France fought one another in Europe and the new world, with the newly established United States also involved from just across the Mississippi River. Ultimately, Spain sought to rid itself of the large and expensive area of Louisiana that was being more and more inundated by Americans, transferring it to France in 1800. Napoleon Bonaparte quickly sold it to the United States in 1803 to fund his war efforts in Europe. Originally part of the Missouri Territory, Arkansas County inhabitants soon petitioned for their own territorial status, which Congress granted in 1819, with the territorial capital at Arkansas Post for a few years before it was moved to Little Rock farther up the river.[4]

The industrial revolution revitalized Arkansas Post's economy, which had been devastated by the move of the territorial capital. What had long been trade based on local Indian inhabitants soon became agricultural in nature as cotton became king and steamboats plied the rivers up and down without trouble, including the Arkansas River. When war came in 1861, Arkansas Post sat on one of the major tributaries of the Mississippi River. Confederate officials saw the need to establish a fortification on the lower Arkansas River to protect Little Rock and the upper Arkansas from Union naval penetration, especially after the fall of Memphis in June 1862 and the almost simultaneous arrival of the Union navy from below.[5]

Lacking a Southern navy, Confederate trans-Mississippi commander Major General Theophilus Holmes ordered fortifications built on the Arkansas River at several points, one of which was Arkansas Post. Colonel John W. Dunnington began the work with slaves and Confederate engineer troops and soon fashioned a star-shaped fortification on a great bend of the Arkansas River, the bend much like a horseshoe that allowed a clear view of the river either upstream or downstream. In the Delta of Arkansas, there was little high ground, but here at the tip of the bend was a bluff about twenty-five feet high that could be utilized to throw plunging shot at enemy gunboats. Captains Robert H. Fitzhugh and A. M. Williams, both army engineers, supervised the work, which was a square-shaped fort a hundred and ninety feet in length on each side, with pointed bastions on each corner. As the bane of every fixed fortification was the turning movement engulfing it, the engineers also constructed three lines of rifle pits and land fortifications, one line starting southward along the river, obviously the direction any enemy would come, as well as an intermediate area; the main line extended from the fort itself northwestward to Post Bayou, a large bayou that covered the flank. But that bayou provided little real protection, one soldier describing it as a mere "12 feet wide and 18 inches deep, and across which were several easy fords."[6]

From this fortification just a few miles from the Mississippi River, Confederate raiders preyed on Union shipping, including taking the *Blue Wing* and all its stores. The Confederates hauled the vessel up to Arkansas Post and took its ammunition for their own. The raiding proved successful to a degree, but not enough to counteract the attention brought on the area for just such depredations. John McClernand would in fact use the raiding of the Union supply lines as a chief excuse to go after Arkansas Post, and by the night of January 10, he was there and ready to attack.[7]

Awaiting the Union onslaught was a motley band of Confederates that numbered only about three thousand effectives. The commander was Brigadier General Thomas J. Churchill, a Kentuckian who studied law at the same Transylvania University that Jefferson Davis and Albert Sidney Johnston attended, although decades later as Churchill was much younger. He had a varied career, including fighting in the Mexican–American War as a lieutenant and serving as Little Rock's postmaster after he settled in the trans-Mississippi state. He was a veteran of Wilson's Creek and the Kentucky Campaign in the fall of 1862, promoted to brigadier general in the process. Tasked with defending the Arkansas River and Little Rock, Churchill arrived at Arkansas Post and quickly saw a less than ideal situation.[8]

Churchill's troops were an assortment of infantry, naval units, and dismounted cavalry organized into three brigades. Colonel John W. Dunnington, actually a former officer in the United States Navy and now a first lieutenant in the Confederate navy (but appointed a colonel and chief of ordnance by

Churchill), commanded one brigade that was fixed in the fort itself, commanding the river. Under his care, logically, was the majority of the force's artillery, particularly that in the fort fronting the river. The 19th Arkansas and Lieutenant Colonel William Crawford's Arkansas Infantry Battalion were nominally under his command, but the bulk of the fort's defenders were Confederate naval personnel from the ram *Pontchartrain*. In addition, Colonel Robert R. Garland of the 6th Texas commanded a Texas brigade consisting of his own regiment and the 24th and 25th Texas Dismounted Cavalry, along with Captain William Hart's Arkansas Battery. West Point graduate Colonel James Deshler commanded the third, consisting of the 10th Texas and the 15th, 17th, and 18th Texas Dismounted Cavalry. None of the units were his originally, he being a staff officer most of the war thus far. In addition were four companies of cavalry sorted out among the brigades and held in reserve.[9]

Word of the approaching danger first came to Churchill on the morning of January 9 when scouts alerted him that Union vessels had moved through the cutoff and were in fact heading up the Arkansas River, not the White River. McClernand's effort to confuse the enemy of his intention until the last possible moment worked, and Churchill had to move fast to meet the threat. He sent Deshler's Texans and Dunnington's Arkansans southward along the river to the lowest set of rifle pits a couple of miles out from the fort, but they manned the intermediate set when it was found that McClernand had landed at Notrebe's that evening, just a mile or so farther downstream and "in the immediate vicinity of the lower pits," Deshler related. The various companies of cavalry and a few of Garland's Texans scouted farther ahead as skirmishers, but the bulk of Garland's troops were posted as a reserve along the river, with Hart's Arkansas Battery on the bank but not daring to engage the enemy gunboats.[10]

Churchill's Confederates spent a nervous night on January 9 wondering what the next day would bring. He nevertheless had his troops hard at work on the main fortifications, extending and strengthening them as well as cutting trees in front to form an abatis. "In this way we worked during the entire night," Deshler reported, but he added that "the want of tools, axes, spades, &c., was a very serious drawback to this work." And as expected, daylight brought enemy movement. McClernand sent Steele northeastward across the bayou, which Churchill correctly interpreted as an attempt to outflank him. When Porter's gunboats opened up as well and the gunners in Fort Hindman itself had so much trouble with powder that they could not even fling a ball to the Confederate position much less the enemy gunboats, he consequently fell back to the fort, leaving Garland's Texans to hold the intermediate line of fortifications. Ultimately, everyone withdrew all the way to the main earthworks connecting with the fort itself, though it was an ordeal; Garland reported that he "was delayed some time in assisting to bring up the artillery and ammunition wagons, the route being exceedingly boggy." The Federals declined to assault the main line that day, although there was some skirmishing and Porter's gunboats made another appearance to bombard the fort that evening.[11]

The various Confederate commanders spent another nervous night on January 10 perfecting their defenses as best they could amid a severe lack of tools. Churchill noted that "I employed the balance of the time till next morning in strengthening my position and completing my intrenchments." Adding to the tension was a telegram received from General Holmes in Little Rock, who fully understood the threat to his headquarters if Arkansas Post fell: "Hold out till help arrive[s] or until all dead." An Alamo-style defense was easy to order from Little Rock but much harder to enact on site at the underwhelming fort along the Arkansas River.[12]

Yet Churchill placed his troops and hoped for the best, he telling his boys, "gentlemen, the fight will commence in a very short time, and we must win it or die in the ditches." Dunnington's Arkansans and naval personnel held the bastion itself, although the 19th Arkansas took a position immediately outside the fort in the earthworks to the west; they would soon be used as a reserve to be sent where needed, as only so many troops could occupy the fort anyway, there being no need to man with infantry the western, southern, or eastern faces. The fort itself contained eleven guns, the three most powerful being on the eastern face fronting the river. Two 8-inch iron guns were enclosed in casemates on the northeastern corner and in the center of the eastern face, with a 9-inch gun en barbette on the southeastern corner. The casemates were eighteen by fifteen feet wide and covered with three layers of sixteen-inch oak timbers enclosed with a "revetment of iron bars." Four smaller 3-inch rifles and four light 6-pound smoothbores were distributed around the fort to cover the other approaches, mainly to the north and west. The parapet of the fort itself was eighteen feet wide at the top, and the ditch in front was eight feet deep and twenty feet wide at the top, although narrower at the bottom.[13]

In the fortifications immediately to the left (west) of the Arkansans and the fort itself, what Garland described as "on a prolongation with the north front of the fort, nearly at a right angle with the river, extending westward toward the bayou," were Garland's Texans, manning the earthworks with the 6th Texas, 24th Texas Dismounted Cavalry, and 25th Texas Dismounted Cavalry from right to left; Colonel Franklin C. Wicks of the 24th Texas had already alerted his men—"cap your guns; shoot low; shoot at their knees." In addition, several guns of Hart's Arkansas Battery held the right of the brigade. Garland ordered that they "proceed immediately to throw up defenses by intrenching and collecting brush, timber, and such material as could be found" even while the enemy gunboats bombarded the position for several hours that evening. The Texans went to work immediately strengthening their works with whatever material they could find. Garland reported that "the command, although unprotected, maintained its position during this trying ordeal with firmness."[14]

By morning on January 11, despite the lack of tools, Garland's Texans had a formidable though nowhere near finished line of defense constructed. But then worse news came as Churchill ordered Colonel Charles L. Dawson's 19th Arkansas, between Garland and the fort, out of line to move to the extreme left where a bigger crisis was unfolding. Worse yet, four guns of Hart's Battery also moved leftward, leaving Garland to make up the difference. He could only order the 6th Texas "to cover the interval thus made, by taking ground to the right with his regiment by extending interval, which consequently rendered this part of the line rather scattering."[15]

The reason the Arkansans were needed to the west was because of what was transpiring in Deshler's brigade that morning. He had fallen back and gone into line west and on the left of Garland's troops, prolonging the line straight westward toward Post Bayou, which ran into the Arkansas River in rear of the Confederate line and upstream from the fort. Unfortunately, the bayou was not a major impediment, it being fordable in many places. On top of that his regiments did not even reach all the way to the bayou, a gap of some two hundred yards separating Deshler's left from the bayou itself, "thus leaving that flank completely open," he complained. Still, Deshler placed the regiments in line, with the 18th Texas Dismounted Cavalry on the right and the 17th Texas Dismounted Cavalry, 10th Texas, and 15th Texas Dismounted Cavalry filling the line to the left. The Texans initially found no earthworks at all but spent the entire night digging and rounding up anything that could be used as an impediment. "We commenced at once to throw up such slight fortifications as circumstances would permit," Deshler reported, including tearing down winter quarter cabins to use the logs for protection and to deprive the enemy of cover. But it was hard work, Deshler describing how his men "were compelled to use pieces of board for shovels."[16]

While the front was covered by daylight on January 11, the looming gap to the left still worried Deshler, so he ordered traverses erected along the line in case he was outflanked; he also ordered the line bent back somewhat. As daylight revealed Federals moving toward that undefended flank, Deshler sent two companies of each regiment to act as skirmishers along the bayou to protect his rear. When he informed Churchill of his predicament, the commander ordered additional cavalry companies to report to him, and Deshler

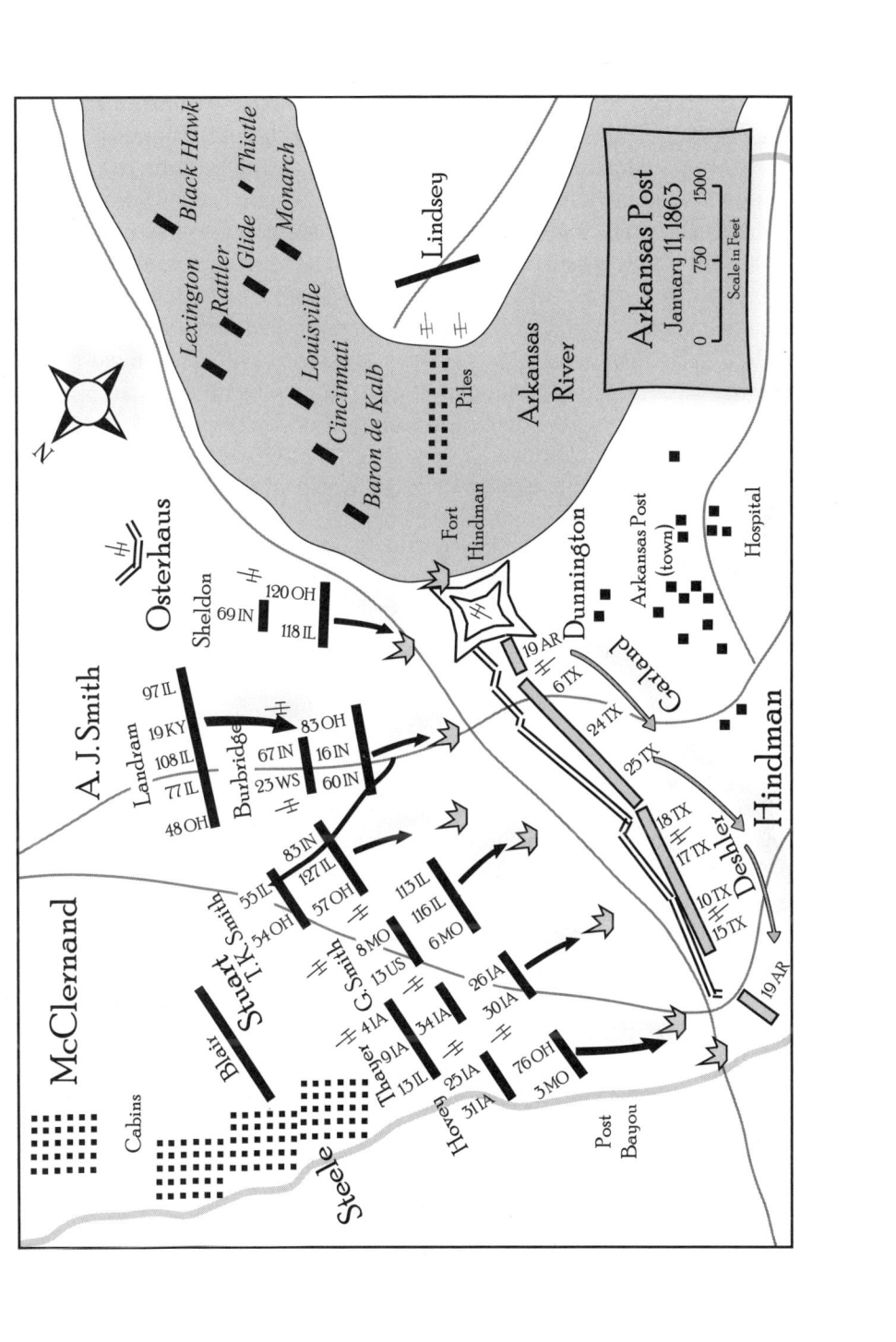

placed them also along the bayou, actually all the way to the river to provide warning if there was a threat to the rear; he also sent some of them across the bayou for more warning. Churchill also sent six companies of the 19th Arkansas to Deshler, causing Garland to have to cover the now-unmanned portion of the line by extending his troops to the east. Deshler kept the Arkansans in position immediately behind his line to be used where needed and placed the four Arkansas guns of Hart's Battery on his main line.[17]

This line was weak and cobbled together to be sure, especially facing some twenty-five thousand Federal troops, but it was all Churchill had. Reinforcements were not terribly promising, although he had ordered Colonel E. E. Portlock at Saint Charles to march to his assistance; only a few hundred actually arrived. With the admonition to hold or die in his mind, Churchill could only wait to see what the heretofore careful Federals would do. As a result, all morning long the Confederates caught only glimpses here and there of the enemy through gaps in the trees: "The heavy growth of timber and brush prevented me from gaining anything but occasional glimpses of their columns," a frustrated Deshler related. But it was enough to know that they were out there and an attack could come at any minute. And soon it did, led by Porter's ironclads on the river itself.[18]

As in most cases with strong fixed fortifications on rivers, the seemingly obvious way to defeat them was to blow them to pieces with gunboats. That fallacy was perhaps started with Flag Officer Andrew H. Foote's significant victory at Fort Henry in February 1862; no army was needed. But the operations since that time told a different story, at Fort Donelson, Columbus, Kentucky, Forts Pillow and Randolph in Tennessee, Island No. 10, and elsewhere, where the vast majority of the time it was not gunboats per se that doomed a fixed position with heavy guns. It was rather an army on land turning the position, cutting it off, and either causing the fixed fortification to surrender or withdraw. Yet naval doctrine at the time still included the push forward by gunboats to the heavy guns of a fort to knock them out of service, and that is exactly what Admiral Porter sought to do on this Sunday, January 11, at Arkansas Post: "There is no Sabbath in the army," an Iowan bemoaned.[19]

Porter prepared his vessels that morning, to the point of covering the iron portions with "tallow or slush; it will make the shot glance." One sailor noted the boats were "greased." He also coordinated with McClernand, telling him "we will move up in a few moments. The moment we hear your shouts of assaults we will cease firing or fire far to the left of you; that is, to the left of your right wing, as we sailors would say." Fortunately, the gunboat commanders knew what lay ahead, they having made the demonstration the evening before with orders to "stick up a mark on the bank" to indicate range and Porter reminding them that "1,330 yards is the bursting point of a 5-second fuse, 10-second, at about 2,700 yards."[20]

By midday on January 11, McClernand was ready for the assault and so sent word to Porter, twice. The admiral accordingly pushed forward with the three ironclads *Louisville*, *Baron de Kalb*, and *Cincinnati*, each assigned specific portions of the fort itself to concentrate on. Behind them were the "frailer vessels," which Porter ordered to "haul up in the smoke and do the best they could." Porter, on the *Black Hawk*, watched with intense excitement as his ironclads closed on the fort and both sides blazed away at one another at an increasingly shorter distance. It was the first such battle Porter was in, and his thoughts must have ranged to his friend Andrew Foote and what it was like at Forts Henry and Donelson nearly a year earlier. But it was his show now.[21]

The three gunboats moved upstream, the bow guns taking the fort under fire. One watching infantryman marveled that "the ironclads came steadily up one after the other [and] when the first one got abreast of us she opened her port guns on the fort right merrily. I tell you as soon as she got out of the way the second came up and also opened and so on until they all engaged." Yet the Confederates did not roll over. The *Louisville*, under Lieutenant Commander Elias K. Owen, sustained the most damage, Owen reporting that the hits, "though serious, have not in the least unfitted her for duty." The vessel had already taken two concerning shots the evening before, one "a large shell hole through the bluff of bow on the port side"; the shell exploded on the gun deck, "tearing both gun and spar deck badly." Another shell had entered one of the ports and exploded, tearing the wood decks severely. This day, the *Louisville* took even more punishment, six shots in all. A couple went through the boat, striking the gun deck and carrying away equipment and rigging. One shell lodged in the escape pipe, and another went through the smokestack. Superficial damage occurred to the rigging and launches on deck, but a fire also broke out on the vessel, unknown by her crew who was concentrated on the fort. The tug *Thistle*, on which Porter spent part of the fight directing movements, came alongside and sent a boarding party to the *Louisville* to put out the fire. They did the same thing for the *Cincinnati* when another fire was reported, but it was a false alarm. In firing 212 shots, the *Louisville* lost eleven casualties, all wounded, although two were considered mortal, they being head and neck wounds.[22]

Meanwhile, the *Cincinnati* moved up and poured its fire into the fort as well, the gunners firing exactly one hundred rounds that day. Lieutenant George M. Bache took the *Cincinnati* toward the fort and concentrated on the "right casemate gun of the fort (the one assigned us)." It was soon silenced, and the *Cincinnati* shifted its fire to the left casemate and barbette gun, later shelling the interior of the fort as well. Yet the ironclad likewise suffered damage above the two shots she took the evening before, one through the "upper works" and a more concerning one "at the water line forward." The *Cincinnati* took nine total shots this day, all "on the bow, casemate, pilot house, and upper works."[23]

The most destructive ironclad by all accounts was the *Baron de Kalb* under Lieutenant Commander John G. Walker, which bored in to within a hundred yards of the fort. Porter later testified that Walker "managed and fought his vessel most beautifully, and I never had to correct a movement of his during the action." But boring in so close brought destruction on the vessel, including a Confederate shot that hit the muzzle of one of the 10-inch guns; "both gun and carriage [were] destroyed." It was later dumped overboard. Another shot hit a 32-pounder carriage and put it out of service. A shot also broke one of the iron plates on the forward casemate. Other projectiles came through the ports, damaging the woodwork, but the only serious harm came from a plunging shell that came through the deck and cut off a "lower deck beam." The other shots mostly glanced off the iron-plated casemate and pilothouse, which Walker had, according to Porter's orders, covered with "slush, which I think was of much assistance in turning the shot, as the vessel was repeatedly struck by 8 and 9 inch shot at very short range, and the iron was in no case penetrated. The loss was from shot and shell entering the ports." Still, in firing a total of 158 times, there was some destruction, the *Baron de Kalb* losing two killed and fifteen wounded, two of which were head and neck injuries and probably mortal. In fact, Frederick Davis, aboard the *Baron de Kalb*, related that it was "as hard a fight as at Fort Donaldson." The bombardment of all three ironclads was nevertheless amazing, future Kansas governor Lyman Humphrey explaining that "it was terrific[.] The deafening thunder of the loud mouthed cannon as they belched forth their rapid discharges of shot & shell and destruction in every shape was extremely heavy."[24]

Porter also had his smaller and weaker vessels in the action, the shot-up *Rattler* and *Glide* adding their shells to the whole. The smaller gunboats put in their fire where they could and suffered some superficial damage. Once he saw an opportunity, Porter ordered the smaller vessels to move past the fort, accompanied by the ram *Monarch* under Colonel Charles Ellet, which was at the front and ordered to "take the lead if a rebel ram appeared." Porter intended to "cut off the enemy's retreat by the only way he had." Thereafter, Porter twice ordered his own flagship *Black Hawk* to close on the fort "for the purpose of boarding it in front," but the vessel was "unmanageable" and

Porter had to suffice with eventually depositing a regiment from Colonel Daniel Lindsey's brigade across the river near the fort. But all knew it was heretofore a navy show, one Federal writing how "we can see the Bombs bursting in and over the Fort and occasionally 3 or 400 feet up in the air."[25]

The Confederates responded with what they could, a mere eleven guns. Churchill boasted that "Colonel Dunnington, who commanded the fort, was ready in an instant to receive him. The fire opened and the fight lasted near two hours." There was of course damage to the Union gunboats, but Porter later argued that his order to coat the casemates and pilothouses with tallow proved the difference. Porter gave examples such as the *Rattler* that was struck on its 3/4-inch iron, but the shells "flew upward without scratching the iron." On the *Cincinnati*, most of the shells "glanced off like peas against glass." Porter stated that only the *Baron de Kalb* had its iron broken, but that was "done by a continuous hammering of three hours with solid shot from the fort." He informed the Navy Department, "I am perfectly convinced that a coating of tallow on ironclad gunboats is a perfect protection against shot if fired at an angle. The experiment is worth being tried."[26]

Ultimately, the heavy naval fire succeeded in silencing most of the guns of the fort, Churchill writing that all but one was put out of action and that was "on the land side," allowing Porter to move past and get in rear. The 8-inch gun in the casemate on the northeastern corner was completely destroyed, one report reading "one-half of the chase of the gun knocked away by a shot through embrasure. Gun totally disabled. Carriage shattered. Embrasure side of casemate forced inwards by numerous shots, several of which penetrated the entire thickness of timber. Roofing badly shattered, but the ceiling of casemate uninjured." To the south in the center of the eastern face, the other casemated gun was damaged less, although in similar fashion. The 8-inch gun itself took a shot directly on the muzzle, which caused some damage as well. The 9-inch gun en barbette on the southeastern corner of the fort was "cut in two in front of reinforce by a 30-pound Parrott shot. Carriage badly broken, completely disabled." In addition, one of the 3-inch Parrott guns had a "large piece of muzzle knocked off. Carriage shattered," and one of the 6-pound smoothbores was also "much broken." Others received slighter damage, and only two of the smoothbores received no harm at all.[27]

Yet silencing the Confederate guns did not necessarily cause the surrender of the fort itself as Porter had hoped, because what was happening on land was much more destructive to the Confederate defense. But getting past the fort did allow what Churchill called a "cross-fire upon the fort and our lines." Still, although Porter had no way of knowing it, the army had indeed assaulted but had done no more to take the fortifications than he had as of yet.[28]

William T. Sherman was up early on January 11—"the moon rose about 1 a.m., when I rode forward and examined the position of the enemy as well as possible." His troops were deployed along the entire line of Confederates from the fort westward, although they soon shifted westward themselves to allow Morgan's troops to move into line between them and the river. Some of Sherman's troops left a fortification they had thrown up in the night, mainly by the muscle power of Colonel Oscar Malmborg (of the 55th Illinois) and the men of the 127th Illinois, leaving it to one of Morgan's batteries. Sherman also perceived the Confederates were hard at work as well, he reporting that "we could hear the enemy all night busy at work chopping and felling trees, and became convinced he was resolved on a determined resistance." Sherman visited the forward pickets at times, within a few hundred yards of the fort itself. Division commander David Stuart reported that "my entire division was under arms and on duty all that night, which they thought no hardship when they saw their corps general himself in their midst and front, despising his own ease and denying himself rest."[29]

Daylight brought some relief, McClernand himself writing that "passing a cold night without fires and tents, our chilled but faithful men were greeted by a bright and genial sun on the morning of the 11th." But it also brought confrontation, one Missourian writing that they could see "the traitor flag saucily floating in the morning breeze directly in our front." By daylight Sherman moved his two divisions "into an easy position for assault." The troops spread out into a wooded area fronted by felled trees and bushes. The Confederates took shots at the Federals they could see through gaps in the brush, but Sherman was not concerned, thinking it "accustomed our men to the sound of rifled cannon." Sherman placed Steele's division of three brigades on the extreme right, butting up against Post Bayou to the west. There, Brigadier Generals Charles Hovey's and John Thayer's brigades waited for the signal to attack, while Brigadier General Frank P. Blair, Jr.'s shot-up brigade (at Chickasaw Bayou) held the reserve, although he still rode his lines and was cheered lustfully. To the left, David Stuart's two brigades under the dual Smiths deployed, Colonel Giles Smith's forward on Thayer's left and Colonel Thomas Kilby Smith's a little to the left and rear, under better cover. The left rested on the Little Rock Road, which led through the Confederate fortifications and to the town in rear of the Confederate lines.[30]

By midmorning Sherman reported to McClernand that he was ready to assault, but a delay ensued as the navy prepared and Morgan's troops took their positions; especially difficult was getting Morgan's artillery up. It was not until 12:30 p.m. that McClernand informed Sherman that the navy was getting started and that he would move forward soon. The heavy firing by the navy would be the sign to start operations, at which time Sherman would unleash all his artillery for a time. After a three-minute pause to make sure all batteries quieted, the infantry would advance.[31]

The gunboats moved forward about 1:00 p.m., although Sherman could not see them. But he could hear as they advanced "at first slow and steady, but [then] rapidly approached the fort and enveloped it with a complete hailstorm of shot and shell." The artillery batteries opened up as well, and Sherman allowed them to fire for perhaps fifteen minutes, prompting Churchill inside Fort Hindman to quip that the enemy "commenced moving upon my lines simultaneously by land and water." On Sherman's front were the two Chicago batteries, Captain Peter Wood's on Stuart's left and Captain Samuel Barrett's between Stuart's and Steele's divisions. Steele also had two batteries on his front, Captain Louis Hoffman's 4th Ohio Battery and Captain Henry H. Griffiths's 1st Iowa Battery, as well as Captain Levi W. Hart's battery (H, 1st Illinois Artillery) that was intended to hold the fortification dug the night before. The Illinoisans went into position farther to the left rear of Stuart's troops, although the men had to cut fields of fire through the trees to be able to bombard the enemy. The artillery fired rapidly but elicited no response from the Confederate line, although Colonel Deshler wrote that "this fire was kept up quite rapidly and continuously, but with scarcely any effect excepting the killing and wounding of some of our artillery horses." He went on: "How many batteries they had playing upon my line I could not tell owing to the intervening brush and timber, and they seemed to shift their positions frequently; I think it probable, however, that there were five or six batteries in my front." The effect was nearly as stark on the Union side, one Missourian in Hovey's brigade explaining that "the very earth seemed to quake under the heavy discharges of those cannon filling a soldier's heart with a strange, unspeakable feeling of courage and eagerness for the fray."[32]

Sherman soon ordered the firing to cease and prepared to send his infantry forward. He reported that the men "sprang forward with a cheer." There was a clear space of a hundred yards or so along much of Sherman's lines, with another three hundred yards of felled timber and brush closer to the Confederate position. The ground was also undulating in this last three hundred yards, with gullies and crevasses, but that would help shield the troops. Nevertheless, Sherman sent his boys forward and reported that they "dashed rapidly" at first but were quickly hit by "the fire of the enemy's artillery and infantry, well directed from their perfect cover." Sherman admitted that it "checked the speed of our advance, which afterward became more cautious and prudent."[33]

Over on the extreme right, Frederick Steele placed two of his brigades on the front line, John Thayer's on the left, next to Giles Smith's of Stuart's division, and Charles Hovey's on the extreme right, butted up against Post Bayou. Frank Blair "properly," Sherman said, held the reserve position and saw little action, he enduring only nine casualties, all wounded, the entire time. Thayer and Hovey, however, did engage, fiercely, and sustained heavy casualties, in fact the most in the corps. One of the Chicago gunners nevertheless exclaimed that after lying under Confederate fire for so long "we commenced to take revenge and got satisfaction."[34]

Charles Hovey led off the advance in Steele's division, he being on the extreme right of the division, corps, and army. After slight skirmishing during which one Missourian dolefully noted in his diary that "we of the infantry could not do anything yet, and only served as a target," the time for an assault neared. Hovey placed the 17th Missouri as skirmishers to the right to guard that flank against any Confederates across the bayou and formed his main line with the 76th Ohio and 3rd Missouri on the front, supported by the 25th and 31st Iowa, the 12th Missouri and Captain Clemens Landgraeber's Battery F, 2nd Missouri Artillery having been left behind. Oddly enough, right in the middle of the chaos, one Ohioan looked rearward and saw a boyhood friend in another regiment who had moved to Iowa; he had not seen him for years but yelled hello, upon which the similarly prone Iowan yelled gladly: "He was delighted to see me but asked to be excused from shaking hands at the time."[35]

The brigade advanced but met immediate problems. The Missourians on the extreme right moved forward but were "attacked on the flank much more violently than was anticipated, and was compelled to divert his whole regiment from its original course to repel this assault." The Confederates opposing him were the reinforcing 19th Arkansas, and they effectively stopped the Missourians. In fact, Deshler deftly handled his open flank in the attack, particularly before the Arkansans reinforced him. He related that a "strong column" came around his line and was "continually pressing toward my left flank, evidently with the intention of passing around it through the interval between it and the bayou." Deshler sent Lieutenant Colonel Augustus S. Hutchinson and his six companies of the 19th Arkansas to plug the gap, although the Arkansans could not fill the entire hole. The regiment placed their left on the bayou and refused the line a bit but was basically parallel with Deshler's main line, only a little farther back. But there was still a gaping hole of a hundred yards or so between its right and Deshler's left, but refusing the line allowed Deshler's Texans to sweep the area in front with a flanking fire. Still, the Arkansans "had no intrenchments whatever, though sheltered in a measure by a heavy growth of timber." Sometime in the midst of the seeming crisis, Union brigade commander Hovey was wounded in the arm by a piece of shell from this Confederate line but refused to leave the field and remained in command.[36]

The problems with the 17th Missouri on the flank reverberated down the line to the left. Hovey ordered the 3rd Missouri, supported by the 31st Iowa, to move ahead; "they moved forward vigorously," Hovey wrote, "and for a time I confidently expected they would enter the works, but the galling crossfire of infantry and artillery bearing directly on their front and flanks . . . checked the charge and at length compelled . . . [the regiments] to resume their original line of battle." Especially unnerved was the brand-new 31st Iowa, which Hovey described "lost much of its effectiveness through lack of discipline." The left of the brigade moved forward as well but met much the same fate. The 76th Ohio in the lead, followed by the 25th Iowa (Colonel George A. Stone of the 25th Iowa placed his hat on his sword and bellowed orders to march), moved at the double-quick through several hundred yards of fallen timber, Ohioan Lyman Humphrey describing how "with a yell we went in on a charge . . . till we got within a few rods of them and they opened upon us one of the heaviest fires I ever heard [and] a perfect hailstorm of bullets grape canister swept through our ranks." He added that "we soon laid down." Deshler on the other side related that "in the repeated charges made by the enemy his ranks seemed actually to wither under our fire. I feel proud to command such men." After temporary advances, Hovey realized he was as far as he could go at this point and simply ordered his troops to try to bring down the enemy artillerymen working the cannon doing so much damage in the Union ranks.[37]

The same basic fate met John Thayer's brigade to Hovey's left. Thayer deployed his brigade in column of regiments because of "the thick underbrush and the want of space for a front of the brigade," he being squeezed in between Hovey to the right and Giles Smith of Stuart's division to the left. Thayer placed the 26th Iowa on the front left, the 30th Iowa to their right. Behind them came the 34th Iowa, and in reserve farther back was the 4th and 9th Iowa and the 13th Illinois. The troops moved forward but met immediate and heavy fire, Thayer himself having his horse shot from under him while Colonel Milo Smith of the 26th Iowa fell wounded even as the colors went down at least three times, only to be taken up again and again. Fortunately, Thayer had another general to aid him in his command, William Vandever, the former commander of the 9th Iowa who had been promoted to brigadier general back in November and had just returned to the army two days before. Vandever took command of his old regiment and aided Thayer in the brigade command as well. Thayer's advance hit the right center of Deshler's brigade, the 10th Texas. Deshler noted that "after this fire had been kept up for about an hour the enemy pushed forward a column of attack of several battalions against that part of my line occupied by the Tenth Texas." The Texans were ready, the four guns of Hart's Arkansas Battery nearby, which in fact attracted a large amount of the Union artillery fire. "We did not open fire upon this column with small arms until its head was within 80 to 100 yards from our line," Deshler reported, "then we gave them a very deadly fire, firing by file with marked effect, as after the first volley those who were not killed or wounded fell back in great confusion to the shelter of the timber, from whence they kept up a very heavy skirmishing fire."[38]

Matters were not going any better over in Stuart's division to the left. The timing was even misplaced somewhat, as David Stuart watched for the artillery to cease fire. Before it had done so completely, he saw a regiment of Steele's division to his right moving forward at a double-quick. He immediately queried Sherman, who was on his front lines, about what to do, and Sherman motioned Stuart forward as well. Giles Smith accordingly moved ahead also at the double-quick, Kilby Smith's brigade following a hundred and fifty yards to the rear. Giles Smith's Federals, particularly the 6th Missouri and 113th and 116th Illinois in the front line (the 8th Missouri and 13th US were in reserve), were immediately hit in the opening they crossed, Stuart writing that "it was opened on by a heavy fire from the right and left as well as the front of the intrenchments and by two batteries, one on its right and the other on its left front." Garland's Texans also provided heavy small-arms fire, and Stuart related how Giles Smith determined that "it was not altogether hopeful to push his assault farther till he could silence or dispose of the enemy's cannon, from which he had begun to fire grape and canister." As a result, Stuart added, Smith "ordered a halt, and the line dropped to the ground to seek the best shelter the place afforded." Smith's Federals simply shot at the Confederate cannoneers from long range for much of the afternoon.[39]

Stuart also had another brigade to utilize as well, and he quickly brought up Kilby Smith's troops from the rear and sent them forward on Giles Smith's left, where a gap existed between Sherman's troops and Morgan's farther eastward. Like Giles Smith, Kilby Smith placed three regiments in the front line, the 83rd Indiana, 127th Illinois, and 57th Ohio, with the 55th Illinois and 54th Ohio in reserve. But Kilby Smith could go no farther than Giles Smith, Stuart writing that "a heavy fire from the trenches" also halted Kilby Smith's brigade. Both brigades took the best possible cover they could find amid the fallen logs and stumps and continued to pelt the enemy as best they could with fire for the next couple of hours, although the well protected Texans of Garland's brigade did not give them much to shoot at. Only the artillerymen of Hart's Battery were exposed enough to be cut down, Giles Smith relating that his skirmishers of the 6th and 8th Missouri "advanced to within 100 yards of the guns, which they effectually silenced, not only picking off every gunner who showed himself above the works, but killing every horse belonging to the battery." There were casualties in the Union artillery as well, however, one 57th Ohio soldier telling of a cannoneer who lost both arms "within four inches of his body." The miserable man cried, "Lieutenant, for the sake of my wife and my six little ones, take your revolver out and blow my brains out. I am no use to them anymore . . . (shaking the bloody stumps) the hands that earned those I love better than life or living are gone and I want to die." The lieutenant obviously refused, but the man soon died anyway. One Illinoisan summed up that "it was pretty hard fighting while it lasted. Almost as hard as it was at Shiloh."[40]

Though stopped, the Union attacks were nevertheless taking a toll primarily on Deshler's Confederates, and he had to once again call on Garland's brigade for aid. Churchill had told Garland to send help to Deshler or Dunnington if they needed it, which Deshler did. Garland again sent reinforcements, tasking every other company in his two dismounted cavalry regiments and two of the 6th Texas companies to head to the left. Deshler was appreciative, although the men were not so enthused. "These companies had to pass through a very galling fire almost the entire length of the line, as it was on my extreme left that I wanted them," Deshler reported, "and it was necessary to crawl on all fours in our shallow trench the whole distance." Garland was not altogether happy either, complaining that "in carrying out these instructions in good faith the most important part of the line was left almost defenseless." He would have been more disturbed had he known that the attacks on Deshler's front were about over and "there was a temporary cessation in the attack on my left." Deshler consequently made his way from his crisis-ridden flank to the right of the brigade to check on its status, he finding along the way that the four guns of Hart's Battery had been basically put out of service during the attacks. He explained that "the enemy concealed in the timber along the front of the line kept up such an unremitting and intensely hot skirmishing fire that it was almost impossible for a man to show himself without being struck." In fact, he added that "out of the horses belonging to the four pieces and their caissons only one or two escaped being either killed or wounded."[41]

Still, it was long-range fire doing the damage, not overpowering assaults made in tandem. In fact, Deshler reported that in these attacks the enemy "did not charge along my whole front at any one time, but in each case pushed forward a column of several regiments." Sherman admitted that his troops reached within a hundred yards of the enemy line after a couple of hours of fighting but went no farther. And there was little he could do about it. In fact, although being up front part of the time and one of his staff officers having a horse shot from under him, Sherman related that Stuart and Steele took care of most of the work, which "left me the comparatively easy task of watching their movements, which were all skillful and correct." At times, however, he could by this point look to the left and see Admiral Porter's gunboats approach the fort, including "the admiral's flag directly under it." The fort had apparently stopped any firing, and only occasional artillery discharges came from the line of extended Confederate works, the heavy infantry fire from the stalled Federals keeping the artillerymen down. But the naval fire did not reach the Confederate infantry, they not wanting to fire near their own troops of course, and so Sherman was on his own in terms of breaking through. But after some three hours of stalling and only inching forward at some places, that did not seem to be possible, Deshler reporting that in all "they made seven or eight distinct charges against my line and were driven back with heavy loss each time. I allowed them to get up within 80 to 125 yards before opening on them with small arms, and as both officers and men were cool and self-possessed the fire was very effective."[42]

Consequently, the Federals of Sherman's corps were no closer to taking Arkansas Post than when they had begun earlier in the day. One of Blair's Federals related that the enemy troops still "bear themselves bravely and fight on without seeming in the least discouraged," and indeed a spattering of Confederates of miniscule numbers compared to McClernand's horde had stopped all Union advances on the western portion of the line. And that line was itself wavering, as skulkers hid any place they could find. One lieutenant threatened to shoot a captain he found who was feigning a wound, and the captain took umbrage, wanting to know by what authority he did so: "You are nothing but a lieutenant." The lieutenant countered, "You are nothing but a coward" and marched the captain to the colonel and told him he would shoot him like a dog if he found him in the rear again. The colonel simply agreed: "Amen." But Sherman's advance, or lack thereof, was not all that was in line and ready to attack. Despite the heavy resistance on his front and the bad blood already growing between them, Sherman could only hope George Morgan was having better success down the line to the left.[43]

The morning of January 11 brought some relief to the shivering Federals of George Morgan's corps. Many of them had struggled through the night to reach their positions while others kept still, making the cold even worse. No fires were permitted during the dark hours, but fortunately Colonel Richard Owen of the 60th Indiana related that the next morning "a few small fires were permitted for the purpose of allowing the men to boil a cup of coffee."[44]

George Morgan had nowhere near the firepower that Sherman had, mainly because many of his brigades were detached on other duty. In fact, Peter Osterhaus's division of three brigades fielded only one in the fight proper, Colonel Daniel Lindsey's being across the river and Colonel John De Courcy's covering the transports, like Blair's in Sherman's corps largely because of the beating it had taken at Chickasaw Bayou a few days ago. But Colonel Lionel Sheldon's was in line closest to the river. Andrew Jackson Smith's two brigades were both present, however, and went into line in Sherman's old position after Sherman shifted to the right late on January 10 and early on January 11. In fact, some of Smith's troops moved through the deployed lines of Sherman's command, still waiting to move to the right, and took a position in front of them. Morgan himself looked around at his potential assault area: "I at once rode forward and made a reconnaissance of the ground to be occupied by me as soon as General Sherman advanced." The signal for Morgan's movement would be when he heard the shouts of Sherman's troops to his right, which were of course based on the movement of the navy back at the river, ironically closer to Morgan.[45]

A. J. Smith's division deployed east of the Little Rock Road, but as there was so little room for the entire corps between Sherman's shifted position and the river, Smith deployed only one brigade up front, Brigadier General Stephen G. Burbridge's. These troops went into line late on January 10 and finished their deployment the next morning as Stuart's troops moved westward. Chaos initially erupted as all went forward in new territory; Burbridge leading the way, in fact, wrote that "owing to a misapprehension of orders only one regiment . . . had followed. I immediately sent back orders for the rest of the brigade to move up, and becoming impatient [I] rode back myself and brought them up at double quick." Three guns of Captain Ambrose A. Blount's 17th Ohio Battery also moved forward and took position inside the fortification that Malmborg had constructed during the night. It was big enough to house only three guns, and Blount kept the other three in the rear in reserve. General Smith, as was his custom often, sighted some of the guns himself during the fighting, and one eventually moved forward with the infantry for a time.[46]

Burbridge eventually deployed his six regiments in two lines, the 60th Indiana at the front right and the others filling in to the left. The 16th Indiana took the center position while the 83rd Ohio filled out the front line to the left, although there was much confusion in that regiment as Lieutenant Colonel William H. Baldwin received several conflicting orders about supporting Blount's guns to the left rear, causing the regiment to change positions several times before renewing its correct position beside the 16th Indiana. Behind lay three more regiments, the 23rd Wisconsin on the right, the 67th Indiana in center, and the 96th Ohio on the left, which soon took a position to the rear supporting the three guns of Blount's Battery in the fortification. Then Burbridge waited for the signal, which had "been agreed . . . should be musketry and cheering from Major-General Sherman's corps, on our right."[47]

The shouting and shooting soon swelled in that direction, and Burbridge sent his troops forward. In the Confederate lines, Garland's Texans waited for the enemy advance, only the section of Hart's Arkansas Battery still left in position here firing at the enemy at first in the distance. Lieutenant G. W. McIntosh commanded the section, and he "commenced firing as soon as he could do so with effect, and on several occasions drove the enemy's sharpshooters from under cover of some buildings several hundred yards in front of his position, as well as otherwise generally annoying the enemy until all his ammunition was blown up by a shell from one of the enemy's batteries in front." The Texas soldiers behind the fortifications waited longer to open up, Garland giving orders that they were not to fire, with the exception of a few sharpshooters, "until the enemy should advance to within fair range."[48]

The Union regiments soon did so, pouring out of the woods and moving forward across the field toward the heavy volleys of Confederate fire. Colonel Richard Owen of the 60th Indiana on the right related how his regiment moved forward "at first at common time through the woods, and afterward in quick and double-quick, with shouts, for about 300 yards through the open field, in which, the ground being swampy, we sank over ankle deep." The front line made it to within a hundred and fifty yards of the Confederate fortifications but could go no farther, the men going to ground, "it being impossible to advance farther under such a fire without destruction to the command," wrote Colonel Thomas J. Lucas of the 16th Indiana. Stalled and his line wavering, some even falling back, Burbridge could only add more weight to the advance and pushed forward the three rear regiments, which moved across the open ground under the same heavy fire and to the same conclusion, although Burbridge reported that "the three front regiments refused to be relieved." Commanders went down quickly, including Colonel Frank Emerson of the 67th Indiana taking a ball through the thigh as well as Lieutenant Colonel John M. Orr of the 16th Indiana, the colonel being sick on a boat back at the landing. When Orr went down with a piece of shrapnel to the head, command fell to Major James H. Redfield, but Colonel Thomas J. Lucas soon got up from his sickbed and made his way to the regiment, taking control amid the fighting. The lieutenant colonel of the 60th Indiana, William J. Templeton, also went down.[49]

Although unknown to Burbridge's Federals finding it hard to move forward, a crisis was emerging in the Confederate line they faced. Garland had by this point received word from Churchill to send Deshler reinforcements to his left. Garland ordered the "alternate companies" of the two cavalry regiments and two additional companies of the 6th Texas to move in that direction, forcing his own troops to extend to cover the undefended ground. And worse, more Federals were on the way toward them in the form of Smith's other brigade, Colonel William Landram's troops. Still, Garland reported, "notwithstanding our line was very much weakened they were promptly and handsomely repulsed."[50]

Landram was indeed moving forward to the same fate as his comrades. He had deployed in a single line in rear of Burbridge the 48th Ohio, 77th Illinois, 108th Illinois, 19th Kentucky, and 97th Illinois right to left (the 131st Illinois being detained in rear to guard the roads back to the landing site). The troops had been told there would be no need for them, but there was. When Burbridge asked for support, Landram sent his left two regiments forward, they bearing to the right, the 19th Kentucky and 97th Illinois. Landram later reported that "at a later hour it became manifest that it was necessary to put the whole brigade into action," and he sent the others forward to take what positions they could find, but none were able to drive past Burbridge's troops or take the Confederate position. "The engagement lasted near two hours at this point," Landram wrote, "all the men having advanced to within 200 yards of their lines." Lieutenant Colonel Job Parker of the 48th Ohio, A. J. Smith himself telling the regiment "Forty-eighth Ohio, go right in!," received a wound in the arm but refused to turn over command, merely having it dressed on the field and returning to duty. Nearly wounded also was Colonel David Grier of the 77th Illinois, he later telling his fiancée, "I am happy to inform you I was not killed at Vicksburg as reports said in Peoria, but came pretty near it at Arkansas Post." Yet Burbridge and Landram as a whole could not move forward, the former complaining that this attack area was "through an open, marshy field, where the enemy had a full and fair range with grapeshot and musketry." Over the course of three or four hours, in fact, Burbridge sustained the highest number of casualties of any brigade in the army, a total of 349. Burbridge was not wrong when he described how "shells, grape, and musket balls rained like hail in a storm."[51]

While Smith's division endured heavy casualties, Peter Osterhaus's division of Morgan's corps saw much less action. One reason was because there was not a lot of room left for it to deploy, and a second was because much of it had been doled out elsewhere for different jobs. John De Courcy's brigade, for instance, which had suffered so at Chickasaw Bayou a few days before, remained in reserve most of the day guarding the vessels at the landing and the roadways forward. Osterhaus called up the unit later in the day, around 3:00 p.m., and although it marched forward the regiments never entered the fight. The brigade did not lose a single casualty in the entire operation.[52]

Lionel Sheldon's brigade of the division did make an appearance, however, on the left of Burbridge's and Landram's troops, between them and the river. Sheldon had only three regiments: the 69th Indiana, 120th Ohio, and 118th Illinois. The Indianans remained in reserve except for companies sent forward as skirmishers, but the Illinoisans and Ohioans advanced to the artillery battery firing near the river: "Our boys give the hoop and in they went," wrote an Indianan. Although delayed and needing "extraordinary efforts on the part of the artillerists to bring their pieces through the swamp," the now-present guns were a section of 20-pound Parrott rifles of Captain Jacob Foster's 1st Wisconsin Battery under Lieutenant Daniel Webster. The gunners found a perfect spot to fire on the Confederate fort, particularly the casemate in the center of the eastern face of the bastion. Evidently, the northeastern casemate was already out of action, and soon this one was as well, Foster writing "whether done by the gunboats or us is but little matter." At Osterhaus's direction, the gunners then shifted their fire to the cannon mounted en barbette on the southeastern corner, that gun soon also ceasing to fire, with Foster writing "this work we claim to have done." Meanwhile the infantry moved forward, and Osterhaus brought up Captain Charles G. Cooley's two sections of the Chicago Mercantile Battery, which "pitched in" and began pounding the fort and rifle pits as well, although requiring thirty infantrymen to assist them because so few men were available due to sickness; despite the men's hatred for him, Captain Cooley reported that he silenced some of the small guns in the fort itself and then "fire[d] diagonally through the lines in rear of their earthworks." One of the cannoneers countered that "we quietly minded nothing whatever about the Captains orders but each gun independently directed by its lieutenant or sergeant." As for the infantry, the Illinoisans took a position on the right of the battery and lost a few casualties, but the Ohioans moved the farthest forward. After a couple hours, Colonel Daniel French led his 120th Ohio toward the fort itself, "in column, doubled on the center." But like so many other Union regiments that day the Ohioans were stopped, primarily at the deep ditch surrounding the fort itself and a connecting huge chasm that opened into the river. The Confederate fire from Dunnington's troops was severe here as well, and the Ohioans had to huddle behind whatever they could find for cover. Lieutenant Colonel Marcus Spiegel expressed his thanks in a letter to his wife: "Oh it is perfectly awe inspiring, terrific, yet most delightedly glorious to get out unhurt."[53]

While the terrain was harsher nearer the fort, as the Ohioans found out, the Union attacks slowly spreading down to the bastion itself caused alarm inside Fort Hindman. Churchill was there himself and had given orders to Garland to provide reinforcements if necessary to Dunnington as well. Of course, Dunnington had lost his main regiment, the 19th Arkansas, to Deshler earlier, and he now called on Garland for help; Garland sent two companies of the 6th Texas inside the fort. "Although one-half of my command was already detached," Garland wrote, "deeming the holding of the fort of vital importance to us, I directed Lieutenant Colonel [Thomas S.] Anderson to throw the two right companies of his regiment into the fort." Worse, by this point the Federal gunboats had made it past the fort and were pouring in a rearward fire and "had complete command of the position, taking it in front, flank, and rear at the same time, literally raking our entire position."[54]

Meanwhile, Osterhaus's third brigade had a little different route to the fighting. Detached as it was across the river, Colonel Daniel Lindsey's brigade (7th Kentucky, 49th Indiana, and 114th Ohio), along with two sections of artillery and a troop of cavalry, moved forward toward the top of the horseshoe bend opposite the fort. Lindsey had arrived at James Smith's Plantation the night of January 9 from his debarkation point at Fletcher's Landing and had held the river in both directions with his artillery, a section of the Chicago Mercantile Battery as well as a section of the 1st Wisconsin Battery. The Confederates detected their presence, some few skirmishing on that side of the river and the fort itself throwing a few inaccurate shells toward them. Still, one of the Illinois artilleryman admitted "it would have amazed you to see us dodge behind the big trees to get out of the way." By 2:00 p.m. on January 11, however, when naval vessels passed the fort and took possession of the river so that he no longer needed to cover it against reinforcing Confederate troops, Lindsey moved to the point opposite the fort and opened up with his artillery. In fact, a naval officer had come ashore yelling "now is your time to do something. Where is the officer in command?" Lindsey met him and after a short conversation ordered the artillery and regiments northwestward into the bend of the river to fire on the Confederates.[55]

Lindsey opened up on the fort and particularly the Confederate line to the west, which he could see plainly from its rear. "We then fired upon them with fuse-shell," Captain Foster of the 1st Wisconsin Battery wrote, "and to my great satisfaction all exploded, causing great commotion among the enemy's troops in the rifle-pits. I feared the time of the fuse was too short, but it seemed to cause such destruction that we continued to use the same length fuse and with great effect. Every shell burst and just at the right point." Lieutenant Frank Wilson's section of the Chicago Mercantile Battery also opened up with their 3-inch rifles on some log buildings in rear of the fort and did good work despite being a new battery that had "never fired but 10 rounds to each piece at target." There was even an attempt to cross over a regiment in rear of the Confederates, the *Black Hawk* taking on board the Kentuckians, but other events intervened before the regiment could make a landing.[56]

Still, by near dark on January 11, the verdict was all but in that none of the Federals would be able to take the Confederate fort by assault. The big guns in the fort itself had been silenced, and most of the smaller ones both inside and along the Confederate fortifications to the west were also out of action, either destroyed or completely commanded by the Union infantry that was in places now no more than one or two hundred yards out. But the fact was that all assaults had been stopped—and quite bloodily. "For two days," Churchill wrote, "did we signally repulse and hold in check that immense body of the enemy." And they did it while causing heavy losses. Some of the brigades, particularly Burbridge's, Hovey's, and Thayer's, had taken hundreds of casualties. None of the Federal commanders had dreamed taking the fort would be this difficult, and it appeared that no game-changer was on the horizon. Likely, the Confederates could hold against additional frontal assaults until nightfall, at which time any number of things could happen, most likely a Confederate escape to the rear; Churchill in fact reported that "my great hope was to keep them in check until night, and then, if re-enforcements did not reach me, cut my way out." Desiring that not to happen, some Federals planned further assaults that afternoon before dark ended any chance of taking the Confederate position.[57]

It was a difficult situation to be in, and McClernand knew exactly what was going on at all times. His staff officer Lieutenant Samuel Caldwell had climbed a tree and "gave me momentary information of the operations both of our land and naval forces and of the enemy." McClernand knew the assaults had failed thus far. But then out of nowhere came a resolution.[58]

Despite having repulsed or deflected, even if barely, every single attack by gunboat and infantry, white flags amazingly began to go up along a portion of the Confederate line. Who authorized them, if anyone, was in question, but the general effect was a spiral out of control. Churchill himself noted that "just at this moment, to my great surprise, several white flags were displayed in the Twenty-fourth Regiment Texas Dismounted Cavalry, First Brigade, and before they could be suppressed the enemy took advantage of them, crowded upon my lines, and not being prevented by the brigade commander from crossing, as was his duty, I was forced to the humiliating necessity of surrendering the balance of the command."[59]

Exactly what happened and who displayed the white flags first was unknown. Churchill added that "I hope and trust that the traitor will yet be discovered, brought to justice, and suffer the full penalty of the law." About all anyone knew was that the flags indeed first appeared in the 24th Texas Dismounted Cavalry, the center regiment of Garland's brigade. And not all the regiment was even there, as half the companies had moved to the left to support Deshler. Garland explained that he had no idea either, writing that "it was during this terrific cross-fire, about 4.30 o'clock p.m., that my attention was attracted by the cry of 'Raise the white flag, by order of General Churchill; pass the order up the line,' and on looking to the left, to my great astonishment, I saw quite a number of white flags displayed in Wilkes' regiment (Twenty-fourth Texas Cavalry, dismounted), from the right company extending as far as I could see toward the left." The order did not pass down the line, Garland reporting that the 6th Texas "refused to raise the white flag or to pass the word up the line," and Churchill later praised "Colonels [Thomas S.] Anderson and [Clayton C.] Gillespie for the prompt measures taken to prevent the raising of the white flag in their regiments." Nor did the surrender flood down to the other brigade: "In the Second Brigade, commanded by the gallant Deshler, it was never displayed."[60]

But the damage was done initially and was compounded by split-second decisions that caused Garland to waffle as to what to do. He explained his predicament in detail:

> being deceived by the sudden and simultaneous display of white flags (for I could not conceive it possible that a white flag could be thus treacherously displayed in any part of our line with impunity), as well as by the cessation of firing on the left and the repeated and emphatic manner in which the words came coupled with the name of the commanding officer, I was convinced at the time that the order had originated from the proper source though not conveyed through the ordinary channel—as at this time the enemy's fire of artillery and small-arms was so intensely hot that no one could have passed from the general's position to mine without being struck—and directed the words to be passed to the fort as they had come to me. As the order did not reach me through the ordinary channel I did not feel authorized to give any order on the subject, and particularly as no order could have been of any avail, the act having already been consummated before it came to my knowledge.

About all Garland could testify to was that the flag had indeed appeared in Colonel Franklin C. Wilkes's 24th Texas Dismounted Cavalry, he adding as well that "the interest of the service, as well as justice to the rest of the brigade, demands a thorough and immediate investigation."[61]

Apparently, there was some physical debate in the Confederate lines whether to raise the flags at all, General Morgan writing that "several times, at different parts of the field, unauthorized white flags were run up and torn down again by the enemy." But it is significant that the flags appeared both as the Federals to the front were clearly, if not easily, held back and as the firing in the rear from gunboats and Lindsey's command across the river erupted. The Texans and Arkansans had showed they could repel the attacks in their front, but as the gunboat and artillery fire from across the river began to take their lines in rear, determination to hold the line seemed to vanish for some. One Confederate told a Union counterpart "you can't expect men to stand up against the fire of those gunboats." Deshler similarly described the rearward fire and related that some of the shooting coming in from the rear was actually so high "I noticed some of their shells pass over our line and fall among their own men in our front." He also noted that some fire hit the hospital even though it was plainly marked; one surgeon of the 15th Texas Cavalry (Dismounted) was mortally wounded by a shell while caring for the wounded there. The Federals certainly thought the rearward fire caused havoc in the Confederate ranks, Captain Foster across the river writing that "we had fired about twenty minutes into the place, when, with indescribable pleasure, we saw the white flag first at the point we had been firing upon." His counterpart across the river Lieutenant Wilson echoed that he had just started firing when the flags appeared: "[We] were just getting warmed up for work." It is certainly a probability that the sudden fire coming in from the rear unnerved some of the Texans in Garland's line and caused them to raise the white flags.[62]

But no one really knew what it meant for certain other than "the white flag took the place of the symbol of rebellion." The net result was mass confusion, although one Illinoisan explained that "they showed the white feather just in time to save a great deal of blood shed for our men were fixing for a grand charge all along their lines." That said, the general response by the Federals was logically to cease firing. That confused the Confederate defenders even more, and one Federal described how they "rose up in great numbers from their rifle-pits in full view." A gentlemanly debate then ensued as to what it meant and how to proceed. Deshler reported that he received word of the flags but dismissed it: "Everything had gone on so well on the left wing, and as far as I knew in Garland's brigade also, and knowing that it was General Churchill's determination to fight to desperation, I did not think it possible that a surrender could be intended, and paid no attention to these flags." But then the enemy stopped firing, logically, "and a mounted officer bearing a white flag was seen advancing toward our line." Deshler had no choice but to order his troops to cease firing. Then, of course, the Federals came out of their cover, Deshler relating that "the enemy showed themselves in immense force in three or four distinct and apparently parallel lines of battle and extending along my entire front and as far to the right and left as I could see." He added that "the whole space in my front, as far as I could see through the timber, seemed almost black with their forces."[63]

Back at the fort itself, Churchill was at a loss to explain the white flags or the stoppage of firing. And worse, Federals across the board were now moving toward his lines not with bayonets but also with white flags of truce. In fact, General Burbridge himself appeared at the entrance to the fort on the western side. Morgan reported that, once the white flags appeared, "General Burbridge was handed a flag, with orders to be first in the fort and plant it." He met a Confederate guard that "presented bayonets and stated that they had not surrendered." Burbridge "told him that they had fought gallantly, but were whipped, and I demanded a surrender." He also pointed to the white flags, and the Confederates allowed him in. Inside, Burbridge met Churchill and Dunnington, who agreed that surrender was the only option; Burbridge then raised the national colors over the fort. Burbridge took Churchill to McClernand, "from whom I received the formal surrender of the post, its armament, garrison, and all its stores," McClernand gloated. The former naval officer Dunnington preferred to surrender to the United States Navy, and Admiral Porter related that "Colonel Dunnington, late of the U.S. Navy, commandant of the fort, requested to surrender to the Navy. I received his sword." Captain J. J. Ennis, one of A. J. Smith's staff officers, captured the garrison flag.[64]

To the west, Deshler went in front of his lines to meet the Federal officers, one of whom was Frederick Steele. He asked what the white flag was for, and a surprised Steele responded that the Confederates had surrendered. Deshler knew better, but Steele convincingly pointed to the white flags along Garland's line and even by now the United States flag atop Fort Hindman itself. Deshler could not see the fort from his own lines but now in front of them could look to his right and see that it was so. Still unconvinced, Deshler stated that he had received no such order to surrender and asked that the Federals remain where they were until "I could hear from General Churchill." Eventually, word came to Steele from Deshler that "though he had not surrendered the forces it had been done by some unauthorized person and the act was now accomplished." Others were surprised as well; Porter was elated when in the act of delivering the Kentucky regiment across the river "the enemy held out a white flag, and I ordered the firing to cease."[65]

Once the surrender was confirmed, Federal troops rushed upon the Confederates lines once more, this time mostly in safety. "Their looks showed that the act was very humiliating to them," one Iowan remembered, "but they had no choice in the matter." That said, a few Federals were wounded by stray shots of probably livid Confederates. Others were more moved, especially at getting through the fight safely with friends still alive, one Federal writing that "I could not help blubbering like a calf to see them & I was not the only one with wet eyes." Sherman himself went forward after an aide made initial contact, and he sent orders for Steele to sweep around the enemy flank to cut off any Confederates trying to escape; he soon found "that the surrender was perfect and in good faith." Sherman asked who was in command at this point, and Garland met him; then he went to the fort and found Churchill and Admiral Porter in conversation and then to the west to help Deshler understand what had happened. Deshler snapped at Sherman when he asked why he was still resisting, stating that "he had received no orders to surrender." Churchill, who was with Sherman, gave the order: "You see, sir, that we are in their power, and you may surrender." Sherman asked Deshler if he was kin to the Deshlers from Columbus, Ohio, which the Texan denied "in an offensive tone." Sherman later recalled that "I think I gave him a piece of my mind that he did not relish." United States flags nevertheless went up, those Federals across the river jubilant that "we saw the flag for which we are ready to waste our last drop of blood proudly waving over the rebel Post Arkansas."[66]

Then there was a free-for-all among the Federals concerning which was the first regiment to reach the works, go inside the works, and enter the fort, many regimental commanders claiming the honor and nearly as many generals claiming it for their respective brigade or division. Others in the rear were too late but also marched in, William Landram noting that his reserve brigade nevertheless went in "with the banners of our country floating in triumph." Others described their regiments entering "with deafening cheers" and "hilarious with joy." Sherman reported his troops marched in "with cheers and hallooing," and even the navy cheered, Frederick Davis, still aboard the *Baron de Kalb*, relating that "all hands were piped on deck, to cheer." A Federal summed up writing home that "it was a real splendid sight to see about 30000 blue coats [march] into the rebels fortifications to the tune of Yankee Doodle."[67]

The mopping-up began immediately and continued for the next few days, one bewildered Illinoisan writing that "we were soon commingling, apparently as friends, with those whom only a few minutes before we had been trying to kill." The honorary assumption of commands for the various areas and the collecting of loot, of which there was plenty, also took place. The 77th Illinois took possession of the fort itself, one touring artilleryman amazed that "I never saw anything so completely riddled as the fort. There don't seem to be a whole spot in it." McClernand ordered what was left of the fort and earthworks destroyed immediately, Captain William F. Patterson of the Kentucky engineers gaining the duty of "destruction of the enemy's magazine, casemates, and the 9-inch gun, which he cut off." Stores of all kinds were also taken, Sherman proudly writing that "I was rejoiced to find the ammunition shipped for me from Memphis for Vicksburg, which had been captured by the enemy on the *Blue Wing*." The captured Confederates were quickly rounded up, and they stacked arms before being corralled near the "landing back of the Post." They were subsequently shipped north, conveyed by the *Lexington*. All of it was done amid horrible cold weather that moved in and produced soldiers around campfires "burning on one side and freezing on the other"; there was also almost bottomless mud, one Ohioan writing that "the members of the 76th Regiment carried portions of the soil of Arkansas Post for months afterwards." With the bad weather incoming, the Federals quickly moved into the comfortable Confederate cabins, one writing that "for the first time since I left Helena I undressed & slept well."[68]

Confederate battle losses were light, Churchill reporting that "my loss will not exceed 60 killed and 75 or 80 missing." Of course, it was in the number captured that the true tale was told, the Federals ferrying some 4,791 Southerners northward to prison camps. Ironically, that number included about two hundred men that Colonel E. E. Portlock had marched forty miles in twenty-four hours to reinforce Arkansas Post; one Confederate explained that he "succeeded in entering our lines amidst a heavy fire from the enemy on his flanks. He was just on the eve of bringing his men into action when the surrender took place." The Confederates were enraged at the surrender, especially given the circumstances, and one Federal attested that "the prisoners are mostly Texas and Arkansas rebels of the deepest dye and they grit their teeth with rage." Illustrating the heavy fighting and terrible assaults the Federals made, as well as the stout defense the Confederates put up, total Federal casualties amounted to 134 killed, 898 wounded, and 29 captured — a total of 1,061 casualties. The dead were buried immediately on the field, but the Confederates were not exchanged until the next May, three months later. Most wounded were likewise shipped north for their grueling recovery, one officer moving through the hospital vessel admitting "the further I went the sicker I got."[69]

"We met the enemy and fought them terribly and took them beautifully," Lieutenant Colonel Marcus Spiegel wrote home the next day, adding that "it is decidedly the most glorious and complete victory of the War." Another

Federal could only compare this result with the last: "We have fought another battle but with far different results than the one at Vicksburg." One relieved soldier wrote that "our boys cheered themselves hoarse for this was our first victory and we had almost become discouraged." A similarly jubilant McClernand was thrilled with his victory. Sherman related that he found him on the *Tigress* shouting "Glorious! glorious! My star is ever in the ascendant!" He quickly sent a message informing Grant of his success: "I have the honor to report that the forces under my command attacked the Post of Arkansas to-day at 1 o'clock p.m., and at 4.30 o'clock, having stormed the enemy's works, took a large number of prisoners, variously estimated at from 7,000 to 10,000, together with all his stores, animals, and munitions of war." Although he fudged a bit and made it sound as though the victory was won by storming the works, now, hopefully, Grant would take him seriously and see exactly what he could do in command of an army.[70]

But McClernand was not yet done in Arkansas. He quickly set about the mopping-up actions, including sending prisoners northward, although a few escaped in the chaos. One Federal described them as "bred to fight Indians and to lasso wild horses and cattle. They have abolished the use of all edger tools about their heads and on the whole present a wild and rough specimen of humanity and if we can take their language as an index of the sentiment of the south we may kill them but can *never* subdue them." The piles of supplies and weapons were also organized, but not before the 97th Illinois swapped out their old Belgian muskets for Confederate Enfields, "saving to the men of three pounds on the gun, and one pound on forty rounds of cartridges." The ordnance officer "made a terrible kick" about it, one Illinoisan explained, because he had no ammunition for the Enfields, but the swap was already made. More important, McClernand also sent additional units up the Arkansas River to gather provisions and drive away any remaining Confederates. The ram *Monarch* moved twelve miles upriver but ran into low water, actually running aground four times. Porter wanted the piles at the fort removed so that his vessels could operate more freely, and he also called for more ammunition and had it brought forward by the *Signal* from the mouth of the White River. It was all part of the plan to continue on up the waterway, perhaps all the way to Little Rock.[71]

All the while, congratulations were certainly in order, one Indianan writing home that "our loss so small & the results so great, make our army pretty proud." McClernand issued a proclamation to his soldiers declaring that this was "an important step toward the restoration of our national jurisdiction and unity over the territory on the right bank of the Mississippi River." One of his soldiers reacted that it was "very high strung and too highly colored, *but sounds swell in the papers.*" McClernand also eventually sent out President Lincoln's good words that the "success was both brilliant and valuable, and is fully appreciated by the country and Government." Porter even commended McClernand, writing that "I congratulate you that we have disposed of this tough little nut, the capture of which is alike creditable to the Army and Navy." But despite Porter's attempt to garner for the navy an equal role, McClernand was already claiming all the work as his own. He wrote Porter that "all the prisoners and materials of war captured testify to the harmonious and successful cooperation of the land and naval forces, and that each nobly emulated the other in the time of patriotic duty." But at the same time, McClernand was informing Grant that the navy "cooperated in accomplishing this complete success." Porter soon countered with his argument that "this has been a naval fight, although the Army attacked with long range, but did not assault." Of course, the casualty figures told otherwise, but a turf war seemingly was afoot. Still, Porter declared that "this was a most beautiful fight."[72]

Porter continued to push his branch's efforts, writing that the navy "disposed of Fort Hindman. . . . In no instance during the war has there been a more complete victory and so little doubt as to whom the credit belongs." He ended with a call for further service: "Let us show these rebels that there is no such thing as a defeat expected by the Navy. You have proved on this occasion that mud forts and railroad-iron casemates will fall before the well-directed fire of American sailors." Many of his officers were just as jubilant and went ashore to examine the Confederate fortifications. McClernand was of course not in agreement, and Porter, under a cloud already because McClernand's version of the affair reached Washington first, complained that McClernand's account simply said "that the Navy cooperated, when in fact it forced the fort to surrender, and then cut off the retreat of the rebels, who were driven back on the Army." He added: "I find that the army officers are not willing to give the Navy credit (even in very small matters) they are entitled to, but you will find that I do not fail in my reports to give my officers and men the credit they justly deserve, even at the risk of hurting the sensibilities of the Army."[73]

There was also disagreement among the army officers, made worse by the deteriorating weather conditions of rain, cold, and sickness, one Federal writing that "it seemed to rain misery." Angst was especially prevalent between David Stuart and Charles Hovey over who silenced the Confederate artillery on Deshler's line. It went as far up as Sherman, who cautioned Stuart that "I regret these conflicts of opinions, but they are always occurring when troops look to neighbors for support and assistance. The true rule is, as you state it, each commander to report his own acts and let a common superior reconcile any seeming discrepancy." Likewise, the seething dislike between Sherman and Morgan continued, Morgan writing that Sherman's lack of effort caused the heavy fighting and casualties. He described a bit of high ground across Post Bayou and added that "had General Sherman succeeded in turning the enemy's left, as contemplated by General McClernand's original plan, and a battery been planted upon that elevation, it would have enfiladed the enemy's line of rifle-pits and driven him from his cover in twenty minutes." Morgan also intimated that Sherman had objected to the idea of troops getting on the bank opposite the fort for fear they would fire into his men, but Lindsey's presence had indeed proved helpful.[74]

There were also Confederate squabbles, despite some admiration among the Federals that the enemy "fought like tigers being mostly Texas troops." Much of the argument revolved around who lofted the white flags. Even while Sherman was with the Confederates, Churchill had ridden with him over to Deshler's position but met Garland on the way. Churchill demanded "why did you display the white flag!" and Garland reported that "I received orders to do so from one of your staff." Churchill angrily denied it, and the two grew more bitter until Sherman himself stopped them, telling them it made no difference now that they were prisoners. Garland took the brunt of the abuse thereafter, he requesting a court of inquiry, which never occurred; he would live with the stain the rest of his life. Debate over relieving Garland as well as Colonel Wilkes, in whose regiment the flags first appeared, as well as even Churchill himself also raged even among the highest of Confederate officials, Jefferson Davis and Secretary of War James A. Seddon. As with Garland, nothing was ever done. For his part, Theophilus Holmes took up for his overmatched general defending Arkansas Post.[75]

Yet Arkansas Post had much larger consequences—enormous, in fact—on the Union high command. While Pemberton, Johnston, and the Confederate commanders east of the Mississippi River made little note of the operation, being concerned more with events east of the Mississippi than in a different department altogether across the river, the whole nature of the Mississippi Valley campaign for the Federals turned on Arkansas Post. McClernand envisioned his victory being lauded, but in fact his accomplishment brought only condemnation and oversight from Grant. Despite his detailed arguments for doing so, his official "Reasons for the Arkansas River Expedition," the simmering dispute and distrust between Grant and McClernand would come full term as a result.[76]

Grant was nervous already about McClernand taking command, but he could not argue with Lincoln and Stanton. But as McClernand's communications and reports of the command grew tardy, perhaps on purpose, Grant began to realize McClernand was now pulling a fast one on him just like he and Sherman had done on McClernand earlier. Perhaps such a victory might just circumvent Grant by impressing Lincoln as well as the general public, who would not dare tamper with a winning general on a roll. Accordingly, when Grant heard of Arkansas Post, he snapped.[77]

"General McClernand has fallen back to White River, and gone on a wild-goose chase to the Post of Arkansas," Grant seethed to Halleck on January 11, the very day McClernand was attacking the fort. Obviously, McClernand had waited sufficiently long enough to act without returning orders from Grant restricting his plans. "I am ready to re-enforce, but must await further information before knowing what to do," Grant continued. The backward move was bad enough, likely causing an uproar in the papers and among politicians that Grant was on the retreat, but to move away from Vicksburg and into an altogether different department to perform needless operations was even worse.[78]

Grant wasted no time lambasting McClernand. The same day he informed Halleck and possibly even while McClernand was in the act of attacking, Grant wrote that "unless absolutely necessary for the object of your expedition you will abstain from all moves not connected with it." He went on to add: "I do not approve of your move on the Post of Arkansas while the other [Vicksburg] is in abeyance." He wanted McClernand to keep the main goal in the forefront, "the capture of Vicksburg." He further added that "unless you are acting under authority not derived from me keep your command where it can soonest be assembled for the renewal of the attack on Vicksburg," and he mentioned Milliken's Bend as probably the best place to return to: "Unless there is some great reason of which I am not advised you will immediately proceed to that point."[79]

The tirade produced some hoped-for change for Grant—not with McClernand but in Washington. The next day brought a short note from Halleck: "You are hereby authorized to relieve General McClernand from command of the expedition against Vicksburg, giving it to the next in rank or taking it yourself." That was all Grant needed, but he still had to be careful. McClernand was, after all, still under the president's direction, and removal might spark a political battle Grant did not want to fight just yet; certainly, McClernand would not go down without a fight. Instead of relieving McClernand outright, in the best Clausewitzian awareness of the political attributes of military operations, Grant simply chose to do what he perhaps should have done all along: defy the theories of supporting columns espoused by Jomini and make the Mississippi Valley operations a one-push effort under one commander (himself) at a time. Grant informed his commanders in Tennessee the next day, January 13, that "it is my present intention to command the expedition down the river in person."[80]

McClernand's sole command had lasted all of a couple of weeks, although Grant later admitted, likely when he heard Sherman's version and that he had been behind it in the first place, that "I was at first disposed to disapprove of this move as an unnecessary side movement having no especial bearing upon the work before us; but when the result was understood I regarded it as very important." In fact, one of Grant's brigade commanders, Kilby Smith, asserted that McClernand "reaped but the harvest that had been sown by Sherman." It would remain to be seen if Grant could work through all the issues, including McClernand remaining with the army as senior commander under Grant, to finally take Vicksburg. But the troops were confident, this victory having boosted morale in a significant way. One Indianan wrote his wife: "We shall start on another expedition immediately probably again for Vicksburg. We hope to close the war soon—God help us."[81]

4

"The Work of Changing the Channel of the Mississippi"

January 14–31

The Mississippi River has been notorious for changing course in its history. Just an examination of any modern map illustrates the fact, as numerous so-called oxbow lakes parallel the current bed. These were once great bends of the river themselves but are now cut off due to the strong forces of nature, particularly water. These changes yielded situations in which portions of Mississippi, for example, now lay west of the river while parts of Louisiana and Arkansas reside east of it. The massive changes also affected how history developed, with once thriving areas now left in the shadow of isolation. Moon Lake in northwest Mississippi is one such example, as is Eagle Lake just north of Vicksburg, now a detached body of water that during the Civil War was the main channel. But no better example is Davis Bend south of Vicksburg, which was once a thriving location owned by the Davis brothers, Joseph and Jefferson, where the president of the Confederacy maintained his plantation Brierfield. With the river cutting through the narrow neck of land that once connected the bend with Mississippi, Davis Bend today is a mere backwater and totally isolated from tourists or travelers, and it is also a little section of Mississippi west of the modern Mississippi River.[1]

The most significant change in the river's course was at Vicksburg itself after the war, in April 1876. The wartime river took the great turn to the northwest of Vicksburg but then took another hairpin turn to the south, paralleling its course just to the east except flowing the opposite direction as it passed Vicksburg, which sat on the high bluffs on the eastern leg of the horseshoe-shaped curve in the river. The result was an extremely narrow peninsula of land that extended up into the horseshoe bend, known then as De Soto Point.

A small town existed there, mainly because it was the terminus of the Vicksburg, Shreveport, and Texas Railroad that ran eastward from the heartland of northern Louisiana to the Mississippi River. Travelers and goods could cross the river there and continue eastward on the Southern Railroad of Mississippi that left Vicksburg heading east to Jackson and the greater Confederacy. In 1876, after years of wearing away at the thin peninsula, the river finally cut through, making the horseshoe-shaped bend backwater and leaving Vicksburg high and dry, no longer sitting on the river itself. Of course, in the years since, Vicksburg has expanded southward to once again touch the river with extended corporate limits while the old channel, through work by the Army Corps of Engineers, has become a port area. But it is ironic that nature did what the Federals tried and failed to do in 1862–1863: find a safe route past Vicksburg and its numerous batteries closing the river to traffic.[2]

But it was not because of a lack of effort, even starting a year earlier. While there in 1862, Thomas Williams declined to attack the city with his small force, prompting mortar commander David D. Porter to complain that Williams "lost his chance." Instead, he began to dig. In fact, Federal commanders as early as the summer of 1862, knowing full well that the river had a tremendous tendency to change course, sought to help that process a little bit and nudge the waterway into doing what it ultimately did in 1876, leaving Vicksburg bypassed. The way to do that, they thought, was to dig a waterway, or canal, across the narrow neck of land to allow water to flow freely. Hopefully once that was done, more and more water would rush through, continually scouring the canal until it grew larger and the river ultimately changed course. It was an ingenious idea, one soldier simply explaining that "it is to cut off Vicksburg, so that we can go up and down without going by there."[3]

Major General Benjamin Butler first mentioned the idea of the canal on June 6, 1862, as Brigadier General Thomas Williams pushed his brigade to Vicksburg. "You will send up a regiment or two at once and cut off the neck of land beyond Vicksburg by means of a trench across . . . making the cut about 4 feet deep and 5 feet wide. The river itself will do the rest for us." Williams made preparations but ran into doubts from Flag Officer David Farragut, who "does not concur." He argued that, to land troops on the upriver cut area, he would have to pass the Vicksburg batteries while working against the current. He had done so at Forts Jackson and St. Philip, but Vicksburg was an altogether different story. While Farragut would eventually do so, he was not on board at this point for the operation.[4]

Williams persevered and by late June started digging, his mostly New England troops unaccustomed to the heat and humidity of Mississippi summers and paying the price in sickness and death. One Federal later wrote that "I saw several graves down there of the Vermont boys." Williams nevertheless first "commenced running and leveling the line of the cut-off canal, and on the morning of [June 27] broke ground." Local slaves gathered by force did much of the work, as many as twelve hundred of them working in parties of twenty each overseen by soldiers; they performed the work of "excavating, cutting down trees, and grubbing up the roots." But Williams was not too confident: "The labor of making this cut is far greater than estimated by anybody. The soil is hard clay as far as yet excavated (6 1\2 to 7 feet), and must be gone through with, say, some 4 feet or more before the water can be let in; for all concur in this, that we must come to sand before the cut can be pronounced a success. The current of the river, however great, will not wash the clay." Still, Williams predicted eventual success, especially with the predicted "June Rise" already being reported in the Northern papers: "We are in good heart. The project is a great one worthy of success." Even Farragut had come around by early July, Williams describing him as "most sanguine and even enthusiastic."[5]

Ultimately, the canal did not divert the river in the summer of 1862, despite Williams's hopes. "I regard the cut-off to be my best bower," he wrote; "should it fail me I shall resort to the next best, to seize and hold the enemy's batteries, or at least spike their guns." There was a temporary setback on July 11 when the canal was actually about a foot or two below the current river level. Williams was almost ready to let water in to begin scouring, but several cave-ins delayed the progress, and in the meantime the river fell dramatically so that it was now below the level of the canal. Williams termed this "at least a temporary failure," but he was not giving up, hoping to cut a crevasse as deep as needed so that even at low water the river would still flow through. That might, he explained, even reach depths of forty feet, which would take months to dig, but he was not giving up.[6]

Williams would not have the chance to continue his work, the falling river also causing havoc with the navy, which had to seek deeper water and thus could not protect the workers sufficiently. Housing was also an issue, and the sick list was growing exponentially as the work in the swampy, miry lowlands continued. Most important, rumblings of Confederate moves southward near Baton Rouge and the Red River emerged, causing Butler to recall Williams, he adding that "besides, you are in the geographical department of General Halleck." Indeed, in a matter of weeks Confederates would attack at Baton Rouge, where Williams would be killed.[7]

Despite some pressure on Halleck to look toward the canal, perhaps in an effort to get him to more contextually look to Vicksburg itself, the War Department suggested strongly that Halleck take over the work in late June and July. "If you have not already given your attention to the practicability of making a cut-off in the rear of Vicksburg I beg to direct your attention to that point," Stanton wrote Halleck in late June. Farragut also got in on the lobbying, writing that Williams's force was too small but that he was nevertheless "cutting a ditch across the peninsula to change the course of the river."[8]

Halleck ultimately burst everyone's hopes, writing that "it is impossible to send to Vicksburg at present, but I will give the matter my full attention as soon as circumstances will permit." Thus languished any hope for a major move on Vicksburg in the summer of 1862, as well as any hope of changing the river's course. As a result, Williams's canal, termed by many as "Butler's Canal," sat cold and miry throughout the fall and winter, a mere eighteen feet wide and thirteen feet deep. It was a start, but not sufficient to change the course of "old man river."[9]

But it was not the last attempt to "leave Vicksburg in the dry" by changing the course of the river at the "celebrated ditch," a decidedly against-the-book effort to win a military campaign.[10]

Before any such renewed military campaigning or even canal-digging took place in late January, however, both sides went about a time of reorganization and refitting that would encompass the middle of January: "The yankeys ar on one side of the Miss river & we ar on the other," one Georgian informed his wife. This period of reorganization saw the Union high command in a state of flux, one Iowan admitting that "this army is not fit for service yet." Although not on site, Grant knew he needed to be down with the army and made plans to make a temporary trip down to Napoleon or Milliken's Bend to see what was going on and to "have a better understanding of matters than I now have." But he also knew McClernand's command would be a while getting resituated for new efforts: "I learn by special messenger sent to the fleet in Arkansas that it will be fifteen days before they can act efficiently again." Meanwhile, Grant also had command issues back in West Tennessee, such as getting rid of Brigadier General Thomas Davies, who had by all accounts (except his own) panicked during Forrest's Raid in December, and replacing him at Columbus, Kentucky, with Brigadier General Alexander Asboth. The corps system being emplaced also brought changes, especially when Hurlbut went on leave and Grant left Charles Hamilton in charge of the XVI Corps assets in West Tennessee and northern Mississippi. Hamilton had been one of his wing commanders in the Mississippi Central Campaign, along with James B. McPherson, but Grant had other special intentions for his protégé McPherson.[11]

The implementation of the corps system created the special work for McPherson, he being one of the four men named to command Grant's four corps back in December. And with Grant intending to soon move southward on the river with John Logan's and John McArthur's divisions, those two, along with Isaac Quinby's that would remain in West Tennessee for the time being, would constitute the three divisions of McPherson's XVII Corps. Grant was already working on transportation for these two divisions, even calling in steamers from the Ohio River for service and cautioning McClernand to send back upriver all he could spare. For his part, the somewhat still naive and inexperienced McPherson wrote Grant upon receiving his orders that "I cannot express to you the gratification it gives me, and I shall most assuredly do my utmost to merit your confidence." But not all were so thrilled at McPherson's ascendance; one Federal wrote that "we are now in the 17th Army Corps commanded by General Macpherson in whom we have about as much confidence as we would in a six month's old baby." The other corps' orders of battle were also working out, with McClernand's XIII Corps (currently under Morgan) consisting of A. J. Smith's and Peter Osterhaus's divisions and Sherman's XV Corps of Steele's and Stuart's divisions. Each would gain new divisions as well once the army coalesced down near Vicksburg, including the newly arrived brigade from the East under Sherman's brother-in-law Brigadier General Hugh Ewing, which went to Stuart's division of Sherman's corps.[12]

By far, Grant's biggest concern was with McClernand, who after his victory at Arkansas Post seemed to take on even more desire for overall command, even challenging Grant and others at times. Perhaps his appearance on the front page (along with Porter, ironically) of *Harper's Weekly* inflated his ego even more. Sherman had received orders to begin referencing his corps as the "XV Corps," but McClernand sent a terse note "to inquire of you by what authority you call the Second Army Corps of the Army of the Mississippi the 'Fifteenth Army Corps.'" Sherman had apparently used the name in correspondence with McClernand, also referencing McClernand's corps, and McClernand took exception to that too, "well knowing that General Morgan is in command of the First Army Corps." The orders had not reached McClernand as yet, and Sherman had to show him Grant's order to absolve himself. Later, McClernand also felt the need to complain to Grant about the apparent disparity of numbers between his own and Sherman's corps, "not doubting in the absence of any good reason to the contrary you will at once equalize the strength of the corps."[13]

The biggest concern was what McClernand might do before Grant could arrive and rein him in. He had definite plans to go on up to Little Rock, orders going out to be on the boats and ready by the morning of January 14 "ready to make a new move." But "want of sufficient water in the channel of the Arkansas River" precluded that advance. Ultimately, by January 14, Grant's orders to move back out to the Mississippi River arrived, and McClernand, still jubilant over his victory, informed Grant "I find that our success here is more extensive than I at first supposed." McClernand, still unaware of Grant's anger, simply ordered his corps eastward, although even that brought some disobedience, he writing General Gorman who was on his own expedition up the White River: "My orders from Major-General Grant require me at once to go to Napoleon, but I shall delay a day or two in order to threaten Little Rock and Pine Bluff as a diversion in your favor." While McClernand did not move on upriver, Admiral Porter did send some of his ironclads up the White River to aid Gorman.[14]

McClernand had an idea he was being superseded, mentioning to Sherman on January 14 that "it is not improbable that orders from General Grant will control the movements of our forces when we reach the Mississippi River." But he was unprepared for the salvo unleashed on him in Grant's note of January 11 (possibly also the one on the 13th), which did not arrive until the evening of January 16. McClernand shot back that "I take the responsibility of the expedition against Post Arkansas, and had anticipated your approval of the complete and signal success which crowned it rather than your condemnation." He again listed many of the reasons for the move, ending tersely: "I accept the consequences of the imputed guilt of using it [the army] profitably and successfully upon my own responsibility. The officer who, in the present strait of the country, will not assume a proper responsibility to save it is unworthy of public trust."[15]

The Illinois politician-general was even more blunt with Lincoln, whom he wrote the same evening. He sent a copy of Grant's note, editorializing that "I believe my success here is gall and wormwood to the clique of West Pointers who have been persecuting me for months. How can you expect success when men controlling the military destinies of the country are more chagrined at the success of your volunteer officers than the very enemy beaten by the latter in battle? Something must be done to take the hand of oppression off citizen soldiers whose zeal for their country has prompted them to take up arms, or all will be lost." He added, "Do not let me be clandestinely destroyed, or, what is worse, dishonored, without a hearing." He also prodded: "How can General Grant at a distance of 400 miles intelligently command the army with me? He cannot do it. It should be made an independent command, as both you and the Secretary of War, as I believe, originally intended."[16]

What came back next, whether in response to this scathing note or earlier ones, was not at all settling. Stanton merely wrote that "I think you need no new assurance of the sincere desire of the President and myself to oblige you in every particular consistent with the general interest of the service, and I trust that the course of events will be such as will enable the Government to derive the utmost advantage from your patriotism and military skill." Lincoln's reply was even more blunt: "I have too many family controversies (so to speak) already on my hands, to voluntarily, or so long as I can avoid it, take up another. You are now doing well—well for the country, and well for yourself—much better than you could possibly be, if engaged in open war with Gen. Halleck. Allow me to beg, that for your sake, for my sake, & for the country's sake, you give your whole attention to the better work." McClernand had already seen his support from Washington begin to erode, and this was more of the same and not at all reassuring. In fact, Lincoln and Stanton had extracted what they intended out of McClernand and were now backing off their deal.[17]

Despite the unevenness from Washington, McClernand's near insubordination continued. At one point he proclaimed that he was "tired of furnishing brains for the Army of the Tennessee." One staff officer later admitted that Grant "was greatly annoyed by McClernand's insubordinate behavior," and several tried to get the general to "give him such a rebuke that he could not effect to misunderstand his position as a subordinate." Grant declined: "No, I can't afford to quarrel with a man whom I have to command." Clearly, Grant had the political implications in mind as he dealt with McClernand— certainly a Clausewitzian line of thought.[18]

Yet Grant and McClernand were thinking alike on at least one issue, although to McClernand's ultimate horror. He had written to Lincoln of Grant's inability to command the Vicksburg operations from West Tennessee, and Grant was of the very same opinion. But his realization brought him to very different conclusions than McClernand, who wanted an independent command. It would be an independent command all right, but not like McClernand envisioned. To his subordinate's horror, Grant was intending to come down himself and take command around Vicksburg, something observers noted was well debated: "Whether it will be successful or not remains to be seen—and is questionable in the minds of those who are best informed."[19]

But Grant was having a hard time just getting downriver in the midst of a severe cold snap: "Citizens say it is the coldest weather they have had for 20 years," one Federal wrote home. Grant was delayed several times, including once by prisoners of war from Arkansas Post showing up at Memphis. He had to deal with where to send them, the obvious choice of the western exchange location at Vicksburg being out of the question: "They would go at once to re-enforce the very point we wish to reduce." A heavy storm that dumped as much as eight inches of snow on Grant's army in northern Mississippi and froze water solid, the same system that pelted McClernand's force on its way from Arkansas Post, did not help either. One Federal simply explained that "wee had to grin and bare it." Grant also had to deal with everyday departmental issues such as trade permits and civilian relations. Of more pressing interest was the supply situation down with the army, McClernand having reported to him of the lack of goods and that "to be caught without such stores, particularly ordnance stores, at so remote a point as the vicinity of Vicksburg, with the river infested by guerillas, would indeed be a dilemma."[20]

There were other command problems as well, which if they did not involve Grant or McClernand nevertheless caused discord within the army. And in fact, much of it centered on Sherman. It was during this time that Sherman became embroiled in the famous squabble with *New York Herald* reporter Thomas W. Knox, who had written disparagingly about Sherman and his Chickasaw Bayou operations. Sherman had him hauled in and ultimately placed under arrest, despite Knox, perhaps unwisely, admitting that he had written his story before the full knowledge of the reports was had. Sherman seethed that "I could hardly believe that a white man could be so false as this fellow Knox." He later went on a full tirade against Knox, asserting that "if he (Knox) cannot get at the truth he must publish falsehood" and that "without further hesitation I declare that if I am forced to look to the New York *Herald* as my law and master instead of the constituted authorities of the United States my military career is at an end. . . . I for one am willing no longer to tamely bear their misrepresentations and infamies, and shall treat Knox and all others of his type as spies and defamers." Ultimately, Lincoln gave in to Knox and allowed him to return if Grant approved it, but Grant would not unless Sherman approved it, which he did not. When asked, Sherman replied "my answer is—never."[21]

Worse for military unity, Sherman brought others into the chaos. He asked Porter to write a note "for the satisfaction of my brother, John Sherman, in the Senate," adding that he would like an answer to the question of "whether I acted the part of an intelligent officer or that of an insane fool." Porter supported Sherman all the way, including disparaging Morgan's division and particularly John De Courcy's brigade, which was already becoming Sherman's favorite place to lay blame for the defeat. Worse, when Knox appeared before Sherman, the reporter named Frank Blair as "authority for most of his general and specific assertions." Sherman wrote Blair a long, nasty letter full of questions, which the former congressman answered in detail. He fully denied being any part of Knox's wrong assertions or negative stories about Sherman, hitting back that "it is a matter of mortification to me to receive such a letter from you," later adding that "I confess myself greatly mortified and annoyed in being called on to answer such interrogatories under such circumstances." Sherman later recanted, and in fact both he and Grant had a change of heart about the politician Blair. Sherman even ended one of his last letters with "I now retract that and assure you of my confidence and respect."[22]

Sherman also seemed to have some explaining to do about Arkansas Post. In the heated back-and-forth with Sherman over Knox, Blair wrote that "I am well aware, also, that you planned and in great measure executed the movement against Arkansas Post." Even Porter wrote Sherman that "it originated with yourself entirely." Now that Grant had let his displeasure be known, Sherman wrote him in defense of McClernand's actions: "I infer from a remark made by General McClernand that you have disapproved the step." He also went through the reasoning behind it, mentioning the supply line threat and that "the capture of the *Blue Wing* was a mere sample." In fact, he went on to state that "I assure you when next at Vicksburg I will feel much less uneasiness about our communications." Grant walked back his protest now that he realized it was primarily Sherman and not McClernand who conceived the idea.[23]

All the while, McClernand and Sherman were moving back to the Mississippi River: "We then steamed off down the river," one Federal wrote home. Another informed his parents that "we have blown the old fort sky high and have returned to the Mississippi." One Illinoisan situated in the comfortable Confederate cabins complained that "this is the way it always is, as soon as we begin to be comfortable, we have to get up and move," adding "we were ordered to put every thing combustible in the houses and fire them, which we did and at 3:00 P.M. we started for the boats, leaving nothing but smoking ruins. The rifle Pits are filled up & the fort being demolished as fast as possible & soon the Fort at Arkansas Post, will remain, only, in History." But worse was to come. The heavy snowstorm hit that very day, making the soldiers out on the transport decks miserable. One Federal related the suffering to his wife: "I have lay down at night wet to the skin, rolled myself in equally wet blankets, lay down so thick crowded that I could not possibly turn myself. Awoke in the morning covered with snow my clothes frozen so stiff I could scarcely unroll myself." An Illinoisan wrote that the hurricane deck of his boat had a sheet of ice and that all they had to cover themselves was a blanket on the ice and two on their bodies. "The boys would spoon up," he added, "some making light of our condition, and others meeting it with curses." Another admitted that "if this is a fair specimen of winters in the Sunny South a very little of it will do me." Worse, men frequently fell overboard as well, some of whom drowned while others were picked up by the small cutters on board the steamers. The flotilla nevertheless arrived at Napoleon by January 16, even though the outlook for permanent camps there was not good either, although a few found comfortable quarters in the vacant houses of the town. "Napoleon is a hard-looking place," Sherman informed McClernand, "and I can see no place where I could form a brigade." And it grew worse, as a fire started in what was left of the town, Sherman himself trying to help extinguish it. He was unable to do so and called for justice for whoever started it, although no one knew anything. He simply accepted that "in some future time the actor will boast of it, when it can be fixed on him." Obviously, the army would need to move on southward, as Grant intended all along. It did so by the morning of January 17, although one Illinoisan admitted, "I hate Steam Boat Soldiering more than anything else."[24]

Grant followed along, arriving at Napoleon while the high command was still there. "I start immediately to the fleet," he had written Halleck the day before; "my design is to get such information from them as I find impossible to get here. I will return here in a few days, and in the mean time reenforcements will be forwarded with all dispatch." Grant met with the senior officers at Napoleon and then immediately sent them on their way back down to Vicksburg, Grant returning to Memphis. But what he found during the visit was not good: "The weather is highly unfavorable for operations," he informed Halleck, "and streams all very high and rising. The work of reducing Vicksburg will take time and men, but [it] can be accomplished." Worse discoveries especially regarded McClernand. Grant informed Halleck once back at Memphis that "I regard it as my duty to state that I found there was not sufficient confidence in General McClernand as a commander, either by the Army or Navy, to insure him success. Of course, all would co-operate to the best of their ability, but still with a distrust." Sherman had written confidentially of his displeasure with McClernand and that "I wish you would come down and see. I only fear McClernand may attempt impossibilities." That was part of the reason Grant did go down, but he found a lot more trouble as well. Grant made sure Halleck understood that he did not ask questions and that the officers of both branches confided in him first. He summed up that it really did not matter since he was planning to take personal command soon, but "I want you to know that others besides myself agree in the necessity of the course I had already determined upon pursuing." Grant used this opportunity to also recommend all four western department commands be put under one commander, much like Halleck himself had back in early 1862. He also perhaps foolishly added: "As I am the senior department commander in the

West, I will state that I have no desire whatever for such combined command, but would prefer the command I now have to any other that can be given."[25]

Despite the trouble with McClernand, some good news arrived when Grant returned to Memphis by the night of January 19: Halleck had finally placed the Helena command and any other Arkansas troops in Grant's vicinity under his charge, something Grant had repeatedly urged. Grant had been chirping about the need for such a move, something the Confederate high command on the ground also saw as a necessity for their own troops. But whereas the Union War Department did so, the Confederates never would. In infusing the Arkansas troops into the Army of the Tennessee, Grant assigned all of Gorman's men at Helena to McClernand's XIII Corps, which would help alleviate some of the disproportion of troops McClernand had been barking about. With the lack of boats and supplies, however, as well as camping ground farther south, Grant told McClernand to leave them at Helena for the time being: "There is no great hurry about starting them [southward]." Nevertheless, Grant now had control of many of Samuel Curtis's troops, especially those along the river, and Grant immediately ordered General Gorman, off on his own White River expedition, to return at once to Helena and send northward the steamers he was using unless there was "any enterprise for breaking up the enemy in his stronghold, if you are near the accomplishment of such a result." Still, he reiterated that "the Mississippi River enterprise must take precedence over all others." Gorman was to wait, however, Grant not yet knowing how the upcoming campaign would look: "I cannot say now how soon that may be, but I am making all the dispatch possible." One Federal watching the proceedings was not worried, writing his brother "at dress parade on Saturday evening a order was read placing all the troops under Gen Gorman under the command of Gen Grant. I do not know that the order has any particular significance to us. It gives Gen Grant the authority to move us [but] probably amounts to nothing." How wrong he would be.[26]

Taking care of everything needed at Memphis, including sending more troops southward, Grant returned downriver for good on January 26, arriving at Young's Point two days later. In one of the regiments sent down from Memphis, an Iowan explained that "we embarked on the Steamer *Minnehaha*, the same, big, old tub that carried us from St. Louis to Pittsburg Landing. By what chance of war we again got this steamer, out of hundreds of others, I never knew." Grant enjoyed his last few days of peace, writing his wife, Julia, that "the trip, with nothing to bother me, makes me feel well. The living on the boat is very fine and my appetite good." But he knew hard work was ahead and informed her that "I shall not return to Memphis until the close of this campaign. . . . Vicksburg will be a hard job. I expect to get through it successfully however."²⁷

Once arrived, Grant began to wield control of the various portions of the army, but that only brought another confrontation with McClernand. When Grant repositioned a unit, McClernand sent a terse but loaded letter on January 30, writing that "if I am to be held responsible for the safety of this camp, I must be permitted to dispose of the forces within it as I may think proper. . . . The enforcement of your order will be the subversion of my authority." Going on, McClernand evidently decided this was the time, now that Grant was on site, to finally decide who was in command. He continued:

> And, having said this much, general, it is proper that I should add one or two other words. I understand that orders are being issued directly from your headquarters directly to army corps commanders, and not through me. As I am invested, by order of the Secretary of War, indorsed by the President, and by order of the President communicated to you by the General-in-Chief, with the command of all the forces operating on the Mississippi River, I claim that all orders affecting the condition or operations of those forces should pass through these headquarters; otherwise I must lose a knowledge of current business and dangerous confusion ensue. If different views are entertained by you, then the question should be immediately referred to Washington, and one or the other, or both of us, relieved. One thing is certain, two generals cannot command this army, issuing independent and direct orders to subordinate officers, and the public service be promoted.

It was highly insubordinate and even more presumptive, especially his leaning on the president and secretary of war, who he knew were already backing away from their deal. Grant simply noted that "it was highly insubordinate, but I overlooked it, as I believed, for the good of the service."²⁸

Yet Grant soon decided he had to make a firm statement to assure McClernand of his place, he telling Washington that if Sherman was still in command "such is my confidence in him that I would not have thought my presence necessary. But whether I do General McClernand injustice or not, I have not confidence in his ability as a soldier to conduct an expedition of the magnitude of this one successfully." Therefore, he wrote, "I determined to at least be present with the expedition." Unknown to McClernand, the matter of command had already been "referred" to Washington, and Halleck had given Grant permission to take command himself. Grant accordingly sent out orders on January 30 that he "hereby assumes the immediate command of the expedition against Vicksburg, and department headquarters will hereafter be with the expedition." He added that "army corps commanders will resume the immediate command of their respective corps, and will report to and receive orders direct from these headquarters." It was unmistakably directed at McClernand, and one of Grant's engineers noted that it was "to the joy of everyone except McClernand." Incidentally, the command would also be designated as the Army of the Tennessee instead of McClernand's Army of the Mississippi.[29]

As expected, these orders brought a vitriolic response from McClernand, who wrote asking whether the orders "relieve me from the command of all or any portion of the forces composing the Mississippi River expedition, or, in other words, whether its purpose is to limit my command to the Thirteenth Army Corps." If so, McClernand argued, it was in violation of the presidentially endorsed War Department order giving him the command. He also quibbled with troop movements ordered by Grant. The department commander responded firmly that "I will take direct command of the Mississippi River expedition, which necessarily limits your command to the Thirteenth Army Corps. . . . I have seen no order to prevent my taking immediate command in the field." McClernand of course would not let it go and railed against the order: "I protest against its competency and justice." But he let it go after that, waiting for another opportunity to complain against Grant and perhaps regain what he thought was his rightful command.[30]

Despite the brainpower wasted on needless command friction, Grant was still thinking of the future at the same time. Even before he arrived for consultations with McClernand, Sherman, and Porter on his first trip southward, he was already conceiving in his mind a plan, and much of the talks centered on the business at hand. In fact, he warned Halleck once back in Memphis that particularly Sherman and Porter, "who have had the best opportunity of studying the enemy's positions and plans, agree that the work of reducing Vicksburg is one of time, and will require a large force at the final struggle." While Grant did not need reinforcements just yet, he did go ahead and ask to know where they would eventually come from so that he could plan better. For his part, Halleck had been telling him of Major General Nathaniel Banks's effort to the south, hoping for his movement up the river, with which Grant was to cooperate. Halleck told him not to rely on Banks but to cooperate if he did show up at Vicksburg: "They will at least occupy a portion of the enemy's forces and prevent them from re-enforcing Vicksburg." But Grant still had a lot of planning to do on his end, even considering at one point a march through the Delta north of the Yazoo River to a point north of Haynes' Bluff where, "once back of the intrenchments on the crest of the bluffs, the enemy would be compelled to come out and give us an open field fight, or submit to having all his communications cut and be left to starve out." It was the same old need to reach the high ground east of Vicksburg, but the rough winter weather, Grant terming it "the intolerable rains that we have had, and which have filled the swamps and bayous so that they cannot dry up again this winter," made it impossible probably for months. "What may be necessary to reduce the place I do not yet know," he informed Halleck from Napoleon, "but since the late rains think our troops must get below the city to be used effectively."[31]

Porter and Sherman were thinking the same thing, Porter arguing that "my opinion is that Vicksburg is the main point." Sherman was a little more detailed, thinking out loud of anything from "we might possibly land right under the guns" at Vicksburg with the navy's help to another try up the Yazoo, although he said nothing would work at Chickasaw Bayou and that the Haynes' Bluff area would be the only possibility. But then he also mentioned, if Federals forces were coming up as rumored from the Gulf, "it may be the approach from the south may be better." Yet Sherman emphasized that "the importance of Vicksburg cannot be overstated, and if possible a larger force should somehow reach the ridge between the Black and Yazoo, so as to approach from the rear." But that was all in the future, as right now everything was almost totally underwater; about all the Federals could do was to throw a few shells now and then from the gunboats to "stir them up." Sherman in fact correctly summarized to his brother that "we must get on land before we can fight." But the overall objective was never far from Grant's mind, and he succinctly summed up the question: "The problem then became, how to secure a landing on high ground east of the Mississippi without an apparent retreat."[32]

Meanwhile, the expectant army moved continually downriver and landed at Milliken's Bend and Young's Point, an Ohioan writing that "the soldiers nearly all got on the hurricane decks with eyes widely opened while looking at the city and its fortifications of Vixburgh." And it did not take long to start the festivities, one Missourian explaining that the artillery soon shelled Vicksburg "to let Johnny Reb know that we were there again." Yet all the common soldier knew was that "I suppose we will soon be trying Vicksburg again."[33]

"The Yankee fleet again appeared in the Miss above Vicksburg," one Alabamian scribbled in his diary in late January. "The Yankees are in sight with their Gunboats," a Louisianan in Vicksburg similarly related to his mother, adding "we can see there tents on the other side of the river. I expect we will have a fight up here soon." With that, all knew the operations around Vicksburg would again be picking up very soon.[34]

For the Confederates, the mid-January reorganization meant making sense of what had occurred at Arkansas Post, how if at all it impacted Vicksburg (Theophilus Holmes could worry about the immediate results in his separate department across the river), and settling on a command system in Mississippi that was workable and effective. All of that took place in the context of a rapidly rising river that only aided in their defenses as it restricted approaches to Vicksburg except by boat. Accordingly, there was a "comparative quiet" in activity but not in sickness; smallpox, varaloid, and typhoid fever broke out in many regiments. One Confederate with smallpox wrote home that "the general has sent us out of the brigade one mile and half, there to die or get well." Amid frequent reports of drill and reviews in the down time, some commanders of local Mississippi units even took the opportunity to allow some of their men to return home: "Col. [Michael] Farrell very generally let the boys of each company off in squads to spend a few days at home, and these returning, other squads would do likewise," related a member of the 15th Mississippi. Others were allowed to return home to recruit.[35]

Morale soon grew despite the winter dreariness and lack of activity. One Louisianan wrote home that "I think that all they can do is what they have already done," adding that he was well fixed for quarters, food, and fortifications. Another wrote that, despite the Federals being on the opposite side of the river and shelling Vicksburg constantly, "I do not think the city can be taken by a *hundred* thousand northerners—so very strong it is." Yet all knew a fight was coming due to the movements that gradually concentrated the Confederate army around the Vicksburg and Jackson areas, one Mississippian complaining of his trip from Grenada down to Jackson: "Cooked three days rations to go to parts unknown."[36]

But there were problems. Command cohesion was seemingly not possible as long as the departmental commander Joseph E. Johnston remained in Mississippi with his thumb figuratively on Pemberton, questioning his every move and making some of his own without Pemberton's input or thoughts. The relationship between the two would never be good, and it would certainly reap negative dividends later in the campaign. But as for now, the two tried their best to work together before Johnston returned to Tennessee to oversee the other part of his department from Chattanooga. Johnston remained in Jackson at least until January 17, but then he traveled cross-country, reaching Montgomery, Alabama, by January 23 and Chattanooga two days later. He remained in telegraphic communication with Pemberton, but it was clear that Pemberton now had sole command of his Department of Mississippi and East Louisiana.[37]

Yet Johnston left the distaste of his presence in Mississippi, particularly by one major move that would come to have significant results for Pemberton. Johnston became fixated it seemed on one specific issue, and that was a new cavalry operation under Van Dorn. Johnston believed concentrating almost all cavalry in both departments of his western command, including that in Mississippi and Tennessee, Forrest included, would allow Van Dorn to do what he had done before: raid the Confederates' way to victory. "I want to combine a cavalry expedition in the two departments," Johnston informed Pemberton on January 11; "please assign General Van Dorn to the same cavalry, with instructions to report to me." He later added that "the object of the expedition under Van Dorn will be to interrupt any movement into Mississippi or Middle Tennessee." Johnston gathered much more than just Pemberton's cavalry, however, including that under Colonel Phillip D. Roddey in Alabama and also asking for much of Major General Simon Bolivar Buckner's cavalry from Mobile. Johnston even worked to arm weaponless individual cavalry units for his plan and sought to have brigadiers appointed to command the units: "I have four brigades of cavalry and but one brigadier-general," he informed Davis in Richmond; "senior colonels incompetent. An important expedition about to move under General Van Dorn."[38]

Pemberton also had trouble from his fellow generals. He had met with Van Dorn and Sterling Price at Jackson on January 21 and had made an astonishing statement that both thought they should write down in a memo for future reference. Both Price and Van Dorn testified that "in conversation two days ago between Generals Pemberton and Van Dorn and myself," Price wrote, "the following statement was made by General Pemberton, viz: That 100,000 men could not have taken Vicksburg, and that since the attack was abandoned by the enemy he had strengthened his works of defense very much; that he could spare General Bragg 8,000 men, but would not make the proposition for fear of accidents." Van Dorn endorsed it: "The above statements were made to General Price and myself in the office of Lieutenant General Pemberton." It is not known whether Pemberton's uncooperative spirit or Price and Van Dorn's conspiring against him was worse. For his part, Johnston, now at Montgomery on his way to Chattanooga, also continued to try to micromanage, telling Pemberton he needed to keep a brigade at Meridian as well as at Jackson, but he later rescinded his order. Even Jefferson Davis got in on the advice from afar; he wrote from Richmond that the old Yazoo Pass route through the Delta should be obstructed as a potential avenue of Union advance, which Pemberton had already ordered.[39]

Pemberton meanwhile took a more department-wide view, even during the lull around Vicksburg, traveling down to Port Hudson on January 11 to examine the conditions there. "All quiet here," he reported; "I think everything will be in good condition in one week." But by far Pemberton's main concern was his northern perimeter, even as far north as Corinth, where he kept out scouts to watch any Federal movements in northern Mississippi. He also kept the bulk of his forces toward the northern sector of his department, with only some ten thousand troops at Port Hudson and nearly twice that many at both Grenada and Vicksburg, fifteen thousand at the former and eighteen thousand at Vicksburg itself, with another eighteen hundred at Jackson in reserve and that many more at Columbus covering the Mobile and Ohio Railroad. Most significant, given the Union withdrawal from Grenada, Pemberton also pushed forward Major General William W. Loring's forces there to take back as much of the lost territory as possible, even up to the Tallahatchie River.[40]

But Johnston conflicted with Pemberton when he took the vast majority of his cavalry and some artillery from Mississippi and sent it to Tennessee in mid-January, when some six thousand cavalry in all transferred east. That left only a small amount of mounted troops in Pemberton's department, and he had to stipulate that some remain, such as Colonel Thomas N. Waul's Texas Legion and Colonel Wirt Adams's Mississippi Cavalry. Johnston's obsession with sending the bulk of Pemberton's cavalry eastward of course set up Van Dorn's rendezvous with Mrs. Peters's jealous husband, who murdered him, but it also stripped Pemberton of the very cavalry he needed to patrol and defend such an extended department stretching for hundreds of miles along the Mississippi River and along the railroads in northern Mississippi and West Tennessee. With the Federals in northern Mississippi watching Van Dorn, one writing that "we have information of a large cavalry force, under Van Dorn, having left Grenada a week since; destination unknown," it was a development that would come back to haunt the Confederate high command immeasurably. The enemy certainly took note of the lack of cavalry in Mississippi.[41]

Though matters slowed down considerably in mid-January, Pemberton remained hard at work. And his administrative prowess came to the forefront. Everything from paymaster to subsistence issues emerged, but he mostly continued his emphasis on collecting supplies inside Vicksburg, he in mid-January having a slim supply at best of pork and bacon; he had an overabundance of peas, nearly seven hundred thousand rations on hand, while having little more than five thousand of bacon and a mere eight hundred of pork. Pemberton's agents and commissary officers were hard at work gathering more, although there was a drastic need for more storage in Vicksburg itself. One agent noted that "I have large quantities of corn, mostly in the shuck, lying on the banks of the river . . . and [it] is liable to damage from exposure to the weather." Pemberton's chief of subsistence, T. B. Reed, was buying everything he could, but without transportation he was likewise afraid it "will be lost from rot by exposure to recent rains." There was also continued concern on Pemberton's part of illicit trade with the enemy, which many officials thought was necessary, as well as personnel moves, including a court of inquiry centered on Brigadier General Lloyd Tilghman's destruction of supplies and equipment during the retreat from the Tallahatchie River back in December; the court found no wrongdoing.[42]

Over time, Reed and other commissary and subsistence agents built up a strong allotment of goods at Vicksburg. By late January, he had over four million rations of peas, plus hundreds of thousands of rations of corn, rice, and salt, shipments from Texas and Louisiana arriving at Vicksburg by steamer. Contracts for huge amounts of goods were let, although for not all that was available despite orders from Major Theodore Johnston that all goods "ought to be taken when possible." Mainly, there was a great fear of a lack of beef; the herd kept in the better pasture areas around Edwards Station and driven into Vicksburg only in needed quantities for slaughter was dwindling. A major effort thus went forward to gather all the cattle that could be had, although a herd driven across the Mississippi River at Rodney was on the way to help ease the burden. Still, the situation was not good; the Edwards beef was bad, and "the troops are complaining very much of the quality of the meat, but as we are not permitted to buy, but directed to consume the Government cattle first, the evil cannot be remedied." One Mississippian, in fact, wrote that "our commissary was very defective, especially the beef department." Soldiers took to calling it "Boogar Meat," and word went around that the cows "die faster than the butcher can git them to us." And by January 23 even that poor beef was running out without anything to replace it. Eventually, an attempt to swap the bad cattle for fattening with planters who had ample meat on their hands was worked out, and Pemberton sought to buy millions of pounds of bacon. Likewise, only a hundred thousand bushels of corn were contracted for along Deer Creek when there was in excess of three hundred thousand available, and that despite warnings that "the levees on the Mississippi River are all down, and the Deer Creek country is subject to from 4 to 6 feet overflow"; it would all be lost in such an event.[43]

One soldier gave the specifics of his food quandary. George Clarke of the 36th Mississippi remained near Snyder's Bluff for much of the winter, having arrived in the concentration in response to the Chickasaw Bayou threat in December. He and the Mississippians had marched right onto the battlefield while the enemy was still active, a cannon firing above their heads as they passed by. "I do not now think that I jumped more than six feet into the air, and I was not the only one that exercised this jumping capacity," he wrote. When matters calmed, he related that "our principal duty, when not on picket, was unloading boats, and shucking corn and shelling corn for the army around Vicksburg." He went on, reporting "at that time we were very poorly fed, as to quality and variety. Our rations consisted only of coarse corn meal, and the very poorest of poor beef. You could take a piece of that beef, throw it against a wall, and it would adhere to it as though it had been glued there. If you broke a bone of it the marrow looked for all the world like the corruption that flows from a blood boil when punctured." The joke around camp was that the cows could not even stand on their own and had to be stood up to kill them. Much of the beef that did reach the troops had to be "condemned, carried off, and buried." The Mississippians working at the Haynes' Bluff landing were thus in a good spot when something better came along, and they had no qualms about surreptitiously taking what they wanted. Such was the case when a boatload of "bacon, hams, sides and shoulders" arrived, causing a "delightful odor." Clarke admitted that "shucking and shelling corn had no longer any charms for us . . . and we thought it would be strange if we went to camp empty handed that night." Others had gotten away with their stash by the time Clark made his move with a shoulder, "when who should I meet at the gangway but General [Louis Hébert], who had come up to the landing to inspect the commissaries." The general barked at him, asking what he was doing with the shoulder. Clarke maintained he was moving it from boat to boat and, when the general smiled and winked, moved on.[44]

The situation became worse in late January, Pemberton himself getting involved. He warned his chief commissary, Theodore Johnston, "there must be rations kept here [Vicksburg] all the time for 25,000 men. The men have no meat at all to-day." He ordered his agents to buy more cattle and hogs. But there was little hope of anything changing in the near future, Reed at Vicksburg reporting that the Big Black River was too high to cross so that cattle on the other side could not be brought in. Likewise, there was a severe shortage of cash to pay with, Reed asking that Pemberton release funds immediately and order vessels to report to him to transport it. Meanwhile, the commissary had to depend on corn and peas; Reed's millers at the Vicksburg mill, with four stones turning, could supply eight hundred bushels in a day, which would feed up to thirty-six thousand men per day. It was not beef, but it was food.[45]

During the mid-January lull, Pemberton also reorganized his army. He had four military districts, Brigadier General Daniel Ruggles's first district in the northeastern part of Mississippi, the second under Major General Carter Stevenson along the river and the northwestern portion of the state, Brigadier

General John Adams's district in southern Mississippi, headquartered at Jackson, and Major General Franklin Gardner's district in Louisiana at Port Hudson. Not all districts had many troops, of course, and where those troops were concentrated needed some reorganization. The force at Grenada was far too small to utilize the corps system any longer, so Pemberton ordered a consolidation of divisions into brigades and corps into divisions, ultimately making two divisions at Grenada. Brigadier General Albert Rust's old division was made into a brigade and put with Brigadier General Lloyd Tilghman's division to make a division for William Loring, Tilghman taking a brigade therein. Brigadier General John S. Bowen's division was likewise shortened to one brigade, and Sterling Price's troops now became one division under him, with brigades under Bowen and Brigadier General Martin Green. Price left the army soon thereafter, going to Richmond to beg to be sent back to Missouri, leaving Bowen in command.[46]

Of course, there were already three divisions at Vicksburg itself, under Carter Stevenson, the ranking division commander, Martin L. Smith, and Major General Dabney H. Maury. Stevenson had overall charge of the Vicksburg defenses while Pemberton oversaw the department as a whole, although he spent some time in Vicksburg when necessary but most of his time at Jackson. Maury commanded the right from Snyder's Bluff down to Chickasaw Bayou, where Martin Smith commanded the Vicksburg front, including the heavy batteries, while Stevenson's brigades stood in gaps and in reserve, with one south of the city. Unlike Johnston's complaints of the cavalry brigade commanders, Pemberton had nineteen brigades in the department, commanded by seventeen brigadier generals. Two others commanded military districts. Only two brigades were commanded by colonels.[47]

As late January emerged, however, Pemberton's attention shifted from reorganization to defense once more. Carter Stevenson began to detect Union movements again, obviously McClernand's return to the Vicksburg area, and had suspicions of coming confrontations. "Hurry on the intrenchments, and have all the river batteries in fighting order," Pemberton ordered on January 21; "report any confirmation of your suspicions." He also alerted Franklin Gardner at Port Hudson "there are indications of another attempt on Vicksburg. It is probable they may make one simultaneously on you. Be on the alert."[48]

News from scouts confirmed the gathering enemy. Word continually came in of steamers heading south to Vicksburg, mostly McClernand's force as well as others from Memphis. Yet with the arrival of more Federal forces in the vicinity, no one knew quite where the enemy would attack, if they even would in this terrible weather. Some thought a renewal of the effort up the

Yazoo would occur, Pemberton telling Stevenson to "strengthen the works at Snyder's Bluff. Put some rifle guns in position there for the defense of that point." Eventually, Snyder's Bluff and the attending works at Haynes' and Drumgould's Bluffs on either side would contain sixteen heavy guns, including Columbiads, with at least seven of them being rifled. Stevenson authorized the taking of slaves to do the work, but the brigade commander in the area, Brigadier General Louis Hébert, reported that "the planters give up their negroes very reluctantly, and hide away their tools." A cave-in at a magazine at Snyder's Bluff did not help. A lot of hope for a defense of the Yazoo went into the raft across the river at Snyder's Bluff, which had been strengthened with chains and booms, but the new fear was that driftwood brought down in the floods would cause such force that it would break. One Mississippian who had to cross the raft on foot at night to conduct picket duty on the other side of the river described it as "nearly in the shape of a letter 'W' . . . the river was high and running like it was in a great hurry, and the raft was swaying at a terrible rate." The barrier ultimately had four crossbars to it, but the concern eased when old man Snyder himself, "who has lived here for a number of years," told them that when the Mississippi was as high as it was, "there is no current in the Yazoo" and in fact "the current runs up in the Yazoo," basically backward.[49]

The news by late January was thus not good, with Federals returning to Vicksburg and no idea of where they would land or attack. But even more troubling was the intelligence that much of Grant's army was abandoning northern Mississippi and moving to Memphis and then down the river. For all his issues with action, Joseph E. Johnston was a good thinker nevertheless and could see what was happening. He had predicted that "should Grant join Sherman at Vicksburg it would be very embarrassing." That seemed to be exactly what was happening.[50]

A mid all the high-level back-and-forth on both sides, there was indeed some movement in the latter half of January, an accompanying newspaper correspondent writing that this was "not a time of positive inactivity." Naval movements on the river kept everyone's attention, including a Confederate vessel, *City of Vicksburg*, which soon tied up at the waterfront. That same day, members of the 13th Illinois captured the small Confederate tug *De Soto* on a fact-finding mission. Confederate scouts and units in the Delta picked up on the larger Union movements, including the shift northward from Vicksburg resulting in Arkansas Post, which they had a hard time understanding. They also reported Grant's later movement of troops southward from Memphis. But in the ever-continuing effort to open the Mississippi River to safe passage, of which Vicksburg was the major sticking point, the idea of rerouting the Mississippi River past Vicksburg again emerged in Federal commanders' minds. McClernand, in fact, on January 8 mentioned the idea of "the practicability of isolating Vicksburg by opening another channel for the Mississippi." Just two days later Grant himself started thinking of the idea, believing wrongly that McClernand's troops were still at Vicksburg and needed something to start working on. "I send Colonel [Josiah] Bissell, of the Engineer Regiment of the West, to report to you for the purpose of surveying the ground and determining the practicability of reopening the canal across the tongue of land opposite Vicksburg," Grant informed McClernand on January 10.[51]

The Arkansas Post interlude, as important as it was in reshaping the Union high command and bringing Grant himself to direct the force near Vicksburg, also delayed the proposed work on the "ditch for our cannon boats," as one Federal likened it. McClernand and Sherman did not return to the Young's Point/Milliken's Bend area just upriver from Vicksburg until around January 20; by that time, Secretary of the Navy Gideon Welles had sent word to Porter that Lincoln himself was "exceedingly anxious" for the work to begin. Still in charge on site until Grant arrived, McClernand put Sherman to work immediately on the effort, and Sherman quickly landed, putting Stuart's division ashore while keeping Steele's troops on their transports for the time being. "I expect to march with Stuart's division, without wagons, by the left flank," Sherman reported on January 21, then "follow the levee to the canal, the canal to the river below Vicksburg, and to reconnoiter very closely the ground between this and Vicksburg." Eventually, Steele's division arrived as well, as did McClernand's corps of A. J. Smith's and Osterhaus's divisions (Morgan soon returning north sick), all around Milliken's Bend, or what more than one Federal wrote as "Mooligan's Bend." But it was not easy: "Unloaded the battery in the afternoon in the rain," one artilleryman scribbled in his diary.[52]

Sherman could see immediately this was not a promising effort. "It is no bigger than a plantation ditch," was his initial reaction. His engineer, Captain William Jenney, did not think much of the plan either, especially when word from McClernand arrived to "blow up the bottom of the canal," and it had to be done that night. Sherman handed Jenney the order with a twinkle in his eye, knowing no more what that meant than Jenney did, and Jenney soon gained an earful from McClernand himself when he attempted to get clarification of how to blow up the water-filled canal. "You can dig a hole, can't you?," McClernand impatiently demanded. "You can put powder into it, can't you? You can touch it off, can't you? Well, then, won't it blow up?" Jenney

"THE WORK OF CHANGING THE CHANNEL OF THE MISSISSIPPI" 105

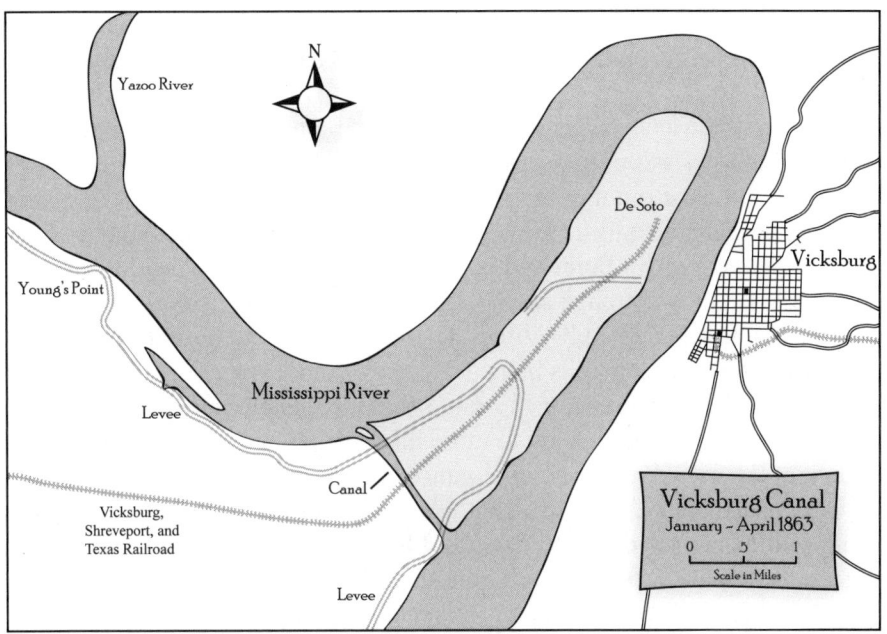

walked away but admitted that "a suppressed 'Damn' was all the 'blowing up' it received that night."[53]

McClernand himself soon arrived at Young's Point and personally reconnoitered the canal, just as many of his soldiers were doing; those off duty wanted to get a sight of the canal, one unimpressed Illinoisan saying it was not big enough "at present to swim a Duck in it." But the Federal soldiers mostly wanted to see "the noted city," Vicksburg itself. Some reported no view because of fog or haze, while others could hear bands playing for reviews across the river and see "very few people were moving round, and those military." Even dogs could be heard barking and the clocks striking in the city, as well as the trains arriving and the "'toot,' 'toot'" of the whistles. One Federal who could get a good view related that "the city looks quite imposing from where we are," and an Iowan wrote in his diary that it reminded him of "Burlington, Iowa — with its bluffs rising in succession — each higher than the preceding one and losing themselves to the eye in the far distance." Brigade commander Thomas Kilby Smith was just as impressed, writing home that "as I write its white towers and steeples and window panes gleam in the light of the setting sun. It's the Gibraltar of America, and we shall have a good time taking it, I guess." One Federal became so excited he wrote it was "as pretty a sight as

I ever seen a city on a hill hurah bully for Vicksburgh," but another kept his frame of mind and noted how "the fortifications can be clearly seen with the naked eye."[54]

Once on site, McClernand sent Grant a brief report of what he found: "The water of the Mississippi River, which is rising rapidly, is in the upper end of the canal, and must run through in a few hours if the rise continues." Further scouting brought the entire canal into Union hands, and Sherman moved Stuart's troops to Young's Point and put them ashore at daylight on January 22, at which time they marched southward to take firm possession. "The line of the canal is now occupied by forces deemed sufficient to hold it," he further informed Grant, adding "it is believed that by to-morrow night all my forces will have gained positions at the same time defensible and commanding." Additional scouting parties led to more information and ground claimed, although at the cost during one exploration of Colonel Warren Stewart of the 15th Illinois Cavalry, who was shot by probing Confederates as he scouted south of the canal. A dying Stewart told his captors "if you can send a message to General McClernand, tell him I died fighting for my country."[55]

Still in Memphis on January 22 but planning to start southward as soon as possible, Grant wrote that "I hope the work of changing the channel of the Mississippi is begun, or preparations, at least, being made to begin." Still not knowing what things were like at Vicksburg itself, Grant retained several divisions, including Logan's and Quinby's of McPherson's XVII Corps at Memphis and Gorman's, at Helena for the time being, although one of Logan's Illinoisans related that "we expect to go to Vicksburg in three or four days and there I look for a big fight."[56]

That fight became more probable as the Confederates geared up to meet this latest threat. Pemberton and his Confederates were immediately apprised of this new danger the canal represented, knowing, as one Federal wrote, that "the ditch will isolate that place from the benefits of the Miss." Stevenson informed Pemberton at Jackson on January 23 that "the enemy have landed quite a force on the peninsula, near the canal." The news was concerning, although Stevenson totally misconstrued the ultimate goal, reporting "apparently with the intention of crossing at Warrenton." A crossing of the Mississippi River south of Vicksburg was a real possibility, although not as easy as other operations, but at this point the Federals had no such ideas. They simply wanted to open the canal for river traffic, bypassing Vicksburg. Still, Stevenson requested reinforcements, in particular one of his own division's brigades at Jackson under Brigadier General Thomas H. Taylor. Pemberton agreed with the threat of the canal but admitted, concerning the Warrenton landing, that "I hardly think they will attempt it." But he started Taylor's troops on the way anyway, cautioning Stevenson that the "railroad is in such bad condition the movement will be slow." He recommended sending other troops for the time being. Also, Pemberton prepared to head to Vicksburg himself, leaving the next morning.[57]

More information came to light the next day, prompting Pemberton to act more decisively. "The enemy is landing his forces on the west bank, 5 miles above Vicksburg," Pemberton informed Richmond. He then gave explicit detail gleaned from "a memoranda book taken on the person of Col. [Warren] Stewart, chief of cavalry, killed yesterday." The book told Pemberton all about the size and scope of Sherman's and Morgan's corps, the reinforcements currently on the way, and that Grant was personally down the river, although it was a reference only to his midmonth temporary trip to Napoleon and not his permanent transfer later. Still, Pemberton now knew a lot more, including the orders to reopen the canal. He finished by stating "this may compel me to withdraw forces from Grenada," which he immediately began doing in the form of Waul's cavalry as well eventually as some of Price's troops even though Price himself was not there. He informed Price, then in Montgomery, of what was up and notified him to return to his command at once. After informing Johnston of the developments, Pemberton also received advice from him to bring the Grenada force southward. Pemberton called off Loring's advance northward from Grenada and began shifting troops, explaining that the enemy was "working hard at the canal."[58]

Meanwhile, with his information in hand from the cavalry scout that disproportionately aided the Confederates, McClernand developed a plan. "I will immediately commence enlarging the present or cutting a new canal for the purpose of diverting the channel of the river, as circumstances transpiring within a few hours may suggest." But he needed tools and asked Grant to send him all he could. Meanwhile, Sherman positioned his troops, by January 24 having Stuart's division occupying the length of the canal. He also had artillery at each end, including where it exited and reentered the Mississippi River. The troops worked on their respective portions, widening the canal itself and throwing the excess dirt on the western bank to build a levee that would keep overflows out of the camps. At the same time, they leveled down any excess dirt on the eastern bank so "it will overflow the other side first." By January 24, Sherman reported "about 2 feet of water is in the canal now, and moving at a current about the same as the main river." Grant related that work went on "with all vigor," although one Ohioan laboring in the mud and slop related "what the object is for doing it is now more than I can tell at present."[59]

Other troops were also taking position in addition to Stuart's three brigades.

Steele landed his division and sent two of the brigades under Frank Blair and John M. Thayer down the canal to a point below it, where Union boats from the south, if Banks passed Port Hudson, could safely connect with them. Hovey's brigade remained in general reserve elsewhere. Likewise, other troops became very important as unforeseen emergencies arose. The major concern was that, with the rising river, crevasses were opening up in the main river levees. Even though they had little to do with the canal itself, these breaches in the levees allowed water to flow into the lowlands where the Federals working on the canal camped. If the rising water from the river flooded out the camps, work on the canal would invariably stop. Other troops were thus tasked with finding and repairing these crevasses and weak places in the levees, Sherman first reporting them and advising that if the river rose and water flowed through, "as I feel assured it will very soon, water will overflow this plain, and we will all be in the levee. . . . [It] may drown us out." McClernand wholeheartedly agreed: "The threatened inundation demands energetic measures, which have been ordered to be taken for the repair of the crevasse above these headquarters. . . . It is hoped that everything will be secure by to-morrow night."[60]

The situation was not remedied the next day; in fact it became worse. By January 26, McClernand reported three large crevasses in the levee in a twenty-mile span south of the canal's reentrance into the river. They let water into the Federal operational area, and McClernand advised that "the country for some 12 miles above New Carthage is being rapidly overflowed." Two others were forming on the other end of the canal near McClernand's headquarters as well, which he said "demand indefatigable labor of details, with the very few implements I have, to mend them." With the threat of flooding their campsites, one observer described how "Grant's big army was stretched up and down the river bank over the plantations, its white tents affording a new decoration to the natural magnificence of the broad plains." McClernand had to keep enough transports on hand to withdraw to if needed, and Sherman made sure he kept roads open enough to get his artillery out quickly in the event he was flooded out. One Federal in fact explained that, as the floodwaters continually crept higher, "there is more of our men there than has room to lye down."[61]

As feared, the floodwaters flowed through the crevasses south of the canal, and the ground between the river, canal, and railroad embankment south of the railroad slowly flooded; "we would have to skedaddle or swim," one Ohioan prophesied. Despite Sherman's intent to keep "a continuous chain of sentinels along the line and canal," he eventually had to withdraw the troops on the southern portion of this effort "in consequence of the great danger of an immediate breach in the levees and flooding of the land between the railroad and lower levee." Blair and Thayer of Steele's division had to withdraw from south of the railroad to north of it, where Hovey's reserve brigade camped. Likewise, Stuart had to withdraw Ewing's and Kilby Smith's troops from the canal also to a point north of the railroad. Sherman now focused his attention on keeping water out of the area north of the railroad, orders going out to keep the canal itself from overflowing in that area.[62]

Obviously, Mother Nature had a lot to do with the crevasses in the levees, as the rising river produced the effects that were not at all uncommon with each rising tide. But the Confederates helped as well. One Southerner noted with rising tension that "the enemy seems to be working on the canal," so Pemberton issued orders to combat the Federal workers in about the only way he could: "Messrs. James Russell and David Reddit will proceed with the utmost dispatch to Point Lookout [11 miles south of Lake Providence], and cut the levee effectually at that place, with the purpose of flooding the country now occupied by the enemy's army opposite Vicksburg." Others were to help as well, and while it is unknown just what Confederate tampering had to do with all the major crevasses emerging now, there is direct evidence that at least some of it was intentional sabotage. If they could not get to the enemy to drive them away, perhaps they could flood them out.[63]

Throughout the latter days of January as the canal process seemed to gain traction, Pemberton also continued to shift troops from Grenada to Vicksburg, orders issued for Jackson staff officers that "all troops arriving here to-night will go forward at once. Four engines in readiness to move." But the movement was very slow, Loring writing that "the command is waiting. Without sufficient transportation; moving very slowly for want of it." Pemberton also made efforts to stop the river traffic that might result from the canal work, including a captured ferryboat that he warned Gardner at Port Hudson to be on the lookout for.[64]

All the while, work went on at the canal as best it could amid the floodwaters and rainy weather. One Indianan wrote that the goal was to make it eighty feet wide and sixteen feet deep, but a Federal reported on January 27 it was a mere twenty feet wide and seven feet deep. Another soldier admitted that the troops did not work themselves too hard, writing that "we had to take our turn digging, about two days in a week, and it was poor work we done, a shovel full of earth would be thrown about every ten or fifteen minutes by most of us."[65]

Grant was of course all this time impatient to get things going, especially with word late in January from Halleck: "Direct your attention particularly to the canal proposed across the point. The President attaches much importance to this." Grant spared no detail as he ratcheted up work on "the canal Grant dug or had dug," even to the "saving of all sacks emptied by the army.... When it comes to erecting batteries, these sacks will come in play most conveniently." He also notified McClernand that he was collecting "mining tools ... for a long siege."[66]

The canal project was more complicated than just widening or deepening the existing one, however. Grant, and others soon on the scene, including engineers James H. Wilson and Frederick E. Prime, realized that Williams had not cut his original canal in the best spot. One Ohioan admitted that it was "a very insignificant affair as originally designed" and that the hope was to "persuade the lazy portion of the Mississippi to take the near cut, presuming that water, like men, could easily be induced to labor saving." Likely, it would need to be altered or scrapped altogether, to be replaced by an entirely new effort. The same Ohioan joked that "it was intimated by some individual unacquainted with military sciences, that a steamboat 40 feet wide could not pass through a canal 20 feet wide." Worse, the location was far off. Grant explained to Halleck that "I propose running a canal through, starting far enough above the old one commenced last summer to receive the stream where it impinges against the shore with the greatest velocity." Williams's work had left the Mississippi "in an eddy," or where the force of the river's current was already moving perpendicular to the canal's entrance. Grant wanted the canal opened at such a place that the current would flow directly in, basically parallel to the current. As concerning, Williams's old canal reentered the Mississippi below Vicksburg but still in front of the high hills, on which Confederate artillery sat. Southern cannoneers could easily command the mouth from the hills, but the new canal would enter the river far below, out of range of the guns. In fact, McArthur's division from Memphis arrived and took a position upstream from the original canal's mouth to start a new opening: "He has permission to change its channel for 200 or 300 yards" and was directed to "sink frequent pits through the clay in order to facilitate its washing." But it would be hard work in a daunting environment; one wide-eyed infantryman of the arriving division confessed "this is a rough part of the world."[67]

By January 26, the new cut was made, but the prognosis was not good. McClernand reported three feet of water in the canal, but it "gives no evidence of diverting the channel of the river." Even the new cut "terminating higher up the river" gave no evidence of working, and McClernand began to have misgivings, writing Grant that "I am doubtful that even this change will prove successful, but as it will cost but comparatively little time and labor, I thought I would try it." McClernand nevertheless had engineers working on surveys for an even newer cut higher up. Little resulted, and by January 30

McClernand admitted that "if they prove unsuccessful, the uselessness of the present canal will have been demonstrated." He nevertheless did not give up on the entirely different cut through the peninsula, but requested more power to do so, even steam-powered dredging machines. "Time presses," he lectured Grant, "and every practicable effort to make this army available for great results should be tested."[68]

All the while, other issues ate at efficiency, not the least of which was a lack of tools. Fortunately, captured shovels at Arkansas Post helped in that regard. Morale among the army also became a matter of concern given the weather, lack of camping ground, and ridiculous amount of disagreeable work on the canal. "I am not over cheerful in regard to matters in general," wrote one of Grant's brigade commanders, Colonel George Boomer. "The constant rains and tremendous rise in the river may operate against us for the time being," Grant himself predicted. When Sherman ordered some of Steele's troops to corduroy the entire swampland road for some two miles across the peninsula, he reported that "I have never seen men work more grudgingly, and I have endeavored to stimulate them by all means." McClernand himself admitted that "sickness has prevailed" among some of the troops, particularly some sent back to the Chickasaw Bayou area. The rainy weather did not help at all either, McClernand reporting on January 26 that "it has rained more or less every day for several days in succession. The rain has been occasionally accompanied by winds, chiefly from the south." Given the tedium, Grant had to close all the bars on the steamboats and outlaw the sale of alcohol to the troops. "Card-playing and gaming is also strictly prohibited," Grant ordered in an effort to keep the troops' minds focused on the work.[69]

One foot soldier explained the low-level morale problem in his diary. On January 26, Ohioan William Willey wrote: "This is a hard old place. Every thing is confusion. We have had scarcely any thing to eat for a week and nothing a sick man could eat for a month. We have been on the go for thirty-six days, on boat and land and had a hard time of it generly. Troops are at work on a ditch to turn the River away from Vicksburgh." He even added: "The weather warm and wet; Bull Frogs bellowing day and night."[70]

Worse, Confederate movement on the night of January 25 caused a stir but resulted in little change. "Five of the enemy's transports have dropped down from Vicksburg to a landing on this side, about 1 ½ miles below," one Federal wrote. It could have been the result of Pemberton's effort to gather any waterborne fighting chance he could. He wrote Louisiana Governor Thomas O. Moore about Captain Beverly Kennon and his boat *Webb*. He asked permission to use it, arguing that with the *Webb* "together with the co-operation of our land batteries, the mouth of the canal on this side can be held."[71]

Also dealt with were Confederate civilians residing along and near the canal and campsites. Grant ordered that no one was to be put out of their houses for headquarters, and in particular Sherman worried over elderly Mrs. Grove, who had a dying daughter to contend with as well. Sherman asked that she be moved despite her complaints being valid. "There is a guard at her house," he noted, "but the poor woman is distracted and cannot rest. She will soon be as prostrate as her dying daughter. Either the army must move or she. Her grievances cannot be alleviated otherwise." One lower-level Federal had much less sympathy, writing of her as "a perfect vixen of a Southerner." Reverend Abraham Hagaman was a different story, he appealing to John McArthur for passage upriver on several grounds including being "a minister of the Gospel—a non combatant & finally I appealed to him as a Mason for relief. I think the last ground of appeal made an impression." McArthur invited him to sit down "at his writing desk" and write a request, which was granted. Peter Osterhaus complained while dealing with one civilian that he was "a good and *if possible* in this latitude a loyal man."[72]

Nevertheless, by January 31, the prospects of the canal were not looking good. One Federal wrote home that "I think it a ridiculous folly in the present plan. They have dug a ditch and then folded arms and expected God to make the river run through and clear it out. It will never do." Grant was beginning to wonder about this canal project as well, not necessarily because of anything Pemberton was doing in response but due to the lack of engineering progress made. He had earlier written Halleck that "water in the canal is 5 feet deep, and river rising. There is no wash, however, and no signs of its enlarging." On the last day of January he similarly wrote, "I am pushing everything to gain a passage, avoiding Vicksburg. Prospects not flattering by the canal of last summer." Still, he kept up work while the water was so high, in the words of Julia Grant, "to amuse the country until the waters should subside." But he was not giving up by a long shot. The very next sentence of his missive to Halleck read that, although work would continue on the canal, "other routes are being prospected."[73]

5

"But Grant Is on Two Other Projects"

February 1–15

"It commenced raining on last Saturday and continued without ceasing up to last night," one Alabamian wrote home amid the winter deluges hitting the Vicksburg area. "This is Thursday morning," he added. His disgust was evident, writing later, "I am literally worn out with this place. We are so miserably situated in the river swamp in mud and water up to our ankles nearly all the time. . . . I am fearful that I will turn to be a regular Mississippi *Hoosier* if I remain in this dismal swamp much longer among the *coons* and *wild cats*." It was no exaggeration when a Texan referred to it as "this most miserable of climates."[1]

Despite many a Northern boy being used to cold weather, although one admitted that "the cold goes harder with me down here than it does up home," the added winter chill during campaigning was not ideal in any sense. Many Federals complained of the weather, especially the bitterest days. Florison D. Pitts described in his diary how the weather was "cold at Jehu. Laid in tent all day with a hot brick at my feet and a blanket over me." Only a few days saw any sunshine, but some were most optimistic, one Iowan calling it "the sun of Austerlitz" on February 9. Obviously, military operations were impacted by all the water and cold, one Federal describing a review by Sherman on February 8: "It was a poor affair as the parade ground was shoe deep in mud."[2]

Liquid dirt was indeed a very present issue. "Pleasant over head but verry unpleasant under foot," one Ohioan scribbled in his diary in early February. Colonel Wirt Adams in the Delta reported that "we have had thirty-six hours of constant rain, and this morning the snow and sleet has commenced falling rapidly. Our march has been temporarily arrested by this weather and the almost impassable condition of the roads." His men had been busy along the river, destroying firewood and rails to impede McClernand's movement to Arkansas Post, but the weather was terrible. "The roads above Rolling Fork of Deer Creek, leading in the direction of the Yazoo, are utterly impassable. In addition to their recent obstruction I learn that the rain water has accumulated so rapidly that it is now swimming to a horse," he explained. In Vicksburg, a Louisianan noted in his diary "we have had a rainy dreary Sabbath day. Notwithstanding the rain the church bells ring at the usual hours." He later added "this is a rainy day; poor soldier, how you have to wade through rain mud and water."[3]

Wind could also be a problem, especially in the frequent storms that rolled through on the tips of weather fronts. "Regular hurricane in afternoon," one Federal scribbled in his diary. In a later episode he described his tentpole being broken and the tent falling around them and how the wind "blew down the smoke stack of the *Universe* and raised cane generally." One Federal even told of the high winds breaking steamboats from their moorings. A Confederate described a windstorm that blew limbs down and killed several in various regiments: "They was mashed all to pieces." Another product of the violent storms was lightning, which struck occasionally and at times killed soldiers too close to the impact site.[4]

One of the main issues the wet weather and swampy terrain brought was sickness such as typhoid, consumption, flux, and measles, although Grant always maintained that reports were severely overplayed. One soldier in fact related that "a great many of the men are sick and a great many pretending except when it comes to eating and then they make full hands." Grant related that "visitors to the camps went home with dismal stories to relate; Northern papers came back to the soldiers with these stories exaggerated." Sherman railed against the weakening Northern morale these stories produced, writing later that "we had to fight a senseless clamor at the North, as well as a determined foe and all the obstacles of Nature." One of his Ohioans could not understand it any better: "I know not what motive would have prompted the reports of the great sickness and mortality in this quarter, for it does not and has not existed." That said, there was definitely sickness and death enough to go around, some of it simply the effects of gathering new recruits. One of McPherson's staff officers confided to his mother that "the mortality among the new regiments is considerable and is greatest in those regiments composed of large strong farmer boys, [and] they can[']t begin to stand what the thin young fellows from the towns do." Much of the sickness was also the result of drinking tainted river water, brigade commander Kilby Smith writing that the troops were "infected with the plagues of Egypt, all but the frogs; and the first sun, I reckon, will make them tune their pipes."[5]

The result was a lot of death, with relatively little place to honorably bury bodies. The only ground above water was the levees, and newspaperman Sylvanus Cadwallader related that the dead were first buried in the intervening ground between the river and levee, but those inadvertently dug up by wagon traffic were either buried deeper or, when the river rose to the levee, in the side of the levee, creating a scene where the levee was "literally honeycombed by such excavations." As the water continued to rise over the spring months, many of these bodies also washed out, creating a gruesome atmosphere. An Ohioan simply declared that "here you find their graves along the side of the river so close to each other that there is no room for another and this for miles. An army of men has been buried along the Mississippi."[6]

Many described the gruesome scenes. One Ohioan wrote that "many die every day in this Army. The levee for three miles is almost one continual Graveyard of new Graves." Another added "we are camped in a perfect graveyard," with an Ohioan providing morbid context: "We were compelled to pitch our tents on newly made graves while we remained on the levee, and in some cases the stench of the decomposing bodies was quite perceptible." Orders went out to "have their respective burial grounds neatly fenced in, and head boards with name and company of deceased." Division commander Osterhaus elaborated, writing that "to bury the remains of the deceased decently is a sacred duty we all owe to our brother soldiers who sacrificed their lives for their country in her hour of peril. The appearance of our cemeteries ought to give evidence that the dead were honored by their comrades and at the same time command the respect of those who may come afterwards." Still, the sickness and death continued, and smallpox also made an appearance later, those contaminated separated into tents "with their red flag hanging limp to the staff."[7]

Numerous efforts took place to offset the threat of sickness in such weather. McClernand ordered that all carcasses and offal of animals be buried to keep down the chance of spreading bacteria and disease. Peter Osterhaus wrote headquarters that "I have the honor to report that all the carcasses and offal within the lines of my division are duly under ground." The remains of humans were more problematic, lining the levees as they did. Policing the camps and even dress parades and guard duty to keep camps clean helped somewhat, although one division commander complained it was done in a "miserable, careless and unmilitary style." Additionally, commanders came and went because of sickness, brigade commands in particular changing frequently. At one time the colonel of the 124th Illinois, Thomas J. Sloan, took temporary command of his brigade in Logan's division, and one of his soldiers complained that his wife was with him and she "has a finger in every body['s] dish."[8]

As bad as mud, sickness, and certainly death was, accumulated water was the main problem for major military movements. "Rain and mud since we landed," George Carrington wrote in his diary; "river rising fast." He added: "Oh! This is a beautiful swamp, the Sunny South." Another mentioned how "the water drove us out of our nasty swampy place where we were camped." Colonel David Grier of the 77th Illinois wrote home that "we are still in camp in our old mud holes." Even Sherman was not immune, he having made his headquarters at the Grove House, "which had the water all around it, and could only be reached by a plank-walk from the levee, built on posts." He noted that the main job was "digging the canal and fighting off the water of the Mississippi, which continued to rise and threatened to drown us."[9]

Almost continuous rains only added more and more water to the soggy campaign area. "It is preparing to rain and it knows how in this country," one Federal wrote home. Grant similarly referred to "the almost continuous rains that fell." He described how "this is a terrible place at this stage of water. The river is higher than the land and it takes all the efforts of the troops to keep the water out." He later wrote that "it is most disagreeable and trying to our men, this weather, but so far as I see they are not wanting in cheerfulness." Grant kept his headquarters on the steamer *Magnolia* but informed Julia he would "go into camp as soon as a definite plan is fixed upon." The little vessel stayed tied up at Young's Point most of the time, guards stationed at the gangplanks. But he kept his confidence through it all; by mid-February Grant was also telling Julia that "a few weeks more I hope will settle the business here favorably." He pushed to have the troops paid quickly, in fact, knowing they would be off on the campaign soon.[10]

Obviously, the weather, in particular the precipitation, had the biggest effect on the level of the water, one Illinoisan writing that "the river is the most dangerous foe we have at present." And that posed a problem for Grant's quick capture of Vicksburg. "The everlasting rains set us back here wonderfully in our work. It is impossible for us to get done more than one day[']s work in three," Grant wrote. It was not only the rain that fell around Vicksburg, as bad as that made tramping around in the mud to be, but also what fell anywhere in the Mississippi River watershed, theoretically from the Appalachians to the Rockies. All that water had to flow southward past Vicksburg and eventually to the Gulf of Mexico, the rapidly rising river backing up into the tributaries and engulfing everything not protected by adequate levees. And that is exactly what happened over the course of the spring. A massive influx of water rushed southward in late January and early February, Engineer Frederick Prime giving the readings as the river rose five or six inches per day around the turn of the month. By February 9, the rise was down to two and a half inches per day and in a couple of weeks, in late February, had actually started to recede slightly an inch or two on average in the course of twenty-four hours. But that was only temporary as early March brought another rise, albeit slowly at first. It was only April when the water level began to recede again slowly, the river falling a half an inch on average in a day on April 17 and 18 and then beginning to fall more rapidly by the end of the month. Still, soldiers reported frequently digging ditches to drain their camps, and the punishment for being late to roll call in the 47th Ohio was bailing water.[11]

Obviously, all this water was going nowhere anytime soon, and that was a major factor that Grant had to take into consideration. Some locals reported the river higher than any year since 1815; old man Snyder, who lent his name to the bluff just up the Yazoo River, did not think the Mississippi would recede for "the next four or five months." Some began to think the entire campaign would be scrapped because of the high water. One Confederate declared to his wife that "whatever route he may choose he will find it a hard road to travel." Colonel Grier added in a later letter that "the taking of Vicksburg will probably be abandoned for the present as the river is so high that it is impossible to land an army on the other side." Some even began to take leaves of absence amid the downtime, brigade commander William Landram going home for several weeks, leaving Grier in command of the brigade. He hoped it would turn into a promotion so that his fiancée could marry a general instead of "only a colonel." Yet Grant had bigger ideas than promotions or marriages and sought to find a way to use the high water to his advantage rather than as an impediment.[12]

One account of a lady visitor to a party onboard Grant's headquarters boat left vivid imagery of his concentration later in the spring:

> on board the head-quarters boat at Milliken's Bend, a lively gathering of officers and ladies had assembled. Cards and music were the order of the evening. Grant sat in the ladies' cabin, leaning upon a table covered with innumerable maps and routes to Vicksburg, wholly absorbed in contemplation of the great work before him. He paid no attention to what was going on around, neither did any one dare to interrupt him. For hours he sat thus, until the loved and lamented McPherson stepped up to him with a glass of liquor in his hand, and said, "General, this won't do; you are injuring yourself; join with us in a few toasts, and throw this burden off your mind." Looking up and smiling, he replied: "Mac, you know your whisky won't help me to think; give me a dozen of the best cigars you can

118   CHAPTER FIVE

find, and, if the ladies will excuse me for smoking, I think by the time I have
finished them I shall have this job pretty nearly planned." Thus he sat; and when
the company retired we left him there, still smoking and thinking.[13]

Alternatively, the high water and terrible mud were also a part of the defense
John C. Pemberton counted on, unless the enemy came by boat. And for much
of the spring, that was about the only option Ulysses S. Grant had. "The real
work of the campaign and siege of Vicksburg now began," Grant wrote. "The
problem was to secure a footing upon dry ground on the east side of the river
from which the troops could operate against Vicksburg."[14]

"I do hope that they would do what they intend to do, and let us get away
from this place," an inpatient Confederate wrote his wife amid all the muck
and mire. He got his wish as the calendar turned to February. It was then
that the campaign began to mushroom into a much larger and more complex
operation than seen heretofore, even in the multicolumn advances during
the Mississippi Central and Chickasaw Bayou efforts. Over the next three
months, the campaign would in fact start to encompass several efforts at the
same time, across a canvas of six or seven states, on both sides of the Mississippi River. It would also include land maneuvers, mounted efforts, naval
operations, and some out-of-the-box thinking. Indeed, few would find these
types of upcoming operations anywhere in the military manuals of the day;
Jomini and Clausewitz had little to say about cutting canals to divert rivers,
breaching levees, flooding lowlands, or amphibious operations. One Federal
went so far as to write home, "I do not know whether we will be successful
or not [but] if hard digging in the mud will do any good I think we will." Another Federal wrote that "we still lay idle before Vicksburg the whole army
doing nothing—To all appearances our generals have given up all thought of
taking the place and are waiting for something to turn up." Obviously, there
was more method than that to the madness, and better yet Grant endured the
suffering with them, one soldier writing in his diary on February 1: "I saw
Gen. Grant this morning riding along the Levie with Gen. Sherman."[15]

As a result, by early February Grant had no less than four simultaneous
experiments going on, three new ones in addition to the canal project that was
looking less and less likely to be successful with each passing day and inch of
rising river. Yet he continued on with the work at the canal despite one Indianan confessing "we are still lying here by the 'Canal' as we call it in front of
Vicksburg, doing, I can scarcely say what." But Grant also soon added in two

more potential efforts on the west side of the river as well. And then there was a major advance east of the Mississippi River. While complaining of the canal work, Sherman quipped "but Grant is on two other projects." Another noted to a superior that Grant "seems to comprehend the great work before us," although there were some who complained of dispersing the forces all over the map, including brigade commander Colonel George Boomer: "I think they ought to be together. Whatever is done the force should never be divided." Grant nevertheless oversaw it all from his headquarters steamer *Magnolia*, where the officers of the army obviously fared better than the common soldiers tramping around in the muck.[16]

The three efforts west of the river were similar in desired effect but very different in scope. The canal was already turning out to be more trouble than it was probably worth, but Grant kept the work going per orders to work "with all possible dispatch." Sherman had control of the canal operations, but he split his time between the canal work and an almost total effort to rid the army, and perhaps the nation if he had his way, of the vile newspaper reporters who had caused him so much grief. Others were on the same crusade; Hurlbut and Hamilton up in Tennessee both had already banned the Chicago *Times* within their commands, some claiming it was "as big a secesh paper as was ever published." Grant had to rescind any such order.[17]

All the while, Sherman kept digging, although he informed one general "our canal here don't amount to much. It is full of water, but manifests no disposition to change the channel. It is a very small affair, and we can hardly work a barge through it for the stumps." He informed his senator brother that he was in sight of Vicksburg, "but the great Mississippi flows between us." An Iowan was more impressed, writing that the canal was "beginning to assume more the appearance of one than it did when we first came here." Then it was only a ten- or twelve-foot-wide "ditch, but now as thirty to thirty-five feet wide." Soon, entire regiments would be assigned sections to dig, and commanders were able to stagger the work the way they saw fit. Sherman had both his present divisions under Stuart and Steele detail five hundred men per day, the two divisions alternating days at work, all under the supervision of corps engineer Captain William Jenney. There was even some high-level advice from Washington regarding how to proceed, engineering-wise: Brigadier General Andrew A. Humphreys had studied the Mississippi River and its channel changes and advised that the channel would not change as long as the river bottom and canal were "composed of a hard, tenacious blue clay, not an alluvial deposit, which even the strong currents of the river wear so slowly as seemingly to produce no effect upon." He recommended borings where the intended change would be to see how deep the clay was and how deep the troops would have to dig to get to sand that would easily wash away. Yet Sherman also realized what Grant was coming to discern: "Even if it succeeds, Warrenton Bluff lies below, next Grand Gulf, next Rodney, and so on."[18]

Consequently, by late in the first week of February, Grant was indeed beginning to have more than just uneasiness but serious doubts. After a personal visit on February 4, he described the canal "at right angles with the thread of the current at both ends, and both ends are in an eddy." McClernand even asked Porter to send a tug "to increase the action of the water in the upper end of the canal by the use of its screws." Worse, the current reopening of the canal was still "under bluffs completely commanding it," and even if successful there were, as Sherman noted, still high-ground bluffs the Confederates could fortify such as Warrenton. But Grant took what the project gave, including "the effect of making the enemy divide his forces and spread their big guns over a great deal of territory."[19]

That said, there was some faint hope attendant to the new canal openings "so that the water will be received where the current strikes the shore, and will be carried through in a current." Yet as the weather continued to deteriorate and the water continued to rise, the canal became more and more of a headache. By February 9, Grant informed Halleck in Washington that "the continuous rise in the river has kept the army busy to keep out of water, and [has] much retarded work on the canal." To better keep the water out so workers could dig, a dam had been inserted at the head using "corn-sacks filled with earth, resting against a wooden framework." A cut in the western levee as well as a steam pump removed the water as best it could so that workers could get in and remove stumps and dig deeper. As many as five hundred contrabands were at work as well, and Engineer Prime reported that "with fair weather and strong working parties, there is a fair prospect of obtaining satisfactory results." Often the slaves did not want to work, but one Federal told how "if he refused some of the boys would take one of the officers swords and whip it out of the scabbard and order cuss to lay hold of the wheel-barrow—taking him to be an officer he would wheel the dirt and sey no more about it." But larger power was needed than just human muscle, even in abundance. From his faraway vantage point, Halleck recommended steam dredges, "four lying idle" at Louisville even then.[20]

Still, it was clear that Grant was losing faith in the canal project, and he cast about for other remedies; in fact, he told Halleck on February 14 "I immediately . . . ordered . . . other routes prospected." One of those other routes was a wider but still local (to Vicksburg) effort to similarly bypass the city and reach the Mississippi River below Vicksburg. Grant sent Captain

John Cornyn and about three hundred cavalry and infantry (8th Missouri) on a reconnaissance to find a way through the bayous west of the river near Vicksburg. Cornyn landed at Buckson's Plantation at Milliken's Bend in early February searching for Big Bayou, but he quickly found that there was a better access point farther up the Mississippi River at Omega Plantation. He moved his force there and found the bayou, and after provisioning his troops he explored the eight miles to Willow Bayou, the nine miles of Willow Bayou itself, and about four miles of the connecting Roundaway Bayou. Ultimately, he went all the way south of the railroad. Cornyn reported that a mere three hundred yards of digging would get transports into the fifteen-foot-deep Big Bayou, which would lead to Willow Bayou, although there were places where the depth would have to be dredged and several points that would have to be cut off so the vessels could get around the sharp turns. There was also a lot of driftwood, logs, and timber that would need to be removed. Once in Willow Bayou, however, the hundred-foot width would allow easy travel, although at the end of it there was a swamp that Cornyn reported would need to be contained with artificial banks or levees to keep the water at a sufficient depth; the three miles of swamp would pose a problem, but it could be done. Once in Roundaway Bayou, which "opens with a fine sheet of water," the seventy-five-foot width and fifteen-foot depth allowed for good movement, although a few trees would need to be removed. Cornyn stopped on Roundaway Bayou because he could not get his troops through on land and because "I was convinced the whole project is impracticable at this season of the year. During low water it would be a matter of labor and time." Despite sending his chief engineer Frederick Prime as well as Colonel George G. Pride to look further into the feasibility of the route, Grant soon gave up on this project for now, but he kept the possibilities in the back of his mind for future reference when the river started to fall and the adjacent areas dried up. He simply informed Halleck that "there is no question but that this route is much more practicable than the present undertaking [canal], and would have been accomplished with much less labor if commenced before the water had got all over the country."[21]

While the canal and Willow Bayou attempts seemed to be going nowhere, Grant writing that "it was found, however, that with the then stage of water some other plan would have to be adopted for getting below Vicksburg with transports," the project that Grant put the most confidence in west of the river was the most expansive of all in that section; in fact, it was an even more long-range path through the bayous and rivers of Louisiana to bypass Vicksburg. The inner ring of projects to bypass Vicksburg was the canal; the intermediate was the Willow Bayou route. The outer ring was the Lake

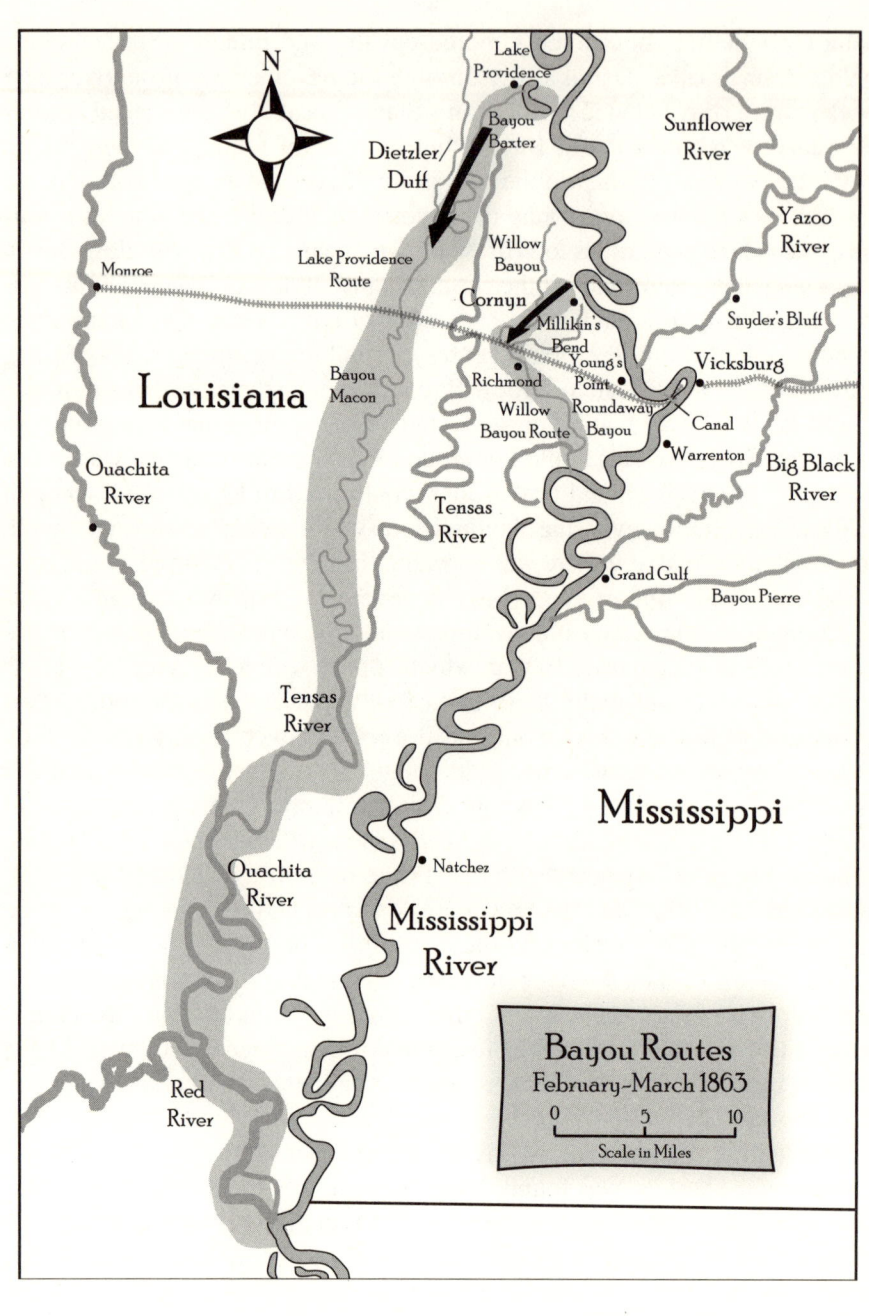

Providence route. "By inquiry I learn that Lake Providence, which connects with Red River trough Tensas Bayou, Washita [Ouachita] and Black Rivers, is a wide and navigable way through," Grant wrote. "As some advantage may be gained by opening this, I have ordered a brigade of troops to be detailed for the purpose, and to be embarked as soon as possible," Grant informed Porter. He asked for "one of your light-draught gunboats" to go with them, "if it can be spared." The major work would require a canal to be dug from the river to the lake, but many were by this time tiring of digging, an Illinoisan at the canal writing that "I wish the Old Concern was finished and we were through with digging ditches. I think our regt has done their share of canal digging." An Ohioan obviously tired of digging canals similarly related that this new effort "clearly belongs to the mania for canals."[22]

In ordering McClernand to send the brigade, Grant added that "the distance to be cut to enter it from the Mississippi [is] not great. With this open, a vast foraging district would be opened, and our gunboats of light draught would be enabled to cut off the enemy's commerce with the west bank of the river. I have determined to make the experiment, at all events, and for this purpose will want a brigade detailed and embarked as soon as possible." McClernand did so, adding that if the Lake Providence scheme failed it perhaps could also be done farther up the river near Lake Village, Arkansas, which would allow access to the Ouachita as well.[23]

McClernand sent one of John McArthur's brigades (McArthur's being the only present division of McPherson's XVII Corps at the time) under Colonel George W. Deitzler to reconnoiter the route near Lake Providence, described by one newspaper correspondent as "a quiet little hamlet, embowered in groves of magnolias and evergreens." There was also a curiosity of sorts in the village cemetery, an exposed grave of eighteen years with a woman in a metallic casket with a glass plate over her face: "The curious can see through the glass, the face in a state of decay. It is a ghastly sight and one that the authorities should remove quickly." Despite heavy fog and the sickness of the engineer in charge, Lieutenant Colonel William L. Duff, Deitzler moved to Lake Providence by February 1, where he was also instructed to send to the canal all the contrabands he could get. After slight skirmishing Deitzler sent about a hundred back, but he informed Grant that "the planters have sent most of their negroes and cotton back into the country, on Bayou Macon." But Deitzler also forwarded good news about the project. After a scout on February 1 and later a lengthier one with about eighty cavalry, Deitzler and Duff informed Grant that the river was eight feet higher than the level of the lake, which would allow for a good flow once the levee was cut, creating a channel a hundred feet wide and five feet deep. It would also ensure a flood of water into the lake and bayous farther down the line to raise their levels as well. He predicted that, once "the water in Lake Providence rises to the level of the water in the Mississippi," there would be no trouble getting through Bayous Baxter and Macon, from which small gunboats and transports would "have a clear coast to Red River." Deitzler concluded that "I look upon the prospect as entirely practicable"; the only thing needed would be to cut a few trees "so as not to interfere with chimneys." He also reported vast amounts of horses, mules, and cattle among the plantations lining the lake that he could "gobble up" if so desired, one plantation (Bellagio) being that of Edward Sparrow, a member of the Confederate Congress. Another was reputedly owned at one time by the 1860 Democratic nominee for president, Stephen A. Douglas, and an Illinoisan got a rooster from the plantation and named him "Old Dug." Deitzler also reported word of large saltworks farther west that would certainly be within striking distance of the expedition.[24]

Lieutenant Colonel Duff agreed wholeheartedly, his report giving more detail of the engineering aspects. There were two possible routes through Lake Providence, one that would need to be straightened and cut free of trees, or another that both Deitzler and Duff agreed would be the best, a canal that the free-flowing water would bore out and widen once the levee was cut. Duff saw the need, whichever route was chosen, to cut off the other with a dyke, but that would be easy work. Deitzler soon had his men working on the canal option, which would provide a depth of five feet when water came through, about all that could be utilized in the downstream bayous anyway. Some of the route went through the town of Lake Providence, which would necessarily destroy it, but Duff reported that "neither Colonel Deitzler nor myself thought this a matter of sufficient importance to interfere with the accomplishment of the object in view," the town being generally deserted already. Duff concluded similarly to Deitzler: "I do not doubt the entire practicability, during high water, of passing with such vessels as the mosquito fleet from the Mississippi to the Red River."[25]

Grant shared the report of the possibilities with Sherman, who was all for the experiment. "I have hastily read the reports of the Lake Providence scheme," he responded; "it is admirable and most worthy a determined prosecution. Cover up the design all you can, and it will fulfill all the conditions of the great problem." He added "this little affair of ours here on Vicksburg Point is labor lost," which probably made the Lake Providence potential look even better. Sherman told another general of his excitement as well: "This is a magnificent scheme, and, if successful, will be a grand achievement." He noted that when completed the route would allow "reaching the sea without approaching any bluff or ground easy of defense."[26]

Grant went up to Lake Providence to take a look for himself on February 5, and he liked the potential so much that he ordered McPherson down with Logan's division that very day. He told McPherson, the former engineer, that he would also send up another brigade of McArthur's division, also now working on the canal, adding that "this bids fair to be the most practicable route for turning Vicksburg." He described the route of the Tensas, Ouachita, Black, and Red Rivers, writing that all the streams were navigable and that "by a little digging, less than one-quarter that has been done across the point before Vicksburg, will connect the Mississippi and lake, and in all probability will wash a channel in a short time." He cautioned McPherson to bring all the tools he could and to try to stop as many cotton speculators as he could from following. McPherson was all on board, writing that "I hope soon to be with you, and aid in carrying out the plan, which strikes me as the best and most feasible that has been presented." Not everyone was so enthused, however, one writing jokingly of how "it is proposed to go through 73 different bayous, thence into Black River, then into Red River, and from that point I know not where."[27]

Yet the work progressed slowly, mainly because of a lack of manpower. Lieutenant Colonel Duff reported on February 9 that work was progressing, with the canal from the Mississippi River levee to Lake Providence nearly done by that time. But work was still needed on the link between the lake and Bayou Baxter. Of course, the levee could not be cut until that was accomplished, and Duff simply did not have enough men; he called for the remainder of McArthur's division to be sent upriver. He also reported a slight inconvenience when Confederates attempted to cut the levee upstream at Bunch's Bend, which would have flooded everything before it was ready, but patrols circumvented the sabotage and made the perpetrators repair the work themselves. They also warned that any additional sabotage would "be visited by the burning of every house in the settlement."[28]

Grant nevertheless had high hopes for the project and accordingly detailed a large number of troops to the effort. Intending to send Logan's entire division down from Memphis to join McArthur's troops just as soon as transports could be found, he also wanted Quinby's division to follow quickly thereafter with as many tools as could be had. McPherson, now with a fair chance of concentrating his entire corps at Lake Providence, celebrated the arrival of orders to move with a proclamation to the men of the XVII Corps: "Our marching orders have come, and it is for us to respond with promptness and alacrity. We move to capture the stronghold of the rebels in the Valley of the Mississippi." He continued, with even greater encouragement: "We go forward to strike a fatal blow against this most unjustifiable rebellion, a blow which will tell with deadly effect, and cause the heart of every true and loyal man in our country to swell with pride. We go to plant our flag upon the ramparts of Vicksburg."[29]

But McPherson was still in Memphis with Logan's troops on February 11, unable to move because of a lack of transportation. Logan's troops in fact had been waiting for ten days to move, Logan himself being sick. But with several vessels frozen in ice at St. Louis, he saw no chance of moving even for the next several days. "I am very much annoyed, but see no help for it," McPherson informed Grant. Also annoyed were some of his troops in Memphis: "The meanest place in the world for an army—too much to eat, too much drink, too many other vice things 'too tedious to mention.'" As a result, the Lake Providence effort ground to a halt much like the canal project to the south, ironically at the very time when the river was high enough to make it work. There was amazingly not enough manpower there while, at the same time, the water was too high at the canal, where sufficient manpower had less and less to do because of the water. With the flooded third-option route around Willow Lake added in, the Federals were stymied in the first half of February west of the river. "I don't believe our troops can ever take it [Vicksburg]," one despondent Indianan wrote home in February.[30]

Grant was stymied personally as well. In making a couple of trips up to Lake Providence only to miss McPherson each time because he was still stuck in Memphis due to a lack of transports, he groaned that "we are not much nearer an attack on Vicksburg now apparently than when I first come down." Worse, he informed Julia on February 11, "I met with a great loss this morning." He detailed how "last night, contrary to my usual habit, I took out my teeth and put them in the wash bason and covered them with water." The next morning the servant, not knowing they were there, dumped the basin overboard, "teeth and all." He had Julia try to get in touch with a dentist who could make him a new pair while he gummed orders for the next several days. The story made the rounds in the army, one Illinoisan writing home that "I heard a good joke on Genl. Grant today. His nigger waiting upon him, threw a bowl of water overboard, in which the Genl. had placed his false teeth, so that he is around now without any upper teeth ha! ha!"[31]

"While this work was progressing," Grant later wrote, "we were busy in other directions, trying to find an available landing on high ground on the east bank of the river." A more promising, and in-depth, attempt to reach Vicksburg safely consequently began on the east side of the Mississippi River as well, the so-called Yazoo Pass (or "Yazoo Cutoff") Expedition. While it would be weeks before any troops or gunboats actually became part of the effort and entered the Mississippi Delta, the exploration necessary for the operation took place in early February and involved a huge amount of engineering and out-of-the-box thinking. And it took place far away from Vicksburg, way out in northern Mississippi, beginning some hundred and fifty straight-line miles north of Vicksburg.[32]

The potential of the route into the Delta was well known, it having been an old trade route for Delta inhabitants for decades before the construction of the levees in the 1850s; in fact it was first explored in the late 1820s when the land was still part of the Chickasaw Nation. Planters utilizing the Yazoo River and its tributaries were able to move goods bound for Memphis through the pass and into the Mississippi River opposite Helena, Arkansas, rather than all the way down to Vicksburg and the Yazoo River's mouth. Access to that route cut off a lot of time and travel but ended with the levee across the pass. But even then, fear of a Union effort through it remained, Pemberton showing concern back during the Mississippi Central Campaign and Jefferson Davis likewise advising a watch over the route. Grant also showed early interest as a possibility if none of the more logical and straightforward advances worked. By February, they had not.[33]

With the probability of reaching high ground on the east side of the Mississippi River strangled at Vicksburg and Snyder's Bluff and all the way between them, another access point had to be found. That is why the Mississippi Central effort was so inviting, as it would place Federal forces on that high ground without battling against either Vicksburg's or Snyder's Bluff's guns. "This route, if practicable, would enable us to get high ground above Haynes' Bluff," Grant wrote, "and would turn all the enemy's river batteries." One Missourian put it more commonly when he wrote home how "by that means we will make a flank movement on Mr. Secesh." If it could be done, moving down the Yazoo River would solve the problem. If it could be done.[34]

Grant wanted to know if it could be done and thus sent some of his best staff officers to experiment with it. Almost immediately after his arrival near Vicksburg, Grant personally ordered Lieutenant Colonel James Harrison Wilson northward. He would go on to become a major player in the war, particularly leading cavalry later in the conflict, but he was an engineer by trade and was now on Grant's staff. In fact, after Wilson had been ordered away to another department Grant had to pull strings to keep him. Accompanying Wilson was Acting Master George W. Brown of the navy, commanding the USS *Forest Rose*, a small gunboat. They had an adventurous trip just to Helena, taking on two women civilians and four children at Lake Providence who claimed to be loyal and said they "would like to get North." Once at Helena,

Brown fired on three Confederate pickets with one of his guns, killing one. Engineer Wilson also "shot another with a rifle." The two nevertheless soon met General Gorman at Helena, and with the general aboard the gunboat they began their exploration the next day, February 2.[35]

Wilson was to explore the route and see what could be done if the levee was breached and the upper Delta flooded. That required yet another canal, one Ohioan also poking fun that "the government, not content with these canals, I understand [has] appropriated largely to the building of another canal in the northern part of Illinois. Verily this is a calamity of canals." Little was known of what lay beyond the levee, although they knew generally that there was an old part of the river that was now known as Moon Lake, which could be reached by the pass once the levee was broken. One Federal described it as "a long sheet of water called moon lake about 1/2 mile wide & near 6 long it is shaped Something like a Crescent with the convex side to the north." Another wrote of the "beautiful silver lake." But a torturous waterway connected Moon Lake with the rivers of the Delta. It all had to be explored, and Wilson and Brown made their way to the pass by 10:00 a.m., accompanied by five hundred troops Gorman provided, although the general soon returned to Helena to await news of the work. Wilson related that he "found a much more favorable state of affairs than I at first anticipated." He found the pass channels to the levee easily navigable, one to the south that was the main route used prior to the levee being built not as good as the upper channel. He came to the levee by early afternoon, describing it as "a very heavy one," and immediately determined where the cut should be made and set men to working on it. He found a gradually sloping levee blocking the waters of the river, still ten feet above the level of the river and sloping more than forty-five feet toward the water. The slope on the east side was steeper and was in fact nearly twenty feet above the waters of the pass. The Mississippi's waters, eight or nine feet above the level of the pass on the other side of the levee, would allow for a rapid current through any breach to widen it to a necessary width and facilitate plenty of flooding, which was already occurring because of crevasses elsewhere in the levee that had not been kept up due to the war. Wilson was very optimistic as he began the work of cutting the levee, writing Grant that he thought boats would be through within three days: "The undertaking promises fine results." Others watching were encouraged as well, an Iowan writing home that "it seems singular but I think he is trying to make a new route to Vicksburg & that he will succeed."[36]

Wilson made two cuts in the levee just south of the pass channel. The two cuts were some twenty feet apart, and he exploded powder in one to open a crevasse. The blast did so, creating a hole about five feet wide at first around 7:00 p.m. on February 3. The rush of water soon took over, and within a few hours, after additional blasts, Wilson happily saw that the gap had widened to forty yards and that "the water [is] pouring through like nothing else I ever saw except Niagara Falls. Logs, trees, and great masses of earth were torn away with the greatest ease." Wilson reported the success to Grant the next morning, telling of a gap of eighty yards in the levee and the waters still rushing through and falling to the level of the Delta. But because of "the great rapidity and fall of the water," the naval officers were loathe to try to run through any time soon; some said it would be four or five days before it was safe to push through, that being how long it would take "to fill up the country so much as to slacken the current." Still, Wilson was upbeat, adding that "the work is a perfect success." Better yet, he had met "a prominent rebel living near Helena, General [James L.] Alcorn," who admitted that they would have no trouble getting into the Delta rivers.[37]

The wait was on for the waters of the river and pass to equalize, and in the meantime the gunboat *Forest Rose* steamed up to Memphis for a few repairs. Brown was back by February 7, and he and Wilson made their run that morning. The passage through the levee was easier than feared, Wilson saying they "entered the Pass with great ease." They also moved another mile into Moon Lake, which afforded all the room and depth they needed. But the outlet of Yazoo Pass itself that connected with the Delta rivers was another matter. Some five miles down Moon Lake was the mouth of the inland pass, but Wilson found it to be "neither so large nor straight as it is nearer the river." Although he did not know this yet, it was a torturous twelve or thirteen miles of winding, narrow pass that would need to be navigated. He later described it as "60 to 80 feet clear, and from 18 to 30 feet deep." Wilson merely went three or so miles this day in a small boat but found obstructions. He also found three men in a canoe who said they were making a salt run. They reported that Confederates on the other end of the pass had figured out what was happening and that a force of some thirty or forty soldiers and a hundred slaves were busy felling timber into the stream "at intervals between its junction with the Coldwater and a point nearly five miles from Moon Lake." Worse, in the process of exploring, Wilson nearly perished or at the least was almost taken captive, as Confederate cavalryman Captain Aaron H. Forrest, younger brother of the more famous cavalry leader, had hidden in the woods with his men ready to pounce. Forrest saw the markings on Brown's uniform and assumed the party contained generals, whereupon the plan changed from planning an attack to trying to capture them. Just at that moment, wild pigs made a ruckus nearby, frightening the Confederates, who thought the Federals had landed troops. The party of officers, although not generals, barely escaped.[38]

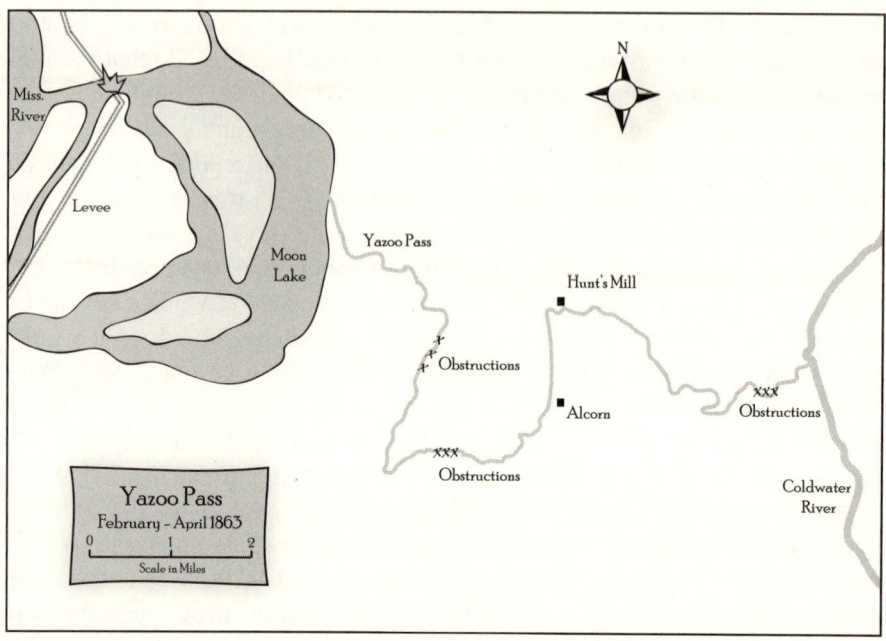

Wilson made a deeper run into Yazoo Pass the next day, February 8, in one of Brown's cutters, some six miles in total. The small party overtook two Confederates who admitted to the sabotage of the pass, but Wilson again found no major obstructions even this far into the area. He saw numerous trees that had been felled into the pass, but these had either sunk in the deep stream or drifted with the current to the bank, prompting Wilson to report to Grant that "I am inclined to think that, although many more trees may have been cut lower down, and at points opposite each other, they will not materially interfere with navigation." The major problem Wilson foresaw was the narrowness of the channel, only some one hundred feet at best, and the low limbs of the trees on the bank overlapping the stream: "It will be necessary to cut out considerable in order to prevent the smoke-stacks of the steamers from being knocked down." Worse, as the banks were mostly underwater at least as far as Wilson explored (there was a little higher ground on down the pass), there was no good way to get at the limbs or trees except by boat, which the limbs stopped. Still, Wilson was upbeat: "[Even] with all these difficulties, no one here entertains a doubt of our being able to work through." That said, Wilson also advised that "no material advantages in the way of a surprise can be obtained." In fact, word was that the Confederates were already "making arrangements for our reception." Wilson did not know where, but

Grant had also gotten word of a battery set up at some point near Greenwood on the Yazoo River, but the best indications he had were that it had been removed. All advised caution in moving forward nevertheless.[39]

Despite some original pessimism, General Gorman at Helena had seen enough to start heavy work. He sent Brigadier General Cadwallader Washburn and two regiments of infantry—a force of a thousand soldiers—with five hundred more added the next day to the pass on February 8 to begin the work of clearing the channel. Washburn later informed his brother, Congressman Elihu Washburne, that "the undertaking was pronounced by many impossible & nearly every body threw cold water upon the project. I said it could be done, and offered to do it if the men could be furnished." Gorman himself continued to explore in the small steamer *Carl*, and three other steamers were on hand to add their power, the *Mattie Cook*, *Luella*, and *Henderson*. But the work quickly proved more difficult than first imagined; in addition to the obstructions the Confederates laid, the pass itself, the Federals learned, had not been used "since 1853, when the levee was made." By February 12, Washburn's force had cleared only about five miles of the pass, and it was the least obstructed, being on the Federal end of the waterway. Some of the troops camped near Hunt's Mill on the north side where some dry land emerged, but even it was soon flooded with the continual rush of river water through the cut levee.[40]

"Two somewhat considerable obstructions of fallen and drifted timber" were already cleared, Wilson reported, though it took large amounts of manpower and all the force the steam capstans could muster on the vessels. But then the workers soon began to run up on more and more obstructions, including driftwood and trees purposefully cut into the stream by Confederates. The overflowed banks in the first half of the pass made footing off the boats almost nonexistent, Wilson describing how "nowhere is there more than a mere strip of land next the bank, and that only a few inches out of the water." Worse, the ropes and tackle on the boats themselves proved to be too lightweight for the work, breaking frequently. Larger, six-inch cables were on the way, but the trees were getting bigger, Wilson finding a new cache of downed trees in a half-mile obstruction up next, in which some of the trees were four feet in diameter and "will weigh 35 tons." He also found that, due to the narrowness of the pass, everything had to be removed that would not sink into the deep channel, although George Brown remarked that "the rebels have saved us the trouble of cutting a number [of trees] by cutting them themselves." Still, Wilson reported to Grant on February 12, "there is no doubt of our ability to remove the obstructions, and make the Pass navigable for the largest boats." But it would take time.[41]

Grant had heard enough at this point to begin plans for a larger incursion. He asked Admiral Porter for all the help he could provide, writing that to get to the Yazoo River above Haynes' Bluff was "the great object of the expedition." He informed Porter of the general plan and his specific wishes, including destroying or better yet capturing all the Confederate vessels on the Yazoo and Sunflower River systems as well as destroying the two railroad bridges at Grenada. He sent six hundred infantry at first "to act as marines to the expedition" but later stipulated that this was a navy show until land operations ensued, hopefully at Haynes' Bluff. Grant warned that, although "the troops will be under the immediate command of their own officers, ... in no instance are they to exercise control over the vessels, or dictate when they are to go or what to do. The troops are designed to give protection to the vessels on which they are, and to operate on land if the necessity arises." He also had to warn, after being notified by Admiral Porter that "the army transports have been in the habit of taking coal belonging to the Navy Department," about taking navy coal except only in emergencies, after which "any coal taken should be returned as soon as possible." He added that "the two branches of service are supplied out of different appropriations; hence the necessity of being particular in this matter." He further assured Porter that "no military commander has a right to direct or order a naval vessel on any duty."[42]

But the entire plan changed as an enthused Grant then decided to send in large amounts of troops. Conflicting messages had resulted from the work in early February, Gorman informing McClernand, whom he more closely identified with than Grant, that the log piles and cut trees were so numerous that he doubted the entire plan's worthiness. "The obstacles become more and more formidable, but not, perhaps, insurmountable, and I am yet fearing that boats as large as the gunboats are will not be able to pass through, and it will take ten days more to get out the drift from the cut-off, and then it is uncertain what further obstructions the fleet will find in the Coldwater." He added that "the scouts I send report unfavorably to taking boats through of any size or as large as gunboats." Perhaps worse, he noted that "secrecy is out of the question, as it is fully known at Grenada what we are doing." Word was that there was even a Confederate armed steamer operating in the area.[43]

Yet Wilson's optimism overmatched Gorman's pessimism. And Grant listened more to Wilson than Gorman, who was already under investigation and would in fact be superseded for trade irregularities that also caught up a naval officer who had deployed a gunboat to guard his son's illegal shipment of cotton. Wilson oversaw the various regiments at work, which for their part had a good time despite the hard labor: "The Lieut Col who had command of the expedition let every man do just about as he pleased." In fact,

Grant wrote a subordinate that requests from Wilson for troops or garrisons should be considered "as if from myself." With a lot of power for a lieutenant colonel, Wilson had nothing but positive reports on the operations, fully confident that a large force could get through. By February 15, consequently, Grant informed Washington that "steamboats through Yazoo Pass have gone to within 6 miles of Coldwater. Express no fear but that they will reach it and the Yazoo." It was time to send in the army, and Grant that very day ordered Brigadier General Leonard F. Ross's entire infantry division to move to Moon Lake so they could enter the Yazoo Pass.[44]

While these major operations were going forward, numerous smaller efforts also came and went, but they kept the soldiers busy and Grant's hopes up. He wrote Julia on February 14: "I hope in the course of ten days more to be making a move. My confidence in taking Vicksburg is not unshaken unless if our people at home will give their moral support." Yet Grant had to oversee numerous matters in addition to his military commands, such as issuing orders that "the enticing of negroes to leave their homes to come within the lines of the army is positively forbidden," although he noted that those already there "will not be turned out." Trade was also an issue, he not allowing it open past Helena. Even then, General Gorman at Helena became caught up in the alleged nefarious activities and had to be replaced. There was also a vast effort to "ferret out" bribery, blackmail, and other crimes in the detective department in Memphis, a military commission being appointed to investigate.[45]

The Memphis area was of special concern, because that was from whence Grant obtained all his supplies and any additional troops to utilize down the river, they continually looking for any "news from below." A lot of hard fighting had taken place to take and then defend this area from Memphis to Corinth, and Grant saw no need to abandon it now, although the numbers of troops were significantly lowered and some places in the rear were almost entirely abandoned. But there was continual patrolling, scouting, and raiding on both sides in northern Mississippi and West Tennessee, particularly fortifying Memphis, resulting in little change but rather continual sparring across what had become no-man's-land around the unwritten demarcation zone that was the Tallahatchie River. Federals along the Memphis and Charleston Railroad probed and scouted down to the river while Confederates raided and demonstrated from safe zones south of the waterway.[46]

The Federal effort in West Tennessee and northern Mississippi was under Grant's XVI Corps commander, Major General Stephen A. Hurlbut. He had been with Grant since Shiloh and was one of the generals named specifically in the orders from Washington to take command of Grant's four corps back in December. With Hurlbut recently on leave up north, Charles Hamilton had filled in, but with Hurlbut now back Hamilton reverted to his command at Corinth, which he said "limits my command . . . and thrown nearly all the trade business into my hands. I find enough to do." In addition to watching for raids on the railroad and keeping track of the Confederate effort to infiltrate the Delta with small steamers to take away all food products available for storage in Vicksburg, a major source of intrigue and news for these Federals was Van Dorn's movement eastward in January and February, moving the bulk of the cavalry to Middle Tennessee. Federal cavalry watched and harassed Van Dorn even as he moved into Alabama and crossed the Tennessee River at Florence, heading out of the department and into Major General William Rosecrans's domain and concern.[47]

But several generals saw the opportunity that the movement of most all the Confederate cavalry in Mississippi entailed. Grant first broached an idea on February 9, writing Hurlbut that "if practicable I would like to have a Cavalry expedition penetrate as far South as possible on the Miss Central R R to destroy it." Hamilton similarly wrote on February 12 that "this movement of Van Dorn's clears our front of all cavalry except that of [Major Green L.] Blythe's, which is operating in the direction of Panola [modern Batesville]. It is time to strike the Vicksburg and Jackson Road." Hamilton envisioned a cavalry brigade moving southward through Mississippi to damage the Southern Railroad of Mississippi near Jackson and perhaps even the Big Black River railroad bridge, which would "completely isolate Vicksburg from the interior." Hamilton recommended Colonel Edward Hatch of the 2nd Iowa Cavalry for the job, but Grant wrote Hurlbut the very next day that "it seems to me that [Colonel Benjamin H.] Grierson, with about 500 picked men, might succeed in making his way south, and cut the railroad east of Jackson, Miss." He added: "The undertaking would be a hazardous one, but it would pay well if carried out. I do not direct that this shall be done, but leave it for a volunteer enterprise."[48]

All the while, Hurlbut was losing manpower in Memphis as the Army of the Tennessee continually shifted southward on the river for "the impending struggle in opening the Mississippi River." One Federal reported his commander at Grand Junction, Tennessee, "rec'd a dispatch asking him if he could hold the place with one Regt. of infantry & two of cavalry." McClernand already had two divisions at Milliken's Bend and Young's Point, and Grant assigned the newly acquired Arkansas troops at Helena (now under Brigadier General Benjamin Prentiss of Shiloh fame because of the trouble with Gorman) to his corps as well, although Prentiss was originally slated to be a division commander under Sherman; the Helena troops were divided into two divisions under Brigadier Generals Alvin P. Hovey and Clinton B. Fisk (a Methodist minister who preached in camp on occasion), giving McClernand four in total. Still, the Helena forces remained stationary for the time, some encamped on a huge sandbar along the river derisively named "Camp Nowhere." The lack of steamers and transports also figured into the delay for the troops at Helena. And certainly there was no need for more men to pile into the limited camping area down at Vicksburg for now. Sherman at the time had two divisions around the canal, he writing that "aside from the canal-digging, we are idle." But Grant began to think of adding to Sherman's force a third division, taken from Hurlbut's forces at Memphis. This would eventually become Brigadier General James Tuttle's division of the XV Corps, though it would likewise be delayed somewhat in heading downriver. McPherson's XVII Corps already had one division under John McArthur down the river aiding on the canal and then at Lake Providence, and McPherson was set personally to head down with John Logan's division soon, but the dearth of transportation delayed his departure for more than a week. Accordingly, Isaac Quinby's division remained in Memphis for the time being as well; Quinby, according to Hamilton in a note to Grant, "seems adverse to going down the river, and wished me to speak to you about it. He must tell you his own reasons." It was largely because of his own sickness, and indeed the division would be swapped among sick commanders for much of the remainder of the campaign.[49]

Another major area of activity occurred in the naval forces Porter had concentrated near Vicksburg. While assets were spread out all over the map with Grant's expeditions, Porter himself opened yet another area of operation, one that would provide huge benefits. "One of the rams ran the blockade this morning," Grant reported to Washington; "this is of vast importance, cutting off the enemy's communication with the west bank of the river." The ram *Queen of the West* had indeed run the batteries of Vicksburg on the morning of February 2, despite what one Confederate called "a severe thumping by our batteries."[50]

Porter had ordered Colonel Charles R. Ellet to run the batteries with *Queen of the West*. There were also infantry companies assigned to the rams, and at least one soldier very much liked the change — "much more easy, nicer and better than in the army." But there was a problem when the pilot, Josiah Reeder, refused to go and was ultimately tried and acquitted because he was not in the service. There was also a delay in moving the wheel to a safer place on deck and then back when it did not work: "An hour or more was spent in rearranging the apparatus, and when we finally rounded the point the sun had risen and any advantage which would have resulted from the darkness was lost to us," Ellet reported. Despite a delay that put him after dawn making the run, Ellet managed to ram the *City of Vicksburg* but did not sink it, the current of the river taking the stern of Ellet's boat and swinging it around so "that nearly all her momentum was lost." Ellet did fire incendiary shot into the steamer, but the Confederates managed to put out the flames and keep the vessel afloat. The *Queen* also was afire by this point, however, and departed quickly, taking as many as fifteen shots, only two being dangerous in the hull but above the waterline. The fires were doused by cutting loose the padding cotton bales, two deep, which were afire. Despite the hits, the Confederate batteries did not put up a good show, one Louisianan writing that "the batteries did very poor shooting; some of them did not fire a gun; they are much censured." Another simply added "our upper batteries were not working well."[51]

"It was a grand sight to see her go through the fire safely," one Federal wrote in his diary. After meager repairs, Ellet continued down the Mississippi with *Chicago Tribune* newspaper reporter Albert Bodman aboard, taking some fire from the guns at Warrenton; Bodman admitted he "sought the starboard of the *Queen*, where the thickness of four bales, & four feet of oak, might be supposed to insure complete safety." Once past Warrenton, Ellet tried to ascend the Big Black River but could not; he then landed opposite Natchez. Bodman reported "we reached the beautiful city of Natchez, and were greeted by a large concourse of her fair inhabitants, as we steamed silently by 'Natchez on the Hill' was ablaze with beauty and senility, but not a shout was raised, or a cheer of welcome. A few negroes 'under the hill' did indeed wave." Ellet next headed up the Red River to interdict any Confederate transportation possible. In all, he captured three Confederate vessels, *A. W. Baker*, *Moro*, and *Berwick Bay*, on which were hundreds of thousands of pounds of goods, including pork, meal, salt, sugar, and flour. He went ten miles up the Red River, but other Confederate steamers fled upstream to get out of harm's way. By February 5, Ellet was nearly out of coal and had to return to the lower canal opening, destroying the captured steamers and their prizes because they could not keep up and he could not wait for them. After arriving there, Ellet strategized with Sherman and other Federals working on the canal. But the mere presence of the ram was enough to deter Confederate shipping, Porter writing that "they [Confederate steamers] will likely not attempt to go out while the ram is about." Indeed, Franklin Gardner at Port Hudson reported that he kept the one boat there tied up to keep it from being captured as well.[52]

The effect was instantaneous, Porter informing Secretary Welles that "the people did not dream of anything of the kind" and assuring him that "if we cannot take just now the 6 miles of river in front of Vicksburg, we can take anything that steams upon that portion of the Mississippi between Vicksburg and Port Hudson." That was true, as long as the ram had power, and the next problem was getting coal to Ellet downstream from Vicksburg. Sherman himself went aboard to discuss options, and he informed Porter that hauling it by land was not an option: "The roads are awful, and to haul the coal in wagons is a simple impossibility. You saw them in fair weather, and can judge of them in foul. No drainage, rain above, and water underneath and all around, and a sticky, slimy clay, all militate against roads." The only options for Sherman were to work coal barges through the canal (which would even at this point be difficult) or to turn loose a barge of coal upstream and let it float southward on the river to Ellet's position. Hopefully, the Confederates would not detect and sink it.[53]

The *Queen of the West* caused so much havoc that Porter soon decided more power south of Vicksburg was needed: "I will re-enforce the *Queen of the West* as soon as an opportunity offers." In addition to positioning mortars on scows to open up on Vicksburg itself, that opportunity came on the night of February 12, when the ironclad *Indianola* also moved past the Vicksburg batteries; the troops said it "ran the blockade." Warning had been given to Sherman to be on the lookout and to show a light to let the crew know where friendly forces were, and Steele and Stuart did so. "The object in sending you is to protect the ram *Queen of the West*," read Porter's orders to Lieutenant Commander George Brown. He also ordered him to "go to Jeff. Davis's plantation and his brother Joe's and load up said steamer with all the cotton you can find and the best single male negroes." The passage was easily made, one Confederate admitting that "it was so dark and cloudy, we had to fire at the sound of her paddles, so she was probably not hit."[54]

It was a good thing the *Indianola* was now between the Confederate fortresses, because the *Queen of the West* met its end before the *Indianola* arrived to protect her. Ellet departed once more on the night of February 10, taking another vessel, the *De Soto*, and a coal barge. He moved up the Red River on February 12, taking stores and breaking Confederate logistical efforts on river and land. He also burned a few plantations and also managed to capture another steamer, the *Era No. 5*. As the small flotilla approached Fort Taylor near Alexandria, Louisiana, however, the treachery of the pilot, a Mr. Garvey, did in the *Queen*. When Ellet began to take fire and ordered Garvey to back the vessel out, the pilot instead managed to run her aground.

Confederate shot raked the vessel: "The enemy's shots struck us nearly every time." Soon, the steampipe was severed, and that was the end. Ellet ordered the crew to abandon the vessel, mostly on cotton bales floating in the river, but he could not burn it because of a wounded officer trapped below. Ellet and some of the crew members who were not captured eventually floated to the *Era No. 5*, which Ellet took command of and set out downstream after burning the *De Soto* and the barge. Back at the Mississippi River, however, Garvey again grounded the vessel he piloted, which caused Ellet, remembering disloyal sentiments he had uttered, to arrest him.[55]

Ellet was about to head back upriver when he fortunately met the *Indianola* heading south. He returned southward with the ironclad, but they failed to meet any action due to the Confederate gunboat *Webb* discerning the powerful *Indianola* and fleeing up the Red River. The *Indianola* decided not to pursue, and Ellet, having had a bad trip all the way around, returned to Vicksburg and the safety of the canal area. Despite the loss of the *Queen*, the coup was still an amazing feat, with first the ram and then the gunboat *Indianola* between Vicksburg and Port Hudson wreaking havoc on Confederate shipping. And it would continue to do that so long as Porter could keep the *Indianola* active. But she was alone amid a sea of Confederates, one of whom assured his wife "they might run them all by but that don't give them possession of the river. We will hold this place if they run every gun boat that belongs to the Yankee government."[56]

Amid all the renewed Union activity, the Confederate high command also lurched back into motion with the developments of the first half of February. A period of momentary ease had overcome the Department of Mississippi and East Louisiana after Sherman withdrew from Chickasaw Bayou and then the entire Federal force withdrew northward, albeit to attack Arkansas Post. That fight was in another department, and although concerned about the whole, Pemberton and his western commander Johnston saw the effort as a different department and for someone else to worry about. It was during such a lull in fact that Johnston left the area and returned to Middle Tennessee while Pemberton returned to his effort to stockpile as many goods in Vicksburg as he could, knowing the enemy would be back. And they soon were, although only experimenting with canals amid the mud. In speaking of the heavy rains of late January and February, one Confederate confessed they might help the canal project but assured his reader that "we will be ready for them even should they succeed. The road down the Miss. River is agoing to be a hard road to tread, as much so probably as the road to Richmond."[57]

The Federals were easily seen from Vicksburg, their white tents and numerous vessels standing out well. "I can see the Yankees gunboats and transports," one Tennessean wrote home; "any amount of them they are knot a very pleasant sight to see." Another explained that all the vessels "look a good deal like a town on the Miss River," and yet another declared they could hear the drums from the Union camps. Confederate gunners accordingly fired at any and everything in range: "The[y] air throwing bums now from Vicksburg at them across the river," one Tennessean wrote home. The canal efforts were obviously on the other side of the river and posed no real immediate threat, although initial assumptions among Pemberton and his officers were that the Federals were doing it to prepare for a landing south of Vicksburg, which was not being considered at this point in the Union plans. Still, the lack of major concern for anything developing on the west side of the river was a pattern that was beginning to develop in the Confederate high command, something that would grow to the point that Pemberton came to depend on the river as an almost unassailable blockade that could not be breached, or at least not quickly. He became more and more fixated on keeping the enemy west of the river and dealing with any Federals who wandered into his actual department east of it.[58]

Even while he watched closely and reacted to the movements to the north, Pemberton continued his main effort at gathering supplies for Vicksburg in case the operations came down to there entirely. "It will take a tremendous force to accomplish anything here," one perceptive Confederate wrote; "we are well fortified and if we are fully provisioned we can hold out for a long time." But just as important a crisis was brewing in Vicksburg itself as anywhere, where the growing number of troops were running out of food. Beef was still scarce at the pastures near Edwards, and by early February corn and other items were also lacking inside Vicksburg. "Send corn forward more rapidly. It is much needed here now," Vicksburg's commissary officer, T. B. Reed, begged departmental commissary Theodore Johnston in Jackson. But there was mass confusion regarding the collection and storage of supplies, including pushback from the railroads, which brought complaints to and reprimands from Richmond. There was also mismanagement and miscommunication among the chartered government vessels operating in the Delta and on the Mississippi River and its tributaries, especially with Federal gunboats on the loose. Even the Confederate departments squabbled with one another over vessels and storage, Reed advising that the government boat *Edward J. Gay* be taken and moored at Haynes' Bluff as a storage boat, with the engines affixed to mills to grind corn: "I think we ought to secure her at once, as the quartermaster's department will take her, if we do not."[59]

The commissary problems of course affected the average soldier the most, which in turn affected morale. "Wagons are passing from morning till night every day hauling corn and other provisions from the depot to the different Regiments in the vicinity," one Confederate wrote. To supply the local depots, he added, "the cars are coming and going day and night, bringing in and carrying out immense quantities of guns[,] ammunition[,] and all kinds of government stores." Of course, sickness also resulted from a lack of supplies and hurt morale, one lowly Louisianan who was actually getting better being cheered only by the surprise arrival of his father: "My father has shown great kindness to me ever since I have been here; he pays no regard to expense when he can give me aid or comfort: he has truly been a father to me all the days of my life, and I should certainly be an ungrateful son, were I ever to forget his kindness." Yet even the hospitals were not totally safe, the same Louisianan describing a fire breaking out next door as well as periodic Union bombardment of the city, which at times came close to the hospitals. He added how "a great panic prevails among the women who remain here, and they are rapidly stowing themselves and children away in their caves which they have dug in the sides of the hills all through town."[60]

Another departmental headache occurred during this time, among other command changes and appointments, as Sterling Price again lobbied for his and his troops' return west of the Mississippi River. His recent trip eastward had succeeded in getting orders for Pemberton and Lieutenant General Kirby Smith, the newly appointed commander of the trans-Mississippi, to swap forces, Smith ordered to meet with Pemberton on his way to his new lair about the plan. Pemberton was to do all he could to swap forces if practicable, but only if losing them would not harm Pemberton's defense of the department and Mississippi River. Obviously, he was loath to lose such veteran troops, and in fact the swap would never be made, at least in regard to the troops themselves.[61]

As a result, few showed much concern for the activities west of the river such as the scout of the Willow Lake route or even the Lake Providence efforts. Pemberton probably did not even know about the former, and there was some pushback against the latter and the canal, mostly cutting levees to allow the river to flood out the Federals when and where Confederates could not act to do so. And it seemed to be working, one Federal admitting that his regiment "skedaddled" ahead of the floodwaters. Carter Stevenson informed Pemberton at Jackson that "from the movements of transports yesterday and to-day, I think the water has forced the enemy to move their camps, which were below the canal, on this side, to Milliken's Bend." Concern was likewise lessened by what Pemberton reported as "large numbers of deserters from

Federal army are daily coming in." That did not sound as if the enemy was capable of doing much anytime soon. Put simply, Grant's operations west of the river were not that much of a concern for Pemberton and his generals, though activities bore watching.[62]

The naval threats on the river were a concern, however. Pemberton had to deal with the waterborne Federal incursions such as the *Queen of the West*. The vessel was originally thought by the Confederates to be the USS *Conestoga*, one of the early timberclads. Although the *Queen* eventually captured three vessels and later destroyed them, in addition to the *Era No. 5*, Confederate officials along the river were able to get word out in time to save others. Still, the idea of enemy gunboats south of Vicksburg was a concern, Pemberton advising Johnston now at Tullahoma, Tennessee, of the developments. Johnston would not return to Mississippi, thankfully for Pemberton, but offered what advice he could from far away. "What do you suppose enemy designs, and can you resist them?," Johnston simply queried. Pemberton could only respond: "Unless the enemy designs landing below Vicksburg and a protracted investment, perhaps first capturing Port Hudson, I can see no purpose in his arrangements." But it was clear that the *Queen*, and then the *Indianola*, had been able to pass the Vicksburg batteries easily, the *Queen* in broad daylight. Colonel Edward Higgins, commanding the heavy batteries at Vicksburg, recommended some changes as a result, placing the heaviest guns on the northern end of the river line so that they could take advantage of the longer field of fire and "command the doublings of the river." Higgins advised that, "if the enemy's iron-clads succeed in passing the upper batteries, they will have little difficulty in passing the others."[63]

In case that was what Grant indeed planned, Pemberton had his departmental engineer, Major Samuel Lockett, busy scouting areas on the Big Black River for batteries and defenses. If the idea was to go south of Vicksburg, Federal transports could move up the Big Black River and land troops directly in rear of Vicksburg. Lockett found little to work with along the lower Big Black River, especially around the major transportation routes and ferries such as Baldwin's, Hall's, and Hankinson's, although he did find some useful high ground to fortify around Regan's and Ivanhoe. Lockett reported, however, "the Big Black River is a very crooked stream, narrow and difficult of passage, and I do not apprehend much danger from the enemy in any attempt to use it against us. It also overflows its bottom to such an extent that it would be extremely difficult for the enemy to land troops along its banks whenever the water is high enough for them to ascend it. They can only ascend when the water is out of its banks."[64]

By far, Pemberton's biggest concern was actual Federal activity on his own side of the river: the breaking of the levee and arrival of Federals at Moon Lake and Yazoo Pass. Word first came to Pemberton in a February 9 note from Captain Isaac N. Brown of the Confederate navy at Yazoo City: "The enemy have cut the Yazoo Pass levee; contemplate, perhaps, assailing us down the Yazoo." He asserted that blocking the pass itself would provide only temporary delay and recommended placing a fortification to stop the incursion if it happened, the most likely place being near Greenwood, where the Yalobusha and Tallahatchie met to form the Yazoo River. The river was narrow there and would limit how many gunboats could advance at a time. Plus, the flooded banks would prevent infantry turning or taking the fortification. He asked Pemberton if he could get a couple of big guns from Mobile to block the river. Pemberton's initial response was less than helpful, saying no guns could be had from Mobile, adding "nor do I think the movement probable."[65]

As more information came in over the next few days, however, Pemberton came to realize just what a threat this was. "Henderson's Scouts reports three gunboats & two transports in Moon Lake & one gunboat in Yazoo Pass," William Loring informed Pemberton on February 10. Loring, having just left Grenada and now at Jackson, was still in nominal command in that area, and more reports flooded in to him on February 11 and 12. The news was not good at all. One of his scouts working out of Panola, simply named Smith, reported two gunboats and two transports entered Moon Lake on February 8 with fifteen hundred troops, although there were as many as ten thousand Federals back at Helena waiting to be sent in. One Confederate engineer, Captain J. A. Porter, likewise reported the entrance into Moon Lake on February 8 and also that the enemy was already exploring into the pass itself.[66]

Not knowing exactly the extent of the Federal effort at Yazoo Pass caused Pemberton a little bit of a quandary. He had just moved most of the troops from Grenada down to Jackson and Vicksburg upon the return of the Federals to Milliken's Bend and Young's Point, albeit slowly due to mismanagement of the railroads, according to Pemberton. Railroad officials conversely complained and said it was army mismanagement. Either way, the bottom line was that much of the army was now concentrated in the Vicksburg/Jackson corridor, while the nearest major threat east of the river was far back up in the Grenada area. How many troops should be kept farther north, where the incursion should be met if it was indeed successful in getting through the pass, and how many troops could conceivably operate in the limited expanses of a flooded Delta were all important questions.[67]

Yet Pemberton saw quickly what enemy success here would do, as the whole goal of Grant's effort was to get to high ground on the east side of the Mississippi River. Moving through Yazoo Pass and ultimately down the

Yazoo River in the Delta would allow the Federals to land on that high ground upstream of Haynes' Bluff, where there were no fortifications. Grant could then not only turn, capture, or cause Haynes' and Snyder's Bluffs to be evacuated but also be on that high ground east of Vicksburg—in fact on the ridge of land between the Yazoo and Big Black Rivers on which Vicksburg itself sat. This was definitely a threat, though using a roundabout route, but Pemberton also realized that Grant did not need to send his entire army along this route. Rather, just enough troops to land and turn or cause the evacuation of the fortifications at Haynes' and Snyder's Bluffs were needed; the Yazoo would then be open and transports could unload the entire Army of the Tennessee on that high ground. The potential was great for Grant, and the danger was just as real for Pemberton.[68]

Still, Yazoo Pass was a long way from Vicksburg, and there was no guarantee that the Federals could even get through. Pemberton therefore did not panic immediately, although in responding he showed a level-headed defense, much like he had been providing ever since he took command back in October. Just as in the Mississippi Central and Chickasaw Bayou operations, Pemberton was able to respond adequately because he had time to react because the Federal moves took so long across the wide chessboard on which he and Grant were matching wits. Pemberton saw no need to change his approach with this new phase of operations in this new year, continuing his Jominian style of defense that had worked well in December, namely meeting each advance by shifting troops quickly along interior lines of communication. It had worked between Grenada and Vicksburg in December, and Pemberton saw no reason to do anything differently now; he actually had even better interior lines of communication now, with both the railroads and the Yazoo River between threatened points.[69]

Without large numbers of troops on site, and with questions as to how many could operate at any given point anyway, for now the defense would be left to small cavalry units, Mississippi State Troops, and partisan rangers already operating in the area. Others were about to be formed from Mississippians in the northern tier of counties near Federal control who were dodging conscription but more than willing to join small home guard units. But as of the time of the initial Federal breach and first moves into the pass, only a few units were available to respond, including Engineer Porter, who soon had work crews felling trees into the pass itself. Porter reported that "the current is swift, and the channel narrow and torturous, and navigation difficult," adding that "opportunities for attack are good." He recommended sending cavalry and artillery directly to the pass to defend it, as the Coldwater River was too big to be defended in such manner; it would have to have "a steamboat and chains" to block that larger waterway, much like the raft down on the Yazoo at Snyder's Bluff.[70]

Supporting Porter were small units under Captain Aaron Forrest, who skirmished with one of the gunboats. There was also a cavalry company under Captain W. C. Maxwell operating in the area, but reports were counterproductive. Scout Smith, for example, reported that "obstructions in Pass said to be impassable," but Maxwell related that "the blockade is thought to be ineffectual." Yet the consensus was that the best place to delay or stop the enemy was in the narrow pass itself; once any Federals broke through and entered the Coldwater, there would be little short of military confrontation to stop them. As a result, Loring quickly ordered more manpower to the pass on February 11, including the nearest larger unit under Major Green L. Blythe, the 1st Mississippi Battalion Cavalry, Minute Men, and alerted the State Troops commander in the region, Brigadier General James Z. George, to send "his ranger cavalry."[71]

Tension built as the days passed and reports of continual Federal progress in the pass arrived. By February 15, in fact, Colonel Robert McCullough, in command of scouts and cavalry in the area, reported that the Federals would reach the Coldwater River that day, which was untrue but concerning nevertheless. Perhaps more concerning was his information that the Confederate vessels in the pass and the Coldwater working on obstructions had given up: "Our gunboat and transport left the mouth of Coldwater this morning for Yazoo City, having given up obstructing the river." It seemed the Federals would indeed be to the Coldwater soon if not there already, and Pemberton had no choice but to start taking this threat much more seriously than he originally had. And it was indeed serious, with the distinct possibility of Federal gunboats, and perhaps transports laden with thousands of Federal troops, potentially running loose in the Mississippi Delta. "It is likely they will attack us at different points," one observant Louisianan scribbled in his diary. "I anticipate a bloody struggle here but I hope we will be able to defeat the northern hordes that are sent against us."[72]

6

"The Prospect of Opening the Pass Is Encouraging"

February 16–28

It has been called "the most Southern place on earth": the Mississippi Delta. Distinct in its geography, culture, society, and environment, the northwestern section of Mississippi is renowned for its food, music, heritage, and history. From its deep roots in the blues and country music to its centrality to the civil rights movement, the Delta's mystique also includes a healthy portion of Civil War history as well. Turned back from every other conceivable approach to Vicksburg, Federal commanders tried to go through the Delta, "tried" being the operative word. Despite an unforgiving environment, the Delta operations nevertheless illustrated well the departure from the by-the-book military operations of the past. Neither Clausewitz nor Jomini, or anyone else for that matter, wrote much about conducting military operations amid such a challenging space. Grant, in fact, explained that "we are going through a campaign here such as has not been heard of on this continent before."[1]

The Mississippi portion of the Mississippi River's alluvial plain sat east of the river and was shaped something like an elongated oval. Bounded by the Mississippi River on the west and a distinctive ridgeline on the east, the flatland is readily apparent to all who see it, especially from the hills to the east known at various places as Walnut Hills, Valley Hill, and so on. Spread out some sixty-five or seventy miles at its widest point, the oval stretched over a hundred and eighty-five miles in height, from near Memphis in the north almost to Vicksburg to the south. The entire flatland is tilted southward, as would be expected following the river itself flowing south, with elevations at Tunica in the north at 197 feet above sea level. The Delta from there gradually sloped southward; at its widest point near the Greenwood/Greenville corridor the elevation fell to 131 feet for both, and by the time the Delta reached Vicksburg the elevation was down to around a hundred feet above sea level. The Mississippi River saw a similar drop in footage, falling from a modern mark of 184 feet at Memphis to 46 feet at Vicksburg. Illustrating the heights of the bluffs at Memphis and Vicksburg, their elevations sat at 338 and 240 feet above sea level respectively.[2]

The slope of the Delta not surprisingly produced waterflow southward, mostly carried by four major watercourses that were nevertheless interconnected with bayous, creeks, swamps, old river runs, and lakes to create a maze of swampy, miry, primordial bottomland. By far, the dominant river system in the Delta lay on its easternmost curve, the Yazoo River. Giving its name at times to the region (explaining its other common name, the Yazoo River Delta), the Yazoo and its tributaries drained the vast majority of the region from near Memphis southward. Although the Yazoo River officially began at Greenwood, the tributaries that flowed into and formed it created the dominant drainage. Several rivers flowed east to west off the higher hills to the east in northern Mississippi, all turning southward in the Delta to reach Greenwood and form the Yazoo. Farthest north, the Coldwater River flowed just north of Holly Springs and roughly paralleled the Mississippi–Tennessee state line until its spilled out into the Delta just thirty miles south of Memphis, where it turned sharply southward and flowed around forty straight-line miles (many more in winding river miles) until it flowed into a larger tributary of the Yazoo, the Tallahatchie River. Coming off the same higher hills to the east, the Tallahatchie paralleled the Coldwater twenty to thirty miles to the south, just north of Oxford, before it also turned sharply southward when it reached the Delta. The Coldwater and Tallahatchie, along with the waters of the Yocona that flowed off the same high hills to the east and joined the Tallahatchie just before its merger with the Coldwater, joined at the small village of Polkville, Mississippi, where the Tallahatchie flowed another forty or so miles until it joined yet another river flowing roughly parallel with the Coldwater, Tallahatchie, and Yocona Rivers, the Yalobusha. It flowed just north of Grenada and after exiting the hills also turned sharply southward once in the Delta, where it joined the Tallahatchie at Greenwood to create the Yazoo River. All these rivers, winding and interconnected with ancient and not so ancient runs of the rivers, clung closely to the eastern hills from whence their waters flowed, and the Yazoo at times along its ninety straight-line mile length would even butt up right against the eastern hills at Yazoo City, Satartia, and Haynes' and Snyder's Bluffs nearer to Vicksburg.[3]

While the Yazoo River and its tributaries were the dominant system in the Delta, other major streams similarly drained the western portions of the

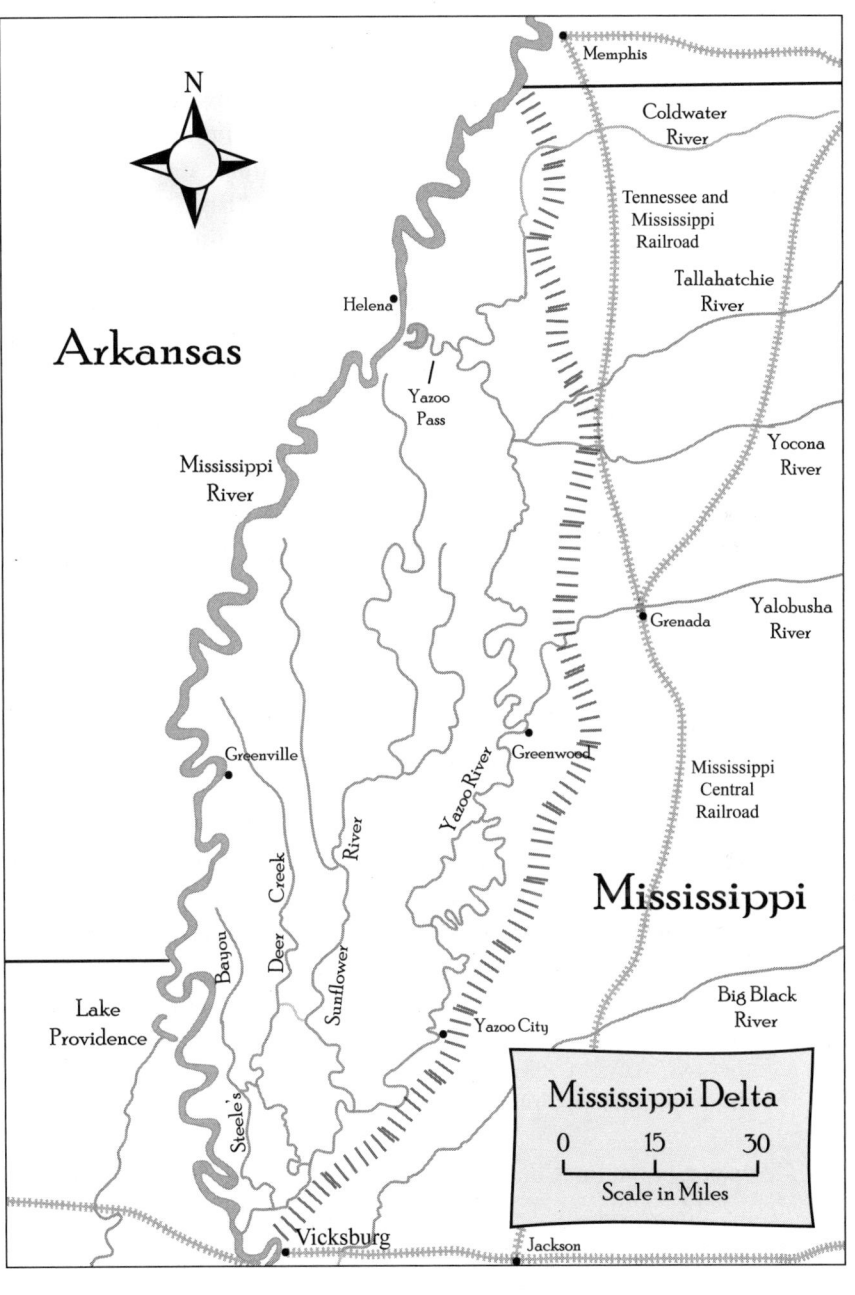

flatland, although none were as significant and fully navigable as the Yazoo River system. Still, the Sunflower River, Deer Creek, and Steele's Bayou offered some navigation on their lower extremities, allowing access into the vast Delta by boat easier than along the few roads through the area. The Sunflower River, with a smaller component sometimes termed the "Little Sunflower River" that often dubbed the main river the "Big Sunflower River," had its headwaters in the northern portion of the Delta just south of Moon Lake and near Friar's Point and the small village of Delta on the Mississippi River itself. The Sunflower River flowed due southward just twenty or so miles to the west of the Yazoo/Tallahatchie/Coldwater path, eventually flowing into the Yazoo some twenty-five straight-line miles northeast of Vicksburg, between Satartia and Haynes' Bluff.[4]

A third major water system, Deer Creek, also had its headwaters near the Mississippi River, beginning just north of Greenville and flowing due south another ten or twenty miles west of the Sunflower River's course. Deer Creek drained the central Delta, flowing into the Yazoo River just north of Haynes' Bluff. The fourth watershed, closest to the Mississippi River itself, was Steele's Bayou, which began well south of Greenville and flowed a mere five or ten miles west of Deer Creek, and not that much more from the Mississippi River itself to the west, at times being no more than a mile or two off the wild turns of the river.[5]

While all these bayous, creeks, and rivers ran southward, they were fed by smaller although at times still substantial and even navigable feeders that literally crisscrossed the Delta, interconnecting these waterways to one another and the numerous lakes and stagnant bayous that did not flow but were filled with collected water. Nevertheless, the overall movement of almost all water was southward, eventually into the Yazoo River itself, which flowed into the Mississippi River just ten or so miles northwest of Vicksburg. And the relatively flat ground made sure that all the water went nowhere fast. One Indianan, in fact, described the Delta as "such a monotonous country. Such a sameness overspreads every thing—No hills—no mountains no valleys—Nothing but one vast plain of plantations—cypress forests and watery Bayous."[6]

While basically flat but tilted southward, there was some small and almost indistinguishable variation of land that could really only be deciphered when the entire region was flooded, when only a few spots of dry ground protruded out of the water. And there was plenty of that. "Rain, Rain, Rain!," wrote a disgusted Iowan on February 16. "Still raining. What weather! The river is rising rapidly." Corps commander James B. McPherson described to his mother how "it never rains in the North as it does here, for there it comes down in drops but here it comes down in streams." These higher areas were mostly along the major waterways in the form of natural levees that appeared over time as the Delta rivers, bayous, and creeks spilled out of their banks. The sediments carried by these overflowing waters slowly sank without the current, the heaviest sediments falling first and creating the slightly higher elevations right at the point of overflow along the streams' banks. Likewise, there were other natural depressions where former channels of the waterways had existed and then filled in but were largely still filled with water. In the arid seasons, however, these could be dry and formed a lower level of ground than normal.[7]

All along the Mississippi River itself were former channels, known as oxbow lakes, where the waterway once flowed but had since cut through the narrow neck of land at the foot of the great bends and built up sandbars to cut them off. One Mississippian described it as "many years ago, when the 'Father of Waters' was much younger than he is now, long years before Lasalle, or DeSoto had looked upon his turbid yellow waters, he, like most other young men, wished to see something of the world. . . . But as he got older he saw the folly of these long bends and corrected them by cutting across, as the Yankees are now to his utter disgust trying to persuade him to do at Vicksburg." These by-product lakes remained full of water and even connected to the river itself in overflow times, and the same occurred on smaller scales with the inland rivers of the Delta as well. Passage throughout the Delta was thus achievable, at least until manmade levies corralled the river as best they could.[8]

All of the Delta was rich and very workable agricultural ground if it was dry. But that was the problem: the Mississippi River as well as the others flooded every winter and spring, overflowing natural banks and even the slight levees that had built up. That made occupation and agricultural work chancy at best unless something could be done to mitigate the danger of flooding and disease; one Mississippian noted that "a man who can stand the malarious nature of the country can produce luxuriant crops of corn, cotton, oats, and all other crops indigenous to the latitude." But that was a huge task, and as a result the Delta remained for many decades after Mississippi's admission into the Union in 1817 a sparsely settled region. In fact, by 1860 these Delta counties were still some of the thinnest-settled areas in the entire nation. Issaquena County, for example, just north of Vicksburg, contained a mere 587 white people, with Tunica County south of Memphis having not many more, just 883. That is comparable to the northern Mississippi hill counties recently opened up with the cession of Indian land in the 1830s, many such as Pontotoc, Tippah, Marshall, Itawamba, or Choctaw having ten to fifteen thousand whites residing there. Tishomingo County in the northeastern corner had a whopping 19,159 population. Elections told the same story. The delegate to the Mississippi Secession Convention from Issaquena County won his election by two votes, 73 to 71; delegates from the northern Mississippi hill counties won vote totals in the thousands. One soldier later confessed, "Oh! What a country for any man who considered himself at least ½ civilized to live in, it is hardly fit for wild beasts."[9]

As the decades passed in statehood, however, planters soon learned to make the Delta pay. The problem of working the fertile land of the Delta without the threat of continual flooding was somewhat solved with a system of levees emplaced along the Mississippi River and elsewhere in the 1850s, which dried out much of the Delta and kept the waterways mostly within their banks. These massive levees, one Federal comparing them to the pyramids of Egypt in scope, first went up around New Orleans in the early 1700s and gradually extended northward into Mississippi and Arkansas, but a concerted effort at building a thorough levee system did not appear until the 1850s. The Delta region of Mississippi produced a paltry thirty-nine thousand bales of cotton in 1840 and only forty-two thousand in 1850. With the advent of levee boards in each river county and an overall state board headed by James L. Alcorn, a politician planter from Coahoma County who lived on the banks of Yazoo Pass itself, by 1860 some 310 miles of levee, built mostly by slave labor and funded by bonds and loans, shielded the Delta from the Chickasaw Bluffs at Memphis nearly to Vicksburg. As a result, cotton production jumped in the partially dried-up Delta to two hundred and twenty thousand bales of cotton in 1860 and two and a half million bushels of corn.[10]

Obviously, the levees stopped many of the continual overflows that made the land so productive in the first place, but in the use-up-the-land-and-move-on mentality of Southern agriculture, that was a small price to pay for a few decades of accumulated wealth. As a result, by the time of the Civil War, the Delta was beginning to be cleared of the vast forests and put under cultivation, protected as it was by the levee system the state initiated. Thus, the same census returns for 1860 that showed a mere 587 white population of Issaquena County also showed a slave population of 7,244. Tunica County's 883 whites compared with 3,483 slaves. Bolivar County had a white population of 1,393 but 9,078 slaves. There were no free blacks to speak of in the Delta.[11]

While there were different classes of whites in the Delta, the most important to politics and war were the large planters, first situated along the Mississippi River, although they soon spread out into the Delta along the waterways as Mississippi learned to fight back against the floodwaters. Huge plantation owners such as James L. Alcorn, Charles Clark, Benjamin Humphreys, Samuel G. French, Wade Hampton, and Jefferson Davis himself a little farther south of Vicksburg owned thousands of slaves and made the Delta pay. Nonetheless, by the time of the Civil War the Delta was largely a wilderness of sorts, only isolated and sparse plantations along the major waterways able to make a profit in the wilderness. One Mississippian who left the area for other posts wrote home, "I am sure you will congratulate us on getting out of Yazoo River swamp alive and well, and if you only could have seen the place you would have thought it impossible for us to have lived there so long." But the Delta posed an altogether different problem to the Union high command, one that they had little education in when Union armies began to push on through the narrow Yazoo Pass and pop out into the vast Delta itself where, one Federal explained, "alligators, lizards, and poisonous snakes abound."[12]

"The enemy have driven us off from the works on the Pass, and are coming through," related the somber message from northern Mississippi. And it was not the only one, as numerous messages came eventually to Pemberton from the small-unit commanders working against time to obstruct the Yazoo Pass and delay the Federals from working therein. Most arrived through subordinates in the area, namely Major General William W. Loring and Confederate navy commander Isaac N. Brown at Yazoo City, although the latter was also active as far up as the pass itself planting torpedoes, or mines. And they all related the same basic message: the obstructions in the pass would not stop the determined Federal advance, and Union forces would soon be operating amid the interconnected rivers of the Delta. One Louisianan had recently jotted in his diary that "no one can account for the delay of the enemy in their attack," but it seemed to finally be happening.[13]

It was a growing crisis for sure, although Pemberton and others still had a hard time believing this was the main Federal thrust. He obviously had to keep his eye on other potential efforts, such as the enemy gunboats below Vicksburg, the canal operations right on Vicksburg's front door, as well as other potential problems such as the efforts west of the Mississippi River, although Pemberton had always been less concerned for what was happening on that opposite side. But even this new threat east of the Mississippi brought doubt to Pemberton's mind: "I do not apprehend anything serious from this demonstration," he wrote. Similarly, Engineer Powhatton Robinson related that "I can't believe the Yankees have got through our obstructions yet."[14]

All the while, Pemberton continued to deal with departmental issues as well, including changing general officers and stockpiling goods at Vicksburg for the final showdown, if it came to that. There was also a widely reported "military execution" in front of the troops at Vicksburg, a "youth—almost a boy—who had deserted from a Tennessee Reg't, and enlisted in the Federal Army." He had been captured at Chickasaw Bayou and court-martialed. "He met his fate with fortitude," William Pitt Chambers related; "it was a solemn and impressive scene." And that was not the only one, others describing similar episodes and one Louisianan writing "there has ben three men shot here in the last 4 weakes the boys all seane one of them shot." An Alabamian described a "man shooting" in March, the entire division drawn up to witness it as the man sat on his coffin and was shot. Most vividly, three were shot for desertion, they having been captured again and recognized when brought to Vicksburg. Their sentence was to be "shot to death with musketry," to be done, which it was, on March 6. Others had lighter sentences, one to "have the right half of his head shaven and receive fifty lashes on the bare back with a common raw hide." Conversely in the Union camps, a 54th Ohio soldier was, for the offense of cowardice, merely made to parade around the camps in the division with a board on his back labeled "coward." He had turned and run at Arkansas Post, but one Indianan admitted, "I'd rather be shot."[15]

In larger strategic matters, Pemberton had a general idea of how the campaign would unfold, Vicksburg probably being the safest zone and logically the last to be tested. But how that would eventually happen was still unknown. With Union gunboats between Vicksburg and Port Hudson, "it is, moreover, possible that the enemy may succeed in opening the canal, or, by taking advantage of the darkness, may even run by some of his transports. . . . Either from above or below there is a possibility that troops may be landed and Vicksburg be invested by land and water." Obviously, Yazoo Pass was but a part of the overall plan, but a part indeed: "Many people believe that the enemy will get through the Yazoo Pass . . . [and] if it be the enemy's purpose to lay siege to Vicksburg, this is doubtless part of his plan to cut off our supplies, and would materially assist the investment of the place." Once again, Pemberton misread the intent, which was to take the big guns closing the Yazoo River in reverse; he thought only of supplies, which he was very concerned about—even ammunition, writing that at the current time "there is now on hand a sufficiency for a battle, but not for a protracted siege." In order to make sure he had everything he needed and to stop "illicit trade," he even asked for the "suspension of writ of habeus corpus in Jackson," which the War Department refused. Another headache in the middle of all the planning was Sterling Price's transfer back to the trans-Mississippi "at his own request," although the orders stipulated that his troops would be sent only "as soon as the exigencies of the service will admit of it." Price's attention was obviously elsewhere, he not even showing up for a scheduled review in early March. But Price addressed his trans-Mississippi troops upon his departure and reviewed them, a sad day for the troops who were not going with him. And the way things were looking, that would not be anytime soon either, but at least one of his trans-Mississippians was not distraught: "As for my single self," he wrote a friend, "I don't care a straw. I am glad we are from under him. He is not such a man as Van Dorn or Bowen."[16]

But as the days moved on and it seemed obvious that the Federals would indeed break through Yazoo Pass and enter the Coldwater River, Pemberton and everyone else saw the potential problems and began to act more swiftly. One of the scouts battling amid the high waters and determined Federals, Lieutenant F. E. Shepperd of the Confederate navy, advised that "hasty obstructions with fortifications may save Yazoo City" before adding, "I have done my best; worked under their noses, till their pickets came in 100 yards of me."[17]

Pemberton in particular began to shift assets northward on the Yazoo River, intending to meet the enemy at the most favorable ground he could farthest to the north that he could. But a lack of time could make any defense north of Yazoo City problematic, depending on how fast the Federals moved. Pemberton first sent Waul's Texas Legion northward to Yazoo City and then on forward, but with the instructions that Loring could stop them at Yazoo City for the main defense if it was already too late to make a stand elsewhere. Pemberton also shifted northward to Yazoo City two large-caliber guns originally intended to go across the river to aid in Major General Richard Taylor's defense of the Red River, a 32-pound rifle and a 30-pound Parrott as well as a lighter field battery. As the big guns would be the ones that could close the river, he added a word of haste to get the two powerful guns on site even before the Texans or field artillery left.[18]

Where to make the defense was the big question, as there were limited opportunities in the flat Delta. There was high ground at Yazoo City, where the range of hills ending the Delta came nearby the river and could be utilized as a defense. But that was seen as a last line of protection, the boatyards there needing to be saved at all hazards. Likewise, if the enemy made it that far and past Yazoo City, they were on the ridge east of Vicksburg, where they wanted to be all along. But if that was the best place, Pemberton gave Loring the discretion to start to assemble troops near Yazoo City, including some from Grenada stopping at Vaughan's Station on the Mississippi Central Railroad.[19]

The only other possible area of defense was west of Greenwood, where a small bluff on the Tallahatchie River allowed for some height dominance; it was also where the Tallahatchie and Yalobusha met to form the Yazoo, which curved around again and flowed at one point within a few hundred yards of the Tallahatchie. A defense across the narrow neck of land could cover everything involved, including the mouth of the Yalobusha, potentially keeping Grenada and its railroad bridges from being attacked or turned. One Confederate already at Greenwood noted that "the river here is very narrow, which, together with some little fortifying already done, it is thought will enable us to hold the place against the force which it is said is advancing." But he did not believe any force would use this route: "Don't you think it rather absurd for them to attempt the accomplishment, with so small a force, virtually of the same thing which Genl Grant failed to do with a large army?"[20]

Confederate navy commander Brown was also involved, getting a defense of manned gunboats ready, but he needed more men and boats. He had two ready to send up the river if a defense could be made in time at Greenwood, the *Mary Keene* and the *Star of the West* of Fort Sumter fame at the start of the war. (In a twist, one of Grant's regimental and future brigade commanders, Colonel Charles Woods, had commanded the infantry on board at the time.) The vessel had moved to the Gulf of Mexico and was captured, the Confederates taking it up the Mississippi River and then up the Yazoo for safety as the Federal navy cut off more and more of the Mississippi. Brown needed crews to fight with the vessels, but in a period of pessimism he wrote that "I regret that we have so little time to make preparations, so little, in fact, that I cannot be answerable for what may happen; in other words, I can give no assurance that we shall be able to stop the enemy, as we cannot tell with what amount or description of force he is coming through. We will do all we can."[21]

Pemberton also decided to send Loring himself to take command of the situation. He directed him to the Yazoo River on February 17, "with a view to finding some suitable place on the Yazoo or Tallahatchie whereat to erect works and place obstructions to the passage down of the enemy." Time was of the essence, and various officers coordinated under Loring began to make a defense. Engineer Robinson thought a gunboat covered with cotton could buy more time in the Coldwater as he planned more obstructions, even in the pass if he had time, which he did not. "Otherwise across narrow neck between Tallahatchie Yazoo, 300 yards wide; impregnable position when fortified and Tallahatchie obstructed. Obstructions worthless unsupported by artillery."[22]

Loring himself arrived at Greenwood on February 21, even as the Federals were still poking their way through the pass sixty-five miles to the north. He had sent Major Minor Meriwether ahead of him to pick a sufficient location for defense, and with the aid of local men in the service Meriwether chose the same neck of ground between the Tallahatchie and Yazoo Rivers that others had described, where Beck's Ferry crossed the river. Loring described it as "the only one offering the slightest advantage for defensive works." He therefore "determined to avail myself of its strong points." Meriwether started fortifications, and when Loring arrived he approved of the site and work, informing Pemberton that the fortifications, "when completed, will do much toward preventing the passage down of the enemy." He also related that "this is the only point short of Yazoo City where any defense can be made on the river." He described the site as two or three miles west of Greenwood, although four miles by river, and the banks were some eight feet above the river itself. The guns would be mounted on parapets of cotton bales gathered up and down the rivers and covered with dirt, which would "place them at an altitude that insures a plunging fire upon the enemy's boat." Loring found Waul's Texans already there, and the general recommended Waul take command of the site already dubbed "Camp Pemberton." To further blockade the river, Loring also planned rafts much like those down at Snyder's Bluff, but if speed was needed, Loring also planned to sink the *Star of the West* "athwart the channel." Nothing, however, would be done until the last minute to allow navigation all the way up into the Coldwater in case the cotton-clad steamboats Brown was fitting out at Yazoo City became operational. Of course, the fort needed guns when completed, and Loring recommended sending the two rifles Pemberton had earlier ordered to Yazoo City on up, they being replaced by others perhaps from Vicksburg. And they needed to be replaced at Yazoo City, Loring argued, "in the event we should be compelled to abandon the works up the river." Despite the rush, the entire hasty defense soon began to take shape, Loring reporting that "these necessary arrangements were prosecuted with the utmost diligence day and night," and once completed the little stronghold gained a more formidable name than Camp Pemberton; it soon became "Fort" Pemberton.[23]

But Loring was not satisfied with just the preparations at Greenwood. Hoping to find additional areas to defend farther north, he set out the next day on a fact-finding trip up the river on the steamer *Hope*, making sure Waul was in contact with authorities farther south by courier to the Mississippi Central Railroad at Vaiden while he was gone. But Loring found few other possibilities; in fact, what obstructions that the Confederates had placed in the Coldwater River were soon washed away. Guarded by a hundred and twenty of Waul's Texans, Loring explored "as far as safe and practicable." By February 24, he had gone some seventy miles but turned around and went back to Greenwood upon word that the Federals had broken through to the Coldwater: "I deemed it proper to return here and hasten the completion of the works at this point."[24]

Meanwhile, Waul continued work on Fort Pemberton under the capable eyes of engineers Captain Robinson and Major Meriwether. The "exceedingly wet weather" delayed progress some days, but Waul reported on others that "to-day the sun shines brightly, and we can proceed rapidly." But he knew works without guns were useless and advised more heavy cannons be sent up, but at the least any guns at all, even mountain howitzers. He reiterated that heavy guns "would render this neck not only defensive, but nearly impregnable," especially as these guns commanded the river for a distance of eight hundred yards toward its turn north of the fort. More troops also began to arrive. Upon his arrival back at Greenwood, Loring similarly ordered another regiment of Tilghman's brigade to Greenwood from Grenada as well as Robert McCullough's cavalry brigade to the Coldwater region in case they could find access to the river to harass the enemy. He also had civilian Thomas Weldon ready to obstruct the river with the rafts, timber for which was already being cut, and Weldon himself had gone after the *Star of the West* to sink in the channel if necessary. All the while, messages continued to come in from the scouts and cavalry companies near the pass, following closely the Federal advance with good accuracy, even concerning the commanders of the Union troops.[25]

Over the latter days of February, Loring continued to build up the defenses, requesting more heavy guns that Pemberton could not send. But Loring assured Pemberton that he would put up a fight at the latter's namesake fort: "If we have five [days] more time, defenses and raft will be formidable." Time would tell if he had that much leeway, as the Federals were continually making progress through the Yazoo Pass and would soon burst out into the larger rivers of the Delta.[26]

As February slipped by, Union workers indeed continued their tasks of clearing the harrowing pass between Moon Lake and the Coldwater River. The obstructions that Porter, Forrest, and Maxwell were placing became larger and more significant on the second half of the pass, as did the torturous bends and turns as the path led in almost every direction. One obstruction was a full mile in length "and composed of the heaviest trees, cut from both sides of the stream, so as to lie across and upon each other." Wilson explained that "the trees were of the largest and heaviest kinds, cottonwood, sycamore, oak, elm, and pecan prevailing, and all, except cottonwood, having a greater specific gravity than water. These, mixed with drift-wood, rendered the barricade of no trifling nature." He added that "various plans were tried for removing them, all attended with the breakage of cables and boat machinery, but finally, by cutting, sawing, and pulling out upon the banks entire trees, the way was opened." And much of the work had to be done "by men standing in boats" because of the flooded terrain. At times when land could be had, as many as four hundred men pulling on six-inch cables removed the largest trunks.[27]

The narrow and winding nature of the pass was also problematic, but the troops made steady progress under Wilson's watchful eye and with the muscles of Washburn's manpower at work both in the pass as well as guarding it so that no more trees could be felled into it. Obviously, the aid of the steam capstans on the vessels did not hurt either in the effort to "snake out" the trees. The groups of as many as five hundred men working a day, that being all that could be squeezed into the narrow front of work and at times less than that, were so frequently exhausted that the men had to work in shifts and be replaced frequently. One Indianan related that "we were put to work hauling logs out of the Pass that had been felled in there by the Rebels to prevent our boats passing through. The weather during the time we were engaged was very disagreeable raining nearly all the time." Fortunately, Washburn and Gorman had plenty of troops at Helena for the task. But it went well, word coming to the main army down near Vicksburg that "the prospect of opening the pass is encouraging . . . General Washburn expected to reach the Coldwater with his transports to-morrow [February 23]."[28]

There had been some Confederate resistance above and beyond the obstructions, Washburn sending three wounded men back to Helena shot on February 16 by Confederate outliers. "They are still hanging around," Washburn reported, "watching our movements and embarrassing us a little." Still, Washburn reported that his men "have taken out a good many very large trees. . . . I am satisfied that they cannot establish any timber blockade that I cannot remove." Once cleared, he boasted, "I am satisfied that we can take as large an army down here as we can find transports for." Grant would take any steamers he could get, but he desired sidewheelers that could navigate the narrow streams better than sternwheelers.[29]

Still, the continuing menace of Confederate cavalry hanging around needed to be taken care of to keep the morale of the workers up, which Washburn also aided by promising them that the paymaster would be held at Helena until they got out of the pass and returned to their camps. An Indianan, who noted that "we were wet and muddy all over," added "the officers took pity on us and issued commissary whiskey to each man. Some of the boys paid twenty-five cents a thimbleful for to make a good drink." The men indeed worked hard, one explaining that "the plan worked on was to fasten two long Ropes to one of the long logs which held the drift 200 or 300 men would then lay hold & out it would come the Boats however did most of the work & before we came away they had got through with cold water." Washburn also requested Prentiss to send him more cavalry and begged, "I wish very much that you would come down here, as I am anxious to have your opinion." He specifically asked that two hundred troopers move from Dowd's Plantation on Moon Lake cross country to Hunt's Mill near the other end of the pass, and eventually part of the 1st Indiana Cavalry did so.[30]

After sending his report to Prentiss, Washburn had another idea, this time to utilize trickery in the effort. In order to "throw the enemy off his guard," he requested Prentiss to telegraph a report to the Associated Press that read: "The attempt to open the Yazoo Pass is likely to prove an entire failure. After expending great labor to remove the obstructions placed in it by the rebels, it is found impossible to open it except for the very smallest kind of boats. Besides, the rapid fall of water, it is reported, has caught a number of boats in the Pass, which, unless strongly guarded, are liable to be destroyed." Washburn noted that, if sent, "such a dispatch would find its way to Vicksburg in two days after it was published in the Eastern papers."[31]

Work continued amid the trickery. By late on February 21, in fact, the working parties neared the entrance into the "long looked for Coldwater," and at last the path was cleared. But it was tough amid the heavy rain, one Iowan describing it as "the most fatiguing work I ever did in my life." The *Henderson*, which had been thoroughly damaged during the work and passage (to the point that Wilson recommended that "it would . . . be no more than justice to put her in repair at the public expense"), and *Mattie Cook* entered the Coldwater the very next day with a regiment of troops on board and proceeded down the comparatively wide and open river southward some two or three miles to the large Cole Plantation. Wilson described the Coldwater as "a considerable stream after its junction with the Pass—from 120 to 150 feet in width inside of its banks; is now quite full, rising slowly, and is easily navigable for any boat that can work its way through the Pass." He in fact thought that vessels as long as a hundred and eighty feet could make the passage in four days as long as water remained in abundance.[32]

The two steamers tied up for the night, the Coldwater, although much larger than the pass, still being a very narrow and winding stream itself and therefore dangerous except in daylight. The next day, February 23, the two steamers and the infantry continued on another ten or twelve miles "through some of the shortest bends," Wilson reported, this time at points actually going all directions of the compass. Washburn informed his congressman brother the next day: "In just two weeks after I commenced the work I sailed with two Steam Boats into Cold Water River, and yesterday I run down that stream for 12 miles, until I became thoroughly satisfied that the route was entirely feasible. The rebels had blockaded the 'pass' which is about ninety feet wide by falling an immense [amount] of timber into it. I have taken it out & the way to take Vicksburgh is clear." Having seen enough to know they had broken through for good, the vessels returned to the safety of the pass itself, stopping for the night at Hunt's Mill nearly midway in the passage, there to await the next phase of the operations. But the hardest work had been done in opening the pass itself, although the Confederates quickly reported the developments to Vicksburg: "The Federals have succeeded in getting through the Pass into Coldwater River," Scout Sam Henderson reported to Pemberton on January 23. "One of their gunboats passed into Coldwater and then went back up the Pass to-day." Other Confederates were nearby as well; there was a small skirmish on February 19 in which the 1st Indiana Cavalry killed, wounded, and captured about twenty-five Confederates with no loss to the Indianans.[33]

Wilson took a moment and reported to Grant the progress on February 24, again stating his optimism: "I am confirmed in the opinions expressed in my previous reports concerning the practicability of this route, during proper stages of water, as a line of military operations." He was not concerned at all about depth of water, as the shallowest on the whole route was the bar where the pass entered the Mississippi River, which occurred at almost all tributaries as they entered larger streams and dropped the sediment they were carrying as the waters entered the current of a different stream. If vessels could pass that bar, they could easily get through the pass, depth-wise. The only real problem was the overhanging trees in the pass, which would cause trouble with the steamers' smokestacks. In that regard, Wilson noted, it would actually be better if the water level was down a few feet. Overhanging limbs would also be a problem, but to a lesser extent, in the Coldwater, but both could be worked around. Unfortunately, there was no real way to deal with it given "the impossibility of cutting them down without letting the whole tree fall into the channel." If there was land on the banks to operate on, perhaps with a lower level, the trees could be cut and pulled to fall inland rather than in the stream, but that was not always the case.[34]

The situation was consequently what it was, and the channel would get no better. Even on the way out, one Iowan in a working party explained that "the channel is narrow & in Some places very crooked. it was quite common for limbs to Rub the side of the Boat Some times glass was broken from the windows." Nevertheless, the pass was open, one Missourian explaining that "the opening of this pass by Gen. Gorman is thought here to be one of the greatest achievements of the war in the West." As a result, Prentiss sent in troops. He ordered Brigadier General Leonard F. Ross to load his division onto twelve transports, taking fifteen days' rations with them and plenty of ammunition.

The division under Ross had two brigades: the 43rd, 46th, and 47th Indiana under Brigadier General Frederick Salomon; and the 29th, 33rd, and 36th Iowa, 33rd Missouri, and 28th Wisconsin under Brigadier General Clinton B. Fisk, who brought along his wife for the expedition, she there to care for the sick and wounded. Also along were a couple of artillery batteries, Company A of the 1st Missouri Artillery and the 3rd Iowa Battery. After loading, Ross was to proceed on February 23 to Moon Lake to meet up with the navy under Lieutenant Commander Watson Smith with his flag on the "cannon boat" *Rattler*. He had with him eventually the ironclads *Baron de Kalb* and *Chillicothe*, tinclads *Rattler*, *Marmora*, *Signal*, *Romeo*, *Petral*, and *Forest Rose*, and rams *Dick Fulton* and *Lioness*. Also along was the towboat *S. Bayard*, with three coal barges. Porter had sent Smith to command the expedition, which at first was to be in Porter's mind a sole navy outing but then was saddled with army troops, which Smith complained delayed the advance. In the first plan, Smith was to move quickly and steam up both the Tallahatchie and Yalobusha Rivers breaking railroad bridges, but Porter soon countermanded those orders. Smith was to move fast on Yazoo City, although only during the daytime. Extended as he would be, Smith was to especially "be careful of your coal, and lay in wood where you can find it." Few common soldiers knew the plan: "From thence the devil and Mr. Grant only knows," one soldier wrote.[35]

The *Baron de Kalb* was familiar to many of the soldiers, they having seen the similar lines of the Pook Turtles (nickname for the City-class ironclads) often in the war from Fort Henry onward; she had helped bombard Arkansas Post into submission just a month or so earlier. But the *Chillicothe* was a different monster altogether, one sailor in awe of its appearance in early January writing that it was "this new novelty of naval architecture." One Indianan wrote home: "One of the gunboats, the *Chillicothe*, is built different from any gunboat I ever saw. It has two large side wheels and a propeller underneath so that it has double the power of any gunboat on the river. It has a turret in the front end with iron four inches thick and has two guns."[36]

Cadwallader Washburn was a little upset he was not along: "If I had the rank I no doubt should have the Command of the Expedition, as every body thinks it belongs to me, I having done the work in spite of croakers all around me." Nevertheless, he bid the force farewell, the only recompense being a letter from Prentiss that "if this Expedition succeeds you are the one to whom the greatest praise should be given." Ross himself tried to get Washburn detailed to go along but failed, although he rode part way on the *Chillicothe*. Perhaps his irritation fed Washburn's private turn against Grant, he informing his congressman brother that Grant was drunk at times and generally not approving of the campaign: "All Grant's schemes have failed. He knows that he has got to do something or off goes his head." Yet not all were so enthused and desirous of going into the wilderness; one Federal related to his diary, "the men are characteristically American—rush to destruction as to a feast."[37]

After some trouble crossing the bar in the mouth of the canal, Ross and Smith met up in Moon Lake on February 23 and two days later set off into the pass itself bound for the Coldwater. One Illinoisan admitted "our difficulties immediately began." Others questioned the future: "What we are intended for I do not know." But he later added: "If we are successful in what appears to be our object, it will be one of the greatest feats of the age, otherwise it will be called the rashest undertaking of the War." Once the totality set in, many of the soldiers were not enthused, one writing a friend that they were heading into the Delta "by a kind of overland steamboat, mud puddle route unheard of but in the philosophy of modern warfare." He added, rhetorically, "can you imagine the consternation which our advent into this unexplored part of Dehaney will create amongst the bullfrogs & Alligators whose peaceful dreams have hither to been undisturbed since this map of clay was sent on its voyage around the sun." Colonel James Slack similarly wrote his wife, "Here we are in the woods winding our way down a narrow track through a dense forest, generally as wild as any impenetrable forest you ever saw." Smith reported that "as the steamers of the army working party came out of the pass this afternoon our advance entered." Some of the gunboats had the three coal barges tied alongside, but these could not possibly make it through the pass abreast, so they had to be towed behind. This made the tight turns even stricter while getting both connected gunboat and coal barge around the tight bends in the pass. Ross related that "these were very difficult to manage, the channel was so extremely narrow and tortuous, often impending our movements very greatly. It was impossible, from the character of the stream to move except by daylight." Smith himself spoke of his speed being "necessarily less than the current of the stream, backing and checking with lines being the only means of rounding the numerous turns and to avoid collision with trees and shore." He also complained of "every vagrant log [having] a chance to foul our wheels, and as many do foul them delays are frequent." He in fact sent a report to Porter that "if we get through this with our casemates up and wheels serviceable, it will be as much as can reasonably be expected." High winds also hurt the efforts to keep moving, Ross writing that he "was detained by high winds and the difficulty in moving coal-barges."[38]

One Iowan admitted to his diary that "it seems as though it will be impossible for us to get through." The trees in the pass, as feared, did a lot of damage to the steamboats, the *Emma* being nearly wrecked and having to be sent back to Helena by the time she reached the end of the pass; the *Key*

West came forward and took her place. And the other transports were not the best vessels afloat either, Ross quipping that "our transports, though perhaps the best that could be procured, were very poor, and frequently delayed us by breakage and derangement of machinery." In fact, all of them endured heavy damage, Ross describing "a number of our transports were more or less crippled." Smith echoed him that "some being without smoke-stacks and with damaged wheels, the woodwork of the light-draft being much torn." One soldier related that "pieces of banisters [were] left all along," and many captains of boats had the soldiers take down their chimneys to keep them from being damaged. "Slow progress today great quantity of drift removed," Frederick Davis of the *Baron de Kalb* related to his diary. Nevertheless, the entire twelve transports and several gunboats and barges made their way successfully, if with much difficulty (one day making only a mile and a half), through the pass by the last day in February. The head of the flotilla plunged out into the broader Coldwater River on March 1 (it would take the rest in the rear several more days to emerge), that river being a better hundred to a hundred and thirty feet wide, although "running through a dense wilderness nearly all the way." Ross was glad but somewhat dumbfounded, "having been five days going the distance of 16 miles." Brigade commander Frederick Salomon described the trip as "a tedious and perilous passage," but at least the units did not have to send pickets out at night in many places: the flooded terrain gave them total security.[39]

The experiences of Iowan Allen Miller are illustrative of the tedious movement through the pass. Aboard the *Lavinia Logan*, he described in his diary that the pass was "narrow and crooked beyond conception." On the first day in the pass, he described how his transport "slides around its thousand crooks with eel-like dexterity. How I admire the skill of pilot John Parish." The next day tested his patience, he writing that most of the day was spent at a standstill as "boats before detain us." He went on to describe "a perfect wilderness, uninhabited by man. Occupied by bear and other wild varmints. So much for Miss., the boast of cottondom. How tedious and yet how novel." The next few days were similar: "Came slowly through the brush and trees. One continued cane break from the lake down on either side, with endless profusion of vines equal to Vineland itself." Then the next day: "Still in the pass and no prospect of getting out soon. An awful undertaking to get through here with a fleet, but we are equal to the task unless sad reverse checks us. Not a rebel showed himself yet. Makes us quite bold to think we can go where we please unmolested." The ensuing days contained entries such as "made but little progress. Still a little toward victory or destruction is so much irretrievable advance" and "still another day's march toward an unknown destiny into an unknown future with all its mysteries, doubts and fears." By March 4 he admitted that "this trip has proved one of the most eventless trips ever taken on this business." But then success came on March 5 when his transport broached the Coldwater River, although Miller sarcastically admitted, "I don't notice that the water is any colder than heretofore."[40]

The local people were just as amazed at what was going on, including Mississippi politician James L. Alcorn, whose plantation, Mound Place, was nearby and to which Federal officers flocked to see the Mississippi statesman. His diary entries read continually of Federals killing his stock and taking over his mill. Yet Alcorn, despite being a Confederate state militia general earlier in the war, was more interested in his own status and was friendly with whomever it was best to befriend at the moment. He was a fierce cooperationist at the secession convention and would later be a Republican governor of the state. Now, as the ironclad *Chillicothe* passed by, he boarded her to discuss the expedition with the Union commanders. An Iowa soldier related that "he has been in the Rebel army, but claims to be a Union man. It is only to save his property." In a later wave, Colonel Green B. Raum of the 56th Illinois met Alcorn and knew there was something familiar about him, only to discover he had known him in Illinois, where Alcorn had been born and raised. Obviously, more worrisome were real Confederates in the area, and many regiments set up barricades on the hurricane decks of the transports to be able to fight them off.[41]

Despite all the delays and issues, many had high hopes for this endeavor, although Colonel Slack confided to his wife that "my judgment dictates that it is a very hazardous undertaking." Still, the Federals were soon through, and by March 1 the lead elements were ready to continue the movement down into the soggy Delta. What they would find was anybody's guess.[42]

While the Yazoo Pass expedition continued to snake its way southward, Grant's other projects were in full swing as well in the latter half of February, although many units took time out to fire a salute on President Washington's birthday on February 22; one Ohioan also noted it was his own birthday. Embracing their shared heritage, even Confederate units fired their own salutes to the former president. The navy fired so loudly that "we thought the Rebel fleet had attacked our gunboat fleet," one Federal admitted. Yet work continued, and down on the "the great Ditch," as one Indianan termed it, patience was running out amid the "excessively bad weather and high water we have had to contend against." In fact, McClernand ordered that "on account of the excessive fatigue and exposure of the soldiers of the 13th Army Corps at work on the canal opposite Vicksburg, it is ordered that an extra issue of one gill of whiskey be made to each man on work, daily." Grant alerted Halleck that "most of the time that troops could be out at all has been expended in keeping water out of our camps." With such high ground at a premium, conflicts arose as to who had which land, Osterhaus complaining that there was a company of cavalry "squatted in the centre of my division." Grant added that, if he had good weather, the task of widening the canal to sixty feet wide and "sufficient depth to admit any vessel here" could be done in five days, but "judging from the past, it is fair to calculate that it will take from ten to twelve days to get those five days." And then he added more because "the work is being done by soldiers, the most of whom, under the most favorable circumstances, could not come up to the calculations of the engineer officers."[43]

Sickness was also prevalent, one Federal writing his wife that "there are a great many sick in the army and a great many dying every day. It in fact is so common to see dead men and new made graves that they attract no more attention than a dead dog would in Salem. I yesterday saw laying in one pile 42 coffins with dead bodies in them waiting burial." Another reported to his wife: "The soldiers['] graves reaching away along the 'Levee' for miles, just as closely as they can be made. My Dear you would count them by hundreds. There they sleep poor boys far from home. They died too without mother, sister or wife to administer to their comfort." Grant rebutted the negative reports of death and sickness as not to the extent that the newspapers reported it, and in fact he argued that "the greatest drawback to the spirits of the troops has been the great delay in paying them." Perhaps because of all the issues with soldiers doing the work, Grant asked Hurlbut to send "with as little delay as possible, as many able-bodied negro laborers as can be had or spared from Memphis and other portions of your command." Grant was having trouble finding them around Vicksburg, as all the planters had withdrawn their slaves into the interior areas.[44]

Work continued as well up at Lake Providence, although the delay in Logan's and Quinby's divisions moving southward kept the progress slow and irritating. McPherson reported that he finally hoped to leave Memphis with Logan's troops by February 19 or 20 and that "I have been annoyed beyond measure at the delay here, but could not help myself." In fact, the quartermaster and commissary supplies for the division had been loaded and waiting for eight days by now. The troops were getting restless as well, Luther Cowan telling his wife of the expectation of leaving: "We will most likely hear a little thunder down there, but I don't believe we will have any more mud to the square acre, that would be impossible." The division did not leave until February 23, and by that time the boats "became very filthy, worse than any hog pen you ever saw." But they finally shoved off, corps commander McPherson moving with them and writing his mother that "each day carries me farther from Home in point of distance but perhaps nearer to it in point of time." Once they arrived at Lake Providence, Logan's troops found McArthur's men from the canal area already there working, Grant assuring Halleck that they were not needed at the canal. "They could not be of any service in helping on the work here, because there are already as many men as can be employed on it, and then he would have to go 5 or 6 miles above to find land above water to encamp on." For their part, the Confederates were wise to the plan at Lake Providence, Richard Taylor, commanding in Louisiana, sending "a staff officer to examine and issue necessary orders to counteract these designs."[45]

Affairs in northern Mississippi and West Tennessee were no more promising, especially at Memphis, where Hurlbut reported "the city of Memphis has more iniquity in it than any place since Sodom." He soon had to ferret out issues of bribery and extortion. The weather was awful there as well, McPherson writing before leaving that "the roads are in a most horrible condition." It did not help that the city was full of troops awaiting transport southward, ultimately three divisions of Logan, Quinby, and the third one scheduled to join Sherman's corps, Hurlbut tasking James Denver's division, they having at one point earlier been under Sherman already. There was no threat, to be sure, but McPherson reported that "the guerillas are very bold and troublesome." And there were also reports that the Confederates had retaken the Tallahatchie River crossings and pushed on even to Holly Springs. That said, McPherson alerted Grant that "Mrs. Grant and Jesse are quite well," something Grant certainly appreciated.[46]

There were some preliminary moves in West Tennessee, however. At Hamilton's suggestion, and "satisfied this [Van Dorn's move] will remove nearly all the cavalry from my front," Hurlbut on February 16 put in motion the cavalry raid deep into Mississippi under Benjamin Grierson and Edward Hatch, ultimately aimed at the Southern Railroad of Mississippi. As part of the diversion for this diversion to Grant's work, Hurlbut also wanted a side raid to aid the Yazoo Pass effort. "It appears perilous," he informed Grant, "but I think it can be done and done with safety, and may relieve you somewhat at Vicksburg." But then, just as quickly, Hurlbut cancelled the raid when Hamilton abandoned his portion of it due to reports of greater strength in Mississippi than before known. Grant was not happy, but little could be done except try again later if the opportunity presented itself.[47]

In fact, more trouble from Hamilton emerged as well. He tried his best to butter up Grant: "The taking of Vicksburg is *your* right, and I hope it may be added to the laurels which belong to you as the most successful general of the war." But at the same time, Hamilton was reporting rumors and acting on them, much like the dispatch that caused the cavalry raid to be cancelled. The problems reached all the way to Grant when Hamilton loudly pronounced the Confederates withdrawing from Vicksburg; Grant simply responded that "it may be that some of the force is leaving Vicksburg, but I have no evidence of the fact." But it can be certain that Grant's estimation of Hamilton was being affected.[48]

Other commanders entered into petty squabbles as well, including Colonel Albert Lee of the 7th Kansas Cavalry, known as the Jayhawkers. Lee found out from a paroled prisoner returning to Memphis that several of his men were being held in irons because of the reputation of the regiment for dirty deeds. Lee asked permission to open correspondence with the Confederates about it and retaliate. Grant approved. Even Grant and Carter Stevenson sparred over a proclamation Admiral Porter issued about guerrillas attacking his vessels on the Mississippi River, saying they would be treated as "highwaymen and assassins, and no quarter will be shown them." Porter eventually became involved as well, asking that Stevenson converse directly with him and not army officers, but admitted "I decline, however, to stand on a point of etiquette." Of course, the continual dance over trade of cotton continued as well, and several soldiers remarked on all the flags of truce that went back and forth across the river on occasion. That said, the lower-level soldiers worked out their own means of communication, one Federal on picket writing that "our boys are down at the Rivers side talking to the Rebels on the other side of the river. We can hear every word they say to us plainly."[49]

Despite a gaggle of operations already ongoing, others were soon developed or at least proposed as well. McClernand and Prentiss worked out another advance up the Arkansas River to Pine Bluff, stating that Arkansas Post had been reoccupied. Grant squelched it immediately: "The forces now here to operate with are assigned to looking to the one great object, that of opening the Mississippi, and to take off the number of men suggested would retard progress." Grant even used a little of McClernand's own tactics against him, reminding him that "I know the President is looking forward with great anxiety to the completion of the canal . . . so as to admit steamers through it. The work requires all the forces here." In true McClernand fashion, he just would not let it go and peppered Grant with plans and possibilities the rest of the month. McClernand also sent a couple hundred contraband "women and children" to Memphis who were "dropped upon the levee." Hurlbut had no idea what to do with them.[50]

When the "one great object" was in need of an expedition, however, Grant did not hesitate to send it. Admiral Porter reported harassment of his transports and vessels around Greenville, with detail that "two regiments of rebels, with artillery, have been sent up the Sunflower to annoy vessels passing Greenville." There was eventually a "Police Fleet" of four vessels carrying all arms that patrolled the river, but in this instance an entire brigade went. Porter sent Grant word asking for aid, and although Grant was gone at the time, McClernand took the initiative and ordered A. J. Smith to send a brigade up the river to clear the Confederates out. McClernand coordinated with Colonel Lewis B. Parsons for transportation and Porter for cover, and Smith sent Brigadier General Stephen G. Burbridge's brigade northward on February 14.[51]

Burbridge led his transports, accompanied around Greenville by the ram *Monarch*, to an initial landing site near Greenville and over the course of the next several days reboarded and landed several times seeking to find and catch the enemy. He was at a disadvantage immediately, however: "The roads were almost impassable, in consequence of rain, which had been falling since we left our transports. . . . I find that there are no road improvements in the country, and it is impossible for infantry to be effective against cavalry in such a country." He added also that "their [Confederates'] information is always better than our own; the citizens all sympathize with them." Still, Burbridge landed at various places such as Cypress Bend and Perkins' Landing, but he could never bring the Confederates under Colonel Samuel W. Ferguson to heel, although they did capture Ferguson's father-in-law and Ferguson's wife went to reclaim him; she was "detained on the boat for two days." There were several small skirmishes, including around Fish Lake and Deer Creek and near a "school house" on February 23, but Burbridge was never able to cut off Ferguson's forces with his own cavalry, the 6th Missouri Cavalry and 2nd Illinois Cavalry. That was because Ferguson's artillery battery, a conglomeration of guns from units from Missouri, Maryland, Mississippi, and Georgia all under Lieutenant R. L. Wood of Bledsoe's Missouri Battery, fought almost by itself when the cavalry company under Captain James Lewers fled the scene; Ferguson called the mounted troops "rabble" and "without exception, the poorest [company] I have ever seen." That was attested to by the Federals who acquired one of their cannons, an Ohioan describing it as a gun "mounted on the fore wheels of a wagon and it was so dangerous to fire it that they had to put a slow match to it." Still, Burbridge could do little, and by February 24 he decided to return, but he did so with cattle, horses, and mules, over three hundred of them. "I found the citizens more willing to give up their negroes than their stock," he noted, "especially horses and mules, and in nearly every instance they had attempted to hide them from us."[52]

For his part, Ferguson remained in the Deer Creek area after Burbridge left, continuing to harass Federal shipping. "I can annoy the enemy exceedingly," he wrote. He also hoped to bring down Mississippi civilians who were being disloyal: "The whole community engaged in trading cotton with the enemy." He even contemplated using torpedoes that had proven so successful against the USS *Cairo* at various landing sites on the Mississippi River, remarking that, "as far as I can learn, they always tied up at the same spot. By using great secrecy, and placing them at night, the plan may succeed."[53]

Perhaps the biggest concern for Pemberton among the already-in-process efforts was the naval presence between Vicksburg and Port Hudson. Porter and Grant soon realized the *Queen of the West* had been captured and put back in Confederate service, Richard Taylor describing her as "scarcely injured" in the fight. That gave the Confederates two rams on the Mississippi. "The *Queen of the West* is now at Warrenton, with the rebel flag flying," Grant informed Halleck on February 25. Worse, heavy firing had been heard to the south during the night—"it is supposed to have been between the *Queen* and *Indianola*. Apprehension is felt for the safety of the *Indianola*." Apprehension was also felt for the canal work, forcing Grant to emplace a battery of heavy guns past the opening south of Vicksburg to defend against the vessels. Of course, an infantry brigade was required there to support the battery, and that meant supplying the brigade. Grant wanted a "plank road" built along the levee to facilitate the logistics.[54]

Apprehension was indeed warranted, because the *Indianola* had met the *Queen* and *Webb* and had been captured. Confederate scouts tracked the whereabouts of the ironclad at every move, allowing a coordinated response by the Confederate naval assets. Rumor was that the *Indianola* had even been sunk, although the Federal high command was still unsure as February dwindled. Porter had the unenviable task of reporting to the secretary of the navy the loss, although still of unknown fate, and chalked it up to "a non-compliance with my instructions." He was understandably concerned about getting new and repaired ironclads southward from St. Louis as soon as possible.[55]

Union fears over the *Indianola* were eventually confirmed. The *Indianola*, under Lieutenant Commander George Brown, had been caught running upriver by the *Queen of the West*, *Webb*, and the lighter steamer *Dr. Beaty*, which had on board two hundred and fifty "gallant spirits" from Port Hudson aiming to board the Union ironclad; she was, however, "a frail steamer" and had to be towed by another vessel, the *Grand Era*. Major General Richard Taylor, commanding in Louisiana, had sent Major Joseph L. Brent to organize the expedition to take the *Indianola*, and throughout February 24 Brent gained on the Union ironclad steadily, overtaking her near midnight twenty five or so miles south of Vicksburg. "The moon was partially obscured by a veil of white clouds," Brent reported, "and gave and permitted just sufficient light for us to see where to strike with our rams, and just sufficient obscurity to render uncertain the aim of the formidable artillery of the enemy." Once in range, despite fire from the *Indianola*, the *Queen* rammed the *Indianola* three times and the *Webb* twice; she was heading for a third blow when Brown surrendered. The Confederate rams used the current of the river on their successive runs as "additional power obtainable from the descending current of the river," and Brown reported that some of the hits were "bows on, with a tremendous crash, which knocked nearly everyone down on board of both vessels." Brent reported how the *Queen* became stuck on its first attempt when "the *Webb* came dashing by us, and plunged, with terrific force, just in rear of his bow." The *Beaty* later arrived and Brent "called out to them that the opportunity for boarding her had arrived." Lieutenant Colonel Frederick Brand began preparations to board but likewise was notified of the surrender, Brand jumping to the *Indianola* himself and accepting Brown's sword after he assured him he was surrendering and "in a sinking condition." After having thrown "both signal books" into the river, Brown surrendered himself and around a hundred others (one Federal was killed), at the expense of two killed and five wounded on the Confederate vessels.[56]

The *Indianola* was indeed sinking: "The water poured in in large volumes," Brown reported, but the "formidable monster" was towed to the east side of the river, no one wanting the hulk to be on the west side, where the Federals could raise the vessel. Ultimately, however, she was towed farther upstream before being abandoned and blown up on the reported arrival of another Union gunboat, which was false; the only thing salvaged from the *Indianola* besides the crew was "the wine and liquor stores." The Union crew was landed at Grand Gulf and taken to Vicksburg and "put in jail as prisoners of war," although Colonel Edward Higgins obtained permission to take Brown, his personal acquaintance, and hold him in his own quarters. The remnants of the vessel thereafter rested in the river just out from Joe Davis's Plantation and close to "His Excellency President Davis' plantation." One Federal remarked that "Col. Ellet who went with the *Queen* gets a good deal of the blame for the capture of both boats."[57]

Without much of anything else to deter the Confederates, Porter resorted to trickery; the fabled gunboat that resulted in the Confederates blowing up the salvageable ironclad was nothing of the sort. Soon, there was tied up near the exit of the canal a "flat-boat rigged up to represent a gunboat. She has a square turret forward, with a mock cannon projecting toward the bow from within. Smoke-stacks made of flour barrels; wheel-house, &c., covered all over with a thick coat of tar." It was the invention of the 8th Missouri, one Illinoisan describing how they "got up a big scare for the rebels. They took an old 'coal barge' and piled up several flower barrels, fastening them securely, and painting them black to represent the smoke stack. Then they built a sham wheel house, or wheel houses. They fixed up a temporary pilot house and thus constructed they set it afloat." Porter reported the effort cost the taxpayers $8.61; on the side was painted "Deluded People, Cave In." It was enough to concern the Confederates of course, and they fired at it, actually putting a hole through the bow. More important, it was this mock gunboat that the *Queen of the West* spotted and fled from, causing the panic that ultimately caused the abandonment and destruction of the *Indianola*. Confederates working on the sunken ironclad panicked and placed the guns muzzle-to-muzzle and fired them with "slow match" to destroy them. Pemberton himself informed Richmond on February 28 that "Confederate fleet abandoned the *Indianola* on approach of what was supposed to be turreted iron-clad. I am not satisfied that it was a gunboat, but have no definite intelligence yet." The truth soon came out, the Vicksburg *Whig* cajoling that "a coal barge is magnified into a monster." One Federal termed it a "sham boat" and another a "quaker gunboat," and an Ohioan confided to his diary that "it was a yankey trick."[58]

But the real problem of renewed Confederate dominance on the river between Vicksburg and Port Hudson left the exit of the canal in a dangerous fix, and Sherman soon removed the brigade guarding the battery, keeping only a regiment there. He also directed the last Union boat south of Vicksburg be scuttled, the *New Era*. Sherman wanted its machinery removed and broken and the vessel itself destroyed "in such a way as to leave no trace." To safeguard the regiment left behind, the 76th Ohio, Sherman sent Colonel Charles R. Woods rockets to warn of the approach of Confederate vessels. Sherman himself went and tested the route the retreating regiment and artillery would have to take if driven away: "I crossed over last night on foot, and the road across the swamp, though passable, is villainous."[59]

The Federal right flank, far south of Vicksburg down at the canal exit, was thus vulnerable if the Confederates could take advantage. It was currently held by four Parrott rifles, a regiment of Ohioans, and a "dummy" gunboat. But that was not the major scene of attention at this point, all eyes seemingly shifting northward to the narrow and treacherous little channel of the Yazoo Pass, where Federal troops were poised to head southward and see what lay around each bend of the river. Awaiting them, of course, around one particular bend just west of Greenwood, was Confederate Fort Pemberton. Only time would tell if it would be enough to stop the massive Federal movement.[60]

7

"The Yankee Boats Are Here"
March 1–15

Just up in the hills of Carroll County, Mississippi, sat one of the most palatial plantation mansions in the state. Built in 1854, Malmaison rivaled anything found in the more affluent plantation country at Natchez or Vicksburg, with its French-style architecture and some fifteen thousand acres of land and around four hundred slaves. Its location just north of Big Sand Creek, and more important just a few miles east of the confluence of the Yalobusha and Tallahatchie Rivers, forming the Yazoo itself, provided an outlet for its major crops. In fact, the owner soon opened a port, Point Leflore, at that confluence as early as the 1830s. Then a town sprang up in the ensuing years, and it took as its own the given name of this opulent plantation owner, Greenwood.[1]

That owner had an interesting history himself. Greenwood LeFlore (who would also give his surname to the county that was established out of parts of Carroll County and others after the war) was a politician, plantation owner, and Unionist during the Civil War, but he was best known as the last of the great Choctaw chiefs east of the Mississippi River. Leflore had been born into a powerful family of Choctaws through his mother's lineage, his father being a French trader, Louis LeFleur. The senior LeFleur had earlier established the hamlet at LeFleur's Bluff on the Pearl River that later became the state capital, Jackson. The younger Leflore rose to be one of the tribe's numerous chiefs and, realizing the dim future Choctaws faced east of the Mississippi, led in the effort of removal in 1830. He pushed heavy for and signed the Treaty of Dancing Rabbit Creek that year, which ceded most Choctaw land to the United States and removed the people to Indian Territory, present-day Oklahoma.[2]

But Leflore stayed, making a fortune in cotton and slaves at Malmaison, ultimately building up his plantation to huge sizes in Carroll County. He also dabbled in politics, serving the county in the Mississippi legislature. And when the new town of Greenwood, first known as William's Landing, was incorporated in 1845, it took the name of the most prominent planter in the area at the time, Greenwood Leflore.[3]

Yet by March 1863 another name dominated the Greenwood area, perhaps not as prominent but certainly more important as the commander of the Confederacy's Department of Mississippi and East Louisiana. As the tiny fort blocking the Tallahatchie River began to appear out of the murky Delta swampland, it first took on the name "Fort Greenwood" but was soon changed to commemorate the departmental commander. Consequently, as the Federals slowly trudged down the rivers of the Delta toward the Yazoo River, awaiting them was the only real defense the Confederates could muster, at Fort Pemberton.

The namesake of the little fort at Greenwood and many of his soldiers were not terribly concerned during the Union's initial Yazoo Pass operations, one of his soldiers stationed at Fort Pemberton even by March 1 admitting "it still remains a matter of doubt as to whether they will come or not." John Pemberton just could not fathom that a Federal flotilla and troops could make it through the pass and actually operate within the flooded and mostly submerged Delta: "I do not think he can effect anything very serious," he assured Joseph E. Johnston as late as March 4, incidentally the same day one of his Confederates remarked to his diary that "President Lincoln[']s time is half out to-day." Pemberton likewise informed Loring up at Fort Pemberton that "Vicksburg and Snyder's Mill are more important than any other points." In fact, over the course of the first week or so of March Pemberton was much more concerned with other threats to his department, including renewed operations around Port Hudson. The canal work still concerned him as well, and the ever-pressing lack of supplies, much less building up a horde of reserve food and ammunition in case the fighting reached Vicksburg itself, was ever present in his mind.[4]

The logistical problems were indeed numerous, Pemberton himself even getting involved in ordering purchases and moving supplies from his headquarters in Jackson; all the while, troops poured over the rail lines as well. In fact, amid all the other issues, even Federals bearing down from several directions, he informed Johnston on March 6 that "my main difficulty to contend with at present is transportation of supplies." The one railroad line into Vicksburg, the Southern Railroad of Mississippi, was in "wretched condition" in Pemberton's words, and the recent heavy rains that had so affected the

Federals likewise caused enormous problems for Pemberton and his troops. One of his foot soldiers who had just traveled over the rail line wrote home, "that road is a dangerous one," and even when operable it was intolerably slow; one Confederate unit took eighteen and a half hours to travel the 125 miles from Meridian to Vicksburg, less than seven miles per hour.[5]

Yet the transport of supplies was most affected. Inventories continued to show large amounts of peas, rice, sugar, and salt only, with little meat in any form available and only a little more stock of corn and flour at the commissary depots at Vicksburg and Jackson. Pemberton himself ordered out purchasing agents, he telling Stevenson amid the lack of supplies in Vicksburg: "You must make your quartermaster and commissaries exert themselves on the Yazoo and Sunflower. What is being done in Sunflower and Deer Creek? I am using every exertion to get corn by railroad. . . . Use your rice and peas." Tasked with the defense of the Vicksburg area, Stevenson asked about the rafts to be placed in the Yazoo and Big Black Rivers, which would stall transportation but provide defense. He asked when exactly they should be placed. Pemberton even lobbied Richard Taylor across the river in Louisiana that "you can do this command as well as myself a great favor if you will take immediate steps to have forwarded all the beef possible, or bacon or salted pork. In this respect, general, no greater service can be done the country than in hurrying forward these supplies, and I wish to impress its vital importance upon you." Taylor later balked at sending so many goods east of the Mississippi, particularly corn that his own troops needed. It did not help that there was also at this time a major squabble among Pemberton's staff commissaries at Jackson and those in the field, including at Vicksburg, over ruined supplies and unwarranted shipments of sugar out of the department.[6]

The uptick in Union activity forced Pemberton to keep a greater eye on his entire department, however, including establishing a fifth military district in northern Mississippi under recently transferred Brigadier General James R. Chalmers. Rumors of an all-out Union assault at the Vicksburg riverfront notwithstanding (the scout reporting such related that "this information comes from a source entirely reliable, who got it directly from high Federal military authority, as a great secret"), there were legitimate concerns; one Confederate admitted "[we] can't tell what they wille do." Another concern was the canal, not so much as a threat to Vicksburg itself but as a threat to allow Federals to position themselves to be a threat to the city. Carter Stevenson reported on March 5 that it looked like the enemy would succeed in opening the canal, which would make Vicksburg irrelevant. He recommended moving some of the big guns southward, some to Warrenton, which the enemy vessels would still have to pass even if the canal worked, and ultimately even to Grand

Gulf down at the mouth of the Big Black River. Dabney Maury had recommended the same thing a month earlier. Stevenson's logic was that "if we do not occupy Grand Gulf the enemy will, and thus be enabled to invest us." Conversely, Confederate occupation of Grand Gulf would force the Federals to land in between, probably at Warrenton, where they would have to "give us battle there under disadvantages." Stevenson recommended sending three or four heavy guns from Vicksburg to the heights at Grand Gulf, along with a part of John Bowen's troops to garrison the place "at once." Pemberton agreed, but he also cautioned Stevenson to watch Bayou Pierre just to the south of Grand Gulf: "Are you aware that Bayou Pierre is navigable at high water? Grand Gulf may be taken in the rear." Stevenson also wanted to fortify Warrenton and set up a battery to play on the lower end of the canal.[7]

The threat to Grand Gulf loomed large in Pemberton's mind as the enemy's canal work progressed. In fact, he ultimately took extralegal actions to help defend it. He notified Richmond of the "great probability of his getting through" the canal and informed the government that he had no big guns to spare to send to Grand Gulf. The only guns available were two moved from Vicksburg itself and three being shipped to Shreveport, Louisiana, two 8-inch and one 32-pound rifle. They actually belonged to the navy, but Pemberton confiscated them and sent them to Grand Gulf, arguing that he had no transportation to spare to send them to Shreveport anyway. Richmond rated his actions as illegal but approved them nevertheless due to the crisis situation. Pemberton also eventually ordered the entirety of Bowen's brigade down to garrison the forts that Bowen quickly began to erect around the destroyed town, a result of the first Federal arrival in 1862.[8]

Over time, despite eventually three dredges "very quietly at work," the fear for the canal subsided, the overflowing banks doing as much as anything to forestall Federal work. "Spade work is stopped for the present," Pemberton informed Johnston. "I begin to hope it may prove a failure," he added on March 14. Tennesseans in the army at Vicksburg offered hope they might now be sent back to their home state, but to no avail. Then action picked up to the south at Port Hudson as well; Pemberton reported to Johnston on March 15, "General Gardner telegraphs me (2 p.m.) that the bombardment at Port Hudson has commenced." It seemed the Federals were coming at Pemberton from every direction.[9]

Other worries added to Pemberton's nervousness, including word of the problems reaching the people; he ordered circulation of several newspapers stopped in Vicksburg on March 6. With reports of the Federals on several expeditions, Joseph E. Johnston also soon reentered the process, writing often and querying about the situation particularly at Yazoo Pass. But his notes betrayed an obvious lack of context for the situation, and his meddling only made matters more complicated for Pemberton. Worse, Johnston then even started to the Mississippi Valley himself. He moved as far as Mobile before important business called him back to Middle Tennessee, a development Pemberton was no doubt glad to see. Nevertheless, Johnston wanted answers, and Pemberton did not always have them.[10]

Worse yet, Richmond also became involved, wanting to know especially about the Yazoo Pass threat. Secretary of War James A. Seddon and even President Davis himself queried Pemberton directly, Seddon writing of Yazoo Pass: "What are the facts, and where are the boats?" Davis took a wider range in his rapid-fire questions, including the possibility of establishing guns and fortifications at other places on the Mississippi River such as Ellis' Cliff south of Natchez. Pemberton responded that Ellis' Cliff was much too far to aid Vicksburg, but he reassured the president that "I think General Loring will be able to repel them" at Fort Pemberton; he later qualified that some, writing, "have enough force, I think, on Yazoo and Tallahatchie to meet any force they may bring," though adding, "if enemy increases his fleets, you will have to increase my guns." Grasping for any help they could get, Seddon even called in Major General Samuel G. French, then commanding in southern Virginia, to give him ideas on how to defend the Mississippi River. Although a Northern-born general, French had come to Mississippi earlier and owned a plantation on Deer Creek in the Delta. He had numerous ideas on how to defend his adopted land.[11]

Matters had, in fact, seemed dire enough to Richmond that President Davis issued a proclamation calling for fasting and prayer later in the month. War Department clerk Jones quipped that "there will certainly be fasting—and prayer also." But he added, "and God has helped us, or we should have been destroyed ere this." Not all were so enthused, at least in the political aspects of prayer and fasting. When announced in one Attala County church, Mississippian Joel Harvey objected: "I have no objection to meeting and praying. That's all right enough. But I don't intend to fast and pray just because Jeff Davis tells me to do so. When they were instigating this war, they didn't call on the Churches to pray them into it; and now they needn't call on them to pray 'em out of it. I don't owe allegiance to Jeff Davis nor Abe Lincoln."[12]

Still, Pemberton was obviously also worried about the Yazoo Pass threat, although initially no more so, and at times less so, than others. Stevenson in fact reported Union troops moving northward (probably McClernand's move to Milliken's Bend) and correctly assumed the flooding west of the river was the cause; he reported the canal itself "overflowed on both sides" on March 12. However, there were also indications from scouts around Friar's Point, before being flooded out of position, indicating large movements down the river. Yet as more word came in about the progress of the Federals in the

Delta, Pemberton began to take a more serious role in supporting Loring. He sent Loring needed ammunition but told him he had no more guns or troops to send; the only conceivable body Loring could pull from was the brigade left at Grenada under Lloyd Tilghman. Loring's troops also had to provide their own wood, with details sent southward along the Yazoo River to bring it up to the fort. That said, as the crisis grew, Pemberton realized he had to send more troops and finally positioned Brigadier General John C. Moore's brigade in supporting distance at Yazoo City if needed upriver quickly. Miscommunication at times also caused confusion, such as scouts reporting that the enemy "has gone down Pass again," which caused Pemberton to ask if that meant "in direction of Moon Lake, or from Moon Lake toward Tallahatchie?"[13]

As time passed, more and more reports of just what a substantial enemy flotilla this was emerged, prompting Pemberton to finally take it more seriously. Early indications were that numerous gunboats, as many as five or six although only two were ironclads, and as many as twenty or so transports with troops aboard had made it through the pass. Some tried to calculate the amount of troops, multiplying the number assumed on board by the number of craft. As the transports were fairly small, it indicated a small number of troops on each, but still, with that large a number of them it totaled a substantial amount. Some estimates reached as many as seven thousand Federals, though there were not that many. As the days passed, reports of the Federal's progress continued to come in along the rivers, marked by their arrival at the various plantations. "The Yankee boats are here; four of them are lying at E. V. Dickens', and two went below and landed at George McRae's place," read one report from the scouts on March 6.[14]

All the while, the tiny force under Loring, Waul, and Isaac Brown at Fort Pemberton watched and waited, deciphering what the various reports meant in terms of timing. Yet the initial enemy was the continuously swarming gnats, which especially bothered the horses and mules, getting in their nostrils: "Smoke from burning decaying wood was our principal way of warding off these pests," one Confederate explained. Another added that "smokes were made all along the line that the horses might stand in them and in some measure be protected from the gnats." But the bigger threat by far was the approaching Federal flotilla, traceable the closer it came by the smoke it emitted. The latest indications gave a pretty accurate count of the force bearing down on them; obviously, the overall lesson was that the Federals were making steady if slow progress. Ultimately Pemberton decided to throw more troops into the defense at Greenwood, including the rest of Lloyd Tilghman's small brigade: 942 men left at Grenada besides militia under James Z. George, which amounted to 488 State Troops but hemorrhaging deserters at a rapid pace. Perhaps it was for the best, as Tilghman and George did not get along, the former actually placing George under arrest at one point. Several of Tilghman's units were positioned at important points while most went on to the fort. Knowing an engagement was imminent, Loring also continued to call for more troops and in particular ammunition, which the confusion at Vicksburg itself had delayed.[15]

By the second week in March, the Federals were nearly on the defenders, as was the rain; Commodore Brown reported on March 10 it was "raining hard, making the weather unfavorable to us." While a herculean task had been accomplished to put anything in the way of the Federals, it was still a mighty small amount of firepower. In slave-built Fort Pemberton itself were ultimately a mere four heavy guns worth fighting, including two 8-inch Columbiads. There was also a 10-pound Whitworth, as well as the best of the lot, a 6.4-inch rifle. The men gave their guns various names such as "Lady Lobdell" and "Whistling Mary," while one already had a name: the "Lady Richardson" had been captured at Corinth the previous October. The fort itself did not extend far in length, although over time it increased up and down the river, prompting one Mississippian to eventually explain that "I am proud to say that we have the best fortifications I have ever seen for protection. I have no fears to go behind them." He added that "the enemy in great force are near our works, and will attack perhaps early to-morrow." Whatever condition they were in, it was all they had against what appeared to be a mighty host arriving, one Confederate infantryman admitting they had "a few large pieces and with a lot of Quaker Guns, doing good service in holding the fleet in check until the Quakers could be exchanged for the real guns."[16]

The large Federal flotilla was indeed bearing down on the little fortification that was all that stood between them and the lower Yazoo River; Grant admitted that "I thought for a time of the possibility of making this the route for obtaining a foothold on high land above Haynes' Bluff." But just because the Union gunboats and initial transports reached the comparatively wider waters of the Coldwater River did not mean the operation was set to speed down the Delta rivers. There was still a lot of nature to be endured and seen, one Federal describing killing a turtle that weighed a hundred and fifty pounds and at one point seeing a bear. A report of a soldier falling off his vessel and drowning also emerged, a frequent occurrence due to all the operations amid such overflowed terrain. And then there were the commanders. In fact, a difference of opinion soon developed as Lieutenant Commander Smith decided to await the arrival of the transports Ross's troops were on to snake their way through the pass, a lengthy operation to be sure, before heading farther southward. Lieutenant Colonel Wilson advised him, and then basically begged

Smith, to send the gunboats and a few of the lighter rams and tinclads on down the rivers to take control of the waterways lest the Confederates use the spare time to erect a defense at some point. General Ross agreed as well, as did, according to Wilson, the commanders of the two gunboats, Lieutenant Commander James P. Foster on the *Chillicothe* and Lieutenant Commander John G. Walker on the *Baron de Kalb*. Foster later agreed, writing that had Smith followed his orders "I have no doubt that the expedition would have been successful." But Smith would not hear of it and awaited Ross's arrival before heading southward. Diaries during this time were filled with notes of "lie at anchor" for the entire day or "we lie still several days to make the most necessary repairs of the wheels."[17]

After a grueling trek through the pass, including much damage to the transports such as punctures to hulls that filled the *Bayard* nearly half-full before being arrested, the head of Ross's transports reached the Coldwater on the morning of March 1, although badly beaten up and several severely damaged. One Federal wrote in his diary "we have made Cold Water at last." Others straggled in over the next few days, but the *Diana* and *Emma* were almost too severely damaged to go on, although Ross had little other option but to try to make them work. Worse news came as well when reports of the enemy establishing a defense farther south began to arrive. Ross reported to Prentiss that "a large force of rebels is reported on the Tallahatchie awaiting our advance. I do not credit the report, but if they are there we shall probably find them in the course of a couple of days, when we shall do just the best we can." It was not a very optimistic outlook, but then Ross was days away from reinforcements while stuck out in the middle of a swamp with his men being transported by a bunch of dilapidated and leaky old boats.[18]

Still, the now-concentrated flotilla set off southward on the Coldwater, slowly making its way around the same kinds of torturous turns and bends that the pass had contained, although a wider river made the movement easier. "It is very crooked," one Federal explained, "but the crooks are long." Rarely could one boat even see the next in line or behind, so circuitous was the river's course. At one point, Ross advised Smith that his two brigades were five miles apart on the river. Lieutenant Commander Smith admitted that "we are advancing but slowly. This stream is not so much wider or clearer than the Pass as to make much difference in either speed or the amount of damage inflicted on these vessels." He reported additional damage in the Coldwater River, even to the hull of his own vessel, and would only make the same speed as the current: "We can only advance with the current; faster than that brings us foul. Our speed is not more that 1 ½ miles per hour, if that." Worse, the winds, even light ones, severely tossed the vessels, being of such light draft.

Smith informed Porter that "we will get through in fighting condition, but so much delayed that all the advantages of a surprise to the rebels will have been lost." The impatient infantry were aware of the problems, and on one of the days an infantryman reported very little movement at all—"in fact some of the boats have not moved." Morale began to plummet with the lack of quick movement and damage taken, as well as the shortages in provisions that began to occur. The word "mutiny" began to appear in diaries.[19]

By the evening of March 6, the flotilla had made its way the eighteen straight-line miles (but more like thirty-five river miles) down the Coldwater to its junction with the Tallahatchie River, which came in from the northeast. It was here that Alvin Hovey and Cadwallader Washburn had crossed the river on their raid in the Confederate rear back in December, Washburn moving on eastward to Mitchell's Crossroads and toward Grenada. It was fifty miles from the Mississippi River, which made a measly six-miles-per-hour average for the flotilla. But the Tallahatchie River was even larger, thankfully, at times a hundred and thirty to a hundred and eighty feet wide, and it "affords fine navigation." Its banks were heavily wooded, causing one Iowan to remark that it "looks here much like Skunk River in Iowa." But at the same time, it potentially allowed Confederates up the river to come down in rear of the flotilla, a constant worry for Smith. At the urging of Ross, Wilson, and the two ironclad commanders, Lieutenant Commander Smith finally agreed to leave the coal barges at the mouth of the Coldwater River with the tinclad *Marmora* and the 29th Iowa while the rest pushed on to where the rumors were coalescing about Confederate resistance: Greenwood. A Confederate deserter even made his way to Helena to give details on the Confederate defense. With Smith still doubting the Greenwood rumors, Wilson and Ross fumed that Smith should have sent the gunboats on southward in late February, but he had not; the Confederates had apparently utilized that time in between to establish their defense.[20]

Ross reported that the plan was to push on southward on the Tallahatchie River and be at Greenwood by March 10, at which time (if in their possession) the entire flotilla would wait for the coal barges to catch up. As a result, foraging and plunder on land was strictly curtailed because of time, although some still took place. While waiting for the barges, the plan was to possibly move up the Yalobusha River and damage the railroad bridges Grant was so interested in at Grenada. Then the entire flotilla would move on southward on the Yazoo River toward Yazoo City and Haynes' Bluff. But there was a word of caution as Ross notified Prentiss of the plan: "Greenwood is represented as being fortified, and we have been very kindly informed that there were from 20,000 to 30,000 troops awaiting our arrival."[21]

Still, there seemed to be little desire on the part of the navy to move swiftly, over and above stopping each night; Ross reported on the morning of March 8: "We have again made a late start this morning, being delayed for the gunboats to complete coaling. The work should have been done by 2 o'clock this morning, and we on our way by 5.30, but it was 7.30 this morning before we started, and then had to leave one of the gunboats to finish her coaling." Ross fumed at other times when "on several occasions the gunboat immediately in my advance stopped and lay to an hour for dinner; and when in motion it seemed that they moved very slowly, as I had no difficulty in keeping up with my transports." He added: "I am a little, yes, considerably, disgusted with these necessary delays. I hope it will be better in the future."[22]

Part of the problem was the condition of the transports and even gunboats, beaten as they were coming through the Yazoo Pass. Smith had to leave the tinclad *Petral* in the Tallahatchie just below the Coldwater's mouth because of a broken wheel due to "accidents and bad management." Several of the transports were badly damaged as well, and Ross even surmised that they would not be able to stand a trip back through the pass and hoped they would be able to remain in the Yazoo until it was opened, at which time they could move on down the widening river to Vicksburg in safety. Worse, he had to send the *Luella* back to Helena because of major damage and it sunk in the pass, partially blocking the channel. Another eventually sank as well in the pass, the *Jenny Lind*, although far enough out of the channel not to block anything. At least one soldier mentioned a third sunken vessel. With so many complaints from the infantry housed on the transports, Ross sent Engineer Wilson to make a study of the "unserviceable condition of some of our boats," and Wilson determined that the *Key West No. 2* was "completely broken down and unable to proceed." The *Diana*, *John Bell*, *Luella*, and *Bayard* were all "(very) unseaworthy, and incapable of making the trip without great risk of their loss." The *Bayard* eventually had to be left behind as well, and two seamen deserted from her, taking pistols with them. Others were in terrible condition though somewhat better, Wilson rating they "might fail at any moment under a stress of work." It was not a good situation.[23]

Wrecks in the river also slowed the progress. Fires were burning on the banks of the rivers as they passed a few plantations, although Wilson remarked that from the pass to the Yazoo River at Greenwood "there are not more than fifty plantations" in the distance of around two hundred miles. Ross nevertheless described it as "well-cultivated country," the owners torching their cotton rather than see it taken. Only portions of the banks were habitable, however, Ross also describing "the wide strips of overflowed country on each side between the river and the hills." Smith noted "all is swamp."

Fortunately, that inundated land made the flotilla's path somewhat safer, as there were only a few spots the enemy could either establish a defense or even reach the river to attack.[24]

On the evening of March 10, the flotilla even ran up on a Confederate vessel, the steamer *Thirty-Fifth Parallel* with a barge, both loaded with cotton and on fire. Commodore Isaac Brown of the Confederate navy had been up the river on the *Parallel* to remove cotton but came a little too close to the Federal advance, at which time he moved to the smaller *Saint Mary* to observe the enemy, sending the laden *Parallel* on southward. Unfortunately the boat, "from the extreme narrowness of the stream, ran into the woods and disabled herself, so that, to save falling into the hands of the enemy, I [Brown] ordered her burned, which was done as the enemy came in sight." Rumor was that there were three thousand bales on the vessel, causing it to drift along the river afire—something many a Federal commented on. Ross reported that he saw equally as many cotton bales on fire on land.[25]

There was also some Union destruction and misbehaving on the route, however. Brigade commander Clinton B. Fisk wrote Ross complaining of the other brigade's troops: "I am pained to witness the pillaging, plundering, and irregular foraging on the part of some of the commands of this expedition." He argued that it was impossible to keep his troops in line "when they discover men from the steamers of the other brigades on shore capturing the delicacies of poultry-yards and pantries." The Methodist preacher-turned-general was so disgusted that he issued an order saying he would stop it with force and told Ross point-blank that, "with the grace of God sustaining me, I will enforce it if I have to shoot men both in and out of shoulder-straps. We cannot make good soldiers of thieves and robbers."[26]

The trip southward in the Delta was thus anything but quick and powerful; in fact it was timid and weak. Many reasons abounded, but this was not the textbook example of combined arms according to which army and navy cooperated and provided beneficial results. Obviously, the army blamed the navy while the navy blamed the army. Probably both were at fault, but the weight of evidence seems to rest on the navy's lack of punctuality, which seemed to revert to the navy's commanding officer, Lieutenant Commander Watson Smith. That said, Smith gave some evidence of the army's neglect as well, especially in food stores brought along. Ross admitted that he had only enough rations to last until March 13 but had more on the way, which would carry him to March 22. But he also noted he had been issuing rations to the navy as well, adding that "I learn that many of the gunboats are about out, and are expecting to get from me." Ross ordered more from Helena, telling Prentiss that, "if I remain to do the work that seems to be before me, I shall want more rations, say 50,000 more"; Prentiss quickly sent them, although communication back and forth over the two hundred or so river miles was slow at best; most boats took three days to make the one-way journey. Lieutenant Commander Smith added that part of the delay was because the column of vessels had to stop frequently for the soldiers to forage where they could on any land that was still above the high water in the Delta. Smith even reported that "this delay has spoiled our chances." That said, it was mostly army officials railing against Smith, especially Engineer Wilson, who reported to Grant of the "many provoking delays." And Smith himself notified Admiral Porter that he had only a month's worth of provisions and needed ammunition as well.[27]

Nevertheless, the Federal flotilla finally arrived just upriver from Fort Pemberton at Dr. Curtiss's Plantation, Shell Mound, on the evening of March 10, slaves on shore indicating that a major fort was just ahead. The force had come some forty-five straight-line miles from the mouth of the Coldwater but a whopping eighty by winding river miles. In all, they had navigated some two hundred and twenty-five winding river miles since leaving the Mississippi. But the next morning "a turn brought us within view of the enemy's work," Smith reported. Ross added that he was "prevented from advancing any farther by a strong fortification, extending from the Tallahatchie to the Yazoo River, across a neck of land." All could see this was not an ideal situation. The lowlands were flooded, making the only real way to approach the Confederates by river; some Indianans had to "wade in water up to their breasts" to get into picket positions. And the river itself was narrow, the rams being unable to move against anything in the river without exposing themselves to the fort's fire. Smith picked up immediately on the fact that "we have these disadvantages—that we must fight down-stream, and that we are all stern-wheelers but one." To aid his chances, Smith had the navy crews bring aboard all the cotton they could to shield the vessels when they approached the Confederate guns, although several could not emplace the cotton at the most significant points, especially around the boilers amidships. But all knew the two ironclads would do the majority of the fighting anyway, the river being too narrow to get much more than that in the fight up front. Accordingly, the sailors aboard the *Chillicothe* and *Baron de Kalb*, themselves covered with cotton bales, figuratively if not literally battened down the hatches and prepared for battle.[28]

Despite the time wasted on the trip southward, the Federal high command in the Tallahatchie River—Lieutenant Commander Smith and Brigadier General

Ross, plus Lieutenant Colonel Wilson providing his vocal opinions—wasted no time in testing the little fort. It looked strong from their vantage point, and it was, enough at least to stall the Federal advance.

But some of the Confederates were anxious to find out just how strong their modest fortification was, Isaac Brown reporting that the questions were legitimate. The lack of ammunition, and the fact "it has been raining hard for two days here, which made it very unfavorable for us," caused concern. He even confided to Pemberton that "I have never been well pleased with our position here, but hope that we may not have to regret taking it up, rather than concentrating our whole force at Yazoo City." Even Loring related that the enemy's arrival found "us but poorly prepared to receive him."[29]

It was too late to do anything about that, so Loring ordered the last precautions taken as the Federals arrived that morning. "The enemy made his appearance before us with nine gunboats and twenty-four transports.... The raft in an unfinished state was hastily swung across the Tallahatchie, and the Confederate States steamer *Star of the West* sunk behind it." The latter was a total loss, as nothing had been removed from the ornate ship, one soldier describing the captain as "very indignant." Two hundred and fifty holes had been bored into her hull and plugged, and when the plugs were pulled she settled quickly, although diagonally across the channel. Still, it was good enough. The gunners in the fort across the neck of land also took their positions, under the command of Loring's inspector general, Captain John D. Myrick. With all preparations made, Loring related that "we awaited the assault."[30]

Fort Pemberton housed eventually eight guns strung across the neck of land between the Tallahatchie and Yazoo Rivers. The cotton bales and earth formed the parapet, through which the guns protruded at the embrasures. An assortment of carriages held the guns, including the Whitworth on a field carriage, the naval gun on a naval carriage, the 32-pound rifle en barbette, and the 12-pound rifles on siege carriages. It was a respectable amount of firepower for so narrow a river, but ammunition was the main concern; some of the guns had as few as sixty rounds per piece. Nevertheless, three magazines, with another under construction, contained what ammunition there was. Most of the crews came from infantry detachments, although naval crews manned two of the guns. Only the Whitworth had a regular artillery crew from the Pointe Coupee Louisiana Artillery.[31]

The Federals soon advanced against this motley assortment of weaponry; "they greeted us with blue pills and we them also," one infantryman aboard the *Baron de Kalb* wrote in his diary. An infantryman in the rear related that "our gunboats pitched into like they were going to take the fort immediately." With Ross and Wilson aboard, Smith poked his gunboats forward as soon as

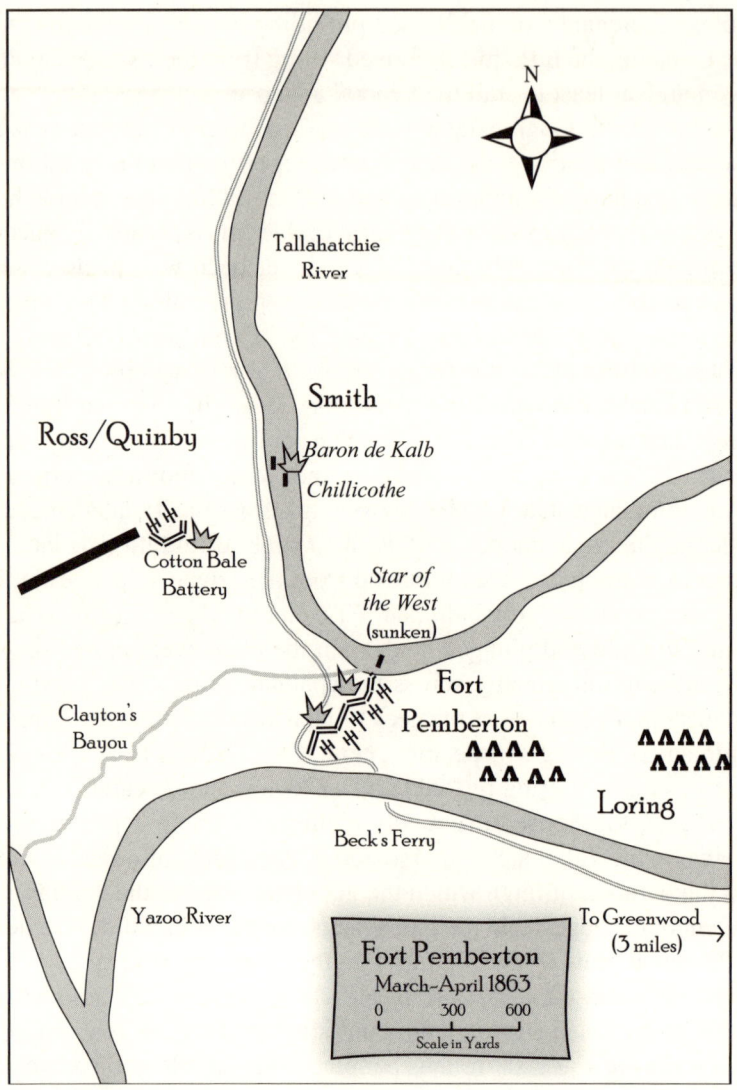

they arrived on March 11 for a "reconnaissance of the fort." Loring related that "at 10 a.m. the formidable iron-clad *Chillicothe* steamed around the bend of the river in our front, as though it was intended to rush upon the raft and destroy it." A couple of heavy shots hit the ironclad, one in the square turret, but did no damage, but it was enough to let the Federals know there was resistance ahead and to tread carefully—as if they were not doing so already. The first shot to strike came from the 32-pounder, and Loring noted "she sensibly diminished her speed." The second shot from the rifle caused the captain to back the vessel "up stream until her hull was hidden around the bend, save her bow and that portion of her which contained the 11-inch guns." A steady fire emanated from Fort Pemberton, Loring himself atop the parapet shouting "give them blizzards, boys! Give them blizzards!" He soon wore the sobriquet "Old Blizzards."[32]

Lieutenant Commander Foster backed the *Chillicothe* out of harm's way, but with the knowledge gained Ross began to land troops, including the 46th and 47th Indiana to locate the Confederate lines. Some small skirmishing took place as some of Waul's Texans moved forward to meet them in skirmish formation west of the river, and there were Confederate troops occasionally operating on the east side as well. Loring reported that they met "a large body of the enemy's infantry and cavalry and drove them back to their transports," and a sailor on the *Baron de Kalb* verified he heard "volley after volley of musketry . . . supposed to be skirmishing." Two Federals were wounded, but the Indianans basically found out that the terrain was mostly flooded and there was no good way to get to the fort by land; Ross reported it was "entirely surrounded by water." In particular, there was a "deep and wide bayou" a half-mile out from the fort that was impassable, Clayton Bayou. With these developments, neither Ross nor Smith were terribly optimistic. Though small, the fort looked fairly strong, and there was no way to approach without sailing right down to it, which the Confederates had, after all, intended by placing it there.[33]

Despite the concern among all involved, plans progressed for the naval attack that afternoon. That was seemingly the first and most important option and, really, the only one. Troops could not get to the fort by land, and for any of the rams to take effect on any Confederate vessels or the raft, the fort that would tear them to shreds if they came in proximity first had to be silenced. There was some thought of moving past the fort on the east side of the river, but troops likewise could not get through that area or even in a position to enfilade it with guns. In fact, the only area high enough out of water to even remotely stake guns or troops was a small spot to the west of the river where a little high ground allowed a dry place to operate. But it was still seven hundred yards away from the fort, and in between was the channel of Clayton Bayou as well as plenty of soggy swampland that was well overflowed.[34]

Without any other recourse, Smith probed ahead again that afternoon on March 11 with the *Chillicothe*, Loring writing that "the fight was resumed." The gunboat under Lieutenant Commander Foster charged ahead but came under immediate fire from the Confederate guns, and she quickly showed her defects. Lasting only about thirty minutes, the *Chillicothe* withdrew when a Confederate shell came shrieking through the left gunport on the bow, exploding within and killing four and wounding twelve of the crew. In fact, it hit just as the piece was being loaded, causing more damage. Smith declared that the *Chillicothe*'s "forward face of her casemate had been nearly destroyed by the enemy's fire of solid conical shot." Other shots hit the pilothouse as well, rattling the pilot. Lieutenant Commander Foster thought it best to back out of the hot fire again and decide on a better course of action. Indeed, the vessel was damaged severely; it would take a couple of days to repair, and the Confederates at Fort Pemberton reported "part of her inner works, with piece of shell sticking in it, floated against raft opposite fort." Wilson admitted "the *Chillicothe* has not stood the work well; that, too, at 1,100 yards. What may be the result at close range must depend entirely upon chance." A watching Federal similarly admitted that "in the afternoon the *Chillicothe* went down and exchanged shots with the rebel . . . but came back with four dead and fourteen wounded."[35]

By the night of March 11, all knew the Union expedition had been stopped, at least temporarily. If the Federals could get no farther than Fort Pemberton at Greenwood, there was no hope of altering the military situation at Vicksburg. As a result, the command trio of Ross, Smith, and Wilson set about finding a new plan, but every option discussed always came back to the fact that they had to obliterate the fort's guns to proceed. Infantry was a nonissue on either bank, although the Federals did camp on the shore as best they could. The fort had to be blasted out of the way, and that brought the ill-equipped *Chillicothe* back into the equation as well as the *Baron de Kalb*, which was much sturdier. To aid in the blasting power aimed at the fort, Wilson also erected during the night a land battery on the only available ground west of the river near Clarke's Plantation, some seven hundred yards out from the fort. It was a heavily wooded area that provided cover, but the only available resource he had in abundance was cotton bales, so the "cotton battery" soon emerged. Without siege guns, Wilson took one of the naval guns off the smaller gunboats, which could not fight anyway due to the narrowness of the river, and emplaced it there. A 30-pounder Parrott rifle soon went into position and began firing on the fort the next day. Two nights later, another naval 30-pounder Parrott joined the one on land and kept the fort under fire, but the Confederates countered the firepower by quickly erecting traverses around the guns inside Fort Pemberton. However, they did not respond to the enemy fire because of a lack of ammunition, Loring wanting to save what he had for the river advances that all could by now see was what would determine victory or defeat. In fact, he reported as early as the afternoon of March 11 that "our 32-pounder shot nearly exhausted; they are our main reliance." Soon, Wilson also placed in the land fort an "8-inch ship gun," actually a large howitzer, and men of the 36th Iowa supported the battery, all volunteering but the officer in command making them count off by twos for the duty.[36]

All hoped for a major attack the next day, March 12, one Federal writing, "[We] will roll up our garments tomorrow and clean out the darned thing if we can." But Commodore Smith did nothing on March 12, Wilson noting simply "the naval forces not . . . ready to attack." The same Federal added to his diary "we didn't clean it out." Most of the day was spent in repairing damage to the *Chillicothe*. But all planned on another major attack the next day, March 13. Both the *Chillicothe* and *Baron de Kalb* would take part this time, as well as the mortar that had been dragged along, in addition to the now three guns in the land battery. It was the best hope the Federals had of breaking through.[37]

But the advance on March 13 was less of an attack than a bombardment, although heard fifty miles away at Kosciusko. The three guns in the naval battery on land opened up a little after 11:00 a.m., and the two ironclads and mortar also surged ahead and opened fire, being careful to not get anywhere near enough to be hit hard again by the Confederate guns. Still, one Confederate gunner inside the fort admitted "we fired two cannon onto them to scare them, which resulted in a bombardment." Because of attacking with the current, Lieutenant Commander Walker ordered the *Baron de Kalb* tied to trees on the bank "to secure *De Kalb* against turning or falling below if disabled; secured her, therefore, so that if necessary she could be drawn out of view against the current." Similarly, the *Chillicothe* was "tied up by her stern and a breast line on the starboard side forward to keep her in position." It was not an optimistic move for taking the fort, and Loring's gunners indeed responded, this time to the vessels but not the land battery. He related that "we promptly responded with every gun we had in position, and the fight raged furiously." For a couple of hours the boats exchanged fire with the fort, creating a heavily smoke-covered river, Loring reporting to Pemberton that the enemy fire was "kept . . . up with great spirit until after sunset." He sent an almost minute-by-minute account to Pemberton: "Terrific fire from enemy; four hours; uninterrupted; from ten to sixteen heavy caliber gunboat guns; two heavy guns on land, and a mortar. . . . Enemy's gunboats and batteries struck constantly; large quantities of burning cotton struck from them."[38]

In the chaos, the Confederate gunners actually hit the *Chillicothe* some twenty times without major damage, although she soon withdrew "for the purpose of filling shell and cutting fuses." With Lieutenant Commander Smith aboard, the *Baron de Kalb* was "also severely handled" but, supported by the mortar fire, kept up the long-range fight until dark, "but with little effect," Ross reported. The Confederate fire shifted to the land battery and was likewise hot, one supporting Indianan writing that "as the enemy opened on us with a number of heavy guns, it made our position a pretty warm one with shot and shell flying around us and cutting off limbs and tree tops over our heads." Yet Ross added that the Federal loss was only a handful of slightly wounded, as he guessed in the Confederate ranks as well. Despite what he called "an immense amount of fighting done during the day. . . . If [the Confederate casualties are] no greater than our own," he wrote, "I may truly say nobody is hurt by to-day's operations."[39]

The Confederates suffered a few more casualties but, as expected, not anything severe. The major blow came against the fortifications themselves, one of Waul's gunners writing that "our trenches constructed of mud walls were severely damaged by direct hits." A few men suffered wounds as well. When one of the *Chillicothe*'s shells penetrated the fort, it "passed through the parapet, displaced a cotton bale, and ignited a tub of cartridges in the magazine of the Whitworth gun. The fire was communicated by the fuse." The shell fortunately did not explode, but the hit and the resulting fire wounded Lieutenant J. Q. Wall, who commanded the nearby gun, and burned as many as fifteen of his men, "some badly," Loring reported. At another gun, a shell exploded directly overhead and wounded three cannoneers, one mortally. Still, Loring was able to report, "thank God, our loss small so far."[40]

As the Confederates repaired the damage during the night and fortuitously welcomed a new supply of ammunition, Engineer Wilson, though nearly prostrated by going "two days and entire nights without sleep, and am almost dead," did his best to determine exactly what the Confederates had and where the guns were located. But from the distance he had to observe them there was no major detail. Ross also had infantry out to reconnoiter as much as they could, including the 33rd Missouri and 47th Indiana again, engaging in a slight skirmish, but there was little they could determine despite probing on both banks of the river. Wilson thought the fort itself was "constructed of cotton bales covered over with sand and earth." He did identify "only two guns of any weight" in the Confederate fort; he decided one was "a powerful rifle, 6.4 inch bore." Command was apparently under either Tilghman or Loring, he thinking Loring had left. How many troops were there was anybody's guess, but he did get word of the *Star of the West* being sunk and the *John Walsh* standing by to also be sunk if necessary or to be used as a ram.[41]

Wilson let his revulsion show in a report he sent that night to Grant. "I'm disgusted with 7, 9, 10, and 11 inch guns; to let one 6 ½ rifle stop our Navy. Bah! They ought to go up to 200 yards and 'make a spoon or spoil a horn.'" In the attack planned for the next day, March 14, he admitted "I have no hope of anything great, considering the course followed by the naval forces under direction of their able and efficient Acting Rear-Admiral, Commodore,

Captain, Lieutenant-Commander Smith. One chance shot will do the work; we may not make it in a thousand." Not knowing reinforcements were even then on their way, he added that no new troops were needed because they could not do anything. All was dependent on the navy: "I think we have troops enough to whip all the rebels in this vicinity if we can only get by the fort. One good gunboat can do the work, and no doubt; the two here are no great shakes." Unknown to him, that task would be harder, as even that night the supply of ammunition that had been so desperately needed at Fort Pemberton finally arrived from Vicksburg.[42]

Despite the pessimism, March 14 finally came and with it hopes from the army for the final showdown. Iowan Allen Miller noted in his diary that "Commodore Smith says he'll knock the fort into the river tomorrow. I'm in hopes he will, but I'm afraid he won't." He added: "We can't get at it with infantry or we would tear it down." And Smith did not fulfill his promise; in fact, he put the attack off that day, Wilson complaining "because the gunboats had not finished their repairs." Only sporadic firing from the land battery shook the silence, but this time Loring, with plenty of ammunition, returned fire. "Lasted but few minutes," he related, "evidently to try strength of our guns." One Federal nevertheless admitted that this expedition was "the first time I ever heard a cannon ball whiz. I can't tell you what kind of noise they make. It is particular." And the attack would not commence the next day either, Sunday March 15, "out of respect for the Sabbath." An Iowan noted that "no one dares to break in upon the solemn silence." Loring similarly noted that the day "was occupied by the enemy and ourselves in adding strength to our respective works," while another Confederate simply wrote "raining as usual." Wilson reported that the attack would actually be made the next day, March 16, but "I am not over sanguine of success, since I can see a disposition on the part of the Navy to keep from a close and desperate engagement." He added that he had done all he could to talk to them "to give them backbone."[43]

As a result, there was a definite air of defeat already hovering over the Union expedition, some soldiers even dying of disease while in front of the fort and being buried on what little dry land that could be found. Even as early as March 13 Wilson was showing signs of defeat. "We are stopped now certain," he wrote Grant. "Ross has done all in his power to urge this thing forward. If what he suggested had been adopted, the iron-clads would have been here fifteen days ago and found no battery of any importance. So much for speed." After the defeat on March 14, he likewise reported that "the game is blocked on us here as well as below." Only a miracle happening in the next day's attack would change things, but the ever-working mind of Wilson could not see that happening—and with dire results: "Should it turn out this way,

Vicksburg becomes subordinate, our department secondary, and Rosecrans' army our hope in the West. Won't we, in that event, be required to furnish 50,000 or 60,000 men?" Ross likewise later reported that, "in my opinion, its fate was decided, and a withdrawal inevitable, as soon as it appeared that the gunboat could not silence the enemy's work."[44]

Wilson certainly knew where to lay the blame: "Smith, you doubtless have understood by this time, I don't regard as the equal of Lord Nelson." He rated the two gunboat commanders Walker and Foster better, but they could only follow orders, although he asserted that they felt the same about Smith as he. In fact, Wilson went so far as to blame Smith for the entire failure, which he predicted: "Commodore Smith is entirely responsible for the detention at this point and the consequent failure of the expedition, and responsible for no other reason than his timid and slow movements." Ross agreed somewhat but wrote "it is but just to say that, while I am satisfied Lieutenant Commander Smith might, by more energy and rapidity of movement, have made the expedition successful, the error was one of the judgment only; that he was, although in very feeble health, after arriving in front of the fort, indefatigable in his labors, and exhibited during the engagement the utmost coolness and gallantry."[45]

Wilson also turned his hatred on the *Chillicothe* as well, writing that the ironclads "have suffered pretty heavily from the effects of the heavy rifle." He described how there were no penetrating shots, but those that hit the *Chillicothe* splintered the soft pinewood behind the iron so that "there is no fun in it." He concluded that the *Chillicothe* "is an inglorious failure." The *Baron de Kalb* was better but had to fight bow-forward to resist the Confederate shells. Still, the Confederates even at 1,100 yards "have battered and hammered the armored crafts sadly."[46]

And there were also potential problems in the rear, where Smith had been forced to leave vessels behind because of cover or breakdown. Pemberton personally had ordered the meager cavalry he had on the scene under Colonel Bob McCullough and State Troops commander Brigadier General James Z. George to move in rear of the Federals and make it to the Tallahatchie or Coldwater Rivers "to cut off messenger or supply boats. Do this at once."[47]

But there was still a faint glimmer of hope that the next day's planned attack on March 16 would pull victory out of the jaws of defeat. Given the status of the two ironclads and the timidity of the naval commander, however, it was but a feint flicker indeed.

As March began, Ulysses S. Grant had more to think about than just the Yazoo Pass effort, as promising as that initially seemed. In fact, Grant was so enthused about it, despite what he later said in his memoirs, that he began to make bigger plans for the operations, ultimately sending in as many as five or six divisions on the route: "If the gunboats are successful in getting into the Yazoo I expect great results," he wrote Admiral Porter, and he explained to a congressman that it "is going to prove a perfect success." It was seemingly a way for him to make the high waters of the winter work for and not against him, as they were in so many other ways such as at the canal.[48]

The desire for a quick victory could also have been the result of a truly interesting message he received from Washington, dated March 1: "There is a vacant major-generalcy in the Regular Army, and I am authorized to say that it will be given to the general in the field who first wins an important and decisive victory." It was stunning, perhaps almost bribery, but it was clearly intended to spur the Union major commanders forward, as it had also gone to Rosecrans in Middle Tennessee and Major General Joseph Hooker in Virginia. At the chance of fueling an unwise and less than prepared movement to gain the rank first, the chance was worth the risk to gain victories. A similar proposal to make Porter an admiral also went out from the Navy Department in return for a victory at Vicksburg.[49]

William Rosecrans blew up, he being offended by the offer: "As an officer and a citizen, I feel degraded to see such auctioneering of honor." Joseph Hooker planned to win his victory by following Major General Ambrose Burnside's failed plan of earlier in the winter, a plan that would result in the debacle at Chancellorsville in a couple months' time, which certainly did not win Hooker the promotion. Grant, for his part, simply pocketed the note for future reference and did little to change what he was already pushing forward on multiple fronts. With the weather situation, the terrain and topography of operating on a river with a giant alluvial plain right in the middle of operations, and the amazing defensibleness of Vicksburg itself all parts of the equation, Grant actually had little choice but to continue what he was doing anyway. If he had wanted to spur things along to win a quick victory he could not have done so.[50]

Grant also had family issues on his mind, including a continuing spat between Julia and his father. That said, Grant reported that he felt well: "Better than I have been for years. Every body remarks how well I look. I never set down to my meals without an ap[p]etite no[r] go to bed without being able to sleep." He felt so good, in fact, that he told Julia he wanted Fred, his twelve-year-old son, to come down and join him for the campaign. Fred ultimately arrived with a staff officer also returning to the army on March 29, Grant promising to make him write his mother and that he would require him "to read and study his arithmetic." He later added that "I doubt not [he] will receive as much permanent advantage by being with me for a few months as if at school." For Fred's part, he later explained that the haste was exacerbated "by my desire to possess myself of a beautiful Indian pony which Colonel [Major Theodore] Bowers of father's staff had provided especially for me." The boy's trip down was a bit dangerous; when told to seek shelter while passing a notorious Confederate ambush site, Fred fixed himself amid a coil of ropes near the boilers but was told as soon as the danger was over: "See here, sonny, if them rebs had fired at us and hit our boilers, you would have gone straight up through the hurricane deck, and there would not have been a piece of you left to send home to your mamma."[51]

Still, Grant's main focus was on military matters, and he certainly kept those multiple operations moving forward, they mainly by early March boiling down to the Yazoo Pass, canal, and Lake Providence efforts along with Admiral Porter's naval contributions on the river south of Vicksburg. But it seemed that March brought a seeming turning point in the campaign. The weather broke somewhat and the rains began to subside, prompting Grant to assure Halleck on March 6, "I will have Vicksburg this month, or fail in the attempt." One of Grant's soldiers marveled that "we have had four clear days and dry, the first this winter I believe of so long duration"; soon he was describing how "the weather is very warm, much the same as in June in our country; the trees begin to look green, the flowers are out in great profusion and the birds sing like summer time." With this warming trend the boys took to the water in sport: "Enjoyed themselves in their leisure time boat rowing and paddling canoes of their own construction, which were altogether too rough and clumsy to draw the admiration of an Indian or a boat builder." While the river would not fall any time soon, the possibility of greater mobility was certainly dawning with the better weather. As a result, Grant began to have a brighter outlook and started to concentrate troops southward along the river for the final showdown. He notified Prentiss at Helena, for example, to constitute a division under Brigadier General Alvin P. Hovey and send it on down to be part of McClernand's XIII Corps. "With a few days such weather as we are now having," he wrote Prentiss, "I hope to be ready for prompt action, and want Hovey, with his old division, with me." Hovey's troops were ready to go, they watching Ross's progress (they were "more than half way to Vicksburg" at one point, one Federal marveled) and afraid they would miss everything. One Iowan confided to his brother, "I am afraid Vicksburg will be captured & our Reg. take no part in the conflict."[52]

In addition, Grant also corralled an entire division from Missouri under Brigadier General Eugene A. Carr, ultimately also to be attached to McClernand's XIII Corps. The two brigades moved southward on the river in March, stopping at Lake Providence ("for exercise") and ultimately went on to Milliken's Bend. One arriving Federal described how the trip was grueling on the flooded river with his vessel loaded "to the very guards, and the lower deck nearly touched the water." An Iowan related that "the water washed over the deck and took everything in its way," including one soldier who was swept overboard but survived after being revived to consciousness. Likewise, even though Logan and Quinby's XVII Corps divisions had moved southward from Memphis to "the beautiful little lake" (Lake Providence) in late February, one of Quinby's Missourians writing home of "gliding down the Father of Waters for Dixey," Grant wanted others brought down from West Tennessee as well. He had already alerted Hurlbut to send down an additional division under Brigadier General John E. Smith for Sherman's XV Corps, Smith writing his wife that "it is no easy matter to get the Rascals on the boats and attend to all their wants." Now he also called for yet another division from Hurlbut, who planned to send the one under Brigadier General Jacob Lauman despite many troops favorably situated and admitting they would rather stay put. But the intent was clear, Grant similarly telling Hurlbut that he wanted paymasters sent down as well to mitigate the lack of pay's "very depressing effect upon the men" because "I hope to be able to make a move very soon."[53]

Losing so many troops, Hurlbut was to constrict his remaining lines and abandon a lot of the area north of him, especially the Mobile and Ohio Railroad that was so torn up in December by Forrest and had still not yet been fully repaired. Hurlbut faced the additional issue of public relations and dealing with civilians that most of Grant's officers did not face farther south, although McPherson had to deal with a Confederate senator's wife and daughters who wanted passes to get back into Confederate lines at Vicksburg "and to take two or three of her female house servants." Hurlbut continually griped about the wickedness of Memphis, in one especially productive moment describing how "as the United States cannot be expected to hire all the cardinal virtues for $13 a month [the common soldier's pay], soldiers on picket are bribed, officers are bribed, and the accursed system is destroying the army. Men are looking for opportunities to make money, and the whole course of the Treasury Department is tending to corrupt and degrade everybody connected with the administration of affairs. I am heartily sick, tired, and disgusted." That was perhaps not the full story, as Chicago *Tribune* correspondent Albert Bodman reported Hurlbut drunk on numerous occasions, and his excoriations also drifted to Quinby and McPherson being drunks and gamblers, although he noted McPherson was not to the degree of the others. Corroboration came from division commander John E. Smith, who was trying to get his division out of Memphis but received snippy word from Hurlbut that "if your command shall not have left this levee before sundown today, I shall be compelled to report you to the Maj Genl Army Dept." Smith simply wrote at the bottom: "Steve was too drunk on this day to remember his verbal instructions, his Quartermaster having failed to provide the necessary transportation to enable one to do so. JES."[54]

Still, Grant depended on Hurlbut to hold the line in northern Mississippi and West Tennessee, as well as to cooperate by sending the long-discussed cavalry raid into Mississippi, which Grant again revived in mid-March. He wrote to Hurlbut that he regretted that the February version of the raid had been doomed by Hamilton, though admitting "the weather, however, has been so intolerably bad ever since that it might have failed." But now he wanted it ready to go again, perhaps even in coordination with cavalry that might leave the Yazoo Pass forces. And Grant wanted Benjamin Grierson to lead it, writing that "I look upon Grierson as being much better qualified to command this expedition than either [Colonel Albert L.] Lee or [Colonel Jacob K.] Mizner." He also stated that he would let Hurlbut know when to send it: "The date when the expedition should start will depend on movements here. You will be informed of the exact time for them to start." Hurlbut in the process also offered his opinions, including that any Confederate general with sense, once Grant reached the high ground on the east side of the Mississippi River, would evacuate Vicksburg: "They will not risk a large army about Vicksburg."[55]

That said, it was still just a little bit early, and soggy, to make a major move beyond what Grant was already doing, and the troops particularly at Vicksburg grew tired and bored. "Everything here is as dull as can be," Colonel David Grier wrote home, "and the only thing that we have had lately exciting is the capture of two of our gun boats by the enemy." Many soldiers reported in their letters and diaries a lot of downtime playing cards or dominoes, pitching horseshoes, or fishing; one related "boys had a dance by moonlight to the merry music of the contraband's fiddle." An Indianan related how some of the boys made miniature one-man gunboats on the bayous, complete with boarded sides and portholes for miniature guns that would fire: "It was a wonder someone did not get hurt or killed." One Federal even explained that "we have great fun playing ball every evening, the Col. plays with us." Another related that "we played Base Ball according to *rule* for the first time today and it was laughable as no one knew exactly how." One such game at Lake Providence did not turn out well: "Play[ed] ball, broke up in a row, had a fight." Others frequently mentioned preaching in the camps, one providing the text: "For what shall it profit a man to gain the whole world and lose his own soul." Some enjoyed going to the riverbank at Vicksburg where the river was narrowest and "holding conversations with the enemy soldiers an citizens." Inspections and drill filled other times to less delight, although it could produce some merriment: "The regiment passed inspection by Gen A J Smith," one Federal wrote in his diary; "the officers got pretty severely reprimanded. Considerable of fun was the result." On another occasion, Job Yaggy of the 124th Illinois took exception to his colonel inspecting everything from blankets to muskets: "He was very rash in throwing back the guns, too. He hurt meney of the Boys."[56]

At the canal itself, Grant was watching closely this effort favored by the president himself: "Mr. Lincoln had navigated the Mississippi in his younger days and understood well its tendency to change its channel, in places, from time to time. He set much store accordingly by this canal." Grant assured Halleck on March 7 of "the near approach to completion of the canal." And it would have been quicker had not one of the bulwarks keeping water out broken and allowed water into the ditch, "filling up where men were at work getting out stumps, and thus setting back work for several days." An Ohioan described the water as "a rushing, grumbling, tumbling, surging, pitching, seething, boiling angry noise" that was comparable only to the falls at Niagara. Even with the damage, the dredges on site were working wonders. Halleck had sent down steam dredges from Louisville, and the "steam dredging boat *Hercules*" arrived at Lake Providence on March 5, McPherson sending it on down to the canal immediately. Another, the *Sampson*, arrived as well, handpicked by Colonel George G. Pride, and Grant reported they "work to a charm" despite one breaking down: it "gave out this afternoon," Grant informed McPherson. A marveling Federal soldier simply scribbled in his diary "they do very fast digging." In fact, with the dam breaking on March 6 and water flowing through the cut made to drain to the west, flooding numerous camps, Grant reported that "all work would have had to be suspended until there was a fall of at least 3 feet (the river is still rising), but for these machines."[57]

To remedy the break, engineers tried to sink a barge in the gap, but it swung around and hit and damaged one of the dredges, to Grant's chagrin. An Illinoisan related that "Genl. Grant and [Lieutenant Colonel John A.] Rollins with others of the staff sat all day to see it work but when it broke they left in disgust." Grant's staff officer John Rawlins was certainly not pleased with the delay, one Illinoisan writing home that he was "down here swearing around because things worked so slow." With the only real hope amid the rising river being the dredging boats and "a pile driver and machine for cutting trees under water," quartermaster officers sought even more dredges. Yet as the river continued to rise, even dredges seemed to be overkill, and Grant soon informed Halleck that no more would be needed for this miserable canal. One Federal explained that "I learnt last night that Gen Grant had give up all hopes of saving it. For some time past, it has been from one week[']s end to another that the leavey has been crowned with Whites and Blacks for over a mile in length working on it. Now it seemes as though there work is all in vane." Soldiers quickly moved their camps, and one Indianan simply wrote home "things look bad at present down here."[58]

As a result, Sherman had to issue orders on March 7 about what to do in the event the flooding continued: "The only safe ground will be the levee in front of our camps till the troops can be embarked." Determining exactly how the water would come into the camps ("the water will enter the swamps to the rear of our camps, and will fill up, slowly advancing up the ditches and over the fields, until the level of the water inside is about 18 inches below the level of the water outside"), Sherman ordered specific zones on the levee for specific parts of the corps to ensure organization in the midst of the chaos. In fact, Grant had to move McClernand's entire corps camps northward to Milliken's Bend because of the flooding, leaving Sherman's two divisions under Steele and Stuart to continue the work at the canal. "We will soon have to skedaddle on board of the boats," one Illinois wrote, and Sherman quipped that the troops were "roosting" on the levees.[59]

Up the river, matters also picked up more on the Lake Providence front as March swept in, especially as the reinforcing troops from Memphis began to arrive. Incidentally, among them was Andrew Jackson Donelson, nephew of the former president, down to look after his plantations in Mississippi. Logan's entire division was now on site and taking in the beautiful plantations along the shore, one Illinoisan describing the people as "immensely rich"; another described how the planters had buried their gold and silver and "there has been some twelve thousand dollars found since we came here." Boats for Quinby's division were also gathered as quickly as possible, and that entire division arrived as well by March 3, the men thinking they were bound for Vicksburg: "We dread it too. We hear so much of the place. It has become a terror." The men to their surprise found their new surroundings ideal, one admitting, "I only wish that they will keep us here during the summer, I have very little inclination to go to Vicksburg." Another Indianan wrote that "there is plenty of game, such as ducks, loons, geese and in fact all sorts of water fowl," and he added that Governor Oliver P. Morton also sent a lot of dried fruit and potatoes and onions "and sent an order in the articles not to give a shoulder strap one single bit of them, and we didn't either." There were plenty of fish as well, but no hooks, one soldier asking his family to mail him fish hooks that could not be procured locally. Many explored, finding the cemeteries fascinating, one Iowan describing a grave marker that stated: "Here sleeps Major Felix Bosworth U.S.A. died Vera Cruz, June 9th 1847, Aged 38 yrs." With so little camping area around the flooded, and soon to be more flooded, areas adjacent to the river levees, McPherson ordered Quinby to land a few miles upriver at Grand Lake and from there to move across to Bayou Macon, where he could cover that route as well as bring in a lot of the area's goods such as cattle, horses, mules, and cotton. There was a slight elevation on the west side of the bayou that Quinby could use for camping, and he was still within supporting distance of the other divisions as well. It was there that something of a revival broke out within the division.[60]

McPherson himself was on site and at work, making his headquarters at the Sellers Plantation. There, he and his staff lived sumptuously, one officer writing that "we have a mess tent and a nigger cook and a full sett of china which I think the boys must have drawn or borrowed some where." His troops fared better than most of the army, camped as they were in what one called "the very Garden of Eden." Once on site, McPherson reverted back to his old engineering days. With high hopes of ultimately reaching the Red River, the Federals managed to get a small steamboat, the *J. A. Rawlins*, into the lake by March 4, and one jealous Ohioan explained in his diary that there were "two brig Genls. one major Gen on board accompanied by their staffs brass band and ladies[;] quite a grand appearance." McPherson personally reconnoitered the various bayous on the route, looking at how long it would take to get them in condition for travel once the levee was cut at Lake Providence itself. The canal from the river to the lake was ready, and McPherson informed Grant he could cut the levee any day but wanted to do a lot of the work inland around Bayou Baxter before cutting it to allow better access for the workers' footings that would be overflowed when the levee was cut. In fact, the land was already almost flooded and soggy from the "recent heavy rains," causing immense problems for McPherson's workers. McPherson sounded a note of pessimism when he admitted to Grant that "the work of cleaning it [Bayou Baxter] out is much greater than I was led to believe from the engineer's reports." He consequently developed an alternate plan of perhaps cutting a new canal from the Mississippi River near Ashton, farther north, over to Bayou Macon, which would also give full access to the intricate network of bayous. He personally reconnoitered that route and, although unsure whether it would work, set Colonel Bissell and his engineer regiment on the task, acquiring blasting powder to blow the levee near Ashton. These canal digs were seemingly getting out of hand, correspondent Bodman writing that "these ditch digging plans of our generals, I frankly confess, have no attractions for me."[61]

McPherson's pressing problem now, whichever route he ultimately chose, was that trees in the bayous would have to be removed regardless, and that meant cutting the trees below the waterline and hoping that breaking the levee would raise the level of the water high enough for boats to get through. The lower the cuts the better, of course, but it was all done in solid water. McPherson also faced the dilemma of low water being more advantageous for cutting the trees lower to the ground, although that in itself precluded steamboats being on site to move the trees with their steam machinery, namely capstans. But if he cut the levee to get the powerful steamboat machinery in to do the work, that would raise the level of the water and make cutting the trees lower unrealistic. "I am a little apprehensive that in cutting them off," he wrote Grant, "as the surface of the water now is, the water, when the levee is cut, will not rise high enough to float the boats clear of the stumps." As the slow work continued over the next few days under Brigadier General Mortimer D. Leggett, McPherson assured Grant that "the work of cleaning out Bayou Baxter is progressing as rapidly as circumstances will admit." But there were continual reports such as "the work of opening Bayou Baxter progresses more slowly than I wish, on account of the great difficulty of getting at it, the low ground being all overflowed." One of the lower-level soldiers agreed, writing that "it will take a while yet, since the whole project is organized poorly and clumsily." He added: "I do not believe that we [will] get enough water to operate steamboats, since the land around us is too flat and the water just spreads into every direction." There were concerns from the local citizens as well; one Indianan declared that "the old planters around here has offered ninety millions of dollars not to cut it through for it will destroy thirty-three counties."[62]

More delay ensued, however, as Bissell cut the levee farther north near Ashton and the flooding began. McPherson went up to see for himself and declared on March 10 that "the water is now rushing like a torrent through several of the crevasses he has made," but he doubted the overall results: "Do not think it practicable as yet." Obviously, several more days would be needed for all the water to level out and to see if boats could be pushed through, but that only brought more delay. Still, Grant was losing interest in the operation, lengthy as it was, and on March 7 informed Halleck that "there is but little possibility of [this] proving successful." He later admitted to McPherson that "I do not expect to use that route but want to know if it can be used in case of necessity." One of the lower-level troops admitted as much, writing home that "we have not done anything at *whipping* Rebels since we came here."[63]

Even the naval operations on the river were not producing anything of great benefit. With the loss of the *Queen of the West*, *Indianola*, and *New Era*, the latter because Grant ordered it scuttled to the navy's chagrin ("no reason was assigned for the disposition of a valuable boat"), Admiral Porter seemingly panicked and determined to send another vessel below Vicksburg immediately. It was still unclear what the fate of the *Indianola* was, so Porter might be facing her as well. He called Colonel Ellet to Vicksburg with the ram *Switzerland* and ordered him to prepare to pass the batteries once more. Better news arrived as Major General Nathaniel Banks, operating to the south around Baton Rouge and Port Hudson, finally made contact and informed Grant that Admiral David Farragut would push past the Port Hudson batteries with his famed *Hartford*, which had already been to Vicksburg once before, thereby interdicting Confederate traffic once again between the Confederate garrisons. All Farragut needed, he informed Grant directly, was coal that could be floated down from the north.[64]

But it was clear that Grant's focus as March came about was the seeming possibility of success in the Yazoo Pass operation, even to the detriment of the other ongoing efforts; in the same March 7 note to Halleck, he added that "the Yazoo Pass expedition is a much greater success." Obviously, word of the halt at Greenwood had not reached him as yet. In fact, as early as March 5, Grant ordered McPherson to "stop Quinby from debarking any more troops where he now is. All transports, no matter what their size, can run into the Pass to Moon Lake, which is about half way from the river to Coldwater. I want your corps to get in there as rapidly as possible, and effect a lodgment at Yazoo City or the most eligible point on Yazoo River from which to operate." In fact, Grant and Porter had worked out that when the gunboats from Yazoo Pass approached Haynes' Bluff they would fire off a certain signal (nine guns one minute apart and then, after five minutes of silence, three guns ten seconds apart), at which time Grant would cooperate from his side of the Yazoo River. Porter mistakenly told Grant he heard the signal on March 6; obviously, both were operating on invalid assumptions and rumors.[65]

Yet shifting Quinby to the Yazoo Pass operations spoke volumes about where Grant thought the best chances of success would be. He added that McPherson should continue work on the Lake Providence effort "with the force you have left," and he wanted the clearing continued and water let in "to see what it will do." But it was clear that the Yazoo Pass expedition would be the priority. In fact, counting Logan's division that would also go up eventually, as well as the two from Memphis coming down, Grant advised McPherson "this will give you five divisions to operate with, which, with the gunboats, I hope will enable you to carry out one end of the proposed programme." The twenty-five thousand troops in the five divisions, interestingly, did not include Ross's currently at Greenwood, a fact Grant was not privy to, he still thinking they were at Moon Lake. McPherson was to replace Ross with Hovey's new division from Helena, Grant writing that it was "composed of old and tried troops, whilst the others are raw, and with rather indifferent brigade commanders, I fear." Quinby would be in charge until McPherson arrived.[66]

The only major issue Grant advised McPherson to look out for was the size of boats. He ordered McPherson to send all vessels at Lake Providence shorter than a hundred and eighty feet to Yazoo Pass, that being the size Wilson had reported could get through the narrow and winding portion of the passage that led to the Coldwater River. With so few vessels of that size to be had, however, Quinby's troops would have to wait until more arrived to head into the pass. Meanwhile, McPherson himself was expected any day in Helena to take command of the Yazoo Pass operations.[67]

Quinby had his division "on board the transports again" by March 7 and headed northward. There was some confusion, caused by Grant's larger confusion, about what Quinby should do once he arrived at Moon Lake (either drive on into the Delta with Ross or await other troops). Obviously Ross was already nearing Greenwood by that point, but McPherson, no nearer Moon Lake that Quinby, could tell him only what he understood: that he was to move on in, as time was of the essence. But he made sure Quinby understood to enter the pass only with vessels shorter than a hundred and eighty feet and to send all those longer back to Lake Providence to bring Logan's brigades northward. Meanwhile, with those of sufficient length, Quinby was to press ahead and find a defensible point in the Delta to hold while the other transports, using the longer vessels he had sent back, brought the other divisions to Quinby's position. "When we get all our troops together, we can then risk the issue of a battle," McPherson explained.[68]

It is obvious that the Federal commanders from Grant on down were working with faulty information. They had no idea Ross was already at Greenwood or that the Delta was so flooded that there was no place that could hold numerous divisions to camp or to operate toward a pitched battle. Even Admiral Porter was confused, reporting to Grant that he had received word that his gunboats had made it all the way to Yazoo City by this point. No wonder Grant was highly excited about this route. But the reality on the ground was nothing like what he envisioned.[69]

McPherson had other problems as he worked to shift northward, planning to move with Logan's troops. "We have here now about 2,400 negroes—men, women, and children. What is to be done with them when the command leaves?" Grant had no answers, writing McPherson that "in regards to the contrabands, the question is a troublesome one. I am not permitted to send them out of the department, and such numbers as we have it is hard to keep them in."[70]

Yet the concentration of troops continued. Arriving at Moon Lake and fearing an entrance because of high winds and fog, and therefore camping his brigades on the west side of the river temporarily on a vast sandbar that was quickly dwindling in the still-rising river, Quinby of course found that Ross was already in the Delta. He quickly sent a message forward to Ross, telling him of the overall plan. "He evidently attaches great importance to the movement down the Yazoo River," Quinby wrote of Grant, "the failure of which would in all probability render it necessary to make a complete change in the present programme.... We cannot afford to fail." He thus ordered Ross to be extremely careful and not to fight a battle until Quinby's troops arrived at the least. "Better fall back a little rather that jeopardize the success of the whole campaign by an untimely reverse."[71]

Word of where Ross actually was arrived on March 10, Ross directing his March 7 and 8 dispatches to Prentiss at Helena, not knowing anything about Quinby taking over. Quinby read the reports with satisfaction but fired off another note to Ross, again urging caution: "We must meet with no reverse, and I therefore urge upon you to proceed with extreme caution." He confided to McPherson that "he has but about 4,000 troops, and evidently does not apprehend the dangers by which he is surrounded." In fact, he wanted Ross to just maintain his position at Greenwood until he could arrive with reinforcements, which he hoped to start by March 12. "The great difficulty we meet with is procuring suitable transports," Quinby explained. He related that the ones he had were not willing to go: "I confess myself very much annoyed by the unwilling and unaccommodating spirit of the steamboat men in charge of the boats which have been thus far assigned to take my division forward. Without exception, all have found some serious defects in their respective boats, which render them unfit for the service, and they resort to all sorts of pleas and subterfuges to get out of it." To that end, not wanting to take the bigger vessels into the pass and have one sunk in the channel, Quinby tried to shake loose every small steamer he could on the Mississippi and Ohio Rivers. He especially wanted those that had not been in government service yet, some of the ones now in service having been so for months and thereby losing the revenue of civilian trade during that time and the worse for the wear on top of that. Bad news arrived, however, that many of the vessels were tied up transporting supplies to Rosecrans on the Ohio River, and he was not likely to release them for service in a different department.[72]

Finally, by March 12, Quinby was able to get enough boats to start with a portion of his division, hopefully even a brigade. He loaded aboard Colonel John B. Sanborn's troops and set out on March 14 for the pass, which brought, in his words, "three days of unremitting toil, and, for me, much painful anxiety." Some of the troops were amused to find messages on barrelheads or other items nailed to the trees along the pass by soldiers who went ahead of them. This next wave of soldiers also met and conversed with James Alcorn, who was becoming something of a luminary among the Federals. Quinby and the brigade finally reached the Coldwater River on March 16, while two other brigades remained behind under Colonel George Boomer, ready to push ahead into the pass as soon as additional boats arrived.[73]

Grant was sweating the delay from Young's Point, writing that "the Yazoo expedition seems to move slowly." Others were impatient as well, one Illinoisan writing that "I expect the Rebs set up on those hills over there [are] laughing at us, but it will be our turn to laugh by & by." Grant became even more afraid when he learned that Ross had gone on down the rivers, and he was very anxious for Quinby to catch up: "I have a great deal of confidence in his judgment," he wrote, something he evidently did not have in Ross, and higher numbers also made the expedition safer. "Have him [Quinby] go in just as rapidly as the transports can take him" were Grant's instructions to McPherson, even if it was a brigade at a time.[74]

McPherson was doing all he could despite the lack of boats. By March 15, he had a couple of Logan's brigades loaded and ready to depart for Yazoo Pass, but they would have to deposit them and return for the rest as well as McArthur's troops. Meanwhile, he reported some good news on the Lake Providence effort: the water let in by Bissel had flooded the bayous, and his engineer, Captain Andrew Hickenlooper, had found "a thoroughly practicable route."[75]

The Lake Providence route was good, but it was evident by this point in mid-March that Grant was not nearly as interested in the efforts west of the river as he was in Yazoo Pass on the east side. Clear evidence was the removal of troops from those western efforts to ones east of the river. On top of that, spring was budding despite many Federals remarking even in February that some of the warmer days were much like summer in the North; one Ohioan related as early as March 10 that "the peach trees are in full bloom." Another admitted he had "spring fever." The army's morale was accordingly building, one Federal writing home that "our generals all appear in good spirits, and as a consequence the men are in better spirits." And on top of that, there was all of a sudden another major possibility dawning, one that Grant could not pass up either. But it was also through the soggy, boggy, flooded Mississippi Delta.[76]

At the turn of the year some two months into the Vicksburg Campaign, Ulysses S. Grant found himself beset by unfavorable political winds, broad Confederate defenses, and most important a landscape nearly underwater. Amid such difficulties, he would spend the next four months seeking a way to reach high and dry ground on the same side of the Mississippi River as Vicksburg. (Library of Congress)

Although a political thorn in Grant's side, the senior corps commander, John A. McClernand, was aggressive in mindset. He competently led in several efforts such as capturing Arkansas Post, the canal to bypass Vicksburg, and most important the dangerous movement southward beyond Vicksburg. (Library of Congress)

One of McClernand's division commanders, German Peter J. Osterhaus led the Army of the Tennessee's march on the west side of the river southward past Vicksburg. His brigades opened the route that the rest of the army would utilize. (Library of Congress)

Grant's favorite subordinate, William T. Sherman became involved in a number of attempts to get past Vicksburg, including the canal and the near-disastrous Steele's Bayou expedition. Although not in favor of the final move past Vicksburg, Sherman gave his friend Grant all his support, even to the point of leading feints that could have been seen as defeats to allow Grant better odds of success. (Library of Congress)

One of Sherman's division commanders, Frederick Steele took part in several of the Vicksburg efforts, leading some independently. His mid- to late April expedition down Deer Creek from Greenville helped divert Confederate attention from Vicksburg itself. (Library of Congress)

Another of Sherman's division commanders, Frank P. Blair, Jr., led the effort in late April to return to the Chickasaw Bayou area to draw attention north of Vicksburg. Though likely to be labeled a defeat, Blair's troops were sufficiently loyal to risk the effort and were accordingly hand-chosen for the job. (Library of Congress)

Grant's young protégé commanding a corps, James B. McPherson oversaw several Vicksburg efforts, including cutting the levee at Lake Providence and sending in troops to the Yazoo Pass expedition. Each failed, although not due to the engineer McPherson's lack of effort. (Library of Congress)

Grant's naval counterpart, David Dixon Porter often came to Grant's aid in so many waterborne efforts. Although nearly losing the backbone of the flotilla in the Steele's Bayou Expedition, Porter was immediately thereafter ready and willing to risk his vessels again in the passage of Vicksburg. (Library of Congress)

Though only a colonel, Benjamin H. Grierson wielded an importance far outweighing his rank. His cavalry raid in mid- to late April through Mississippi diverted Confederate attention at a critical time, helping Grant cross the Mississippi River unopposed. (Library of Congress)

One of Grant's chief engineers on his staff, James H. Wilson was the brainchild of the Yazoo Pass Expedition. He cut the levee and then accompanied the forces all the way to Fort Pemberton, complaining about the navy the whole way. (Library of Congress)

Confederate commander John C. Pemberton utilized the high water and vast expanses well until he became disoriented because of so many expeditions, raids, and feints. These distractions took Pemberton's attention away from Grant at a critical time, during Grierson's Raid, and that allowed Grant to cross the Mississippi River virtually unopposed. (Library of Congress)

Pemberton's senior division commander, Carter S. Stevenson had charge of Vicksburg itself while Pemberton remained at department headquarters at Jackson. Much of the defense of the city and on both flanks fell to him. (Library of Congress)

Pemberton's roving division commander, William W. Loring first defended Fort Pemberton in the Yazoo Pass Expedition and then shifted his focus to Grierson's Raid. Eventually, the troops that would make up his division coalesced around Jackson and were sent to the new crisis point in late April, the Grand Gulf area. (*Miller's Photographic History*)

Division commander Dabney H. Maury was liked by his troops, who manned the upper reaches of the Yazoo River near Vicksburg. Defense of the Delta fell to him, and his commands opposed the Steele's Bayou Expedition as well as several Federal forays along Deer Creek. (Library of Congress)

John H. Forney became a division commander when Maury transferred to East Tennessee. Forney then took command of the area to the northeast of Vicksburg along the Yazoo River. (Library of Congress)

The longest serving division commander at Vicksburg, Martin L. Smith had been there since mid-1862. He commanded much of the city's defenses. (Library of Congress)

Formerly a brigade commander whom Pemberton sent to fortify and hold Grand Gulf, John S. Bowen became a division commander with the addition of another brigade to his defenses. He would hold Grand Gulf but could not stop a Federal landing farther southward. (*Miller's Photographic History*)

A member of the Mississippi Secession Convention and a former militia general earlier in the war, James L. Alcorn lived on a plantation along the banks of Yazoo Pass. He met and conversed with many Federals making their way along the route. (Library of Congress)

A favorite task of President Abraham Lincoln, the Vicksburg canal sought to change the course of the mighty Mississippi River. It failed, but later in 1876 the river changed course on its own. (Library of Congress)

The City-class ironclads played a major role in the bayou operations in the vicinity of Vicksburg. The USS *Louisville* participated in several efforts such as Arkansas Post, Steele's Bayou, the passage of Vicksburg, and Grand Gulf before helping ferry Grant's army across the river at Bruinsburg. (Library of Congress)

Admiral Porter passed the Vicksburg guns on the night of April 16, as depicted in this postwar painting by James E. Taylor. Porter later wrote of reminiscing while viewing the work of art, even describing it in a letter to a group of his naval veterans on the twenty-fifth anniversary of the passage. (Ohio Historical Society)

Smith Coffee Daniell II built a magnificent mansion atop the bluffs near Bruinsburg, and the leading Federals rested in its spacious surroundings as McClernand's XIII Corps pushed inland on April 30. The house burned decades later, and the only known illustration is by a Federal soldier in the 20th Ohio, Henry Otis Dwight. (Ohio Historical Society)

8

"The Enemy Press Me on All Sides"
March 16–21

At one of the most critical points of the Civil War, a civilian engineer came to the nation's rescue. In late 1861 when the Northern public pushed for an offensive, and President Lincoln himself set a date by which all forces would move forward early the next year, the Union had a decided advantage if it could seize the initiative. Riven with watercourses that bisected and drove deep into the heart of the Confederacy, the West was a golden opportunity for advancement, which played out in the early battles of 1862. The commanders were important, the geography essential, and even weather played a role. But one of the most significant contributions was a flotilla of ironclad gunboats that an almost miraculous building effort produced in record time. Essentially, this is where the North gained its greatest advantage over the Confederacy in the West.[1]

The City-class ironclads were the dream of James B. Eads, river architect, salvager, engineer, and shipbuilder. Taking a design by Samuel Pook, which later brought the nickname "Pook Turtles" for these low, tortoise-like vessels, Eads told the Navy Department he could build seven of them in a matter of weeks. He was well known to the bureaucrats in Washington, and the contracts were let in August 1861, with a delivery date of October. In fact, the timber that would go into the ironclads was still growing in the forests when Eads signed the contracts for the gunboats that August. Eads subcontracted with sawmills, rolling mills, and railroads to build the vessels at shipyards in Missouri at Carondelet (*Carondelet*, *St. Louis*, *Louisville*, and *Pittsburg*) and Illinois at Mound City (*Mound City*, *Cincinnati*, and *Cairo*). While Eads did not meet the deadline totally, he did deliver by around the new year, although the navy itself had numerous problems trying to crew the new vessels. "You have no idea how much work is required to improvise, as we are doing, a navy here, with our limited means," one naval officer explained.[2]

Mounting thirteen guns each inside the casemate plus an added howitzer on the deck, each vessel was 175 feet long and 51 feet wide, with a crew of 175. Two-and-a-half-inch thick iron covered the sides around the guns, boilers, and engines as well as the bow guns, but the decks were constructed of wood and vulnerable to plunging fire. These vessels proved their worth early on at Forts Henry and Donelson even if shot up a bit, and then on the slow push down the Mississippi River the rest of 1862. They also became the backbone of the navy's activities in the later Vicksburg Campaign, and by March 1863 all were on different and widely varying operations. Named after river cities on the Mississippi and Ohio, these ironclads took the war deeper into the Confederacy than it had ever been, even into the bowels of the Mississippi Delta. In fact, one of them, the *Baron de Kalb* (formerly *St. Louis* but changed when the ironclads became navy instead of army property in the fall of 1862, as there was already a *St. Louis* on the rolls), was even then biding its time with the different-class *Chillicothe* in front of Fort Pemberton, readying to make an all-out attack on March 16. Five others were actually on a new mission into the Delta by a different route, one that if successful could also spell doom for Vicksburg. If unsuccessful, however, it could spell defeat for the vessels themselves in such constricted waterways and territories.[3]

Sadly, one of the vessels was completely out of commission by this point. While some had been sunk and raised in previous action, including the *Cincinnati* and *Mound City*, others would also be sunk and raised as well, including the *Cincinnati* again during the siege of Vicksburg. But the *Cairo* had been sunk for good in the Yazoo River just above Chickasaw Bayou back in December, the result of a torpedo, or mine, in the river. It would not see daylight again until a hundred years later, raised and eventually put on display at Vicksburg National Military Park. Later in 1863, the *Baron de Kalb* would meet the same fate farther up the river at Yazoo City. It would never be raised, however, and lies there today.[4]

But for a brief moment in time, these Eads ironclads, though not perfect and certainly not invincible, were nevertheless forces to be reckoned with, as they were showing even now as they trudged along the narrow waterways of the Mississippi Delta in Grant's effort to reach the high ground east of the Mississippi River. Grant termed it "the ground I so much desire," and he was learning that he could never get that coveted ground without the help of the United States Navy.[5]

L**ittle** was heard from the expedition through Yazoo Pass in the first half of March, only sporadic reports from Brigadier General Leonard F. Ross of nearing the Yazoo River itself at Greenwood. With his stoppage there on

March 10, it took a while for word to get back to Helena. In fact, Benjamin Prentiss, commanding at Helena, wrote Grant on March 16, the very day the all-out attack would take place at Fort Pemberton, that "I may be too confident, but I am of the opinion that [General Ross's] expedition ere this has taken Yazoo City." In an addendum to his letter later that day, Prentiss added that a scout just reported that the Confederates had withdrawn to Yazoo City: "This information is reliable." In actuality, Ross was stopped at Greenwood, not even yet in the Yazoo River proper. Federal officers could look through their glasses and see the Confederate flag still flying defiantly over little Fort Pemberton and the garrison inside.[6]

But March 16 was the day that would decide victory or defeat here. Loring, commanding at Fort Pemberton itself, certainly thought so, relating to Pemberton that "[I] am of opinion it is but the advance of a very powerful force." In fact, thinking more Federals would be on the way, he ordered more troops up from Yazoo City to Greenwood and placed his primary regiments, Waul's Texans, the 2nd Texas, and the 20th and 26th Mississippi, the former Mississippi regiment under Colonel Daniel R. Russell from Carrollton—just fifteen or so miles up in the hills to the east, along the parapets. He also asked for an engineer officer to be sent up the Yazoo at once. But it was soon evident that "Monday . . . was fixed by the enemy for a grand assault with their entire force upon our works."[7]

The Federals were indeed ready to attack once and for all. Naval commander Smith had spent the last couple days preparing his vessels, with Wilson adding to his armament on land. All were intent on an all-out attack that, if unsuccessful, would likely be the end of the effort, as no other way past could be readily conceived. Ross loaded "the three best regiments of his command" on several of the tinclads, and they prepared to head quickly to the fort if the ironclads were able to silence the big guns; Colonel James M. Lewis of the 28th Wisconsin would lead the assault. All hands prepared the vessels as a result and by midmorning began the slow movement around the great bend of the river to the familiar position some thousand yards away from the tiny Confederate fort. But despite Wilson's constant barking, Smith would go no farther.[8]

In fact, he barely got that far. Despite being ready around daylight, the land battery did not open up until about noon, and the navy advanced a little bit after that. The land battery, now reinforced with an 8-inch gun, pelted the Confederate works, dueling also with some outlying Confederate batteries that had been emplaced during the lull of the last couple days. Infantry also moved forward as far as it could to skirmish with the defenders but could get only to within about four hundred and fifty yards. The Confederate gunners obviously concentrated on the gunboats, however, they being the looming threat. Consequently, as the *Chillicothe* steamed forward and was again tied in position with a stern line, having had her powers of endurance increased by "packed cotton bales on the forward portions," she began to take hit after hit on the bow turret. The situation quickly became serious. Captain John D. Myrick, Loring's aide, had command of the Confederate guns and directed them with "courage, coolness, and efficiency," Loring noted, he adding that "he stood unfalteringly." Wilson described how the *Chillicothe* "was struck with great violence several times." The gunboat fired only seven shots before the Confederate fire silenced the two forward guns due to damaging the port covers: "Neither could be opened til they were lifted off and hammered out." After only fifteen minutes or so, Smith had seen enough and pulled the *Chillicothe* back. Despite Wilson's almost frantic appeals, the *Baron de Kalb*'s commander, wanting nothing of the Confederate fort by himself, declined to advance alone.[9]

The result was a sputter when most had anticipated an all-out fight. Smith admitted that "in seven minutes she was compelled to back up the river and out of range." The great attack, some several days in the making, was over almost before it began. Likewise probably was all chance of now getting past the Confederates at Fort Pemberton. Still, the Confederate earthworks took a pounding, one cannoneer admitting that "our trenches were in bad condition and we had to work by day and by night on them." He added: "I never had an idea just what cannon balls could do, but have now seen enough where trees from 2 to 3 feet in diameter were cut away as were they blades of grass." But the Federals suffered more. The *Chillicothe* was a near wreck, Wilson describing how in all she had been hit fifty-two times and was crumbling; he described the vessel as "now almost incapable of further active service." Wilson further described the boat as "a great cheat and swindle upon the Government" in the first place, the iron affixed to the nine inches of soft pine backing with metal spikes instead of bolts. Obviously, the Confederate fire did not help, and it literally almost caved in the forward portion of the vessel to where the deck had to be "propped up in order that the steering-wheel may be turned." Another shot in that area would likely have caved in the entire forward deck, turret and all. Ross confided to Prentiss that "I don't believe our two iron-clads can stand the terrific fire of the guns now on the fort for one hour without total destruction." He blatantly told him there would have to be new gunboats "sent us, if it is expected to accomplish anything." Even the *Chillicothe*'s commander, James P. Foster, admitted that "she is almost a failure and will remain so until alterations are made," and later he declared her "a perfect failure as a fighting vessel." As a result, the *Marmora* sped northward to bring additional aid; one Mississippian crowed that "we ruined the gunboat *Chillicothe* and drove the army back."[10]

Only the land battery kept up the fight, sporadically until nightfall. The Confederates merely watched as the Union gunners fired, taking cover and watching carefully as more guns deployed. But Loring would not allow the Confederate guns to respond, he being "fearful of not receiving more ammunition in time." Much work instead went toward creating yet another raft in the river to block access to the fort. Loring related to Pemberton the next day that, "if I can hold the enemy back a week, [I] will have another raft constructed in Yazoo River opposite this and works thrown up on the other side."[11]

A distraught Wilson wrote Grant again that night, informing him that "I am sorry to say we are no nearer the accomplishment of our object to-night than we were yesterday." But Wilson was not giving up, and he began to work on new ideas. One was to bring in more troops and building material, including pontoon bridges, to get troops across the river in rear of the fort so that they could attack Fort Pemberton from behind. He used the word "siege" and admitted that it would take weeks to reduce the fort in this way, although there was a chance that also in that time a fall in the river might strand the flotilla now in the Delta and the vessels would have to be burned. Accordingly, he also began to devise a plan to cut the Mississippi levee wider to allow in more water, if nothing else than to flood out the Confederates. Cutting the levee "will let in an immense volume of water, but whether enough to produce the desired effect is the problem to be solved. It's worth trying, I think." He also advocated cutting the levee farther upriver at Austin to let in even more water. This was done, Prentiss writing that "it will do us no harm, and can do the enemy no good," but this likewise did not produce the necessary effect. Still, while awaiting the outcome "of enlisting the elements on our side," Wilson requested more of everything, including guns and ammunition, and Grant ordered a battery of four 30-pounder Parrots from McClernand's corps to go to Greenwood. "There is a great chance yet for us," Wilson concluded.[12]

Not to be outdone, Confederate commander Loring knew what the enemy was probably thinking and was just as concerned about his flanks as the Federals were interested in turning them. In fact, he ordered three additional regiments from Yazoo City northward "to protect my flanks by preventing the crossing of the Tallahatchie in my rear and reaching Yazoo in my front." Obviously, doing so would take some time and engineering, Loring adding that "both are difficult for the enemy to do, owing to overflows." But if the time and material were available, the enemy would have an advantage. Loring could build new fortifications only at the threatened points for now. At some points, Loring even constructed fortifications "on the other side of the river," but his main concern was his left front along the Yazoo River to his south: "Principal fear is that they may turn one of my flanks, particularly my left front." He quickly sent the reinforcing regiments of John C. Moore's brigade to that area, though notifying Pemberton that "as heavy additions are reported being made to their force, it will take one correspondingly large to successfully meet them." Meanwhile, Loring assured Pemberton that he and his troops "have made up our minds to fight it to the bitter end. You may look for nothing but a series of hardly fought battles throughout the whole length of the Yazoo." But he still needed more guns and ammunition to make the defense solid, and he likewise added: "Send also artillerists for our guns; we need them badly, and have none at all." Pemberton could reply only that he had none to spare: "Train some of your men to the guns."[13]

Unknown to Loring, however, there were no additional plans among the Federals to try again. With the shock to morale and the chances of victory evaporating (the *Chillicothe* herself had endured twenty-two "killed, wounded, and drowned" and the *Baron de Kalb* had suffered as well—including an officer arrested "for drunkenness on duty, in action"), the next few days saw little renewed effort. One Iowan correctly noted, "O! Delay, thou hast lost many brilliant victories." Many were understandably disgusted, brigade commander Clinton Fisk, not a fan of this operation to begin with, apparently storming around in a rage. "Brig. Gen. Fisk is bustling around like an insane person with his long train of guards at his heels," one diarist explained. He also added that Fisk's wife was also present on the expedition: "Mrs. Gen. Fisk, dear innocent creature had better go home and stay there with the children if she has any. I guess the fact of her having none is the secret of her being here. She divides the time of our general."[14]

Loring reported that "a significant silence characterized [the Federals'] movement the three following days, although we could see them plainly at their batteries." But there was a lot going on inside the Union high command in those intervening days. The major development was that Smith left the flotilla, turning over command to Lieutenant Commander Foster of the *Chillicothe*. Smith had been sick even before leaving the Mississippi River to take part in this operation, and it only became worse while stuck here in the Delta. Finally, he asked the surgeons to declare him in need of leave, which they did. He soon departed on his flagship *Rattler*, one of many vessels plying back and forth carrying messages and soldier mail. Also aboard were other sick, including George Yost, formerly of the sunken ironclad *Cairo* and who explained in his diary: "I was well cared for by my Sailor friends the most of whom had belonged to the gunboat *Cairo*." The *Rattler* and others ran into numerous Confederate guerrillas on the return trips and had one killed and one severely wounded, alongside three who died of sickness on the trip. Some thought Smith himself "in, I fear, a dying condition," and indeed he passed away the next year, though not stemming directly from these events. It was no secret that Wilson and Ross were not happy with Smith, and he knew he was at terrible odds with the army's high command. Wilson was glad enough to see him go, reporting that "his excellency Acting Rear-Admiral Commodore Smith left to-day for a more salubrious climate, very sick." But the glee that accompanied getting rid of Smith turned to more horror as Lieutenant Commander Foster immediately reported his intent to withdraw his forces from the Delta. Wilson protested. Ross waffled but finally agreed, first intending to stay, although all soon saw that without the gunboats the army could not remain. Even Wilson termed it "childish folly" to continue on without naval support.[15]

As a result, on the morning of March 20 all began the slow trek upstream on the Tallahatchie toward the brutal path through the Yazoo Pass, prompting Loring to report "thus was conducted the battle of the Tallahatchie." The intervening days had convinced everyone but Wilson that it was time to get out; no land approach could be had, the gunboats were battered and nearly out of ammunition, and the promised reinforcements were nowhere in sight. A distraught Wilson, reporting to Grant that the only way to win was with navy commanders who would charge head-first up to the fort to batter it with gunboats, nevertheless began dismantling the land battery and preparing for the return trip. "We have thrown away a magnificent chance to injure the enemy," he wrote, all because of the navy's incompetence: "It's provoking beyond measure to think that everything we undertake must be marred by incompetency and stupidity! I am intensely disgusted to-night." He later added, "I can't begin to give you an idea of my disgust."[16]

But there was need to be careful even in withdrawing, as the Confederates were diligent to follow up. Some at the fort itself went out and got all they could from the abandoned Union camps, causing some trouble for one Confederate who fell in the river; about the only help he received was unappreciated advice from the shore to "put our money in our mouth for it might get wet." The commanders were also quick about pushing cavalry to the banks, trying to harass the transports as best they could. Loring and the district commander in northern Mississippi, James Chalmers, worked to stalk the Federals on their retreat, using the cavalry of Colonel Bob McCullough as well as James Z. George's State Troops. There was a real fear among the Federals that barges or vessels moving down the Tallahatchie from Panola could intercept or at least tamper with the flotilla, and indeed Loring had ordered cavalry to harass as much as possible and also for Confederates in the upper Delta "to have round rafts made and floated down the river into fleet, covered with burning cotton." One Confederate even filled a flatboat with highly flammable "pine knots" to light and send among the wooden Union vessels. None made a major difference, but Loring was able to inform Pemberton that "the enemy have commenced a precipitate retreat up the Tallahatchie, abandoning the position of their land batteries. I have ordered pursuit upon their rear and both flanks." He followed up later: "Enemy in full run, as fast as steam can carry him, and my men after him." Pemberton was elated, writing Davis that "I think they will not return."[17]

Unknown to almost all on either side down near the fort at Greenwood, however, more Federals were on the way. Quinby had left Helena back earlier on March 14 and made the grueling trip through the pass in three days with one of his brigades, "moving slowly all day from one tree to the other, backing up nearly as often as going ahead," one artilleryman explained. The officers of this next wave again called on James Alcorn before entering the Coldwater River on March 17. They met other Mississippians as well, one Illinoisan describing a planter who "pretended to be a Union man but I think he would be Secesh if there was any of them around." The narrow pass attracted a lot of attention, one Illinoisan writing that "it is so narrow that the boats would drag on boath cides," and that did not even take into account the trees. "It was awful," one Indianan wrote; "did not see land all day." The steamers became separated and the lead vessel, *Prima Donna*, had to await the others catching up. Missourian Joel Strong wrote of the ordeal how "every stanchion on both sides was knocked out by sweeping against obstacles, and only those at the bow and stern were left standing. Some of the troops, who were quartered on the hurricane deck, had to vacate for fear it might be swept away, as sometimes the boat would suddenly strike an obstacle and be brought to a complete stop." Others reported hitting snags and breaking rudders, wheelhouses, and other critical parts of the steamers, one captain declaring he would "take us to Coldwater or sink before dark." A Missourian explained how "we went tearing and smashing boats saplins and other timber at a woful rate," and a Federal on the *J. S. Pringle* explained the "hurricane deck stove in from the trees." An Illinoisan added that "it was very exciting[;] the limbs of trees would strike across the steamer and we had to run from one side to the other to keep from being brushed into the water." The overflowed banks were confusing as well, he adding that "the stream was so very crooked and made such short bends that the steamer would run out into the timber, then they would take long rope and run back and tie to a tree and pull the steamer back into the channel by winding the capstan." Accordingly, the boats would stop each night, and "the boys would scatter on shore" from the several boats guarded by cavalry sent ashore from Helena. One Illinoisan marveled that they could see steamers across the bends one evening, and that was exactly where they stopped the next night; the steamers in sight were a full day ahead of them. Unfortunately, some died along the way and were buried on the banks where dry ground could be found.[18]

Quinby in the meantime wrote a memo stating that, if much of this was to take place, he would recommend the construction of flatboats that could navigate the pass much easier and safer than steamers. He thought twenty or so flatboats a hundred and twenty feet long and fifty feet wide pulled by tugs could get through the pass in a day, whereas it took three days for steamers. Fortunately, Quinby received some advance news about Ross's expedition when the mailboat *Carl* arrived from Fort Pemberton, bearing news of what was occurring deeper in the Delta. Quinby eventually passed the gunboat *Petral* on station at the mouth of the Coldwater River and soon reached the Tallahatchie River.[19]

But whether the Yazoo Pass effort, even with reinforcements, would prove worthwhile was still to be determined, although if Grant had anything to say about it the operations on the Tallahatchie would take a back seat. As he wrote on March 17, he had yet another project in the works: "The necessity of a large force descending the Yazoo, I think, has ended by the discovery of a route into the Yazoo from here by the way of Steele's Bayou and other cross bayous."[20]

While the effort at Yazoo Pass was sputtering to a standstill and even reversal, Grant saw another opportunity and took it. One of his engineers admitted that Grant "was always ready to listen to anyone who would talk sense and was ready to try any scheme that promised a grain of success." This possibility, also on the east side of the Mississippi River, had the chance of doing the same basic thing the Yazoo Pass operation was doing: positioning troops on the high ground around Vicksburg on the east side of the Mississippi River. Grant, in fact, notified Washington that the goal was "to find a practicable passage to the Yazoo River without passing the enemy's batteries at Haynes' Bluff, . . . to enable me to land most of my forces east of the Yazoo, at some point from which Haynes' Bluff and Vicksburg could be reached by high land." But like the other expedition, this one involved a roundabout path that was as restrictive, if not more so, than the Yazoo Pass route. But Grant saw great possibilities, not only to put troops ashore on the high ground but also to get forces in between Vicksburg and the Confederates at Fort Pemberton.

If the Federals managed to get gunboats and infantry in the Yazoo River south of Yazoo City, it would cut off all the Confederate shipping in the Yazoo as well as the defenders at Greenwood; Grant informed Quinby, even then going into the Delta to support Ross at Fort Pemberton: "I cannot promise success to this expedition, but it is probable that, if it does get through, such consternation will be created among the inhabitants and the troops on the Yazoo that you will hear of it." Grant even declared the plan "perfectly practicable" and foresaw a time when success would "justify me in sending all available forces through by that route." It was a chance Grant had to take.[21]

The idea actually came from Admiral Porter, who later admitted: "I really do believe I thought I was sure of getting in the rear of Vicksburg." On a tip from a contraband, he had scouted up Steele's Bayou in mid-March with Lieutenant John M. Murphy of the *Carondelet*, finding after he swapped to a smaller tug, the *Jessie Benton*, that it was mostly navigable well northward into the Delta despite calling it "at low stages of water nothing but a ditch." It was indeed narrow, but it was deep, with "5 fathoms of water in it." He also found that there was a convoluted route through connecting bayous over to the Sunflower River, which was navigable and fed into the Yazoo River between Yazoo City and Haynes' Bluff. The route led through Black Bayou to Deer Creek, which presented a choice to Porter, as he could go south on Deer Creek and come out at Haynes' Bluff or go north to Rolling Fork and pass over that waterway into the Sunflower River and come out on the Yazoo much farther up from Haynes' Bluff. It was understood that it was better not to tamper with Haynes' Bluff while debouching into the Yazoo, so the northern Rolling Fork option was preferable. Grant had no preference, simply telling Sherman the overall goal was "determining the feasibility of getting an army through that route to the east bank of that river [Yazoo], and at a point from which they can act advantageously against Vicksburg."[22]

Porter liked the possibilities so much that he informed Grant of the route; both then explored northward along Steele's Bayou with five of the City-class ironclads, all Porter had with him since the *Baron de Kalb* was at Greenwood with the Yazoo Pass expedition and the *Cairo* was still in her Yazoo River grave. Porter and Grant explored the bayou on March 15 on the tinclad *General Price*, Grant going around thirty miles up in "a large gunboat, preceded by four of the old 'turtles.'" One ironclad, the *Louisville*, was left behind to guard the route and would catch up later. The thirty miles to Black Bayou was far enough for Grant to be convinced that this was certainly doable. He returned that evening while Porter stopped for the night just short of Black Bayou, Grant ordering Sherman to put David Stuart's division, including at least one section of artillery, in motion while he gave Porter the go-ahead and

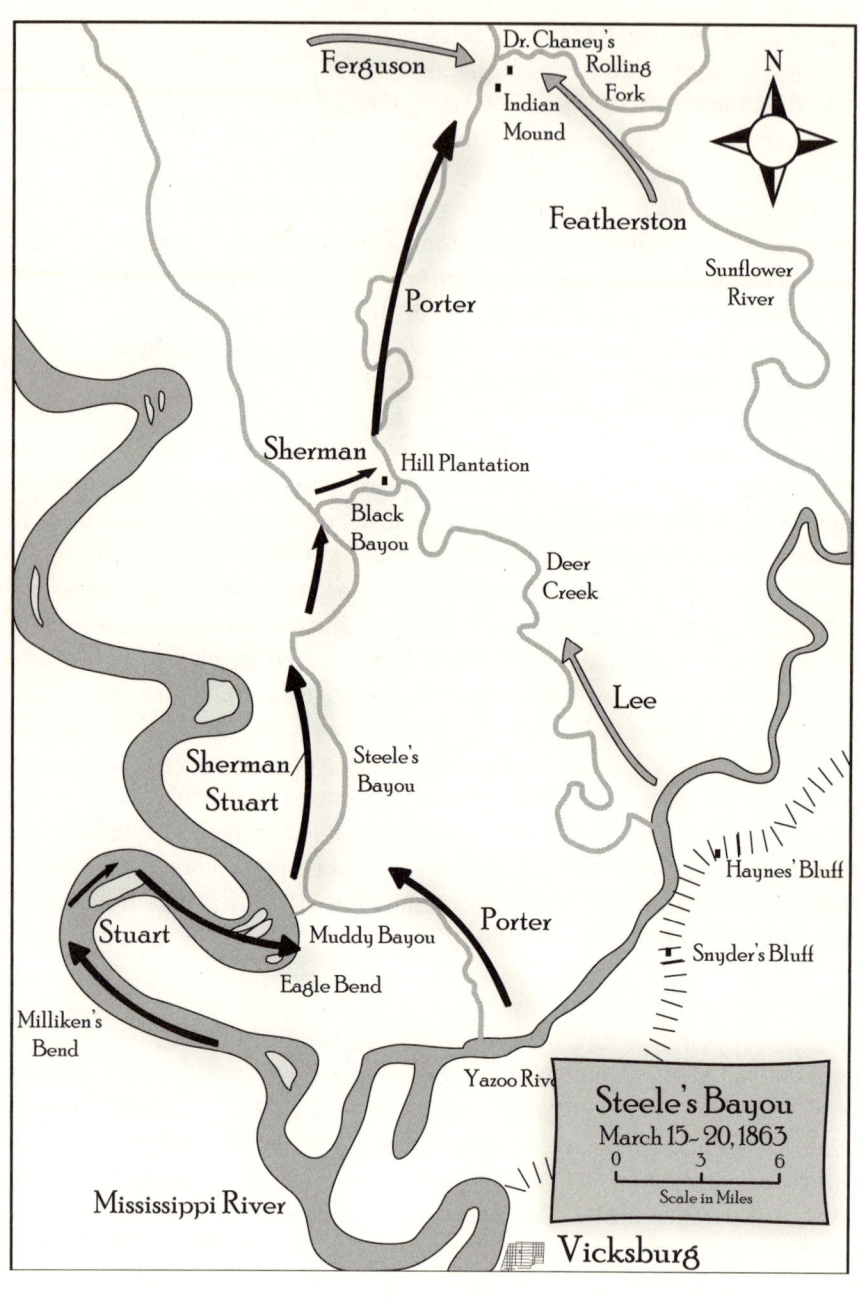

assured him Sherman's XV corps would be along to help. Porter, anxious to get on with the advance knowing time was of the essence, just as in the Yazoo Pass effort, pushed on forward in his "expedition into the enemy's country." But soon the vessels began to hit trees as the bayou narrowed and the trees converged even more. One officer on the *Cincinnati* related that "our decks are covered with limbs broken from trees by the pressure of our boats in crushing their way along." He added that the flagstaff was also broken. Pushing forward soon became a real chore. Newspaper correspondent Sylvanus Cadwallader, tagging along, reported that "in many instances great notches from one to two feet deep had to be cut into cypress trees on each side of boats to allow the guard rails to slide through."[23]

Knowing the transports that followed later would have a much harder time, Grant also sent in a working party on the *Diligent* and *Silver Wave*, the former with the 8th Missouri ("being many of them boatmen") to push on to Black Bayou to open that route while the *Silver Wave* and its troops cleared the other stretches of Steele's Bayou. Those who did not make the trek watched as the Missouri regiment shoved off, one Illinoisan explaining that "there is something up on the Yazoo." Grant assured Sherman that little work was needed in this manner, simply to cut out a tunnel through the thick trees overhanging the bayou. Most of the work would need to be done in the first few miles of Black Bayou: "There is but little work to be done in Steele's Bayou, except for about 5 miles midway up the bayou. In this portion many overhanging trees will have to be removed, and should be dragged out of the channel." Grant also sent an engineer to oversee the work, Captain William Kossak. To make it easier on the following troops themselves, Grant ordered Sherman to send his brigades to Confederate senator William M. Gwin's plantation at Eagle Bend on the Mississippi River, where Steele's Bayou approached within a mile or so; there was also a connecting bayou, Muddy Bayou, although a lot of work had to be done to open the road on the bank across its mile-long extent; one Federal complained that there was "much delay and disappointment in consequence of misapprehension of Gen. Grant, supposing the crossing from Mississippi River could be made on dry land 1 mile." The 47th Ohio led in the effort to build the road and to bridge some of the gaps in the levee, and one soldier was impressed that "no grumbling is heard, as our officers, including General Stewart [Stuart], are wading in too, and working with good will." Grant himself came up on March 18 on his headquarters boat *Magnolia* and crossed over to Steele's Bayou to see the area himself.[24]

By this time Sherman's forward troops were at work, with detailed instructions to the crews on both the *Diligent* and *Silver Wave*. Steele's Bayou was "now full and deep," he related, and he wanted all trees overhanging the bayou cut "for the navigation of steamboats of ordinary size and draught." He reminded the *Silver Wave* detachment that "Admiral Porter has already passed through this bayou, and is now at a point beyond, working his way through to the Yazoo, and it is of vast importance that this part of the channel be cleared as fast as possible; therefore use all dispatch." Sherman sent similar orders to the *Diligent* and her onboard Missourians, telling them to enter Steele's Bayou across from Walter Johnson's Plantation, "where we landed on the 26th of December last." He told Lieutenant Colonel David C. Coleman commanding the 8th Missouri to also take ropes and "a keg of spikes" so he could make rafts "on which the men are to stand whilst cutting away the tree tops." Soon, Sherman's advance troops were in position and clearing out the channels for the rest of the division to move forward on their transports.[25]

Porter moved forward slowly in the ensuing days, he in the lead ironclad *Cincinnati* ramming trees and bridges alike to move them out of the way, slowly moving his ironclads through the choking bayou by force. One sailor related that at one point the flotilla "came to a forest of very large trees—old monarchs of the woods—whose branches were so dense that a ray of sun rarely penetrated them. Here the line of battle was broken. The boats could not squeeze through the trees, and as a last resort the experiment of ramming them down with the heavy ironclads was tried and proved successful. In the thoroughly soaked earth the roots gave way and the boats butted their way through." But it was at the expense of the tree-dwellers. The same sailor wrote that "the animals of the forest that could climb had taken refuge in the immense trees as their only arks of safety. Coons, wild cats, mice and reptiles were everywhere seen clinging to the limbs overhead and looking down in apparent wonder and alarm at the singular intrusion." He added: "Sometimes rat, mice, squirrels, lizards and snakes would fall upon the decks or upon the head of some luckless sailor who was trying to keep the decks clear and dodge the falling limbs at the same time. An old gray coon fell upon the deck, and although stunned by the fall recovered himself and fought his way overboard."[26]

Porter reached Black Bayou by March 17, its water dark and murky— "properly named," said one Illinoisan. Another Federal explained that "the water here is as black as a wicked man's heart, or my boots." The going was not too difficult for the ironclads, which were sturdy and could push away driftwood and limbs and even large trees with no great damage, although more effort was needed to push through Black Bayou because of the overhanging trees. "The boats crawl along the narrow bayous," one Federal explained, "tearing up the dirt and pushing over trees." One surgeon explained that "our men are stationed forward, pushing our boat's bows off from the timber as we proceed. Our deck is covered with twigs and limbs swept off from trees and bushes as we pass them." Porter likened it to "cutting our way through the woods (which are all under water)." The turns in Black Bayou were also shorter for the long gunboats, and he admitted that "we found that by removing the trees we could heave the vessels around the bends, which were very short and left us not a foot to spare." While the ironclads made it fairly well, one officer still noting that "the trees meet over our heads, and there is great danger of knocking down the chimneys at every revolution of our wheels," there were tense moments. The same officer noted that several ironclads became stuck: "Have several times pushed out the *Carondelet* when wedged fast between trees."[27]

But all this advance was not done in a vacuum, and the Confederates at Vicksburg and up the Yazoo River toward Haynes' Bluff quickly picked up on the movement. Scouts in that area under Colonel Samuel W. Ferguson, as well as some civilians, soon brought in news of a major Federal movement, and the overall Confederate commander in the area, Carter Stevenson in Vicksburg, had remarkably good knowledge of the Union components: "The expedition consisted of five iron-clad boats, three armed sternwheel boats, four transports, three tugs, and nine barges, all heavily laden with troops." He added that "the importance attached to it by the enemy may be estimated by the fact that the boats were commanded by Acting Rear-Admiral Porter and the troops by General Sherman." Despite being what Dabney Maury explained as a "vigilant and daring young officer," Ferguson initially laughed at the preposterous idea, but soon he found out it was for real. In response, Stevenson in no time had three columns, though mostly uncoordinated, moving against the threat.[28]

Already operating in the Deer Creek area, although farther up toward Greenville, was Ferguson's cavalry and artillery, fresh off their tangle with Stephen Burbridge back in February. He was now augmented by a battalion of infantry under Captain John H. Morgan, some two hundred and fifty men arriving on a steamer. Now with Federals approaching the rich area from the south, Ferguson sent the cavalry and artillery overland and moved in that direction with the infantry battalion on the steamboat and was the first to respond, actually arriving at Rolling Fork on March 19, prior to the Federals. Ferguson took quick stock and pronounced the situation "gloomy enough," although he reported that he "will make every effort to hold the enemy in check long enough for re-enforcements to reach me." He accordingly began the obstruction of Deer Creek and Rolling Fork, although he had a hard time getting troops in position, especially his artillery "over the bad portion of the road, yesterday deemed impassable." Ferguson first concentrated on Rolling Fork, creating an obstruction so that by the next day there was "already enough ... done to detain the boats two or three days," and he also started working some on Deer Creek near Rolling Fork's mouth. Porter and his ironclads would soon meet the results of the indefatigable Ferguson's work, Maury writing of Ferguson that "his only fear has been lest the enemy should escape."[29]

While Ferguson was already on site and at work, Stevenson was sending reinforcements as fast as they could get there. He ordered his right-flank commander at Haynes' Bluff to send troops, and Dabney Maury ordered Brigadier General Winfield S. Featherston to head northward immediately with a portion of his brigade. It was not a ringing endorsement when Pemberton informed Loring that Featherston was sent: "It is hoped and believed that General Featherston will act with energy and judgment." Featherston had with him two regiments, the 22nd and 33rd Mississippi, along with a section of an artillery battery, and these troops moved by boat up the Yazoo and Sunflower Rivers and part of the way up Rolling Fork to a point where they could land amid the overflowed countryside. Once Featherston arrived at Deer Creek on March 20, he of course met Ferguson and worked out the details, taking command as the senior officer; Ferguson kept his own command under him, while Featherston gave the infantry command to Colonel D. W. Hurst of the 33rd Mississippi, he taking charge of the whole. But because of Ferguson's work in obstructing Rolling Fork, Featherston's men could not reach solid ground and had to "march through water three quarters of a mile before reaching land."[30]

There was a third column moving as well, that under Brigadier General Stephen D. Lee, also from the Vicksburg area. Lee of course had been the commander at Chickasaw Bayou back in December, and now he requested to be allowed to lead a force up Deer Creek from its mouth on the Yazoo. As the Federals had an option of moving up Deer Creek to Rolling Fork and then into the Sunflower or straight down Deer Creek to the Yazoo River, this passage had to be guarded as well, although it also was largely underwater at the time. Lee took his troops and nevertheless began to work his way northward along Deer Creek, the men at times poling the boats forward. William Pitt Chambers of the 46th Mississippi related in his diary that "after a great deal of bumping and thumping to the imminent danger of our smoke stacks, scape pipes and Jack-staff of the steamer as well as the hats of those of us who were on the hurricane deck, we debarked at the plantation." By March 20, all Confederate columns were converging on Deer Creek, particularly the stretch between Black Bayou and Rolling Fork, along Hill's and Fore's Plantations.[31]

The Federals were consequently moving into a litany of Confederate commands. Yet as the supporting troops gathered at Eagle Bend, Porter unwisely pushed on into this swelling Confederate vortex, stopping each night and sending out pickets for security. "We are having a fine time, pioneering these inland brooks with our heavy gunboats," one of the Federals explained sarcastically. After moving the twenty-eight miles on Steele's Bayou from Eagle Bend to Black Bayou, Porter entered Black Bayou by March 17, a narrow channel but passable. Soon, he reached the J. C. Hill Plantation another four and a half miles forward where the bayou joined Deer Creek, although one Federal mistook it for Confederate general A. P. Hill's plantation. It would then simply be a few miles to make the run up Deer Creek and across the ample waters of Rolling Fork until Porter would be in free water, able to use the easily navigable Sunflower River to get to the Yazoo. It was at Hill's Plantation, Hill himself absent and the slaves "in charge of the place," that Sherman reached the flotilla by running up Steele's Bayou in the *Black Hawk* and then through Black Bayou in the tug *Fern*. He set up his headquarters at the plantation. It was the first solid ground he had come across since leaving the Yazoo, almost all the land along Steele's Bayou and Black Bayou being underwater, and the little that was not along Black Bayou was thick with cane and forest. And even Hill's Plantation was "not more than 3 feet above water, and is the same kind of ground we have on the Mississippi."[32]

After Porter and Sherman explored three or four miles up Deer Creek in a tug, actually all the way to Fore's Plantation, Porter moved on with four of the ironclads up Deer Creek toward the mouth of Rolling Fork. He left the *Louisville* behind to guard the area before moving on up to rejoin the others "the moment I can get a guard through to this point," Sherman reported. Sherman sent the ironclad on ahead when the 8th Missouri disembarked to work on Black Bayou, which he described as "narrow, crooked, and filled with trees." In an effort to find a more practicable route, Sherman explored the intricate web of bayous and creeks over the next day or two but found nothing better, so he redoubled the work on opening Black Bayou.[33]

But then bigger problems emerged. At times alone at the Hill Plantation until Giles Smith's troops arrived, prompting Smith to describe him as "exposing himself beyond precedent in a commanding general," Sherman immediately began to have his doubts. He informed Grant as early as March 16 that "I don't think we can make a lodgment on high land by this route, on account of the difficulty of navigation." Deer Creek narrowed the farther north it went, and the boats had to go much slower through the less navigable creek, soon making only a mile an hour and later less than that; plus, falling limbs wounded crewmen on deck. Sherman related that it was "not as large nor has it as much current as I expected, but the water is deep and narrow." One of the sailors admitted, "Had anyone have told me that these mud turtles (gunboats) would have climbed trees I would have thought him crazy, but I have seen it and must believe it." Sherman went so far as to advise Grant that taking Haynes' Bluff would have to be done by regular transports "directly up the main Yazoo." Still, he added, "I will push the work."[34]

And he did. Fortunately, the Missourians aboard the *Diligent* were hard at work clearing the path mainly through Black Bayou, Sherman reporting that "the iron-clads push their way along unharmed, but the trees and overhanging limbs tear the wooden boats all to pieces." The Missourians had to work their way through on rafts pulled by tugs "whilst cutting trees," and the tugs took a beating as rudders broke and smokestacks came toppling down from contact with tree limbs. But that freed up the *Diligent* to return and bring forward another regiment, which it did. Better yet, after Sherman returned to Eagle Bend himself on March 20, he brought back two more transports, the *Silver Wave* and *Eagle* with the 6th Missouri and 116th Illinois. These vessels deposited the regiments and again moved southward to bring up even more troops that were gathering at Eagle Bend.[35]

The sight was nevertheless ludicrous, but not as much to the Federals as was the entire operation to the local civilians and their slaves. "The inhabitants looked on in wonder and astonishment," Porter related, "and the negroes flocked in hundreds down to the banks of the creek to see the novel sight." The reactions were endless but mainly included some form of "Glory to de good Lord" or "Bress de Lord." Despite parties of Federals foraging freely, the slaves also sold the Federals turkeys and chickens and traded for tobacco. One soldier noted, "You may bet your bottom dollar old Co. G don't starve where anything is running around hunting an owner." The same soldier told of a comrade who, among others chasing a pig, was in the right place at the right time as the pig leaped over his head at the bank of a levee: he "threw his arms around piggy in a loving embrace, and down to the bottom they rolled together." The man later declared he could "catch pigs or dig a ditch with any man in the army." As soon as the Confederate government agents in the area learned of the enemy presence, they set fire to the cotton nearby, which added a pall of smoke to the odd scene. Many dwellings caught fire as well, both from purposeful Federal sabotage as well as Confederates burning cotton, leading to "many remarks made not at all complimentary to the Confederate Government." Porter was just as amazed, later writing that, "as to the ironclads themselves, I beg to withdraw everything I may have said to their disparagement, for I never yet saw vessels so well adapted to knocking down trees, hauling them up by the roots, or demolishing bridges."[36]

The expedition was consequently making progress as the infantry played catchup to the navy, which was miles farther forward. But the gap between the two, and between Sherman and Porter, was real, the winding Deer Creek needing thirty-two miles of turns to get to Rolling Fork while the nearby straighter road was a mere twelve miles. But the mileage did not matter if Sherman's troops were not there to march, and meanwhile Porter found out just how lonely it was for his gunboats to be without infantry protection. Hearing the Confederates were cutting trees into the creek ahead of them, often using the "negroes, with muskets at their breasts," Porter sent Lieutenant John M. Murphy on the tug *Thistle*, armed with a boat howitzer, on ahead to find out what was happening while he slowly followed with the ironclads. The news was not good as crews began clearing the obstructions, Porter admonishing that "there is nothing that can not be overcome by perseverance." That was a statement the now converging Confederates would question as much as possible.[37]

"There is evident indication of considerable excitement in Vicksburg," Grant informed Halleck on March 17, right in the middle of both the Yazoo Pass and Steele's Bayou expeditions. And indeed there was, rumors swirling about frequently, and at more than just Vicksburg where one Tennessean informed his wife that a battle was expected daily. At department headquarters in Jackson, John Pemberton was certainly feeling the effects of all these Union movements seemingly coming at him from every direction. To the west, the enemy was still working on the canal and the even wider loop of Lake Providence to get vessels and probably troops south of Vicksburg. On the river itself, possibly as an indicator of just how badly those efforts were going, the Union navy continually sent gunboats past the river batteries, and more were coming up from below Port Hudson as well. East of the river was where the bigger problems lay, the enemy coming down not only the Tallahatchie River to the Yazoo but now also moving through the lower Delta with several ironclads and troops to reach the Yazoo River. There were even raids down in Louisiana near Ponchatoula. No wonder Pemberton confided in late March that "the enemy press me on all sides."[38]

All these efforts convinced the Confederates that "Grant was in deep earnest, and not easily discouraged." But about all Pemberton could do was to keep up what he was already doing: shifting his meager number of troops around to meet the greatest and most recent threats and call on neighboring departments and Richmond for more of everything from troops to guns to supplies. It had worked remarkably well so far, probably less a testament to

Pemberton's brilliance than to the tough geographical situation an advancing enemy faced. But Pemberton had thus far performed credibly. Even Joseph E. Johnston realized as much from Middle Tennessee, where he officially moved his headquarters in March, writing that "your activity and vigor in the defense of the Mississippi must have secured for you the confidence of the people of the State; that of the Government you have previously won." But Pemberton had to continue that close-run defense.[39]

Yet changes were coming, and that was not a good sign for Pemberton. As long as the enemy continued their far-flung efforts, hundreds of miles away from Vicksburg, it gave the Confederates time to react, something the habitually indecisive Pemberton needed. But now it seemed these expeditions were beginning to be waged ever closer to Vicksburg, cutting down on the reaction time Pemberton had. In fact, the response to the Steele's Bayou incursion came only when Porter was well up into the Delta, and Ferguson and Featherston barely got ahead of the gunboats as it was. Carter Stevenson realized as much (though Loring logically differed), writing Pemberton that "the route by which the Deer Creek expedition is to proceed is so much shorter than any other that I regard it as by far the most important movement that the enemy are making against us." Worse, the Mississippi River now seemed to have crested and was beginning to fall, reported as dropping three-quarters of an inch in twenty-four hours on March 19. If the river fell and the drying of spring came quickly, it would provide the enemy innumerably more choices about how to get to Vicksburg.[40]

Pemberton would have to worry about that when it came, because there were enough troubles for now. The still-high waters aided his defense in some ways but hampered it in others; one Alabamian wrote home that "our pickets are compelled to fall back from the swamp on account of the back water. They had to wade waste deep on yesterday to get to their post." As a result, Pemberton methodically continued to oversee the shifting of guns and troops wherever they were needed most, acting through his major generals who commanded the various garrisons on his basic line of defense. Carter Stevenson was of course the ranking general under him and commanded at Vicksburg, including the defenses all the way down at Warrenton up through Vicksburg itself and its guns and on up the Walnut Hills to Snyder's and Haynes' Bluffs. Troops under Martin Smith and Dabney Maury reported to him directly. This basic line that had been held all winter was extended on each end during this spring, however, as the Federals appeared in Yazoo Pass as well as below Vicksburg on the river. Pemberton had sent Loring to Greenwood to coordinate the defense of the upper Delta and the Yazoo River. Likewise, he had sent John Bowen, soon detached from Stevenson's command because of distance much like Loring at Greenwood, to Grand Gulf to establish the defense there and to try to halt Union naval movement, especially with the canal looking like it might be ready any day now. Of course, the trouble was that these detached posts at Grand Gulf and Fort Pemberton could be cut off and destroyed if the Federals moved between them and the main defense from Haynes' Bluff down to Warrenton. There was plenty of space for them to do it, and in fact that was one of the intentions of the expedition through Steele's Bayou.[41]

Consequently, Pemberton advised a careful watch on all approaches, especially to the extended garrisons that were detached. At Grand Gulf, John Bowen not only had to watch the riverfront; Pemberton also continually demanded he be careful of Bayou Pierre to his south as well as the Big Black River to his north, even placing guns on the Big Black to stop Federals from using it to get in Bowen's and, more important, Vicksburg's rear. He even ordered a raft built on the river, much like those on the Yazoo and Tallahatchie. Fortunately, "five heavy guns" arrived on March 20, although Bowen's command was woefully provisioned. Still, using slaves from the area alongside his troops, he erected the guns, placed firewood on the riverbank opposite to illuminate any enemy passage at night, and set up signal scouts across the river at Hard Times to allow for warning of an approach. He also built a furnace for heating shot, although he only had shell to fire, which he planned to fill with "clay or brick dust." But Bowen still faced big odds, including Admiral Farragut and his big-gunned *Hartford*, which was prowling north of Port Hudson; the reports from the mouth of the Red River and Natchez indicated throughout mid-March that he was progressing northward. Pemberton accordingly advised to "mount heavy guns as rapidly as possible." Bowen admitted, "I am satisfied that if they attempt a bombardment they will be sorry for it, but fear they may be able to run by without material damage or injury."[42]

The recent movement up Steele's Bayou caused the same concern for Loring, and Pemberton obviously sent troops under Featherston and Lee to counter that threat as well, Stevenson in Vicksburg declaring that "this is without doubt regarded the important expedition." Pemberton ordered all vessels on the Delta rivers to move southward "between our batteries at Snyder's and Haynes' Bluff, where they will be safe." Despite citizens of the area assuring Pemberton that the route was "absolutely impracticable," it was a tense time as he watched from his headquarters at Jackson while the Federals plodded along, he having little else to send to repel them if he was to keep the rest of the line safe as well. Still, later in March Pemberton decided that the northern area was the weakest link in his defenses and had to be held if other places were less safe. As a result, he began to send additional ammunition, guns, and troops to both Rolling Fork as well as Fort Pemberton, where more troops were reported moving through the pass. "I will endeavor to send up another 8-inch or 42-pounder, but it will take time," Pemberton informed Loring on March 16 even as the latter faced the renewed Union attack. About all he could do now was to shift the two cottonclad gunboats *Magenta* and *Mobile* under Captain Isaac Brown of the navy back and forth from Deer Creek to Fort Pemberton as needed. With the Federals soon gone from Fort Pemberton, it seemed the boats were no longer required there, so Pemberton ordered them, as well as other assets, southward. He hoped they would meet and board the Union ironclads, cautioning Loring that with the Steele's Bayou effort he had no other resources for him: "You must hold the position you have selected."[43]

Yet still concerning amid all the other threats were the operations around Vicksburg itself, including the canal where dredging boats were plainly working. Batteries could reach a portion of the canal's length on the southern end and kept the dredges away, prompting one Confederate to feel sorry for the "poor, deluded, ignorant, minions of old 'Abe.'" But work continued despite the contrabands running away every time a shell approached. "Come back you black curs and go to work," the Federal officers would shout, the contrabands crying, "Massa dye kill us all shuah." It was indeed nerve-racking when Confederate shells landed amid the workers, knocking over planks, wheelbarrows, and other tools. Yet there was some sort of movement across the river northward as well, Stevenson reporting that "close observation with the telescope for the last two days confirms the report." Pemberton told Stevenson if true to be prepared to send some of his troops, no longer necessary there in such numbers, up to where they were actually needed. The enemy navy's actions were also a concern, Stevenson reporting that "I think that Farragut is waiting for an interview with Porter, with the view of running some of his iron-clads past." Grant of course was doing the same thing, using any good day to get as close to Vicksburg on a tug as possible to "observe all that can be seen."[44]

All the while, Pemberton kept his peers and superiors calm about the situation in Mississippi. He alerted Kirby Smith and Richard Taylor in the trans-Mississippi that he had commandeered the guns being sent to them: "The heavy guns sent for by you have been detained by me, and I shall be compelled to retain them. . . . I have been compelled to establish several new batteries to meet the enemy in his several different approaches, and these transfers have by so much weakened the defense of Vicksburg. The holding of this place, you are aware, is as important to you as to myself."[45]

Johnston was concerned but remained fairly oblivious to the situation, being more anxious about Middle Tennessee and sometimes lobbing generic advice on specific placements of troops. In fact, some of the problems in Mississippi were his doing, such as sending Earl Van Dorn to Braxton Bragg's army at Tullahoma. Pemberton needed additional cavalry, particularly in northern Mississippi "to protect the planters in putting in their crops," and he had none to send. He queried Johnston if Van Dorn's movement was a permanent separation from his department, adding that "it very much diminishes my ability to defend the northern portion of the State." Johnston replied that it was not, no more so in fact than Stevenson's separation from Bragg's army. It was not news Pemberton needed to hear, that a large part of his infantry defending Vicksburg could conceivably be sent back to Tennessee at any moment. Specifically, about the cavalry, Johnston told Pemberton that Governor John J. Pettus of Mississippi was supposed to have six thousand State Troops for that purpose. Pemberton thus had to scramble to get more cavalry, even asking Simon Bolivar Buckner down at Mobile for a regiment. He fortunately promised to send one.[46]

Pemberton also dealt with Richmond, where Davis was understandably concerned. Pemberton's frequent request for more guns brought action, the president reporting he sent four Columbiads from Alabama and two rifles from Richmond itself. He added, "[I] await further intelligence from you with great anxiety." But it is doubtful whether Davis's anxiety was any higher than Pemberton's right in the middle of it all. "The enemy is now using every effort to get possession of Vicksburg," he wrote.[47]

And that anxiety would not lessen over the coming weeks as the Federals continued their probes. "We are sending troops to meet them at every available point," an Alabamian informed his wife back home. But all the while the chessboard upon which Grant and Pemberton were playing out this campaign was growing smaller and smaller, which would benefit only one side.[48]

9

"We Intend to Take the Boats"
March 21–31

While few if any realized it, the Vicksburg Campaign was, at least theoretically, in a state of change. The first episodes of the struggle were conducted, by both sides, completely within the thinking of Henri Jomini and his ideas of maneuver, supporting columns, interior lines of communication, secure supply lines, and securing geographic points. This next phase beginning in 1863 continued much of that theory of warfare. Some components such as McClernand's Arkansas Post endeavor easily fit well within those lines, but most especially did John Pemberton's command of his Department of Mississippi and East Louisiana. The Southern commander had thwarted Grant's two advances in the fall and winter of 1862 while holding secure geographical points and well-guarded supply lines by utilizing basic tenets of Jominian warfare, including maneuvering raids on the enemy's supply lines and taking advantage of his own interior lines. Indeed, Pemberton had performed well if not spectacularly in shifting troops from one point to the other in time to thwart both Union advances. While many of the ideas that won the Mississippi Central and Chickasaw Bayou confrontations had come from subordinates, Pemberton had nevertheless implemented them; they were enough to provide the victory over the similar Jominian efforts of Ulysses S. Grant.[1]

And though many on the Federal side saw only the need to continue those same principles to eventually win the victory, change was in the offing. One Federal wrote of his thoughts: "I am anxious to get to Vicksburg and see what can be done in taking the place." But he also knew larger forces were at play: "I think there has been some news received from Gen. Grant, which is likely to change the program of our play . . . I have abiding faith and confidence that whenever Gen. Grant sees the right sign of the weather and gives the order to *charge*! We will go right in." Most important, in changing his approach somewhat, Grant ran afoul of Halleck on many issues, including Halleck continually badgering him to send vessels back northward so the armies in both Mississippi and Tennessee could be supplied—a clear dependence on Jominian-style secure supply lines. But Grant needed many of those vessels, explaining that "I found the river rising so rapidly that there was no telling what moment all hands might be driven to the boats." Halleck also reminded Grant to report on the developments more often than he was; Halleck had more military advice as well, including being very careful about these far-flung experiments:

> In operating by the Yazoo, you have, no doubt, fully considered the advantages and dangers of the expedition. Our information here on that subject is very limited and unsatisfactory. There is one point, however, which has been discussed, and to which I would particularly call your attention; it is the danger, on the fall of the water in the Mississippi, of having your steamers caught in the Upper Yazoo, so as to be unable to extricate them. In the present scarcity of steamers on the western rivers, this would be a very serious loss. Another danger is, that the enemy may concentrate a large force upon the isolated column of McPherson without your being able to assist him. I mention these matters in order that you may give them your full attention.

Halleck then went further, advising the time-tested Jominian type of warfare that he had always espoused but that Grant was turning away from:

> When the operations of an army are directed to one particular object it is always dangerous to divide forces. All accessories should be sacrificed for the sake of concentration. The great object on your line now is the opening of the Mississippi River, and everything else must tend to that purpose. The eyes and hopes of the whole country are now directed to your army. In my opinion, the opening of the Mississippi River will be to us of more advantage than the capture of forty Richmonds.

To Halleck, geographical places and secure supply lines were the definite way to go.[2]

But Grant was on the ground and could see the need to change the way he was conducting this Mississippi Valley warfare. Securing geographical supply lines and moving in tandem were not always an option, and Grant had consequently begun to implement against-the-book operations such as cutting canals to divert rivers, flooding vast stretches of countryside, and clearing and steaming through jungle wildernesses on roundabout routes to get where he needed to go. "Troops are moving around us in all directions," one of his officers accurately explained. Obviously, these were not tenets of Jominian theory, and were even diametrically opposed as to supply and logistical concerns, but Grant saw no other recourse and thus began to change his way of doing things.[3]

John Pemberton never made any similar change and would actually continue to command along the age-old and proven techniques of Jominian warfare. Accordingly, the Vicksburg Campaign was shaping up to be a gargantuan struggle between old and new ways of fighting, ultimately between the old Jominian and the new (to Americans) Clausewitzian manner of operating, which actually had not even arrived in full form. It would be a study in contrasts. But who would come out victorious was still anyone's guess as late March arrived in the wilderness of the Mississippi Delta.

By the third rainy week in March, the river was still high and more water flowed from the heavens. Diarist Kate Stone near her Louisiana plantation noted "storms and rain for two days. There has been almost constant rain since Christmas. The oldest inhabitants say they never saw such persistent rains. It might be the rainy season of the tropics." She had a theory, shared by many: "Some think the cannonading at Vicksburg brings on the rains. It is seldom we hear the cannon that it is not succeeded by showers or a downpour, and often it is difficult to distinguish between the burst of thunder and the roar of the guns." Yet it was fortunate that the temperature was warmer, Major Luther Cowan of the 45th Illinois describing his boys "running around barefoot in their underwear. Swimming in the river like frogs."[4]

Despite the rain, it seemed readily apparent to everyone involved that the Yazoo Pass expedition was over and defeat had been declared. That was apparent to everyone except Isaac F. Quinby, that is, who was on his way southward through the pass. A classmate of Grant's at West Point who later became a college professor, Quinby wanted nothing more than to please his old friend and produce the stellar hammer blow that would bring Vicksburg to the Union. That could not be done by retreating, however, and Quinby was in no mood to do so. He wanted to push forward, not letting one little fort along a nearly submerged landscape stop the march on Vicksburg. Colonel James Slack wrote home that Quinby was "determined to take this rebel strong hold."[5]

Accordingly, a major surprise resulted around noon on March 21, when Foster's withdrawing flotilla and Ross's troops spied more vessels looming upriver in the Tallahatchie. It was Quinby with the lead brigade of his division coming to reinforce the expedition. In actuality, it was also a surprise to Quinby. "What we will do now I can't say," one Federal wrote home of the development.[6]

In addition to reinforcing Ross, Quinby also came to take command, and he had his mind made up, solidified by Wilson, on returning and giving the effort another try. But he had to convince the commanders to return with him, many of whose nerves were already frayed in Ross's column as well as his own from the harrowing trip through the pass; many of these frayed nerves spawned arguments between navy and army, even between pilots and crews on the transports. Quinby could order Ross, of course, which he did, naval commander Foster writing that Ross simply "remains quiet" on the issue of returning. But Quinby had to ask the navy nicely. He wrote Foster, "in view of the depressing effect which a virtual abandonment of the Yazoo expedition would have upon our army, our navy, and our country, I most earnestly request you to return with your fleet, notwithstanding its disabled condition, to your former position above Fort Greenwood." He continued: "I ask this in the hope that by land operations we may accomplish the reduction of the fort, and in the belief that the mere moral effect of the presence of the gunboats will go far to insure our success." Ross had to obey orders, but Foster assented, and "our whole fleet was turned around and down we go again down stream," one Federal explained. However, one infantryman wrote that "judging from appearances they do not like it any too well."[7]

Quinby's combined force reached Fort Pemberton once more on the rainy afternoon of March 23, whereupon Quinby started taking stock of the situation, relating that "it is evident that they intend to make a determined stand at this point." The gunboats fired a few shells, but the Confederates did not respond. "Here we are again," wrote one exasperated Federal, "in front of the rebel army of this part of Jeff Davis' kingdom." Mother Nature also let loose, a storm pushing through and toppling several trees and limbs, killing several Federals. A Confederate was beside himself, admitting that "our rejoicing was altogether too soon, as we had hardly done crowing when, the yankee gunboats returned and opened on us again." Another cannoneer in the fort admitted: "You should have heard the triumphant shouting! It sounded as if we already had won everything. But when the Yankees came back on the 23rd of March all was as if no one could utter a sound, all was become silent."[8]

"The enemy in force with their gunboats have again made their appearance," Loring informed his commander from Fort Pemberton on March 23, "opening fire at 2.15 and immediately ceasing fire." So began the second part of the confrontation at Greenwood, where Loring and Pemberton had thought they had driven the enemy away for good. Consequently, there was a mad scramble to get ammunition, guns, and troops, in addition to the cottonclads, back up to Fort Pemberton from the Steele's Bayou area. But the ensuing days brought only confusion, as the Federals did little to nothing except bide their time. Obviously, the rain that fell in torrents during those days made travel on land impossible, and the gunboats were in no condition to test the fort anymore. Consequently, the days were spent with Quinby and Ross exploring any avenue by which Fort Pemberton could be neutralized, they waiting for the rain to stop and the roads to dry out to begin any movements. But first they had to find a way; some marveled at the numerous Indian mounds in the area and wondered why they were not used for artillery.[9]

Ross and Quinby meanwhile went to the again-manned land battery and watched, but they saw little movement in the fort. Quinby ultimately realized that there was little a land force could do due to the "present stage of the water." Still, land forces went as far forward as they could until they reached the vast bayou in front of the Confederate position, where periodic skirmishing took place and at times some conversing; one Mississippian wrote of encountering a few Federals less than a hundred yards away: "Very good naturedly, they did not shoot me." The Federals seemed more afraid of the numerous snakes than the Confederates: "The mosquitoes, gnats, flies, insects and reptiles are in abundance; snakes a common thing," one explained. Scouting on the east bank provided more hope, Quinby evidently influenced by Wilson, who had already determined this might be the best way to succeed. Quinby quickly reported that moving across the Tallahatchie between the fort and the mouth of the Yalobusha River would put land forces in rear of the Confederate garrison. Meanwhile, as the lines stretched all the way eastward to Point Leflore where the Yalobusha and Tallahatchie joined to create the Yazoo, Confederates of the 35th Mississippi conversed easily with their counterparts across the river: "Our pickets meet the Yank pickets and talk. They propose to trade whiskey & coffee for tobacco, so you see that the pickets are friendly." In one instance, an Illinoisan related that the Confederate pickets wanted their counterparts to come across the river to talk, which the Federals declined. The Confederates then dropped their weapons and began to come across to the Union side, whereupon when about halfway across "our men fired into them and killed two of them." He added, "I think such acts are barbarous and should not be allowed."[10]

Quinby needed a pontoon bridge to get across the river in force, and that would take time. And he had very little of that, because Lieutenant Commander Foster soon announced that, unless he received opposing orders, he would pull out by April 1, if not before, if he heard from Admiral Porter in the meantime. That put Quinby in a bind, of course, in that he could not hope to stay safe without naval cover. He ultimately induced Foster to leave a few of the tinclads, but Foster was adamant that he was leaving. The navy's departure obviously also put the timing in jeopardy, as Quinby could in no way have his pontoon bridge on site by the first day in April. And even his plan to send the transports back to Helena to get his other two brigades in the division was put on hold because of the need to get those present aboard if he had to withdraw quickly. "It is one of the great evils of our service that the land and naval forces are left, in a great measure, independent of each other," Quinby complained.[11]

Yet as the days passed and Quinby came to a conclusion about what should be done, the Confederates countered his every move. Quinby and his staff and soldiers scouted every conceivable approach, at one point an Indianan writing that "some of the Gens aids got a close call and one lost his hat." He decided where he would cross once he got a pontoon bridge, but then the next day a Confederate fortification and battery appeared exactly there. "Every move we make is answered by one from them," Quinby grumbled. The weather did not help. He planned to emplace guns on the east bank of the river in rear of Fort Pemberton, but the rains in late March precluded almost any land travel. Delay ensued. Still, Quinby was out personally reconnoitering the possibilities, although few could tell in the Confederate lines. One Southerner wrote home that the enemy "have done nothing in the way of fighting since their return." He added that the boredom as a result was palpable: "I have come to the conclusion that soldiering is about the laziest life in the world."[12]

Unknown to Quinby, by this time Grant was having second thoughts as well. He ordered John E. Smith's division, scheduled to go into the pass, to proceed on down the river if they had not entered as yet; if they had they were to go on. Many were glad, as one Northerner described some of the boats coming out of the pass: "It is a rather hazardous undertaking from what I hear, and by the appearance of the boats that come out from the pass I should think they had been badly used; nearly all their outer works are completely torn off, from the thumps they receive in coming in contact with floating and stationary trees, etc." Grant informed Quinby that he would have to make the decision about how much more to push, largely with the desires of the navy: "We cannot order them, but only ask their co-operation." Meanwhile, the other troops scheduled to go into the pass built up at Helena, John Merrilies of Smith's division describing his camp on "Chuckaluck Island—that game being about the only species of amusement indulged in." Worse, with the rising river, even the island was disappearing: "The river is rising and overflowing everything. Our interesting island is getting smaller by degrees, the waters prevailing over it at the rate of two inches every twenty four hours, the bank washing away constantly." The highest ground on the entire island was a mere foot above the river.[13]

The big problem regarding sending more of Quinby's troops into the Delta — or Smith's or Logan's or anyone else's for that matter — was the lack of boats. They were extremely hard to come by, certainly ones short enough to operate in the narrow and twisty turns of the pass. The culprit was mainly the need of all departments for boats, Lewis B. Parsons, the western superintendent of transportation, informing Grant "everybody is complaining of me here for want of boats." Even Major General John Pope fighting Indians in Minnesota was calling for vessels "to chase up those poor devils, the Indians, &c." In fact, Prentiss at Helena, with the arrival of Smith's division from Memphis, was at an impasse about what to do and finally sent division commander Alvin Hovey to Memphis and elsewhere to find more. He eventually went all the way to Cincinnati but was unsuccessful in finding many boats of sufficient size for use on the Vicksburg waterways operations.[14]

Parsons asked Grant to send all boats down at Vicksburg back to move more troops, but Grant just could not release all his vessels, mainly because he was moving his own troops and had to keep some ready to house the divisions at the canal and Young's Point in case of extreme flooding. Rosecrans in Middle Tennessee was not willing to give up any tonnage either, but he did offer to swap his steamers less than two hundred feet long for larger steamboats Grant may have, as long as Rosecrans got the same amount of tonnage in return. Even Halleck became involved from Washington, he declining to authorize taking boats in emergency situations: "General Grant's last dispatches to me do not indicate any necessity for violent seizures."[15]

The boat issue also affected the expedition itself, it being in one Indianan's words "practically cut off from all the world." The *Luella*, in fact, sank during this time, taking with her a lot of the 29th Iowa's equipment. But Quinby was eager to get the rest of his division on site. He decided on the plan of beaching his troops currently at Fort Pemberton and sending the transports back for more, which brought loud protests from some of Ross's commanders. Clinton Fisk, for example, objected that taking some of his vessels would leave the infantry in danger, and if they had to evacuate quickly it would cause them to be horded into the remaining boats, "crowding them into dirty, rotten transports, as closely as slaves in the 'middle passage.'" Sickness, already rampant, would be even worse. Plus, the navy had made it well known that if they did not receive orders to stay by April 1 they would "weigh anchor for the Mississippi River." Ross endorsed Fisk's arguments, but Quinby sent it on to Grant, stating that Fisk "was opposed to this expedition from the beginning" and that "it is not probable, to say the least, that he discouraged" the navy in their actions.[16]

As a result of the lack of boats of proper size, Grant made the monumental decision not to send any more troops into the Yazoo Pass, even as concern grew about the safety of the expedition even then inside the Delta. Hurlbut opined that "Ross should never have been out of supporting reach, but he is, though, and must be saved, if it be possible." Prentiss had less concern, writing that "I do not understand from his dispatches that the enemy could advantageously assume the offensive." The lack of ammunition was the biggest concern, and Prentiss sought to have Quinby supplied at once. Even Grant showed concern, news having filtered in that Ross was stopped. He pushed the Steele's Bayou effort as a result: "If we can get our boats in the rear of them in time, it will so confuse the enemy as to save Ross' force. If they do not, I shall feel restless for his fate."[17]

Quinby seemed to be the least concerned of all and actually sought to restart the effort, even branching out and sending land patrols to nearby villages such as McNutt. But it was still painfully obvious that there was no way for the infantry to get to the fort and that the gunboats were all but worthless under timid commanders. This left only the flanking option, and Quinby sent a request for a pontoon bridge to Prentiss at Helena. He needed one at least three hundred feet long. He also sent workers to a sawmill the flotilla had passed to see if it could be put in operation to make the desired boats. Quinby still had some confidence even at this point on March 27, writing that, although the enemy met every move he made with new fortifications, "I do not doubt of our success here, unless the gunboat fleet withdraws on the 1st proximo, as is now threatened." But nerves were fraying between the branches even more by then, including over accusations of cotton mysteriously showing up on the various transports. Matters were not so sanguine back at Moon Lake either, where George Boomer was finally ready with more transports to bring the other two brigades of the division through the pass: "This expedition will prove a failure, I fear. My opinion has been expressed to General Grant and General McPherson in advance. I shall try my best, however, which is all the satisfaction from it that I look forward to. I am well and in good spirits," he wrote home.[18]

There were similar raw nerves in the Confederate high command as Loring continued to call for more resources. Pemberton curtly responded on March 25, "I told you long since that I have not the means of defending both Fort Pemberton and Yazoo City." He added that he was sending ammunition, but "[I] have already sent more than can be spared from other places. You must husband it most carefully, and remember that I have many other calls upon me." One staff officer in Loring's division later wrote of the problems beginning here: "There is quite a feud existing between Loring and Pemberton—so far as Loring is concerned I heard several expressions of disrespect at Greenwood. . . . In fact it amounted to that degree of hatred on the part of Loring that Capt. Barksdale and myself agreed that Loring would be willing for Pemberton to lose a battle provided that he [Pemberton] would be displaced." The same occurred with Lloyd Tilghman during the process of defending Fort Pemberton, and Pemberton biographer Michael Ballard explained that Loring and Tilghman, and others, "formed an anti-Pemberton clique." As for troops, Pemberton would do what he could, but he was down to reenforcing Loring with the meager State Troops under James Z. George then at Vaiden and Winona, just in the hills to the east. Poor water on site also ironically created problems for those garrisoning the little fort amid the floodtide.[19]

But the only real opinion that mattered was Grant's. With the problem of so few transports, he quickly began to lose faith in the Yazoo Pass operations. By March 18, he had received word "both from my own means of knowing and from Southern papers" that Ross was stopped at Greenwood. Later, he informed McPherson that "it is now clearly demonstrated that a further force, in by way of Yazoo Pass, can be of no service. The party that first went in have so delayed as to give the enemy time to fortify. I see nothing for it now but to have that force return the way they went in." He similarly told Admiral Porter that "the expedition by the way of Yazoo Pass seems to have come to a dead lock at Greenwood. More forces are on the way to them, but I doubt of their being of any service." But he was willing to "let them try Greenwood a short time longer," especially with another possible route nearby opened up in the Confederates' rear.[20]

But by March 28 Grant had seen enough and called the Yazoo Pass expedition to an end: "The troops that have gone down Yazoo Pass are now ordered back." Lieutenant Colonel Wilson himself had come out of the Delta and traveled down to see Grant, where he no doubt gave the general an earful about the navy; one infantryman meeting him on the return voyage wrote that he "talked animatedly of the plans of the campaign, a little depreciatingly of the part the navy took." Grant listened to Wilson eagerly, writing that Wilson was someone "in whose judgement I place great reliance." Grant even gave orders for what to do with the troops once they escaped the Delta, Quinby's moving back to McPherson's corps area and Ross replacing Hovey at Helena as the garrison so that Hovey could move down and join McClernand's corps: "I do not much like taking troops that have been so long on board steamers, as General Ross's command has, immediately into the field."[21]

Plans were thus made at headquarters, but it took a while for those orders to filter in to Quinby in the middle of the flooded Mississippi Delta. Meanwhile, he continued his exploration for a way, any way, past Fort Pemberton.

Unknown to Quinby in the upper Delta, help was possibly on the way in the form of the Steele's Bayou effort taking place some sixty miles to his southwest. Admiral Porter and Sherman themselves had dived off into this same Delta with five ironclads and a division of troops. But what seemed to be a safe approach at Fort Pemberton was something altogether different down on Deer Creek. Some of the problems were natural, such as the willows that grew in the bottom of the creek that had to be cut away to continue forward. Slaves aided the effort, even when warned by owners that they would be punished; that said, one slave woman "gave Genl Sherman 'ginger' because the boys took her chickens when there was plenty that the white folks left." Then, vessels also literally hit snags, such as the *Cincinnati* hitting a tree that "knocked off 6 feet of our port smokestack." That was about 6:00 p.m.; the diary entry related "and at 7 we got aground."[22]

The main problem was Confederate resistance, however, and a crisis was indeed brewing on this wing of the effort to reach Vicksburg. After moving some twenty-one miles up Deer Creek, to within a few hundred yards of Rolling Fork near Dr. W. J. Chaney's residence, Admiral Porter finally met Ferguson's Confederates on the afternoon of March 20. He also met the major obstructions Ferguson had been placing in the creek. In particular, one huge cottonwood tree had been felled across the creek just south of the mouth of the Rolling Fork, which stopped all progress. Lieutenant Murphy and his party, sent ahead to "hold Rolling Fork" until Porter could get there, took a position on a sixty-foot Indian mound, but Porter never made it that far. All forward movement was stopped by the obstructions, allowing the Confederates to take the initiative, which Ferguson did. He opened up from the Widow Watson Plantation with his artillery under Lieutenant R. L. Wood of Bledsoe's Battery and small arms and sharpshooters, forcing the Federals on the mound to flee. Porter himself explained that "I saw the sides of the mound crowded with officers and men. They were tumbling down as best they could; the guns were tumbled down ahead of them; there was a regular stampede." He added, "Murphy hadn't found the top of the mound a fine strategic point."[23]

The Federals retreated inside their boats, but the sharpshooters "approached the very bank of the stream" and fired into the portholes when opened. Ferguson had also managed to get two pieces of artillery through the overflowed ground and in action, although the artillery's ammunition soon began to play

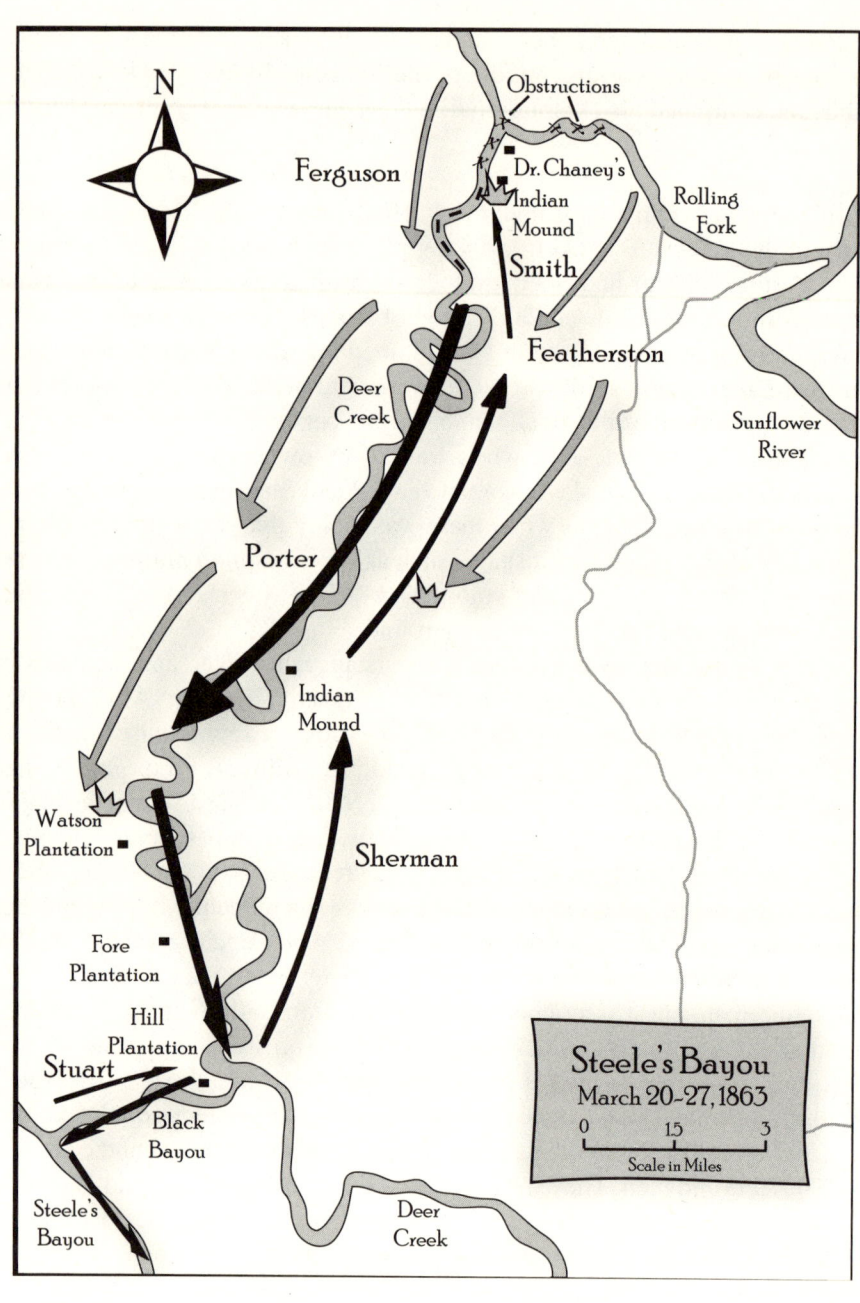

out. And what did hit the gunboats "rolled harmlessly upon the backs of the ironclads," one Maryland artilleryman explained. Fortunately, Featherston soon arrived and met Ferguson, who told him the situation and "urge[d] him to hurry up and attack." Featherston had a 3-inch rifle and 24-pounder howitzer with him under Lieutenant A. P. St. John, so he could fire from a good distance. As more of Featherston's artillery came up, the ammunition was spread around and the firing continued, but it soon ran out as well. To stop the enemy's withdrawal and under Ferguson's heavy persuasion, according to Ferguson, Featherston then sent his two Mississippi regiments to the south on the east bank of the creek, "rather in rear of the enemy," while Ferguson's troops moved across to take control of the west bank, all in preparation that "a rush should be made for the boats." Amid the chaos, the Federals on land were driven back to their vessels, the Confederates taking several small yawls in the process. By the evening of March 20, Featherston had his troops in place and alerted Maury "we intend to take the boats to-night or early in the morning." But, he added, "you had better send me the balance of my brigade." He also requested more of everything from guns to ammunition and tools to "construct a levee across Deer Creek." Meanwhile, Ferguson waited for the boarding, which never came that night, Featherston informing him later that it would be done at daylight.[24]

Porter could only reply with his big guns, which he did, clearly heard by both sides all the way in Vicksburg. But even that was troublesome, as the banks were higher in many places than the guns. With reports of a contraband warning officers on the *Louisville* that the Confederates were still blocking the way forward as well as now behind him, causing Porter to remark in understatement that "this looked unpleasant," Porter decided he should go no farther without protection and sent Sherman a note that he was stalled and that he needed ten thousand troops to protect the gunboats. Back at Hill's Plantation, Sherman obviously had no way to get that amount of troops to him anytime soon, but upon receipt he sent word for division commander David Stuart, who had accompanied him up Steele's Bayou, to go back to Eagle Bend to hurry forward the division. Worse news came later when another note arrived from Porter in the early-morning hours of March 21, about 3:00 a.m., this time spelling out an obvious crisis. Porter was stuck, with no troops to aid in his defense, and he was nearly surrounded by Confederates. Word in fact filtered back to Grant that Porter had ordered his ironclads "smeared . . . with turpentine preparatory to abandoning them and setting them afire."[25]

Fortunately for Porter, the attack and boarding of the boats never came, Featherston explaining that "there was no hope of boarding the boats at this time by the infantry, as they were in the middle of the stream, and could not be reached without passing through water from 10 to 20 feet deep." He later added that "the visionary absurdity of the over-sanguine expectations of capturing gunboats entertained by some military men becomes apparent when it is considered that from 12 to 15 feet depth of water, with a width of from 6 to 10 feet, is always interposed between the assailants and the object assailed, and the boats well nigh incapable of entrance when boarded, and each arranged with reference to the protection of the other." Ferguson was not convinced, later writing that Featherston "blundered.... Featherstone was brave enough but he had never before had a separate command or been thrown upon his own resources, but had fought in the midst of a large army where he had only to obey orders. This was certainly one of the lost opportunities of the lost cause." Ferguson attacked anyway on the morning of March 21, "expecting at every moment to hear General Featherston's regiments open." He was not happy, however, later writing that "all the boats should have been captured or destroyed by a vigorous attack." Conversely, Featherston's troops never got close enough to even try on March 21, because, he reported, "the country from the head of Rolling Fork down Deer Creek to Black Bayou is nearly a continuous chain of plantations, cleared on both sides, and but few points of woods running to the bank of the stream to serve as a cover and protection for sharpshooters."[26]

Still, Porter was in real trouble. Sherman reported that Deer Creek was "deep but channel narrow, crooked, and filled with young willows, which bind the boats and make navigation difficult, and the banks along the whole length are lined with heavy trees and overhanging branches that tear down chimneys and carry away pilot-houses, stanchions, and all wood-work." Porter described how "we have been delayed by obstructions which I did not mind much, and the little willows, which grow so thick that we stuck fast hundreds of times." Sherman related that Porter's "iron-clads move like snails, but with great power, forcing all saplings and bushes and drifts aside." Despite plantations at the slightly higher elevations along Deer Creek itself that offered plenty of provisions, Sherman concluded as a result that "the channel is useless to us in a military way," he later elaborating that it was simply too difficult to move troops quickly while "managing detached boats in small, crooked streams, where overhanging boughs and submerged trees obstruct their progress at every quarter of a mile."[27]

Sherman also had concerns about the southern stretches of Deer Creek, which was the right turn at Black Bayou rather than the left turn all were making. In fact, he informed Porter, enemy "scouts and spies are feeling up their way from Haynes' Bluff, but I will watch them." If Confederates came up that channel, then they could get in behind the Federals once in Deer

Creek. And there were Confederates on the way, under Stephen D. Lee, who had requested the job. His orders were to make it to the slight high ground at Hardee's Plantation and fortify, stopping any advance in that direction and covering another navigable bayou that branched off to the east and led to the Yazoo River. If he could cut off the enemy's retreat at Hill's Plantation, even better. But Lee made it only to the Wilson Plantation some six miles up Deer Creek before high water forced him to stop there and erect any kind of fortification he could. He had with him the 3rd Louisiana, later augmented by the 26th Louisiana and others as well, and once he arrived met the 1st Mississippi Battalion already there felling trees into Deer Creek. There was little room to operate, however, Lee reporting that the dry ground was a mere "1 ½ feet above the creek and overflow from high water." A Mississippian reported that "we soon learned that our progress was slow, whether it was sure or not. Indeed, for a time it seemed that it was not sure, for the wind blew up out of 'our reckoning' and deposited us on a partly submerged 'May-Haw Tree." Lee soon stopped the tree-cutting, arguing that, because of the high water, "in my opinion, the creek was more obstructed by the standing timber than by the timber felled." He sent a small detachment farther north to Hardee's, but it was so underwater that no large group could operate there because of the obstructions and the water being too deep for poling and the meager boats too high from the water for oars to be used. It was not needed anyway, as the Federals never seriously contemplated using the lower stretches of Deer Creek, although Sherman sent a few Federals of Hugh Ewing's arriving brigade southward to scout what they could and to make sure no Confederates came in behind them. The 30th Ohio went southward past the Reality and Good Intent Plantations and all the way to the Omega Plantation before heading back, never meeting the Confederates.[28]

It was obvious that the main threat was to the north, as Sherman could hear cannon fire from that direction, which he took as Porter's vessels shelling the banks to protect his workers. The gunboats were indeed firing rapidly, although one Mississippian in Featherston's brigade explained that it "did us no harm as we were near and behind the levee. They shot over us all the time." Yet the more Sherman heard, he admitted it was "more frequently than seemed consistent with mere guerilla operations." In actuality, Porter was firing at Confederates, who had arrived in force and were now cutting trees into the creek behind Porter's gunboats. Without any army support, Porter was vulnerable to whatever the Confederates wanted to do out of range of his big guns. He had to have help: "Our difficulties increase," Porter wrote.[29]

It was a crisis to be sure, and Porter knew it even if Sherman was not totally cognizant of just how much of a crisis this now was. Sherman at the same time was writing Grant that "I take it for granted the five iron-clad gunboats can fight anything that can be brought against them, and land forces are only needed to cover the ground, to enable them to clean out obstructions." He also wrote Porter himself, "I have no doubt your channel will be obstructed, but no large force can assail you." The message never reached Porter, however, and probably that was a good thing, as Porter was certainly more concerned than Sherman realized. The Confederates captured the contraband courier and note, the slave mistaking a Confederate for a Union soldier and gladly breaking open the plug of tobacco it was hidden in and revealing the note despite Sherman having "promised to pay him $50 if he reaches you and returns safely." Sherman even asked for a receipt from Porter to prove the courier had been faithful. But Porter took nothing for granted, as Sherman did. Porter needed troops, but the only regiments Sherman had with him initially were the advance units of Giles Smith's brigade, the 6th and 8th Missouri and 116th Illinois. With Porter seemingly in such a quandary, however, Sherman slowly becoming convinced, especially when Porter's second message arrived deep in the night. He wisely chose to send forward immediately what troops he had, leaving himself alone with just a couple of staff officers at Hill's Plantation; he sent ahead, he said, "every man with me." Sherman ordered Giles Smith, after crossing over a rebuilt bridge the gunboats had knocked down, to march rapidly on the east bank of Deer Creek the twenty-one miles up to Porter's position. Smith left at daylight on March 21, and Sherman reported to Grant that "the admiral is, doubtless, concerned for the safety of his gunboats, and with propriety." One of Smith's Illinoisans was not thrilled, however, writing that it was a "very hot march."[30]

Meanwhile, Porter was getting desperate, one Federal describing the gunboats as "surrounded by the enemy." All he could do at this point was to back out the way he came: "We dropped down again, unshipped our rudders, and let the vessels rebound from tree to tree." He also ordered his officers to prepare for the worst in case the Confederates attempted to board; Porter ordered the vessels "covered thick with slush" and issued procedures to meet boarders. The worst-case scenario was that he would have to burn his vessels to keep them from being captured, and he gave explicit orders, including how to light fires, to keep the magazines open and strewn with powder, and to aim the loaded and primed guns at the decks so they would go off and sink the vessels. "Every precaution must be taken to defend the vessels to the last," he ordered, "and when we can do no better we will blow them up." Porter later admitted that "I never knew before how much the comfort and safety of ironclads, situated as we were, depended on the soldiers."[31]

The slow withdrawal consequently began, Porter explaining that "after an hour's hard pull we slipped off the willows into soft water." He went on: "Then went forth the orders to unship the rudders and let the vessels drift down stern foremost, and away we all went together with a four-knot current taking us—bumping badly down at the rate of two miles an hour—which was twice as fast as we came up." Yet more problems emerged, including a towed coal barge sinking behind the column and delaying farther progress.[32]

All the while, Smith's troops marched through the day on March 21 to Porter's aid, guided by a slave, they hearing the Confederates as they drew closer. The wagon road along the natural levee was fine for marching and much shorter than the curving creek's path, although Sherman, becoming more and more disillusioned at this being a viable way forward, saw that wagons would churn the road quickly into a mess; the wagons would "cut to the hubs in the damp, low places." All along the route, Smith saw evidence that the Confederates had been obstructing the channel behind the gunboats, and slaves reported they were sent to do the work. Smith simply gathered the slaves and took them with him, warning the local plantation civilians that they would be held responsible if any more obstruction took place.[33]

Fortunately for Porter, Smith arrived before great damage was done and rescued the navy, ultimately providing a cordon of defense around the ironclads, which continued the process of backing down the narrow channel until they could turn around. One of the Illinoisans explained that the "gunboat men [were] very glad to see us," despite one sailor admitting the land soldiers jabbed at them with jokes and friendly jabs: "Jack, you'd better stick to the briny" and "How do you like playing turtle anyway?" Porter nevertheless, again in understatement, remarked that "we were quite pleased to see him." Smith reported that he met little opposition except a few shots from across the creek, but he had no way to get over and thus kept them at rifle distance. "I found the fleet obstructed in front by fallen trees and in rear by a sunken coal barge, and surrounded by a large force of rebels with an abundant supply of artillery, but wisely keeping their main force out of range of the admiral's guns." But, he added, "every tree and stump [was] covered [by] a sharpshooter." As per Sherman's orders, Smith reported to Porter, who told him to hold a position along the line of gunboats and for several miles to the south to keep the enemy from obstructing the getaway route. Smith did so, extending southward all the way to an Indian mound that a portion of the 8th Missouri held. It was a tedious process to withdraw, especially with the sunken barge (rammed and sunk by the *Louisville* when the backward movement began) in the rear of the column. It had to be removed (blown up, according to the *Louisville*'s logbook), and it was gone by daylight on March 22. All the while, Smith's troops skirmished while the gunboats backed down Deer Creek.[34]

Fortunately, more troops were on the way, at least to Hill's Plantation. The three transports sent southward in multiple trips returned by dusk with more regiments from Eagle Bend, something the Confederates scouts were keeping an eye on. They were quickly moved from the mouth of Black Bayou to the first high ground some two miles in. Thomas Kilby Smith described the passage: "Great skill and constant vigilance on the part of the navigators was required to keep these from irreparable injury; the sinking of a boat would have been fatal to the expedition and resulted in disaster to the gunboat fleet." Black Bayou was worse, of course, Sherman writing that "the crooks and turns are so short that boats cannot navigate it with speed." After having moved down Black Bayou in a canoe by himself during the night, Sherman met the arriving troops and "conducted them through the dense canebreaks, by lighted candles, up to the plantation [Hill's] that night." Sherman immediately led them forward the next morning at daylight (March 22) toward the ironclads and Smith's brigade, taking the same road east of the creek, although it passed through swamps at places; Sherman related that the soldiers had to carry their cartridge boxes around their necks and the drummer boys carried their drums on their heads. With Sherman were the 13th US Regulars, 113th Illinois also of Smith's brigade, and the 83rd Indiana, 116th Illinois, and 54th and 57th Ohio of Thomas Kilby Smith's brigade, which, because Smith was (due to a mix-up) absent down the bayou, were under the command of Lieutenant Colonel Americus V. Rice of the 57th Ohio. Sherman pushed forward all morning on March 22, the sounds of cannonading becoming louder and more intense, causing him to realize that the crisis was more substantial than he had known and that Porter was probably shooting at actual Confederates rather than just those tampering with obstructions and sharpshooting at the Union workers. As the force drew closer, the infantry stopped and loaded their weapons for the work all knew was ahead.[35]

Before these troops could get up to the gunboats and while only Giles Smith's Federals defended them, the Confederates made one major attempt to stop the withdrawal, which resulted in what Featherston described as a "sharp skirmish." Giles Smith related that the Mississippians came forward in the plantation fields with infantry and cavalry, with artillery behind. "We discovered a long line of the enemy filing along the edge of the woods and taking position on the creek," Smith reported, "about 1 mile ahead [south] of our advance." His forces skirmished with them, and the gunboats opened up with their big guns, driving away the Confederates. The Mississippians also approached Smith's other troops farther ahead and even to the rear, but they never came close enough to do any damage, though Smith was very worried that the Missourians down at the Indian mound might be cut off. Those three companies fought hard while Smith advanced to the rescue, and even Captain Elias K. Owen of the *Louisville* attempted to push through the obstructions to lend the weight of his guns. Meanwhile, Ferguson, after hours of waiting on the boarding, saw Featherston's troops falling back and knew it was too late to succeed.[36]

By the time Smith reached the mound, Sherman was there too: "Instead of our three companies referred to engaging the enemy, General Sherman had arrived at a very opportune moment with the two regiments . . . and the Second Brigade." Sherman's reinforcing troops from Hill's Plantation were a welcome surprise indeed if tired out; having moved on foot himself, Sherman sat down on the sill of a cabin to rest. Sherman first encountered the 8th Missouri, holding the Indian mound south of the gunboats, there to guard against any Confederate effort to fell trees behind the ironclads. He pushed on and soon encountered the Confederates themselves, Captain Edward Washington of the Regulars leading the way and the brigade under Lieutenant Colonel Rice moving on the left of Giles Smith's troops, between them and the creek. Sherman's men pushed the Confederates back away from the flotilla and plantation fields for some two miles ("with but little resistance") while Sherman himself went to the fleet, meeting on the way Giles Smith, who was moving southward to clear out these same Confederates between the two wings of his force at the northern and southern ends of the gunboats. After riding bareback up to the flotilla on a recently captured horse, Sherman, with sailors cheering him "most vociferously as I rode by," soon met Admiral Porter himself. He was overjoyed at the relief that came in the form of Sherman and his troops. "Halloo, Porter," he shouted. "What did you get into such an ugly scrape for?"[37]

A grateful Porter informed Sherman, who soon went aboard the *Cincinnati*, of all that had happened, how the willows and obstructions had stopped his advance, and that he had decided this was no route to take. He added, "I do not know when I felt more pleased to see that gallant officer." Lieutenant Colonel Rice could see the appreciation, writing that the navy was "much pleased that we had come to their assistance, for they were in a critical situation, the enemy having surrounded them." Now Porter could back out safely the way he had come in, all the way to Black Bayou, which Sherman labeled "this slow and tedious process." And it was, it taking the rest of that rainy day as well as all day on March 23 and a good portion of March 24, until the gunboats reached the Fore Plantation. Featherston and Ferguson, now reinforced again with the 40th Alabama, which had to wade "1/4 of a mile backwater waste deep" just to reach land from Rolling Fork, merely pressed their rear while "they were still getting out of the way as rapidly as possible." Confederates followed the withdrawal on both banks of Deer Creek and only occasionally tried to still envelop the new front of the column to the south. At one point the 31st Mississippi, having gone two days without any rations, found "a fine fat ox," and Colonel Marcus D. L. Stephens gave the men ten minutes to "kill, skin, cook and eat the ox," which the famished Mississippians accomplished. The gunboats also responded "most cordially" to all efforts; with plenty of ammunition, the gunboats "fired furiously at everything which could be seen," although Ferguson reported it as "an amusing display of pyrotechnics." But the Union ironclads were well protected by this time, the regiments under Smith and Rice following along on the bank beside the vessels much of the way until they reached safety, at which time the infantry boarded the gunboats themselves for the ride down to Hill's Plantation. There, David Stuart had arrived with even more troops of the division, mainly Hugh Ewing's brigade, the 4th [West] Virginia welcoming the tired troops and gunboats near the Fore Plantation. The Confederates followed but did not attack, Sherman simply reporting that "the enemy hung upon the rear of our column, but would not come within reach."[38]

During the slow march back rain pelted the Federals, but the infantry stuck with the gunboats as they meticulously backed downstream. "It was one of the most disagreeable marches we ever had and at the same time one of the most important ones," an Ohioan admitted. But they made steady progress backing down Deer Creek, Porter remarking that the *Louisville*, initially in the rear but now in the lead, "cleared away [the trees] almost fast enough to permit us to meet with no delay." Right there among them were the guarding infantry, one sailor describing them as "presenting a ludicrous appearance, covered with cotton, adhering to their hair and clothes from planks of a cotton gin upon which they had slept the night before; still they were generally cheerful as larks." Columns of slaves "following closer to us than the whites" also meandered along the bank, proclaiming "Going to freedom, sure" and "Go 'long, dar, old fool hoss, don't know nothing; your's gwine to freedom, too." Also there was Sherman himself, Major Cyrus W. Fisher of the 54th Ohio remarking that "the major-general commanding the Fifteenth Army Corps was himself on foot, and marched part of the time at the head of the Fifty-fourth, and this exhibition of carelessness of personal comfort on the part of one so high in command filled the men with enthusiasm, and it is saying but very little to say they all believed in General Sherman." At this point, only the sick were allowed on the vessels, some hundred and twenty-five crowding on the *Carondelet*, but all soon managed to catch a ride for the final stretches down Deer Creek.[39]

The Confederates made little effort to stop the withdrawal at this point despite the arrival of more ammunition and men, including the 31st Mississippi of Featherston's brigade, Colonel John A. Orr, who ranked Colonel D. W. Hurst, taking command of all the regiments. The heavy rains that pelted both sides alike caused much of the lack of effort. Featherston continued to call for more ammunition and boats, although he deemed there were enough troops already, certainly more than could be evacuated if an emergency came: "The *Arcadia* runs badly in daylight," he wrote of one of his boats, "and cannot run at all at night." He ended his note, "I shall do the best I can, and leave the result to the Almighty."[40]

Sherman and Porter took a day to rest on March 25 now that it seemed they were in safety. And the troops needed it, one describing "mud, rain, slip, slop, slap you go into the water, through cane brakes and thickets, among alligators, mud turtles, snakes, lizards, thousand-legged worms and frogs." Sherman kept land units three miles to the north at Fore's Plantation, where one member of the 83rd Indiana was killed as the Confederates followed the withdrawal through "an immense cane swamp and marsh," but the Confederates did not approach beyond skirmishers. In fact, Porter returned down Steele's Bayou that day, desiring to meet with Grant and get on to other more important work. Sherman remained until the next day, when orders from Grant for him to return came as well. Stuart and the naval captains then oversaw the exodus starting on March 26, and the "exciting passage through the bayous into the Yazoo" was accomplished by the next day, many of the regiments now aboard the gunboats themselves. The fleet and troops again found their way to waters where they could proverbially breath cleaner and fresher, and more abundant, air; one Federal explained that he "shaved and changed underclothes for the first time for 12 days—felt much better." But there were still dangers even in better waters, one Federal writing how the *Mound City* "pushed over big oak trees[,] one of which broke and fell over bow of boat and knocked a few men overboard." Despite the continual dangers, the expedition lost a mere two men, one from the 6th Missouri and the one from the 83rd Indiana. Others were wounded, in addition to the assistant surgeon of the 4th West Virginia, "who was severely injured by a limb falling on his head, wounding him severely and injuring him otherwise." Confederates also reported finding a grave marked "Engineer United States tug *Dahlia*; died March 22, 1863."[41]

The Confederates lost two killed and a few more wounded. There were accounts of burning and of pillage, including Ferguson reporting one gunboat shell hitting "in the chamber of an invalid woman, in which the women and children had taken refuge." The woman was not hurt, but a slave woman was and nearly killed. A two-year-old child was burned badly as well. On some plantations, nearly all buildings were burned.[42]

Word of the repulse and near crisis filtered back to Grant, at which point he began to scramble to get more troops into the Delta to save the gunboats. He alerted McPherson at Lake Providence to send troops down to Eagle Bend in case they were needed. McPherson readied Logan's division, especially advising that Mortimer Leggett's brigade lead the way: "He is well provided with tools for building bridges, &c., and is a driving fellow." Although some moved to Eagle Bend, Logan's troops never entered the Delta, but McPherson did send in his own and Logan's and McArthur's escort companies of cavalry to scout where Logan would go if they did; only a few troops actually made the trip. By that time, Stuart's infantry had gotten the navy "out of a tight place they had got into."[43]

But it was clear that this hundred-and-forty-mile round-trip experiment was no more possible than the others. "If ever an army skedaddled from danger in good faith," admitted one Ohioan, "it was the Rolling Fork expedition." But it was unique, Porter writing that "altogether this has been a most novel expedition. Never did those people expect to see ironclads floating where the keel of a flat boat never passed." Yet nothing else really developed besides "annoying the enemy and causing him to expend his resources," as well as taking out cotton "enough to pay for the building of a good gunboat." But Porter did not blame Grant or Sherman, describing them as "never yet any two men who would labor harder . . . to forward an expedition for the overthrow of Vicksburg." Yet Sherman himself had flatly told Grant as early as March 21 that the idea of getting to the Yazoo "I pronounce . . . impossible by any channel communicating with Steele's Bayou." Grant confided to Sherman his disappointment, even asking if something could still be done by going south on Deer Creek rather than north: "I regret that the chances look so gloomy for getting through to the Yazoo by that route. I had made so much calculation upon the expedition down Yazoo Pass, and now again by the route proposed by Admiral Porter, that I have made really but little calculation upon reaching Vicksburg by any other than Haynes' Bluff." Grant related that there was such delay that "the enemy got wind of the movement in time to blockade the creek just where the boats would leave it." He further lamented that "the admiral was forced to desist from further efforts to proceed when within a few hundred yards of clear sailing to the Yazoo."[44]

It was all a grand expedition, and the newspaper correspondents tagging along each wanted to get the scoop, or the "beat," as Sylvanus Cadwallader termed it. He requisitioned a skiff and "selected three of the ablest darkies I could find" and rowed his little craft all night back to Eagle Bend, where he hurried across the mile of land to catch the mail boat heading to Memphis the next day. He got his story off, getting the scoop, and bragged that "the Chicago *Times* [was] three days ahead of all competitors."[45]

Meanwhile, the Confederates soon retook the entire area, Ferguson moving down Deer Creek and making contact with Lee, who soon returned to Haynes' Bluff. Additional brigades, such as a Georgia one commanded by Colonel Abda Johnson of the 40th Georgia, also arrived, but one of the Georgians related that "ere we reached Deer Creek, the Yankees had gone into a hole, and taken the hole in after them." Still, they had enough of the "tortuous, serpentine windings" of the waterways, although marveling at the overflowed nature of the ground; one Georgian remarked on houses on stilts and the stock kept on "rafts or artificial mounds, and brought up and milked or fed in flat boats." Ferguson held the Black Bayou area for a while longer, until another incursion farther north called his attention in that direction. Even William Loring, once the Federals left Fort Pemberton the first time, informed Pemberton that "I will, if you wish it, go to the Sunflower and stop him." Porter was not wrong when he advised that the Confederates would never be surprised in this area again: "They will guard every ditch leading into the Yazoo."[46]

But few besides the top leaders knew much of what had happened or even where it occurred. One Federal now back safely at Young's Point entered Engineer William Jenney's office and explained that he had to make a report of the operation: "I want you to tell me where I have been, how I went there, what I did, and if I came back the same way I went, or if not, how I did get back." Yet one surprise was still to be had. Days or weeks after the expedition, a large explosion took place, Ferguson assuming his troops had been surprised by another enemy attack. It was merely a large cannonball shot from the gunboats that exploded while the local slaves burned off a plot of brush for spring planting. The effects of the Steele's Bayou expedition lived on, but fortunately no one was hurt.[47]

It soon became evident that this was a real crisis averted for the Federals and a real missed opportunity for Pemberton, whose biographer criticized him for not going personally to take command of the defense. After initial rumors that the Federals had been successful, even capturing Yazoo City and the entirety of Featherston's brigade, Stevenson at Vicksburg reported that "the damage done their boats was so great that it could easily be discovered from the lookout station." Grant realized as much. These seemingly low-risk experiments with the potential of high reward involving only microscopic portions of the army at any one time had not worked—and probably never would. And this time, the seemingly low risk had almost turned into an unmitigated disaster that could have seen an entire division cut off and potentially destroyed or captured. More important, the loss of five ironclads would have been an almost unrecoverable setback. Grant thus began to realize that these experiments were not working and could possibly even cause severe loss. He had begun to gradually lean more toward decisive operations instead of busywork waiting for the water to go down. Now that April was nearing and, with it, the possibility of the river falling significantly, he began to warm even more to the idea of a decisive move.[48]

Despite dealing with the fallout from defeated and changing plans, Grant kept up his other work while also overseeing numerous smaller efforts and possibilities—all with the goal of finding the right combination that would capture Vicksburg. But that combination was not forthcoming, one Federal sent up to the mouth of Yazoo Pass admitting: "So here we are, but what we are here for, or where we are going or what we are going to do is more than I can tell, and I guess it would puzzle General Grant himself to tell." Not the least of Grant's worries were command issues up the chain and down. Fortunately, relations with McClernand seemed to be smoothed out for now, Grant indicating in late March that, "feeling every desire to gratify General McClernand in every possible [way] consistently with the good of the service," he even worked on a request of McClernand's to have a favored regiment, the 18th Illinois, sent to his corps. But where one area of trouble lessened, others opened. More issues emerged with damages to Southern property, the payments often taken out of payrolls. Likewise, the treatment of contrabands continued to be an issue, they being refugees Grant did not welcome inside his lines because of the lack of living space and of supplies. But Halleck had to correct him, lecturing that "the character of the war has very much changed within the last year." He added that "every slave withdrawn from the enemy is equivalent to a white man put *hors de combat*." He went on that sending back the slaves "is not only bad policy in itself, but is directly opposed to the policy adopted by the Government." Grant had no choice in this matter.[49]

Similarly, a major command development saw Charles Hamilton resign and leave Grant's army. Besides clandestinely informing on Grant's drinking, Hamilton had gotten in a row with Hurlbut over date of rank. Because neither of their major-generalships were approved when Congress adjourned, they reverted back to their brigadier-general commissions, which put Hamilton ahead of Hurlbut. Hamilton wanted to know Hurlbut's date, but Hurlbut declined to state it. Hamilton demanded to be moved or given Hurlbut's position, but the presidential order of Hurlbut commanding the XVI Corps was all Grant needed to keep him. Hurlbut seethed: "I warn you very frankly, if you attempt to exercise independent authority, you will at once be arrested and sent to Vicksburg," to which Hamilton responded that "your letter to me . . . seems unnecessarily harsh and peremptory as coming from a junior to a senior officer." Hamilton also schemed to get command of McPherson's XVII Corps, but Grant stopped that as well: "I am led to believe, and think there is no doubt of the fact, that Maj. Gen. C. S. Hamilton is making indirect efforts to get General McPherson removed from the command of his army corps, and to get the command himself," he informed Halleck. "If this is so, I wish to enter my solemn protest. There is no comparison between the two as to their fitness for such a command." Grant described Hamilton's "natural jealous disposition, which influences his military conduct and acts prejudicially upon the service." Then Hamilton demanded an autonomous command separate from Hurlbut, but Grant gave him the choice of a division under McClernand (who was well satisfied with his current division commanders and wanted no part of Hamilton) or to await orders. Hamilton resigned. Halleck commented that "no doubt he resigns to get a higher command. This game sometimes succeeds, but it also sometimes fails."[50]

Another odd occurrence during this time was a report-writing episode that dated back to a year earlier. Major General Lew Wallace had never been reinstated to a field command, largely because he was seen as a cause of failure on Sunday at Shiloh, he having marched all day instead of coming directly to the battlefield. Wallace now requested an investigation to clear his name, and the War Department asked Grant and the others who were involved, such as McPherson and staff officer John Rawlins, to write their accounts. It seemed very odd that all lined up directly with one another a year afterward, indicating that there may have been some collusion to get their stories correct and to make Wallace out to be the scapegoat of Shiloh.[51]

Even odder was what one McPherson staff officer described as "some little fun at head quarters." A female soldier was found out in the 31st Illinois, one of four who had joined the regiment months before because "she had a lover in the Gallant 31st." The other three had either died or been found out, and now the fourth was, although she demanded her pay up to the time of her discharge "and can't see why she is not entitled to it." The officers "passed around the hat" and collected thirty dollars for her, but the officer reflected that "if the girls want to go to war so bad it is time to let us go home and have them try it a while."[52]

But Grant's real attention was on the military efforts, including continuing work on the canal. Labor there had picked up for a while due to the arrival of the steam-powered dredging machines, a grateful Grant writing that "but for his [George Pride's] personal attention to the selection of them, old and worn-out ones would have been sent, and the result probably would have been that they would have given out before their work was half done." That said, the work slowed thereafter due to the flooding as well as a Confederate battery emplaced to command at least half the canal and certainly its exit. "We had instructions to fire on them every opportunity we had," explained one Southern gunner. One Ohioan took umbrage, writing that "to obstruct or change the natural channel of a watercourse in Putnam County, we'd be attended with a learned dissertation of the law, and a long array of witnesses—not so in this country, the citizens gather together and amuse themselves by throwing 15-inch shells among us for making the attempt." Ultimately, the work on the canal, except on the breakthrough at the dam at the upper end, had to be suspended as the Confederates shelled the dredging boats out by late March. "The canal may be useful in passing boats through at night, to be used below," Grant wrote, "but nothing further." A lower-level Federal took more humor in the situation, writing of "this world renowned canal which is to turn the mighty Mississippi and leave Vicksburg away off in the country." He added that "this canal is done but the old river refuses to leave its course and so we have to let it go."[53]

Lake Providence promised no more success by then either. McPherson had cut the levee at Lake Providence on March 16: "Water is flowing in at a tremendous rate, filling up the lake and bayous." One of his soldiers described that it was "literally drowning out the whole state of Louisiana." The first boat to go through the turbid waters "reeled like a drunken man" but made it through; others were not so fortunate afterward, with some deaths. By March 22 McPherson reported that "the water has risen steadily in the lake until the shore is all overflowed, except in a few high points." He moved Logan's still-present division, not having boats to get them to Yazoo Pass, up the river a bit to higher ground (to the chagrin of the troops leaving their beautiful camps) and also contemplated doing the same with McArthur's also-present division. By a few days later the route seemed open, and Grant pondered its use, perhaps even sending a corps of his army southward to cooperate with Nathaniel Banks at Port Hudson, after which time the whole would come north and assail Vicksburg. Still, despite asking Porter his views on the idea of "get[ing] out all the forces we have attempting to gain possession of the Yazoo River, and use them in the way here indicated," the lack of boats precluded anything in the near future. There was also still some work to do along the route,

McPherson waiting on "the sawing-machine to come from Memphis" to cut the stumps below the waterline. Grant informed Halleck that, although boats could soon get through, "I make no calculations upon using this route for the present, but it may be turned to practical use after effecting present plans. The same may be said of the canal across the point." Plus, the Steele's Bayou effort was starting about that time, Grant writing that "this one, to get all our forces in one place, and that where it will be in striking distance of the enemy's lines of communication north, is the most important until firm foothold is secured on the side with the enemy."[54]

Also promising was renewed naval action around Vicksburg and the idea of shelling the Confederate batteries south of the city, most especially at Warrenton. But with Porter out of the picture while floundering in Steele's Bayou, Grant had to take up some of his oversight, including providing coal for Farragut below Vicksburg. Admiral Farragut had steamed up to the city on March 19, passing Grand Gulf and Bowen's new Confederate fortifications there, including the battery of four Parrott rifles under Colonel William Wade. These had inflicted two killed and six wounded on the ship at the cost of only the Federals damaging "a battery flag staff." But Farragut was about to depart downriver to oversee operations at Port Hudson, he having heard that some of his vessels were damaged or sunk. Farragut passed Grand Gulf again on March 31 going south with only one killed, while one of Wade's 20-pounder Parrotts exploded and killed two and wounded eight, one mortally. In his absence, Farragut requested some of the rams to run the Vicksburg batteries again to take up the task of preventing Confederate commerce from the Red River. It was clear that he was leaving the inter-river miles to Porter's provenance.[55]

While Farragut was still around, however, Grant decided on March 23 to "take advantage of the offer" Farragut had made to transport troops between Vicksburg and Port Hudson. Grant was especially concerned about the Warrenton batteries and wanted to send two regiments to cooperate with the navy's big guns to "destroy effectually the batteries at Warrenton." Grant related that "this is a bad day for troops to be out, but in that particular it may be favorable to us." Captain Henry Walke, in charge with Porter going up Steele's Bayou, also talked of sending a couple rams to cooperate if he could get army cotton to pad his vessels. Grant "promised him anything in the world the army has," reiterating his idea that "it is of vast importance that we should hold the river securely between Vicksburg and Port Hudson."[56]

Farragut shelled Warrenton's four iron-encased Parrott rifles, doing little damage, but the cooperation of the rams was a different matter. Walke would not send a gunboat without Porter's permission, but Alfred Ellet took the responsibility to send two of his rams. The entire plan was delayed, and Grant had to prod to get Ellet to move any of his rams southward. Intending on moving during the early-morning hours of March 25 with the *Switzerland* and *Lancaster*, their crews cut to a minimum (although several of the sailors had earlier passed these same batteries on the *Queen of the West*), it was daylight before the rams got around the bend north of Vicksburg. By then, their escape pipes had given their advance away anyway. Colonel Charles Ellet, commanding the run, noted that, in the dim daylight, "the flashing of the enemy's signal lights from battery to battery as we neared the city showed me that concealment was useless." Both rams put on steam, and the Confederate fire was wild at first, but when the vessels reached the middle of town "the fire became both accurate and rapid." Ellet lost the *Lancaster*, it being holed numerous times, one shot even taking the steering wheel away while not hurting the pilot. The ram sank and Ellet finally burned what was left to dispose of it, he remarking that it was "a very rotten boat." One Confederate wrote home that "I saw her go under[.] The men got [off in] shifts and some . . . jumped [into] the river." Aboard the *Switzerland*, another reported he looked back and "could see the splinters fly from her at every discharge." Soon the water was over the deck and the ram went down, "bow foremost." Cheers roared from the Confederate gunners, especially when the *Switzerland* also took a hit in the boilers, letting all the steam escape and making the Confederates feel sure they had destroyed that ram too. "It would [have] done you a heap of good to hear the Louisiana boys hallo when the boat was sinking," a Louisianan wrote his mother; "it done me so much good to see it go to the bottom. I saw a good many of the Yanks jump overboard. I hope every one drowned." But the *Switzerland* floated to safety and was soon repaired, now another Union vessel between Vicksburg and Port Hudson. The feats soon became material for *Harper's Weekly*, the third week in a row Vicksburg had covered the front page.[57]

Once out of Steele's Bayou, Porter demanded to know "by what authority" Ellet had sent the vessels, and Farragut himself apologized, writing Grant that "I blame myself very much for not insisting on General Ellet's waiting for a dark night. . . . But I never for a moment supposed that he would come down in the day-time." Grant shrugged it off, informing Halleck that the *Switzerland* was below with only a hole in her boiler that could easily be fixed and that the *Lancaster* "received a shot, and immediately went to pieces. A large part, containing the machinery, tipped over, spilling it in the river. . . . She was very rotten and worthless."[58]

But despite getting another gunboat below Vicksburg, it was clear Grant had to come up with a new plan. With both the Yazoo Pass and Steele's Bayou expeditions thwarted and the canal and Lake Providence longshots to begin with, Grant's bag of tricks was just about exhausted. In fact, by March 27 Grant realized neither the Yazoo Pass nor Steele's Bayou expeditions would prove worthwhile, he informing Halleck that "the moment I heard that Admiral Porter had started on his return, I sent orders for the return of the Yazoo Pass expedition from Fort Greenwood."[59]

But Grant was already working on larger, more substantial plans. In a letter to Banks that Grant sent by the returning Farragut, he informed the commander downriver of his larger plans. With almost all experiments blocked or stalled because of a lack of transportation, Grant brought Banks up to date on his activities, mainly of the river flooding "and the nature of the country almost precluding the possibility to land a force on the east bank of the Mississippi anywhere above Vicksburg." He related that the canal was nearly flooded out: "It is exceedingly doubtful if this canal can be made of any practical use, even if completed." He was also souring on the Yazoo Pass expedition by this point and even as early as March 22 adding that "this enterprise promised most fairly, but for some cause our troops delayed so as to give the enemy time to fortify." Even the Steele's Bayou effort was going nowhere: "They got in as far as Deer Creek without any great difficulty, but I fear a failure of getting farther."[60]

Yet there were other options. Grant discussed freely the idea of sending Banks some of his troops to take Port Hudson, when all would move northward and cooperate against Vicksburg. But the absence of steamers to transport the troops was the key, and they would likely not be available anytime soon. More important, he also, as he wrote on March 29, began to think of operating south of Vicksburg himself: "I am about occupying New Carthage with troops, and opening the bayous from here to that place." From there, if Grant could cross the river, he could first operate against Grand Gulf or Warrenton, although occupying New Carthage south of Vicksburg hinged on the water level falling. At any rate, the idea was still to get his troops on the high ground east of the Mississippi River, from which he thought the rest would be easy: "I do not anticipate any trouble, however, if a landing can be effected." With the definite idea of moving troops across the Mississippi River somewhere south of Vicksburg in mind, he asked Porter his opinion: "Will you be good enough, admiral[,] to give this your early consideration, and let me know your determination?" He added that "without the aid of gunboats it will hardly be worth while to send troops to New Carthage, or to open the passage from here to there."[61]

It was certainly an option, although a last resort because of logistics and all the other many moving parts; certainly, the navy's concurrence was the key. Porter was not terribly happy with the idea, confidentially writing to Secretary of the Navy Welles that "the batteries at that place [Vicksburg] could destroy four times the number we have here and not receive any damage in return." Fortunately for Grant, Porter responded positively, although with a caveat:

> I am ready to co-operate with you in the matter of landing troops on the other side, but you must recollect that when these gunboats once go below we give up all hopes of ever getting them up again. If it is your intention to occupy Grand Gulf in force it will be necessary to have vessels there to protect the troops or quiet the fortifications now there. If I do send vessels below it will be the best vessels I have, and there will be nothing left to attack Haynes' Bluff, in case it should be deemed necessary to try it.

That was plain enough. Porter was willing if not excited, but this was the proverbial last straw. This one, unlike the others, could not be undone.[62]

There were other options as well floating around in Grant's mind, possibly because of the seriousness of the southward proposal and Porter's honest analysis. In a moment of weakness rarely seen in Grant, he seemed to grasp at straws and related that "there is nothing left for me but to collect all my strength and attack Haynes' Bluff. This will necessarily be attended with much loss, but I think it can be done." Yet it could not be done quickly, he adding that, because of his spread-out forces, "an attack on Haynes' Bluff cannot possibly take place under two weeks, if so soon. My forces are now scattered, and the difficulty of getting transportation is very great."[63]

But the process was started, and as early as March 22, when Grant informed McPherson "I want concentrated as near here as possible all the troops now scattered from Young's Point to Helena." Division after division consequently made plans to move on down the river, including Smith's, which never made it to the Yazoo Pass but moved on and became part of Sherman's XV Corps eventually under a new commander, Brigadier General James Tuttle. But the going was slow, one Ohioan relating that "we are hourly expecting boats to take us somewhere. But these boats are a slow institution and it would be vain to predict when they may be on hand." In the meantime, while at another stop, they passed the time in the "plundering of a little Jew sutler that had his canvas pitched on the bank"; another that was similarly robbed exclaimed, "I makes more monish in Chicago!" McPherson related to Quinby that he had no idea how bad the Yazoo Pass route was but that Grant "has made a change in the programme." Under immense pressure, Grant admitted that the delays were aggravating, but "it may all be providential however and I shall expect a change of apparent luck soon."⁶⁴

And it was time indeed to do something—anything—as the pressure was building, he feeling pressure not just from Halleck about his far-flung operations. At almost the same time, Lincoln was writing the nearest officer in telegraphic communication with Washington, that being Hurlbut at Memphis: "What news have you? What from Vicksburg? What from Yazoo Pass? What from Lake Providence? What generally?"⁶⁵

10

"This Is the Only Move I Now See as Practicable"
April 1–12

Decision time was here. Spring had begun, the Mississippi River was beginning to fall, and the countryside would soon dry out. But with the media and political spotlights on Grant, not to mention continual word arriving in Washington of his drunkenness—even from McClernand in March, he had to do something quickly. The Copperhead movement at home (as well as with the army; one report of an Illinois state legislator in the camp with "incendiary documents" did not help) was growing, and the focus was increasing on Grant all the time: "Grant himself is on very bad odor, everybody abusing him, and the administration for keeping him where he is." Especially odious was the delay in taking Vicksburg, about which of course nothing as yet could be done. Nevertheless, it was time to make a final decision on how to get to Vicksburg despite the problem that there were no good options. "I presume some great strategic movement is in contemplation," one Ohioan wrote; "another canal probably." Grant had tried just about everything—by the book and outside it—thus far, and nothing had worked. Worse, some of these efforts had almost caused unfathomable damage. Grant was obviously aggravated, admitting to Julia "I am very well but much perplexed. Heretofore I have had nothing to do but fight the enemy. This time I have to overcome obstacles to reach him." To an acquaintance he admitted "the problem is a difficult one, but I shall certainly solve it. Vicksburg can be taken. I shall give my days and nights to it, and shall surely take it." The time had thus come for a tough decision, but then that was nothing new in the course of military history.[1]

Both Jomini and Clausewitz had dwelled at length on the ideal commander and the needed coup d'oeil, Jomini also emphasizing a good chief of staff and general staff while specifying the actions commanders should employ, such as massing against an inferior force of the enemy and taking decisive points. Jomini also delved into the makeup of the commander, writing that two main attributes were necessary—"a high moral courage, capable of great resolutions," and "a physical courage which takes no account of danger." He summed up that a good general "must know how to arrange a good plan of operations, and how to carry it to a successful termination."[2]

Clausewitz went farther and, in examining what he termed military "genius," considered the makeup of the commander, providing a wide range of attributes—what he called "a harmonious combination of elements"—that were essential to success. These elements included courage, intellect, presence of mind, strength of will, energy, staunchness, character, and ability for quick understanding of terrain and situations, the coup d'oeil Jomini had also pondered. But there was a significant continuation in Clausewitz's discussions of these attributes, all of them having to do with steadiness, quickness, and boldness. Timing was also key for him, especially as military activities were so tied to political efforts, as was the case here at Vicksburg.[3]

It is clear that both Jomini and Clausewitz emphasized the strength of a commander's mind, Clausewitz more so than Jomini, and determined that a man of firm belief in a plan and the execution of that plan, even with adaptations, was very much necessary. Obviously, so many Civil War commanders from George McClellan to Joseph Hooker did not make the mark, but Ulysses S. Grant was one who did and in much more Clausewitzian form made a decision, even if it was risky and unpopular, and stuck by it. One veteran called this Grant's "critical point," and he himself admitted the larger stakes than just his own well-being: "I thought that war anyhow was a risk; that it made little difference to the country what was done with me. I might be killed or die from fever."[4]

Early April was just such a crisis time that required this type of leadership to be shown. "There has been something stirring around here in the last week," one Federal wrote home. Grant notified Julia that "it is hard to tell when the final strike will be made at Vicksburg," but "I am doing all I can and expect to be successful." Grant did not shy away from making the big decision, which all understood would be final indeed, one way or the other. By early April, Grant had fully committed himself to a roundabout southern approach to Vicksburg, he informing Halleck on April 2 that "in two weeks I expect to be able to collect all my forces and turn the enemy's left." It was a gamble to be sure, but like so many other times it was a gamble out of necessity. At this point, there was no other option left but to leapfrog past Vicksburg. Grant could not go back to West Tennessee to restart the Jominian, by-the-book type of campaign Sherman desired; that would possibly end his career amid the media coverage and even chirping from within his own army. Likewise, he had tried every conceivable route through the murky bayous and creeks in the Mississippi Delta on both sides of the river to either get on that high ground east of the Mississippi River or past Vicksburg to the west. None worked, and a couple brought problems such as shot-up gunboats, Steele's Bayou even seriously threatening the backbone of the naval force around Vicksburg. And Grant could not stay still where he was much longer with the prime operational weather on him, Halleck himself writing that, "as the season when we can do very little on the lower Mississippi is rapidly advancing, I hope you will push matters with all possible dispatch." The only other option—the final one that would force a conclusion one way or the other—was to move on forward, which would propel his army past Vicksburg.[5]

Grant later admitted that he had been thinking of just such a move all winter, if it came to it. "From the moment of taking command in person, I became satisfied that Vicksburg could only be turned from the south side," he wrote in his report. After the war, he added he had been thinking as much "the whole winter," writing that because it "could not be undertaken until the waters receded[,] . . . I did not therefore communicate this plan, even to an officer of my staff, until it was necessary to make preparations for the start." After the war, James H. Wilson tried to take for himself and Rawlins the credit for planting the idea in Grant's mind, but it is clear that Grant had been thinking in those terms all along, he, contrary to his statement of silence, even mentioning the possibility back in January and February. Rawlins's biographer in fact admitted that "it seems more likely Rawlins's role was as a 'persistent advocate' for the idea." Either way, historian Terry Winschel has described Grant's decision as "a crossroads in his military career."[6]

As Clausewitz would argue, perhaps the political issues before Grant were even more important than the military at this point, and Grant certainly worried over them. In fact, a visitor to the army, Frederick Law Olmstead, wrote that both Porter and Grant "looked to me like disappointed and anxious men." Some newspapers had been ruthless: "Our noble army of the Mississippi is being wasted by the foolish, drunken, stupid Grant." The impatience for something to happen was also clear, another newspaper editor writing that "Grant is getting along at Vicksburg with such rapidity that, in the course of fifteen or twenty years, he will be ready to send up a gunboat to find out whether the enemy hasn't died of old age." There was particular worry in Washington. An increasingly concerned Halleck, and Stanton and Lincoln himself, watched the delay and experiments with growing alarm, Halleck referring to Grant's experiments as "several eccentric operations." He admitted that they were possibly valid "for the purpose of reconnoitering the country," but he cautioned Grant that, when he made his ultimate move on Vicksburg, he should have his army "concentrated to make that blow effective. The division of your army into small expeditions destroys your strength, and, when in the presence of an enemy, is very dangerous." Halleck even called for concentration of troops with Banks. Obviously, Halleck knew very little of the wet and soggy ground Grant had to work with despite acknowledging that "I know you can judge of these matters there much better than I can here." Grant in fact retorted that "the embarrassments I have had to contend against on account of extreme high water cannot be appreciated by any one not present to witness it" and that, specifically concerning Steele's Bayou, "my force had as well be there as here until I want to use them."[7]

The reports of sickness in the army did not help, although again this was a result of the wet and nasty weather; one Federal even reported he had chicken pox. Fortunately, the Sanitary and Christian commissions were on site doing wonders in terms of medical care and offering supplies. Even down with the Union forces was the widow of Wisconsin Governor Louis P. Harvey, who had drowned after Shiloh on his own "mission of mercy" to the troops. Now his wife continued the work. All the while, Grant worked through changing medical directors to get as much medical supplies as possible to the army. Still, some sickness remained, one Missourian writing of having the "Mississippi Quickstep."[8]

Ruminations from Halleck were one thing, but Halleck also sent more worrying concern from Lincoln himself. Halleck asked several questions, relaying that "the President, who seems to be rather impatient about matters on the Mississippi, has several times asked me these questions, [and] I repeat them to you." Seven days later, Halleck added "you are too well advised of the anxiety of the Government for your success, and its disappointment at the delay, to render it necessary to urge upon you the importance of early action. I am confident that you will do everything possible to open the Mississippi River. In my opinion this is the most important operation of the war, and nothing must be neglected to insure success." Grant later mused that "we were, all of us, more or less, on probation," but Lincoln had patience with his out-of-the-box commander: "I rather like the man, and I think I will try him a little longer." But how long was not known.[9]

So a gamble it was, and many read Grant's mind. Although one likened it to a "change of base," one Indianan wrote home, "my impression is that Gen Grant intends to take Vicksburg without a battle if possible. He will use every endeavor to surround them, cut off communications, and force a surrender or an open fight, either of [which] would be very acceptable to the majority of the troops under his command." Another noted, "Grant goes to win before he quits, that is the way."[10]

But naval cooperation was key, Grant admitting to one of his generals that "we cannot order them but only ask their co-operation." Grant of course corresponded frequently with Admiral Porter, including a warning that a Vicksburg paper had called for planters to send their small boats to Vicksburg, perhaps to be used in an attack on the fleet. But if Grant was going to cross the river south of Vicksburg, he had to have naval cooperation. Porter promised it if that was the way Grant wanted to go, but the major problem was that the flotilla had to get past the Vicksburg batteries intact, something the *Lancaster* found difficult only recently. But that was not the major concern or determinant for this being the last effort, succeed or fail. The navy could likely pass the batteries at Vicksburg, although they would no doubt suffer damage and even perhaps lose a few vessels. But the major decision came with putting the navy south of Vicksburg, from which it could never return. Going down the river with the current would be dangerous enough, but coming back up if Grant somehow decided this was not what he wanted to do after all was impossible. There was no way at all the gunboats could survive passing the Vicksburg batteries at an extremely slow pace going against the current. While Grant had troops already heading southward, they could be recalled. Once he sent the navy past Vicksburg, however, there was no turning back. This attempt would decide the fate of Vicksburg, win or lose. "This is the only move I now see as practicable," Grant wrote Halleck, adding that "I will keep my army together, and see to it that I am not cut off from my supplies, or beaten in any other way than in a fair fight."[11]

The resolution was evident to the War Department moles sent to Grant's army to check up on him. Adjutant General Lorenzo Thomas, ostensibly on an African American regimental recruiting tour (he had already spoken to the troops at Lake Providence on April 8, one of the soldiers there remarking of several generals speaking and "one from Washington"), was already there to watch Grant. The story later came out that he had orders to relieve Grant if he thought it necessary, but some historians have pushed back on the claim because there is no verifying corroboration. If he was there to watch Grant, he nevertheless became so enthused at recruiting Black soldiers that he seemingly forgot his oversight mission; he went up and down the river speaking and recruiting, although at Lake Providence a gun went off prematurely during his thirteen-gun salute and it took off an arm of one of the cannoneers and a thumb of another. But Thomas was not the only one. In addition, Congressman Elihu Washburne was on site; Grant owed the politician his rise in rank, and Grant often went to him for guidance and help with promotions and such: "I have selected you to write to on this subject because you have always shown such willingness to befriend me." Grant knew how to play the political game, and in writing Washburne he was always careful to brag on his brother Cadwallader C. Washburn, one of Grant's generals. Yet Washburne now also arrived to see how Grant was doing; with the hurtful letters from his brother, even Grant's guardian congressman was beginning to doubt. Most important, now Charles A. Dana, a newspaperman recently turned bureaucrat working for the War Department, arrived as well, ostensibly to check out paymaster operations in the Mississippi Valley. But he was actually there to check up on Grant, who perceived the mission and made him an insider at his headquarters. In a classic example of keeping his friends close and enemies closer, Grant gave Dana complete access and won him over, with the added boon that Dana was to report in writing nearly every day to Washington, which alleviated the task for Grant, who hated writing letters. Soon, the reports going back to Washington were highly congratulatory of Grant. In fact, Dana's first message from Milliken's Bend, where he arrived on April 6, was laudatory. "General Grant is very confident that Vicksburg will soon be taken." He laid out the plan to land south of Vicksburg and threaten Jackson and the Big Black River railroad bridge: "The enemy will be compelled to come out and fight."[12]

Grant was indeed confident despite what he described as being "sorely afflicted at this time scarsely being able to sit, lay, or stand. Biles are the matter." He nevertheless wrote Julia: "Ten days will probably take me away from here and I hope then soon to have the river open." It was a gamble Grant was more than willing to take, in large part because there were no other acceptable options. Bruce Catton has described the decision to go south as "one of the two or three important decisions of the Civil War." One of his soldiers realized as much, writing in early April of entering "the more active part of the campaign." Another simply informed home: "We will try Vicksburg again."[13]

"What is the 'next' plan in Gen. Grant's crochety brain, it is impossible to indicate," one of his soldiers admitted. "His ways, like the ways of Providence, are past finding out." And even Grant waffled at times at the momentous decision. In fact, he had in a weak moment decided he would just throw his entire army, all of it he could concentrate on the swampy ground and transports, in one giant assault at the Confederate works at Snyder's and Haynes' Bluffs on the Yazoo River. Grant and Fred even went up in a flotilla of transports and gunboats with Porter and Sherman to get a good look at the ground on April 1. In such dangerous areas, he left the "quite disappointed"

Fred behind on a transport and went on farther in a gunboat, only to have Fred go ashore where "we drew marked attentions from the enemy and had to retreat to the steamer." "Not aware of anybody being April-fooled," one of Grant's soldiers scribbled in his diary that same day, but Grant was fooling himself if he thought he could attack at such a defensible place.[14]

After throwing a few shells at the enemy, Grant quickly decided against making the attack: "After the reconnaissance of yesterday," he told Admiral Porter, "I am satisfied that an attack upon Haynes' Bluff would be attended with immense sacrifice of life, if not with defeat." He likewise informed Halleck that "with present high water the extent of ground upon which troops could land at Haynes' Bluff is so limited that the place is impregnable"; he later added "the hillsides are lined with rifle pits, with embrasures here and there for field artillery. To storm this, but a small force could be used at the outset." Although it was unknown to him that the Confederates rushed troops to Snyder's Bluff as a result of his exploration, he just could not send his troops to the slaughter, recognizing quickly, in the best coup d'oeil mentality, that success was not possible or practicable given the casualties that would be endured. "I have no idea of being driven to do a desperate or foolish act by the howlings of the press," he assured his father. There was consequently only one choice left, and that was to go below Vicksburg. He informed Admiral Porter as much on April 2: "Having, then, fully determined upon operating from New Carthage either by the way of Grand Gulf or Warrenton, . . . I would, admiral, therefore renew my request to prepare for running the blockade at as early a day as possible." Grant apparently even went aboard Porter's flagship to discuss it, taking Fred with him, but Porter asked one of his sailors to give Fred a tour of the vessel while the officers talked. It was only later that Fred realized the tour was not all in good taste: "The Admiral, doubtless remembering the old saying that 'little pitchers have long ears,' called a man to show me all over the ship—everywhere but in the cabin. Not then appreciating the reasons for this special courtesy, I enjoyed my explorations very much."[15]

It was also during these ventures, probably on April 1, that Grant suffered a thumb wound while trying out a new "machine gun" on one of the vessels, "a new invention, which it was determined to test when General Grant returned to the boat." A piece of shell struck Grant on the thumb and, according to Fred, made "a painful wound which caused him much suffering for some weeks, and greatly distressed me."[16]

Once his mind was made up, however, Grant pushed hard for the effort south of Vicksburg, unpopular though it was. Some of his generals agreed with the move, while some others remained mostly silent, but a few were surprisingly aghast at the idea. Hurlbut, safely at a distance, agreed with the plan despite wishing to resign (Grant talked him out of it), writing that it looked like something was about to be done, as "General Grant has ordered down the regimental and headquarters transportation, which looks as if he expected to be on hard land again." Then he added: "It is my opinion that the right mode of attack has been at last attempted." McClernand likewise approved of the plan, he likely supporting anything that would get the operations going once more. Dana in fact related that he "entered zealously into the plan." McPherson coyly remained mostly silent, the junior of the corps commanders perhaps thinking this was a little beyond his pay grade. Admiral Porter, however, privately to Secretary Welles, was for going back to the book and doing it the way Grant had started, moving from Memphis along the railroad to Grenada: "Had General Grant not turned back when on the way to Grenada he would have been in Vicksburg before this."[17]

Surprisingly, and despite common perception in the army that Grant and Sherman always "pulled together," it was mostly Sherman who railed against the idea, both personally to Grant and then on April 8 in a letter that outlined his concerns and recommendations. He asked that all Grant's corps commanders be put on record regarding the plan, mostly to protect Grant from McClernand's scheming, he around the same time writing that McClernand had held back his report of Arkansas Post "for a long time, that he might twist and turn his own to his own honor and glory." Giving his own ideas, concerned as he was mainly with supply issues south of Vicksburg, which had not been a concern given all the efforts north of the city, Sherman desired a complete restart of the entire effort, including going back to Memphis to move down the railroads in another, but safer and more comprehensive, by-the-book operation with secure supply lines and acquisition of decisive points. He recommended that "the line of the Yalobusha be the base from which to operate." It was the Mississippi Central campaign all over, which Sherman believed Grant had called off too quickly and thereby given up a golden opportunity; Sherman even wrote his wife confidentially that "I have no faith in the whole plan." That said, he ended by stating that "whatever plan of action he may adopt will receive from me the same zealous co-operation and energetic support as though conceived by myself." Grant heard Sherman's concerns and literally pocketed them, later relating that Sherman had argued "I was putting myself in a position voluntarily which an enemy would be glad to maneuver a year—or a long time—to get me in." Grant did not see it that way; he just needed the roads and bayous to dry up some to get started. And now was that time. Others were similarly unimpressed with the idea, brigade commander Kilby Smith writing home that "the army is on the eve of what I consider a desperate enterprise. I believe the movement is forced by the folly and madness of politicians at home."[18]

Accordingly, with the leadership resolve right out of Clausewitzian theory, Grant began the movements southward on the west side of the river even before April arrived. He also ordered the rest of the army southward from Yazoo Pass and Lake Providence. "Grand Gulf is the point at which I expect to strike," he informed Halleck on April 11, a Confederate deserter having given division commander Peter Osterhaus a good idea of what defenses were there. Grant also corresponded with Nathaniel Banks to the south, still thinking in the back of his mind of making a lodgment on the east side of the Mississippi River and then sending a corps down to operate against Port Hudson before all turning their attention to Vicksburg. But a return note from Banks indicating he was going off on a chase up the rivers and bayous of Louisiana gave him pause; Banks indicated he would not be ready to cooperate until May 10.[19]

Meanwhile, Grant had to figure out whose troops to utilize in the delicate movement southward west of the river, what historian Terry Winschel has labeled as "arguably . . . the most important assignment of the campaign." McClernand's XIII Corps was the nearest corps to the south, so it "naturally fell to its lot," McPherson's troops still mainly up at Lake Providence and Yazoo Pass and Sherman's just returned from Steele's Bayou and one division headed northward for another raid. Sherman was not that supportive anyway (Dana reported he "doubted and criticized"), so the job would go to McClernand, who, if not a Grant crony, was never at a loss for energy or nerve. He had proven that. But given their history, McClernand would need watching closely, he still showing his prickly side at times. On one such occasion after McClernand had started the movement southward and Grant called on him for further details of men, he responded, "I think it probable that you would not have ordered it with a fuller knowledge of my operations. . . . I hope you will find it consistent with your general views to leave me to prosecute my present undertaking with all the resources at my disposal." The decision to use McClernand, who was "exceedingly desirous of this command," caused some ruffles, Admiral Porter and some of his staff opposing it and even Dana relating that "I have remonstrated, so far as I could properly do so, against intrusting so momentous an operation to McClernand." That brought a swift rebuke from Secretary of War Stanton: "Allow me to suggest that you carefully avoid giving any advice in respect to commands that may be assigned, as it may lead to misunderstanding and troublesome complications." Still, Vicksburg historian Michael Ballard has come to the conclusion that Grant trusted McClernand with the operation.[20]

Once the larger movement was decided upon, there were a couple of options for moving troops and goods, one of which was another canal dug from the Mississippi River at Duckport to Walnut Bayou, which connected with Roundaway Bayou at Richmond, which one Federal explained was "not the famed capital of the so called Rebel confederacy which so many have tried to reach but failed." One soldier remarked that "the idea looks feasible enough, but the canal business has failed so repeatedly that there isn't much confidence in it. . . . This canal is evidently his last resource. . . . If this fails it is difficult to imagine where the next one *can* be cut." Another speculated in his diary, "I wonder how many more canals are we going to dig before we get [to] Vicksburg." The canal was dug nevertheless, Grant keeping heavy drafts of men mainly from Sherman's XV Corps working continuously and engineers exploring the ability to float troops through the bayous; even the steam dredges from the main canal at Vicksburg were brought up to work on the Duckport Canal, and Grant gathered all the flatboats and barges he could find, even calling for more from the North as well as small tugs to pull them. The only concern was that cutting the levee again to let in water might flood the very area he was trying to open roads in, but Grant reasoned that with so many other breaks in the levee "I cannot see that this additional crevasse is going to have much other effect."[21]

Perhaps a bigger problem attending the Duckport venture was the massive amount of trees in the bayou, which had to be cut away. Engineer William Jenney utilized a crosscut saw on an A-frame that could cut trees underwater, but it was what was in those trees that scared the soldier the most. "Poisonous snakes were very numerous at that season of the year in that region, and [they] frequently hung from the trees which stretched their branches across the water," Jenney explained. "A slight tap on the branch and the snake would fall, so that, in order to keep them out of our boats and rafts, we were obliged whenever we moved to station men forward with long poles to clear the track from snakes." Eventually, one small boat made it through the canal, but by then the water level was falling, and so did the level of the bayou. At the same time, that made the adjacent roadways appear out of the murky water and once dried out would provide a similar path through the wilderness. One Illinoisan nevertheless quipped that their work was on the "last ditch."[22]

The other option provided more initial excitement: a land route across to Richmond and thence down the bank of Roundaway Bayou. It would obviously be much better to march the troops on dry land rather than shuffle them through snake-infested bayous on flatboats. McClernand admitted that the land route was encouraging, "perhaps more so than that afforded by the Duckport enterprise." Accordingly, Grant gave the orders and McClernand started his troops southward by land as well in a slow opening of territory against slight Confederate resistance and more substantial geographical impediments. But the river was steadily falling, and the ground would soon be ready for a major movement southward, McClernand's initial efforts being only the leading wave that literally opened the route the rest of the army would travel. McClernand gave the task to division commander Peter J. Osterhaus, who oversaw it himself using Brigadier General Theophilus T. Garrard's brigade, specifically Colonel Thomas W. Bennett's 69th Indiana.[23]

Colonel Bennett received orders in late March to move with his Indianans and a portion of the 2nd Illinois Cavalry from "Camp McClernand" at Milliken's Bend to Richmond, some twelve miles, with a view of making that place the base for further movements southward along the bayous and levees to New Carthage on the Mississippi River. McClernand himself gave the orders: "The main purpose of the expedition is to open a practicable communication for our forces via Richmond, La., between this camp and New Carthage." It would literally be an exploration, as few knew what was out there. "It is . . . believed that there is a road along the bank of Roundaway Bayou almost the whole distance," McClernand's orders read. Bennett moved on March 31 and reached Roundaway Bayou, on the other side of which sat Richmond. Confederates held the town, but Bennett took them under fire and sent the cavalry across the bayou on a few skiffs found nearby; with McClernand himself watching, the Illinoisans paddled "across the bayou with the butts of their carbines" and drove the enemy away and secured the town. Osterhaus himself came down the next day and became convinced that Richmond, despite being "not much of a town" (as one of his Ohioans described it), provided what was needed as a base to continue on; he was also convinced of the adaptability of this route to New Carthage. In the ensuing days, as Bennett's 69th Indiana secured the town and even probed ahead three or four miles to the Stanbrough Plantation, the cavalry moved southward all the way to T. C. Holmes's Plantation, named Trinidad (which some of the Federals confused with Confederate general Theophilus Holmes), where they skirmished with some of the enemy under Major Isaac F. Harrison of the 15th Louisiana Cavalry Battalion. Osterhaus sent forward new troops, the balance of Garrard's brigade including the guns of the 7th Michigan Battery, to garrison the town. Also sent forward were Patterson's Kentucky engineers, who had a two-hundred-foot pontoon bridge completed across the bayou by the evening of April 3.[24]

With the bridge built and troops up, Osterhaus led a reconnaissance the next day, April 4, southward along the road to New Carthage, which followed the west bank of Roundaway Bayou nearly all the way to the Mississippi

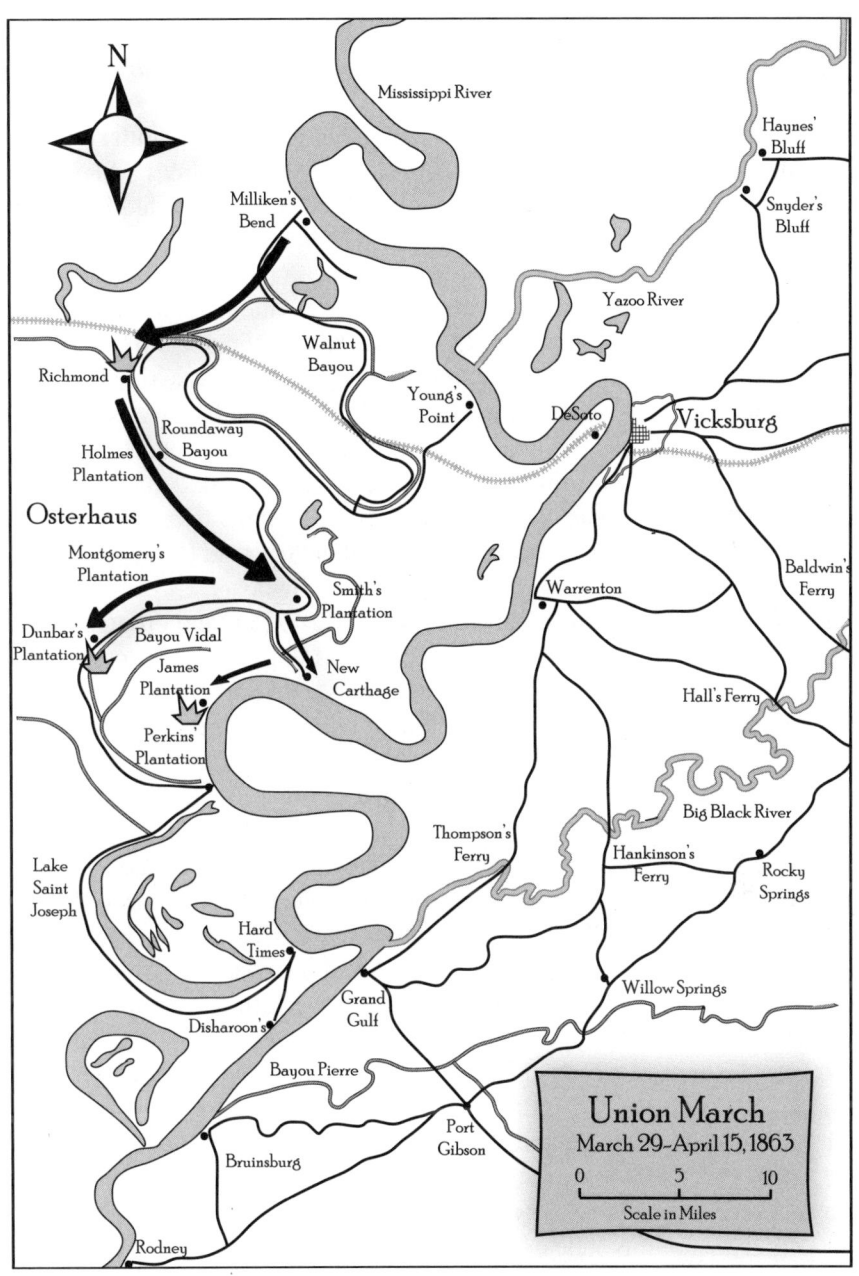

River. McClernand had wanted Osterhaus himself to lead the effort: "I think it expedient that you should personally conduct the expedition." Osterhaus took with him portions of the 2nd and 3rd Illinois Cavalry and 6th Missouri Cavalry, along with the 49th and 69th Indiana and a few artillery pieces. He made quick progress, though moving cautiously at Holmes's Plantation, where the Confederates had been fought earlier. The enemy fled before the Union column, Osterhaus reporting that they "remained all day at a safe but observing distance." The movement was so easy on the levee and dry ground in fact that he made it all the way to Smith's Plantation, where Roundaway joined Bayou Vidal. Roundaway Bayou met Bayou Vidal at Pliney Smith's Plantation, named Pointe Clear, a couple miles short of New Carthage, and some of the road there was still underwater at the time and the landscape back of it to the west was totally inundated. Still, Osterhaus had made it to within a couple miles of New Carthage and the river, but the Confederates were still in his front; worse, the backwater completely flooded the two miles between Smith's and New Carthage. Osterhaus noted that "the road [was] totally submerged, the only possible communication being by boats." So would be the route back to Richmond if the levee broke, and McClernand ordered guards all along the route to keep the enemy from breaking it and the waters "ingulfing us." The Federals also worried over civilian saboteurs on the route, Grant quipping that "about the only loyalty in this region is possessed by the mules and contrabands."[25]

Unable to proceed across the water to New Carthage, which Grant referred to as an "island," Osterhaus instead chose to continue on the dry road north of Bayou Vidal to "find out, if possible, the locality of the rebel camp." He went as far as Montgomery's Plantation with cavalry ahead all the way to R. Dunbar's Plantation another six miles down the bayou. The cavalry reported that the Confederates scampered across Bayou Vidal on a flatboat, which secured the northern bank. Osterhaus then moved back to Smith's to camp that night, McClernand himself having arrived by this time. Osterhaus left cavalry and pickets as far out as Dunbar's, with cavalry camped at Montgomery's, while the main force camped at Smith's Plantation. All were safe, Osterhaus related, with "volumes of water separating and protecting me from them."[26]

Yet the Federals were probing blindly to a large degree. Osterhaus informed McClernand that "notwithstanding the closest searches I could not find a good map of this state or of the neighboring parishes (Tensas, Franklin, Catahoola etc). If there is any thing of the kind at your Hd Qrs I should be happy to be favored with a copy." He added also that "maps of or sketches of the mouths of Big Black and adjacent lands in Mississippi would be very desirable!"[27]

Illustrating the extent of the blind probes, Osterhaus and McClernand personally examined the levee south of Smith's, the only thing above water, and made it much of the way to New Carthage. McClernand staff officer Lieutenant Colonel Henry C. Warmoth gave detail on the generals' adventures, including McClernand forcing "an old secesh" to push him along in a skiff. Warmoth took the skiff back across to get Osterhaus, who panicked when the small boat dipped to one side. Warmoth described how "Genl. Osterhaus got scared and jumped out. His hand reached the shore but his feet stayed in the boat, and there he remained . . . for some moments until he finally had to fall into the river. I don't think I ever laughed more than at this proceeding." Osterhaus tried to wade across, but the current was too swift, so he had to catch another ride on the tipsy boat. The party continued to New Carthage with just McClernand, Osterhaus, Warmoth, and three infantrymen, all six armed with a musket and cartridge box. "It was a military sight to see a Major Genl., a Brig. Genl., and a Lt. Col. with 3 soldiers, all with muskets and cartridge boxes, marching along on a reconnaissance," Warmoth explained. Suddenly, a bullet flew between them; Warmoth and others pushed McClernand behind the levee, although he thought all were going into the water. "Genl. McClernand thought we were going to run, so he very excitedly exclaimed: 'Damn you, stand fire, don't you run, stand fire, damn you!'" Despite the seriousness, all had a good laugh again.[28]

The unusual high-level reconnaissance found that three giant crevasses, "each from 300 to 500 feet wide," according to Engineer Frederick Prime, broke through the levee, and the two generals were able to traverse two of them but ran into the Confederate pickets on the other side of the third, which they declined to cross; McClernand informed Grant that the enemy "came very near hitting me. One of the balls whistled between the members of my little party." But they could see New Carthage and the Mississippi River and knew they were close. Yet they also realized that, at this stage of water, a boat would be needed to get to New Carthage. Osterhaus thus ordered a patrol to capture a flatboat he had heard was on Bayou Vidal past Dunbar's, the information having come from "an intelligent negro, who came into my lines with 4 of the same complexion." The contraband agreed to go take the boat, so Osterhaus sent him the next day, April 5, with a patrol of soldiers from the 3rd Illinois Cavalry to do so, which they did. The Confederates fired into the party as they were moving back to Smith's but were unable to stop their progress.[29]

Now with a boat, Osterhaus planned his attack on New Carthage. Engineer Patterson, finished with his bridge work at Richmond, had come forward and was surprised that "there is no land dry save the levee." He soon built bulwarks on the flatboat to protect the occupants, Osterhaus describing it as "sided up with 3-inch planks in gunboat style." The flat was big enough to carry a cannon and infantry, and Patterson worked through the night to get it ready for action. He was done by the next morning, Osterhaus himself writing the name on the side with a chunk of charcoal: *Opossum*. Osterhaus himself and a gun and several companies of the 49th and 69th Indiana then moved out for New Carthage, some following in skiffs as well. The Confederates abandoned the place on their approach. Landing at the only spot above water where New Carthage itself sat and positioning the gun and two companies of troops there, Osterhaus then led the Indianans on southward along the bank of the Mississippi River to chase the Confederates, they doing so for nearly a couple of miles, all the way to the Joshua James Plantation named Ione. Osterhaus described the plantation house and gin, with other outbuildings, as sitting on twenty acres of dry ground, all that was above water on this side of the levee. The gin commanded the entire area, and there the Confederates made a stand. Osterhaus directed the Indianans to attack, and after an hour's fight the Confederates fled and Osterhaus took control. He moved the Indianans on up to the plantation to safeguard it, relating that they were "perfectly secure, as only the levee is out of water, and they cannot be flanked."[30]

Joshua James, "an old gentleman," Osterhaus reported, desired to get out of the way and move to another plantation "where his negroes are." Osterhaus had no problem with him leaving, especially since "he has not seen anything of our forces," but he wanted permission from McClernand to let him go. Meanwhile, James jawed with the leading Indianans, who declared themselves to his amazement simply the "entering wedge" of a long line of Federals who would soon move through his place. But another local civilian drew more interest than Mr. James. In reporting that from New Carthage he could see the hulk of the *Indianola*, Osterhaus also added that "the plantations of Joseph and Jefferson Davis are also opposite—a very tempting view."[31]

Through the quick and efficient work of Osterhaus and his Indianans, McClernand had New Carthage and the surrounding area in hand by April 6, the same day many of these troops on both sides (Sherman included) noted as the one-year anniversary of Shiloh. Never failing to tout success, McClernand issued a congratulatory message. But it was a tenuous hold, as the Confederates were known to be in force just to the south at Judge John Perkins's Plantation, named Somerset. Also of concern were the Confederate gunboats *Queen of the West* and *Webb*, known also to be prowling around. Osterhaus consequently arranged his troops to protect the entire route from Milliken's Bend, with Garrard's regiments spread out along the line from Richmond to Smith's with troops still out the Bayou Vidal Road and frequently skirmishing with the enemy there, it being plainly heard even by the forces up at Vicksburg.

Colonel Lionel Sheldon's brigade moved forward to man the Richmond area and the road back to Milliken's Bend. Osterhaus's entire division accordingly manned the entire route from Milliken's Bend on the Mississippi River above Vicksburg to New Carthage and the James Plantation on the river south of the city. "Everything is excitement today," one Federal wrote in his diary amid all the sudden movement at Milliken's Bend.[32]

Despite some skirmishing along the leading edges of the force, specifically at James's Plantation on April 8, Grant was convinced that this was a practicable route and thus sent in even more troops; he needed only a boat to ferry them from Smith's to New Carthage, or "if piles could be driven and a way made over the crevasses in the levee, that would be another way," McClernand reported. But it could definitely be done, so McClernand started the troops that had been at Milliken's Bend, they actually being reviewed on April 9 by Grant himself; the troops had shined their equipment for the show, including washing artillery carriages. Despite news that a newspaper editor had published the plan to move via New Carthage to Grand Gulf, Grant then pushed on. (Grant laid the blame for the leak on "that incoragibly gassy man Col. [Josiah] Bissell of the Eng Regt. . . . His tonge will have to be tied if there is anything going on where he is which you don't want made public.") By April 12, Eugene Carr's division had arrived, allowing Osterhaus to concentrate his two brigades specifically between Holmes's and Smith's Plantations on Roundaway Bayou, still with the advance forces at New Carthage as well. The 120th Ohio specifically held the Holmes Plantation, Lieutenant Colonel Marcus Spiegel relating that it was "one of the nicest, grandest and most tasty plantations I ever saw"; he also explained to his wife that, for a day or so, "my boys live in clover; they all eat off of china dishes, gold striped, and have their tents carpeted. I occupy a Parlor and Bedroom furnished in 5th Avenue style, have my office in the Library and Staff and field Officers all have very nice quarters." But it did not last long, and the Ohioans were soon off into the wilderness again. Despite muddy roads, with one Iowan declaring "many wagons had to be abandoned, and the roads were literally lined with wrecks," the rest of the corps began to congregate at the ample camping- and resource-rich ground north of Smith's Plantation, awaiting the open way southward. McClernand, in fact, was down at Smith's Plantation already looking toward the Mississippi River crossing, asking Grant for guidance on whether it should be done up the Big Black River or at Grand Gulf.[33]

Grant was ecstatic but kept his eye on the goal, informing McClernand that "it is no part of my present intentions to bring back the troops you have sent to Carthage ever by the route they went over." He added that Porter would soon be passing the batteries at Vicksburg but admitted, "I have been more troubled to know how to supply you with ammunition, until water communication is established, than on any other subject." Obviously, he could not send ammunition with Porter, like he did rations, for fear of explosions, and neither could he send it on unmanned drifting barges like he did coal for the same reasons. And McClernand calculated the needed amount, which obviously could not be gleaned from the countryside like food: McClernand needed nearly five million rounds besides what the soldiers carried, plus artillery ammunition. Just to get it to New Carthage would take three hundred wagons (he only had a hundred and fifty available) and thirteen days for both small arms and artillery. It was such a dire need that McClernand recommended sending some by using ironclads or even on barges piled high with wet hay bales. Nevertheless, Grant wanted McClernand to keep moving, even as he worked out the ammunition issues. "It is my desire that you should get possession of Grand Gulf at the earliest practicable moment," Grant ordered McClernand on April 12, again mentioning the idea (before Banks's delaying letter arrived) of sending forces then to Port Hudson.[34]

Later on, Grant would also bemoan the lack of ability to send medical supplies southward: "We are necessarily very destitute of all preparations for taking care of wounded men." This was over and above the problems Grant had with reported sickness among the troops and turnover in the head of the Medical Department (as well as the quartermaster, who Grant removed because "he is not up to his present duties"), although Grant boasted later that "no Army ever went into the field better provided with medical stores and medical attendants than is furnished the Army now in front of Vicksburg." The change in the weather obviously helped, one Ohioan writing that "the weather is very warm and since it ceased raining incessantly, the health of the men is improving and they are getting more cheerful." But that was a risk Grant was willing to take in his continual move from the Jominian philosophy of war to a more Clausewitzian type of operation: getting at the enemy no matter what. "I foresee great difficulties in our present position," Grant warned Sherman later on, "but it will not do to let these retard any movements." The irony of course was that with the hoped-for warmer and drier weather came temperatures almost too hot to campaign in. One Federal wrote that it was already getting "quite warm enough to remind us of what we may expect when summer comes."[35]

Certainly, the issues with getting supplies to the army were real; it was even more important since the army was leaving much of its equipment and baggage, and the sick, behind on the Louisiana side. Grant faced other such conundrums as well; for example, if he broke the levee to allow bayou transport of supplies, the break would threaten to overflow adjacent roads. The frequent rainstorms also did not help, Dana reporting of one on April 11 that "made the road very muddy, prov[ing] that a storm of twenty-four hours would render it impassable for days." But Grant continued on even with the logistical issues still somewhat unsettled, and that was a classic example of Grant foregoing the standard book of operations (mainly Jomini's) that touted a secure line of supply. This was anything but that, and it even advanced toward a more Clausewitzian view of warfare, Clausewitz having written that "warfare based on requisition and local sources of supply is so superior to the kind that relies on depots, that the two no longer seem to be the same instrument."[36]

Despite a bad case of diarrhea, Lorenzo Thomas was impressed with the effort, reporting to Washington that Grant had a route opened that only in one place "has got to be raised 10 inches." He added that, once the river fell a mere two feet, he would have a dry road all the way through. It was all very promising, Thomas reporting that "this army is in fine condition, unusually healthy, and in good heart." He also sent the top-secret news that Porter would soon pass the batteries at Vicksburg "about three nights hence." It was good that Thomas was reporting so favorably if indeed he carried in his pocket Grant's relief orders, to be exercised if Thomas saw the need. Fortunately for Grant, even if Thomas did have orders to relieve Grant in hand, so far he did not see any need to use them. It was a very discerning move on Thomas's part.[37]

While the major move was occurring west of the Mississippi River, Grant had other probes and expeditions still out and even more beginning. One was a full division moving northward to Greenville to secure river transportation there. Another was the still-continuing Yazoo Pass expedition, which was soon winding down. In the midst of all that, Grant also had to oversee command changes and administrative duties. The most problematic change occurred when David Stuart left the army, his brigadier general's commission, though appointed, being rejected by the United States Senate and he having already resigned his colonel's commission. He had just led the division up Steele's Bayou and was now out of a command; Grant promoted Frank Blair to take command of the division in Sherman's corps. Other promotion problems disrupted his plans as well, Grant pushing Lincoln himself for Logan to be promoted ("he is entitled to and can be trusted with a command equal to what increased rank would entitle him to"), as well as having unwanted officers foisted on him; he wrote that Brigadier General Napoleon Buford "would scarcely make a respectable Hospital nurse if put in petticoats, and certain[ly] is unfit for any other Military position."[38]

Blair in particular posed a problem, being a former congressman and a brother to a Lincoln cabinet official. One staff officer noted that Blair was a "tricky ambitious politician" and "had a regular cleaning out at Head quarters" when he assumed division command. He added that only trouble could ensue, as "he and Grant don't like each other. Sherman quarrels with him." In fact, Sherman admitted "Frank Blair is a 'disturbing element.' I wish he was in Congress or a Bar Room, anywhere but our Army." But Grant later found reason to walk back his initial thoughts. In his memoirs, he confessed, "I dreaded his coming; I knew from experience that it was more difficult to command two generals desiring to be leaders than it was to command one army officered intelligently and with subordination." He continued: "It affords me the greatest pleasure to record now my agreeable disappointment in respect to his character. There was no man braver than he, nor was there any who obeyed all orders of his superior in rank with more unquestioning alacrity. He was one man as a soldier, another as a politician."[39]

Much of Grant's immediate military concern was getting out the forces now in the Tallahatchie River, the affair having boiled down, in Porter's words, to "a kind of duel between batteries and ironclads, in which shell and powder are expended without any use." Unknown to Grant, and undesired if his wishes had been fully known, Quinby had restarted the entire operation upon his arrival, prompting one Confederate to admit "we had hardly done crowing when, the Yankee gunboats returned." But Quinby found a watery mess once he arrived again at Fort Pemberton, causing several days of delay. Movement restarted in the Union forces only in April. Loring reported them building a new battery on April 1, once the ground had dried to the point they could operate on land. He also reported the departure of the enemy steamers to bring in more troops and asked Pemberton for a corresponding set of soldiers, namely Featherston's brigade fresh off its defense of Rolling Fork. They soon arrived, one Mississippian relating that the boat "was packed full of soldiers and body lice." Loring also wanted more guns, which Pemberton did not have to send. Perhaps in a fatalistic mood, Loring notified him nevertheless that "this fight, from the preparations making by the enemy, will be desperate." Meanwhile, the Federals pitched tents on any ground they could find and appeared to be ready to wait out the Confederates.[40]

Loring reported that "during their short absence we greatly strengthened our lines, and were fully prepared to give them a warm reception." A lot of the help came from the infusion of those new troops on April 1, including Major

General Dabney Maury and the entirety of Featherston's brigade fresh up from below, Featherston being told "there is immediate need of your brigade in another direction." Maury was amazed at the place, writing later that "I could scarce find dry land enough on which to form a line of battle." Loring related that "we waited a short time after their arrival, in the hope that they would muster courage to attack us, but it seems that it failed them in the critical moment." He then added that "we then commenced the offensive."[41]

With fresh troops and ammunition, Loring felt confident in going on the attack. "All quiet with a cloudless sky and a prospect for fair weather," he reported. Lloyd Tilghman had by this time also arrived and plotted on his map the direction of the lone house in the area, which he surmised was the Union headquarters. The civil engineer by trade aimed a cannon by compass at the house and shelled it. Loring also contested the Federal workers erecting new fortifications and batteries and fired on the camps and transports now that he had ample ammunition. "We commenced shelling their camps and transports," he wrote, "and kept it up for two days and at intervals during the night." He also sent out infantry as best he could: "Yesterday we made a reconnaissance in force from our left flank, alarming them very much." Loring also had troops along the river behind the Federals, even with an artillery piece that, he reported, fired into a transport and damaged it. Colonel Arthur E. Reynolds's 26th Mississippi even devised canoes that could carry men with small arms to fire into transports, and one was big enough to even carry the cannon. The Confederate shelling continued over the course of April 2, 3, and 4, but Maury related that "the enemy was very quiet during this whole time." That was questionable, at least to the extent that Grant's engineer James H. Wilson arrived back at the fleet on April 3.[42]

Also arriving were the two other brigades of Quinby's division under the combined command of Colonel George Boomer. They had endured the same old trek through the pass, Boomer writing home that "on the trip down, while one morning in the pilot-house of the *Belle Creole*, a limb burst suddenly through, and cut my right eyelid badly. You would be amused to see our boats—nothing but a photograph could describe them." A lower-level soldier admitted that "the 'pass' today has been but a repetition of the pass of yesterday." But they were here now, ready to add to the weight bearing on Fort Pemberton, although some of these reinforcing Federals had also heard the effects of Sherman's and Porter's entrance into the Delta to the south. Unfortunately for those who made the long trek to Fort Pemberton, also arriving in the scramble were Grant's orders to let go of the operation and head out to the Mississippi River.[43]

Despite getting more troops of his division up to his position, Quinby left

Fort Pemberton on April 5, Easter Sunday, although one Indianan reported in his diary "no eggs." One of Quinby's Missourians admitted that "weather our commanders got skeard at the fort or the fort skeard them I can not tell." One Confederate was not convinced this time, writing that "we are all conjecturing as to their movements.... It may be that it is a Yankee trick to get us away from our works so that they can slip in & occupy them in our absence. I hope that our commanders will be awake to their duty and be sharp enough so as to thwart all of their movements." But it was no Yankee trick; the Federal flotilla was indeed trudging northward. And it was a grueling three-day journey back out the rivers and pass to Helena. "Just as I feared we are on the fall back again," one Federal of Ross's division wrote home, while one of his Iowans simply noted "the fleet on a retrograde movement—bound up the River." Loring gleefully reported to Pemberton that "the enemy commenced embarking last night at 10 o'clock, and before day this morning [they] were in rapid retreat." He did not fully know what was up, as the Federals had left one time before and then came back, but he suspected they "are going to the Mississippi River. The probability is that it is their intention to do so." And it was. "The Yankees, it seems, have given up the trip altogether by this route," one Confederate wrote home.[44]

The trip was indeed just as grueling getting out as it was getting in. The transports led the way, the navy following in rear. There was trouble even before reaching the treacherous pass, however, one Federal telling of the captain of his transport being shot by a guerrilla on shore. The Federals burned the man's house in return. The natural obstacles were worse at the pass itself. The ill-fated *Chillicothe*, her logbook reported, "ran on some hidden obstruction, staving our starboard bow badly." It took a while to get the ironclad free, and when it was freed "she began to leak very badly." The logbook continued that "all hands manned pump and buckets." Once the leak was stopped and the gunboat continued on, she ran against a tree limb overhanging the pass, "badly dashing [the] port wheelhouse." The transports fared none too well either, caving in wheelhouses and breaking all sorts of critical parts; one Illinoisan admitted that "several times today the boat got pretty hard thumps against the trees but she was so badly broken up that she could not be impaired much more than she was." An impatient Quinby nearly snapped, yelling at one captain "this transport has troubled me a great many times during this Expedition. I have a mind to take this Regt. off & set fire to this steamer." Eventually, despite as many as three vessels having sunk in the pass, by April 10 all were back into the more spacious Mississippi River, Confederate scouts gleefully reporting that the Yazoo Pass was "abandoned." The Federals were just as gleeful, one writing that they "bid the Yazoo Pass 'good bye' & not sorry were we to leave it having had a hard trip of it." Another added that the Federals could "breathe freer than in that trap where we had been all the while before," yet another admitting that "the fleet was little else than so many dismantled hulls." Unfortunately, some of the Federals who had gone through the pass to Fort Pemberton found their camps rifled through and possessions stolen once they returned; the culprits were soldiers of their own army who had remained behind.[45]

Loring was able to alert Maury that "my services were no longer required near Fort Pemberton," and he headed back down to Vicksburg. But Maury was struck by the listlessness of the Federals he encountered: "The operations of the enemy were characterized by a great want of energy, but by the usual disregard of the claims of humanity and of the usages of manly warfare; women and unarmed, helpless men were insulted, private dwellings and plantations were destroyed and plundered, and stock stolen or wantonly killed, the fruit trees belted, and every other means taken to gratify the cowardly instincts of base natures." Obviously, Maury was not a fan of the Federal war machine. Other troops were similarly paired away as other places became more problematic, although there was too little transportation to move the men and equipment; one dolefully admitted "we lost a great many of our things at Greenwood on account of not having transportation furnished us for them." Unfortunately, there was a terrible accident among those who remained, as some of the 33rd Mississippi were working with a torpedo, or mine, that exploded: "Cilled 3 of them and wounded 4 others very badley."[46]

Loring added that "I would here remark that this expedition was the prominent one of a great plan for the attack of Vicksburg in rear," the plan also including the Steele's Bayou effort as well as a push up the Yazoo from its mouth. Loring gave Grant more credit that he deserved, as none of the plans were totally in tandem, although Grant saw Steele's Bayou as a possible way to cut off the Confederates at Greenwood. Still, Loring crowed that it was a "check which will undoubtedly prevent a further invasion of the State of Mississippi by the way of Tallahatchie and Yazoo Rivers." In that observation he was correct, but by that time all Union attention had been transferred southward to the movement west of the Mississippi River. Unfortunately for them, Confederate attention would remain focused primarily to the north and east of Vicksburg, with even yet another expedition emerging into the soggy Delta north of Vicksburg "to attract the attention of the enemy in that direction."[47]

Others were confused as well. James Z. George wrote "they disappointed me in leaving without having first made greater efforts . . . to reach the rear of Vicksburg through this channel." But he was not totally giving up on them and this odd new way of warfighting totally against the book: "When they will turn up next, I cannot tell." A Federal was thinking the same thing, writing, "Gen. Grant is not done with his strategy yet. I guess he thinks that he will catch them napping yet."[48]

"Greenville has been a favorite point from which to assail our passing boats," Sherman wrote in new orders, "and one object of your expedition is to let the planters and inhabitants on Deer Creek see and feel that they will be held accountable." As a result, Grant sent an entire division under Frederick Steele to Greenville in the first week of April on "some secret expedition," one Federal complained, to clear out Confederate resistance along Deer Creek as far as "two or three days' easy marches." In addition to reaping benefits concerning secured shipping as well as gathering supplies, Steele's Expedition to Greenville and along Deer Creek would also provide large dividends in sowing confusion among the Confederate high command. One Iowan in fact admitted in his diary a few days later: "It dawns upon us now that the front is marching for Vicksburg, and that our chase up Deer Creek was not a wild goose chase"; "it was done to divert the enemy's attention." These April demonstrations and diversions clearly kept John Pemberton alerted to threats to his north while the real crisis came south of him. Steele's Greenville operations helped in that effort.[49]

Unfortunately for him, Steele was under a cloud at this point, complaints showing up against him in Helena as well as newspapers about his lack of loyalty to Lincoln's administration. He was less than solid on the abolitionist question to be sure, but Grant vouched for his loyalty to the Union, especially when the complaints loomed large amid Steele's confirmation as major general by the Senate. Grant avowed that he and Steele had been classmates at West Point and that "Gen. Steele is one of our very best soldiers as well as one of the most able. He is in every sense a soldier, one who believes, as such, his first duty is obedience to law and the orders of his superiors." Grant enlisted his go-to congressman, Elihu Washburne, in an effort to keep Steele's nomination on track. Perhaps Steele's resulting bad mood was the result; one Illinoisan described how "Gen. Steele became wrathy with the actions of the 13th and to wreck his vengeance, he placed guard upon shore opposite our boat and confined both officers and men on board until further orders." The promotion finally came, just after Frank Blair's, Steele's former brigade commander refusing to wear his second star until Steele's came through as well.[50]

Steele's orders were secret, one of his Federals writing, "I have no idea where we will go, or whether there is any prospect of a fight." Actually, they were going to track down the Confederates under Samuel W. Ferguson fresh

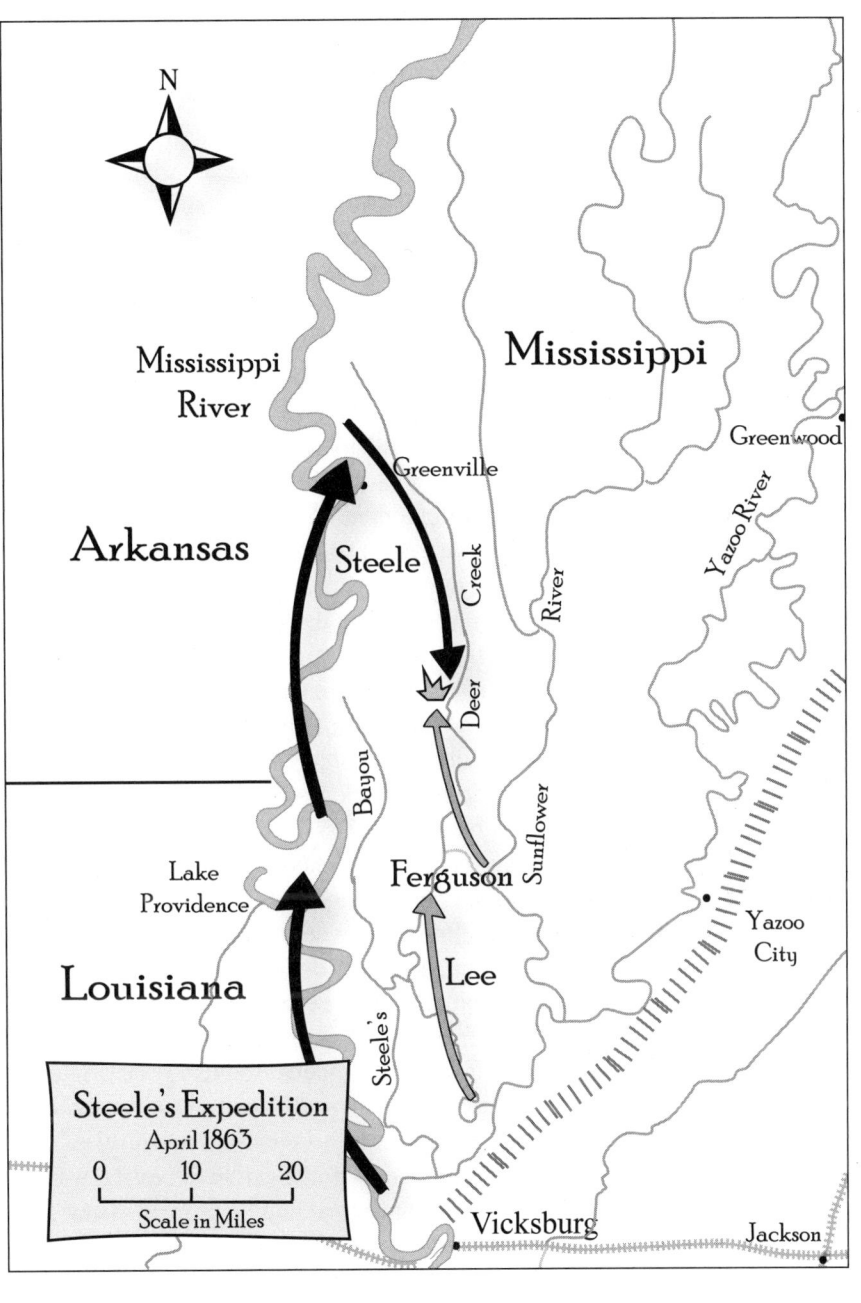

off their defense of the same area from the incursions from the south as well as to gather all the supplies that were available in this rich region. If the planters in the area "remain at home and behave themselves, molest them as little as possible," Steele's orders read. But if they were absent, indicating disloyalty, or if cotton was marked "C.S.A.," then Steele was to take what was needed. Sherman even envisioned Steele moving as far as "the mouth of Rolling Fork, . . . where Admiral Porter's fleet turned back."[51]

Steele moved his three brigades up to Greenville in the first days of April and after trying several routes ultimately landed for good about a mile north of Greenville on April 5, "Easter Day" one of his German Missourians reflected in his diary. "Greenville is a pleasant and picturesque little town about one hundred inhabitants," Henry Seaman of the 13th Illinois related. The various landings netted little besides visitation of the local plantations, where on April 4 one group enjoyed singing "The Star Spangled Banner" in the parlor of one house, accompanied by a Missouri lieutenant on the piano. Once landed for good the next day, Steele then set out southeastward on April 6 toward the plantation-rich Deer Creek country, where Burbridge had operated earlier, leaving a small gunboat and two regiments at the landing site to protect the transports. He first had to cross Black Bayou, the most substantial tributary of the waterway in this region. The bridges were out by this time, Ferguson's men having burned them and driven what stock they could southward to keep it out of the Federals' hands. Steele accordingly had to take time to build bridges before moving on. He bridged Black Bayou near the plantation of Confederate general Samuel G. French.[52]

By this point, Confederate scouts had detected the movement, and Ferguson, the only real Confederate force operating in the area now that Featherston had shifted northward to Fort Pemberton, moved to counter it; aside from a paperwork mess Featherston's commissary and quartermaster left unfinished, Ferguson still retained the 40th Alabama. But Ferguson was still vastly outnumbered, simply falling back in front of the entire Union division as it advanced, although gathering significant intelligence about the enemy force. Ferguson sent repeated requests about how to proceed: "Please let me know at once what to do; whether to hold the country to the last extremity, awaiting re-enforcements, or shall I endeavor to get my force safely out of the way and give the country up?" Meanwhile, the Confederate high command once more began to shift troops to the problem spot, prompting Stevenson at Vicksburg to again send reinforcements into the Rolling Fork/Deer Creek area. He again moved Stephen D. Lee, who had just been presented with a "fine horse" by the 17th Louisiana in recognition of his defense at Chickasaw Bayou, with a force of six regiments and light artillery but unfortunately only a smattering of cavalry, which was most needed. Others were positioned at Snyder's Bluff and even into the Sunflower River in case more force was needed, specifically John C. Moore's brigade from Fort Pemberton. The cottonclad gunboats under Captain Brown were again brought southward as well. Stevenson also asked that Pemberton "order back the intrenching tools" that Featherston had taken with him in his movement to Fort Pemberton.[53]

There was also some terrain exploitation as well. When Ferguson first heard of Steele's arrival, he sent troops to Millar's Bend on the Mississippi River south of Greenville to cut the levee where Black Bayou began. That would flood the area slowly, hopefully after the Federals pushed inland across some of these major bayous. "In about ten days," he related, "the swamp they have crossed on a dryland road will all be overflowed, and their line of communication very seriously obstructed." He betrayed his Jominian mindset as well, writing that "we will, therefore, have the great advantage of operations on an interior or shorter line by water communication."[54]

Despite the gathering Confederate resistance, Steele marched his troops hard on April 6, meeting a vast horde of slaves, some of them as white as the soldiers were ("a man as white as myself with straight hair, regular features[,] and light whiskers," an Iowan marveled). One black woman admitted: "'Laws Sakes,' where did you uns all come from, why you uns aint got no hons, they had been told and believed it that the Yankees had horns on their heads." The Federals were winded to say the least, one admitted, "not being used to marching." More important, Steele met Ferguson on April 7 at the Thomas Plantation some eighteen or twenty miles up Deer Creek from Rolling Fork. It was noted that this area was the same place Burbridge had operated in before, even passing the same "school house" Burbridge had passed. Ferguson deployed what little strength he had in front of a huge canebrake, "just as Mahan in his field Engineering prescribed, for passing a defile to the rear," he noted, even while again frantically calling for reinforcements: "if the country is to be held, more cavalry in indispensable." Meanwhile, Steele deployed in line of battle with some seven or eight regiments—an entire division—backed with several batteries of artillery. Ferguson reported that he repulsed the slight cavalry advance, but then the Union guns opened up on the Confederates, who had a few artillery pieces themselves, and then Steele sent the infantry forward across the plantation fields. Steele reported that the enemy "fled before the infantry became engaged." One of his soldiers simply noted—"but they would not stand," while another explained they were "mere showing fight." The operation was small but interesting, as Captain Axel Silversparre maneuvered his battery so oddly that Steele admitted amid the action, "Well, Captain Silverspeare may know where he is going, but I do not." Having marched a long way that day, Steele allowed his tired troops to bivouac that night where the Confederates had initially taken their position, one Iowan writing that "my feet are badly blistered tonight and before the attack I could barely walk, but the excitement seemed to drive away the pain but *now* I feel it sensibly." The orders were to "go into camp and catch chickens," and one Iowan admitted "we obey orders with alacrity." For their part, the Confederates described the event as "such a check with his small force that they were deterred from a farther advance."[55]

Steele sent out scouts the next morning to determine where the enemy force was, and they learned that Ferguson had fallen back toward Rolling Fork, from whence was coming his reinforcements. But Steele was getting nervous, and well he should. Confederate plans were for Lee to move up the Sunflower River and a parallel connecting bayou, Bogue Phaliah, and get in the Federals' rear to cut them off from Greenville. Under such cover, of course, Confederate boats were also evacuating all the foodstuffs they could from the region. Steele chose not to follow on but instead concentrated on gathering supplies and damaging the infrastructure as much as he could where he was. Plantation after plantation as a result was stripped of its goods, and some were burned, Steele reporting that his officers estimated five hundred thousand bushels of corn destroyed, certainly much of it the very commodities Pemberton had been so eager to gather and horde in Vicksburg. Only after a thorough job of destruction and the realization that the bridge across the creek some three miles ahead was burned did Steele turn back on April 8.[56]

In the column heading back northward, Steele counted some thousand head of cattle, horses, and mules, he adding "there are also a number of ox-wagons, carts, buggies, &c." Also along was what he termed "a great many negroes," prompting one of his soldiers to write home that they went "foraging & taking mules and Darkies." One Illinoisan declared that much of the goods and animals were hidden, "but we are generally informed by 'Sambo' who is the most thoroughly posted man we have in this latitude as to the whereabouts of the mules, cattle, meat, and other contraband goods." More sinister discoveries also occurred, including that "the Rebs hung one of the negroes . . . this morning on the corn crib for saying something disagreeable to Rebel ears. He is buried near the crib." Steele told those "that asked my advice to stay on the plantations where they belonged, except two engineers and a blacksmith," and he requested of Grant to "please send me instructions as to what shall be done with these poor creatures." Much destruction nevertheless occurred, one Confederate even posting a British flag in hopes of saving his assets. One Iowan quipped that "the British flag did not protect his rebel corn." In all, one Federal estimated the damage done at two or three million dollars.[57]

The Confederates merely watched and waited even as reinforcements arrived. Lee himself moved by the evening of April 8 as far north as the Thomas Plantation where the little fight had occurred, learning that Steele had turned back after "destroying everything eatable before them." All Lee could do with the slow infantry and artillery, which could not subsist on the parched land the Federals left behind, was to order Ferguson to follow and harass them as best he could with his mounted forces. Despite starting to break down himself due to work and exposure, Ferguson followed the Federals all the way to Black Bayou, where Steele's troops were again bridging the stream and made a demonstration on the plantation owned by Confederate general French. Only one man was wounded in the affair, and the Federals moved on along, but not before Steele placed a heavy guard on the plantation; he and French had both graduated from West Point in the same class in 1843.[58]

Meanwhile, more Confederate forces moved into the area, although they were late and unneeded by this point. There was a semblance of a merchant shipping system still available on the Delta waterways to shift troops fairly quickly, including the steamboats *Arcadia*, *Dew Drop*, *Golden Age*, *Emma Bett*, and *Hope*. Also restarted were raft projects across almost all the major streams, swung back to allow shipping but ready to be stretched across the waterways in case of emergency, including on the Sunflower River and Rolling Fork. There were even the earthen fortifications that had worked so well at Fort Pemberton; by mid-April, when Lee and many of his troops were preparing to head back to Vicksburg as events picked up there, Lee himself was overseeing a "line of fortifications which . . . will, when completed, be very strong, and can easily be held by the force under the command of Colonel Ferguson." At Rolling Fork itself was a fortification made of cotton bales and earth much like at Fort Pemberton, its parapet fifteen feet thick. Obstructions in the waterways themselves also reemerged to a greater extent than before, Mississippian Sidney S. Champion describing working to block the bayous despite the "gloomy country and full of mosquitoes and snakes." There was also thought of damming up Deer Creek south of Rolling Fork "in order to turn all the water into the latter," thereby draining the bayous Admiral Porter had used earlier. This would prevent any more threat in that direction, something the Confederates feared would occur simultaneously. But Ferguson would have a hard time doing that, as he reported "the water is so much higher now than it was when the last expedition came."[59]

By April 10, Steele was back at Greenville despite a delay when the large cattle herd broke the rebuilt bridge on the route. That allowed Confederates to catch up and skirmish with the rear of the column, but Steele had moved a total of forty-three miles in one direction along Deer Creek. He had lost only a member of his escort killed and a cavalryman wounded, although he admitted that "we have lost a considerable number of stragglers, some of whom were taken because they wished to be, no doubt." Ferguson related that he found four pairs of handcuffs linked by chain and thought they "would well ornament them." And despite rumors circulating among the forces at Helena that Steele had captured Fort Pemberton, Steele nevertheless concentrated around Greenville until further orders arrived, in the meantime going after a bulk of cotton bales he heard was nearby. The division remained near the transports for several more days according to Grant's orders, some even quartering in Greenville's buildings. The Federals remained, in fact, all the way until the latter part of April, during which there was "constant skirmishing" with Ferguson's troops. As they waited in "constant excitement," as one Missourian wrote in his diary, division after division passed them on the way southward to the concentration taking place at Young's Point and Milliken's Bend. Eventually the division also steamed away southward to join the main efforts at Vicksburg.[60]

For his part, Ferguson reported his loss at one trooper captured and two of the 40th Alabama deserted. But he also meted out punishment on the slaves caught in the middle of this devastating war. One was flagrant enough to be hanged: "I yesterday hanged a negro man, slave of William F. Smith," Ferguson reported, "who, mistaking two of my men for the Abolitionists, hailed them across the creek, and volunteered to conduct them to the rebel camp, so as to surprise it; informed them of my strength and position, asked for a gun to kill his master, and said that he would knock down and rape any white woman." It was most likely the man the Federals found at the corn crib. There could also be loss at the hands of the Union soldiers, one Iowan reporting "the firing last night was occasioned by a poor negro woman unknowingly trying to pass the pickets. She was shot through the heart and killed instantly."[61]

But Steele also left a wasteland, the plantations stripped bare, so much so that there was concern for provisioning troops remaining in the area. Lee himself, who returned to Rolling Fork, described how the "planters and negroes are much demoralized on the Mississippi, . . . and on some of the places the negroes are almost in a state of insurrection." Some estimates ranged that as many as two or three thousand slaves had followed Steele back to Greenville. It did not help that word soon filtered in that the United States' adjutant general, Lorenzo Thomas, was in the Mississippi Valley making speeches about how all the slaves would soon be put into the United States Army under white officers. Finally, the heavy rains of mid-April did not help either, especially Ferguson following up behind Steele's withdrawal and again planning to use his artillery on the Federal shipping in the Mississippi River.

The soggy terrain delayed him, something the Federal incursion seemed not to be able to do.⁶²

Although intended as little more than a diversion and as security for river transport, the operation was seen by some in the larger context. One Federal captured on the raid told his captors all they needed to know. When asked "what in thunder Grant expected to do in there," the soldier replied simply: "Take Vicksburg." The Confederate officer explained that Grant had tried "five times already and failed," to which the talkative Federal explained "yes, . . . but he has thirty-seven more plans in his pocket, and one of them will get there now, you bet."⁶³

John C. Pemberton was in full react mode by the first day of April. Although he was rectifying the meat shortage for the troops and was building a horde of supplies at Vicksburg itself, the enemy's movements were starting to get closer and closer. "Enemy is constantly in motion in all directions," he advised Richmond in early April—everywhere, that is, except at Vicksburg itself. "No one knows what the enemy are doing, or how to account for their delay in making their long threatened attack," one Confederate griped, although another in Vicksburg had confidence in his commanders: "I think our generals wood see these hills running down with blood before they will give it up." With Federals coming at him and moving in almost every direction, however, it was not hard to understand Pemberton's concern, and the common soldier felt the tension. "There are a good many leaving this regt every night," one Confederate confided to his sister. Indeed, Federals were still confronting Loring at Yazoo Pass and had reappeared on Deer Creek in the Steele expedition, which prompted some to think there would be another thrust up Steele's Bayou in concert. Others were moving around in northern Mississippi, and they were still working on the various canals on the river, although labor had seemed to stop on the main canal across from Vicksburg in the prior few days because of the Confederate artillery's domination of the mouth. On top of that, the driftwood and higher current in the Yazoo River, because of the breaches in the levee and strong storms in late March, caused part of the raft barrier at Snyder's Bluff to break apart and was even then being strengthened with chains. And then there seemed to be new moves, certainly something going on across the river, as well as, unexplainably, Union troops in seemingly large numbers going northward to Memphis. Effort was also picking up on the river itself and even down around Port Hudson. Pemberton could only continue to shuffle his limited forces around to the most threatened points, although that job was getting more difficult the more Federal moves that took place and the closer they were to Vicksburg itself, limiting Pemberton's reaction time. But the worst result was that Pemberton totally misread several of the enemy moves, leading him to completely wrong assumptions and corresponding countermoves.[64]

The departure of Federals from Port Hudson in early April led Pemberton to shift troops from that locale. Banks had gone west, and Pemberton asked Franklin Gardner at Port Hudson to "ascertain, if possible, at once whether enemy has considerably reduced his force at Baton Rouge, and let me know. I require [A.] Rust's brigade for operations in this direction." Ultimately, Pemberton would call two brigades northward from Louisiana, Albert Rust's and Brigadier General Abraham Buford's. Another brigade was also borrowed from Buckner down at Mobile, despite Pemberton already having a brigade of his and a cavalry regiment.[65]

Loring's isolated position at Fort Pemberton was still a concern to say the least, and Pemberton had recently shifted large numbers of troops northward when Quinby and company reappeared in late March. "I am very much weakening other points to re-enforce you," Pemberton informed Loring while the Federals were still confronting him. Maury himself, though "laid up with rheumatism," as well as entire brigades made the trip up to Greenwood, where nothing happened over the course of the first week in April except minor skirmishing. Then the Federals pulled out on April 5, allowing Loring some breathing space and Pemberton the chance to again shift troops to a more threatened sector. Also moved at his own request was Maury, who Richmond sent to command in East Tennessee. Confederate officials needed a major general and judged that "you can spare one of the major-generals of your command for this purpose, and designates Major General Maury." Pemberton responded that he was "very sorry to lose General Maury, but can spare him if necessary." The troops were also sad to lose the well-liked general.[66]

As concerning were the renewed Deer Creek operations under Steele, this time from Greenville. As part of the misreading of intentions, Pemberton and particularly Stevenson at Vicksburg viewed Steele's incursion down Deer Creek as another attempt to get into the rear of Haynes' Bluff by way of Deer Creek, Bogue Phaliah, or farther north on the Hushpuckanaw River, which led into the Sunflower River. While there was no intent whatsoever of doing so among the Federals, Pemberton shifted troops to the Deer Creek area and Sunflower River, including the cottonclads, for the renewed effort there. Confederate scouts also infiltrated all the small waterways of the Delta between Deer Creek and the Sunflower River to make sure there was no route available across. Fearful of another movement up Steele's Bayou at the same time, Pemberton's major concern was that Federals would this time actually get in rear of Loring, cutting him off and potentially destroying his force. Ultimately, however, Steele withdrew as well back toward Greenville, although he hung around the area for several more days, which only continued to focus Pemberton's and Stevenson's attention to the north.[67]

Closer to Vicksburg, the odd maneuvers of the enemy also brought false assumptions. "They seem to be very slow about making the attack," one confused Confederate wrote home. Grant's reconnaissance to Snyder's Bluff on April 1 was heavily watched, it including several ironclads and transports, and was determined to be a diversion in favor of Steele's efforts to the north. At the canal, Pemberton still wanted artillery coverage despite the dredge boats leaving and going upriver (actually to work on the Duckport Canal), telling Stevenson in the midst of sending big guns elsewhere to "remove nothing that bears on the mouth of the canal." But the Federals, it was feared, knew as much about him as he did about them; he instructed Stevenson at Vicksburg: "Tell the newspapers to keep strict silence."[68]

Yet the two biggest misreads of Federal moves came with one actual effort and one that was blown far out of proportion. McClernand's movements southward to Richmond and Roundaway Bayou to New Carthage were duly noted at Pemberton's Jackson headquarters, John Bowen at Grand Gulf reporting frequently of the continual push and the Confederates' response, which included initially cavalry under Major Isaac F. Harrison but, upon his urgent call for help, eventually three regiments and artillery across the river under Colonel Francis M. Cockrell of the 1st Missouri. This was a violation of the Confederate departmental system, but Harrison needed the help and Bowen needed the information. Taking station at the John Perkins's burned-out plantation, the judge being a member of the Confederate Congress, Cockrell misinterpreted the movement, writing that "their object doubtless is to cut off Vicksburg from supplies by river." When Bowen reported McClernand at Richmond, he also misinterpreted, saying he was headed for Natchez. Cockrell kept his commander Bowen well informed nevertheless, and Bowen did the same for Pemberton now with a new telegraph line extended. But Pemberton, too, seemed to miss the hints. The movements southward, in numbers unknown but led by small forces, did not seem to interest him nearly as much as those enemy movements on the same side of the river as Vicksburg. When Bowen asked if he should commit large numbers of his troops across the river to oppose the movement, Pemberton replied that he could if he could take a safe position and get them out quickly and easily: "I do not regard it of such importance as to risk your capture," he told Bowen. Later, he confided to Richmond that "also reported, but not yet confirmed, movement under McClernand, in large force, by land west of river and southward. Much doubt it." It was a pattern of ignoring evidence that would continue to his own unraveling.[69]

The biggest misinterpretation of the facts, however, came as report after report arrived of Union transports going up the river to Memphis (mainly the Mississippi Marine Brigade being sent to the Tennessee River and Steele's division moving northward to Greenville), coupled with some sort of movement eastward across West Tennessee and northern Mississippi. The district commander in the area, Brigadier General Daniel Ruggles, again called for more troops, but Pemberton curtly replied once more, "I repeat to you, I have no more troops to send you." Probably spying the movement of the Marine Brigade moving up to operate on the Tennessee River, scouts nevertheless reported large chunks of Grant's army moving north and then east, which of course was not happening. But Pemberton and company, and even Joseph E. Johnston and Richmond officials, somehow determined that Grant was giving up the Vicksburg effort and was sending his army to Middle Tennessee to reinforce Rosecrans in that sector. The misunderstanding proved to be hurtful in that both Johnston and Richmond began to call loudly for Pemberton to match the movement and send troops to Bragg's aid in Tennessee, particularly Carter Stevenson's division, officially still a part of Bragg's army. Pemberton was so convinced that he agreed to send as many as eight thousand troops in three brigades (Rust's, Abraham Buford's, and Tilghman's) from his department, although he still railed against the removal of his cavalry under Van Dorn and requested that they be sent back in exchange. Johnston would not hear of it, although Pemberton also addressed his concerns directly to President Davis: "It is indispensable that I have more cavalry." Johnston replied that "General Van Dorn's cavalry is much more needed in this department than in . . . [yours], and [it] cannot be sent back as long as this state of things exist." He reminded Pemberton as well that "you now have in your department five brigades of troops . . . belonging to the Army of . . . Tennessee. This is more than compensation for the absence of General Van Dorn's cavalry command."[70]

Taking everything together, by the end of the second week in April it seemed that Pemberton had once again parried all the threats—yet another misreading of the actual events. At one point Pemberton had informed President Davis that "I see nothing unfavorable in present aspect of affairs" and by April 10 was convinced he could spare troops to send to Bragg; the next day he informed Richmond that "so far enemy has gained nothing toward opening the Mississippi." The Yazoo Pass force had turned back, this time seemingly for good, as they were soon reported back out in the Mississippi River. Steele's Greenville expedition was likewise turned back and the Delta rivers once more defended. Work on the canal seemed to be stopped even though it was front-page news in that week's *Harper's Weekly* (as were the bayou operations the next week), and even down at Port Hudson the Federals had left, Banks moving westward on his march eventually to Alexandria, Louisiana. Pemberton felt a certain degree of confidence that he had yet again thwarted each Federal jab successfully and that he was as safe as he ever was on that high ground east of the Mississippi River. Even better, although his supply situation had hit bottom in mid-February, one commissary officer reporting that the Vicksburg commissary stores were "almost exhausted" except for sugar and peas, Pemberton's agents had worked an almost-miracle in gathering food from the bountiful Delta; by early April they were reporting "a supply that will enable us to stand a six month's siege." Millions of rations of rice, peas, and sugar were on hand, plus hundreds of thousands of pork, bacon, flour, and molasses as well. Only corn and beef were still in short supply, but those were being hurriedly removed from the Delta areas, especially those vulnerable to Union activity.[71]

What Pemberton did not know was that the seemingly insignificant enemy movement southward on the west side of the river would be his undoing; he was not nearly as safe as he thought. Carter Stevenson could see only two alternatives: "Their entire failures on the flank have reduced them to a direct attack or abandonment of the expedition." But there was a third option, a gamble to say the least. In fact, in the very next week, everything would start to come apart for Pemberton as Grant wagered everything on one final attempt to get to the high ground east of the Mississippi River.[72]

11

"They Are About to Execute Some Plan"

April 13–23

"I feel confident now that they will never take this place unless they can do so by a flank movement," a Louisianan at Vicksburg wrote in his diary. Only the latter would be a problem, as it would "cut off our supplies, and I think they can be prevented from effecting this, though they will doubtless make a desperate effort." Now across the Mississippi River in Louisiana, Grant was even then contemplating that very effort, although concerns abounded. The Union army itself faced several miles of inhospitable and flooded terrain on the west side of the river, but that could be overcome; Peter Osterhaus was, in fact, already doing so, although by April 20 the general reported his entire command out of rations; fortunately, the land abounded with foodstuffs. But troops at New Carthage would be useless if stuck on the west side of the river, and that brought the navy into the equation. Grant had to have boats south of Vicksburg in enough number both to cover the landing on the east side, wherever it occurred, and to be able to land a sufficient force at the same time to keep from being repulsed piecemeal. Consequently, Grant had to have ironclads as well as transports south of Vicksburg, and because of the lack of success on the canal and Lake Providence efforts, the only way to get them there was to pass directly by Vicksburg's river defenses. And that was a daunting prospect: standing in the way of a movement south of Vicksburg for the critical naval component were several miles of Confederate batteries fronting the river.[1]

Obviously, passing the batteries had been done before. In fact, Admiral David Farragut had accomplished it several times, even while going upstream. And the trickle of Union vessels sent south of Vicksburg in the interim proved it could be done as well; one Confederate surmised that "some times they sink the boats and some times they pass." But Farragut did it much earlier when the defenses were not as strong as they were now, and sending isolated boats by themselves or as a small group was certainly a different prospect than sending an entire flotilla along. Porter realized the danger and told Grant so, but he was more than willing to make the run if that was what Grant needed. But it is doubtful whether Porter would have done so for a general he was not as fond of, such as McClernand.[2]

The Confederate defenses along the river, under the overall command of Colonel Edward Higgins, were in three basic groups, spread out instead of massed for effect. The upper batteries on the north side of Vicksburg sat at various places on and down the bluffs fronting the river, between Mint Spring and Glass Bayous. Colonel Andrew Jackson, Jr., commanded these guns, arranged in six different artillery sites, all manned by his 1st Tennessee Heavy Artillery. The Water Battery was only thirty or so feet above the river near Mint Spring Bayou, and mounted five guns: three 32-pound rifles, a 32-pound smoothbore, and a 10-inch Columbiad. Four more separate batteries to the south (simply given numbers as names) contained a gun apiece except for the one next to the Water Battery; it containing two. Situated together in these batteries were five guns: two 10-inch Columbiads, a 42-pound smoothbore, a 7-inch Brook rifle, and a 9-inch Dalghren. One of the most powerful batteries came next, near Glass Bayou: the Wyman's Hill Battery. It contained seven guns: three 10-inch Columbiads, an 8-inch Columbiad, a 32-pound rifle, a 2.71-inch Whitworth rifle, and a 3-inch Armstrong rifle. The Water and Wyman's Hill Batteries were a mere thirty feet above the level of the river, with most of the others anywhere from sixty to a hundred and ten feet above, the 42-pound smoothbore at Devil's Backbone being a whopping hundred and sixty feet above and therefore too high to participate much at all, being unable to depress the gun low enough to fire closer to the bank on the east side.[3]

The middle group contained only two batteries near the city itself, under the command of Major Fred N. Ogden of the 8th Louisiana Heavy Artillery. The Whig Office Battery near the city landing had two guns: a 10-inch Columbiad and a 32-pound smoothbore. South of that position was the Depot Battery near that landmark, containing one 10-inch Columbiad. Both were lower to the waterline and thus able to take vessels closer to the bank under fire.[4]

The five batteries south of the city fell under Lieutenant Colonel Daniel Beltzhoover of the 1st Louisiana Heavy Artillery. Immediately south of the railroad was the Railroad Battery a hundred feet above the river, containing

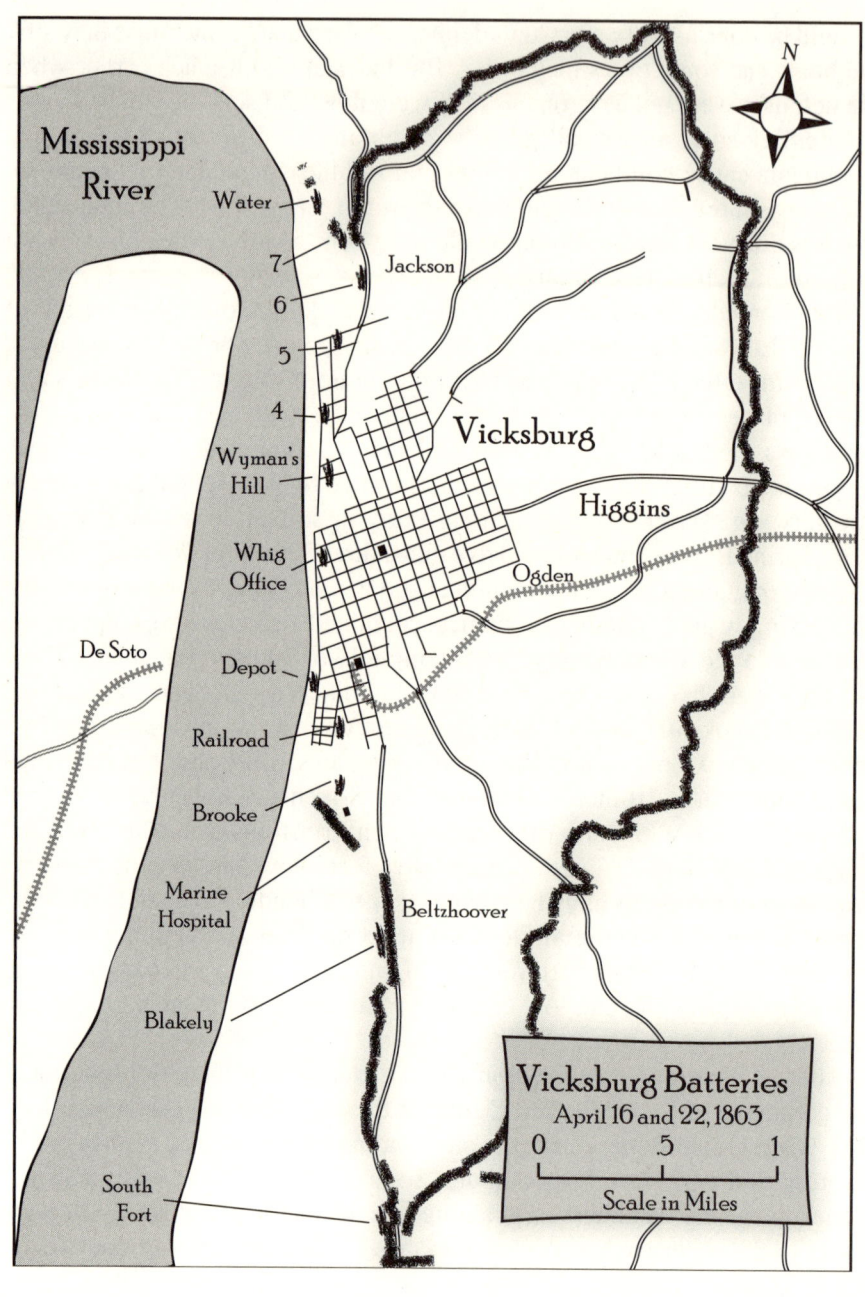

an 18-pound rifle named "Whistling Dick" and a 20-pound Parrott rifle. Just north of the Marine Hospital was the Brooke Battery containing a single 6.4-inch Brooke rifle. Also near the hospital was the Marine Hospital Battery forty feet above the water and containing seven guns altogether: three 42-pound smoothbores, two 32-pound smoothbores, and two 32-pound rifles; a portion of the 22nd Louisiana also helped man these guns. Farther south, the Widow Blakely Battery contained three 32-pound guns and a 7.4-inch Blakely rifle that lent its name to the battery. This group sat a hundred and thirty feet above the river. Finally, at South Fort, a hundred and seventy feet above the water, a 10-inch Columbiad, a 10-inch mortar, and a 30-pound Parrott rifle ended the defenses except down at Warrenton, where four Parrott rifles, 20- and 30-pounders, were encased in cotton bales and earth covered with iron.[5]

In addition to these thirty-seven mostly heavy guns were thirteen field pieces scattered around to repel a river assault. The artillerymen of Company L, 1st Mississippi Light Artillery and the 14th Mississippi Light Artillery manned these guns, and infantry with small arms also covered the more than four miles of defended riverfront. Few thought Grant would be foolish enough to send infantry in an all-out attack against these guns and the defenders of the city itself, but a passage of the batteries by naval vessels was not out of the question. An elaborate system of signals and alerts accordingly went into effect, with lookouts far to the north, obviously the way most any Union approach would come.[6]

But these were not the only guns on the riverfront. In addition to the signal corps that kept Porter and the various wings of the army connected, and also kept an eye on "everything of interest occurring in the town," Grant himself set up a battery of two 30-pound Parrott rifles "in casemate battery opposite the town." By mid-April, these guns were firing on the courthouse and railroad depot despite an unsuccessful Confederate attempt to land from across the river and spike them. The first shots were errant, one Federal writing of "wast[ing] ammunition and do[ing] no damage" (he even mentioned a Confederate who taunted the gunners from the top of the courthouse "swinging his flag all the morning"), but later shots seemed to be right on the mark: "The shells apparently bursting at the height and distance of the dome of the courthouse, and at the very center of the ridge pole of the depot." A Louisianan wrote that the firing was heavy and at one point "killed 7 government mules"; it "set the Depot [on] fire but it was put out before it got too far." These would obviously not be part of the attempt to close the river to traffic, being in support of such an effort rather, should Grant and Porter be foolish enough to try to pass the batteries.[7]

Grant was that foolish, or bold, depending on the point of view. There had been several attempts of course, as well as other alarms that turned out to be only skiffs or flatboats. And many saw it as foolish, one Indianan writing after the last debacle: "This makes the third boat given to the enemy in this manner and I should think good sense would dictate better generalship than to send our rams and ironclads below Vicksburg singly and unsupported to be captured by the enemy without a decent show of resistance—destroying our fleet by piecemeal—by detail. We had as well go down to Vicksburg to capture it with one regiment as to send the boats below one at a time." This move would obviously be different, and Grant gave Porter the go-ahead to make the run and the admiral, though autonomous as he was, complied with the army's wishes. But Porter would do it on his own terms, as he told Grant, sending the best vessels he had and when he so chose. He also advised Grant that "I have received a communication from the Department which will compel me to go below the batteries with the fleet sooner than I anticipated"; Washington had ordered him to move below anyway to take Farragut's place between the Confederate bastions. Porter originally planned to move as soon as the night of April 15 but was delayed. Still, all through the day the crews stayed busy placing hay bales around pilothouses and additional iron on the bows. Although the run was called off that night, all hands piping down in the wee hours of the morning, the time came on the next night, the near moonless darkness of April 16. It was just two nights prior to the new moon and when what moon there was did not rise until about an hour before sunup the next morning. Porter prepared the gunboats to make the run with barges lashed to their sides for fuel and provisions, with three additional transports following in their wake. It was do-or-die time—not only for the navy but also for Grant.[8]

Porter readied eight gunboats, seven of them ironclads, to run the "blockade." One artilleryman watched as toward dark there was "a great stir among the shipping." The converted *Benton*, flagship for Admiral Porter, as well as the City-class ironclads *Pittsburg*, *Carondelet*, *Mound City*, and *Louisville* were in the column, as well as the recently arrived new ironclads *Tuscumbia* and *Lafayette* and ram *General Price*. All except the flagship *Benton* had some type of coal barge attached on the port sides shielding the gunboats from the Confederate batteries on the eastern bank of the river, each barge carrying ten thousand bushels of coal for use south of Vicksburg. Following as well were the transports *Silver Wave*, *Henry Clay*, and *Forest Queen*, the latter having been Sherman's headquarters boat in the Chickasaw Bayou effort while the *Henry Clay* had formerly been used as a prison boat; the *Silver Wave* had been up Steele's Bayou back in March. All these were packed with provisions to be used south of Vicksburg. Having learned lessons from previous runs past these and other batteries, such as at Island No. 10, cotton, logs, and wet hay bales were loaded and positioned on the boats and barges, especially on the more vulnerable port sides where the enemy fire would come, mainly "to protect the hull and machinery against any accidental shot." Porter also ordered that all vessels have their fires well stoked beforehand, "so that they will show as little smoke as possible," and also ordered that all exhaust be let out "in the wheel, so as to make but little noise." He also wanted all lights doused and ports closed "until such time as the vessels open fire." As far as the run itself, Porter issued orders about spacing, firing of guns, what to do in the event a vessel found itself "in a sinking condition" (run to an island below and beach), and once clear of the shoal water around the bend to "hug the shore enough (on the side opposite Vicksburg) to get into the shade of the trees and hide the hulls of the vessels."[9]

It was certain to be a show in the dark night, and numerous officers positioned themselves to watch. Grant himself steamed down to a close but safe point on the former hospital boat *Henry Von Phul*. Also along were Julia and the children, who had just arrived despite orders that families could not be with the army. Grant's officers had in fact turned back one father of two sons in the 120th Ohio at Memphis. Grant gave his apologies, writing that "my orders are against citizens visiting the army in general but I would always make an exception in favor of those who have children in the service." Aboard the *Henry Von Phul* was also Mrs. McClernand and one of his staff officer's wives. But Julia was the center of attention, having arrived that day, and she wasted no time in telling Grant what to do. He was, she recalled, "greatly amused," but told her that "I'm afraid your plan would involve great loss of life and not insure success.... You must not forget that each and every one of my soldiers has a mother, wife, or sweetheart, whose lives are as dear to them as mine is to you. But Vicksburg I will take in good time." Once night fell, the entire family now watched as the show began, the littlest baby sitting in staff officer James H. Wilson's lap. Others also watched. Sherman moved south of Vicksburg to be ready to meet survivors if need be, and even the army's adjutant general Lorenzo Thomas took a position some four miles south of Vicksburg to watch.[10]

The vessels pulled out into the darkened river at the mouth of the Yazoo around 9:15 p.m. and soon made their way to the big bend north of Vicksburg, still undetected. The *Pittsburg*'s log book recorded the boat "beat to quarters" at 10:00 p.m. and readied for the run. Admiral Porter led the way in the *Benton*, with the others in line behind at fifty-yard increments. Tied to the *Benton* was the tug *Ivy* on the starboard side, away from Vicksburg's guns. The *Lafayette* came next, with the vulnerable *Price* likewise lashed to the starboard, or opposite, side from the Vicksburg guns for protection. The turtles *Louisville*, *Mound City*, *Pittsburg*, and *Carondelet* followed in line thereafter. Behind were the three transports, with the ironclad *Tuscumbia* bringing up the rear, largely to make sure the transports did not turn back when the fire became heavy. Each vessel basically floated with the current until discovered, Lieutenant Byron Wilson of the *Mound City* relating that "we continued drifting down, never turning a wheel."[11]

That mere floating down did not last long. The flotilla began its run around 11:00 p.m., the Confederate batteries soon discovering them and opening up as soon as the line of vessels came in range. Several Confederate yawls were on picket duty in the river, though not far enough northward to give ample warning, and while one was rowed to the east shore to alert the gunners at Vicksburg others went to the Louisiana shore to set fires to light up the river. Despite some of the artillery officers attending a dance, one Confederate officer explained that "the upper batteries opened promptly and soon the firing became general along the line." While some initially thought the flashes were lightning, one nearby infantryman of the 46th Mississippi knew what the chaos was about: "Another battery running enterprise was on foot." He quickly went to the river bluffs and watched the "impressive scene." Once alerted, the Confederates set fire to structures prepared for just this very occasion, both on the Vicksburg side as well as on De Soto Point opposite the city. In addition to the lively fire of the Vicksburg guns, the fires on the banks lit up the night sky; additional Confederates had been positioned there for months to light fires unless "there will be moon enough to enable the cannoneers to work their guns with effect." There were even ordered pits "so that the fire guard can be secure when the guns open on any of the enemy's passing boats," although once the Federals took the peninsula these pickets manned the river in small boats and were ordered to land on the Louisiana shore and light the fires in the event of a passage. Not only did the fires light up the river for all to see better, but Porter also reported that "the pilots were deceived by a large fire started on the side opposite to Vicksburg by the rebels for the purpose of showing the vessels more plainly, fire being started on both sides of the river at once." He later mentioned the "great difficulties to contend with—strong currents and dangerous eddies, glaring fires in every direction, that bothered the pilots, smoke almost enveloping the squadron, and a very heavy fire on vessels that were fair targets for the enemy." In reporting the Confederate fire as "not near as heavy as I anticipated," Lorenzo Thomas nevertheless described the burning buildings that "lighted up the whole river," and a sailor on the *Mound City* related the night was "almost as light as day."

Admiral Porter himself, years later, wrote of the vessels "groping their way through the fire and smoke."[12]

Under the command of Lieutenant Commander James A. Greer, the *Benton* led the way, unnoticed until reaching the upper batteries north of Vicksburg. The boat's logbook noted "the lights of Vicksburg plainly in sight." Musketry first peppered the ironclad after discovery, and the crew could hear the long roll being sounded in the Confederate lines. Only minutes later did the Confederate artillery open up, Porter explaining that "every fort and hilltop vomited forth shot and shell, many of the latter bursting in the air and doing no damage, but adding to the grandeur of the scene." Once discovered and the flames lit up the river, Porter ordered all ahead and the *Benton* moved southward swiftly, firing her guns at whatever she could. The first Confederate guns opened at 11:16 p.m., Porter noted, and *Benton* returned fire immediately, followed by all the vessels in the flotilla. The *Benton*'s pilot had already passed these very batteries before, so he knew somewhat what to expect. The *Benton* ultimately fired more than eighty shells at Vicksburg, but damage was unknown at the time, although Greer reported they passed so close to Vicksburg that, in the confusion—within forty yards—they "could hear the rattling of falling walls after our fires." There was damage to the *Benton*, however, Porter reporting that most of the wounded were hers, "which, being ahead, received a concentrated fire." At least five shots took effect on her, several passing through the iron plating and bouncing around inside the vessel. But she was past the batteries within a little more than thirty minutes, the Confederates shifting their fire to the other rearward vessels at 11:52 p.m.[13]

Trouble emerged as the next vessel came under fire. The *Lafayette* had the *Price* tied to its starboard side and a coal barge on its Vicksburg side, which made the vessel extremely unwieldy. Porter explained that she "did not manage very well," and in fact the twice-afire coal barge was intentionally severed from the ironclad in the middle of the passage. The *Price* also became loose as a result of a collision with the following *Louisville*, and Commander Selim E. Woodworth on the *Price* sped southward to "make the rest of the trip alone." Yet the small ram took thirteen shots "and many musket balls," mostly damaging the ram on the deck and causing fires that were quickly doused. But the *Lafayette* was in a fix. Captain Henry Walke shouted orders, but the pilot became confused amid "the smoke, fire, and noise," and the *Lafayette* soon ran toward the Vicksburg shore, bringing her well within point-blank range of the Confederate guns. Walke reported that the ironclad "came near running into the bank under the batteries at Vicksburg, which enabled the enemy to take unerring aim for the short time we were there." Nine shots ultimately hit the vessel, many of them going straight through the iron plating. Yet the gunners opened up with all the guns that would bear, and soon the vessel sped downriver, later rounding up its wayward barge near New Carthage, it having floated downstream without incident.[14]

Louisville came next and found the Confederates ready for her. In fact, she also lost the coal barge lashed to her side, although like *Lafayette* she was able to regain control of it during the passage even while under fire. But the fires on the west side of the river terribly confused the pilot and, "in consequence of being misled by the bright light on the right hand shore, I was compelled to make two full turns in the river abreast the light," Lieutenant Commander Elias K. Owen admitted. As a result, the *Louisville* fired only six shots the entire night as the swirling vessel did circles in the middle of the river. The *Louisville*'s troubles also affected others, during one of the circles the ironclad running into the *Lafayette* and *Price*, causing their separation. In all the commotion, however, the Confederates landed only four shots on the ironclad, with "no shot doing any damage whatever," Owen reported.[15]

The *Mound City* and *Pittsburg*, now with so many targets for the Confederates, fared better and went straight ahead. In fact, they made straight-line runs through the fire, never even running into any issues and suffering little damage. Lieutenant Byron Wilson on the *Mound City* reported that he actually passed the *Lafayette*, *Price*, and *Louisville* "in order to keep from turning around or becoming unmanageable, as they appeared to be." Still, the *Mound City* was hit five times, one 10-inch shot going clear through the ironclad's plating on both sides. The *Mound City* gave as good as she got, however, and fired grape into Vicksburg as she "passed so slowly and leisurely that we could not help getting good aim." The *Pittsburg* was similarly hit seven times, mostly in the upper works, with two shots landing in the logs positioned on the port side for protection. Lieutenant William R. Hoel, commanding, related that had the logs not been there one of the shots would have been disastrous, as it would have hit the magazine. The *Pittsburg* likewise fired forty-three rounds of shell and grape into Vicksburg.[16]

The *Carondelet* finished the line of gunboats but experienced more trouble. Acting Lieutenant John M. Murphy commanded the vessel, but the pilot became confused because of the burning buildings on De Soto Point as well as the nearness of the *Pittsburg* dead ahead. The ironclad "drifted under these batteries near a point above Vicksburg." Murphy "immediately headed the *Carondelet* pretty well across the river, but the coal barge on one hand and the proximity of the *Pittsburg* on the other, prevented her from coming to as we designed, and we were compelled to turn her completely around before proceeding farther." The ironclad made an entire circle in the river under heavy fire. Murphy reported that "although we were exposed to a heavy concentrated fire for nearly an hour, I attribute to this fortunate pirouette the destruction of the enemy's ranges at us." Indeed, the *Carondelet* was hit only twice.[17]

The transports did not fare as well, and in fact two manned by their regular civilian crews began to turn back shortly after making the turn in the river north of Vicksburg. Conversely, the *Silver Wave*, having survived the Steele's Bayou expedition and now manned by a crew from Ewing's brigade of Sherman's corps, surged ahead and somehow passed without incident. But the *Tuscumbia* was there to make the other two return to the line, exactly what it was intended for. "Lieutenant Commander [James] Shirk drove them back and stayed behind them," Porter reported, Shirk describing his job as "the whipper-in to the fleet." He related that soon "I saw that two of the transports had their bows upstream and were going ahead." Shirk turned around the *Forest Queen* and *Henry Clay* and headed southward himself, prompting an exasperated Grant to report to Halleck that "two of the steamers were drawn into an eddy, and ran over a part of the distance in front of Vicksburg three times." But these transports, packed with rations, were much more vulnerable than the ironclads and began to take damaging shots almost immediately. The *Forest Queen* was heavily damaged with a shot in the hull "between wind and water," plus one in the steam drum, which made it seem worse than it was. Nevertheless, the steamboat had to drift southward for a while before the gunboat *Tuscumbia* took her in tow the rest of the way to safety, fourteen inches of water being in the boat "and her machinery . . . disabled." But she was afloat. The *Henry Clay* was not so fortunate. In veering to miss the damaged *Forest Queen*, she exposed her stern and took a shell in the hull, rapidly filling the boat with water. The captain abandoned ship, although the pilot would not, but when the transport caught fire her fate was sealed. The pilot also abandoned and floated downriver on a piece of plank, staying beside the burning boat for hours. Others manning the vessel did likewise, having positioned planks specifically for escape if necessary. Some of the crew moved to the accompanying barge and cut it loose: "Oh! how they peppered all our vicinity," wrote one Illinoisan onboard. "It seemed, when the bluffs of the town were lighted by the blaze of artillery, like going down into the Lower Regions, and to float down gradually, as we were doing, instead of rushing through seemed terrific." He added how, "after entertaining us from half to three quarters of an hour, after we left the *Clay*, with their disagreeable music, the rebels stopped their concert. We had floated out of range, or they were out of wind." By the time the *Henry Clay* drifted to safety she was a total wreck, along with the fifty thousand rations she carried; the government later paid her owners $10,836.25 for the loss while in government service. Reporting the scene "sublime," Sherman spied the burning wreck passing but admitted that "the loss of the *Henry Clay* is not material, as her load was small, and the boat itself a poor old concern."[18]

The *Tuscumbia* brought up the rear and had her own troubles. Shirk ordered the crew belowdecks for safety but then called them to the main deck: "Captain then ordered all hands under the casemates, guns run in, and ports closed." After turning the transports, the *Tuscumbia* veered westward and "struck the Louisiana bank," causing a leak. Shirk ordered her backed off the bank, but the *Tuscumbia* then ran into the damaged *Forest Queen*; the two boats then drifted together for several minutes, making a good target for the Confederate gunners. The collision also increased the leak, which required the men to man the pumps. Shirk related that "this collision caused the rebels great rejoicing, and was made evident to us by their loud cheering, apparently right over our heads." While in such a predicament, a shot hit the *Tuscumbia* below the waterline in the bow, which started more flooding. Shirk ordered the pumps there manned as well, which controlled the flooding for the time being. Another shell did little damage; remaining astern of the *Forest Queen* the entire way, even at a drifting speed due to the damage on the transport, Shirk was soon out of range and took the *Forest Queen* under tow. Those "saucy gunboats," as one Federal had earlier described them, had made it.[19]

All the while, thousands of Confederates watched the show from the banks, one describing how "the whole surface of the stream was lighted up and far out on its broad bosom was a fleet of five or six steamers and two gunboats. The latter were firing as rapidly as their guns could be worked, while our batteries were sending forth a stream of shot and shell. The dense smoke that partially concealed the flashes of sulphureous flame, added to the weirdness of the scene." Above it all could be heard "the wild hurrahs of our men ... and the agonizing wails of the drowning wretches on the water were faintly heard amid the exultant tones of the victors' shouts." One Mississippian admitted that it was "the grandest, most solemn, and awful scene that I ever beheld." Even citizens watched the show, one staff officer describing "during the bombardment the other night the ladies, instead of seeking safety in flight, repaired to the most prominent positions about town and witnessed the magnificent scene, conducting themselves with the utmost coolness." Many Union troops on the west side of the river could also hear the ruckus, and one Vicksburg lady was not wrong when she complained that "resting in Vicksburg seemed like resting near a volcano."[20]

Ultimately, despite wild rumors inside Vicksburg of multiple sunken vessels, the flotilla made it past the batteries after being under fire for a total of two hours and thirty minutes, audible even to Lake Providence where one

Indianan declared "it fairly shook the ground." But they made it: "We still live," one reporter who went along notified the public. But then each vessel had to pass the guns at Warrenton as well, but they were minor compared to Vicksburg's defenses and proved to be minor indeed, one shot merely hitting the *Mound City*. Damage from the Vicksburg guns was nevertheless widespread but mostly "trifling," and Porter related that "all vessels were ready for service half an hour after passing the batteries." Once the entire flotilla arrived by stages, the *Benton* first, Sherman moved out in a skiff and went aboard Porter's flagship to meet the admiral; several of the other vessel's commanders gathered on board as well. All were joyous despite the loss of the *Henry Clay* and twelve total casualties, although most of them, Porter related, "are walking about." All came on the *Benton*, *Carondelet*, and *Mound City*, the others suffering no losses. Only two seemed dangerous, one sailor on the *Benton* having a leg shot off. But it was worth it, all knowing that the prerequisite step of getting a major naval force south of Vicksburg was accomplished. "I ran the batteries of Vicksburg last night," a jubilant Porter informed Washington the next morning. Secretary of the Navy Welles responded that "this successful movement, accomplished with such trifling loss, reflects credit upon yourself and the officers and men under your command." Better yet, now Grant's seventh and final, either way, attempt to get to that high ground east of the Mississippi River could proceed. "There is a prospect of active movement before long," an eager Federal wrote home.[21]

McClernand down at New Carthage was relieved as well, some of his troops mistaking the fighting as flashes of lightning in the moonless night. But he was initially unaware of the results even early on the morning of April 17 when an ominous sign appeared: "The wreck of the steamer *Henry Clay* was seen floating past New Carthage, on fire." Then three lone barges appeared, two of which McClernand managed to bring in, sinking the third when it could not be handled and threatened to get away downriver for the Confederates to use. The burning cotton and the wreckage of the *Henry Clay* made all wonder whether any vessel had gotten through; plantation owner Joshua James seemed very happy at the initial indications. But then around noon, McClernand staff officer Henry C. Warmoth, atop the Ione Plantation House with a spyglass, yelled "Gun Boat in sight." There was much celebration: "The consequence was yelling, dancing and drinking." The eight gunboats soon arrived, significantly changing the feelings at New Carthage. One Indianan remembered that "we threw up our hats and cheered." McClernand went aboard the first one to arrive, the *Pittsburg*, and met Lieutenant Hoel, asking him to go downriver some five miles and shell the Confederates out of their camp at Perkins's Plantation. Hoel wanted Porter's permission, and the admiral himself soon arrived on the *Benton*. McClernand went immediately on board her to strategize as well, the German Osterhaus tagging along and gleefully shouting "now . . . dose dampt fellers, dey'll catch it; give dem gunboat soup!" Porter agreed to McClernand's wishes and sent the *Tuscumbia* to shell the Confederates, McClernand also sending a portion of Osterhaus's troops "to pursue and harass the enemy."[22]

Grant knew the biggest obstacle had been passed, that of Vicksburg itself, by the gunboats, and his son Fred marveled at just how Grant knew the way was clear even that night. He stood by his father's side on the hurricane deck: "He was quietly smoking, but an intense light shone in his eyes. The scene was as vivid on my mind today as it was then to my eyes, and will remain with me always." In fact, Grant wanted to see the result himself and on April 17 rode the thirty or so miles down to New Carthage, spending the night and returning to Young's Point the next day. Fred was with him as well, Grant informing Julia that he "enjoys himself hugely. His pony gets but little rest." Years later, Fred remembered how Grant had displayed his equestrian skill by jumping a large slough. "The rest of us preferred to wait our turn at crossing by the bridge, over which a wagon train was slowly passing." Fred added that the delay "gave Colonel Rawlins an admirable opportunity to display a talent which he exhibited on occasions,—that of ornamental profanity." Yet Rawlins surprised them all farther along in crossing a waterway, where his horse "laid down under him, and began to roll, but this elicited no outburst from the Colonel, who quietly made his way to shore and forbade any interference with the animal's enjoyment."[23]

On the opposite side of the river, the passage was a real problem for the Confederate defenders of Vicksburg and elsewhere as well. Personally, it was a disaster for the elderly James Elzy of the 27th Louisiana, who was hard of hearing and did not hear the sentinel call for him to stop; he was "shot by one of his own men on picket last night during the excitement." Farther away, one Tennessean at Port Hudson wrote that "if this be true the thought is that they will heat us pretty hot at this place in a few days." On a more tangible level, Carter Stevenson, commanding the district at Vicksburg while Brigadier General Seth Barton stepped up to command Stevenson's division, reported that "our ammunition for heavy guns is nearly exhausted." And that was after the somewhat meager Confederate response had provided only an estimated seven shots on average per gun. The guns could not possibly defend against other passages if they had nothing to fire with. Stevenson argued that, "as there is no need of guns at Fort Pemberton, I wish the lieutenant general would let me have them." Jefferson Davis even recommended using "fire-rafts set adrift . . . covered with pine or cypress." But the larger context was the biggest issue, one Confederate explaining that "the character of the defense of Vicksburg ... was changed." Confederate intelligence on the affair was quite accurate, down to the names of the individual gunboats and transports that made the run, making, as Pemberton frequently warned anyone who would listen, nine enemy vessels by his count south of Vicksburg "available for crossing troops." But they knew they had done some damage, Bowen at Grand Gulf reporting "the river yesterday and last night filled with burning cotton, fragments of boats, etc." Stevenson's damage assessment was also fairly accurate, although the Confederates reported two transports sunk rather than one, probably mixing up the damaged *Forest Queen* with another seen still bobbing helplessly along south of Vicksburg while they were in fact the same vessel. Such overreporting was extremely common in war, even as late as World War II. Word of the run was quickly relayed to Pemberton in Jackson, who sent it on to Richmond the next day without elaboration. But everyone knew what it portended. One Federal who felt the ground shaking amid the passage, although ten miles away (another at Lake Providence sixty miles away declared they could also feel the "jar"), wrote in his diary: "This success is really miraculous, and everybody is in high spirits. It will doubtless set our Vicksburg friends to thinking." Colonel James Slack simply wrote his wife "this flanks them badly."[24]

Perhaps the most tangible effect was on the Missourians of Cockrell's brigade stuck across the river from Grand Gulf in Louisiana. I. V. Smith explained that "one morning ... we looked out on and up the river and the gunboats were in sight about five miles away," adding "then there was great excitement in camp." Another admitted that "it caused great confusion for a little bit." A Federal similarly declared in his diary, "I expect we will have lively times soon."[25]

Even as John Pemberton stewed in his Jackson headquarters about the gunboat passage of Vicksburg the night before, another headache was brewing far to his north as a small Union cavalry brigade left La Grange, Tennessee, at dawn on a raid southward into Mississippi. With the decision made to go below and cross the river perhaps in the face of opposition, Grant needed all the diversions he could get, and now was the time to unleash Benjamin Grierson. The cavalry raid to the east had remained in the back of his mind throughout the winter, and Stephen Hurlbut now informed his commanders, namely Brigadier General William Sooy Smith who would oversee the raid, that "the time for our projected cavalry movement is rapidly approaching." Hurlbut had telegraphed Grierson, who was home on leave in Jacksonville, Illinois, to return at once but ordered Smith at La Grange to get ready to send the regiments southward in any event to do "all the mischief they can." He also planned "corresponding movements" to divert attention away from the cavalry raid, which itself was a diversion for Grant. One of the diversions would be the famed "Mule March" under Colonel Abel Streight into Alabama and Georgia, along with a supporting infantry column out of Corinth under Brigadier General Grenville Dodge. The others under Sooy Smith and Colonel George E. Bryant were infantry movements out of Memphis and La Grange westward and southward to the Tallahatchie River. Hopefully, Streight would pull Confederate attention to the east while Smith and Bryant pulled attention to the west. "Under cover of this movement," Hurlbut assured Grant, "I shall sweep down with cavalry." Grierson could hopefully dive down the seam in between the divided Confederate attention and make his way to the Southern Railroad, Hurlbut later adding that "these various movements along our length of line will, I hope, so distract their attention that Grierson's party will get a fair start and be well down to their destination before they can be resisted by adequate force." The date to leave was Friday, April 17.[26]

Despite the intended coordination, it was nevertheless not an exact science. A former music teacher and store owner, Grierson related that "no one knew my plans any more than they did those of Gen. Grant—nor did either of us have predetermined (or definitely detailed) plans before starting on our hazardous undertakings. [But] the two movements, though widely separate at the time, were in conjunction. . . . I simply knew from previous conversation with the general, and afterwards by letter from an officer of high rank and in close relations with him, of his general contemplated movements." Still, what was done was done in great secrecy. "The direction and number of the expedition are, for the present, contraband," one newspaper reported.[27]

But Grierson was nowhere to be found at La Grange. The message to return arrived while he was playing with his two boys in their Illinois home, and it read simply: "Return immediately. By command of General Hurlbut." Grierson related that he left Jacksonville "in high glee," but he also knew the danger and confided such to his wife. Hurlbut ordered that, if he did not make it in time, Colonel Edward Hatch of the 2nd Iowa Cavalry would lead the raid, the troopers already preparing: "We are turning over a lot today, preparing for hard work again." But Grierson arrived in time, with only hours to spare, and made what few preparations he could in the meantime for what Hurlbut described as "the long dash." He reported that "I had a busy night of it and found myself too much engaged with official duties to gain time enough to write another note to Mrs. Grierson." He nevertheless left on time the next morning, April 17, at the head of three regiments of cavalry, his own

6th Illinois Cavalry now under Lieutenant Colonel Reuben Loomis, Colonel Edward Prince's 7th Illinois Cavalry, and Hatch's 2nd Iowa Cavalry. Also along was a battery of small 2-pound Woodruff artillery pieces, Battery K, 1st Illinois Artillery. It was a force of about seventeen hundred men, those who were unfit being left behind.[28]

The plan was for Grierson to get down into Mississippi and send one regiment to the left to break the Mobile and Ohio Railroad and cause a diversion while sending another to the right to break the Mississippi Central and create more confusion. Grierson himself would take his own regiment on the dash for the railroad around Meridian or Chunky. But plans did not work out as envisioned, and by the time Grierson moved into Mississippi with only a Colton's pocket map and a compass to guide him, he realized he did not need to break the Mississippi Central, as it was not operable north of the Yocona River anyway. And he would probably need the additional force because he met Confederate resistance as he moved through Ripley and neared the Tallahatchie River. Breaking his column into three separate forces so that at least one could (hopefully) get across this first impediment he would meet and then outflank the defending Confederate at the others, Grierson actually got across the Tallahatchie easily at all three, the only real skirmishing coming at New Albany. He thereafter trudged on southward through Pontotoc on muddy April roads soaked by "torrents all night," Grierson related. Along the way he bivouacked at plantations such as William D. Sloan's place, who was beside himself at the enemy taking his goods, even hidden horses, and "fairly foamed, rushed towards me, and for the fiftieth time demanded that we should 'take him out and cut his throat and be done with it.'" Tiring of the drama, Grierson the performer winked at his officers and told the burly orderly to do so. "Then a general hub-bub began," Grierson confessed, although Sloan calmed down considerably thereafter. South of Pontotoc, Grierson sent back the broken-down horses and men, the "least effective portion of the command" dubbed the "Quinine Brigade." He sent one cannon with them as well, hoping that the Confederates would think the entire column turned back. The orders were to "pass through Pontotoc in the night, marching by fours, obliterating our tracks, and producing the impression that we have all returned."[29]

The Confederates were on the trail by this point in what one participant described as "a *game* of strategy and speed," but they did not take the Quinine Brigade bait. Lieutenant Colonel Clark R. Barteau had concentrated his 2nd Tennessee Cavalry to the east to cover the Mobile and Ohio, which all thought was the aim of the raid, but Grierson skirted southward to the west and got behind Barteau as the Confederates concentrated around Chesterville. Sprung from the only enemy in the area that could catch him because of the

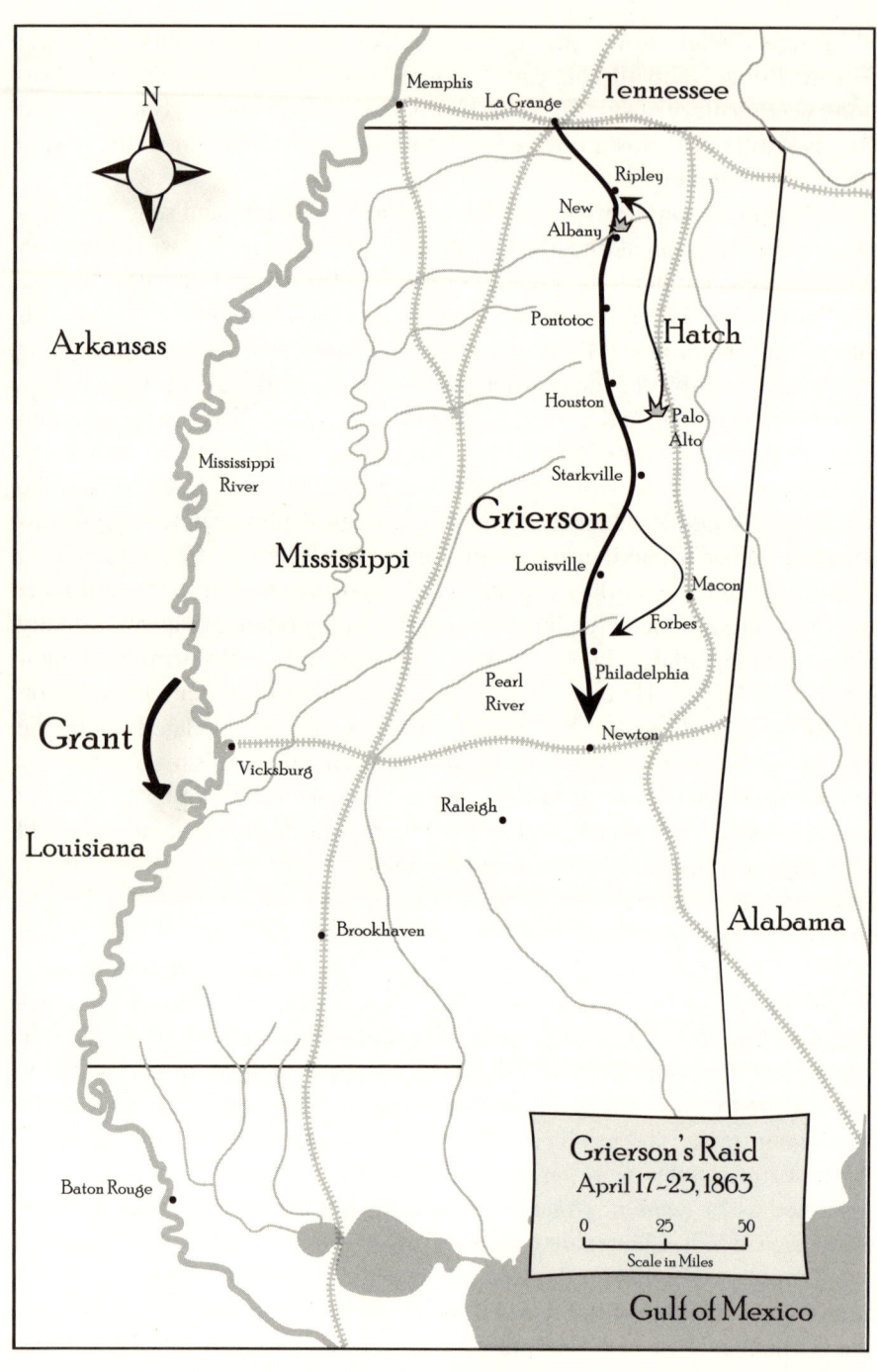

Confederate attention on Streight and the other diversions, Grierson plunged southward with Barteau now on his trail and gaining, coming to within two hours of him on the morning of April 21. When Grierson left his bivouac at the Benjamin Kilgore Plantation that morning, he decided it was time to create a real diversion and sent Hatch and his entire 2nd Iowa Cavalry back northward to Tennessee amid an attempt to break the Mobile and Ohio to the east. A lot of trickery took place at the forks in the road where Hatch went east and Grierson continued southward, including some of Hatch's Iowans following a short distance and then returning so tracks would indicate a turn-around; the Iowans even made four cannon tracks with the lone piece of artillery sent with them. "These detachments were intended as diversions," Grierson reported.[30]

As Barteau reached the fork in the road and studied the tracks, he chose to follow the trail eastward, thinking that was the main body. "The freshest tracks pointed northward," Grierson gleefully explained, and they were Hatch's. Barteau and several small commands of State Troops caught and fought Hatch at Palo Alto and thereafter in a running fight northward as Hatch made his way ultimately safely back to La Grange despite Barteau pursuing and trying to "succeed in gobbling up this force." Hatch had been the bait, something he was not terribly happy with being, but the trickery had worked. Grierson was sprung for good with Barteau's misreading of the tracks, and he and the two Illinois regiments continued southward toward the Southern Railroad. Hatch later boasted that "the fight at Palo Alto, and diverting the enemy from Colonel Grierson, has undoubtedly given him thirty-six hours' start."[31]

The ruse was so good that the Confederate commander in the district, Brigadier General Daniel Ruggles, reported the Federals' "main body" was "falling back before our cavalry" and later stated they had been "routed and driven back by my troops." He later added that "reliable information has just been received that the enemy were passing Houston this morning, going toward Pontotoc." Militia commander Major General Samuel Gholson likewise informed Governor John J. Pettus that the "enemy that were here have been driven back." Certainly Hatch had been, if not routed then nevertheless turned back northward, heading back up to Tennessee. Pemberton at Jackson, who first received word of the raid on April 19, two days after it began, breathed a sigh of relief, thinking one less incursion had to be dealt with. But he was less than thrilled with his district commander Ruggles, who had been a thorn in his side all along, repeatedly asking for troops Pemberton could not send and then causing some disruption with controversies with State Troops officials. Pemberton even sent a terse note on April 20: "I hear from several sources, but not your headquarters, that enemy is approaching Pontotoc."[32]

Yet Grierson was very much still moving southward with around nine hundred and fifty men, undetected except by local people who encountered them. But he knew he was out of contact now, as no one else would be heading back northward; he even penned a final note to his wife and sent it back with the Iowans: "Dear Alice—All well. Apl 21st Tuesday—6 O'clock a.m." Many Mississippi civilians thought Grierson's troopers were Confederates dressed in blue; lies that the cavalry had captured the nice blue uniforms at Holly Springs aided the sham. Grierson, in fact, related that "the inhabitants through this part of the country generally did not know of our coming, and would not believe us to be anything but Confederates." At one point while talking with a miller who was less than thrilled at Confederates again taking his goods, the old man shouted, "Why don't you go after Grierson instead of hanging around here." Meanwhile, led by a group of scouts who were his eyes and ears dressed in civilian clothing and called the "Butternut Guerrillas," their leader a wily sergeant named Richard Surby, Grierson moved on through Starkville and Louisville despite encountering terrible weather and roads as he crossed the Noxubee River bottoms between the two towns. He had heretofore met good fortune most of the way in moving down Pontotoc Ridge, skirting all major waterways once across the Tallahatchie River, but the "dismal swamp" in the Noxubee bottoms caused a lot of delay and toil, as did other watersheds south of Louisville. Most significant was the Pearl River just north of Philadelphia, which the column barely was able to cross through the guile and skill of the scouts. They clandestinely took control of the flooded Pearl River bridge and its civilian defenders, Grierson reporting that "hearing of our approach, their hearts failed, and they fled to the woods."[33]

By and large, the Union raiders treated the civilians with respect and kindness—to a point. Obviously, forage and provisions were needed and acquired on the various plantations, but few houses were burned or civilians offended. "They had expected to be robbed, outraged, and have their houses burned," Grierson confessed. "On the contrary, they were protected in their persons and property." That said, the column left no good horses or mules uncaptured, and most troopers switched mounts as many as two or three times over the course of the raid.[34]

Grierson himself sent out additional diversions as well, including a two-man scout eastward to the Mobile and Ohio at Macon as well as a larger effort to the same place, the entirety of Company B of the 7th Illinois Cavalry under Captain Henry C. Forbes. The small detachment caught back up easily, but Forbes's company began an odyssey that would take them days to catch up to the main column, which had actually given them up as a useful sacrifice to divert any attention away from the main column. "We found ourselves in the midst of the left hand crest of the panic-stricken overflow from the main march," Forbes wrote, "a stampede [that] as we afterwards learned extended 20 to 30 miles in either direction. As our march cut through this crest diagonally, near evening we got outside it and approached Macon." Meanwhile, other than the local civilians who encountered them in person, Grierson's raiders were moving stealthily southward undetected, especially by Confederate authorities who thought they were back near Tennessee by this point.[35]

Grierson moved on through Philadelphia and Decatur on the way to Newton Station on the Southern Railroad. There, he planned to make his attack on the rail line on the morning of April 24, he driving his troops through a forced march of around forty-eight hours with barely enough time to stop and feed. Although undetected at this point, Grierson planned to be entirely detected at Newton Station, both in order to damage the railroad but, more important, to attract Confederate attention to the east and north, away from what Grant was doing to the south and west. The more show Grierson could make and the more attention he could attract the better, and he set his sights on doing just that at daylight on April 24.[36]

While Grierson rode through the Mississippi countryside almost undetected, Grant continued with his gamble: the seventh and final push to get on the high ground east of the Mississippi River. With the overall intent to make an amphibious crossing of the river, Grant clearly saw he needed more vessels to make the passage successful. McClernand, who would make the crossing, lobbied heavily for more transports that would allow more troops to be landed at the initial movement; McClernand in fact asked Grant in no less than three letters across three days for more transports "to carry my whole command at once." Porter had stated he could get about a division over at one time with his gunboats, two transports, and the barges. But if the Confederates were in force on the opposing bank, and there was no reason to believe otherwise, or even just on the high hills back from the bank of the river, then he would need a lot more than a division to make the initial landing. A singular division could be destroyed in the time that it took the flotilla to return to the west bank and retrieve another, which then likewise put in piecemeal could also be defeated before more reinforcements followed. When Grant made the landing, he needed to be able to do so with large numbers at a single time, and the lift power of what he currently had south of Vicksburg just could not provide it.[37]

Given the success of Porter's run, Grant was not above sending another flotilla past, he informing Halleck on April 19 that "our experiment of running the batteries at Vicksburg, I think, has demonstrated the entire practicability

320 CHAPTER ELEVEN

of doing so with but little risk." He therefore ordered a second round of passage as soon as possible, but due to delay it ultimately moved on the night of April 22. And though the April 16 passage of the ironclads was in totality a navy show, the subsequent April 22 movement was all army. No naval vessels made the trip that night, the ironclads and gunboats that remained north of the city being needed to cover that area as well as the Yazoo River. Mainly left behind were the City-class ironclads *Cincinnati* and *Baron de Kalb*, the latter still enroute from the Yazoo Pass operations. Fortunately, others were scheduled to arrive soon, including the ironclad *Choctaw*. Instead, six civilian transports whose crews refused (two captains agreed) to make the run made the attempt, crewed with volunteers from army regiments in nearby brigades. One Illinoisan wrote that "there is plenty of them in ours and Logan's divisions," possibly pushed by the promise of a thirty-day furlough for all who survived. Ultimately, around five hundred men from regiments such as the 7th Missouri, 45th Illinois, 20th Illinois, 23rd Indiana, 11th Illinois, 31st Illinois, 124th Illinois, and 2nd Indiana Cavalry all participated. The pilots were also enlisted men, some of whom wanted the pilothouses removed so that splinters would not hurt them. They feared the splinters from the wood more than the effects of the Confederate shells and "stood exposed," one witness related. One of the volunteers explained that the sailors, once they were assembled, "began to question . . . if they knew the bells and how to shift the cans and what they would do in such cases if things would happen."[38]

The six transports, *Tigress*, *J. W. Cheeseman*, *Moderator*, *Horizon*, *Empire City*, and *Anglo Saxon,* were manned with the smallest crews possible but the most provisions that could be packed onboard, "600,000 rations and a very considerable quantity of forage," including cotton bales and other defenses particularly on the port sides. Also lashed to the transports were twelve barges carrying provisions as well, mostly coal. The lead vessel was the *Tigress*, Grant's old headquarters boat at Shiloh, with Grant's staff officer Colonel Clark B. Lagow, who volunteered for the job, on board in charge of the entire flotilla. While intending to go beforehand, the passage was delayed to the night of April 22, orders that day stating to be ready at 9:00 p.m. that night at Young's Point to proceed. George W. Graham, commanding the transport fleet, cautioned everyone involved to be careful and do their job: "This is an important movement, and I trust every officer and man will do his duty."[39]

With the night "black as the bottomless pit," just four nights after the new moon, the vessels and their attendant barges met up around 9:00 p.m. at the mouth of the Yazoo River at Young's Point and began their trek downstream, departing six minutes apart. Dana reported that "the sky is now cloudy, and a very favorable night is promised." The moon set around 11:00 p.m., so they made plans not to be at Vicksburg until thereafter. By 11:30 they were approaching Vicksburg around the long turn to the south, and the Confederates, now expecting anything, once again lit up the river and opened up with everything from small arms to the big guns, one Indiana volunteer telling that "only ten cannon balls went through his boat and ten thousands Rifle balls." Colonel Andrew Jackson, Jr., commanding the river batteries north of Vicksburg, reported that "the alarm was given at 11:30 p.m., and, soon after, a boat appeared rounding the point above, and was followed by five others at short intervals. The first two . . . side-wheel boats [were] well protected at the sides by barges loaded with coal, bales of hay, or cotton. Their boilers and machinery were also protected by cotton bales." Confederate Vicksburg commander Martin L. Smith had sent across the river Captain Claiborne J. Foster of the 27th Louisiana with several men of the 1st Tennessee Artillery, and they again fired houses to provide the lighted backdrop to the river. Grant had actually earlier sent soldiers to the point to burn the houses beforehand so the Confederates would have nothing to burn during the passage, but the troops had not been able to reach the area due to high water and Confederate fire; a second try under cover of darkness found the houses defended by Confederate troops.[40]

The Confederates were indeed ready this time, not fooled for a second, or actually a third or fourth time now; in fact, they bettered the meager showing on the first run, averaging an estimated fourteen shots per gun this night. "At 11 oclock last night we were aroused by our pickets on the river, giving timely notice of the approach of some of the enemy's fleet," one Louisianan wrote. Pemberton had called for more guns, arguing to Davis himself that the earlier passage "shows conclusively that we have an insufficient number of guns. There are so many points to be defended at this time—Vicksburg, Grand Gulf, Port Hudson, Snyder's Mill, and Fort Pemberton." But ammunition, a real concern after the run back on April 16, had arrived and was distributed to all the guns. New shipments had been on the way from Alabama even before the first passage, but Pemberton also hurried additional resources to Vicksburg, desiring two hundred rounds per gun. Fortunately, it arrived in time, even by April 18. It was such a crisis that Pemberton ordered the shipment be done even "to the neglect of forms, regulations, allowances, &c., as the exigencies of the case do not admit these for a moment to be considered." That was quite a concession for the administrator Pemberton.[41]

The *Tigress* was the lead vessel and flagship, although once on the run the next in line, the *Empire City*, somehow caught and passed the lead vessel. Up front, the *Tigress* was also one of the most vulnerable because she was initially one of the only targets for many of the guns and what one Federal described as the "disagreeable music" coming from the Vicksburg batteries; once the line fully reached the guns, Confederate artillerymen had a plethora of choices for targets, but the *Tigress* up ahead was the only one for a while at each gun. And it told. Colonel William S. Oliver of the 7th Missouri, commanding the *Tigress*, reported that "a few moments afterward the enemy fired their signal guns and made lights by setting fire to two houses on the Louisiana side, so that when opposite the city it was as light as day on the river, and we could see the men at their batteries and the streets in the city plainly." The vessel endured as many as thirty-five hits, fourteen to the hull, the most heavy when it was right in front of the courthouse, where the soldiers on the *Tigress* witnessed a Confederate gun burst near the center of town. But many other shots hit their mark, Oliver noting "they [were] throwing a shower of missiles of all shapes and kinds, from Minie balls to 200-pound shot and shell." The 7th Missouri detachment on board did what they could to put out fires and keep the vessel moving. One Federal related that "as we heard their shots come crashing through our timbers, we wondered how she could live a moment under the raining fire of shot and shell."[42]

Most of the shots hit the upper-deck woodwork and tore it to pieces, "throwing splinters all around," but one of the shots took out several planks in the stern that started massive flooding. The vessel had nearly passed all the batteries, but one of the last shots at them punctured the hull. By this time, the crew had cut away the barge and let it float, it starting to pull the *Tigress* toward an eddy. With a hole in the hull four feet wide, the men stationed below to stuff cotton bags into punctures could do nothing and the vessel began to settle fast even with the pumps hard at work. Oliver ordered the *Tigress* to ground on the west bank several miles below Vicksburg, and Lorenzo Thomas, again watching from a distance, described how she "rounded to . . . , grounded, and sank, breaking amidships. She is a total loss." The crew scrambled above when ordered, they "being in water up to their knees before being relieved." Oliver and his men all escaped, and the pilot and others scrambled aboard a passing vessel that had made it in better shape past the blazing guns. Unfortunately, the *Tigress* had on board much of the army's medical supplies, something Grant had already been heavily concerned about getting southward to the army. Troops from the 30th Iowa who boarded the hulk later only found tables and chairs from her cabins floating in the wreck. Eventually, like the *Henry Clay*, the government paid the *Tigress*'s owners $22,500 for the loss.[43]

It was a gauntlet to be sure, the Confederate gunners firing rapidly despite Colonel Jackson's description: "The atmosphere was hazy and close, and the smoke settled down over the river, often completely concealing and obscuring the boats, and rendering it almost impossible to fire with accuracy." All on both sides could see or at least hear the ruckus. A watching Louisianan wrote that "our pickets fired houses on the La. Shore which enabled us to see the boats very distinctly, and we could also see where the balls struck the boats or plunged into the turbid Mississippi." Perhaps because of the smoke, the transports and their attached barges looked to the Confederate gunners like ironclads, one Southerner arguing they were "so prepared as to have the appearance of gunboats." There was also damage in the Confederate batteries; one 10-inch Columbiad in Captain John P. Lynch's battery "jumped the pintle at the twelfth discharge" and was put out of action temporarily. Worse, Major Fred N. Ogden's 10-inch Columbiad exploded as a result of a "premature discharge," killing one and wounding two others. Jackson laid the blame on "the inferior cartridge bags furnished," although he also complained that "the friction tubes were, as usual, a great source of annoyance, and caused much delay in firing almost every shell, frequently five, six, and eight failing in succession."[44]

Still, the firing intensified as the other boats came within range. To the listening Union troops on the Louisiana side it sounded devastating: "One would suppose from the noise that old Satan himself had been let loose." Next in line, and at times ahead, was the *Empire City*, which was about as badly cut up as the *Tigress*. Lorenzo Thomas labeled it "totally disabled" but still afloat, the critical hit coming in the steampipe, cutting all steam to the engines. Indianan James McLaughlin had volunteered to man the vessel and was at the wheel with the pilot when the hits started coming. He rang the bell for more power, but there was no response from the engine room; next he shouted through the "trumpet" but likewise got no response. Finally, McLaughlin went below while the shaky pilot, who had already left his post once but came back, manned the wheel. Somehow the vessel made it past the batteries, but it needed the assistance of other boats to get down the river and safely past the Warrenton guns, which peppered the transports as they passed as well. Similarly damaged was the *Moderator* next in line, the Confederate guns pounding her with shot and shell. She, too, was put out of running order and drifted helplessly downriver with several wounded aboard. A passing vessel from the rear came alongside and tried to take her under tow, but the connection was never made and the *Moderator* floated helplessly downstream, eventually on past Warrenton.[45]

The latter vessels came through some better, probably the result of the smoke and distortion due to the fires and flames. The *J. W. Cheeseman* was fourth in line and made the passage much easier. In fact, she was in such good shape that she came to the assistance of the others less fortunate. It was this vessel that picked up the *Tigress*'s crew and pilot as she passed below Vicksburg, and she also took the immovable *Empire City* alongside. But as they came near Warrenton around daylight, the *Cheeseman*'s crew, with Colonel Oliver now aboard, realized that she could not maneuver well and cut the *Empire City* loose to float down on her own. Both moved past Warrenton around daylight, neither vessel receiving any further damage despite three shots hitting the *Cheeseman*. The vessel then aided the *Empire City* once more down to New Carthage, arriving about 8:00 a.m. on April 23.[46]

Next to last was the *Anglo Saxon*, which passed through the melee with about the same kind of damage. She had drifted down with the others until the Confederates opened up then began "putting on all the steam she would allow." The upper Confederate batteries hit her in the bow, cutting a line to the barge she was ferrying, which caused the transport to veer to the right and actually "strike the bank opposite the city," Captain Leander B. Fisk of the 45th Illinois reported. Confederate artillery commander Colonel Jackson noted that "one of them ran into the Louisiana shore opposite Wyman's Hill battery, . . . was abandoned by her men, and floated down the river apparently in a disabled condition." The Illinoisans, not abandoning her, quickly cut the stern rope to the barge and "rounded back on her, and headed down stream." Meanwhile, shells continued to pepper the boat, including one in the pilothouse that blew the pilot out of the structure, "stunning him considerably," but two more pilots rushed in only to find the transport unmanageable. A shot also hit the right engine and put it out of service. There was nothing to do but float it out, which they did, and when they came to Union pickets below Vicksburg the Illinoisans threw out the anchor. But the connection to the boat had been shot away so that the chain held nothing. One of the surviving boats that could still maneuver went to her assistance but could not get control of the *Anglo Saxon* before reaching the Warrenton guns, so she floated past them too. The vessel received no damage there, "they only firing six shots at us" despite it being daylight already. Thereafter, others came to her assistance, including the *Silver Wave*, which had made the first passage with the ironclads.[47]

Last came the *Horizon*, she also floating until the enemy opened up, at which time "she put on a full head of steam." Two shots hit her at the upper batteries, while the others continued to pelt her, ultimately with sixteen shots altogether. Yet Captain George W. Kennard of the 20th Illinois related that all were "forward and above boiler deck, except one through her cabin midships." Little damage was done to any critical parts, and she continued on past the batteries, trying to take the damaged *Moderator* in tow but being unable to do so. The *Horizon* also tried to take the crippled *Anglo Saxon* under tow but could not get her stable before reaching the Warrenton guns and therefore let her loose to float past. Ultimately, *Horizon* also passed the Warrenton guns about daylight with only a hit in the rudder, and then she returned to *Anglo Saxon*'s aid again.[48]

Confederate gunners fired around four or five hundred shots at the transports, as well as infantry on the banks of the river firing small arms. "Heavens! What a roar they made! The whole earth seemed to be shaken," one Illinoisan wrote his wife. With so many shots flying through the air, it was a miracle that any of the transports survived, much less the barges, Colonel Jackson admitting that "all the transports were riddled, and the escape of any seemed miraculous, considering the number of large projectiles sent crushing through them." Like the six transports, some of the twelve barges succumbed, with some being cut loose and floating freely, making their way on past Warrenton to be rounded up and readied for service as soon as the army prepared to cross the river. The *Tuscumbia* tried to save one that was filling quickly: "Got all hands pumping, bailing, but could not save her. . . . cut the lines and let it go."[49]

The Federals south of Vicksburg were wise to the happenings by this point, although the heavy firing, one Indianan declared, rattled the windows and doors of the house he was occupying that night. Sherman was again south of Vicksburg to meet the vessels and had surgeons to go aboard to care for the wounded. He soon met Colonel Lagow: "I think he was satisfied never to attempt such a thing again." Yet it was another feat of bravery as well as gambling, and Grant was elated that five of the six unarmored and defenseless transports had made it past. There was heavy damage to some of the vessels in addition to the *Tigress*'s demise, especially to the *Moderator* and *Empire City*, but they were afloat and fixable. That was all Grant could ask for: "I look upon this as a great success," he informed Halleck. There were also some casualties, including two mortally wounded, one a pilot wounded in the gut.[50]

The Confederates tried to make sense of the development, rejoicing in the success of sinking at least one vessel: "One boat is visible this morning, sunk, her smoke-stacks and the upper part of her wheel-houses being visible." It was obviously the *Tigress*. Reports were that another had sunk as well, although no others had; the report of at least two others "disabled" was very much true, however. Stephen D. Lee explained that "all the boats were struck, and repeatedly, and more or less damaged." He added that the fires on the other side helped immensely and that "the firing was generally good, though much interfered with by the smoke of the guns settling in front of the batteries." One staff officer in fact complained that with so much smoke "I could see nothing on the river. . . . We rode home in the dark, considerably disappointed, resolving not to go the next time."[51]

"After this came the calm that as usual follows the storm," a Confederate admitted. Yet as good as some of the news was, still several more transports and barges had gotten past the Vicksburg batteries to join those already below. And with that lesson, Grant wanted more, another tug, the *Rumsey*, moving south on April 26. It was a clear indication of where the campaign was moving, if only the Confederates would take the lesson to heart.[52]

The heightened movements of the Federals, both from their scattered experimental efforts farther north to the southward slide west of the Mississippi River, were unmistakable signs of what was to come. But the Confederate high command largely missed the hint, at least for a time. Even while McClernand was on the move across the river, there were plenty of diversions going on to the north and east, and more began in midmonth, namely Grierson's Raid. But even as McClernand inched southward, Pemberton and company still believed Grant was sending reinforcements to Rosecrans and planned to send their own corresponding troops to even the odds in Middle Tennessee, Pemberton issuing orders for yet another brigade to make the movement, Brigadier General John C. Vaughn's. Pemberton accordingly spent a confused several days in mid-April assuring Richmond he was sending troops and arguing with his own commanders, and even Governor Pettus, about the authority of Confederate verses state militia officers: "There cannot exist over one body of troops two commanding officers, who may issue orders and exact obedience independently of each other," he lectured Pettus.[53]

That said, much of the confusion evaporated with the events of April 16 and 17. Carter Stevenson advised Pemberton from Vicksburg that "every movement of the enemy indicates that they are about to execute some plan," and he described Vicksburg as threatened "on three sides." One Mississippian who had taken the rumors as truth corrected his mistake to his wife, writing: "I told you that the Yanks was all gone from hear but it was a mistake. They are hear as thick as Buffalo nats & they are plenty of them." Most important, Porter's passage of the Vicksburg batteries completely changed Pemberton's ideas about threats to his own department even while Grierson's Raid, the farther south it dove, laid the interior of Mississippi wide open. Pemberton began to warn Richmond and his departmental commander Johnston of the effects, all the while becoming more worried about Grierson's growing threat than McClernand's and Porter's. Still, the naval passage worried him, he declaring as early as April 18 that "I regard the navigation of Mississippi River as shut out from us now." And the "complete breaking up and destruction of the raft" at Snyder's Bluff amid the strong current and piles of driftwood did not help at all, Stevenson declaring that they now had to "depend upon heavy batteries at Snyder's and Haynes' [Bluffs]." Pemberton thus began to waffle and then actually counter the orders to send the troops away, even recalling Abraham Buford's brigade that had made it as far as Chattanooga, Tennessee, and Montgomery, Alabama. "Indications of an attack on Vicksburg are so strong," he notified Johnston on April 17, "I am not warranted in sending any more troops from this department." But even in realizing the change, Pemberton misjudged the cause once more, informing Johnston that the "arrival of Lorenzo Thomas has changed [the] enemy's plans." Nevertheless, the troops returned, passing again through Mobile, where several came across a large lot of oysters and filled their sacks or haversacks with them so that all along the route, when the train stopped to refuel, one could hear them "cracking oysters like they would walnut for they kept up a continuous knocking."[54]

Pemberton dealt with all the concerns, including Steele's presence still in the Delta near Greenville as well as the Duckport Canal, which Confederates in Vicksburg watched "by observation with the telescope." Federals also reported some type of very bright light to watch the river at night, a "Drummond light, which at intervals during the night they turn upon the river." But the two main concerns were the raid in Mississippi and the Federal movements southward, west of the river. In the latter, Pemberton gave the defense over to John Bowen entirely, who gained semi-independent command in a larger shakeup of Pemberton's officers. When Maury transferred to East Tennessee, Pemberton, amid other command changes on lower levels, put Major General John H. Forney (his wife in tow until he took division command in the field) at the head of Maury's old division around Snyder's and Haynes' Bluffs and elevated Bowen to command of a division around Grand Gulf, Martin Green's brigade having been sent southward to reinforce Bowen's troops upon the navy's passage of the Vicksburg batteries. Bowen was ecstatic that Forney, his West Point classmate, was elevated from above him so that he could have the Grand Gulf command all to himself, even to the point of icily meeting Forney on an inspection trip: "His reception of us was far from gratifying," one of Forney's staff officers wrote. But Bowen was now commander of the division there as well as the post at Grand Gulf. Additional reinforcements also moved southward as the threat grew, including the 6th Mississippi and the 1st Confederate Battalion, as well as the Pettus Flying Artillery. Pemberton also sent his engineer Samuel Lockett to sturdy the defenses there.[55]

Bowen kept Pemberton apprised of the developing events, including the Confederate force under Colonel Cockrell, now somewhat isolated across the river with the arrival of the Union navy. Bowen ordered Cockrell back to the James Plantation, where he was to make a stand, but worked to get the three regiments back across to Grand Gulf as soon as possible. Bowen himself crossed the river to take a look at the situation on April 16, and when a safe occasion presented itself when the Union gunboats were known to be out of the area, he brought Cockrell's trapped Missourians that had fallen back continually from the James Plantation to Hard Times across to safety, effectively giving McClernand sole possession of the west bank. One Missourian remembered the crossing was made in haste, an enemy gunboat appearing in the middle of the passage: "Our boat ran up to the landing and we got off in short order; the boat ran up Black River and we marched to camp." Only less than a hundred skirmishers now remained across the river, but in the larger picture Bowen himself misjudged the Union effort, informing Pemberton it was likely only to "cut Vicksburg off from supplies." That said, others such as Stephen D. Lee warned as early as April 15 of a Union crossing and attack "on our left up Bayou Pierre, in rear of Grand Gulf." Pemberton likewise worried about a movement up the Big Black River in rear of Vicksburg and told Bowen, "I look upon Grand Gulf as more to defend Big Black than to prevent passage down. Fire only deliberately." He accordingly also ordered a raft to stop traffic on that river.[56]

More concerning to Pemberton after initially waving them off ("this is a mere raid, but [it] should not be unmolested by you," he told Ruggles at Columbus) were the massive raids that seemed to be coordinated from Tennessee. Pemberton described them on April 20 as "strong raids from three points on Memphis and Charleston Railroad between Memphis and Corinth." Obviously, two of the three were diversions or coordinated with Streight's Mule March, but Grierson's was the real deal. In formulating a response, Pemberton utilized Buford's brigade returning from Alabama, and the brigade just happened to arrive at Meridian and Enterprise right in the midst of the Federal incursion. Loring, now unneeded at Fort Pemberton, moved eastward to coordinate a defense if needed, with Tilghman's brigade moving down to Jackson as a central reserve and Featherston's to the Mississippi Central Railroad around Duck Hill. In the hasty moves, Colonel Arthur E. Reynolds of the 26th Mississippi commandeered a train on the Mississippi Central to move his regiment, which brought the ire of railroad officials, but it was seemingly needed in the response to the Federal raid. Some of the heavy guns at Fort Pemberton, now unneeded as well because "that post will soon be high and dry," Stevenson advised, were sent southward to Vicksburg; indeed, Thomas

Waul still at the fort reported the water falling precipitously, down about four and a half feet from its high mark. Suddenly, with Federals poised in every direction, the Big Black River railroad bridge became extremely important, and Pemberton sent troops there to guard it as well.[57]

In all the chaos, Johnston was little to no help and had actually caused some of the trouble by pulling much of Pemberton's cavalry to Middle Tennessee. Pemberton would not let him forget it either, writing on several occasions, such as when Johnston called for help from Pemberton to aid his own cavalry in Alabama to combat Streight's force, "you are aware I have but feeble cavalry force.... I have virtually no cavalry from Grand Gulf to Yazoo City, while the enemy is threatening to cross the river between Vicksburg and Grand Gulf, having twelve vessels below Vicksburg." Later, he wrote that "heavy raids are making from Tennessee deep into the State. One is reported now at Starkville, 30 miles west of Columbus. Cavalry indispensable to meet these raids." For his part, Johnston simply chirped from Tullahoma about what should be done, including contacting the trans-Mississippi department commander Kirby Smith for help. He also showed his lack of understanding of the threats in Mississippi, writing Pemberton on April 21 "the enemy cannot be in force near Vicksburg and on the three routes you mention. Can you unite troops upon one of them, or destroy bridges?"[58]

Despite his earlier action on rumors of the Federals' departure, by April 21 Pemberton was again convinced that Vicksburg was the main target, with the second naval passage confirming it the next day. Exasperated with Johnston over the cavalry issue, he wired Richmond directly that "I have so little cavalry in this department that I am compelled to direct a portion of my infantry to meet raids in Northern Mississippi." But he had Loring on the defense at Meridian and up the Mobile and Ohio to Macon, although catching cavalry if they came that direction with infantry was a long shot. And then he may need some of Loring's infantry at Vicksburg, he ordering him to "keep me hourly informed, as troops may be required here at any time. Six boats passed Vicksburg last night." The Federals were seemingly coming from all directions: "There is no doubt that their whole energy will be concentrated to take the Mississippi," Stevenson advised. The walls were closing in fast on Pemberton and his prized possession, Vicksburg.[59]

With all the gears in motion, Grant continued to prepare the main movement, that of shifting the Army of the Tennessee southward along the river and down past Vicksburg to New Carthage. By this time the "weather is perfect for either marching or fighting," Dana reported, "and the spirit of the troops is all that could be desired." The weather was indeed warming and drying, one Illinoisan declaring April 19 as "a regular August morning" and another admitting it was "hot enough to melt a man." Grant soon published orders on April 20 "for the information and guidance of the army in the field in the present movement to obtain a foothold on the east bank of the Mississippi River, from which Vicksburg can be approached by practicable roads." He had all divisions still up the Mississippi River boarded and sent southward to Milliken's Bend, including Hovey's and Quinby's from Helena and Logan's from Lake Providence, one Indianan writing that "these orders seemed to suit the boys pretty well for they were getting tired of Helena." Less welcome was a near accident on the way down in which a pilot became turned around in the heavy fog and nearly hit another boat, which would have been catastrophic for the men aboard both. Steele's division remained near Greenville for a few more days simply as a diversion as well but also ultimately received orders to head southward. Sherman admitted that the Deer Creek plan had been to damage the resources of the area and to "demonstrate the fact that we can reach the interior of the country when necessary," but he deemed that "the Deer Creek country has been afflicted enough to make them, in the future, dread the Yankees' visit." With all troops moving southward now, Grant was firm on the plan to cross and take a stronghold such as Grand Gulf and then send a corps to neutralize Port Hudson before going after Vicksburg, still not knowing that Banks had headed up the Red River and was not operating around Port Hudson any longer.[60]

Other units arrived as well to reinforce the army, prompting one Illinoisan to muse that there was now "plenty of force to take Vicksburg and I think that the next time is bound to bring it." One of the arriving units was the newly reconstituted 12th Iowa, most of which had been captured in the Hornet's Nest at Shiloh. Out of prison now and joined with the remnant that had escaped, the Iowans moved down the Mississippi River to Vicksburg, but not without incident. Aboard their transport were Confederate officers' wives trying to get past St. Louis but who were turned away. More interesting were "a large number of rough coffins piled upon the deck." The new recruits were wide-eyed, but the old veterans knew an opportunity when they saw one. They "appropriated the boxes for sleeping apartments, claiming that it was best to make use of them when they could, for it was not likely that they would be fortunate enough to 'draw' such things when they needed them." Sleeping conditions were worse when they arrived near the canal and joined Sherman's corps: "Camps was established in a cornfield, behind the levee, where the ground surface was at least six feet lower than the surface of the river. The furrows between the corn rows were full of water and could be drained only by digging holes for the water to run into and using the dirt from the holes to level up within the tents." One of McClernand's artillerymen reported how "water stood about 2 inches deep in our tent."⁶¹

Meanwhile, Osterhaus still held the front at New Carthage and the James Plantation father south, although it was a tenuous grip. James himself was very unwelcoming, Osterhaus and company sparring with him and making him look at the United States flag they raised over his house. "He is very bitter," one staff officer related. James felt much better on April 15, when Confederates (before being removed east of the river) attacked both at the James Plantation and at Dunbar's Plantation to the west on Bayou Vidal. The 1st Missouri under Colonel Cockrell was a part of the attack at Bayou Vidal, which evidently was supposed to dispose of the Union force at Dunbar's and then cross over and take the Federals at the James Plantation in rear while the main force attacked there in front. The Union cavalry at Dunbar's deflected the attack at the cost of one man mortally wounded and one other wounded, which broke up the entire plan. At the James Plantation, on the Mississippi River, the much larger Confederate force deployed but fell back without launching an attack, evidently because of the lack of cooperation from the force at Dunbar's. Osterhaus explained "they thought . . . that I was a very poor general." Still, his hold was tenuous at best, although Osterhaus found plenty of food in the region and managed to get out hundreds of bales of cotton as well, which they were supposed to give receipts for "upon satisfactory proof of their loyalty." Most concerning was the potential of Confederate gunboats to operate against New Carthage, and on the evening of April 16 "a black-looking vessel, supposed to be a rebel ram, showed herself for a moment around the point below New Carthage." All concern evaporated on April 17, however, when Porter's eight gunboats arrived, securing the area for good. Osterhaus was overjoyed, as were McClernand and Grant. Porter brought the area under firm Union control and also began testing Grand Gulf for strength. Apprised by McClernand that the wreck of the *Indianola* was nearby, Porter also wanted to see the hulk, which he found "much shattered." He soon had crews aboard to salvage what they could, the *Mound City* tying up alongside while the crew "commenced taking the iron plating from the wreck."⁶²

With the naval presence securing New Carthage, McClernand began concentrating his corps in that area despite Grant describing how "the roads, though level, were intolerably bad, and the movement was therefore necessarily slow." One Iowan admitted that "it must have been on this trip that the government mule-driver got his everlasting reputation for exhausting the vocabulary of all words that could be used as prefixes or suffixes to the word 'damn.' The newly coined nouns, proper and very improper, the verbs, adverbs[,] and adjectives that he created will last to the end of time." Nevertheless, McClernand called all his present divisions, Hovey still being on the trip southward from Helena, down to the area, camping them between Holmes's Plantation and New Carthage, a mere six-mile length. There, soldiers put the Holmes Plantation sawmill in operation to build skiffs to cross the flood to New Carthage. Logan's division followed "out in the country," one Illinoisan describing a beautiful scene of the camps and how "at sunset the fifes and drums of the regiments, the brass band of the division, the bugle notes from the cavalry and the artillery corps, all chiming in at retreat."[63]

Eventually McClernand pushed Osterhaus farther down to Perkins's Plantation, where there was slight skirmishing, allowing Carr's following division to be ferried over the crevasses to New Carthage. At the same time, Grant sought out a land route around Bayou Vidal from Smith's to Mrs. Perkins's that would alleviate the water crossing to New Carthage. Soon, Alvin Hovey's arriving division traversed that route despite bridges being washed away. Grant had argued that "another route had to be found," although few if any of the lower-level troops knew where the march would take them; one Indianan marveled that "Regiment after Regt, Battery after Battery file past, looking as though nothing in the shape of human power could resist their force." Oddly enough, Hovey and Osterhaus met up on the far ends of each division's path, Hovey reporting, "I met General Osterhaus coming up from the river on the same business, and on comparing notes the route was deemed practicable." At the same time, Grant ordered McPherson to likewise move southward and take over the defense of Richmond, where they found a thousand of McClernand's sick soldiers without adequate care, as well as the area back to Milliken's Bend, but to "keep closed up" on McClernand to be able to move fast once the crossing came. Sherman remained in rear, perhaps because of his lack of interest but also because he was most trusted for independent operations. Sherman admitted to Steele that "I confess I don't like this roundabout project, but we must support Grant in whatever he undertakes."[64]

Opening the land route around Bayou Vidal was critical, Grant not liking the watery gap in the road between Smith's Plantation and New Carthage, especially the three major crevasses causing the troops to have to be ferried amid the turbulent waters of the bayous and river. Hovey's division with Engineer Wilson thus did yeoman's work while out opening the route around Bayou Vidal. Along the western bank were a series of major bayous that were unbridgeable, so the route had to cross the main Bayou Vidal to get by these and then recross to get back on the main road. But it was soon done, with one bridge nearly four hundred feet long and the other five hundred and fifty made of flats and connected barges. The men, Hovey reported, "worked for hours up to their necks in water." But the "great military route through the overflowed lands" from Smith's Plantation to Perkins' was soon open, McClernand marveling that the division "had to construct nearly 2,000 feet of bridging out of materials created, for the most part, on the occasion." One Indianan noted that all the material was floated "to where the bridge was building," and an Iowan was amazed at the intricacy of all the bayous: "These Bayou's are altogether different from any thing we have in the north. They are not Swamps but chanels with steep Banks. Some of them are very large. Some of them have no outlet but most generally they communicate with some other Bayou thus forming a kind of net work over the country." The bridges were imperfect, however; the big 24-pound howitzers and 30-pound Parrotts "submerged" portions of the bridges as they moved across, one big gun being lost in the process.[65]

With Sherman's troops remaining idle for the moment as Steele's division returned and McClernand continued to open the route southward, Blair's division and others consequently were the recipient of a major speech by Adjutant General Lorenzo Thomas about the "policy of the war," namely enlisting Black troops, and the men were to be drawn together "dressed in their best uniforms." The troops were normally drawn up in hollow squares or circles around a wagon on which Thomas stood, and they heard from Thomas and other generals, Sherman even giving his unfervent blessing couched in the need to obey orders; some accounts included Grant himself making a speech. One Federal reported Thomas as "a tall gray haired and imposing old man," and an Ohioan reported that the troops afterward gave three cheers to the president, the policy, as well as the adjutant general. When Thomas addressed the 8th Wisconsin's division, he particularly pointed out the mascot "Old Abe," the war eagle, who spread his wings at the very time he mentioned that he hoped the eagle would spread its wings over all the rebellious states. One division Thomas apparently did not address was anti-abolitionist A. J. Smith's, who "swears he will hang old Thomas if he comes into his camp making such a speck." Still, word filtered back to Grant's headquarters that Thomas "makes bad speeches to troops, but that they shall obey orders, nevertheless." Ultimately, Grant assigned Brigadier General John P. Hawkins to "the command and organization of all troops of African descent in this department," and the recruiting and formation "goes on bravely," one Illinoisan wrote, adding that it was "fun to see the black boys get their sat'ridge boxes on upside down, they don't know a belt from a hole in the ground. But seem very willing to learn."[66]

At times down as far as New Carthage and Smith's Plantation on Roundaway Bayou, and enduring a night voyage on the river to Porter's flagship that alarmed the staff who thought the commanding general may have capsized and drowned, Grant planned to move his headquarters to New Carthage itself on April 22 as the road along Roundaway Bayou continually dried out and the water in the river and bayous fell. He also kept the idea of running troops and supplies by the bayous through Duckport Canal, which was opened on April 13, and Willow and Roundaway Bayous, even calling for Patterson's engineers to work on cleaning out the bayous. The soldiers of course hated the work but loved the benefits, one Iowan writing his sister: "We can go out fishing the boys gig a great many the greatest thing here is a large bull frog and they are the nearest a bull of any thing I ever saw they are as big as a large duck and make a noise very near alike a bull it is about as big a noise if not quite the same I am going to display my french some day by having a mess of the fellows." All the while, with the route open for good, Grant began to prepare for a crossing of the river, Porter informing him that he could carry around two hundred and fifty infantrymen in each vessel (the second wave of transports not arriving as yet), plus what could be moved on the barges. Grant wanted an entire division at the least thus boarded for the movement, warning McClernand to make sure the men, unaware of the ways of the water, to "keep cool, and to avoid getting too much on one side, or, in other words, to keep the barges trimmed." But at the same time, he repeated that "possession be gotten of Grand Gulf at the very earliest possible moment."[67]

Porter himself was already testing the defenses there, as early as April 20 and in the days following, moving down with the *Tuscumbia* and *Price* and taking the Confederates under fire. He related to Grant that the defenses were not yet impregnable but soon would be: "My opinion is that they will move heaven and earth to stop us if we don't go ahead." In fact, he thought he could go ahead and disable the guns but demurred, wanting it to be done when the infantry troops were ready to cross: "I think it should be done together." He also admitted that "I wish twenty times a day that Sherman was here, or yourself, but I suppose we cannot have all we wish"; still, it was a backhanded slap at McClernand. But McClernand was all about moving on himself, ordering Osterhaus to board what boats he could and to accompany Porter to Grand Gulf for a try. Porter reconnoitered again on April 22 without troops and planned to go again the next morning. McClernand ordered Osterhaus to go along "on such boats as he could find" and, "if the gunboats succeed in silencing the batteries, either with or without your aid, you will, if you think yourself strong enough for the purpose, take and hold the place."[68]

Porter went down on April 23 with the entire squadron, "feeling that something was going on at Grand Gulf that should be stopped." Osterhaus was ready, but Porter ran across a civilian who informed him the position contained four forts and twelve thousand troops, although there were actually only about four thousand men of Bowen's division. The admiral deemed his and Osterhaus's force too small to combat all that, yet he warned Grant that they had better do something quickly: "These forts are only partly finished; in a week they will be formidable."[69]

Porter had a point: with the decisive and irrevocable decision made to go below, especially with the navy, it would be unwise to waste any more time in crossing the river and getting to that coveted high ground to the east.

12

"Attracting Attention from Grant"
April 24–29

Ulysses S. Grant had been slowly drifting from the Jominian concept of war to one, if not totally Clausewitzian at this point, nevertheless much more similar to the Prussian's ideas than Jomini's. Certainly, his use of naval craft amid all the high water to move portions of his army through swampland and near wilderness terrain, his attempts to change the course of a major river to bypass "decisive points," and his seemingly growing disregard for safe supply lines in his movements southward in Louisiana were all examples of moving away from the by-the-book processes that were accepted and venerated in America, especially by Henry Halleck.[1]

As the end of April came, however, Grant moved even farther away from the Jominian book in a number of ways, including planning an amphibious assault, about which Jomini had very little to say. But no better example of doing things differently than Jomini would have liked was in his heavy use of diversions and feints. While both Jomini and Clausewitz discussed these diversions, both had concerns about their use, viewing them as dangerous. Clausewitz gave much more potential to diversions than Jomini, who described them as extremely dangerous and to be utilized only when absolutely necessary. In fact, he termed them "necessary evils" and was if anything unenthusiastic toward their use. Especially repulsive was a large diversion by portions of one's army. Supporting columns was one thing—the idea that the supporting column could take care of itself if necessary—but sending a portion of a whole army on a diversion far away from the army was courting disaster according to Jomini. Certainly, he would not have approved of Grant's use of Frederick Steele up at Greenville, Hurlbut in West Tennessee, or other pending movements about to be employed. "Armies have been destroyed for no other reason than that they were not kept together," Jomini wrote bluntly. Small diversions in the form of raids, such as the one Benjamin Grierson was conducting even at this point, were better suited for good results with low risk if destroyed.²

But Clausewitz saw the potential for such "cunning" movements, though at the same time he expressed reservations about their use. Basically, Clausewitz approved of diversions if done the right way, at the right time, and under the right circumstances; otherwise, he wrote, "one may be digging one's own grave." But under the correct circumstances—and Grant obviously thought he had them—these diversions could produce ample dividends: "Diversions can obviously be useful," Clausewitz opined, "but this is not by any means invariably so."³

Obviously, the United States military has long thought these types of diversions were useful in the right contexts, one of the nine principles of war being economy of force: "Commanders allocate only the minimum combat power necessary to shaping and sustaining operations so they can mass combat power for the decisive operation." Similarly, the principle of maneuver "concentrates and disperses combat power to keep the enemy at a disadvantage. It achieves results that would otherwise be more costly. Effective maneuver keeps enemy forces off balance by making them confront new problems and new dangers faster than they can counter them." Another principle—surprise—which Clausewitz argued was very much a part of cunning, was a necessary ingredient. It is significant that Grant realized as much having never read or probably even heard much about Clausewitz, doing it a full four or five decades before the United States military codified the principles of war. It is just as significant that Grant saw the need to throw away the accepted book on how to do things, whether that be Jomini's or Halleck's.⁴

Benjamin Grierson's blue-clad cavalry poured into Newton Station at daylight on April 24, taking everyone by surprise just as he had hoped. And the Federals came in waves, first the scouts and an advance party under the bold lieutenant colonel of the 7th Illinois Cavalry, William D. Blackburn. An hour later Grierson arrived with the main body. Later, Captain Henry Forbes's Company B would also pass through, giving the inhabitants an idea of almost continual Federal waves moving through Mississippi. The initial group was the most destructive in terms of surprise, they taking control quickly and actually catching two trains that happened to arrive at the wrong place at the wrong time. The Illinoisans secured everything and began the destruction, added to when the others arrived shortly thereafter. Damage to the railroad was significant in both directions as parties moved eastward to Chunky and westward toward a small bridge. But the real effect was the news getting out quickly that Grierson had not been turned back at Starkville and was still moving undeterred.[5]

The entire Vicksburg Campaign changed on that morning of April 24. Although a small part of the entire operation, Benjamin Grierson's raid through the bowels of Mississippi paid large dividends that morning as Grierson suddenly popped out of nowhere at Newton Station, for all to see. He had taken great measures to move as stealthily as possible up to this point, but now he desired to be seen. Obviously, his rail-breaking activity would do so anyway, he for the first time since leaving La Grange being in the general neighborhood of a telegraph that could spread the news quickly. But the other goal of the raid in addition to damaging the single rail line feeding Vicksburg was to show himself and divert attention from whatever Grant was doing to the southwest. While timing was more problematic than split-second coordination, he knew Grant was about to cross the river and so wanted to be the diversion to take Confederate attention toward his direction.[6]

In the first goal Grierson succeeded, although the Confederates had the railroad repaired within a few days, Pemberton writing of the break remaining "for more than a week." But in the second—"this celebrated raid," as Pemberton termed it—was even more than helpful to Grant down in Louisiana. Numerous Confederates around Vicksburg commented on the events, one even writing home that the raid moved "between Jackson & Meridian burning depots & doing other damage." He added, "I think it would have been a good thing for the Confederacy if they had come to Jackson & taken Pemberton—for it does seem that he is determined that the enemy shall have every opportunity to commit their depredations." Most important, for the next five days, from April 24 to April 28, Pemberton's attention was almost exclusively on the now-found Grierson, the actual threat within range of him at Jackson instead of Grant west of the Mississippi River. In reality, Grant was by far the greater potential threat, but Pemberton misread the entire situation as he had been doing for a while now and because of his fixation on Grierson he let Grant nearly get across the river before responding. Once Pemberton pivoted back to Grant's threat at the end of April, it was too late to stop or even barely to slow it.[7]

With the damage done at Newton both physically and mentally, Grierson's goals then shifted. He could still do damage and divert, but his main objective became to get his troopers out safely. To do that, he opted for an unconventional move: to flee southward. Most expected him to turn around

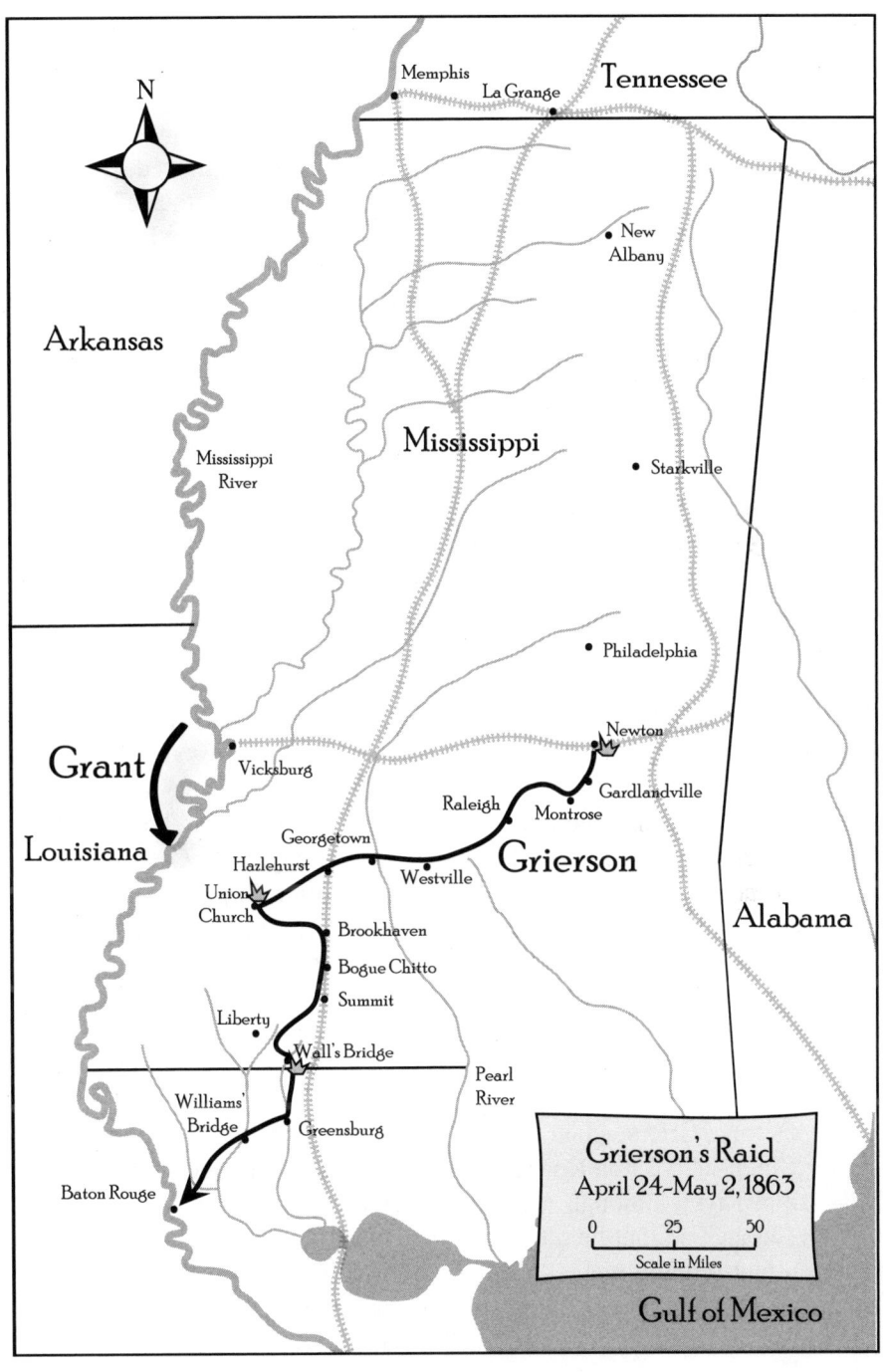

and go out the way he had come in, including Loring, who had by this point positioned himself at Meridian to coordinate the response. But all Loring had was infantry, and he called on Pemberton to send cavalry: "I have no hope of catching them on foot." Loring did the next best thing: move infantry by rail northward, the direction of supposed escape. But Grierson moved southward that afternoon to Garlandville, where citizens "venerable with age" opposed him temporarily, and then he moved on southward to the Griffin Bender Plantation. Given the long two days of forced march he had required of his troopers and then a day of destruction, he took the next day to rest his command, ambling along rather than moving quickly and a long distance. "The forced marches which I was compelled to make, in order to reach this point successfully," Grierson explained, "necessarily very much fatigued and exhausted my command, and rest and food were absolutely necessary for its safety." After a day of rest and "a very easy march," he began moving on April 26 more swiftly westward through Raleigh and Westville to the Pearl River. He would have to cross it wherever he went, which was still undecided.[8]

The Pearl River consequently became a major obstacle for the second time on the raid. This far down its watershed, past Jackson, it was a large river, unfordable with no bridges. There was a ferry at Georgetown, but if it was destroyed, then the Federals would be trapped east and south of the curving river. For a second time, Grierson thus sent troops forward on a forced march to secure the ferry so that the entire command could get across safely. Colonel Prince himself led the forward group and tricked the ferry owner into thinking they were Confederates and moving them across, whereupon they took control of the ferry site and moved the arriving main body under Grierson across as well, although slowly. "He arrived in time," Grierson proudly added, "to capture a courier who had come to bring intelligence of the approach of the Yankees, and orders for the destruction of the ferry." At the same time, the leading Federals now across the river moved on into Hazlehurst and secured the telegraph there, the Union raid again nearing civilization where they could be easily located and swamped by Confederates moving to catch them by train.[9]

By this time, Grierson had narrowed his choices of escape to either heading for Union-held Baton Rouge or joining Grant's army once it crossed the Mississippi River, although details of what was going on with Grant were sketchy, enough so that he ultimately concluded Grant had not yet crossed. Grierson had actually rushed, thinking he was late: "I had hurried forward fearing that I might be too late, but unfortunately [I] had travelled a little too fast and was a few days ahead of time." In actuality, he was early and missed a linkup with Grant, even moving into the Port Gibson–Union Church area by April 28, two days before Grant arrived. But he was able to do more destruction to the New Orleans, Jackson, and Great Northern Railroad around Hazlehurst as he meandered around the area waiting to see if anything developed with Grant. When fires to legitimate government stores got out of hand at Hazlehurst, however, the Federals sought to put them out, Grierson himself in the midst: "The citizens who had arrived to resist us, hearing of this, returned and were greatly astonished at our action and complimented us upon our good conduct."[10]

By April 28, Grierson was beginning to get pursuers from several directions, most notably Colonel Wirt Adams's Mississippi Cavalry but also even mounted infantry; he even had to fight a small skirmish at Union Church. Grierson soon decided that he could not wait any longer to meet up with Grant and, after making "a strong demonstration toward Fayette with a view of creating the impression that we were going toward Port Gibson or Natchez, while I quietly took the opposite direction," he turned southward for good, hoping to make Baton Rouge. "Hearing nothing more of our forces at Grand Gulf," he admitted, "I concluded to make for Baton Rouge." Grierson moved through Summit, where "we found much Union sentiment in this town, and were kindly welcomed and fed by many of the citizens," and toward Liberty as a feint before heading south. All the while, the troopers were exchanging their worn-out mounts for new horses and mules: "We wore out one set of horses, but we captured another set just as good as the old ones, if not better. I have got as fine a young mare as ever traveled and she did not cost me anything," trooper William Dunaway wrote his wife. Wirt Adams could never overtake the Federals as a result, admitting that, "owing to their use of the most skillful guides and unfrequented roads, I found it impossible, to my great mortification and regret, to overhaul them." But more than just Adams's cavalry were concentrating against Grierson by this point. In fact, he met Confederates of the 9th Louisiana Partisan Rangers under Major James De Baun on the lookout for him at Wall's Bridge, southeast of Liberty, on May 1. His impetuous lieutenant colonel of the 7th Illinois Cavalry, William D. Blackburn, led a charge with "undaunted courage" that cost him a mortal wound, with several others killed or wounded, including the chief of the Butternut Guerrillas, scout William Surby. "Had the colonel been as discreet and wary as he was brave," Grierson lamented, "it is very probable that not a man would have been wounded." After sending in more troops, Grierson captured the bridge and moved on, leaving the wounded with locals. He pushed on, through Greensburg and toward Williams' Bridge over the last impediment that could trip him up, the Amite River, "a wide and rapid stream," according to Grierson.[11]

By this point, Confederates were coming at Grierson from literally every direction, but the most concerning was a column sent out by Franklin Gardner from Port Hudson to block Williams' Bridge. Messages ran with haste between the Confederate commanders in the area, one advising that "to stop them at Williams' Bridge is the last chance." If it was defended, the game was up and Grierson would be caught east of the river with no place to go. For the third time in the raid, he consequently called on his troopers to make a forced march, not stopping for nearly two days as he raced between the seams of the Confederates concentrating on him. When Grierson reached the bridge, he was overjoyed to find it guarded by only a couple of Confederates; he was several hours ahead of the column sent to stop him. "It was not long until the welcome sound of our horses' hooves were heard reverberating as we went gaily marching on over the raging torrent," he explained. From there, the Illinoisans trudged on southwestward toward Baton Rouge with many of the men asleep in the saddle, in the process gobbling up a couple of Confederate camps and even the Confederates who were opposing the Baton Rouge forces, taking them in rear. The Confederates there had no idea the enemy was behind them and joked to the Baton Rouge Federals once captured that "they never could have captured them; that the United States government had to send Illinois soldiers clear from Tennessee into their rear before they could be taken."[12]

Soon, Grierson's tired troopers entered Union lines, followed by a stream of contrabands who had seen their chance at freedom and took it. Once in safety, most fell to the ground to sleep. Only Grierson did anything different, wandering over to a nearby plantation house, where, finding a piano inside, the musician-turned-cavalryman sat down and played a tune. "I felt that we had nobly accomplished the work assigned us, and no wonder that I felt musical. Who would not under like circumstances?"[13]

Grierson quickly became a national hero for the feat, the results lasting long after the raid ended. Newspapers across the nation picked up the story and printed accounts in vivid detail, Grierson even making the front page of *Harper's Weekly*. Yet some ramifications were more tangible, a Mississippian back near Garlandville even the next year describing in his diary how "[we] went out of our way to cross a creek called Jarlow, the Grierson raid having burnt the bridge last spring." Most notably, the raid did what it was intended to do, especially taking attention away from Grant's activities to the south. One Vicksburg artillerist queried his diary: "Where are our authorities? 'Asleep?'"[14]

If there was ever a general who took the bait of a diversion it was John C. Pemberton. While numerous lower-level Confederates displayed their assumption that Grant would be the major threat moving south of and then in rear of Vicksburg, Pemberton seemed never to realize as much. Then Grierson's effort completely took his mind off Grant. In the five days between Grierson's reappearance on April 24 and Grant's firm arrival at the Mississippi River crossing on April 28, Pemberton almost completely turned his attention northward and eastward, mainly toward Grierson's imminent threat. But there were many other fears in that direction as well, including the numerous rumors of Federals appearing all over the map in places such as Kosciusko, Carthage, Bankston, and Paulding, some of them nowhere near any body of Federals, much less Grierson. In fact, Pemberton admitted that "it was impossible to obtain any reliable information of the enemy's movements, rumor placing him in various places at the same time." But the combined effect resulted in massive reports of Federals to the east and north, while Grant was still across the Mississippi River. Pemberton went wholeheartedly for the immediate threat.[15]

Pemberton himself began coordinating the response to Grierson's sudden reappearance, embarrassed a bit that such a column could do this to him. Embarrassment was one thing, but actual destruction was another. That Grierson hit the one complete rail line that fed Vicksburg with both food and ammunition, and indeed all supplies, was worse. Pemberton was even then within the monthslong compulsion of storing supplies for a siege at Vicksburg, and the Southern Railroad of Mississippi was the main supplier. In terms of ammunition, Vicksburg had nearly run out of heavy ordnance after the April 16 Union passage; new supplies were even then on the way from the east, to be carried over this very railroad. To have it broken at such a critical time was unacceptable.[16]

Worst of all was the threat that Grierson posed to areas unaffected as yet. While the real threat from Grierson was negligible (the Union colonel was in fact just seeking to get out as best he could at this point), the presumed threat was very real. Word quickly spread among Confederate soldiers who commented freely in letters and diaries about the significance, one staff officer writing in his diary on April 25 that "today we recd news of a bold & dashing cavalry raid made by a portion of the enemy's force, some 1500, under command of Col. Grierson of Illinois. . . . This is certainly a gallant exploit & deserving the praise of both friend and foe." Obviously, Grierson could do more damage to other railroads such as the New Orleans, Jackson, and Great Northern, which he was already doing, but that damage was of a lesser concern. While that rail line would actually be damaged heavier than the Southern Railroad, remaining broken until after the war in fact, the line led nowhere in terms of Confederate territory. Its use was lopped off by the Federal presence in Louisiana, much like the Mississippi Central's use in northern Mississippi. Neither thus connected with the greater Confederacy like the Southern did. And therein lay Pemberton's concern: Grierson might somehow turn north again and hit perhaps even Jackson, the state capital and Pemberton's current headquarters. Of even more concern was the Southern's railroad bridge over the Big Black River between Vicksburg and Jackson. It would be a major problem if the Pearl River bridge at Jackson were destroyed, but even then trains could still connect in Jackson from the Mississippi Central and New Orleans, Jackson, and Great Northern, both of which ran west of the Pearl River. But if the Big Black River bridge fell, Vicksburg would be entirely cut off from everything. And there was some talk of it in the Union army, an Illinoisan in Louisiana who obviously had inside connections describing to his niece how "already an enterprise is on foot for the seizure of that bridge" at Amsterdam, probably a reference to Grierson's Raid, although Grierson never intended to go there.[17]

The tunnel vision Pemberton suffered regarding Grierson is easily discerned in his correspondence. For the period between April 24 and 28, Pemberton sent sixty-nine messages as recorded in the *Official Records*, certainly not all but all those deemed significant enough to be included in the publication of the records after the war. Of those, 92.7 percent dealt exclusively with Grierson. Pemberton literally took a hands-on approach to coordinating the response, even to the point of corresponding from his Jackson headquarters with officers as low in rank as majors and captains, he telling several to "get on his rear, and plant ambush and annoy him."[18]

Pemberton's main response was to send troops chasing after Grierson. Loring in Meridian by this time conveniently had Abraham Buford's brigade to hold that critical rail junction as well as the Mobile and Ohio northward and southward from there. It was a good thing, because Captain Forbes's Company B actually tested one of those railroad stations at Enterprise in his continual attempt to catch up with Grierson. Obviously, he was going the wrong direction, and with a company of a mere thirty-something men he could not tamper with the regiment-size garrisons. With some trickery Grierson himself would have been proud of, Forbes bought time to talk with his commander about, of all things, the Confederate garrison's surrender, and he hurriedly left the scene before the Confederates found out they were contemplating surrendering to a mere thirty or so men. Forbes then moved fast toward Grierson and in an almost miraculous feat of travel finally caught up with him near Westville before the brigade crossed the Pearl River. Operating on foot, Loring was quickly and badly outdistanced, though Pemberton ordered him to "telegraph every hour your position." Ultimately, when Grierson was known to be out of the Meridian/Newton Station region, Pemberton ordered Loring eastward to Jackson.[19]

Pemberton sent more forces eastward from Jackson, hopefully to make contact with Loring across the gap in the rails and telegraph at Newton Station. He also readied reserve units of Tilghman's and Featherston's brigades along the Mississippi Central to respond wherever they were needed. Brigadier General John Adams brought Pemberton's ire in the process, writing those on the other side of the break, even Buckner at Mobile, that if they did not send help "all was lost." Pemberton seethed that "I never authorized you to use such an expression." Pemberton likewise alerted Ruggles and Chalmers in northern Mississippi to be ready to close in the rear if the Federals returned that direction, although it soon became clear that Grierson was heading southward. But other supporting raids from La Grange (the Federals did not know which way Grierson was heading either) took their attention nevertheless. As Grierson clearly entered southwestern Mississippi, Pemberton likewise sent any small command he could scrape together after him, including mounting infantry (begging Governor Pettus for horses and men) and sending what he could by rail. He even released a colonel he had ordered under arrest so that he could lead a chasing column. And as Grierson continually moved southward toward Louisiana, Pemberton admitting "he has studiously avoided meeting our infantry," he had units down there in action as well, including ordering Franklin Gardner to intercept the Federal raiders before they moved to Baton Rouge.[20]

Lost in the chaos of chasing Grierson with just about all he had was the Mississippi River defense; one Confederate at Vicksburg even related that "our regiment was greatly excited over reports of a Federal raid led by Col. Grierson, which passed nearly through the entire state." Yet some could see the problems, especially with the movement of Union vessels south of the city; Carter Stevenson shifted troops from the Snyder's Bluff area to Warrenton in the days after the passage. One staff officer at Vicksburg even confided to his diary, "I have always been afraid of the flank movement at some point below Warrenton, and that a powerful effort would be made to cut off our communication with Jackson—a step, which, if successful, would be fatal to this place." But the troops at Vicksburg itself and up the Yazoo had little to confront, one Louisianan writing that on April 25 "I have just been taking [in] a game of ball with the boys."

There was no such leisure down at Grand Gulf, where John Bowen was loudly proclaiming alarm at the Union buildup and activity in his area.

Stevenson at Vicksburg did the same, his line stretched thin with his division holding the area from Warrenton to the city and beyond, Martin L. Smith's division the city itself and John H. Forney's division from the city up to Snyder's and Haynes' Bluffs. In fact, there was some debate as to which should reinforce the other because both feared an imminent attack, Stevenson writing on April 24 that "there is no information in my possession which induces me to believe that the larger force is not above us. I respectfully submit my opinion that no re-enforcements be taken from Vicksburg for Grand Gulf until it is ascertained definitely that the main force of the enemy is opposed to it." Obviously, Bowen had a better argument, with Grant poised right across the river from him near New Carthage and continually moving southward. The presence of the Union navy was telling as well. But Stevenson had his own troubles, including another naval contingent north of Vicksburg and presently in the Yazoo River. Worse, the defensive raft there had broken at Snyder's Bluff, had been repaired temporarily, but then had broken again for good, and all right about the time that Federals showed up again in the area; the drama with the raft only served to further fix Confederate attention on the vulnerable Yazoo River corridor. The worst-case scenario, of course, was what Stevenson wrote as "if the enemy are well informed as to our positions, and I have no doubt that they are, they would attack right and left simultaneously."[21]

Meanwhile, Bowen was having his own problems at Grand Gulf, prophesying to Pemberton on April 27 that "all the movements of the enemy during the last twenty-four hours seem to indicate an intention on their part to march their army still lower down in Louisiana, perhaps to Saint Joseph, and then to run their steamers by me and cross at Rodney." Bowen went himself and later sent an engineer with the idea of "selecting a line of battle south of Port Gibson." While he assured Pemberton he could deflect an attempted landing at Grand Gulf itself, "if they get so far to my left and rear, continuing to threaten my right and front, I must either imperil my whole command by too great an extension of my line or else submit to a complete investment, with Port Gibson in their possession."[22]

Both Bowen and Stevenson thus reported their problems, but by this point Pemberton was in complete react mode regarding Grierson and barely even heard them. He simply ordered that Bowen and Stevenson keep open communications, especially across the major stumbling block between them, the Big Black River; Stevenson accordingly began work on "a boat-bridge" at Hall's Ferry. Yet nearly all his messages from April 24 to April 28 involved Grierson, and the two or three that included other issues were simply warning in nature and did nothing to actually reinforce the Mississippi River front. For instance, on April 25 he ordered Stevenson to put some of his field artillery armed with incendiary shells on the banks of the river to fire at any more vessels that might pass the city.[23]

Worse, and perhaps the key stroke in the unraveling defense, those actions taken to catch Grierson actually hurt Bowen and Stevenson's attempt to block any Federal landing on the Mississippi shore. On April 27, Pemberton warned Bowen that "it is possible they may be making for Hazlehurst and Grand Gulf, to fall on your rear," and he ordered Bowen to "collect Wirt Adams' cavalry and send them out to meet the enemy. . . . Annoy and ambush them if possible. Move rapidly." It was Adams who then fought Grierson at Union Church and chased him into Louisiana, but it was at the cost of leaving the entire southern Mississippi River front uncovered by cavalry, as Adams was all the mounted force Bowen at Grand Gulf had to depend on.[24]

By April 28, Bowen was almost in a panic. He messaged Pemberton that day, reporting "an immense force opposite me," and later advised that "every man and gun that can be spared from other points be sent here." Pemberton wired both Davis, who was sick in Richmond, and Johnston that "a demonstration is now being made in large force at Hard Times," but he was still in Grierson mode when at the end of both messages he renewed his request for more cavalry to deal with these types of raids. In fact, he responded to Bowen, "have you force enough to hold your position? If not, give me the smallest additional force with which you can. My small cavalry force necessitates the use of infantry to protect important points." That sounded like his attention was still on Grierson, and Pemberton did not in fact send any troops that day but instead merely ordered Stevenson and his Jackson commanders only to be prepared to send troops, as many as five thousand of them, upon further word. Stevenson received the order but reiterated his idea that "it is not improbable that the force opposite Grand Gulf is there to lay waste the country on that side, and is a feint to withdraw troops from a main attack here."[25]

But Bowen was convinced Grand Gulf was the real enemy target and again alerted Pemberton of the possibility of Federal landings. But Pemberton did not or would not hear it, or at least take it for the real threat to him that it was. And Pemberton even responded to Stevenson's call for aid to Vicksburg with the warning that "it is indispensable that you keep in your lines only such force as is absolutely needed to hold them, and organize the remainder, if there are any of your troops as a movable force available for any point where it may be most required." Furthermore, he received little help from his superiors, Johnston in Tullahoma again showing his lack of grasp on the entire situation, writing simply: "Is there not a regiment of cavalry at Columbus to intercept that of the Federals just reported at Newton Station?" It was obvious Johnston was totally out of touch with reality, but Pemberton reminded him every chance he had that a lot of this was Johnston's fault for taking his cavalry: "These raids cannot be prevented unless I can have more mounted men." In a fit of desperation the next day, he even told Johnston that, "however necessary cavalry may be to Army of Tennessee, it is indispensable to me to keep my communications." Later, when Johnston admonished him for not reporting Grierson's raid earlier, Pemberton nearly snapped, writing a long letter explaining how he had done just that on April 20. Pemberton wrote that Johnston's message "may seem to imply censure, which I feel is undeserved." Off-base as it was, however, even Johnston's message indicated the main area of concern for the highest of the Confederate command, and it was not below Vicksburg.[26]

As April waned and all the diversions were in place, Grant and Porter planned the final crossing of the Mississippi River. "We are nearing the moment of the grand decisive blow," one of Grant's observant soldiers wrote home. Grand Gulf was the logical place, allowing access to the high ground inland immediately and a clear path toward Vicksburg, blocked only by the Big Black River. But the presence of the Big Black was a benefit in this case, essentially shielding the landing from Vicksburg. If Confederates wanted to resist with their Vicksburg forces, it would be much easier to do so at Warrenton, if Grant chose to land there. But Grand Gulf, on the south side of the Big Black River, gave Grant an advantage both in having a shield arrayed in front of his own movement as well as an obstacle to Confederate resistance. Yet at the same time Grand Gulf was obviously well defended; one Federal later described how it "is (next to Vicksburg) the strongest natural bastion I have ever seen—The bluffs rise out of the river like mountains & it seems almost impossible that it could have been taken at all."[27]

But Grand Gulf emerged as only one of several places to land. Grant talked of it early on in the campaign, and it was certainly a needed locale once the Federals landed. But the invasion did not have to take place there, right in front of the heavy guns Bowen was erecting. Grant scouted the area north of Grand Gulf and even up the Big Black River but found no promising sites above water. Conversely, a landing farther south would get the Federals on the high ground in probably much easier fashion even if defended, as there would be no large guns to silence before a landing. There was also the matter of getting the ironclads and transports past Grand Gulf's batteries if a landing farther below would happen, but then these guns had proven unable to stop any of the boats passing regularly. That said, a landing farther south would also bring more geographical issues, certainly if below Bayou Pierre, which had all the same attributes of the Big Black River at Grand Gulf. If a landing below the mouth of Bayou Pierre took place, that waterway would shield the tedious operation from Confederates at Grand Gulf, but at the same time it would add yet another major waterway Grant would eventually have to fight his way across to get to Vicksburg.[28]

Thus the logical place to land at this point was Grand Gulf, and no one feared any repercussions. In fact, Porter naively assured Grant as early as April 11 that he could take on troops at New Carthage "and be upon the rebels at Grand Gulf before they know it, shell them out, and let the troops land and take possession." That may have been so on April 11, but John Bowen had been hard at work since then. Even as late as April 24, however, Grant, who had moved forward all the way to Smith's Plantation near New Carthage the night before, assured Sherman that "if an attack can be made within the next two days, the place will easily fall." He had made a reconnaissance, and Charles Dana related that the inspection "has convinced him that the place is not as strong as Admiral Porter supposed." Yet Grant explained that "the difficulties of getting from here (Smith's plantation) to the river are great." Nevertheless, the attack was scheduled for the end of the month, as early as April 27, but delay after delay emerged, and it was not until April 29 that the attack came. Primarily, despite the weather being "very hot, causing much suffering among the men," according to Major Francis C. Deimling of the 10th Missouri, a major storm system moved through on the night of April 26 and all the next day, soaking the roads and landings and causing huge logistical issues for the moving army; many of the roads had to be corduroyed because they were so slippery. "Mud, mud, mud," one exasperated Federal wrote in his diary, another writing of "teams by the dozen stuck some cannons having from 12 to 14 horses hauling them." Nerves frayed in the confusion, one Federal writing of "a fight between Captain Thompson and a private the Captain striking him over the head with his naked sword then tying him behind the wagon and dragging him along for miles." Even those moving by water were affected, Colonel Theodore E. Buehler of the 67th Indiana writing that his regiment was on a barge "in about 7 inches of stinking water, and keeping the pumps steady at work to keep the barge from filling."[29]

In addition to the storms causing significant delays, Dana laid a lot of the blame on McClernand's head. He reported to Washington as early as April 25 that "there is much apparent confusion in McClernand's command, especially about his staff and headquarters, and that the movement is delayed to some extent by that cause." Grant went himself on April 26 to hurry up matters and found, according to Dana, that "the steamboats and barges were scattered about the river and in the bayou as if there were no idea of the imperative necessity of the promptest possible movements." Grant fumed aboard Porter's flagship *Benton* and called for McClernand, telling him to get his troops embarked immediately. But there was more delay, McClernand holding a review of Illinois troops that afternoon so that visiting Illinois governor Richard Yates could make a speech (he had also addressed the troops at Lake Providence on the way down); one Illinoisan did not even recognize him and had to be told who he was. Others arrived as well, including wounded general and politician Richard J. Oglesby, still recovering from his injury at Corinth the year before. Other governors were also rumored to be "in these parts somewhere." Congressman Elihu Washburne was there as well and spoke to the men. McClernand had the artillery fire a salute, which also took time and wasted ammunition, which he had been stringently ordered not to do. Even Lorenzo Thomas became agitated, telling Dana that he believed McPherson's corps would be loaded before McClernand's. Indeed, one Federal documented a lot of fishing in his diary throughout these days—"had fisherman's luck," he added.[30]

Worse, there were also personal issues involved, Dana reporting that "though it is ordered that officers' horses and tents must be left behind, McClernand carries his bride along with him." He later added that there was delay in the shipping of troops southward because one of the boats "was also somewhat delayed by carrying General McClernand's wife, with her servants and baggage." While Dana was not a McClernand fan to be sure, there were certainly Mrs. McClernand sightings by others all around the army, including on the night of the Vicksburg passage on April 16 aboard Grant's steamer. An Illinoisan likewise wrote of being out foraging and "passed Genl. [John A.] McClernand and wife riding out in a chaise." More humorous, one Illinoisan told of her passing, remaking that she was "quite young & beautiful," and she happened to pass when many of the boys were moving logs across a bayou, "swimming & nude as our first parents in the garden of Innocence." McClernand himself was in bad humor much of the time, one of his own staff officers writing in his personal diary that "there is no necessity for a man to be so dictatorial and especially so disagreeable and unreasonable." For his part, Grant admitted to Julia that "I have been fretting here for several days to get ready to attack Grand Gulf with weather roads and water all against me." And Grant was not the only one fretting. Of the prospect of attacking Grand Gulf, a 33rd Illinois soldier wrote in his diary: "O God, protect us."[31]

In the meantime, John Bowen was making Grand Gulf nearly impregnable from the west. Obviously, that it faced the Mississippi River helped, but the Big Black River likewise shielded the northern face, the river's mouth creating the "gulf" just north of the old townsite. Two major forts complete with bricked magazines had emerged by this time, Fort Wade down near the old townsite and Fort Cobun father north near "Point of Rock," the high ground just to the east. Fort Cobun to the north was situated on a plateau forty feet above the river and contained two 7-inch rifles, an 8-inch rifle, and a 30-pound Parrott rifle, the latter on a field carriage. There was room for three or four more guns, including in an adjacent triangular work, but there was such a lack of weaponry that Pemberton did not have any more to send. And one that was on the way had been captured by Grierson around Gallatin. Nearly a mile to the south was Fort Wade, connected with Fort Cobun by a covered way and defended with rifle pits full of Francis Cockrell's Missourians, some of whom were tapped to carry ammunition to the big guns. Fort Wade "commands the river in all directions," one observer noted, and mounted four guns, two 30-pound Parrotts, an 8-inch rifle, and a 100-pound Blakely rifle. In between and on the hills in rear were several 20- and 30-pound Parrott rifles on field carriages. Admiral Porter later admitted that "this is by far the most extensive-built work, with the exception of those at Vicksburg, I have yet seen." But he tested the strength continually, one Confederate of Bowen's division writing a friend that "enemy from their gunboats have shelled us every day."[32]

Ultimately, McClernand began his movement toward this Confederate bastion on April 27, one of his Ohioans relating that they marched through "corn knee high." Grant himself went down that day (his forty-first birthday in fact) to rush the effort, he writing McClernand "a very severe letter." Upon arriving and finding the troops loading, however, he declined to send it. Evidently, the movement was finally beginning.[33]

The Grand Gulf attack contained two parts. One consisted of transports full of troops ready to land once the navy silenced the Confederate forts. And that took getting the army's forces to the area, most especially to the landing at Hard Times on the west bank of the river where a sign denoted the standings in days and hours of the famous steamboat race between the *Eclipse* and *Shotwell* in 1861. One Federal described how "this place is called Hard Times, there is no town, only a plantation and some negro huts. It is Hard times sure enough." Another noted that "it had been hard times all the way from April 15 when we started." Grant ordered McClernand to load all the transports available with portions of his corps, Osterhaus's and Carr's divisions, and send them southward to Hard Times to be ready to land. It took some time, and Grant became even more agitated at the delay. "Moving troops from Smith's plantation has been a tedious operation; more so than it should have been," he informed Halleck on April 27. But the troops were aboard and ready by the evening of April 28, spending the night onboard to be ready early the next morning. But not all were enthused with their

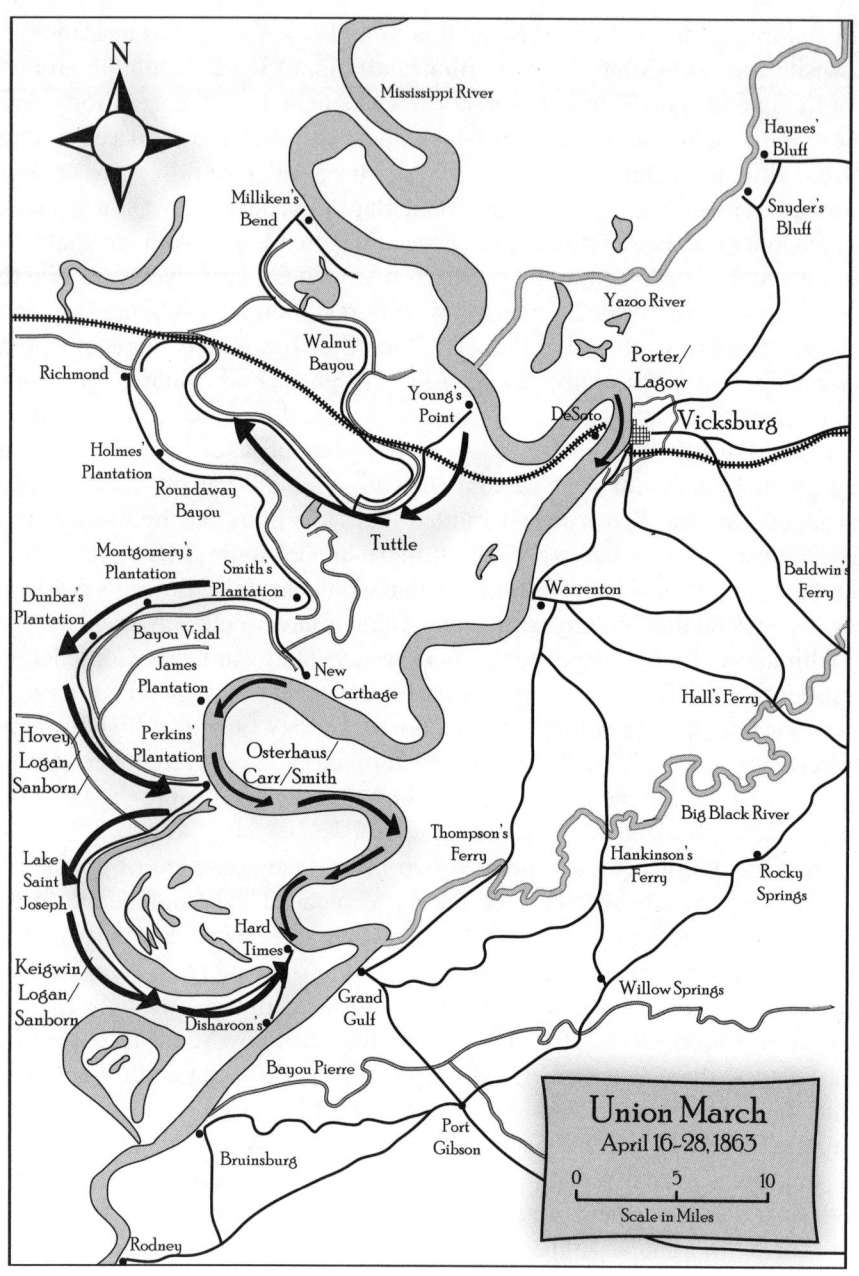

transportation: "They had a good many marks from running the Blockade," one nervous Federal explained.[34]

But this tedious waterborne route would not suffice for the rest of the army, slow as it was and Grant needing the troops up quickly; he also could not depend on the bayous to get supplies through, in which water levels were falling drastically. He needed a firm wagon road. Now that the land route was open around Bayou Vidal, Grant consequently looked to opening another land route to Hard Times as well. McClernand sent one of Osterhaus's brigade commanders, Colonel James Keigwin, to examine the road around Lake Saint Joseph to Hard Times. Keigwin set out on the morning of April 25 "for the purpose of making a reconnaissance on the Lake Saint Joseph Road to a point opposite the mouth of Bayou Pierre, for the purpose of ascertaining whether a practicable road could be found at or near that point that would let us in position on the flank or in rear of Grand Gulf." He had with him the 49th Indiana, 114th Ohio, part of the 2nd Illinois Cavalry, and two guns of the 7th Michigan Battery. His division commander Osterhaus admonished him to rush the effort: "Hurry up—I want you in the fight!" Keigwin moved forward but met bayou after bayou on his route along the western bank of Lake Saint Joseph; one Illinoisan wrote home that these bayous "I suppose up there would be called a creek" but nevertheless reported seeing two tenfoot alligators. Some soldiers made rings from the bones of dead alligators, although one Ohioan found up a tree by his comrades wanted no part of them—he declared an alligator had chased him up the tree. Another Federal reported seeing "some of the biggest snakes I ever saw, some of them are 4 to 6 feet long." These bayous all had to be bridged, and it took several days to make any progress using "timber taken from barns in the immediate vicinity." Harrison's Confederate skirmishers also impeded the Federals.[35]

Keigwin first came to Holt's Bayou, which he bridged, the Confederates having burned the original one. Then he came to another, Du Rossett, which he also bridged despite it being a much larger bayou of a hundred and twenty feet wide and "was bank full, with a swift current." It took the rest of the day and night, but a bridge finally went up. Moving on the next day, April 26, the column came to Phelps Bayou, also missing its bridge, and here Keigwin also encountered Confederate pickets. The main body, in fact, lay just across the next bayou down, Clark Bayou, where the Confederate artillery and main line were. Slight skirmishing "caused them to saddle up and leave in great confusion," however, and Keigwin ordered the two bayous bridged as well, with help from cavalry that had located ample resources due to "their experience in foraging." But it took the rest of the day and the next. In the meantime Keigwin sent a portion of his command forward to follow the Confederates, who left the main road and disappeared to the west. Keigwin soon followed with his entire command, concerned that they might come back in rear of the column and destroy the bridges that had been left under a mere sergeant and ten men each. He followed as far as Lake Bruin and drove the Confederates away with some artillery fire. Satisfied that the enemy would pose no further problem, Keigwin returned to the main road and moved on to Hard Times, reaching it the next day, April 28. The road around Lake Saint Joseph was now open with new bridges, and much of the following army would use this route to get to Hard Times and eventually cross the river. In all, the land route from Milliken's Bend to Smith's, then around Bayou Vidal to Perkins's, and then around Lake Saint Joseph to Hard Times, was a seventy-mile journey.[36]

At the same time, other components of the army were also moving despite the heavy rains, sometimes with lightning, hail, and thunder that caused many to think the boats were running the batteries again. These appeared frequently throughout April 22–27, many of these same rains affecting Grierson's trek to the east. Mosquitoes and gnats, a result of the wet environment, were also problematic, Colonel Manning Force relating that "the air became a saturated solution of gnats." But the army's operations did not slow, one Federal reflecting that "Gen. Grant acted as if he thought a wet soldier was as good as a dry one." While taking Osterhaus's, Carr's, and part of A. J. Smith's divisions with him on transports to Hard Times in what many described as "unseaworthy" vessels, McClernand also had his other divisions on the move. To make sure Keigwin was supported, he sent a brigade of A. J. Smith's division around Lake Saint Joseph, which marched across the four new bridges Keigwin's troops had constructed. Hovey's troops remained at Perkins's to await transport by water down to Hard Times.[37]

As McPherson and Sherman were ordered to start southward as well, they eventually took the land route, although McPherson described it as extremely difficult: "heavy rains had rendered the roads across the rich alluvial bottoms on the Louisiana side almost impassable, and it was only by the most strenuous exertions on the part of the men, and by doubling teams, that the artillery and trains could be got along." Nevertheless, Logan's division of McPherson's corps moved out on April 25 followed by the other two divisions, Quinby's temporarily under Colonel John B. Sanborn because of Quinby's sickness and medical leave. Quinby, in fact, had never even left Helena. Grant initially planned to place the division under Brigadier General Jeremiah C. Sullivan commanding the area west of the river but would soon hand it to Brigadier General Marcellus M. Crocker, who was a brigade commander in McArthur's division. The "order for marching was hailed with pleasure by all," one Illinoisan related, despite heatstrokes and cramps and the attendant straggling endured on the long marches; one Wisconsin artilleryman admitted that the men "were all soft after nearly two months' packing on the boat." Brigadier General Thomas E. G. Ransom's brigade of McArthur's division that had moved down from Lake Providence remained behind temporarily to cover the roadways (other brigades of this division were likewise left as far back as Richmond and Milliken's Bend), but it was tough going for those up front. Colonel David B. Hillis of the 17th Iowa related his troops moved through "mud from 4 to 6 inches deep," and an Illinoisan explained that "the bottom of the ground, if there ever was any, had surely fallen out or so far settled down that it couldn't be reached." Still, the soldiers marveled at the beauty of the plantations they passed through. Brigadier General John E. Smith, now in command of a brigade in Logan's division, related to his wife that "we have passed through a lovely country since leaving Milliken's Bend, flowers of all kinds and hedges for miles composed of Roses. It seems to me I have never seen the Queen of flowers in greater perfection." Others described the beauty as well, especially the roses.[38]

Left behind as McPherson's troops moved southward, one of Sherman's Federals remarked on how "lonesome" it was getting above Vicksburg. Sherman initially received orders to follow "and keep closed up on the rear of General McPherson's Corps," but he was later halted to act up the Yazoo River as well as to build more connecting roads, mainly Tuttle's division creating a road along Walnut Bayou from his Duckport Canal camps. One disappointed soldier of Sherman's corps mused simply "orders to march countermanded. Prospect of staying here for the mosquitoes to feed on a week or two longer." A sad incident occurred in the 72nd Ohio in the midst of the work: a soldier bathing in the canal was drug below with the strong current and drowned, more of the continual process in operations so dependent on water.[39]

Back up at the front, McClernand was finishing his preparations to cross the river and ordered eighty rounds of ammunition issued to each man. The troops embarked on the five working transports, the *Anglo Saxon* because of its damaged wheel being lashed to the side of the transport flagship *General Price*. The barges, some of which were likewise in no working order, nevertheless were put in service to get as many men across at one time as possible. The loading went slowly, however, continuing on into the morning of April 28. But the troops seemed upbeat: "Everybody is jolly and each one has a good word of cheer for his friend or comrade—all are in a bustle; every one is confident of victory in the coming contest." Osterhaus even gave his troops a pep talk in his orders, writing that we are about to attack the enemy and we must conquer him. You are brave—be cool. Perhaps we may have a hard struggle. Be careful in firing. Don't waste your ammunition. Take good aim and see that your balls hit. Whether in dispersed order or in line of battle keep your proper places and never straggle away, but always remain within the hearing of your commanders and obey all orders promptly. When advancing, be lively, when falling back, retire slowly and never cease firing except ordered to do so.[40]

Ultimately, many of the troops landed at Hard Times to allow the vessels to return to Perkins's Plantation for Hovey's division, although a couple of units in Burbridge's brigade remained behind to garrison the area. The slaves on the shore were jubilant at the Union army's arrival, one Illinoisan testifying that "when we were landing there were some Negroes near by who appeared to be very happy indeed upon seeing us. They clapped their hands in joy, prostrated themselves, shook hands with each other, and thanked the Lord as a Negro only can. 'Twas interesting, affecting, and impressive to witness these manifestations of joy." One proslavery officer even admitted, "I was never more tempted to be an abolitionist."[41]

Despite the social ramifications, all knew this was the critical time of Grant's critical gamble—the crossing. Grant needed every man he could get, and on April 28 issued a very odd order:

All deserters who have returned voluntarily and reported for duty from the 1st day of April, 1863, to the present date will be mustered for pay from the date of joining their companies. They will, however forfeit all pay and allowances for the time of their absence, and will be required to make good the time lost by desertion. This clemency is extended to this class of delinquents, subject to approval of the President, and to insure future good conduct on the part of those who avail themselves of it. They will, however, be held subject to trial for desertion, for twelve months from the date of joining their companies, should their conduct within that time frame prove them unworthy of such clemency.[42]

The other component of the Union attack on Grand Gulf was the navy itself, which was on station and ready to go as soon as the army arrived. They had been there, in fact, for several days, Porter stopping Confederate river traffic especially in and out of the Big Black River and testing the defenses at Grand Gulf, warning by the day almost that it was getting stronger. "The rest of the squadron is now at Grand Gulf waiting for the army to make a move," Porter informed Secretary of the Navy Welles in Washington on April 24, later reporting that the rains on April 27 might also delay the proceedings. But when the time came, now that the Confederates had definitely upgraded their defenses, Porter was not that sanguine. He added how, "at present, I see no certainty of a successful landing of our army on the Mississippi side, yet nothing will be left undone by me to facilitate it." By April 29 all was set nevertheless, and Porter issued his elaborate orders about what would happen. Thinking there were four distinct Confederate forts, although there were only two about a mile apart, Porter wanted the four City-class ironclads to concentrate on silencing the southernmost Confederate fort, Fort Wade, named after its commander Colonel William Wade, while the three others would pummel the northernmost work, Fort Cobun (also known as the aforementioned Point of Rock). Porter was careful to remind his commanders not to ground their boats in the fight so close to the shore: "The water is falling; no vessel will anchor for the present in less than 4 fathoms water, and the lead must be frequently used." He also added that when, or if, the batteries were silenced, the troops of McClernand's divisions aboard their transports off Hard Times would move in and land the troops.[43]

With Grant watching from the tug *Ivy* back nearer to Hard Times and an Illinoisan describing "thousands of eyes are looking upon," Porter steamed forward early on the morning of April 29, about 7:00 a.m., and began his attack about an hour later. Waiting near Hard Times were ten thousand troops of Osterhaus's and Carr's divisions on the transports and barges, ready to surge ahead as soon as the Confederate guns were silenced; they had boarded as early as April 27 with an admonition: "'Success' must be our motto!" There were troops aboard the ironclads as well, several companies of the 58th Ohio and some of the 29th Illinois as marines and possibly to land first and take control if feasible. The four City-class ironclads accordingly moved forward, about a hundred and fifty yards between them, and made a great loop south of Fort Wade and then passed close to the eastern bank to take the fort under fire. A watching Confederate Missourian related that "they circled around, one after the other, and kept up a continuous fire," although he admitted "they did not do much damage, and our guns did not seem to have much impression on them; they were not heavy enough." The three other ironclads did the same thing farther north at Fort Cobun. But it quickly proved to be hard work, Porter relating later that day to Welles that he had attacked the Confederate works, "which were very formidable." The currents in the river at the big bend, plus where the Big Black River emptied into the river, made keeping station treacherous, Porter writing that "it was the most difficult portion of the river in which to manage an ironclad; strong currents (running 6 knots) and strong eddies turning them round and round, making them fair targets."

And with the vessels being so close to the Confederate guns, many shots went clear through the iron and at times completely through entire boats.[44]

The firing soon began to become rapid, and the Confederates evacuated the slaves still at work on the fortifications via a covered way. The Missourians manning the trenches could not help but have some fun with the obviously frightened slaves, they telling them that the enemy was firing at them specifically. "They just fell over one another making their escape from the ditches," a Missourian explained. Of course the slaves had the proverbial last laugh, as it was the Missourians who had to stay and stand the brunt of the bombardment.[45]

The four City-class gunboats pounded Fort Wade for nearly four hours and managed to silence the guns. "It was a beautiful sight to see the Gunboats go sailing along as it were into the jaws of destruction," one watching Indianan marveled, "sometimes enveloped in a cloud of smoke [and] at others [we] see them tremble under the terrific shock of the broadside they were discharging." The *Pittsburg*, *Mound City*, *Louisville*, and *Carondelet* took little damage in their fight at Fort Wade, Lieutenant Commander Elias K. Owen of the *Louisville* reporting receiving "but seven shots, four in the hull and three in the light works of the ship," although the carpenter reported that one of the shots in the fantail caused "us to leak badly." The *Carondelet* suffered less than that, a mere five hits all day. The *Louisville* and *Carondelet* suffered no casualties whatsoever, and the *Mound City* one man, although the *Pittsburg* had six killed and ten wounded, including three members of Company H, 58th Ohio onboard as marines as well as a contraband. The ironclads kept up a steady fire nevertheless, seeking to move slowly to maintain a "steady range," according to the *Pittsburg*'s logbook.[46]

Meanwhile, the other three gunboats took Fort Cobun under bombardment in much the same way, the Confederates responding with artillery and even with musketry since the gunboats bore in so close to the bank. But Fort Cobun was more difficult to silence, Porter writing that it was "high, strongly built, had guns of very heavy caliber, and the vessels were unmanageable in the heavy current." Nevertheless, the flagship *Benton* (with Charles Dana aboard), *Tuscumbia*, and *Lafayette* pummeled the fort despite taking major casualties. Hit especially hard were the *Benton* and *Tuscumbia*, which were closer in, the *Lafayette* "lying in an eddy and fighting stern downstream." She endured some forty shots throughout the day anyway, five of which were serious; that said, the *Lafayette* only had one man "slightly wounded."[47]

The *Tuscumbia*, Porter related, "was cut up a great deal (and proved herself a poor ship in a hot engagement)." Much of the problem proved to be its hasty construction and poor design, her carpenter admitting "the outrageously bad

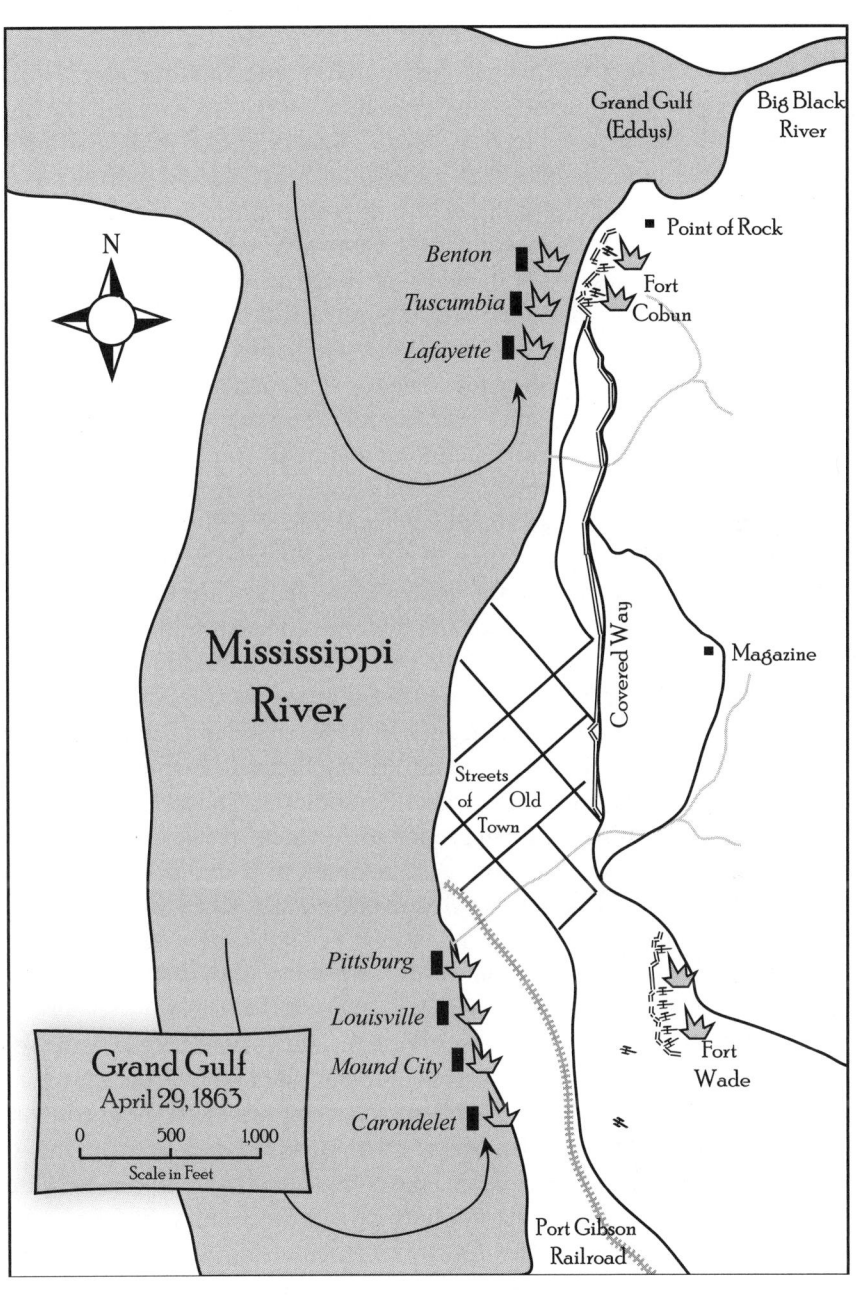

manner in which the armor of the turret has been fastened to the backing." Also problematic were the currents turning her "round and round, exposing her at every turn." In all, some eighty-one shots hit the *Tuscumbia*: "The light woodwork on deck is completely riddled." Others caused leaks that made the vessel settle an inch and a half forward and seven and a half inches by the stern. But she remained in the fight until a shot disabled the port engine. Lieutenant Commander James Shirk tried to stem the current with one engine but could not do so and slowly drifted southward out of the fight. She would need "very extensive repairs" before going into action again, Shirk reported.[48]

Similarly, the *Benton* was put out of action temporarily. She had pounded the enemy works despite getting into an eddy that spun her around; the pilot, drifting downstream, purposefully ran her into the bank "to aid us in turning around." She charged forward once more, and in all some forty-seven shots hit the vessel "in her hull alone, not counting the damage done above her rail." The most telling was a Confederate shot that tore through the *Benton*'s pilothouse and took away a portion of the wheel while wounding the pilot; Admiral Porter was also hit in the head with a piece of shrapnel at the time but not seriously wounded. A new pilot took the unmanageable vessel downstream to repair the damage, although she fired on the silenced guns at Fort Wade while undergoing those repairs. The *Pittsburg* steamed northward to take *Benton*'s place and suffered the consequences, taking in all some thirty-five hits, the most telling being one to the pilothouse, "carrying away two spokes and part of the rim of the wheel." Another exploded at the bow and started some concerning leaks "that increases whenever we are underway." But *Pittsburg* remained on station and continued to pound Fort Cobun, and eventually the other City-class ironclads came northward as well. Lieutenant Byron Wilson on the *Mound City* noted that he "steamed around in a circle several times immediately in front of it . . . passing within 300 yards [and] using all of our guns in succession."[49]

While the chaos was extreme on the ironclads, the Confederates were likewise pummeled with flying shrapnel, debris, and earth. One infantryman manning the adjacent works wrote that "the firing beat Oak Hill, Elkhorn, Corinth, Hutchin's [Hatchie] Bridge, or anything else I ever heard." One Arkansan wrote how "they sent one gun boat right after another, about 100 yards apart." Around midmorning, the flagstaff went down from a shot, but it was soon repaired and the flag flew again. Confederate casualties were surprisingly small so far, although including Fort Wade's namesake and commander, Colonel William Wade, the same Arkansan explaining that "one gun shell bursted right at the gun." One of his staff was also killed, with otherwise around fifteen wounded. In larger context, the pummeling was noteworthy outside Grand Gulf as well, being clearly heard upriver at Vicksburg.[50]

Obviously unable to silence all the guns, Porter peeled off a little after noon to steam upriver to talk to Grant about the lack of progress. The admiral himself had been wounded by a piece of shell on the back of the head, but he believed that a landing could be made as Fort Cobun was able to manage "what was rather a feeble return to our fire." Grant came aboard the *Benton* and remarked that "the sight of the mangled and dying men which met my eye as I boarded the ship was sickening." Fred was with him, and the wide-eyed boy declined an invitation from Porter himself, whose "face showed the agony he was in," to join his crew as a replacement for some of the dead still lying in puddles of blood. Fred responded simply, "I do not believe that papa would allow me to serve in the navy." Despite Porter's urging, Grant would not dare to land troops with Confederate guns still firing, McClernand having earlier advised that "frail transports, laden with men and munitions of war, could not be advanced under the hostile fire to the shore." Grant concluded it could not be done this day. Heavy casualties in the navy added to the need to break off and try something else. Indeed, casualties had been heavy, with twenty-four killed and fifty-six wounded, mostly on the *Benton*, *Tuscumbia*, and *Pittsburg*. In issuing his thanks to the sailors, Porter added that "we have met losses which we can not but deplore; still, we should not regret the death of those who died so nobly at their guns." He also complained that "ours is the duty to silence batteries; it can not be expected that we shall land and take possession."[51]

By 1:30 p.m., Porter realized Grant was not interested in crossing at Grand Gulf and called off the assault, unable to completely silence the Confederate guns despite what Grant described as moving up within "pistol-shot." Fort Wade was no longer responding, and Porter sent the *Lafayette* down to continue fire until dark to keep it out of action, but Fort Cobun's defense still registered. And although Porter's gunboats managed to silence all but one gun, that one gun, even if it "fired but feebly toward the last," still represented a defense; landings could not be made under such circumstances. Porter gave credit where it was due, writing that "the enemy fought his upper battery with a desperation I have never yet witnessed, for though we engaged him at a distance of 50 yards, we never fairly succeeded in stopping his fire but for a short time. It was remarkable that we did not disable his guns, but though we knocked the parapets pretty much to pieces, the guns were apparently uninjured." As a result, Porter informed Welles that it was only a "partial success." A Missouri Confederate agreed, writing that "for the time taken up and the amount of ammunition wasted, I would say it was almost a failure as to results."⁵²

Obviously, a new adaptation if not new plan was needed, and Porter advised Washington that Grant "concluded to land the troops and march over to a point 2 miles below Grand Gulf." That landing, of course, would be on the west side of the river, Grant intending to march southward to find another point to embark the troops and cross. Indeed, he found that "the top of the levee afforded a good road to march upon," as he could not move the transports full of troops past Grand Gulf's guns, damaged as they were. One hit would be disastrous. So he landed the troops again, moved them down the levee to Disharoon's Plantation, and sent the transports in a run past the batteries much like those moves past Vicksburg on April 16 and 22. Porter's gunboats preceded them and kept Confederate attention while the vulnerable transports passed. Grant later explained that "I had intended to make this request, but he [Porter] anticipated me."⁵³

Around 9:00 p.m., Porter consequently again engaged the Confederate batteries, some of which had been repaired and were once more in working order, several of the ironclads taking nonthreatening hits; the pummeled *Benton*, for example, sustained six more shots. But while the ironclads took all the attention, the transports, led by the *General Price*, which actually towed a couple of them that were in bad shape, made their way to safety below. Commander Selim E. Woodworth of the *General Price* reported that "as soon as I saw all the ironclads hotly engaged with the enemy, [I] made all speed, passed the enemy's works, and was soon out of the range of their fire." Porter was ecstatic, the transports having made the run successfully: "Under cover of the fire all the transports passed by in good condition." Lieutenant Byron Wilson of the *Mound City* reported that "we gained our object, keeping the batteries so well employed that probably not a transport was even fired at."⁵⁴

While Byron was correct in spirit, there was some fire directed at the transports. The *Price* itself was hit three times, "causing considerable damage to the vessel," one shot going clean through. One of the transports carrying horses was also hit, killing five of the animals. The same shell crashed into the *Price* (lashed beside the transport) and bounced around inside, even going through the firebrick in the furnace. But it did not explode, Woodworth attributing the reason as "the fuse being extinguished in passing through the horses." And although the ironclads suffered little to no damage from the Confederate fire, there was also some miscommunication, such as when "the worst injury the hull of this vessel [*Mound City*] received was from the *Louisville* running into the port side, she heading down the river while I was heading up."⁵⁵

Meanwhile, word reaching Pemberton was mixed. That Grand Gulf had held was cheering, but the wire went dead soon after word of the fight came and Pemberton spent a nervous day wondering what was happening. More news filtered in throughout the day and night, and Pemberton sent word to Richmond of the ominous development, writing that "repairs are being made, expecting a renewal of attack to-morrow." But the attack shook Pemberton out of his Grierson-induced malaise, placing his attention firmly once more on Grant's threat, albeit too late to respond decisively at such a distance. On the ground itself, Bowen was cheered by the defense as well, including the departure of the Union forces from in front of Grand Gulf after six and a half hours of bombardment. Likewise, he could see at least one enemy ironclad, the *Tuscumbia*, damaged to the point of falling out of the fight. But the simple departure of the Federals from Hard Times and Grand Gulf, satisfying as it was, meant only one thing, particularly with the transports having passed in the evening fight: Grant was obviously heading south to find another crossing point. One of Bowen's Confederates was not fooled, writing on April 30 that "it is their object to effect a landing on this side of the river, and move round in rear of Vicksburg." He admitted tersely: "I fear they will make it."[56]

13

"We Land the Army in the Morning"
April 30

The Union crossing of the Mississippi River has been labeled as the largest amphibious military operation in American history up to World War II. Despite some caveats over semantics, that is fundamentally true. The term "amphibious landing" is normally defined as an invasion by boat from the sea. Technically, the Mississippi River crossing was not a sea operation, but the river was neither bridgeable nor fordable, so it meets the definition; boats had to be utilized. And while there had been amphibious operations throughout history, since the invention of the boat in fact, none were so large in America as the pending one across the Mississippi River.[1]

The British had nearly perfected the use of amphibious assaults in their worldwide empire, and Americans had employed some of the knowledge gained as British citizens in the beginning. George Washington himself utilized the idea in his crossing of the Delaware River during the Revolutionary War, although on a small scale. The most notable American amphibious operation, again on much smaller scale than Grant's plan, was at Vera Cruz, Mexico, in 1847. There had been other water-related crossings, but utilizing pontoon bridges such as those at Fredericksburg or later across the James River in the Petersburg operations, or crossing fords such as on the Rapidan River in the Chancellorsville or Wilderness Campaigns, did not qualify. Actual smaller-scale landings on hostile territory came along the Eastern Seaboard in North Carolina and elsewhere earlier in the war, and the largest (larger even than what Grant had in mind) was the landing of the Army of the Potomac at Fortress Monroe at the start of the Peninsula Campaign. But

Fortress Monroe was not enemy territory and offered a friendly zone to land troops, disqualifying it as an amphibious landing into hostile territory.[2]

Large-scale amphibious landings in American history were uncommon until the early and mid-twentieth century, when the United States created a branch of service dedicated to that effort. While the United States Marine Corps, part of the Department of the Navy, had been around since the 1770s, it was only in the interwar years (between the two world wars) that the Marines became amphibious-oriented. In fact, the first amphibious assault doctrine manual did not appear until 1934, *Tentative Manual for Landing Operations*. In studying the plans and wargames for combat with the Japanese, American military planners soon realized that a war in the Pacific Ocean would require such a force and therefore set the Marines on a course to become amphibious assault troops.[3]

Obviously, both the army and Marine Corps performed amphibious assaults in World War II in the European and Pacific theaters in North Africa, the Mediterranean, across the English Channel on D-Day, and on the numerous Pacific islands that ring in Marine Corps history: Tarawa, Iwo Jima, and Okinawa, among many others. Doctrine called for heavy naval and air support to soften up the beaches as the troops flooded ashore, and corresponding Japanese doctrine changed over the course of the war to switch from defense at the beach to an inward defense on the high ground behind, basically conceding the landings to the enemy to catch them on land in a more vulnerable position.[4]

Like his counterparts late in World War II eighty years later, Grant did not know what he would face when he sent the Army of the Tennessee across the Mississippi River by boat. He knew not whether the enemy would contest the actual landing on the shore or if a defense would come farther inland, along the range of hills that was the exact high ground east of the Mississippi River Grant had been targeting all this time. It depended on where the assault came, and current thinking had been at Grand Gulf, where the heights were closer to the riverbank than elsewhere. And the navy would be his chief support in the effort, there obviously being no airpower at that time. Still, it was plain to see that, no matter what defense the Confederates provided, Grant's forces would not be secure, even with naval support, until they took a foothold on the heights beyond the river itself.

Yet in planning the crossing of the Mississippi River, Grant was also largely going against the book, certainly the Jominian theories he had been violating for several months now. Jomini said very little about amphibious-type operations, which he called "Descents," mainly because of the dominance of the British navy at the time he wrote and because of the invention of artillery. What he did write, however, was decidedly lukewarm due to the many factors involved, such as weather, naval participation, enemy defenses, and vulnerability. He also wrote a chapter on river crossings, in which he always depended on a bridge to cross the troops. Vessels could be involved, but mainly in the effort to get a functioning bridge in place to cross the army. It apparently did not occur to Jomini that operations of this nature were needed. As he had been doing for a while now, Grant was making his own theories as he went along, throwing the book away more and more at every step. The side effect, of course, was that Grant had very little history to lean on; he did not know what to expect once the crossing commenced.[5]

If Grant had no idea what to expect from the unconventional move he was about to undertake, it was clear that he needed diversions to make the chance of Confederate resistance as slim as possible regardless of where he landed. As a result, he had numerous raids and diversions out even now, including the just-concluded Frederick Steele occupation of Greenville as well as Grierson's Raid, which included numerous supporting diversions itself. All took place, and therefore diverted Confederate attention, to the north, directly opposite of where it needed to be. Now as a final act, Grant fostered yet another diversion, one that was actually broached earlier by McClernand. But this time it came much closer to Vicksburg.[6]

The idea was to send some of Sherman's troops, he being in the back of the line, up the Yazoo River to threaten an attack at his old fighting ground around Chickasaw Bayou. That was the direct opposite direction from where Grant was planning to cross the river, and such a move would threaten Vicksburg immediately. The ruse would come at Snyder's Bluff a little farther up, where the raft across the river had just broken and the Confederates were in crisis mode as a result. It was a perfect place to divert attention: "We must do all that is possible to make the enemy believe that the movement is a real attack, though it would be bad management to attempt a lodgment here and at Grand Gulf both, as the enemy could fall on one or the other," a supportive Sherman explained.[7]

But there were concerns over and above Sherman's lack of confidence in this whole plan; he wrote his brother on April 26 "I feel in its success less confidence than in any similar undertaking of the war, but it is my duty to co-operate with zeal, and I shall endeavor to do it"; he even labeled the larger operation "hazardous in the extreme." One major concern was separating a piece of the army while the rest was heading away from it, but that was manageable; again, Grant went against the book and Halleck's continual warning about separation of forces. The more pressing concern was public opinion. Grant was concerned that a show of force north of Vicksburg and then a withdrawal would be construed as another defeat, similar to the one back in December. As a result, Grant was careful how he approached Sherman about it: "If you think it advisable you may make a reconnaissance of Haynes' Bluff, taking as much force and as many steamers as you like.... The effect of a heavy demonstration in that direction would be good, so far as the enemy are concerned, but I am loth to order it, because it would be so hard to make our own troops understand that only a demonstration was intended, and our people at home would characterize it as a repulse. I therefore leave it to you whether to make such a demonstration." Worse, sending Sherman of all people to do it would make the public remember what had happened just four months before—equivalent to rubbing salt in Sherman's wounds. If Sherman did it, Grant advised issuing an order beforehand conveying that it was just a demonstration "for the purpose of calling the enemy's attention from movements south of Vicksburg, and not with any intention of attacking."[8]

For Sherman's part, despite telling his own wife to "prepare yourself for another blast of Sherman blundering and being repulsed," he was adamant at least to Grant that he would do whatever it took. "We will make as strong a demonstration as possible," Sherman assured Grant. "The troops will all understand the purpose, and will not be hurt by the repulse. The people of the country must find out the truth as they best can; it is none of their business. You are engaged in a hazardous enterprise, and for good reason wish to divert attention; that is sufficient to me, and it shall be done." He later added that he would "hang about Benson Blake's" and not worry about the response of the nation: "I will use troops that I know will trust us, and not be humbugged by a repulse. The men have sense, and will trust us. As to the reports in newspapers, we must scorn them, else they will ruin us and our country. They are as much enemies to good government as the secesh, and between the two I like the secesh best, because they are a brave, open enemy, and not a set of sneaking, croaking scoundrels." That said, Sherman privately described the duty as "inglorious," and one of the naval officers involved told a different story. He related to Porter that Sherman "seems to think a strong reconnaissance (amounting to an attack) should be made, but I don't feel willing with such a force to risk it, and only for a demonstration." He added that "even General Sherman says he can hardly see the use of so far as attracting attention [away] from Grant is concerned."[9]

Still, Sherman went with all of Frank Blair's division on ten transports, accompanied by eight gunboats, rams, and smaller armed vessels (*Tyler*,

Choctaw, Baron de Kalb, Signal, Romeo, Linden, Petral, and *Black Hawk*), along with three mortars. It was a formidable expedition, which is what was needed to make the Confederates think there really was something to it. A regiment went ashore "near the old battleground" of Chickasaw Bayou for security purposes, but the rest moved on forward. All made their way up the Yazoo River, still careful to watch for torpedoes (mines) that had sunk the *Cairo* back in December in these very waters. In fact, the flotilla passed the ironclad's grave on the mission, although few probably knew it. Sherman thus landed troops at Benson Blake's Plantation a little upriver from Chickasaw Bayou on April 30 while the navy's gunboats headed on up to the high ground and traded shots with the Confederates there. Miles down the river, and unknown to Sherman, Grant was starting his attempt to cross the Mississippi River as well.[10]

Porter had in no way intended for his vessels to get into a fight, but the commander of the expedition, Lieutenant Commander Kidder R. Breese, did so despite earlier assuring Porter that "I shall be mighty cautious, I assure you, and expose the vessels as little as possible." That said, the brand-new *Choctaw*, fresh from the shipyards via Memphis and apparently carrying some "rubber" armor, led the way. Lieutenant Commander Frank M. Ramsay reported that "the greater portion of the crew had only been eight days on board when the engagement took place, and, owing to the unfinished state of the vessel, had had only three days' exercise at the guns." That did not stop Breese from heading toward the Confederates: "The demonstration was considered so important by General Sherman, I felt compelled to make it appear as much of a real attack as possible without too great risk." He even issued orders for his vessels to bombard "as if it were preliminary to a night attack of the troops."[11]

The bombardment commenced, but one Mississippian behind the fortifications at Snyder's Bluff admitted that "we among the hills, look on with merriment at the harmless grand pyrotechnical exhibition." The Confederate general in command at Snyder's Bluff, Louis Hébert, reported that, although the river was too narrow to allow multiple vessels to attack at once and although the Federals did not come any closer than two thousand yards, the guns still hit hard. "Scarce a moment but a jet of water was thrown up near her or a shot struck her," Breese reported of the *Choctaw*. In the lead "considerably in advance of the others," according to Confederate division commander John H. Forney, the *Choctaw* took a grand total of fifty-three hits, Breese adding that there was "no great damage, but much cut up." Hébert wrote that "at 2:30 p.m. this boat had been so injured as to be compelled to draw out of the fight for repairs, and our firing against the boats ceased." The *Baron de Kalb* suffered little damage, but the venerable *Tyler* took a Whitworth shell in the hull near the waterline, "causing her to leak badly, but [she] was soon ready for action again." There was also some damage in the Confederate works, a shell exploding among the 21st Louisiana soldiers manning the big guns. One Louisianan had a leg injured and it had to be amputated, while another had several ribs broken "and the flesh torn from his side."[12]

Meanwhile, Blair's troops landed at "Blake's negro quarters, and made disposition as for attack, which was kept up till dark, drawing heavy fire," Sherman related. The troops moved up the levee, which was about the only thing above water at this point, "making quite a display, and a threatening one also." Most of the Confederate forces outside the fortifications fell back to their cover, although the 3rd Louisiana remained out front and suffered a few losses. Hébert related that the only infantry threat came on his left, where "a few shots from our guns on our left wing soon made them desist, and although the shelling continued until dark, the enemy's troops (with the exception of the skirmishers) fell back to their transports, and all became quiet for the night." One of his Mississippians described how "several regiments landed, all in bright uniforms—their burnished rifles glistening in the morning sun and altogether presenting a fine display of martial pomp." He added that "this began to look like war again."[13]

The Union troops reembarked overnight but had trouble convincing their captured cattle to board the vessels. One Federal playing cowboy explained that "half of the cattle escaped before they came near our boat and the balance, about 18 head, were got to the gang planks and were surrounded entirely by bayonets, but they were afraid to go aboard and being pricked considerably the largest one made a dash into the crowd and cleared the way. The balance followed, and it was a comical sight. Four or five were shot and five or six got on the steamer alive." He added: "We had fresh meat for our dinner and supper."[14]

But the division advanced again the next day, a regiment on each side of the river in fact. The one on the west side was stopped by high water and a bayou, and the one on the east did not dare tangle with the beefed-up Confederate fortifications. A watching Confederate explained that "dressing their lines, they began to advance towards our position. Our artillery had been ordered not to fire until they came sufficiently close to use grape on them." They never did. Sherman remained throughout this day as well and opened a huge artillery barrage from the flotilla around 3:00 p.m., which lasted until after dark. It was, according to Hébert, a "rapid and terrific bombardment on our batteries on the left.... The shelling of the enemy was at times general along our entire line." Sherman wanted the troops and the navy to stay in place until nightfall, at which time they would be withdrawn, but staying until dark assured the Federals of at least several more hours of the ruse, at least until their departure could be detected the next morning. "I want to prolong the diversion as much as possible in your favor," he wrote Grant on May 1. After dark Sherman pulled out and headed back to the Mississippi River to follow Grant southward. "By daylight," Hébert reported, "not a boat was left in the Yazoo River." There were no additional casualties, although one of the Confederate guns had a malfunction, which was easily repaired.[15]

Sherman did exactly what Grant wanted, and his soldiers understood the game, although one of his orderlies (some said an orderly of brigade commander Kilby Smith) "rode directly into the enemy[']s line deserting our army, or was a spy." Another explained that the man ordered the pickets withdrawn and then swam across a bayou to the cheers of the Confederates. But most understood the reasoning for the diversion and supported it; one Ohioan wrote home it was "to draw the attention of the Rebs and a portion of their forces. While we were doing this Grant was operating below Vicksburg." But Breese was in trouble with Admiral Porter for doing such a good job. He wrote of the demonstration: "[What] you call a feint . . . I consider an unnecessary exposure of the vessels. . . . A feint means a pretended attack, whereas yours was a real one. When I told General Grant that he might have the squadron above to make a feint I never intended the vessels to go under fire, otherwise I would have written you." He added: "Under no circumstances, during my absence, will you permit the vessels to make any attack on land batteries without orders from me."[16]

There has been speculation as to how effective the "feigned attack upon Drumgould's Bluff" was and whether Carter Stevenson at Vicksburg (Pemberton still maintained his headquarters for now at Jackson) was fooled at all. One Forney staff officer admitted to his diary on April 29 that "this is probably a demonstration to divert our attention from Grand Gulf where appearances indicate the real attack." A lower-level Tennessean added "they will not be apt to fool anyone as that is undoubtedly a feint." But the only person Sherman needed to fool was Pemberton, and it was not hard to fool someone who was already thinking the way Grant and Sherman wanted him to, especially with Pemberton being so heavily influenced by Stevenson. Clearly, the rumble of the big guns was distinctly heard at Vicksburg, even as the same rumbling from the south at Grand Gulf on April 29 told a similar tale down there. Stevenson thought it initially just a ruse, informing Pemberton that "the display made in moving them showed a desire to attract our attention." But as Sherman continued on for another day, the Federal effort seemed to get more serious. There is also evidence of the Confederates reinforcing at Snyder's

Bluff, Herbert reporting that "during the night of the 30th, a few additional guns were added to our batteries on the left." One of his common soldiers related that "the command was carried to the trenches at a double-quick; and all looked for an attack by land and water the river being dotted with transports and gunboats." Union naval commander Breese similarly related that "it was observed in the morning that new works had been thrown up in the night, some of the old ones extended, and several new and apparently heavy guns placed in position." He later (May 3) added that "it is considered that the demonstration up the Yazoo was a success, as large bodies of troops were seen to move in that direction from Vicksburg, thereby engaging the rebels' attention from Grand Gulf and vicinity." Sherman himself wrote of his "ostentatious movement up the Yazoo" and that "we could see them moving guns, artillery, and infantry back and forth, and evidently expecting a real attack." Perhaps most telling was Carter Stevenson himself, who informed Pemberton on April 30: "The gunboats have been engaging Snyder's since 9 o'clock. Have sent reinforcements to that point."[17]

But arguable as the results of Sherman's diversion were, Grant was moving forward the very same day with his crossing of the Mississippi River. Only time would tell if the various diversions had been enough.

Disappointment reigned in the Union Army of the Tennessee before the sun rose on April 30. "At this point, officers and men were a little disheartened upon learning that the Navy had found it impossible to reduce the Grand Gulf batteries," Colonel John B. Sanborn admitted. Engineer James Wilson similarly wrote that "our advanced division commander [probably Osterhaus] had begun to criticize and grumble." Yet Grant was not giving up and ordered a new landing site be found. But where to land was the main question. Grand Gulf had been the focus all along, but with that out of the question, at least in Grant's mind, the time for adaptation came. But it was not out of the blue, as for days McClernand and Grant had tossed around the idea of landing elsewhere, even as far south as Rodney. And the nearer McClernand came to the crossing, he advised several ways it could be done, including landing directly at Grand Gulf or even skirting it to the north and moving up the Big Black River for a landing in rear of the Confederate forts. But most attention developed south of Grand Gulf. That put the large watershed of Bayou Pierre in play, and since there was so little room for deployment between Grand Gulf and Bayou Pierre itself, the landing would have to come either up the bayou or south of it if anywhere except Grand Gulf. Just like before, that allowed another shield between the landing army and Confederate forces at Grand Gulf, but it also required another leap of a major waterway to get to Vicksburg.[18]

What lay on the other side of the river, something of a mystery, also mattered. McClernand had his commanders scout with cavalry and "make diligent inquiry" about roads leading to Port Gibson or across Bayou Pierre, all in order to outflank Grand Gulf. Grant even sent his staff engineer Wilson with another engineer and a regiment of infantry across the river to examine the area north of the Big Black River, which Bowen quickly detected; Wilson found a road, but it was totally swamped with several feet of water. Grant also asked Admiral Porter to send a gunboat up the Big Black River to scout. Despite Grant writing that Porter "was and is ever ready to afford all the assistance in his power for the furtherance of the success of our arms," on this particular occasion Porter demurred, Wilson reporting that "the admiral declined to risk his vessel in so narrow a stream." Nevertheless, even before the repulse at Grand Gulf, Grant had scouts out down as far as Disharoon's to "ascertain, if possible, from persons in the neighborhood the character of the road leading to the highlands." He also had "a complete map of the East bank of the Mississippi made for you," he informed McClernand.[19]

These various scouts, eventually also including Osterhaus "in person, to a point on the Mississippi opposite the mouth of Bayou Pierre, and a short distance below," ultimately reported that a crossing below Bayou Pierre could be done and that the closest landing was at Bruinsburg. Confirmation came from some of the other scouts. Captain Richard H. Ballinger of the 3rd Illinois Cavalry had taken a few men and landed north of Grand Gulf to scout out roads. They found a slave who told them all they wanted but refused to go with them across the river until forced to do so, he not wanting to leave his family. "After some delay he was landed in the boat," one of the Federals explained. The slave eventually wound up at Grant's headquarters, where the general had maps spread all around. After explaining that most of the roads near Grand Gulf were underwater, he added: "Dar is only one way, Gineral, and dat is by Bruinsburg, eight miles furder down. . . . Dar you can leave de boats and the men can walk on high ground all de way. De best houses an' plantations in all dis country are dar, sah, all along dat road." Grant later wrote that the slave's testimony convinced him "that there was a good road from Bruinsburg to Port Gibson, which determined me to land there."[20]

Bruinsburg had been at one time a bustling river town, even host to Andrew Jackson and Aaron Burr (who was ultimately captured just across the river), but now was a sleepy community, not even a village, on the bank of the river; one Federal who landed there admitted "I saw nothing there worthy of any name." Another explained that "Bruinsburg had no inhabitants, and not even a house, a few old sheds and three or four straggling fig trees showing that perhaps at one time some person or persons here had a home." But it was a long ten miles south of Disharoon's, which meant the transports and gunboats would have to make long voyages in their transfers of troops back and forth, which would take time. And time was of the essence. Yet it was the only choice Grant had, and it was better than a landing at Rodney even farther south.[21]

Grant had to have Porter's help to make the leap, he later remarking that "I could not order him." But Porter was again more than willing to help, Grant explaining that "he turned his gun-boats into ferry-boats." By the night of April 29 the decision was made: troops would land as early as daylight the next morning. Porter reported that night that "we are now in a position to make a landing where the general pleases," adding in fact that "I should have preferred this latter course in the first instance; it would have saved many lives and many hard knocks." He later added "we land the army in the morning on the other side, and march on Vicksburg."[22]

With the adaptation decided, Grant ordered all his troops forward, as well as more barges past the Vicksburg batteries with supplies. Grant informed Sherman that "I shall be able to effect a landing to-morrow, either at the lower end of Grand Gulf or below Bayou Pierre, with all of McClernand's corps and Logan's division. Have also a second division of McPherson's command that can be landed next day." Grant similarly notified Halleck that "the army and transports are now below Grand Gulf. A landing will be effected on the east bank of the river to-morrow. I feel that the battle is now more than half won."[23]

The troops marched the few miles southward along the levee from Hard Times to Disharoon's during the night and got what rest they could before loading onto the transports and gunboats. "The generals, colonels, and privates all lie down together, one faring no better than another," one Illinoisan explained. Many no doubt wondered what they were doing now as they disembarked off the boats at Hard Times, many ironically referring to it as "Hard Scrabble" (Grant's old homeplace), to march across the neck of land in the bend of the river to Disharoon's. But they marched "across the point," Grant reported, to Disharoon's, where they would again board the transports and barges. Word eventually got out that the goal was Bruinsburg, "the first point of land below Grand Gulf from which the interior can be reached." At Disharoon's, officers made provision for the sick to be left behind as well as much of the army's equipment that was now back along the road to Richmond. Only the barest of essentials was to go across initially, such as forage for the corps headquarters animals.[24]

Grant also made the trip, though not without incident. Dana related that,

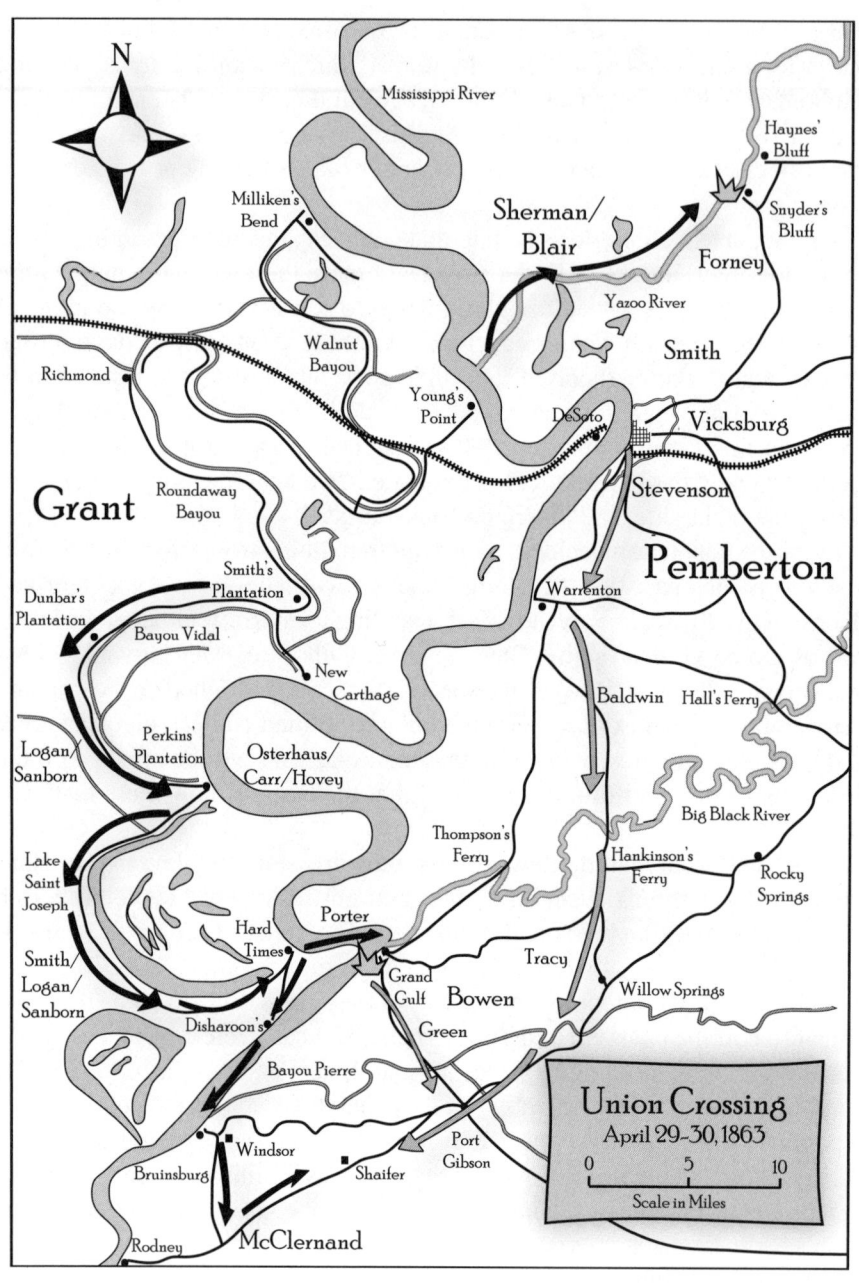

at one point in the darkness, Grant's horse stumbled, and "I expected to see the general go over the animal's head." Horseman that he was, Grant stayed mounted. Dana also expected some cursing, but Grant denied him that as well: "I had been with Grant daily now for three weeks, and I had never seen him ruffled or heard him swear." Dana was sure this would be the occasion, but Grant simply moved on. "And it is a fact that though I was with Grant during the most trying campaign of the war," Dana wrote long afterward, "I never heard him use an oath."[25]

The advance was to begin at daylight on April 30, "the gunboats as well as transports being used for the purpose," Grant explained. "Great excitement in the morning preparing for a fight," one Illinoisan jotted in his diary. But the navy did not beat to quarters until 4:00 a.m., and loading did not commence until after 5:00 a.m. Charles Dana related the confusion during the night, reporting around midnight that "General McClernand's corps are all ready to embark, but it seems to me doubtful whether they will get on board before daylight, though General Grant has given the most urgent orders." The operation was not as fast as Grant wanted, and Dana, certainly not a McClernand fan by this point, laid the problems at the politician's feet. In fact, troops did not begin loading until after daylight. And when they did it became a bottleneck; one artilleryman scribbled in his diary he "saw lots of Major & Brigadier Genls." But the loading soon began, one Federal describing being on the vessels: "As transports were scarce, men were crowded on boats as close as they could stand." Another wrote that "they drove us on the boats just as if we were a flock of sheep, until there was not standing room for one more man."[26]

Grant certainly had many concerns on his mind, namely what his first troops would meet as they bounded down the gangplanks and set foot on Mississippi soil. If Bruinsburg was defended, it would be an ordeal, although the gunboats could likely make quick work of whatever was near the bank of the river, assuming the banks were not too high. There were no reports of any big guns like those that had stopped them at Grand Gulf, so even if resistance was met it would likely not be catastrophic. Grant also worried about transportation east of the river and issued orders for quartermasters, once across, to "seize for the use of the army in the field, during the ensuing campaign, such wagons and teams, as may be necessary for transportation, belonging to the inhabitants of the country through which they may pass."[27]

In fact, there was not a lot of concern about the initial landing, simply because of the gunboats that could cover it well. Rather, the concern was over a Confederate defense at the heights, away from the point the gunboats could aid the inland-moving army. In that case, it would be much like Chickasaw Bayou back in December, when the landings themselves on the riverbanks were uncontested. The Confederate defense came farther inland where the naval guns could not reach, at least not with pinpoint accuracy. So if there was an enemy defense, Grant presumed it would come farther inland, and the logical place was where the river bottom met the highlands a couple miles east. That is exactly where the Confederates had defended at Chickasaw Bayou, albeit at the base of the range of bluffs. If there was stout resistance it would likely come there, so Grant's main concern after getting troops ashore was to get them quickly inland to establish a foothold on the high ground. It was, after all, this high, dry ground that he had been after for months now.[28]

Grant had more going for him than he perhaps realized, however. He certainly had not planned to coordinate with anything; in fact, Grant did not even originally plan on this being crossing day. Yet April 30, 1863 (the same day Joseph Hooker and the Army of the Potomac were crossing another river, the Rapidan, in Virginia) was the very day President Abraham Lincoln had set aside weeks ago as "a day of national humiliation, fasting, and prayer." Lincoln noted the country had "been the recipients of the choicest bounties of Heaven; we have been preserved these many years in peace and prosperity; we have grown in numbers, wealth, and power as no other nation has ever grown. But we have forgotten God." As a result, he declared: "I do hereby request all the people to abstain on that day from their ordinary secular pursuits, and to unite at their several places of public worship and their respective homes in keeping the day holy to the Lord and devoted to the humble discharge of the religious duties proper to that solemn occasion." Perhaps unknown to most, the prayers of hundreds of thousands of Americans would go ashore with them that day. At least one Ohioan marked the event, however, offering a prayer in his diary: "May we be successful in our undertaking . . . may God protect us in our effort."[29]

For all the planning, scouting, and praying that day, the crossing did not get off to a good start. Given the loading delay and the ten-mile trip southward on the river, troops did not land at daylight as desired. In fact, the ironclads, followed by the transports laden with troops, left Disharoon's only at 9:20 a.m. Never one to miss a dramatic moment, an enthused McClernand nevertheless wrote dramatically that his troops were in motion "to plant your colors in the State of Mississippi." But there was still disgust with McClernand for the delay that morning. Dana reported to Washington that "all seems now to be going on well, though had any other general than McClernand held the advance, the landing would certainly have been affected at daylight."[30]

Both transports and gunboats were utilized in the crossing, Colonel

Theodore Buehler of the 67th Indiana writing that he "re-embarked . . . on the gunboat *Carondelet* for Bruinsburg, Miss." Only the severely damaged *Tuscumbia* did not participate, one Iowan writing that nearby "the Gunboat *Tuscumbia*, disabled in the fight yesterday[,] lay tied to the Shore[.] Across the Levee are five open graves dug for the poor fellows who were killed on the Boat yesterday"; the coffins were draped in the American flag. He added that his regiment "went on a Barge at 8 oclock at 8 35 min the Steamer *Moderator* made fast to us & a few minutes the entire fleet of Six Gun Boats & Seven Transports all loaded with troops pushed off from Shore." The flagship *Benton* led the way with the 24th Indiana assembled on the upper deck and the 46th Indiana on the gundeck below. The others followed, with Porter and Grant both aboard the *Benton* to watch for any sign of trouble, both taking station in the pilothouse.[31]

One member of the 46th Indiana gave a detailed account of the crossing:

> The *Benton* ran up a signal and put out into the stream. She was immediately followed by all the gunboats, transports and barges—all heavily laden with infantry and artillery. As the fleet rounded out, a band at the quarters of General Grant played "The Red, White and Blue." The cheers from the boats and the shore, the heavy masses of soldiers on the vessels, with the busy preparations on the gunboats for action, produced impressions on the spectators that will never be forgotten.

The festivity ended as the *Benton* neared Bruinsburg, however:

> On the wheel-house of the *Benton* stood General Grant and Commodore Porter, closely watching the shore. Nothing, however, was visible on land that indicated that the enemy was prepared for the movement. The decks were covered with anxious soldiers, the guns were cleared for action, and the crews were at quarters. Opposite Bruinsburg the *Benton* signaled, 'Prepare to land,' and slowly rounded to. As soon as the boat reached the bank the Forty-sixth and Twenty-fourth Indiana were on shore the first to land. Only one man was seen on the bank. He was supposed to be a spy of General Grant's and was sent on board.

The *Benton* reached Bruinsburg at 9:50 a.m., and the disembarkation started ten minutes later.[32]

One wide-eyed Illinoisan described the terrain he was approaching as "a delightful landing, innocent of any houses that we saw, but covered with a rich carpet of hitherto untrodden grass, that furnished a charming camping ground, with the river and its puffing steamers on one side, and the heavily wooded Mississippi hills on the other." The 24th and 46th Indiana soon rushed ashore on Grant's order. "We threw out skirmishers and advanced half a mile across the plantation to a cypress swamp," one of the Indianans related. "Finding no enemy," he continued, "the skirmishers were withdrawn." More troops then began to flood ashore, one Illinoisan explaining that "they hustled us off the boat in short order and went back for another load." But the Indianans were merely the tip of the spear. Simultaneously, the remainder of the army was snaking its way around the various bayous and over the bridges to this same area to be taken across, the army extending all the way back to Young's Point and Sherman's corps.[33]

Fortunately for Grant, there was no one at Bruinsburg but a civilian, who confirmed the good road into the hills. The Confederates had not defended the landing, and more and more Union troops rushed ashore to take full command of the foothold. Why there was no resistance was a matter of conjecture, but it obviously had something to do with the naval presence. More significant, it also had to do with the lack of emphasis Pemberton had placed on Bowen's defense south of Vicksburg. With Sherman operating even this day north of Vicksburg and Carter Stevenson advising that the attack would come there or at the city itself, Bowen at Grand Gulf had precious little to defend with, and most of that was at Grand Gulf and only beginning to move southward in response to Grant's latest chess move. Most significant, Bowen did not have enough troops to cover the river that far down, and he did not even have cavalry to scout and picket the river south of Grand Gulf to provide information and delay. Wirt Adams's cavalry, Bowen's only mounted troops, had been called away eastward to chase Grierson, who was only a few miles to the east (although by this point heading for Union lines at Baton Rouge). His diversion had worked miracles, and Grant was the benefactor who met no resistance whatsoever upon landing in Mississippi. But still in the back of Grant's mind was a possible defense of the high ground inland.[34]

All the while, other regiments flooded ashore at different spots. The soldiers of the 22nd Iowa had been the first to go ashore in their landing area, causing some to think they were actually the first Federals to land anywhere. Gangplanks were extended from the decks for the soldiers to land on, and one proud Iowan declared that "the 22nd Iowa was the first regiment to plant its feet upon the soil of Mississippi." They quickly sent out a company as skirmishers while the rest of the regiment formed in line of battle to hold the critical foothold. But there was no one there to dispute their landing site. Similarly, Joseph Myers of the 120th Ohio claimed to be the first off the boat in his landing area, the transport *Silver Wave*. As the call came to "shove out a plank," Myers darted forward even before the landmen secured the boat.

Myers being ashore alone, an officer called for him to "go up the bank and see what is behind the levee," which Myers did. He found no levee but called back that there was "a fine meadow on which to camp," the only barrier "a fence overgrown with weeds and bushes." Others similarly claimed for their regiments the honor of being the first to land, and they probably were, at least from their specific vessel at their specific landing area.[35]

Fred Grant was there, too, watching as the troops went ashore and noting that "now not a house was to be seen,—fire had destroyed the whole town." He watched throughout the day as the troops crossed, but the youngster grew tired and bored and, finding a good area on one of the vessels, he noted, "I fell asleep on deck." He did not awake until the next morning, by which time Grant was long gone to the front. But the general had left orders with Lorenzo Thomas that the boy was to remain with the navy and not come forward into the danger all knew was ahead. Fred nevertheless got away "to join a party in chasing a rabbit on the land."[36]

"We expected to get into a little fight," one Federal explained, "but after sending out some scouts and finding no rebs we stacked arms and cooked dinner." With the first troops going ashore around midmorning without resistance, the Federals then began to flood ashore as additional waves brought more of the army to Bruinsburg. The logbooks of the gunboats gave an indication of the day's work with trips back and forth. The *Tuscumbia*, damaged the day before at Grand Gulf, did not ferry any troops, but the others headed back upriver the ten miles against the current, making slow progress on the return trips as a result. The *Benton* likewise did not make as many trips that day, but the other gunboats did. The *Carondelet*'s logbook, for example, reported that troops of Brigadier General George McGinnis's brigade started loading at 6:30 a.m.; the gunboat departed Disharoon's at 9:10 a.m. The troops went ashore at Bruinsburg at 11:00 a.m., whereupon the *Carondelet* went back upriver, taking two hours. She landed at Disharoon's at 1:00 p.m. and started back downriver with two full regiments at 2:30 p.m. Those troops disembarked at 3:30 p.m., whereupon the gunboat then lay "alongside the levee at Bruinsburg." Similarly, the *Louisville*'s logbook reported that troops came on board at 7:00 a.m., she leaving Disharoon's at 8:45 a.m. The *Louisville* landed troops ("rounded to and made fast to Mississippi shore, astern of flagship") by 11:15 a.m. and then moved upriver for another load. Landing at Disharoon's at 2:00 p.m., troops began coming aboard twenty-five minutes later. She landed the troops at Bruinsburg at 3:15 p.m. but likewise did not return upriver that afternoon. The *Mound City* similarly made two trips that day, taking on the 56th Ohio at 7:10 a.m. and depositing them at Bruinsburg by 10:50 a.m., when she returned upriver. A second load consisting of the 124th

Illinois boarded at 2:20 p.m. and were moved southward. The *Pittsburg* also made two trips, carrying first the 47th Indiana and then the 23rd Indiana and "27 boxes Infantry ammunition." The other ironclads and transports worked in similar fashion, amid some of the sailors finding barrels of whiskey aboard the transports when they stopped to coal, and continued the process all night and the next day as well. One Illinoisan being shuttled across explained they were "bidding good by to La after a residence of three months and nine days." The navy sailors also found time to hold burial services throughout the two days for those killed at Grand Gulf. One Federal explained: "I watched them bury their dead . . . they left their clothes on & rapped a blanket around them & put them in & covered them up poor fellows."[37]

With some 22,000 troops ashore by 4:00 p.m. after the first two passes, confusion became rampant. And it continued throughout the night as more and more troops made the trip between Disharoon's and Bruinsburg. The worst result was a collision between the transports *Horizon* and *Moderator* deep in the night of April 30. The 8th Illinois had already crossed on the *Horizon*, one of the "blockade runners" an Illinoisan related, when the accident occurred on a following voyage. The *Horizon* went down quickly, taking with her an entire Illinois artillery battery as well as several horses and two or three men who drowned. One member of Battery G, 2nd Illinois Artillery explained: "We had a very narrow escape from being drowned. We lost all our guns, nearly all our horses, except which broke away and swam out, but all our battery was saved except two men, who were in the stern of the boat with the horses and could not get out." Having been one of the batteries with close calls on the march when its guns "submerged the bridge over the bayou," the Illinoisans now lost all their guns, limbers, and caissons. Worse for the infantry was the loss of rations, one Illinoisan explaining that there were none to be had—"sunk on the *Horizon* with a battery and all the horses." The government later paid $18,500 for the steamer's loss.[38]

Despite the confusion on the river, there was more onshore. The plan was for troops to move forward immediately to the high ground Grant was so concerned about, but moving at all soon became problematic. Missing among the landing troops were almost all the support vehicles and even officers' horses, everything from camp equipage to supply wagons being left behind because of the fragile route of advance through Louisiana and the delicate crossing of the river itself. Alvin Hovey reported that "the horses of all officers, except those commanding divisions, and all kinds of transportation, were left behind." McClernand staff officer Henry C. Warmoth even described division commander Eugene Carr atop "a great big ugly poor mule, his sword and belt hanging on the horn of his saddle," and Wilson declared that he had to borrow a couple cavalry horses for himself and Grant. Wagons that transported food were commandeered to carry more valuable ammunition, and Colonel John E. Tourtellotte of the 4th Minnesota reported that all the vehicles his regiment had were two ambulances, a medicine wagon, and another wagon.[39]

Worse, once ashore Grant found that McClernand had not issued the five days' provisions (which the soldiers would be told to make last longer) as yet and had to stop to do so that morning. Further delay ensued, Osterhaus reporting that "the issue of these stores delayed the march of my division till 4 o'clock p.m." Grant ordered the men fed quickly and to move on, he being especially concerned with getting the high ground: "I deemed it a matter of vast importance that the highlands should be reached without resistance." Over the course of late morning and early afternoon, however, the rations were issued and the troops prepared to head eastward. Division commander Carr related that "after drawing three day's rations, which were to last for five, we moved out." There being few wagons allowed across until all the troops were landed, one Indianan realized that the commanders "expect us to steal or starve." Nevertheless, McClernand moved out about 4:00 p.m. "for the bluffs, some three miles back." He arrived around sunset.[40]

Thus came the real test for these invading Federals. If there was going to be a Confederate defense, it would most likely come here at the high ground, either at the base as at Chickasaw Bayou or on top of the range of hills. These bluffs, while extremely steep, were not as vertical as those of the Walnut Hills at Chickasaw Bayou, so the defense could conceivably be better situated at the top or along the face on the military crest. A stiff Confederate defense, or worse yet a stoppage of movement, would result in a bottleneck in the river bottom as more and more divisions crossed that day and night, and any delay might give the Confederates time to bring in reinforcements. It was paramount that Grant take the heights as soon as possible.[41]

Because of the concern, troops led by the 11th Wisconsin moved out immediately after gaining rations, and one Indianan complained that his regiment did so even before provisions could be issued. "The General said we had done without anything to eat for a week & we could do it again if there was any chance for a fight," one chagrined Indianan wrote home. Most got at least some type of provision, however. Another related the experience of most of the soldiers coming ashore: "Long piles of bacon, barrels of salt pork with the heads knocked in and cords of boxes of hard bread were thrown open from which the troops, Major General and private alike, helped themselves without requisition to three days' rations. These it was understood must last seven." Nevertheless, one Ohioan related, they "started after the secesh"; another wrote similarly that they "started back into the country." One admitted: "What a comical looking sight it was to see that brigade of men, each man with his hunk of bacon on his bayonet and arms at will."[42]

For all the concern, there was likewise no Confederate resistance at the top of the bluffs either, a relieved Grant finally reaching that coveted high ground as his blue-clad troops marched up the deep and narrow road toward Port Gibson that evening. The road was nevertheless not very friendly, one Federal writing that "a roadway, walled in with high vertical banks, cut through the bluff, led from the river bottom up to the table land above." He added that "a small force could have held this pass against an army; but it was left unguarded, and the army marched up." Grierson's diversion and Pemberton's resulting inattention were complete, allowing Grant to steal a march while the Confederate general's mind was elsewhere. Even though heaved back into reality with the activity at Grand Gulf the day before, Pemberton just did not have time to recalibrate and move sufficient troops to this point to resist the invasion. It was consequently a complete success, one Illinoisan writing that the Confederates "were too late, for we were now on the bluffs on equal footing, a long sought for position."[43]

At the top, the perimeter was pushed forward all the way to the Smith Coffee Daniell II plantation house, named Windsor, which staff officer Warmoth described as a "splendid mansion" and another explained was "a stately villa which stood embowered in trees at the crest of the hill"; one soldier related that the Federals even captured a Confederate who was watching the landing from atop the cupola. Daniell himself had died a couple of years back, but his widow still inhabited the home. There, the troops stopped to rest, many taking a break around the marvelous mansion, but they were soon formed again and pushed forward. Osterhaus, for instance, reported that "at the place of Widow Daniels', I received further orders and instructions from the Major-general for the night, and agreeable to them, I proceeded as fast as circumstances admitted." McClernand himself arrived and established his headquarters at Windsor, remaining until about 2:00 a.m., although in the ensuing hours politicians Elihu Washburne and Governor Yates managed to gather some of the Illinois troops and again gave them a speech: "They both gave us a great deal of encouragement," one Illinoisan admitted. But having taken a foothold on the high ground, Grant was not about to let slip any advantage the missing Confederates were giving him; quickly he pushed the troops onward.[44]

After the rest at Windsor, the XIII Corps moved forward. Two roads led to Port Gibson, the first crossing point of Bayou Pierre. The northernmost Bruinsburg Road led along Bayou Pierre and was feared flooded, while the southernmost Rodney Road was farther inland. McClernand pushed his troops to the south to Bethel Church before heading eastward on the Rodney Road, many units taking their line of march deep in the night, even after midnight: "We made a bold dash into the interior, with one of the finest armies the world ever saw," an Indianan wrote his wife. In the lead was Eugene Carr's division, Colonel Charles L. Harris's brigade in advance with the 21st Iowa leading it. Following Carr was Osterhaus's, Hovey's, and A. J. Smith's divisions. John Logan's division of McPherson's XVII Corps was right behind them, having marched around Hovey's and Keigwin's route in Louisiana through the terrible weather on April 26 and 27, making the seventy miles in five days to be at Disharoon's in time to make the trip with the XIII Corps. Major Luther Cowan of the 45th Illinois related to his diary "night cold, got plenty of whiskey here. Good many soldiers tight." The division nevertheless loaded and moved across around sundown. Still, McClernand pressed on. "I determined to push on by a forced march that night as far as practicable," McClernand reported, so that he might occupy Port Gibson and the more important bridge over Bayou Pierre. "I thought the result justified the risk, although I was convinced that if disaster or defeat followed I would be ruined."[45]

One of McClernand's Indianans was overjoyed, writing that

> We [had] struck high, dry ground, for the first time in five long weary months during which we had been marching, scouting and fighting through mud and water; wading Bayous and swamps; camping upon boggs, and sleeping in wet and mouldy blankets; while sickness death and funeral marches were daily occurrences. And now, when our feet struck the solid, firm roads, it seemed to give buoyancy to our limbs and stimulate our spirits as we marched along these narrow defiles among the hills, and through the dark, over-hanging forests, of tall magnolia trees, whose sweet-scented blossoms perfumed and lent an enchantment to the cool night air, as it kissed our cheeks and cooled our brows.[46]

Away the soldiers marched in the darkness, one Iowan in the lead alternately writing that none of the usual cheerfulness was present near him due to the ticklish circumstances. "On the march through the hills no one was allowed to speak above a whisper," he noted. "The thrill of presentiment swept through the mind of each one, and there was eagerness of manner, and veiled excitement, but no disposition for humorous remarks." He added that "the army was slowly feeling its way in the darkness—moving like specters, and halting on the narrow yellow-clay road-side every two or three minutes.... The lonesome hills closed in and around on every side." Only occasional stops were made to eat, and off they were again heading toward Port Gibson, although Harris in the lead became sick with stomach cramps and Colonel William M. Stone of the 22nd Iowa took command of the brigade and the advance.[47]

The rest of the army followed, one Indianan explaining that the deep night march was hard on all: "I was terrible sleepy and would catch myself marching in my sleep being a file closer marching on the side of the column I was in no ones way but there was a many of the boys that was like me almost tiard out on our way." He added that as the column passed several plantations "the Negroes all turned out to see us from one year to 100 years old the Children up to 15 or 18 years old and all women (colored) wore those dirty colored white dresses. . . . How they do grin as we pass along and we cheer them & that makes them show their ivory they know their day of Jubille has come."[48]

McClernand notified Grant that night of his plan to take Port Gibson: "I am pushing forward the Thirteenth Army Corps, with the hope of seizing the bridge across Bayou Pierre, near that place. Please cause all that belong to the corps in the rear to follow rapidly." The tepid Confederate response actually allowed McClernand several miles of freedom to move inland, but finally, contact was made deep in the night (actually in the early-morning hours of May 1 even as the crossing continued back at the river, Grant putting a total of 30,244 men ashore in the initial landing). Confederates held a position southwest of Port Gibson, and minor skirmishing began even in the night. "At 1 a.m. of May 1, we could hear the boom of artillery in our advance," Lieutenant Joseph G. Strong of the 28th Iowa related. "We quickened our pace."[49]

John C. Pemberton was violently shaken out of his lethargy and Grierson tunnel vision on April 29 with the sudden action at Grand Gulf. Heavy firing was clearly audible in Vicksburg, prompting Stevenson to finally admit he needed to start troops in that direction. Word then came from Bowen of the mass attack on Grand Gulf that morning, but then the wires went dead — an ominous development. Pemberton attributed it to either the enemy having "landed on this side of the Mississippi River, or they have been cut by Grierson's cavalry." But what he heard before the breakdown in communication was not good: several enemy ironclads attacked for several hours, with "transports loaded with troops in sight, but inactive." Pemberton informed Richmond and Johnston in Tennessee of the developments, and the fog of war was clear in his messages: "Do not know whether the enemy has made a landing on this side of Mississippi River." But what was clear was that Pemberton pivoted that day from any concern about a small cavalry raid numbering in the hundreds running wild in his rear to major concern about an entire field army supported by numerous gunboats crossing the river on his left flank. Significantly, it was only on April 29 that Pemberton first started ordering units and supplies to reinforce Grand Gulf. By that time, of course, it was too late.[50]

Bowen's frantic messages throughout the day, whether or not they arrived quickly, told of the fight. "Six gunboats, averaging ten guns, have been bombarding my batteries terrifically since 7 a.m. They pass and repass the batteries at the closest ranges," he related, also admitting that his works were "badly torn to pieces." He called for help, mainly ammunition, and explained that "I cannot tell the result, but [I] think that re-enforcements would hardly reach me in time to aid in the defense if they attempt to land." By nightfall after the renewed commotion, Bowen reported that his loss was small but included Colonel Wade. After some three thousand shots at him and his men, who "behaved like veterans (as they are)," they were hard at work repairing the damage done for a renewed action the next day. Worse, he late in the night also related that "six gunboats, with two transports lashed to them, passed my batteries to-night between 9 and 10 o'clock. Enemy on Louisiana shore, below. Hurry up re-enforcements. My lines very much extended."[51]

Bowen continued his barrage of messages throughout the night and into the next day, stating that he could see the transports below loading for future moves. "Cannot tell whether they will attack our left or front," he wrote deep in the night, but he mentioned the possibility of them moving on down as far as Rodney. Ultimately, with news of the landing at Bruinsburg, he alerted Pemberton that "I will fight them the other side of Port Gibson," but gunboats appearing at least partway up Bayou Pierre made him concerned about losing the bridge at Port Gibson, which was his only connection with his now-separated wings. "Shall I remove all to this side, severing all communication by telegraph, or make the best of it?" he queried Pemberton, but he soon decided to make his stand south of Port Gibson with his own troops and the oncoming brigades of Brigadier Generals Edward Tracy and William Baldwin, which were arriving. But farther movement out toward Bruinsburg was impossible given their "jaded condition." Tracy's Alabama brigade, for instance, had marched forty miles in twenty-seven hours, quite the change from their earlier activity just ten or so days before when one Alabamian related in his diary: "Gen Tracy and Col Garrott go fishing."[52]

Behind in the correspondence that was cut at times, Pemberton returned his thanks to Bowen: "In the name of the army, I desire to thank you and your troops for your gallant conduct to-day. Keep up the good work by every effort to repair damages to-night. Yesterday I warmly recommended you for a major generalcy. I shall renew it." By that point communications were down, and

Pemberton, with messages cut to Grand Gulf, spent a nervous couple days trying to get what news he could. "Is anything going on at Vicksburg or Grand Gulf," he impatiently queried Stevenson, who would not respond. Pemberton then wired the next in command, Martin L. Smith. By the evening of April 30 he knew enough that this was the real deal, even with Stevenson reporting Sherman appearing up on the Yazoo as well: "The enemy have been shelling Snyder's at long range most of the day," Stevenson reported. "Forney thinks that five regiments have landed at Blake's lower quarters," which they had. Pemberton ordered reinforcements to Bowen nevertheless: "Hurry forward re-enforcements to Bowen to-night," he wrote.[53]

But then came the worst news of all: "Three thousand Federals were at Bethel Church, 10 miles from Port Gibson, at 3 p.m., advancing," Bowen reported on April 30; "they are still landing at Bruinsburg." An incredulous Pemberton knew full well that Grand Gulf had "itself lost most of its value," and he could only notify his commanders as he began to draw them in for what was obviously becoming the next phase of the struggle: "Enemy is landing just below Grand Gulf."[54]

All Pemberton could do at that point was too little and too late to address the situation south of Bayou Pierre. Ironically, Stevenson at Vicksburg reported simultaneously that "all quiet here," and worse yet Jefferson Davis replied that he was working on getting Pemberton more cavalry. But the time was long past when he needed it. Pemberton could now merely continue to concentrate his forces nearer to Vicksburg; in fact he soon moved his own headquarters from Jackson to the river city—a clear indication of where his priorities lay. He also continued the vast effort of filling the city with supplies for a siege he now envisioned as more than probable. He had griped to the president of the Southern Railroad that "the shipment of Government supplies and stores to Vicksburg is much too slow for the requirements of the service," and then Grierson's breakages caused even more trouble: "Employ such a force on the work that the necessary repairs may be completed in the shortest possible time, as a great portion of the supplies for this command must now come over your road."[55]

Although late, Pemberton had started reinforcements southward, including Tracy's brigade as well as a few odd other troops and, later, Baldwin's troops. One of Baldwin's Mississippians related that "we formed the Brigade in the city, and about dark, started on the Warrenton Road." They crossed the Big Black River at Hankinson's Ferry on the steamer *Charm* about noon the next day (April 30) and, after a rest, moved on toward Port Gibson, where Colonel Claudius W. Sears recorded in his diary "[we] went through town as rapidly as possible—people brought out water for us as we passed." Pemberton later started William Loring himself southward with troops of his newly amalgamated division of brigades that had been defending northern and eastern Mississippi and then chasing Grierson. He also sent Major J. D. Bradford to Grand Gulf to replace the deceased Colonel Wade. Pemberton informed Bowen of his moves but warned "you had better whip them before he [Loring] reaches you." But Pemberton did not undertake a full defense to the south, even with reports of Grant's crossing. Sherman was, after all, still on the Yazoo River north of Vicksburg at this point, and Pemberton admitted "it was impossible for me to form an estimate of his absolute or relative strength at the two points." He added that "to concentrate my whole force south and east of Big Black for the support of General Bowen against a landing at Grand Gulf, or any point south of it not yet apparently even threatened, would, I think, have been unwise, to say the least of it." The lack of cavalry certainly hamstrung him more than anything else.[56]

With so little to work with, Bowen did what he could. He had discerned the possibility of Grant crossing below Bayou Pierre and had himself scouted southward from Port Gibson to find the best place to challenge him. He took Pemberton's engineer Lockett with him, and both concurred with the need to do so as far out as possible, Bowen estimating it would take as many as twenty-thousand troops to hold back the enemy. After the Federals failed to land at Grand Gulf, Bowen put his plan in motion and began to shift troops southward as indications became more and more certain that Grant was crossing at Bruinsburg. But still needing to defend Grand Gulf as well, he was stretched too thin, "and [it] left me no hope to fight the enemy on the spot selected unless the promised re-enforcements should reach me in time." One of those reinforcements admitted: "We were too late."[57]

Some did arrive south of Port Gibson in time to meet the Federals, however. Bowen first sent a portion of Brigadier General Martin E. Green's brigade southward to Port Gibson to cover the two roads leading from Bruinsburg to Port Gibson; one of his Arkansans noted they were ordered to cook three days' rations but wondered: "I never could tell why three days rations was always the order,—why not two or four." Later, as Edward Tracy's brigade arrived, Bowen ordered it to halt at the town itself to rest a bit after its grueling march and to report to Green when needed. The Alabamians were surprised to be heading to a land battle, one of them, upon leaving the Vicksburg vicinity, remarking in his diary "orders to leave—I recon to hunt them gun boats." Bowen himself went out the afternoon of April 30 "and established Green in his position" while placing other regiments of his own brigade now under

Colonel Cockrell in position to cover Bayou Pierre from the threatened naval incursion. Much of the rest of Bowen's force remained in reserve "to be ready to move at a moment's notice."[58]

Meanwhile, Green arrived at Port Gibson early in the morning on April 30 and began to scout ahead "to reconnoiter the country and choose location for the battle." But divining that the enemy could approach on the Rodney and Bruinsburg Roads, Green held his command closer to Port Gibson to cover both until Tracy's troops arrived and he could move forward in force on both. Green ultimately sent Tracy's Alabamians out the Bruinsburg Road closer to Bayou Pierre while he held the Rodney Road with his own force augmented with the 6th Mississippi and an assortment of other troops such as the 4th Mississippi ("we marched 50 miles in ½ day and a night") and unmounted companies of the 20th Mississippi. William Baldwin's brigade had arrived in the vicinity as well, spending the night at the "beautiful stream, spanned by a new suspension bridge," Bayou Pierre. But they were famished. The troops had started the march eagerly: "The air seemed purer and the spirits of the men were wonderfully elated. . . . Jest and repartee were heard on every side." Yet he then related: "But physical fatigue will dampen the ardor of the most elastic spirit, and as long hours dragged by with, no orders save 'close up!' the enthusiasm seemed to die away, and a great weariness of limb overtook us."[59]

Ultimately, Eugene Carr's lead brigade ran into Green's pickets near the Abram K. Shaifer House on the Rodney Road deep in the night of April 30. Skirmishing began quickly in the darkness as April turned to May. Also begun with the change in month, and more particularly with those first shots, was the next phase of the Vicksburg Campaign.[60]

Epilogue
"But I Was on Dry Ground"

"The great fight has now commenced on the Mississippi," one Tennessean declared as April rolled over into May and Grant struck inland. One Confederate had predicted peace by May 1, but that was obviously not happening. Rather, Grant had landed on Mississippi soil and was heading toward a confrontation on that date. The wild turn of events led most to reconsider the campaign and future, even Grant himself describing in one of the most quoted passages of his memoirs his feeling of relief that at last something was going to happen either way:

> When this was effected I felt a degree of relief scarcely ever equaled since. Vicksburg was not yet taken it is true, nor were its defenders demoralized by any of our previous moves. I was now in the enemy's country, with a vast river and the stronghold of Vicksburg between me and my base of supplies. But I was on dry ground on the same side of the river with the enemy. All the campaigns, labors, hardships and exposures from the month of December previous to this time that had been made and endured, were for the accomplishment of this one object.[1]

The four months since the new year turned were part of that process, and the period definitely had its effects. Obviously, a lot of the impact was on the personal level, which could be small or large depending on the end result. One Federal admitted, "I have found a nice Lady down here and am afraid I will have to take a *rib* down in this part of the Confederacy." Others kept romance in mind as well, a Confederate staff officer writing frequently of games and dancing with the ladies, even to the point that "they have a good joke on me about trying to kiss one of them. I must confess I did try and tried very hard too but without success. But it was all her fault."[2]

Most of the effects were more permanent and costlier, however, certainly when death visited. And most realized that, given the new developments of crossing the river, a new and likely more deadly phase of the campaign was just starting. While the past four months were dreary enough, many considered them easy, especially compared to what lay ahead. It was the end of easy times, if that could be said of it. One Confederate stated that this period was "the most pleasant period of my army life. Our principal occupation was eating and sleeping." But he added that by the end of April all things changed and that "the great maelstrom of war was again beginning to whirl and soon we will be swallowed in its inexorable vortex."[3]

How involved the fighting would be as this new phase began was a question to ponder, and most had their opinions. Many—Grant included—thought just crossing the river was the hardest part. In a bout of continual overconfidence that seemed to plague Grant for much of the war (certainly at Belmont, Fort Donelson, and Shiloh), Grant had told his troops back in late April that "we should be in Vicksburg in twenty days." He similarly told Halleck, "If I do not underestimate the enemy, my force is abundant, with a foothold once obtained, to do the work." He also wrote that "once there [Grand Gulf], I do not feel a doubt of success in the entire cleaning out of the enemy from the banks of the river." Perhaps his most overconfident musings came in his private correspondence with Julia, wherein he wrote that "foot once upon dry land on the other side of the river I think the balance would be of but short duration." Later he added that "once landed on the other side of the river I expect but little trouble." By April 28 he continued that "possession of Grand Gulf too I look upon as virtual possession of Vicksburg and Port Hudson and the entire Mississippi River." He would certainly learn differently as May plodded along—and June and into July as well.[4]

Many of his soldiers were confident too. One wrote that "when we get there [Vicksburg] we will take the 'durn thing,' bag and baggage." Even the lowliest could see what was happening: "Gen. Grant is likely to place his troops fairly in the rear of Vicksburg and thus effectually cut off all communications and supplies. Surely the Rebels will not be caught in this trap." Even the colonel of the 77th Illinois, David Grier, was overcome with overconfidence, writing his fiancée: "I think the Rebels will evacuate the place without a fight." Others made bold predictions of what the capture of Vicksburg, as if it was a done deal, would mean: "As soon as we get Vicksburg I think that the rebellion is about played out."[5]

But not all were so sure. One Indianan wrote that "all is quiet at Vicksburg. Some think they are evacuating the place but that is all in the eye. I don't believe the half of it. If ever we get Vicksburg we will have to fight for it." One

German Federal wrote home that "we hope we do not fare like the fox in Aesop's Fables, 'the grapes that look so inviting turned out to be sauer grapes.'" Whether the campaign would be successful or not, many knew a fight or two was coming. "It is my opinion that the next six weeks will tell a tale that all will have a pretty good idea how long this war will continue," one explained, and another informed his wife on April 17: "I think ere you get this we'll shall have been in deathly conflict with the enemy and if victorious will be couped in Vicksburg." One Federal even predicted in April that "the city will Be ours against the 4th of July 63."[6]

While all looked ahead to the next phases of the campaign, the four months just passed were ever present in many minds. On the surface, it looked like wasted time and a severe defeat for the Federals. But the end result was Grant's Army of the Tennessee gaining the ground he wanted so badly, albeit far from where he intended. But he was now on that high ground nevertheless. Consequently, it was not so much a defeat as a delay, one of Grant's engineers, William Jenney, explaining that "many of these moves on the Vicksburg chessboard were very bold in their conception, made with secrecy, energy, rapidity, and all failed from a combination of natural causes, very materially assisted by an active and watchful enemy." But it ultimately turned to the path of victory, Confederate general Stephen D. Lee admitting that in these wet and dreary months Grant actually "groped to success." Grant himself later thought the earlier failures "may have been providential in driving us ultimately to a line of operations which has proven eminently successful."[7]

But these four months of novel operations were important in their own right, one veteran writing of "a campaign that revolutionized modern warfare." Certainly, in the sense of the accepted theories of war, they were new, bold, and revolutionary. Grant's operations clearly went against the standard book at the time, the evolution of the Jomini-to-Mahan-to-Halleck version of warfare, which prized secure supply lines, coordinated supporting columns, and gradual maneuver-based advances along solid ground. These four months of operations were anything but that. And while Grant certainly went against the book in many ways, he also started the process, to a lesser degree, of acquiring the more Clausewitzian art of war. Indeed, Grant's resolve in the face of opposition from his most trusted subordinates testified to his Clausewitzian leadership abilities. One of Grant's earliest biographers in fact wrote how, in clear Clausewitzian form, Grant "believed that Vicksburg was only to be won by hard fighting, and by destroying armies."[8]

There were, of course, still those who even now questioned the logic of this new move, Sherman especially. Engineer Wilson later wrote that Sherman "quoted Jomini in favor of the policy of concentration. He pointed out the danger of cutting loose from our base.... All this was in accordance with the books and the precedents." But Grant himself explained his reasoning best:

> When I determined on that campaign I knew, as well as I knew anything, that it would not meet with the approval of the authorities in Washington. I knew this because I knew Halleck, and that he was too learned a soldier to consent to a campaign in violation of all the principles of the art of war. But I felt that every war I knew anything about had made laws for itself, and early in our contest I was impressed with the idea that success with us would depend upon our taking advantage of new conditions. No two wars are alike, because they are generally fought at different periods, under different phases of civilization. To take Vicksburg, according to the rules of war as laid down in the books, would have involved a new campaign, a withdrawal of my forces to Memphis, and the opening of a new line of attack. The North needed a victory.

In essence, Sherman was most concerned about the logistical aspects, and Grant essentially traded a secure supply framework via the river when all his efforts were on the north side of Vicksburg for a much better tactical scenario, which he did not have above Vicksburg, but with a much less secure logistical lifeline. It would obviously have been better if both a good tactical and logistical context could have been attained, but in this curious and unique environment it was not possible.[9]

For his part, John Pemberton never made such a change. But then he did not need to at this point. The fact that most of the Federal operations were either on the opposite side of the river, which was administratively in another department, or far to his north or south gave him the time and opportunity to meet each threat with those same Jominian principles Grant was already shunning, namely interior lines of communication that allowed him to concentrate and shift troops. Many touted Pemberton's success if not his generalship, Lee stating that the "energy and sagacity of Gen. Pemberton" had defied Grant in the bayou operations.[10]

But there were concerns, especially that Pemberton was firmly on the defensive, his biographer Michael Ballard arguing that Pemberton "had developed a strictly defensive state of mind." It was a dangerous thing to give Grant the initiative, but in the Jominian mindset that he had been taught and that he observed, Pemberton preferred to wait and react rather than take control and mold the situation. He certainly could have benefited from more Clausewitzian ideas such as counterattacking at the enemy's "culminating point," definitely in the winter operations around the Mississippi Central and even Chickasaw Bayou but also in the bayou operations at Yazoo Pass or Steele's Bayou. And allowing Grant to march inland uncontested while at the end of a long and tedious line of advance, perhaps a true "culminating point," was unfathomable.[11]

Nevertheless, the Confederates had been able successfully to meet each earlier threat while playing on such a large canvass. But as the chessboard grew smaller, which it certainly did when Grant crossed the river within thirty-five miles of Vicksburg itself, Pemberton found it harder and harder to react in time. In fact, that already became an issue in some of the bayou expeditions. The reaction to the closer-in (to Vicksburg) Steele's Bayou effort was actually much tardier than anyone wanted and almost did not arrive in time simply because it took place much closer to Pemberton's Vicksburg/Jackson base; the reaction time was therefore much shorter. And Pemberton certainly did not have time, once he figured out what was happening, to react to Grant's river crossing. No doubt some wondered what would happen now that Grant was on the same side of the river as Pemberton and within thirty-five miles of Vicksburg itself.[12]

Even though not as well known or decisive as some of the other more glamorous parts of the Vicksburg Campaign, these four months of bayou operations, culminating in the big development of Grant crossing the river, were immensely important. And the old veterans who lived through them and the rest of the war certainly thought back on them perhaps not with fondness but rather amazement. "I often think of those old times and wonder what all my comrades are doing," one Confederate explained years later. "Many of them have gone over the river," he reminisced, "and it will not be many years until all will be gone."[13]

Specific events were well remembered. One Illinoisan wrote of the effect of Grierson's Raid well after the fact: "We who marched with Grant to the rear of Vicksburg (I was in the 72nd Ill. Infty.), realized as never before the help your raid was in keeping the enemy away from us." But perhaps Admiral Porter illustrated it best when he was asked in 1888 to address a reunion of naval personnel from the Mississippi Squadron in Cincinnati. He wrote a long and passionate letter that obviously took him back to the dramatic passage of the Vicksburg guns so many years before. In fact, the reunion was being held on that very date, April 16, but twenty-five years later.[14]

Porter wrote by way of introduction that he was glad "that there are enough survivors of the Mississippi Squadron to observe the anniversary," but he likewise knew full well that many "have long since gone to the undiscovered country from whose bourne no traveler returns." Then he began his trek back in memory: "As I write you, I am looking at a representation of the passage of the fleet by Vicksburg, the original study of a painting by James E. Taylor of New York, and it brings the whole scene vividly before me." He described how

> There is the sturdy old flagship *Benton* (Lieutenant-Commander Greer) having passed the last battery, straightening up to give room to those in the rear; the *Lafayette* (Captain Walke) with the *General Price* alongside, just taking a sheer to clear the way for the *Louisville*, which is crowding her closely. Then comes the *Mound City* (Lieutenant Commander Byron Wilson) still delivering her broadsides, close to the left bank of the river; the *Pittsburg*, under the gallant William R. Hoel . . . managing his vessel with the coolness of a veteran naval officer; the *Carondelet* (Lieutenant Commander J. McL. Murphy) coming on in the distance, belching forth her port broadside; the *Tuscumbia* (Lieutenant Commander Shirk) bringing up the rear and taking care of the army transports that were fitted up to pass the batteries, and the *Henry Clay* close alongside all in a blaze, some of her crew pitching cotton bales overboard, some jumping into the water to escape the flames, while her brave pilot, standing at his post, is steering his vessel through the advancing gunboats till driven overboard by the heat,—all are there.

He added: "Though it is now a quarter of a century since that exciting scene was enacted, I can see it all as plainly as though it was the occurrence of yesterday."[15]

Porter took a shot at the army, adding that all the veterans who would hear this letter read "have the satisfaction of knowing and handing down to your children the knowledge that it was the passage of the fleet by Vicksburg that sealed the fate of the stronghold." He praised the former sailors "with hearts of oak, in Western iron walls." But then he gave the army its due as well, writing of "the soldiers ready to dare any risks that their brave general chose." He ended with the congratulation that "the day will come when the children of those who did their duty so nobly in those great scenes of hardship, can with pride point to the names of their fathers and say—'They helped to break the backbone of the rebellion and opened up "The Father of Waters" so that commerce of the states re-united and of the world, could float once more in safety upon its bosom.'" Finally, he added, "congratulate yourselves that it was greatly owing to your exertions, patriotism[,] and bravery that we are indebted for a united and happy country."[16]

Appendix A

Union Order of Battle for Arkansas Post, January 11, 1863

ARMY OF THE MISSISSIPPI
    Major General John A. McClernand

FIRST ARMY CORPS
    Brigadier General George W. Morgan

FIRST DIVISION
    Brigadier General Andrew J. Smith

Escort
        4th Indiana Cavalry, Company C

First Brigade
    Brigadier General Stephen G. Burbridge
        16th Indiana
        60th Indiana
        67th Indiana
        83rd Ohio
        96th Ohio
        23rd Wisconsin

Second Brigade
    Colonel William J. Landram
        77th Illinois
        97th Illinois
        108th Illinois
        131st Illinois

19th Kentucky
48th Ohio

Artillery
Chicago Mercantile Battery
17th Battery Ohio Light Artillery

Cavalry
6th Missouri (squadron)

SECOND DIVISION
Brigadier General Peter J. Osterhaus

First Brigade
Colonel Lionel A. Sheldon
118th Illinois
69th Indiana
120th Ohio

Second Brigade
Colonel Daniel W. Lindsey
49th Indiana
3rd Kentucky
114th Ohio

Third Brigade
Colonel John F. De Courcy
54th Indiana
22nd Kentucky
16th Ohio
42nd Ohio

Artillery
7th Battery Michigan Light Artillery
1st Battery Wisconsin Light Artillery

SECOND ARMY CORPS
Major General William T. Sherman

FIRST DIVISION
Brigadier General Frederick Steele

Escort
    Kane County (Illinois) Cavalry

First Brigade
    Brigadier General Francis P. Blair Jr.
        13th Illinois
        29th Missouri
        30th Missouri
        31st Missouri
        32nd Missouri
        58th Ohio
        4th Ohio Light Artillery

Second Brigade
    Brigadier General Charles E. Hovey
        25th Iowa
        31st Iowa
        3rd Missouri
        12th Missouri
        17th Missouri
        76th Ohio
        Battery F, 2nd Missouri Light Artillery

Third Brigade
    Brigadier General John M. Thayer
        4th Iowa
        9th Iowa
        26th Iowa
        30th Iowa
        34th Iowa
        1st Iowa Light Artillery

Cavalry
    3rd Illinois Cavalry

SECOND DIVISION
    Brigadier General David Stuart

First Brigade
    Colonel Giles A. Smith
        113th Illinois
        116th Illinois
        6th Missouri

8th Missouri
13th United States, 1st Battalion

Second Brigade
Colonel Thomas Kilby Smith
55th Illinois
127th Illinois
83rd Indiana
54th Ohio
57th Ohio

Artillery
1st Illinois Light Artillery, Battery A
1st Illinois Light Artillery, Battery B
1st Illinois Light Artillery, Battery H
8th Ohio Light Artillery

Cavalry
Thielemann's Illinois Cavalry Battalion (Companies A and B)
10th Missouri Cavalry, Company C

Appendix B

Confederate Order of Battle for Arkansas Post, January 11, 1863

ARKANSAS POST GARRISON
    Brigadier General Thomas J. Churchill

First Brigade
    Colonel Robert R. Garland
        6th Texas
        24th Texas Cavalry (dismounted)
        25th Texas Cavalry (dismounted)
        Hart's Arkansas Battery
        Denson's Louisiana Cavalry Company

Second Brigade
    Colonel James Deshler
        10th Texas
        15th Texas Cavalry (dismounted)
        17th Texas Cavalry (dismounted)
        18th Texas Cavalry (dismounted)

Third Brigade
    Colonel John W. Dunnington
        19th Arkansas
        Crawford's Arkansas Battalion
        CS Navy Detachment

Unattached
        Nutt's Louisiana Cavalry Company
        Richardson's Texas Cavalry Company
        Johnson's Texas Cavalry Company
        24th Arkansas

NOTES

ABBREVIATIONS

Abraham Lincoln Presidential Library	ALPL
Alabama Department of Archives and History	ADAH
Archives of Michigan	AM
Atlanta History Center	AHC
Auburn University	AU
Augustana College	AC
Butler Center for Arkansas Studies	BCAS
Chicago History Museum	CHM
Civil War Documents Collection	CWD
Civil War Times Illustrated Collection	CWTI
De Kalb County Historical and Genealogical Society	DCHS
Duke University	DU
Emory University	EU
Filson Historical Society	FHS
Gettysburg College	GC
Gilder Lehrman Institute	GLI
Grenada Public Library	GPL
Harrisburg Civil War Roundtable Collection	HCWRT
Harvard University	HU
Huntington Library	HL
Indiana Historical Society	IHS
Indiana State Library	ISL
Indiana State University	ISU
Indiana University	INU
Iowa State University	ISU
Library of Congress	LC
Louisiana State University	LSU

Minnesota Historical Society	MNHS
Mississippi Department of Archives and History	MDAH
Missouri Historical Society	MHS
National Archives and Records Administration	NARA
Newberry Library	NL
Ohio Historical Society	OHS
Old Courthouse Museum	OCM
War of the Rebellion: A Compilation of the Official Records of the Union and Confederate Armies	OR
The Official Records of the Union and Confederate Navies	ORN
Papers of Ulysses S. Grant	PUSG
Southern Illinois University	SIU
Stanford University	SU
State Historical Society of Iowa, Des Moines	SHSIDM
State Historical Society of Iowa, Iowa City	SHSIIC
State Historical Society of Missouri	SHSM
State Historical Society of Wisconsin	SHSW
Supplement to the Official Records	*SOR*
Tennessee State Library and Archives	TSLA
Tulane University	TU
United States Army History and Education Center	USAHEC
United States Naval Academy	USNA
University of Alabama	UA
University of Arkansas	UAR
University of California, San Diego	UCSD
University of Colorado Boulder	UCB
University of Illinois	UIL
University of Iowa	UIA
University of Memphis	UMEM
University of Michigan Bentley Library	UMB
University of Michigan Clements Library	UMC
University of Mississippi	UM
University of Missouri	UMO
University of North Carolina	UNC
University of South Carolina	USC
University of Southern Mississippi	USM
University of Tennessee	UTK
Vicksburg National Military Park	VICK
Western Kentucky University	WKU
Western Reserve Historical Society	WRHS
Wisconsin Historical Society	WHS

Preface

1. J. F. C. Fuller, *The Generalship of Ulysses S. Grant* (Bloomington: Indiana University Press, 1958), 135–136.
2. Kenneth W. Noe, *Through the Howling Storm: Weather, Climate, and the American Civil War* (Baton Rouge: Louisiana State University Press, 2020); Judkin Browning and Timothy Silver, *An Environmental History of the Civil War* (Chapel Hill: University of North Carolina Press, 2020).
3. See also Timothy B. Smith, *The Union Assaults at Vicksburg: Grant Attacks Pemberton, May 17–22, 1863* (Lawrence: University Press of Kansas, 2020), and Timothy B. Smith, *The Siege of Vicksburg: The Climax of the Campaign to Open the Mississippi River, May 23–July 4, 1863* (Lawrence: University Press of Kansas, 2021).
4. Fuller, *The Generalship of Ulysses S. Grant*, 135.
5. Timothy B. Smith, *The Real Horse Soldiers: Benjamin Grierson's Epic 1863 Civil War Raid Through Mississippi* (New York: Savas Beatie, 2018); Timothy B. Smith, *The Decision Was Always My Own: Ulysses S. Grant and the Vicksburg Campaign* (Carbondale: Southern Illinois University Press, 2018), 43–101; Timothy B. Smith, *Champion Hill: Decisive Battle for Vicksburg* (New York: Savas Beatie, 2004).

Prologue: Vicksburg *Not* by the Book

1. Timothy B. Smith, *Early Struggles for Vicksburg: The Mississippi Central Campaign and Chickasaw Bayou, October 25–December 31, 1862* (Lawrence: University Press of Kansas, 2022); Henri de Jomini, *Summary of the Art of War, or, A New Analytical Compend of the Principal Combinations of Strategy, of Grand Tactics and of Military Policy* (New York: G. P. Putnam & Co., 1854); Henri de Jomini, *The Art of War* (Philadelphia: J. B. Lippincott & Co., 1862).
2. Allan R. Millett, Peter Maslowski, and William B. Feis, *For the Common Defense: A Military History of the United States from 1607 to 2012* (New York: Free Press, 2012), 119.
3. Carol Reardon, *With a Sword in One Hand & Jomini in the Other: The Problem of Military Thought in the Civil War North* (Chapel Hill: University of North Carolina Press, 2012), 5–9; John H. Brinton, *Personal Memoirs of John H. Brinton, Major and Surgeon U.S.V., 1861–1865* (New York: Neale Publishing Company, 1914), 239; John F. Marszalek, David F. Nolen, and Louie P. Gallo, eds., *The Personal Memoirs of Ulysses S. Grant: The Complete Annotated Edition* (Cambridge, MA: Harvard University Press, 2017), 292; *War of the Rebellion: A Compilation of the Official Records of the Union and Confederate Armies* (Washington, DC: U.S. Government Printing Office, 1880–1901), Series 1, Volume 17 (Part 2):119. Hereafter cited as *OR*, with all references to Series 1 unless otherwise noted, followed by volume and part number. Ira Payne to parents, March 28, 1863, and Ira Payne Diary, March 26, 1863, Ira A. Payne Papers, ALPL.
4. For the campaign, see Smith, *Early Struggles for Vicksburg*.

5. Paul L. Schmelzer, "Politics, Policy, and General Grant: Clausewitz on the Operational Art as Practiced in the Vicksburg Campaign," in *The Vicksburg Campaign: March 29–May 18, 1863*, Steven E. Woodworth and Charles D. Grear, eds. (Carbondale: Southern Illinois University Press, 2013), 214–228; Bruce Catton, *Grant Moves South* (Boston: Little, Brown, and Company, 1960), 407.

6. Carl von Clausewitz, *On War* (London: N. Trubner and Co., 1873), 403; Schmelzer, "Politics, Policy, and General Grant," 214. For Grant's Clausewitzian thought, see Paul L. Schmelzer, "A Strong Mind: A Clausewitzian Biography of U. S. Grant" (PhD diss., Texas Christian University, 2010).

7. Marszalek, Nolen, and Gallo, eds., *Personal Memoirs of Ulysses S. Grant*, 374; *The Official Records of the Union and Confederate Navies in the War of the Rebellion*, 30 vols. (Washington, DC: Government Printing Office, 1894–1922), Volume 24:479.

8. Marszalek, Nolen, and Gallo, eds., *Personal Memoirs of Ulysses S. Grant*, 307–309.

9. "Ulysses S. Grant," April 9, 1885, *National Tribune*; William Kennedy to unknown, January 21, William J. Kennedy Papers, ALPL; Dick Ransom to unknown, January 4, 1863, Dick Ransom Collection, BCAS; John Ruckman to John Kinsel, February 16, 1863, John Ruckman Letters, VICK; William Rand to father, April 12, 1863, Rand Family Papers, ALPL; Sheldon Treat to mother, February 1, 1863, Sheldon C. Treat Correspondence, UA.

10. Schmelzer, "Politics, Policy, and General Grant," 217; Henry Steele Commager, ed., *The Blue and the Gray*, 2 vols. (New York: Meridian, 1994), 2:65; Payson Shumway to friend, June 17, 1863, Z. Payson Shumway Letters, NL.

11. John B. Sanborn, "The Campaign Against Vicksburg," in *Glimpses of the Nation's Struggle, Second Series: A Series of Papers Read Before the Minnesota Commandery of the Military Order of the Loyal Legion of the United States, 1887–1899*, 6 vols. (St. Paul, MN: St. Paul Book and Stationary Company, 1890), 2:125.

Chapter 1. "We Were Out-Generaled Some Way"

1. Merrill D. Peterson, *Thomas Jefferson & the New Nation: A Biography* (New York: Oxford University Press, 1970), 752–753.

2. Robert V. Remini, *Andrew Jackson and the Course of American Empire, 1767–1821* (New York: Harper & Row, 1977), 127.

3. Robert V. Remini, *Andrew Jackson and the Course of American Freedom, 1822–1832* (New York: Harper & Row, 1981), 218.

4. *OR*, 31(3):459. For Mississippi's secession, see Timothy B. Smith, *The Mississippi Secession Convention: Delegates and Deliberations in Politics and War, 1861–1865* (Jackson: University Press of Mississippi, 2014).

5. "Sixth Day," Jackson *Weekly Mississippian*, January 16, 1861; Alex W. Randall to John J. Pettus, January 21, 1861, "Joint Resolutions of the General Assembly of the State of Ohio, January 12, 1861, "Joint Resolutions on the State of the Union," February 2, 1861, Oliver P. Morton to John J. Pettus, unreadable date, and Unknown to John J. Pettus,

February 2, 1861, all in Mississippi Governor, John J. Pettus, Correspondence and Papers, 1859–1863, Series 757, MDAH; Untitled Articles, Vicksburg *Evening Citizen*, January 14, 1861; "From the Seat of War," Vicksburg *Evening Citizen*, January 14, 1861; Charles D. Fontaine to Sally Ann, January 12, 1861, Fontaine Family Papers, MDAH; Michael B. Ballard, *Vicksburg: The Campaign That Opened the Mississippi* (Chapel Hill: University of North Carolina Press, 2004), 9; B. L. C. Wailes Diary, January 19, 1861, DU.

6. James B. McPherson, *Battle Cry of Freedom: The Civil War Era* (New York: Oxford University Press, 1988), 333–336.

7. Marszalek, Nolen, and Gallo, eds., *Personal Memoirs of Ulysses S. Grant*, 306. For the history of the Mississippi River, see Stephen E. Ambrose and Douglas Brinkley, *The Mississippi and the Making of a Nation: From the Louisiana Purchase to Today* (Washington, DC: National Geographic, 2002).

8. For Union naval operations on the inland rivers, see Barbara Brooks Tomblin, *The Civil War on the Mississippi: Union Sailors, Gunboat Captains, and the Campaign to Control the River* (Lexington: University Press of Kentucky, 2016) and Gary D. Joiner, *Mr. Lincoln's Brown Water Navy: The Mississippi Squadron* (New York: Rowman & Littlefield, 2007); Robert Gudmestad, "Elusive Victory: The Union Navy's War along the Western Waters," *Civil War History* 67, no. 2 (June 2021): 79–109. For corresponding Confederate naval efforts, see Neil P. Chatelain, *Defending the Arteries of Rebellion: Confederate Naval Operations in the Mississippi River Valley, 1861–1865* (El Dorado Hills, CA: Savas Beatie, 2020).

9. Timothy B. Smith, *The Union Assaults at Vicksburg: Grant Attacks Pemberton, May 17–22, 1863* (Lawrence: University Press of Kansas, 2020), 5.

10. Warren E. Grabau, *Ninety-Eight Days: A Geographer's View of the Vicksburg Campaign* (Knoxville: University of Tennessee Press, 2000), 14–15; George B. Davis, Leslie J. Perry, and Joseph W. Kirkley, *Atlas to Accompany the Official Records of the Union and Confederate Armies* (Washington, DC: Government Printing Office, 1891–1895), Plates 154 and 155.

11. M. R. Banner to wife, April 5, 1863, Banner Family Letters, OCM; Davis, Perry, and Kirkley, *Atlas*, Plates 154 and 155; James Carlisle Diary, January 2, 1863, VICK.

12. Davis, Perry, and Kirkley, *Atlas*, Plates 154 and 155.

13. Matthew Adams to sister, January 31, 1863, Matthew R. Adams Letters, OCM; Ted Ownby and Charles Reagan Wilson, eds., *The Mississippi Encyclopedia* (Jackson: University Press of Mississippi, 2017), 327.

14. *OR*, 1, 17(2):351, 356.

15. Richard L. Howard, "The Vicksburg Campaign," in *War Papers Read Before the Commandery of the State of Maine, Military Order of the Loyal Legion of the United States, Volume 2* (Portland, ME: Lefavor-Tower Company, 1902), 2:29–30; Davis, Perry, and Kirkley, *Atlas*, Plates 154 and 155.

16. *OR*, 10(2):430; Edward Reichhelm Memoir, undated, Edward P. Reichhelm Papers, LC, 21.

17. *OR*, 4:419–420; *OR*, 6:823, 826; *OR*, 7:880; Grabau, *Ninety-Eight Days*, 17; Charles Bracelen Flood, *Grant and Sherman: The Friendship That Won the Civil War*

(New York: Farrar, Straus and Giroux, 2005), 149; J. C. M. to editor, April 23, 1863, E. Merton Coulter Collection, UGA; James Slack to wife, April 14, 1863, James R. Slack Letters, ISL; Clarkson Fogg to unknown, March 1, 1863, Clarkson Fogg Letters, VICK; W. R. Eddington Memoir, undated, ALPL, 7.

18. *OR*, 4:419–420; *OR*, 6:823, 826; *OR*, 7:880; Grabau, *Ninety-Eight Days*, 17; James Slack to wife, April 14, 1863, James R. Slack Letters, ISL Flood, *Grant and Sherman*, 149; J. C. M. to editor, April 23, 1863, E. Merton Coulter Collection, UGA; W. R. Eddington Memoir, undated, ALPL, 7; Clarkson Fogg to unknown, March 1, 1863, Clarkson Fogg Letters, VICK.

19. *OR*, 4:419–420; *OR*, 6:823, 826; *OR*, 7:880; Grabau, *Ninety-Eight Days*, 17; W. R. Eddington Memoir, undated, ALPL, 7; James Slack to wife, April 14, 1863, James R. Slack Letters, ISL.

20. Timothy B. Smith, *Grant Invades Tennessee: The 1862 Battles for Forts Henry and Donelson* (Lawrence: University Press of Kansas, 2016), 30.

21. For Johnston, see Charles P. Roland, *Albert Sidney Johnston: Soldier of Three Republics* (Austin: University of Texas Press, 1964).

22. For operations around Forts Henry and Donelson, see Smith, *Grant Invades Tennessee*.

23. William Preston Johnston, *The Life of Gen. Albert Sidney Johnston: His Service in the Armies of the United States, The Republic of Texas, and the Confederate States* (New York: D. Appleton and Co., 1879), 568–571, 583–584, 613; A. P. Stewart to William H. McCardle, April 30, 1878, William H. McCardle Papers, MDAH; *OR*, 10(1):671; Marszalek, Nolen, and Gallo, eds., *Personal Memoirs of Ulysses S. Grant*, 291. For Shiloh, see Timothy B. Smith, *Shiloh: Conquer or Perish* (Lawrence: University Press of Kansas, 2014). For Corinth, see Timothy B. Smith, *Corinth 1862: Siege, Battle, Occupation* (Lawrence: University Press of Kansas, 2012).

24. *OR*, 10(2):579; *OR*, 6:867, 877, 883–885; *OR*, 15:13; James Snell to wife, July 19, 1862, James C. Snell Letters, TSLA; John Crenshaw to May Crenshaw, July 15, 1862, John Crenshaw Letter, USC; Earl Van Dorn to Daniel Ruggles, July 22, 1862, Frederick M. Dearborn Collection, HU; Edward Potter to unknown, June 29, 1862, Edward E. Potter Papers, NC; E. T. Eggleston Diary, June 29, 1862, VICK; David Farragut to wife, July 4, 1862, David G. Farragut Papers, UTK; David Porter to sir, July 3, 1862, David Dixon Porter Correspondence, VICK. For the first action around Vicksburg, see Edwin C. Bearss, *Rebel Victory at Vicksburg* (Vicksburg: Vicksburg Centennial Commission, 1963).

25. James Snell to wife, July 19, 1862, James C. Snell Letters, TSLA; Spencer B. Talley Memoir, 1918, TSLA, 10; P. B. Starke et al to M. L. Smith, July 26, 1862, John G. Devereux Papers, UNC. For Halleck, see John F. Marszalek, *Commander of All Lincoln's Armies: A Life of General Henry W. Halleck* (Cambridge, MA: Harvard University Press, 2004).

26. McPherson, *Battle Cry of Freedom*, 510–545.

27. McPherson, *Battle Cry of Freedom*, 510–545.

28. Ron Chernow, *Grant* (New York: Penguin Press, 2017), 220.

29. Marszalek, Nolen, and Gallo, eds., *Personal Memoirs of Ulysses S. Grant*, 289.
30. *OR*, 17(2):278–279, 285, 294, 296.
31. Matthew Adams to sister, January 31, 1863, Matthew R. Adams Letters, OCM; Davis, Perry, and Kirkley, *Atlas*, Plates 154 and 155.
32. *OR*, 17(2):296; William Foster to Sir, June 15, 1857, Robert Jemison Jr. Papers, UA; N. G. Bryson to A. J. McCoonico, April 10, 1861, Southern Railroad Company Letter, USM.
33. Robert C. Black, III, *The Railroads of the Confederacy* (Chapel Hill: University of North Carolina Press, 1952), 1; "The First Meeting of the Board of Directors," January 7, 1854, Mississippi Central and Tennessee Railroad Subject File, MDAH; "Our Rail Road," Jackson *Mississippian and State Gazette*, October 27, 1858; "Mississippi Central Railroad," Hinds County *Gazette*, November 16, 1859; "Railroad Line Changes Names Back to Mississippi Central," Holly Springs *South Reporter*, February 18, 1993. See also the A. J. McConnico Papers, DU.
34. *OR*, 17(1):467; *OR*, 17(2):314–315; John Russell Young, *Around the World with General Grant: A Narrative of the Visit of General U.S. Grant, Ex-President of the United States, to Various Countries in Europe, Asia, and Africa, in 1877, 1878, 1879. To which are Added Certain Conversations with General Grant on Questions Connected with American Politics and History* (New York: American News Company, 1879), 615.
35. *OR*, 17(2):348; John Y. Simon and John F. Marszalek, eds., *The Papers of Ulysses S. Grant*, 32 vols. (Carbondale: Southern Illinois University Press, 1967–2014), 6:354, hereafter cited as *PUSG*; Seneca Thrall to wife, November 6, 1862, Seneca B. Thrall Papers, SHSIIC; *OR*, 17(1):467.
36. *OR*, 17(2):348; *OR*, 17(1):467; Simon and Marszalek, eds., *PUSG*, 6:354; Seneca Thrall to wife, November 6, 1862, Seneca B. Thrall Papers, SHSIIC.
37. *OR*, 17(1):530, 538; *OR*, 17(2):409, 744–746, 779; Charles Dickinson to father, November 30, 1862, Charles Dickinson Correspondence, NL; Thomas K. Mitchell Diary, November 30, 1862, OCM; John Given to family, December 10, 1862, John G. Given Papers, ALPL; Edward Wood to wife, November 26, 1862, Edward J. Wood Papers, IHS.
38. *OR*, 17(2):385, 387, 771.
39. Joseph Stockton Diary, December 5, 1862, VICK, copy in Coco Collection, HCWRC, USAHEC; Smith, *Early Struggles for Vicksburg*, 162.
40. A. F. Brown, "Van Dorn's Operations in Northern Mississippi—Recollections of a Cavalryman," *Southern Historical Society Papers* 5, no. 4 (October 1878): 154.
41. *OR*, 17(1):742; *OR*, 17(2):351, 356.
42. *OR*, 17(2):282; T. Harry Williams, *Lincoln and His Generals* (New York: Alfred A. Knopf, 1952), 192.
43. *OR*, 17(2): 412, 434, 436, 787–788; *OR*, 17(1):592, 602–603, 614–615, 626–627; *OR*, 52(2):398; Brown, "Van Dorn's Operations in Northern Mississippi," 159–160.
44. *OR*, 17(1):594; Thomas Jordan and J. P. Pryor, *The Campaigns of Lieut.-Gen. N. B. Forrest, and of Forrest's Cavalry, with Portraits, Maps, and* Illustrations (New Orleans: Blelock & Company, 1868), 204, 206; Smith, *Early Struggles for Vicksburg*, 308; N. B. Newkirk to mother, January 4, 1863, Jack K. Carmichael Papers, ISL; Joseph Hotz

to wife, January 5, 1863, Joseph Hotz Letters, IHS; Vincent Wicker to friend, January 28, 1863, Vincent Wicker Papers, IHS.

45. *OR*, 52(2):408; Battle Report, January 4, 1863, George H. Daniel Correspondence, AHC; George W. Morgan, "The Assault on Chickasaw Bluffs," in *Battles and Leaders of the Civil War*, 4 vols. (New York: Century Company, 1884–1887), 3:463; W. H. H. Monroe, "A Battle in the Bayous," *National Tribune*, October 5, 1899; Stephen D. Lee, "Details of Important Work by Two Confederates Telegraph Operators, Christmas Eve, 1862 Which Prevented the Almost Complete Surprise of the Confederate Army at Vicksburg," *Publications of the Mississippi Historical Society*, 13 vols. (Oxford: Mississippi Historical Society, 1904), 8:52–53; Phillip Fall to William Mickle, January 6, 1905, Civil War Collection, EU.

46. *OR*, 17(1):613; Smith, *Early Struggles for Vicksburg*, 363; Alexander McGahey to family, January 7, 1863, Alexander F. McGahey Letters, OCM.

47. *OR*, 17(1):607, 672, 681; William Hays to father, February 23, 1863, William B. Hays Letter, OHS.

48. Isaac O. Shelby Diary, January 3, 1863, UNC; Smith, *Early Struggles for Vicksburg*, 368, 380–381; Stephen Lee to Paul Hamilton, January 14, 1863, Paul Hamilton Papers, USC; Dempsey Ashford Diary, January 1, 1863, VICK; Henry Morgan to Ellen, January 4, 1863, Henry T. Morgan Letters, CWD, USAHEC.

49. David Dixon Porter, *Incidents and Anecdotes of the Civil War* (New York: D. Appleton and Company, 1885), 129; Isaac O. Shelby Diary, January 1, 1863, UNC.

50. Smith, *Early Struggles for Vicksburg*, 416–428; John Smith to Teresa, December 20, 1862, John M. Smith Letters, CWD, USAHEC.

51. Curtis P. Lacey Diary, January 2, 1863, NL.

Chapter 2. "Can the Enemy Intend Another Attempt to Approach Vicksburg?"

1. E. B. Long, *The Civil War Day by Day: An Almanac, 1861–1865* (New York: Doubleday, 1971), 306.

2. J. B. Jones, *A Rebel War Clerk's Diary: At the Confederate States Capital, Volume 1: April 1861–July 1863*, 2 vols., James I. Robertson, Jr., ed. (Lawrence: University Press of Kansas, 2015), 1:202.

3. C. W. Burgess to Mr. Dykes, May 10, 1863, Dykes Family Papers, OHS; John Boucher to Mr. Sawyer, March 2, 1863, Boucher Family Papers, CWD, USAHEC; Mather Oakhurst to Jerry, March 1, 1863, Tallman Family Letters, Civil War Collection, MHS; James Burton to parents, February 14, 1863, James R. Burton Letters, TSLA; William Lewis to family, March 18, 1863, William E. Lewis Letters, SHSMC; Jean Powers Soman and Frank L. Byrne, eds., *A Jewish Colonel in the Civil War: Marcus M. Spiegel of the Ohio Volunteers* (Kent, OH: Kent State University Press, 1985), 230; Allen C. Richard, Jr., and Mary Margaret Higginbotham Richard, *The Defense of Vicksburg: A Louisiana Chronicle* (College Station: Texas A&M University Press, 2004), 108; Jonas Roe to wife,

April 30, 1863, Jonas H. Roe Papers, ALPL; Hovey Manuscript, undated, IU, 38; Andrew Sproul to wife, January 26, 1863, Andrew J. Sproul Papers, UNC; Cyrus Miller to sister, March 25, 1863, Cyrus K. Miller Letter, VICK; Simon Helmick Diary, February 24, 1863, VICK; Townsend Heaton to Jack, February 11, 1863, Townsend P. Heaton Papers, OHS.

4. Smith, *Early Struggles for Vicksburg*, 416–428.

5. Marszalek, Nolen, and Gallo, eds., *Personal Memoirs of Ulysses S. Grant*, 294; Ernest A. Warden Diary, February 18, 1863, OHS; Richard L. Kiper, *Major General John A. McClernand: Politician in Uniform* (Kent, OH: Kent State University Press, 1999), 21, 149, 153–155; Smith, *Early Struggles for Vicksburg*, 316, 318; Lionel Sheldon Memoir, undated, Lionel A. Sheldon Papers, HL.

6. Michael B. Ballard, *Pemberton: The General Who Lost Vicksburg* (Jackson: University Press of Mississippi, 1991), 128–129; Richard and Richard, *The Defense of Vicksburg*, 110; Rowland Chambers Diary, January 2, 1863, LSU. For Pemberton, see also Michael B. Ballard, "Misused Merit: The Tragedy of John C. Pemberton," in *Confederate Generals in the Western Theater*, 4 vols., Lawrence Lee Hewitt and Arthur W. Bergeron Jr., eds. (Knoxville: University of Tennessee Press, 2010), 103–121, and Michael B. Ballard, "Misused Merit: The Tragedy of John C. Pemberton," in *Civil War Generals in Defeat*, Steven E. Woodworth, ed. (Lawrence: university Press of Kansas, 1999), 141–160. See also the John C. Pemberton Papers, UNC, VICK, MDAH, and NARA.

7. *OR*, 17(2):724, 726–728; M. R. Banner to wife, January 22, 1863, Banner Family Letters, OCM; A. S. Abrams, *A Full and Detailed History of the Siege of Vicksburg* (Atlanta: Intelligencer Steam Power Presses, 1863), 9.

8. Mansfield Lovell to G. W., October 26, 1862, Mansfield Lovell Papers, HL; Dabney Maury to Walker, December 23, 1862, Dabney H. Maury Letter, GLI; Jones, *A Rebel War Clerk's Diary*, 1:208, 226, 266.

9. *OR*, 17(2):728, 732, 742; Ephraim McD. Anderson, *Memoirs: Historical and Personal Including the Campaigns of the First Missouri Confederate Brigade* (St. Louis: Times Publishing Co., 1868), 245; Smith, *Early Struggles for Vicksburg*, 27.

10. *OR*, 17(2):727, 733, 788–789; *OR*, 52(2):381–382; Harry Pflager to friend, October 16, 1862, Harry W. Pflager Letters, MHS; M. V. Lovell to Josie, October 22, 1862, Mansfield Lovell Letter, Lionel Baxter Collection, CWTI, USAHEC, copy in Baxter Collection, UM. For Van Dorn, see Robert G. Hartje, *Van Dorn: The Life and Times of a Confederate General* (Nashville: Vanderbilt University Press, 1967) and Arthur B. Carter, *The Tarnished Cavalier: Major General Earl Can Dorn, C.S.A.* (Knoxville: University of Tennessee Press, 1999).

11. *OR*, 17(2):815–816; William C. Davis, *Jefferson Davis: The Man and His Hour, A Biography* (New York: Harper Collins, 1991), 492; Terrence J. Winschel, "The Absence of Will: Joseph E. Johnston and the Fall of Vicksburg," in *Confederate Generals in the Western Theater: Essays on America's Civil War*, 4 vols., Lawrence Lee Hewitt and Arthur W. Bergeron Jr., eds. (Knoxville: University of Tennessee Press, 2010), 2:80; Craig L. Symonds, *Joseph E. Johnston: A Civil War Biography* (New York: Norton, 1992), 193.

12. *OR*, 17(2):815, 823, 827; Robert K. Krick, "'Snarl and Sneer and Quarrel': General Joseph E. Johnston and an Obsession with Rank," in *Leaders of the Lost Cause: New*

Perspectives on the Confederate High Command, Gary W. Gallagher and Joseph T. Glatthaar, eds. (Mechanicsburg, PA: Stackpole Books, 2004), 188.

13. *OR*, 17(2):823, 826; General Orders 23, January 8, 1863, Orders and Circulars, 1862–1865, RG 109, E 94, NARA.

14. *OR*, 17(2):815, 822; *OR*, 52(2):403; David Spigener to sister, January 5, 1863, David Spigener Letter, VICK.

15. *OR*, 17(2):816–817, 820–822.

16. *OR*, 17(2):816–817, 820–823, 826–827.

17. William P. Chambers, "My Journal," *Publications of the Mississippi Historical Society*, *Centenary Series*, 5 vols. (Jackson: Mississippi Historical Society, 1925), 5:257; John Meriwether to wife, January 6, 1863, Meriwether Family Papers, UA; Samuel Addison Whyte Diary, January 1, 1863, UNC.

18. *OR*, 17(2):816–821, 823, 826–828.

19. *OR*, 17(2):817, 819, 823, 830–831.

20. William Rorer to Susan, January 15, 1863, W. A. Rorer Letters, DU, copies in MDAH; John Wilson to Lizzie, January 3, 1863, John A. Wilson Letters, MDAH; Matthias Murphy to Floyd, January 18, 1863, Matthias Murphy Letter, OCM.

21. *OR*, 17(2):824–825, 828–829, 831; John Wilson to Lizzie, January 11, 1863, John A. Wilson Letters, MDAH.

22. *OR*, 17(2):830; *OR*, 52(2):404; Chambers, "My Journal," 257.

23. Wilson E. Chapel Diary, January 1, 1863, Dekalb County Historical and Genealogical Society; Adoniram Withrow to wife, January 1 and 3, 1863, Adoniram Judson Withrow Papers, UNC; Curtis P. Lacey Diary, January 2, 1863, NL.

24. Luther Cowan Diary, January 3, 1863, Luther H. Cowan Papers, TSLA; W. R. Eddington Memoir, undated, ALPL, 4.

25. *OR*, 17(2):518.

26. *OR*, 17(2):518; Luther Cowan Diary, January 3 and 5, 1863, and Luther Cowan to family, January 4, 1863, Luther H. Cowan Papers, TSLA.

27. *OR*, 17(2):518, 526, 530–531, 544; Simon and Marszalek, eds., *PUSG*, 7:163, 171; David Palmer to parents, January 3, 1863, David James Palmer Papers, UIA.

28. *OR*, 17(2):518–519, 525, 533; Luther Cowan Diary, January 3, 1863, Luther H. Cowan Papers, TSLA.

29. *OR*, 17(2):521, 523–525.

30. *OR*, 17(2):523, 525, 530–532, 540–541.

31. *OR*, 17(2):542; Luther Cowan to family, January 4, 1863, Luther H. Cowan Papers, TSLA.; Bela St. John to father, January 9, 1863, Bela T. St. John Papers, LC.

32. *OR*, 17(2):527, 544–545, 548, 550–551; Thomas White to sister, January 21, 1863, Thomas K. White Papers, OHS; George Hildt to parents, January 31, 1863, George H. Hildt Letters, OHS; G. B. Thurston to R. B. Mitchell, January 13, 1863, Hugh Ewing Papers, RG 94, E 159, NARA. For the Ewings, see Kenneth J. Heinman, *Civil War Dynasty: The Ewing Family of Ohio* (New York: New York University Press, 2012).

33. *OR*, 17(2):545, 548–550; Simon and Marszalek, eds., *PUSG*, 7:191, 226; John Sullivan to wife, January 4, 1863, John M. Sullivan Papers, OHS.

34. *OR*, 17(2):551; Thomas Crawford to H. R. Gamble, January 20, 1863, Hamilton R. Gamble Papers, MHS.

35. *OR*, 17(2):545, 548–550, 552.

36. Adoniram Withrow to wife, January 8, 1863, Adoniram Judson Withrow Papers, UNC; John Higgins to Nancy, January 4, 1863, John A. Higgins Papers, ALPL.

37. *OR*, 17(2):528.

38. *OR*, 17(2):534; Soman and Byrne, eds., *A Jewish Colonel in the Civil War*, 220; Porter, *Incidents and Anecdotes*, 131.

39. *OR*, 17(2):519, 528; Soman and Byrne, eds., *A Jewish Colonel in the Civil War*, 217–218.

40. *OR*, 17(2):528–529.

41. *OR*, 17(2):529; Virgil Moats to Eliza, January 3, 1863, Virgil H. Moats Papers, UMC.

42. *OR*, 17(2):530, 534, 538–539, 540; *OR*, 17(1):700–701; Mary Bobbitt Townsend, *Yankee Warhorse: A Biography of Major General Peter Osterhaus* (Columbia: University of Missouri Press, 2010), 69; Soman and Byrne, eds., *A Jewish Colonel in the Civil War*, 218; Abraham Lincoln to Frederick Steele, January 22, 1863, Frederick Steele Papers, SU; Peter Osterhaus to E. D. Sanders, January 8, 1863, Letters Sent, RG 393, E 3221, NARA; Special Orders 6, January 6, 1863, General Orders, RG 393, E 5545, NARA.

43. *OR*, 17(2):535–536; Rachel Sherman Thorndike, ed., *The Sherman Letters: Correspondence Between General and Senator Sherman from 1837 to 1891* (New York: Charles Scribner's Sons, 1894), 181–182.

44. *OR*, 17(2):536, 883; *OR*, 17(1):701; Bjorn Skaptason, "The Chicago Light Artillery at Vicksburg," *Journal of the Illinois State Historical Society* 106, nos. 3–4 (Fall/Winter 2013): 428; Joseph Fardell to parents, January 3, 1863, Joseph A. Fardell Papers, Civil War Collection, MHS; James H. St. John Diary, January 6–7, 1863, ISL; Sidney Little to mother, January 11, 1863, Sidney Little Papers, UMC; Dick Ransom to friends, January 9, 1863, Dick Ransom Collection, BCAS; Don Pardee to unknown, January 4, 1863, Don Pardee Papers, TU.

45. William T. Sherman, *Memoirs of General William T. Sherman: Written by Himself*, 2 vols. (New York: D. Appleton and Co., 1875), 1:296–297; Porter, *Incidents and Anecdotes*, 131; Samuel Gordon to wife, January 10, 1863, Samuel Gordon Papers, ALPL; Edward Reichhelm Memoir, undated, Edward P. Reichhelm Papers, LC, 23.

46. *OR*, 17(2):541; *OR*, 17(1):701; William Rand to father, January 13, 1863, William L. Rand Letters, ALPL; Dick Ransom to friends, January 9, 1863, Dick Ransom Collection, BCAS.

47. *OR*, 17(2):537, 546, 553; William L. Shea, *Union General: Samuel Ryan Curtis and Victory in the West* (Lincoln, NE: Potomac Books, 2023), 139–161.

48. *OR*, 17(2):536–538; *ORN*, 24:98; R. B. Beck Diary, January 5, 1863, Mrs. Douglas W. Clark Papers, LC.

49. *OR*, 17(2):547; Isaac O. Shelby Diary, January 4, 1863, UNC; James Boyd Diary, January 8, 1863, ALPL; Edward Reichhelm Memoir, undated, Edward P. Reichhelm Papers, LC, 22.

50. *OR*, 17(1):702, 722, 745, 754; *ORN*, 24:100, 102–103; Edwin C. Bearss, *The Vicksburg Campaign*, 3 vols. (Dayton, OH: Morningside, 1985), 1:364; Soman and Byrne, eds., *A Jewish Colonel in the Civil War*, 219; S. W. Bishop, "The Battle of Arkansas Post," *Confederate Veteran* 5, no. 4 (April 1897): 151–153; Leo M. Kaiser, ed., "The Civil War Diary of Florison D. Pitts," *Mid-America: An Historical Review* 40, no. 1 (January 1958): 30, copy in Florison D. Pitts Papers, CHM; James C. Sinclair Diary, January 7, 1863, CHM; R. R. Hall Diary, "Diary of Pioneer Wichitan Reveals Horrors of War," January 5, 1863, OCM; Isaac O. Shelby Diary, January 8, 1863, UNC; Edward Reichhelm Memoir, undated, Edward P. Reichhelm Papers, LC, 22; R. B. Beck Diary, January 8, 1863, Mrs. Douglas W. Clark Papers, LC.

51. *OR*, 17(1):702, 722, 745, 754; *ORN*, 24:100, 102–103; Soman and Byrne, eds., *A Jewish Colonel in the Civil War*, 219; Bishop, "The Battle of Arkansas Post," 151–153; Kaiser, ed., "The Civil War Diary of Florison D. Pitts," 30; James C. Sinclair Diary, January 7, 1863, CHM; R. R. Hall Diary, "Diary of Pioneer Wichitan Reveals Horrors of War," January 5, 1863, OCM; Isaac O. Shelby Diary, January 8, 1863, UNC; Edward Reichhelm Memoir, undated, Edward P. Reichhelm Papers, LC, 22; R. B. Beck Diary, January 8, 1863, Mrs. Douglas W. Clark Papers, LC.

52. *ORN*, 24:99–101; R. B. Beck Diary, January 9, 1863, Mrs. Douglas W. Clark Papers, LC; Frederick Davis to parents, January 11, 1863, Frederick E. Davis Papers, EU.

53. *ORN*, 24:100–101.

54. *OR*, 17(1):703–704, 719, 722, 733 754–755, 765, 771; Adoniram Withrow to wife, January 15, 1863, Adoniram Judson Withrow Papers, UNC; Special Orders 34, January 10, 1863, Benjamin Spooner Letters, ISL; Edward Reichhelm Memoir, undated, Edward P. Reichhelm Papers, LC, 24, 26; John Bowman to friends, January 17, 1863, John A. Bowman Letters, OCM; R. B. Beck Diary, January 10, 1863, Mrs. Douglas W. Clark Papers, LC.

55. *OR*, 17(1):703–704, 722, 754–755, 765, 771; *ORN*, 24:104, 107–108; Sherman, *Memoirs*, 1:298; William Royal Oake, *On the Skirmish Line Behind a Friendly Tree: The Civil War Memoirs of William Royal Oake, 26th Iowa Volunteers*, Stacy D. Allen, ed. (Helena, MT: Farcountry Press, 2006), 68; Curtis P. Lacey Diary, January 10, 1863, NL; George R. Yost Diary, January 10, 1863, ALPL; Frederick Davis to parents, January 11, 1863, Frederick E. Davis Papers, EU.

56. *OR*, 17(2):552; Soman and Byrne, eds., *A Jewish Colonel in the Civil War*, 218; William Rand to father, January 13, 1863, William L. Rand Letters, ALPL.

Chapter 3. "We Have Disposed of This Tough Little Nut"

1. Roger E. Coleman, *The Arkansas Post Story: Arkansas Post National Monument* (Santa Fe: Southwest Cultural Resources Center, 1987), 1–3. For a huge amount of historic Arkansas Post information, see the Core Family Papers, UAR.

2. *OR*, 17(1):705; Coleman, *The Arkansas Post Story*, 3–16; Soman and Byrne, eds., *A Jewish Colonel in the Civil War*, 219.

3. Coleman, *The Arkansas Post Story*, 19–49; Kiper, *Major General John A. McClernand*, 156.

4. Coleman, *The Arkansas Post Story*, 51–93.

5. Coleman, *The Arkansas Post Story*, 95–101.

6. Coleman, *The Arkansas Post Story*, 103–106; *OR*, 17(1):721.

7. *OR*, 17(1):709.

8. *OR*, 17(1):780; Ezra J. Warner, *Generals in Gray: The Lives of the Confederate Commanders* (Baton Rouge: Louisiana State University Press, 1959), 49–50; "Gen. Thomas J. Churchill," *Confederate Veteran* 15, no. 3 (March 1907): 122–123.

9. *OR*, 17(1):780, 783, 790–791; Bearss, *The Vicksburg Campaign*, 1:371, 419; Bruce S. Allardice, *Confederate Colonels: A Biographical Register* (Columbia: University of Missouri Press, 2008), 136; "Arkansas Post," *Southern Historical Society Papers* 22 (1894): 10–13; "Capt. John W. Dunnington," *Confederate Veteran* 4, no. 3 (March 1896): 84.

10. *OR*, 17(1):780, 790.

11. *OR*, 17(1):780, 783, 790–791.

12. *OR*, 17(1):781.

13. *OR*, 17(1):705, 755, 760, 781, 783–784; Bearss, *The Vicksburg Campaign*, 1:351; Bishop, "The Battle of Arkansas Post," 152; William Jolly to family, January 17, 1863, William H. Jolly Letters, Keen Family Papers, SHSIIC, copy in VICK.

14. *OR*, 17(1):781, 783–784; L. V. Caraway, "The Battle of Arkansas Post," *Confederate Veteran* 14, no. 3 (March 1906): 127–128; L. V. Caraway, "The Battle of Arkansas Post," *Confederate Veteran* 36, no. 5 (May 1928): 171–173.

15. *OR*, 17(1):784.

16. *OR*, 17(1):791.

17. *OR*, 17(1):792.

18. *OR*, 17(1):781, 792.

19. Isaac O. Shelby Diary, January 11, 1863, UNC. For Fort Henry, see Smith, *Grant Invades Tennessee*.

20. *ORN*, 24:104–106; Frederick Davis to father, January 29, 1863, Frederick E. Davis Papers, EU.

21. *ORN*, 24:108; *OR*, 17(1):706.

22. *ORN*, 24:112–113, 119; William Rand to father, January 13, 1863, William L. Rand Letters, ALPL.

23. *ORN*, 24:111, 115–116, 118.

24. *ORN*, 24:106, 109–110, 118; R. R. Hall Diary, "Diary of Pioneer Wichitan Reveals Horrors of War," January 11, 1863, OCM; Frederick Davis to parents, January 11, 1863, and Davis to unknown, January 14, 1863, and Frederick E. Davis Diary, January 13, 1863, Frederick E. Davis Papers, EU; Lyman Humphrey to mother, January 19, 1863, Lyman U. Humphrey Correspondence, KHS.

25. *ORN*, 24:108, 110, 118–119; *OR*, 17(1):779; R. B. Beck Diary, January 11, 1863, Mrs. Douglas W. Clark Papers, LC.

26. *OR*, 17(1):780; *ORN*, 24:106, 116.

27. *OR*, 17(1):760.

28. *ORN*, 24:108; *OR*, 17(1):781.

29. *OR*, 17(1):755, 772, 778.

30. *OR*, 17(1):704, 755–756, 772; *Military History and Reminiscences of the Thirteenth Regiment of Illinois Volunteer Infantry in the Civil War in the United States 1861–1865* (Chicago: Women's Temperance Publishing Association, 1892), 290–291; Wilson E. Chapel Diary, January 11, 1863, De Kalb County Historical and Genealogical Society; Edward Reichhelm Memoir, undated, Edward P. Reichhelm Papers, LC, 29; R. B. Beck Diary, January 11, 1863, Mrs. Douglas W. Clark Papers, LC.

31. *OR*, 17(1):755–756.

32. *OR*, 17(1):756, 765, 769, 772, 781, 792; Skaptason, "The Chicago Light Artillery at Vicksburg," 429; Edward Reichhelm Memoir, undated, Edward P. Reichhelm Papers, LC, 30; Charles J. Sauter Diary, January 11, 1863, VICK.

33. *OR*, 17(1):756; William Hays to father, February 23, 1863, William B. Hays Letter, OHS.

34. *OR*, 17(1):717–718, 757; Edward Reichhelm Memoir, undated, Edward P. Reichhelm Papers, LC, 26; Israel P. Rumsey Diary, January 11, 1863, NL; Israel Rumsey to parents, January 16, 1863, Israel P. Rumsey Papers, NL.

35. *OR*, 17(1):766; William G. Bek, ed., "The Civil War Diary of John T. Buegel, Union Soldier, Part II," *Missouri Historical Review* 40, no. 4 (July 1946): 504, original in SHSMC; Elisha Coon to family, January 13, 1863, Elisha Coon Letters, SHSIDM; Isaac O. Shelby Diary, January 11, 1863, UNC; Robert Moyle to parents, January 13, 1863, Robert J. Moyle Letters, UIA; Charles Miller Memoir, undated, VICK, 34, later published as Stewart Bennett and Barbara Tillery, eds., *The Struggle for the Life of the Republic: A Civil War Narrative by Brevet Major Charles Dana Miller, 76th Ohio Volunteer Infantry* (Kent, OH: Kent State University Press, 2004).

36. *OR*, 17(1):757–758, 766, 793; Bek, ed., "The Civil War Diary of John T. Buegel, Union Soldier, Part II," 505.

37. *OR*, 17(1):766–769, 795; Isaac O. Shelby Diary, January 11, 1863, UNC; Calvin Ainsworth Diary, January 11, 1863, UMB, copy in VICK; Bek, ed., "The Civil War Diary of John T. Buegel, Union Soldier, Part II," 505; Charles A. Willison, *Reminiscences of a Boy's Service with the 76th Ohio, In the Fifteenth Army Corps, Under General Sherman, During the Civil War, By That "Boy" at Three Score* (Menasha, WI: The George Banta Publishing Company, 1908), 40–43; Lyman Humphrey to mother, January 19, 1863, Lyman U. Humphrey Correspondence, KHS; Charles Miller Memoir, undated, VICK, 32–36.

38. *OR*, 17(1):757, 769–770, 793; *Supplement to the Official Records of the Union and Confederate Armies*, 100 vols. (Wilmington, NC: Broadfoot Publishing Company, 1994), 3:349–350, hereafter cited as *SOR*; Ezra J. Warner, *Generals in Blue: Lives of the Union Commanders* (Baton Rouge: Louisiana State University Press, 1964), 523; Oake, *On the Skirmish Line*, 67–70; Adoniram Withrow to wife, January 12, 1863, Adoniram Judson Withrow Papers, UNC; Joseph Child Diary, January 11, 1863, UIA.

39. *OR*, 17(1):772–773, 775–776; U. G. McAlexander, *History of the Thirteenth Regiment United States Infantry, Compiled from Regimental Records and Other Sources* (N.p.:

Regimental Press, Thirteenth Infantry, 1905), 31; *In Memoriam: Charles Ewing* (Philadelphia: J. B. Lippincott, 1888), 43; Unknown to parents, January 13, 1863, John and Alexander Harper Papers, ALPL; James Boyd Diary, January 11, 1863, ALPL; Charles Bullard Memoir, 1918, CWD, USAHEC, 3.

40. *OR*, 17(1):773, 774, 776–777, 793; Walter George Smith, *Life and Letters of Thomas Kilby Smith, Brevet Major-General United States Volunteers, 1820–1877* (New York: G. P. Putnam's Sons, 1898), 30, 258–260; *The Story of the Fifty-fifth Regiment Illinois Volunteer Infantry in the Civil War, 1861–1865* (Clinton, MA: W. J. Coulter, 1887), 199–204; Robert J. Van Dorn and Daniel A. Masters, eds., *The 57th Ohio Veteran Volunteer Infantry* (Perrysburg, OH: Columbian Arsenal Press, 2021), 132; "Military History of Captain Thomas Sewell," 1889, DU; James H. St. John Diary, January 11, 1863, ISL; William Kennedy to wife and mother, January 8, 12, and 16, William J. Kennedy Papers, ALPL; Andrew McCornack to parents, January 18, 1863, Andrew McCornack Letters, Wiley Sword Collection, USAHEC; Thomas R. Latimer to parents, January 12, 1863, Latimer Family Collection, USAHEC; William Jolly to family, January 17, 1863, William H. Jolly Letters, SHSIIC.

41. *OR*, 17(1):786, 793.

42. *OR*, 17(1):756–757, 759, 795.

43. Eric Michael Burke, *Soldiers from Experience: The Forging of Sherman's Fifteenth Army Corps, 1862–1863* (Baton Rouge: Louisiana State University Press, 2023), 111; Van Dorn and Masters, eds., *The 57th Ohio Veteran Volunteer Infantry*, 133; R. B. Beck Diary, January 11, 1863, Mrs. Douglas W. Clark Papers, LC.

44. *OR*, 17(1):733; George W. Morgan Biographical Sketch, undated, George W. Morgan Papers, LC; George Russell to friend, January 18, 1863, George W. Russell Papers, ALPL.

45. *OR*, 17(1):722–723; F. H. Mason, *The Forty-second Ohio Infantry: A History of the Organization and Services of That Regiment in the War of the Rebellion; With Biographical Sketches of Its Field Officers and a Full Roster of the Regiment* (Cleveland, OH: Cobb, Andrews and Co., Publishers, 1876), 171–179; Enos Pierson, *Proceedings of Eleven Reunions, Held by the 16th Regiment, O.V.I.* (N.p.: n.p., 1887), 72; Andrew Sproul to Fanney, January 14, 1863, Andrew J. Sproul Papers, UNC.

46. *OR*, 17(1):725–726, 729, 731, 733.

47. *OR*, 17(1):729–730, 736; George Chittenden to wife, January 14, 1863, Chittenden Family Papers, ISL.

48. *OR*, 17(1):784.

49. *OR*, 17(1): 716, 723, 730–731, 732–735, 736–738; T. B. Marshall, *History of the Eighty-third Ohio Volunteer Infantry, The Greyhound Regiment* (Cincinnati: n.p., 1912), 55–58; R. B. Scott, *The History of the 67th Regiment Indiana Infantry Volunteers, War of the Rebellion* (Bedford, IN: Herald Book and Job Print, 1892), 18–21.

50. *OR*, 17(1):784.

51. *OR*, 17(1):716, 730–731, 733–734, 737–742, 744; *OR*, 24(2):237; John A. Bering and Thomas Montgomery, *History of the Forty-Eighth Ohio Vet. Vol. Inf.* (Hillsboro, OH: Highland News Office, 1880), 65–68; Terrence J. Winschel, ed., *The Civil War Diary of a Common Soldier: William Wiley of the 77th Illinois Infantry* (Baton Rouge: Louisiana

State University Press, 2001), 32; W. H. Bentley, *History of the 77th Illinois Volunteer Infantry, Sept. 2, 1862–July 10, 1865* (Peoria, IL: Edward Hine, Printer, 1883), 115–118; David Grier to Anna, January 30, 1863, Grier Family Papers, MHS; W. R. Eddington Memoir, undated, ALPL, 5.

52. *OR*, 17(1):754; Frank H. Mason, "Arkansas Post," August 28, 1884, *National Tribune*; Townsend, *Yankee Warhorse*, 73; William A. Sypher Diary, January 11, 1863, CHM; Asa Sample Diary, January 11, 1863, ISL, copy in IHS; Peter J. Perrine Diary, January 11, 1863, OHS.

53. *OR*, 17(1):717, 728, 746–747, 749–750; Soman and Byrne, eds., *A Jewish Colonel in the Civil War*, 221; Kaiser, ed., "The Civil War Diary of Florison D. Pitts," 31; Carolyn S. Bridge, ed., *These Men Were Heroes Once: The Sixty-ninth Indiana Volunteer Infantry* (West Lafayette, IN: Twin Publications, 2005), 89–95; William Brown to father, January 12, 1863, William L. Brown Papers, CHM; George Roberts to wife, January 13, 1863, George W. Roberts Collection, ISL; George B. Marshall Reminiscences, 1912, ISL, 33–36; Chase Dickinson to father, January 12, and Chase Dickinson to Louise, January 17, 1863, Chase H. Dickinson Correspondence, NL; William Rand to father, January 13, 1863, William L. Rand Letters, ALPL; Dick Ransom to friends, January 9, 1863, Dick Ransom Collection, BCAS.

54. *OR*, 17(1):784–785.

55. *OR*, 17(1):722, 749, 751, 753; William Brown to father, January 12, 1863, William L. Brown Papers, CHM.

56. *OR*, 17(1):749, 753; Thomas Buchanan to parents, January 29, 1863, Thomas Buchanan Letter, CWD, USAHEC.

57. *OR*, 17(1):781.

58. *OR*, 17(1):708–709.

59. *OR*, 17(1):781.

60. *OR*, 17(1):781, 785.

61. *OR*, 17(1):785.

62. *OR*, 17(1):724, 749, 753, 773, 776, 795–796; *ORN*, 24:108.

63. *OR*, 17(1):748, 770, 794; William Rand to father, January 13, 1863, William L. Rand Letters, ALPL.

64. *OR*, 17(1):707, 724, 726, 731; *ORN*, 24:106, 108, 116; Henry Walke, *Naval Scenes and Reminiscences of the Civil War in the United States, on the Southern and Western Waters During the Years 1861, 1862 and 1863* (New York: F. R. Reed, 1877), 343.

65. *OR*, 17(1):794; *ORN*, 24:108.

66. *OR*, 17(1):724, 726, 731–732, 734, 740, 742–743, 748–749, 756–757, 771; Sherman, *Memoirs*, 1:300–301; Oake, *On the Skirmish Line*, 71; Joseph Lesslie to wife, January 20, 1863, Joseph Lesslie Letters, VICK; Adoniram Withrow to wife, January 12, 1863, Adoniram Judson Withrow Papers, UNC; R. B. Beck Diary, January 11, 1863, Mrs. Douglas W. Clark Papers, LC; Henry Shubert to sister, January 14, 1863, Henry A. Shubert Letter, VICK.

67. *OR*, 17(1):724, 726, 731–732, 734, 740, 742–743, 748–749, 756–757, 771; R. B. Beck Diary, January 11, 1863, Mrs. Douglas W. Clark Papers, LC; Sherman, *Memoirs*,

1:300–301; Frederick Davis to parents, January 11, 1863, Frederick E. Davis Papers, EU; Oake, *On the Skirmish Line*, 71; Henry Shubert to sister, January 14, 1863, Henry A. Shubert Letter, VICK; Joseph Lesslie to wife, January 20, 1863, Joseph Lesslie Letters, VICK; Adoniram Withrow to wife, January 12, 1863, Adoniram Judson Withrow Papers, UNC.

68. *ORN*, 24:111, 126; *OR*, 17(1):708, 724, 757, 764, 771; Wilson E. Chapel Diary, January 12 and 13, 1863, De Kalb County Historical and Genealogical Society; William Brown to father, January 12, 1863, William L. Brown Papers, CHM; "Military History of Captain Thomas Sewell," 1889, DU; Charles Miller Memoir, undated, VICK, 36; W. R. Eddington Memoir, undated, ALPL, 5.

69. *OR*, 17(1):719, 757, 781–782, 787; *OR*, 17(2):557; Van Dorn and Masters, eds., *The 57th Ohio Veteran Volunteer Infantry*, 134; Chase Dickinson to father, January 12, 1863, Chase H. Dickinson Correspondence, NL.

70. *OR*, 17(1):699; Sherman, *Memoirs*, 1:301; Soman and Byrne, eds., *A Jewish Colonel in the Civil War*, 221; Leonard Loomis to wife, January 12, 1863, Leonard Loomis Letters, Douwe B. Yntema Collection, AM; "Memoir of Chickasaw Bayou and Arkansas Post," 1888, Richard M. Hunt Collection, USAHEC, 8.

71. *OR*, 17(1):700, 720–721, 764; *ORN*, 24:111, 120, 126; "Frank M. Bell," *Confederate Veteran* 11, no. 1 (January 1903): 32; Leonard Loomis to wife, January 15, 1863, Leonard Loomis Letters, Douwe B. Yntema Collection, AM; W. R. Eddington Memoir, undated, ALPL, 5; Carlos Colby Memoir, undated, Bilby Collection, USAHEC, 1–2.

72. *ORN*, 24:113–115; *OR*, 17(1):710; George Chittenden to wife, January 17, 1863, Chittenden Family Papers, ISL; Israel P. Rumsey Diary, January 17, 1863, NL; General Orders 28, February 13, 1863, General Orders, RG 393, E 5541, NARA.

73. *ORN*, 24:117–118, 127, 697.

74. *OR*, 17(1):721–722, 774; Chase Dickinson to Louise, January 17, 1863, Chase H. Dickinson Correspondence, NL.

75. *OR*, 17(1):782, 786–790; Sherman, *Memoirs*, 1:300; Leonard Loomis to wife, January 12, 1863, Leonard Loomis Letters, Douwe B. Yntema Collection, AM.

76. *OR*, 17(1):709.

77. *OR*, 17(1):763.

78. *OR*, 17(2):553.

79. *OR*, 17(2):553–554.

80. *OR*, 17(2):557.

81. Marszalek, Nolen, and Gallo, eds., *Personal Memoirs of Ulysses S. Grant*, 304; Brooks D. Simpson, *Ulysses S. Grant: Triumph Over Adversity, 1822–1865* (Boston: Houghton Mifflin Company, 2000), 169; Smith, *Life and Letters of Thomas Kilby Smith*, 31; George Chittenden to wife, January 14, 1863, Chittenden Family Papers, ISL.

CHAPTER 4. "THE WORK OF CHANGING THE CHANNEL OF THE MISSISSIPPI"

1. Davis, *Jefferson Davis*, 70–73.
2. Bearss, *The Vicksburg Campaign*, 1:449; Marszalek, Nolen, and Gallo, eds.,

Personal Memoirs of Ulysses S. Grant, 308; "Again in Vicksburg," June 7, 1894, *National Tribune*.

3. *OR*, 15:25–26; David Porter to Gustavus Fox, June 30, 1862, David Dixon Porter Correspondence, VICK; Theodore St. John to Janie, January 27, 1863, Theodore E. St. John Papers, LC.

4. *OR*, 15:25–26; "Let's Call it Williams' Canal, Not Grant's," Jackson *Clarion Ledger*, October 20, 1990, copy in Grant's Canal File, MDAH.

5. *OR*, 15:27–28, 31; Theodore St. John to Janie, January 27, 1863, Theodore E. St. John Papers, LC.

6. *OR*, 15:31–32.

7. *OR*, 15:31–32; Warner, *Generals in Blue*, 564.

8. *OR*, 15:494, 514–515, 517, 519.

9. *OR*, 15: 514–515, 517, 519; Adoniram Withrow to wife, January 23, 1863, Adoniram Judson Withrow Papers, UNC; Curtis P. Lacey Diary, January 22, 1863, NL.

10. Soman and Byrne, eds., *A Jewish Colonel in the Civil War*, 227; Israel P. Rumsey Diary, January 22, 1863, NL.

11. *OR*, 17(2):554, 560, 564–565, 569; William Rogers to Manerva, February 13, 1863, Antebellum and Civil War Collection, AHC; James Giauque to family, January 23, 1863, Giauque Family Papers, UIA; Special Orders 10, January 10, 1863, Charles S. Hamilton Papers, RG 94, E 159, NARA.

12. *OR*, 17(2):556, 559, 564, 568–569; Lewis Van Tuyl to cousin, March 11, 1863, Lewis Van Tuyl Papers, UMC; James McPherson to George Cullum, December 25, 1863, James B. McPherson Papers, RG 94, E 159, NARA; Elizabeth J. Whaley, *Forgotten Hero: General James B. McPherson* (New York: Exposition Press, 1955), 126; Cyrus Delany to brothers, January 17, 1863, Cyrus M. Delany Letters, TSLA; General Orders 21, January 18, 1863, General Orders, RG 393, E 6305, NARA.

13. *OR*, 17(2):556, 560, 563–564, 574; *Harper's Weekly* front page, February 7, 1863; General Orders 9, January 14, 1863, Orders and Letters, RG 393, E 3227, NARA.

14. *OR*, 17(2):560–563; Frederick Davis to unknown, January 14, 1863, Frederick E. Davis Papers, EU.

15. *OR*, 17(2):564, 567.

16. *OR*, 17(2):566–567, 579; Kiper, *Major General John A. McClernand*, 182.

17. *OR*, 17(2):566–567, 579; Kiper, *Major General John A. McClernand*, 182.

18. Albert D. Richardson, *A Personal History of Ulysses S. Grant* (Hartford, CT: American Publishing Company, 1868), 284; Schmelzer, "Politics, Policy, and General Grant," 218; Simon and Marszalek, eds., *PUSG*, 7:225; Adam Badeau, *Military History of Ulysses S. Grant, From April, 1861, to April, 1865*, 2 vols. (New York: D. Appleton & Co., 1881), 1:151; James H. Wilson to Adam Badeau, March 9, 1867, James H. Wilson Papers, LC, copy in Vicksburg file, USGPL.

19. *OR*, 17(2):567; Thomas Crawford to H. R. Gamble, January 20, 1863, Hamilton R. Gamble Papers, MHS.

20. *OR*, 17(2):566, 569, 574, 578; *OR*, 24(3):3; Luther Cowan Diary, January 16–17, 1863, Luther H. Cowan Papers, TSLA; Cyrus Delany to brothers, January 17, 1863, Cyrus

M. Delany Letters, TSLA; Unknown to father, January 15, 1863, Rowland-Shilladay Papers, IHS; Francis M. Johnson Diary, January 15, 1863, ALPL; Andrew Bush to Mary, January 20, 1863, Andrew Bush Letters, OCM; W. A. Gordin to Don Pardee and Peter Osterhaus to W. B. Scates, February 9, 1863, Letters Sent, RG 393, E 3221, NARA.

21. *OR*, 17(2):580–581, 587–588; Simon and Marszalek, eds., *PUSG*, 8:30–32. For more on Sherman's war against newspapers, see John F. Marszalek, *Sherman's Other War: The General and the Civil War Press* (Kent, OH: Kent State University Press, 1999).

22. *OR*, 17(2):581–590, 882–883; William E. Parrish, *Frank Blair: Lincoln's Conservative* (Columbia: University of Missouri Press, 1998), 161; Sylvanus Cadwallader, *Three Years with Grant*, Benjamin P. Thomas, ed. (Lincoln: University of Nebraska Press, 1996), 45–46; Missouri Legislature Petition, February 1863, Civil War Collection, MHS.

23. *OR*, 17(2):570–571, 586, 883.

24. *OR*, 17(2):568, 571–572, 575; Sherman, *Memoirs*, 1:302; William Dupray to family, February 23, 1863, Morgan Family Papers, UW; Oake, *On the Skirmish Line*, 92; Thomas H. Johnson to wife, 1863, Thomas H. Johnson Letter, Chapman University; Carlos Colby Memoir, undated, Bilby Collection, USAHEC, 3; Wilson E. Chapel Diary, January 13 and 15, 1863, De Kalb County Historical and Genealogical Society; Richard Puffer to sister, January 12, 1863, Richard R. Puffer Papers, CHM; Adoniram Withrow to wife, January 15, 1863, Adoniram Judson Withrow Papers, UNC; Charles A. Dunn Diary, January 24, 1863, Frank E. Gunn Collection, AM; John Jones to parents, January 18, 1863, John G. Jones Papers, LC; Curtis P. Lacey Diary, January 19, 1863, NL; Israel Rumsey to parents, January 16, 1863, Israel P. Rumsey Letters, NL.

25. *OR*, 17(2):570–571, 573; *OR*, 24(1):8–9; Don Pardee to unknown, January 20, 1863, Don Pardee Papers, TU.

26. *OR*, 24(3):5–6; *OR*, 24(1):8–9; Simon and Marszalek, eds., *PUSG*, 7:230; Donald Stoker, *The Grand Design: Strategy and the U.S. Civil War* (New York: Oxford University Press, 2010), 245; David Massey to sister, January 26, 1863, David T. Massey Letters, Civil War Collection, MHS; William Rigby to brother, February 11, 1863, William T. Rigby Papers, UIA.

27. *OR*, 24(3):18–19; *OR*, 24(1):10; Marszalek, Nolen, and Gallo, eds., *Personal Memoirs of Ulysses S. Grant*, 306; Simon and Marszalek, eds., *PUSG*, 7:253, 270; Oscar E. Stewart Memoir, undated, OCM, 17.

28. *OR*, 24(3):18–19; *OR*, 24(1):10; Simon and Marszalek, eds., *PUSG*, 7:253, 270; Marszalek, Nolen, and Gallo, eds., *Personal Memoirs of Ulysses S. Grant*, 306.

29. *OR*, 24(1):11; William L. B. Jenney, "With Sherman and Grant from Memphis to Chattanooga: A Reminisce," in *Military Essays and Recollections: Papers Read Before the Commandery of the State of Illinois, Military Order of the Loyal Legion of the United States*, 5 vols. (Chicago: Cozzens and Beaton Company, 1907), 4:200; Charles to friend, March 15, 1863, Letter from Charles, VICK; General Orders 13, January 30, 1863, Ulysses S. Grant Papers, RG 94, E 159, NARA and Orders and Letters, RG 393, E 3227, NARA.

30. *OR*, 24(1):12–13; Simon and Marszalek, eds., *PUSG*, 7:264.

31. *OR*, 17(2):570, 573; *OR*, 24(1):8–9.

32. *OR*, 17(2):571, 889; Thorndike, ed., *The Sherman Letters*, 184; Marszalek, Nolen, and Gallo, eds., *Personal Memoirs of Ulysses S. Grant*, 308; George D. Carrington Diary, January 26, 1863, CHM.

33. *OR*, 17(2):570, 573; *OR*, 24(1):8–9; Steven E. Woodworth, *Nothing but Victory: The Army of the Tennessee, 1861–1865* (New York: Knopf, 2005), 287; General Orders 11, January 17, 1863, Watson Smith Papers, USNA; Bek, ed., "The Civil War Diary of John T. Buegel, Union Soldier, Part II," 506; Thomas Butler Gunn Diary, January 24, 1863, MHS; Adoniram Withrow to wife, January 22, 1863, Adoniram Judson Withrow Papers, UNC; General Orders 11, January 17, 1863, Orders and Letters, RG 393, E 3227, NARA.

34. Richard and Richard, *The Defense of Vicksburg*, 112; John Meriwether to wife, January 24, 1863, Meriwether Family Papers, UA; Isaac Coleman to wife, January 24, 1863, Isaac B. Coleman Letter, ADAH; Edmund Pettus to wife, March 21, 1863, Edmund W. Pettus Papers, ADAH; William Lowery Diary, January 6, 1863, ADAH; Elbert D. Willett Diary, January 23 and 25, 1863, ADAH; Isaac Coleman to wife, January 24, 1863, Isaac B. Coleman Letter, OCM; J. A. S. Milligan to Postmaster, January 9, 1863, D. D. Hammack Letters, OCM; William Montgomery to sister, March 7, 1863, William A. Montgomery Letters, Ann Sturdivant Collection, CWD, USAHEC; Luke Roberts to unknown, January 24, 1863, Luke R. Roberts Letters, HCWRTC, USAHEC.

35. J. A. S. Milligan to Postmaster, January 9, 1863, D. D. Hammack Letters, OCM; Thomas Gore Memoir, undated, USM, 67; John Meriwether to wife, January 24, 1863, Meriwether Family Papers, UA; Isaac Coleman to wife, January 24, 1863, Isaac B. Coleman Letter, ADAH; Edmund Pettus to wife, March 21, 1863, Edmund W. Pettus Papers, ADAH; Richard and Richard, *The Defense of Vicksburg*, 112; William Lowery Diary, January 6, 1863, ADAH; Elbert D. Willett Diary, January 23 and 25, 1863, ADAH; Luke Roberts to unknown, January 24, 1863, Luke R. Roberts Letters, HCWRTC, USAHEC; Isaac Coleman to wife, January 24, 1863, Isaac B. Coleman Letter, OCM; William Montgomery to sister, March 7, 1863, William A. Montgomery Letters, Ann Sturdivant Collection, CWD, USAHEC; General Orders 6, January 22, 1863, Orders and Circulars, 1862–1865, RG 109, E 97, NARA.

36. Raymond Trahan to Elizabeth, January 30, 1863, Raymond Trahan Letter, OCM; Jared Sanders to unknown, January 23, 1863, Jared Sanders Letters, OCM, copy in VICK; Joel C. Watson Diary, January 29, 1863, Grenada Public Library.

37. *OR*, 17(2):838; *OR*, 24(3):597, 602; *OR*, 52(2):410.

38. *OR*, 17(2):832–833, 838.

39. *OR*, 24(3):596–597, 608.

40. *OR*, 17(2):832–833, 835–836, 841; *OR*, 24(3):591.

41. *OR*, 17(2):833–835, 838–839; *OR*, 24(3):8, 598; Special Orders 19, January 20, 1863, Orders and Circulars, 1862–1865, RG 109, E 97, NARA.

42. *OR*, 17(2):837, 839–840, 846–847; *OR*, 24(3):591, 596, 610–611; General Orders 33, February 1, 1863, Orders and Circulars, 1862–1865, RG 109, E 94, NARA.

43. *OR*, 24(3):591, 593–595, 598–599, 602, 607–610; *OR*, 52(2):438; George Powell Clarke, *Reminiscence and Anecdotes of the War for Southern Independence* (N.p.: n.p.,

n.d.), 75; Henry Morgan to Ellen, February 20, 1863, Henry T. Morgan Letters, CWD, USAHEC; William L. Roberts Diary, January 31, 1863, ADAH; John Pemberton to W. A. Broadwell, January 14, 1863, Letters and Telegrams Sent, RG 109, Chapter II, Vol. 57, NARA.

44. Clarke, *Reminiscence and Anecdotes*, 75, 77–79.

45. *OR*, 24(3):607.

46. *OR*, 24(3):592–593, 596, 599, 611.

47. *OR*, 24(3):593, 600–601, 604; Arthur W. Bergeron, "Martin Luther Smith and the Defense of the Lower Mississippi River Valley, 1861–1863," in *Confederate Generals in the Western Theater: Essays on America's Civil War*, 4 vols., Lawrence Lee Hewitt and Arthur W. Bergeron Jr., eds. (Knoxville: University of Tennessee Press, 2011), 3:74; John Pemberton to J. R. Waddy, January 7, 1863, John C. Pemberton Papers, RG 109, E 131, NARA.

48. *OR*, 24(3):593.

49. *OR*, 24(3):594–595, 600, 603, 606; Bearss, *The Vicksburg Campaign*, 2:262; Clarke, *Reminiscence and Anecdotes*, 86–87; J. H. Jones Account of Wilkinson Guards, undated, J. H. H. Claiborne Papers, UNC, 2.

50. *OR*, 17(2):823.

51. *OR*, 17(2):547, 551–552, 836–837, 839; Chester G. Hearn, *Admiral David Dixon Porter: The Civil War Years* (Annapolis: Naval Institute Press, 1996), 181; *Military History and Reminiscences of the Thirteenth Regiment of Illinois Volunteer Infantry*, 296–297; Albert H. Bodman Memoir, undated, Albert H. Bodman Papers, CHM, 26.

52. *OR*, 24(3):4–5, 8; *ORN*, 23:181; James C. Sinclair Diary, January 24, 1863, CHM; Arnold Rickard Diary, January 21, 1863, CHM; Andrew Sproul to wife, February 27 and March 15, 1863, Andrew J. Sproul Papers, UNC; Nicholas Ollemar to Lisette, January 23, 1863, Nicholas Ollemar Letter, VICK; Don Pardee to unknown, January 29, 1863, Don Pardee Papers, TU; Unknown to Jeanie Beery, January 23, 1863, Samuel S. Miner Papers, OHS.

53. William L. B. Jenney, "Personal Recollections of Vicksburg," in *Military Essays and Recollections: Papers Read before the Commandery of the State of Illinois, Military Order of the Loyal Legion of the United States*, 5 vols. (Chicago: The Dial Press, 1899), 3:252–253.

54. *OR*, 24(3):5, 7, 13–14; *SOR*, 3:343–345; James C. Sinclair Diary, January 29, 1863, CHM; John Merrilies Diary, March 31 and April 20, 1863, CHM; Adoniram Withrow to wife, January 23, 1863, Adoniram Judson Withrow Papers, UNC; Isaac O. Shelby Diary, January 22, 1863, UNC; George Russell to friend, January 29, 1863, George W. Russell Papers, ALPL; Andrew McCornack to parents, February 1, 1863, Andrew McCornack Letters, Wiley Sword Collection, USAHEC; Smith, *Life and Letters of Thomas Kilby Smith*, 266; Clarkson Fogg to unknown, March 1, 1863, Clarkson Fogg Letters, VICK; James Giauque to family, January 23, 1863, Giauque Family Papers, UIA; John Jones to parents, January 30, 1863, John G. Jones Papers, LC; Isaac Jackson to unknown, February 8, 1863, Isaac Jackson Letters, UMC.

55. *OR*, 24(3):5, 7, 13–14; *SOR*, 3:343–345; L. A. Wailes, "A War Mystery,"

Confederate Veteran 29, no. 2 (February 1921): 65; James C. Sinclair Diary, January 29, 1863, CHM; John Merrilies Diary, March 31 and April 20, 1863, CHM; John Jones to parents, January 30, 1863, John G. Jones Papers, LC; Adoniram Withrow to wife, January 23, 1863, Adoniram Judson Withrow Papers, UNC; Isaac Jackson to unknown, February 8, 1863, Isaac Jackson Letters, UMC; Isaac O. Shelby Diary, January 22, 1863, UNC; George Russell to friend, January 29, 1863, George W. Russell Papers, ALPL; Andrew McCornack to parents, February 1, 1863, Andrew McCornack Letters, Wiley Sword Collection, USAHEC; Clarkson Fogg to unknown, March 1, 1863, Clarkson Fogg Letters, VICK; James Giauque to family, January 23, 1863, Giauque Family Papers, UIA.

56. *OR*, 24(3):6, 11; *OR*, 24(1):10; Simon and Marszalek, eds., *PUSG*, 7:231; Luther Cowan to wife, January 21, 1863, Luther H. Cowan Papers, TSLA; John D. Brownley Memoir, undated, Anders Collection, USAHEC, 1.

57. *OR*, 24(3):597; George Chittenden to wife, January 21, 1863, Chittenden Family Papers, ISL.

58. *OR*, 24(3):598–602, 604–606; *SOR*, 3:344–345.

59. *OR*, 24(3):7, 9–10; *OR*, 24(1):44, 117; Van Dorn and Masters, eds., *The 57th Ohio Veteran Volunteer Infantry*, 141.

60. *OR*, 24(3):10; Andrew Sproul to wife, January 26, 1863, Andrew J. Sproul Papers, UNC.

61. *OR*, 24(3):12; Cadwallader, *Three Years with Grant*, 28; Charles A. Dana, *Recollections of the Civil War* (New York: D. Appleton and Co., 1898), 28; Joseph Skipworth to wife, March 26, 1863, Joseph Skipworth Papers, SIU.

62. *OR*, 24(3):16–17; Soman and Byrne, eds., *A Jewish Colonel in the Civil War*, 231.

63. *OR*, 24(3):604; George Hildt to parents, January 31, 1863, George H. Hildt Letters, OHS.

64. *OR*, 24(3):605, 607, 608–609.

65. George B. Marshall Reminiscences, 1912, ISL, 37; James H. St. John Diary, January 27, 1863, ISL; William Jolly to family, March 7, 1863, William H. Jolly Letters, SHSIIC.

66. *OR*, 24(3):6, 11; *OR*, 24(1):10; Simon and Marszalek, eds., *PUSG*, 7:231; Luther Cowan to wife, January 21, 1863, Luther H. Cowan Papers, TSLA; John D. Brownley Memoir, undated, Anders Collection, USAHEC, 1.

67. *OR*, 24(1):8; *OR*, 24(3):9; Cadwallader, *Three Years with Grant*, 46; Van Dorn and Masters, eds., *The 57th Ohio Veteran Volunteer Infantry*, 142–143; John W. Chambers Diary, January 20, 1863, ISU.

68. *OR*, 24(3):12, 19.

69. *OR*, 24(3):10, 13, 15; *OR*, 24(1):10; Mary Amelia (Boomer) Stone, *Memoir of George Boardman Boomer* (Boston: Press of Geo. C. Rand & Avery, 1864), 242; Van Dorn and Masters, eds., *The 57th Ohio Veteran Volunteer Infantry*, 143; Parker Leeper to father, January 26, 1863, Parker Leeper Letter, OCM.

70. William F. Willey Diary, January 26, 1863, OHS.

71. *OR*, 24(3):10, 608.

72. *OR*, 24(3):9–11; Curtis P. Lacey Diary, January 25, 1863, NL; Louisa R. Conner

Memoir, 1905, MDAH, 11; Abraham Hagaman Memoir, 1873, MDAH, 30–31; Peter Osterhaus to W. B. Scates, April 8, 1863, Letters Sent, RG 393, E 3221, NARA.

73. *OR*, 24(1):10; Chase Dickinson to father, February 1, 1863, Chase H. Dickinson Correspondence, NL; Thomas H. Barton, *Autobiography of Dr. Thomas H. Barton, The Self-made Physician of Syracuse, Ohio* (Charleston: West Virginia Printing Co., 1890), 96; John Y. Simon, ed., *The Personal Memoirs of Julia Dent Grant [Mrs. Ulysses S. Grant]* (New York: G. P. Putnam's Sons, 1975), 111.

CHAPTER 5. "BUT GRANT IS ON TWO OTHER PROJECTS"

1. John Meriwether to wife, February 19, 1863, Meriwether Family Papers, UA; L. D. Bradley to wife, February 21, 1863, L. D. Bradley Letter, UNT; Civil War Diary, January 21, 1863, ALPL.

2. Kaiser, ed., "The Civil War Diary of Florison D. Pitts," 32; John Higgins to wife, January 17, 1863, John A. Higgins Papers, ALPL; Isaac O. Shelby Diary, February 9, 1863, UNC; Curtis P. Lacey Diary, February 8, 1863, NL.

3. *OR*, 17(2):836; Richard and Richard, *The Defense of Vicksburg*, 117, 120; Reuben H. Falconer Diary, February 6, 1863, OHS.

4. Kaiser, ed., "The Civil War Diary of Florison D. Pitts," 32, 34; John Barnes to uncle, March 29, 1863, John W. Barnes Letters, DU; Isaac Vanderwarker Diary, March 5, 1863, CWD, USAHEC; Charles Miller Memoir, undated, VICK, 37; Cyrus Randall to mother, April 2, 1863, Cyrus W. Randall Papers, ALPL.

5. Marszalek, Nolen, and Gallo, eds., *Personal Memoirs of Ulysses S. Grant*, 317; Price F. Kellogg Diary, January 15–February 28, 1863, ALPL; Sherman, *Memoirs*, 1:319; Daniel A. Masters, ed., *Sherman's Praetorian Guard: Civil War Letters of John McIntyre Lemmon, 72nd Ohio Volunteer Infantry* (Perrysburg, OH: Columbian Arsenal Press, 2017), 110; Sidney Little to brother, February 8, 1863, Sidney O. Little Papers, LSU; Soman and Byrne, eds., *A Jewish Colonel in the Civil War*, 238; Charles Miller Memoir, undated, VICK, 38; David Grier to Anna, March 1, 1863, Grier Family Papers, MHS; Smith, *Life and Letters of Thomas Kilby Smith*, 271; John B. Fletcher Diary, January 25, 1863, ALPL; Frank Tupper to mother, March 24, 1863, Frank W. Tupper Papers, ALPL; Adoniram Withrow to wife, January 26, 1863, Adoniram Judson Withrow Papers, UNC.

6. Cadwallader, *Three Years with Grant*, 54; Oake, *On the Skirmish Line*, 93; Van Dorn and Masters, eds., *The 57th Ohio Veteran Volunteer Infantry*, 150; Daniel Roberts to family, March 23, 1863, Daniel Roberts Correspondence, ISL; Flavius J. Thackara Diary, March 29, 1863, OHS; Regimental Orders 1, February 14, 1863, Ohio Knox Papers, OHS.

7. Marszalek, Nolen, and Gallo, eds., *Personal Memoirs of Ulysses S. Grant*, 317; Bridge, ed., *These Men Were Heroes Once*, 99, 110; Price F. Kellogg Diary, January 15–February 28, 1863, ALPL; J. Grecian, *History of the Eighty-third Regiment, Indiana Volunteer Infantry. For Three Years with Sherman* (Cincinnati: John F. Uhlhorn, Printer, 1865), 22; Sherman, *Memoirs*, 1:319; Masters, ed., *Sherman's Praetorian Guard*, 110;

Sidney Little to brother, February 8, 1863, Sidney O. Little Papers, LSU; Peter Osterhaus to Colonel, March 11, 1863, Letters Sent, RG 393, E 3221, NARA; Soman and Byrne, eds., *A Jewish Colonel in the Civil War*, 238; R. L. Howard, *History of the 124th Regiment Illinois Infantry Volunteers, Otherwise Known as the "Hundred and Two Dozen," From August, 1862, to August, 1865* (Springfield, IL: H. W. Rokker, 1880), 68; Charles Miller Memoir, undated, VICK, 38; David Grier to Anna, March 1, 1863, Grier Family Papers, MHS; John B. Fletcher Diary, January 25, 1863, ALPL; Frank Tupper to mother, March 24, 1863, Frank W. Tupper Papers, ALPL; Adoniram Withrow to wife, January 26, 1863, Adoniram Judson Withrow Papers, UNC; General Orders 15, February 16, 1863, and General Order 19, February 24, 1863, General and Special Orders, RG 393, E 3230, NARA.

8. Peter Osterhaus to W. B. Scates, February 11, 1863, and Peter Osterhaus to W. B. Scates, February 20, 1863, Letters Sent, RG 393, E 3221, NARA; James Boyd Diary, April 6, 1863, ALPL; Cyrus Randall to mother, March 9, 1863, Cyrus W. Randall Papers, ALPL; Field Orders, February 4, 1863, General Orders 21, March 2, 1863, General Orders 26, March 22, 1863, General Orders 28, March 25, 1863, and General Orders 40, April 24, 1863, General and Special Orders, RG 393, E 3230, NARA.

9. Sherman, *Memoirs*, 1:305; Soman and Byrne, eds., *A Jewish Colonel in the Civil War*, 236; George D. Carrington Diary, January 26, 1863, CHM; David Grier to Anna, February 4, 1863, Grier Family Papers, MHS.

10. *OR*, 24(1):44; Simon and Marszalek, eds., *PUSG*, 7:270, 309, 331, 351; Robert J. Burdette, *The Drums of the 47th* (Indianapolis: The Bobbs-Merrill Company, 1914), 141–142; George W. Gordon Diary, April 12, 1863, USAHEC; Cadwallader, *Three Years with Grant*, 54; Frank Blair to Christine, February 16, 1863, Frank and Montgomery Blair Papers, MHS.

11. *OR*, 24(1):81, 119, 121–122, 125; Simon and Marszalek, eds., *PUSG*, 7:368; Marszalek, Nolen, and Gallo, eds., *Personal Memoirs of Ulysses S. Grant*, 306; Kaiser, ed., "The Civil War Diary of Florison D. Pitts," 33; Lisa M. Brady, *War Upon the Land: Military Strategy and the Transformation of Southern Landscapes during the American Civil War* (Athens: University of Georgia Press, 2012), 50–52; Joseph A. Saunier, *A History of the Forty-seventh Regiment Ohio Veteran Volunteer Infantry, Second Brigade, Second Division, Fifteenth Army Corps, Army of the Tennessee* (Hillsboro, OH: The Lyle Printing Company, 1903), 120; George D. Carrington Diary, February 5–6, 1863, CHM; George Chittenden to wife, February 5, 1763, Chittenden Family Papers, ISL.

12. *OR*, 24(3):606; Noe, *Through the Howling Storm*, 243; John Wilson to Lizzie, March 2, 1863, John A. Wilson Letters, MDAH; R. A. Wilson to wife, February 21, 1863, R. A. Wilson Letter, OCM; David Grier to Anna, February 9 and 13, 1863, Grier Family Papers, MHS.

13. Richardson, *A Personal History of Ulysses S. Grant*, 292–293.

14. *OR*, 24(1):81, 119, 121–122, 125; Simon and Marszalek, eds., *PUSG*, 7:368; Marszalek, Nolen, and Gallo, eds., *Personal Memoirs of Ulysses S. Grant*, 306.

15. John Meriwether to wife, February 19, 1863, Meriwether Family Papers, UA; Curtis P. Lacey Diary, February 1, 1863, NL; Chase Dickinson to father, February 13, 1863,

Chase H. Dickinson Correspondence, NL; Thomas R. Latimer to parents, February 1, 1863, Latimer Family Collection, USAHEC.

16. *OR*, 24(3):35, 37–38, 42; Stone, *Memoir of George Boardman Boomer*, 245; Smith, *Life and Letters of Thomas Kilby Smith*, 280; John W. Chambers Diary, February 3, 1863, ISU; William Jolly to sister, February 11, 1863, Jolly Family Papers, IHS.

17. *OR*, 24(3):41, 50; *OR*, 17(2):889–897; Thorndike, ed., *The Sherman Letters*, 187–188, 197; Jeffrey N. Lash, *A Politician Turned General: The Civil War Career of Stephen Augustus Hurlbut* (Kent, OH: Kent State University Press, 2003), 122–124; Joseph Lesslie to wife, February 1863, Joseph Lesslie Letters, VICK; Special Field Order 1, February 11, 1863, Orders and Letters, RG 393, E 3227, NARA; F. H. Bruce to mother, April 21, 1863, Bruce Family Papers, ALPL; Hezekiah Clock to brother, February 15, 1863, Hezekiah C. Clock Letters, Anders Collection, USAHEC.

18. *OR*, 24(3):38, 40, 51–52; Thorndike, ed., *The Sherman Letters*, 191; Samuel Gordon to wife, March 1, 1863, Samuel Gordon Papers, ALPL; Isaac O. Shelby Diary, February 7, 1863, UNC.

19. *OR*, 24(1):14; John McClernand to David Porter, January 28, 1863, David Dixon Porter Papers, MHS.

20. *OR*, 24(1):14, 17, 119–120; *OR*, 24(3):37; George Russell to friend, January 28, 1863, George W. Russell Papers, ALPL; William Rand to brother, February 28, 1863, Rand Family Papers, ALPL; David Grier to Anna, February 17, 1863, Grier Family Papers, MHS.

21. *OR*, 24(3):33–34; *OR*, 24(1):14, 44–45; Simon and Marszalek, eds., *PUSG*, 7:268.

22. *OR*, 24(3):17; *OR*, 24(1):44; Curtis P. Lacey Diary, February 11, 1863, NL; Van Dorn and Masters, eds., *The 57th Ohio Veteran Volunteer Infantry*, 145.

23. *OR*, 24(3):18; "Grant's Failure at Lake Providence," *Confederate Veteran* 22, no. 10 (October 1914): 459–460.

24. *OR*, 24(1):15–16; *SOR*, 3:345–346; Woodworth, *Nothing but Victory*, 299; William W. Belknap, *History of the Fifteenth Regiment, Iowa Veteran Volunteer Infantry, from October, 1861, to August, 1865, When Disbanded at the End of the War* (Keokuk, IA: R. B. Ogden and Son, Print., 1887), 90; Simon and Marszalek, eds., *PUSG*, 7:278; Cyrus Randall to mother, March 8, 1863, Cyrus W. Randall Papers, ALPL; Kaiser, ed., "'In Sight of Vicksburg,'" 212, 215, 219; George D. Carrington Diary, March 23, 1863, CHM.

25. *OR*, 24(1):16; Wales W. Wood, *A History of the Ninety-fifth Regiment Illinois Infantry Volunteers, From its Organization in the Fall of 1862, Until Its Final Discharge from the United States Service, in 1865* (Chicago: Tribune Company's Book and Job Printing Office, 1865), 56.

26. *OR*, 24(3):32, 38.

27. *OR*, 24(3):33, 40; *SOR*, 3:346; Marszalek, Nolen, and Gallo, eds., *Personal Memoirs of Ulysses S. Grant*, 311; Van Dorn and Masters, eds., *The 57th Ohio Veteran Volunteer Infantry*, 145; John W. Chambers Diary, February 9, 1863, ISU.

28. *OR*, 24(3):41–42; George D. Carrington Diary, February 9, 1863, CHM; General Orders 31, March 1, 1863, General Orders, RG 393, E 6305, NARA.

29. *OR*, 24(3):43–44; James McPherson to soldiers, February 10, 1863, General Orders, RG 393, E 6305, NARA.

30. *OR*, 24(3):44; James Pickett Jones, *Black Jack: John A. Logan and Southern Illinois in the Civil War Era* (Carbondale: Southern Illinois University Press, 1967), 151; Luther Cowan to wife, February 7, 1863, Luther H. Cowan Papers, TSLA; George Roberts to wife, February 15, 1863, George W. Roberts Collection, ISL.

31. Simon and Marszalek, eds., *PUSG*, 7:311, 314, 321, 323; Marszalek, Nolen, and Gallo, eds., *Personal Memoirs of Ulysses S. Grant*, 311; Israel P. Rumsey Diary, February 18, 1863, NL.

32. William Vermilion to wife, February 4, 1863, William F. Vermilion Papers, UCSD; Marszalek, Nolen, and Gallo, eds., *Personal Memoirs of Ulysses S. Grant*, 310. For the expedition, see Timothy B. Smith, "Victory At Any Cost: The Yazoo Pass Expedition," *Journal of Mississippi History* 67, no. 2 (Summer 2007): 147–166.

33. *OR*, 24(1):10; *Journal of the Senate of the State of Mississippi at their Twelfth Session* (Jackson: Peter Isler, 1829), 18–19; "Official Report," June 21, 1828, Broadsides, MDAH; "The Siege of Vicksburg, Its Approaches by Yazoo Pass and Other Routes," 1863, LOC and LSU.

34. *OR*, 24(1):14; John Boucher to mother, March 14, 1863, Boucher Family Papers, CWD, USAHEC.

35. *ORN*, 24:228; *OR*, 24(1):371, 386; Woodworth, *Nothing but Victory*, 304; Simon and Marszalek, eds., *PUSG*, 7:246.

36. *OR*, 24(1):371–373; Van Dorn and Masters, eds., *The 57th Ohio Veteran Volunteer Infantry*, 145; William Rigby to brother, February 6 and 24, 1863, William T. Rigby Papers, UIA; Allen W. Miller Diary, February 25, 1863, LC.

37. *OR*, 24(1):373; *ORN*, 24:249; James Harrison Wilson, *Under the Old Flag: Recollections of Military Operations in the War for the Union, the Spanish War The Boxer Rebellion, Etc.*, 2 vols. (New York: D. Appleton and Co., 1912), 1:151–152.

38. *OR*, 24(1):374–375, 388; Larry A. McCluney, *The Yazoo Pass Expedition: A Union Thrust into the Delta* (Charleston: History Press, 2017), 64; George W. Brown, "Service in the Mississippi Squadron, and Its Connection with the Siege and Capture of Vicksburg," in *Personal Recollections of the War of the Rebellion: Addresses Delivered before the Commandery of the State of New York, Military Order of the Loyal Legion of the United States, 1883–1891*, 4 vols. (New York: The Commandery, 1891), 1:308–309.

39. *OR*, 24(1):374–375; *OR*, 24(3):36.

40. *OR*, 24(1):374–376, 387; *ORN*, 24:251, 258; George Ditto Diary, March 15, 1863, ALPL; Alexander Ewing to parents, February 14, 1863, Alexander K. Ewing Papers, ALPL; *History of the Forty-sixth Regiment Indiana Volunteer Infantry, September, 1861–September, 1865* (Logansport, IN: Press of Wilson, Humprheys and Co., 1888), 47; Cadwallader Washburn to Elihu Washburne, February 24, 1863, Abraham Lincoln Papers, LC.

41. *OR*, 24(1):374–376, 387; *ORN*, 24:251, 258; Cadwallader Washburn to Elihu Washburne, February 24, 1863, Abraham Lincoln Papers, LC; Alexander Ewing to parents, February 14, 1863, Alexander K. Ewing Papers, ALPL; George Ditto Diary, March 15, 1863, ALPL; *History of the Forty-sixth Regiment Indiana Volunteer Infantry*, 47.

42. *OR*, 24(3):36, 38–39, 55.

43. *OR*, 24(3):55–56.

44. *OR*, 24(1):17; *OR*, 24(3):55–56; Hearn, *Admiral David Dixon Porter*, 203; Simon and Marszalek, eds., *PUSG*, 7:347; William Vermilion to wife, February 4, 1863, William F. Vermilion Papers, UCSD.

45. *OR*, 24(3): 46–47, 49–51; Simon and Marszalek, eds., *PUSG*, 7:325; Special Orders 28, February 24, 1863, General Orders, RG 393, E 6305, NARA.

46. *OR*, 24(3):54–55; *OR*, 24(1):331–335, 339–341, 349, 356–360; Hugh Bay to wife, March 18, 1863, Hugh Bay Letters, IHS; Townsend Heaton to Jack, February 11, 1863, Townsend P. Heaton Papers, OHS.

47. *OR*, 24(3):30, 35, 38, 41, 45, 50, 54.

48. *OR*, 24(3):30, 35, 38, 41, 45, 50; Simon and Marszalek, eds., *PUSG*, 7:307.

49. *OR*, 24(3):22, 30, 35, 38–39, 42, 49; William Vermilion to wife, February 8 and 15, 1863, William F. Vermilion Papers, UCSD; William Rigby to brother, February 11, 1863, William T. Rigby Papers, UIA; Stanley D. Buckles, *Not Afraid to Go Any Whare: A History of the 114th Regiment Illinois Volunteer Infantry* (Bend, OR: Maverick Publications, 2019), 24; Israel Rumsey to parents, February 8, 1863, Israel P. Rumsey Letters, NL; Special Orders, February 8, 1863, and Special Orders 34, February 30, 1863, Orders and Letters, RG 393, E 3227, NARA; Hezekiah Clock to brother, February 15, 1863, Hezekiah C. Clock Letters, Anders Collection, USAHEC.

50. *OR*, 24(1):14; *OR*, 24(3):39, 160–161; William Merriman to Kittie, February 15, 1863, William H. Merriman Letters, TSLA; William Jolly to sister, February 11, 1863, Jolly Family Papers, IHS.

51. *OR*, 24(1):336–337; *ORN*, 24:217–219; Frederick Davis to mother, February 4, 1863, Frederick E. Davis Papers, EU; Richard and Richard, *The Defense of Vicksburg*, 115; Joseph D. Alison Diary, February 10, 1863, UNC, copy in MDAH and OCM; George Townsend to Ellen, February 5, 1863, George E. Townsend Letters, SHSM; Ellet description, undated, William F. Warren Papers, ALPL; Samuel Bartlett to brother, March 16, 1863, Bartlett Family Papers, TU; Isaac O. Shelby Diary, March 3, 1863, UNC.

52. *OR*, 24(1):17, 338–339; *OR*, 24(3):32–33; *ORN*, 24:223–224; Albert H. Bodman Memoir, undated, Albert H. Bodman Papers, CHM, 27–28; Curtis P. Lacey Diary, February 2, 1863, NL.

53. *OR*, 24(3):32–33, 36–37; Mary Cabell to George Corkhill, April 21, 1883, Mary Ellet Cabell Letter, TSLA.

54. *OR*, 24(3):39, 45, 49; *ORN*, 24:375–377; James C. Sinclair Diary, February 13, 1863, CHM; Joseph D. Alison Diary, February 24, 1863, UNC.

55. *OR*, 24(1):342–348.

56. *OR*, 24(1):343–344; John Wilson to Lizzie, February 1863, John A. Wilson Letters, MDAH.

57. N. J. Lillard to Crate, March 13, 1863, Lillard Family Papers, TSLA.

58. Wiley Bartlett to wife, January 26, 1863, Wiley Bartlett Letters, TSLA; George Jones to mother, February 18, 1863, George Jones Letters, TSLA; William Merriman to Kittie, February 15, 1863, William H. Merriman Letters, TSLA; Sam Bayless to wife,

February 11, 1863, Samuel D. Bayless Letters, TSLA; "Army Correspondence," February 18, 1863, Knoxville *Daily Register*.

59. *OR*, 24(3):614–616, 619, 624–625, 627–628, 1068–1069; Bearss, *The Vicksburg Campaign*, 1:597–613; Elijah Hall to parents, February 27, 1863, Elijah Hall Letters, TSLA; Harry P. Owens, *Steamboats and the Cotton Economy: River Trade in the Yazoo-Mississippi Delta* (Jackson: University Press of Mississippi, 1990), 54; N. J. Lillard to Crate, March 13, 1863, Lillard Family Papers, TSLA; John Wilson to Lizzie, February 25, 1863, John A. Wilson Letters, MDAH; Henry J. Reynolds Memoir, undated, CWTI, USAHEC, 4.

60. Wiley Bartlett to wife, January 16 and February 6, 1863, Wiley Bartlett Letters, TSLA; Richard and Richard, *The Defense of Vicksburg*, 115–118; William Merriman to Kittie, February 15, 1863, William H. Merriman Letters, TSLA; John Bond Diary, February 3, 1863, OCM.

61. *OR*, 24(3):615–616, 618, 622–623, 625.

62. *OR*, 24(3):616, 620, 626; Myers to colonel, February 13, Benjamin Spooner Letters, ISL.

63. *OR*, 24(3):615, 618, 621–624; *OR*, 52(2):421; Elijah Hall to father, February 27, 1863, Elijah Hall Letters, TSLA.

64. *OR*, 24(3):621–622.

65. *OR*, 24(3):620; L. D. Bradley to wife, February 21, 1863, L. D. Bradley Letter, UNT.

66. *OR*, 24(3):622–623; William Loring to John Pemberton, February 10, 1863, John C. Pemberton Papers, RG 109, E 131, NARA.

67. *OR*, 24(3):614, 619–620; Samuel Meek to Lula, February 22, 1863, Samuel M. Meek Papers, MDAH.

68. *OR*, 24(3):620.

69. Smith, *Early Struggles for Vicksburg*, 425–428.

70. *OR*, 24(3):620–622.

71. *OR*, 24(3):622–623; Dunbar Rowland and H. Grady Howell, Jr., *Military History of Mississippi: 1803–1898, Including a Listing of All Known Mississippi Confederate Military Units* (Madison, MS: Chickasaw Bayou Press, 2003), 529; Timothy B. Smith, *James Z. George: Mississippi's Great Commoner* (Jackson: University Press of Mississippi, 2012), 64.

72. *OR*, 24(3):626; Richard and Richard, *The Defense of Vicksburg*, 115; C. Y. Ford, "Pot Shot," *Confederate Veteran* 24, no. 4 (April 1916): 167–168.

Chapter 6. "The Prospect of Opening the Pass Is Encouraging"

1. James C. Cobb, *The Most Southern Place on Earth: The Mississippi Delta and the Roots of Regional Identity* (New York: Oxford University Press, 1992); Ownby and Wilson, eds., *The Mississippi Encyclopedia*, 327–328; Simon and Marszalek, eds., *PUSG*, 7:410.

2. Ownby and Wilson, eds., *The Mississippi Encyclopedia*, 327. The elevation and river level data also comes from online searches, particularly from the National Oceanic and Atmospheric Administration.

3. Davis, Perry, and Kirkley, *Atlas*, Plates 154 and 155; "The Siege of Vicksburg, Its Approaches by Yazoo Pass and Other Routes," 1863, Confederate Collection, Boston Atheneum.

4. Davis, Perry, and Kirkley, *Atlas*, Plates 154 and 155.

5. Davis, Perry, and Kirkley, *Atlas*, Plates 154 and 155.

6. Davis, Perry, and Kirkley, *Atlas*, Plates 154 and 155; George Chittenden to wife, February 25, 1863, Chittenden Family Papers, ISL.

7. *SOR*, 3:361–362; Arthell Kelley, "The Geography," in *A History of Mississippi*, 2 vols., Richard A. McLemore, ed. (Hattiesburg: University & College Press of Mississippi, 1973), 1:8–9; Isaac O. Shelby Diary, February 16, 1863, UNC; James McPherson to mother, February 26, 1863, Wilfred S. Foerster Collection, Rutherford B. Hayes Presidential Center.

8. Grabau, *Ninety-Eight Days*, 17; William Rorer to Susan, February 22, 1863, W. A. Rorer Letters, DU.

9. Joseph C. G. Kennedy, *Population of the United States in 1860: Compiled From the Original Returns of the Eighth Census Under the Direction of the Secretary of the Interior* (Washington, DC: Government Printing Office, 1864), 264–265; Clarke, *Reminiscence and Anecdotes*, 89; Smith, *The Mississippi Secession Convention*, 222–226; Election Returns, 1817–2007, Secretary of State Records, RG 28, Vol. 34, Box 2445, MDAH; Alexander Ewing to parents, March 6, 1863, Alexander K. Ewing Papers, ALPL.

10. Dunbar Rowland, *Mississippi; Comprising Sketches of Counties, Towns, Events, Institutions and Persons, Arranged in Cyclopedic Form*, 3 vols. (Atlanta: Southern Historical Printing Association, 1907), 2:91–96; *Military History and Reminiscences of the Thirteenth Regiment of Illinois Volunteer Infantry*, 299. See also Robert W. Harrison, "Levee Building in Mississippi Before the Civil War," *Journal of Mississippi History* 12, no. 2 (April 1950): 63–97, Robert W. Harrison, "Early State Flood-Control Legislation in the Mississippi Alluvial Valley," *Journal of Mississippi History* 23, no. 2 (April 1961): 104–126, and Lillian Pereyra, "James Lusk Alcorn and a Unified Levee System," *Journal of Mississippi History* 27, no. 1 (February 1965): 18–41.

11. Kennedy, *Population of the United States in 1860*, 264–269.

12. *OR*, 24(3):701; Ownby and Wilson, eds., *The Mississippi Encyclopedia*, 327–328; William Rorer to Susan, April 22, 1863, W. A. Rorer Letters, DU; John Hipple to granddaughter, undated, John Hipple Letter, OCM.

13. *OR*, 24(3):629, 636–637; Richard and Richard, *The Defense of Vicksburg*, 119; L. A. Fitzpatrick, "Obstructing Grant's Advance," *Confederate Veteran* 25, no. 1 (January 1917): 25.

14. *OR*, 24(3):629–632; Ben Giddens to wife, March 2, 1863, Ben Giddens Letters, OCM.

15. Chambers, "My Journal," 258; Richard and Richard, *The Defense of Vicksburg*, 120, 128; Wiley Bartlett to wife, March 12, 1863, Wiley Bartlett Letters, TSLA; John

Meriwether to wife, March 6, 1863, Meriwether Family Papers, UA; William Lowery Diary, March 6, 1863, ADAH; W. H. Tunnard, *A Southern Record: The History of the Third Regiment Louisiana Infantry* (Baton Rouge: n.p., 1866), 220; Charles Swift Northern, III, ed., *All Right Let Them Come: The Civil War Diary of an East Tennessee Confederate* (Knoxville: University of Tennessee Press, 2003), 65; M. R. Banner to wife, March 7, 1863, Banner Family Letters, OCM; Isaac Herring to wife, March 8, 1863, Isaac E. Herring Letters, OCM; John Barnes to sister, March 8, 1863, John W. Barnes Letters, DU; John Wilson to Lizzie, March 6, 1863, John A. Wilson Letters, MDAH; G. H. Burns to wife, March 12, 1863, George H. Burns Letters, VICK; General Orders 43 and 44, February 25–26, 1863, Orders and Circulars, 1862–1865, RG 109, E 94, NARA; William Jolly to family, February 21, 1863, William H. Jolly Letters, SHSIIC. Four had also been executed in June 1862 at Vicksburg. See E. T. Eggleston Diary, June 20, 1862, VICK.

16. *OR*, 24(3):629–632, 634–635, 639–640, 642–643, 646; *ORN*, 24:629; Philip Thomas Tucker, *Westerners in Gray: The Men of and Missions of the Elite Fifth Missouri Infantry Regiment* (Jefferson, NC: McFarland & Company, 1995), 110; Isaac Herring to wife, March 6, 1863, Isaac E. Herring Letters, OCM; Albert Castel, *General Sterling Price and the Civil War in the West* (Baton Rouge: Louisiana State University Press, 1968), 139; William A. Ruyle Memoir, undated, HCWRTC, USAHEC, 12; R. S. Bevier, *History of the First and Second Missouri Confederate Brigades 1861–1865 and From Wakaruse to Appomattox, A Military Anagraph* (St. Louis: Bryan, Brand and Company, 1879), 168; Dabney Maury to unknown, January 27, 1863, Frederick M. Dearborn Collection, HU; John Wilson to Lizzie, March 2, 1863, John A. Wilson Letters, MDAH.

17. *OR*, 24(3):629.

18. *OR*, 24(3):629; Brandon Franke, "Waul's Texas Legion: Towards Vicksburg," *East Texas Historical Journal* 53, no. 1 (2015): 6–7.

19. *OR*, 24(3):633.

20. *OR*, 24(3):629; L. D. Bradley to wife, February 21, 1863, L. D. Bradley Letter, UNT.

21. *OR*, 24(3):629–630; F. W. Merrius, "The 'Bones' of the Star of the West," *Confederate Veteran* 7, no. 10 (October 1899): 457–458; "History of the 'Star of the West,'" *Confederate Veteran* 2, no. 4 (April 1894): 120; Hannis S. Smith, "The Futile Star of the West," *Journal of Mississippi History* 14, no. 1 (January 1952): 63–66; Audrey Glenn, "A Vanderbilt at Greenwood: The Star of the West," *Journal of Mississippi History* 16, no. 4 (October 1954): 258–267; Frank Blair to unknown, January 17, 1863, Blair Family Papers, LC.

22. *OR*, 24(3):630; *OR*, 24(1):415.

23. *OR*, 24(3):638, 644; *OR*, 24(1):415; Owens, *Steamboats and the Cotton Economy*, 56; McCluney, *The Yazoo Pass Expedition*, 72–73; William Loring to John Pemberton, February 21, 1863, John C. Pemberton Papers, RG 109, E 131, NARA.

24. *OR*, 24(3):639–640, 643; Isaac Brown to John Pemberton, February 24, 1863, John C. Pemberton Papers, RG 109, E 131, NARA.

25. *OR*, 24(3):641, 643–646; Larry J. Daniel, *Engineering in the Confederate Heartland* (Baton Rouge: Louisiana State University Press, 2022), 78–79; S. H. Lockett, "The

Defense of Vicksburg," in *Battles and Leaders of the Civil War*, 4 vols. (New York: Century Company, 1884–1887), 3:484–485; William Loring to John Pemberton, March 13, 1863, John C. Pemberton Papers, RG 109, E 131, NARA.

26. *OR*, 24(3):644–645; Map of Yazoo Pass, 1956, Yazoo Pass File, MDAH.

27. *OR*, 24(1):360–361, 378, 381, 387–388; Hovey Manuscript, undated, IU, 45; William F. Hollingsworth Diary, February 22, 1863, OCM; Harry Watts Reminiscence, 1915, ISL, 63; Cadwallader Washburn to Elihu Washburne, February 24, 1863, Abraham Lincoln Papers, LC; Augustus Sinks Journal, undated, ISL, 27; James L. Alcorn Diary, February 11, 1863, MDAH.

28. *OR*, 24(1):360–361, 378, 381, 387–388; Cadwallader Washburn to Elihu Washburne, February 24, 1863, Abraham Lincoln Papers, LC; William F. Hollingsworth Diary, February 22, 1863, OCM; Harry Watts Reminiscence, 1915, ISL, 63; Augustus Sinks Journal, undated, ISL, 27.

29. *OR*, 24(1):401–402; Simon and Marszalek, eds., *PUSG*, 7:442.

30. *OR*, 24(1):402; 49; Richard J. Fulfer, *A History of the Trials and Hardships of the Twenty-Fourth Indiana Volunteer Infantry* (Indianapolis: Indianapolis Printing Company, 1913), 49; Scott, *The History of the 67th Regiment Indiana Infantry Volunteers*, 26–27; William Rigby to brother, February 24, 1863, William T. Rigby Papers, UIA; Oliver Scott to John Noble, 1863, Oliver H. P. Scott Letter, BCAS; William Rigby Journal, February 20, 1863, William T. Rigby Papers, UIA.

31. *OR*, 24(1):402.

32. *OR*, 24(1):377–378; Harry Watts Reminiscence, 1915, ISL, 64; Alexander Ewing to parents, February 28, 1863, Alexander K. Ewing Papers, ALPL; William Rigby Journal, February 16, 1863, William T. Rigby Papers, UIA.

33. *OR*, 24(1):360–361, 376; *OR*, 24(3):642; Sam Henderson to John Pemberton, February 19, 1863, John C. Pemberton Papers, RG 109, E 131, NARA; Cadwallader Washburn to Elihu Washburne, February 24, 1863, Abraham Lincoln Papers, LC.

34. *OR*, 24(1):376–378.

35. *ORN*, 24:244–245, 265; *OR*, 24(3):62; Charles Dana Gibson and E. Kay Gibson, *Assault and Logistics: Union Army Coastal and River Operations, 1861–1866* (Camden, ME: Ensign Press, 1995), 268; Mrs. Clinton Fisk to my dear madam, March 23, 1863, Frederick E. Davis Papers, EU; Bearss, *The Vicksburg Campaign*, 1:591, 593; Milt Shaw to Alf, March 10, 1863, Milton W. Shaw Letter, USM; James F. Mallinckrodt Diary, February 25, 1863, OCM; William Rigby Journal, February 23, 1863, William T. Rigby Papers, UIA; John Boucher to wife, March 18, 1863, Boucher Family Papers, CWD, USAHEC; George R. Yost Diary, February 20 and 25 and March 2, 1863, ALPL; Paul Dorweiler Diary, February 25, 1863, CWTI, USAHEC.

36. Thomas Lyons Diary, January 10, 1863, LC; James Fogle to family, March 8, 1863, James S. Fogle Papers, ISL.

37. John Rawlins to Elihu Washburne, May 26, 1863, William S. Hillyer Papers, University of Virginia; Catton, *Grant Moves South*, 387; Cadwallader Washburn to Elihu Washburne, February 24, 1863, Abraham Lincoln Papers, LC; Allen W. Miller Diary, February 25, 1863, LC; James L. Alcorn Diary, February 26, 1863, MDAH.

38. *OR*, 24(1):397–399; *ORN*, 24:245, 259–260; William Vermilion to wife, February 25 and March 1, 1863, William F. Vermilion Papers, UCSD; Milt Shaw to Alf, March 10, 1863, Milton W. Shaw Letter, USM; George Ditto Diary, March 14, 1863, ALPL; James Slack to wife, February 28, 1863, James R. Slack Letters, ISL.

39. *OR*, 24(1):388, 397–400; *ORN*, 24:246; William A. Russ Jr., ed., "The Vicksburg Campaign as Viewed by an Indiana Soldier," *Journal of Mississippi History* 19, no. 4 (October 1957): 265; William Vermilion to wife, March 1, 1863, William F. Vermilion Papers, UCSD; William Vermilion Diary, February 26 and 28 and March 2, 1863, UCSD; Frederick E. Davis Diary, February 27, 1863, Frederick E. Davis Papers, EU.

40. Allen W. Miller Diary, February 26–March 5, 1863, LC.

41. James Slack to wife, February 28, 1863, James R. Slack Letters, ISL; Green B. Raum, "With the Western Army," December 12, 1901, *National Tribune*; Pereyra, "James Lusk Alcorn and a Unified Levee System," 20; Timothy B. Smith, *Mississippi in the Civil War: The Home Front* (Jackson: University Press of Mississippi, 2010), 135–136; James L. Alcorn Diary, February 12–15, and 26–27, 1863, James L. Alcorn and Family Papers, MDAH; William Vermilion Diary, February 27, 1863, UCSD; Augustus Sinks Journal, undated, ISL, 28; George R. Yost Diary, February 28, 1863, ALPL.

42. James Slack to wife, February 28, 1863, James R. Slack Letters, ISL.

43. *OR*, 24(1):18; *OR*, 24(3):65; Peter Osterhaus to W. B. Scates, February 24, 1863, Letters Sent, RG 393, E 3221, NARA; Kaiser, ed., "The Civil War Diary of Florison D. Pitts," 32; Tunnard, *A Southern Record*, 219; James C. Sinclair Diary, February 22, 1863, CHM; William A. Sypher Diary, February 22, 1863, CHM; Adoniram Withrow to wife, March 10, 1863, Adoniram Judson Withrow Papers, UNC; William Jolly to family, February 21, 1863, William H. Jolly Letters, SHSIIC; Samuel Lougheed to wife, April 30, 1863, Samuel D. Lougheed Papers, UW; Special Orders 276, February 25, 1863, General Orders, RG 393, E 5545, NARA.

44. *OR*, 24(1):18; *OR*, 24(3):65; Peter Osterhaus to W. B. Scates, February 24, 1863, Letters Sent, RG 393, E 3221, NARA; Kaiser, ed., "The Civil War Diary of Florison D. Pitts," 32; Tunnard, *A Southern Record*, 219; James C. Sinclair Diary, February 22, 1863, CHM; William A. Sypher Diary, February 22, 1863, CHM; Adoniram Withrow to wife, March 10, 1863, Adoniram Judson Withrow Papers, UNC; William Jolly to family, February 21, 1863, William H. Jolly Letters, SHSIIC; Samuel Lougheed to wife, April 30, 1863, Samuel D. Lougheed Papers, UW; Special Orders 276, February 25, 1863, General Orders, RG 393, E 5545, NARA.

45. *OR*, 24(1):18; *OR*, 24(3):59–60, 637; Luther Cowan to wife, February 18, 1863, and Luther Cowan to Mollie, February 25, 1863, Luther H. Cowan Papers, TSLA; Eugene Duncan Memoir, undated, OCM, 3; James McPherson to mother, February 26, 1863, Wilfred S. Foerster Collection, Rutherford B. Hayes Presidential Center.

46. *OR*, 24(3):58–61, 73; George R. Lee Diary, March 3, 1863, ALPL.

47. *OR*, 24(3):58.

48. *OR*, 24(3):41, 59, 62–63, 71.

49. *OR*, 24(3):61, 66–67, 69, 77–78, 636; Curtis P. Lacey Diary, February 25, 1863, NL; Israel P. Rumsey Diary, March 4, 1863, NL; Thomas White to mother, March 6,

1863, Thomas K. White Papers, OHS; Dabney H. Maury, *Recollections of a Virginian in the Mexican, Indian, and Civil Wars* (New York: Charles Scribner's Sons, 1894), 181–182; O. B. Brumback to Lucius Wing, January 30, 1863, Lucius B. Wing Correspondence, OHS; *SOR*, 3:350–352; Jonathan Beach to wife, February 28, 1863, Jonathan H. Beach Letters, OHS; William T. Mumford Diary, March 1, 1863, OCM; Archie Thompson Diary, April 15, 1863, OCM.

50. *OR*, 24(3):54, 56–57, 68, 73.

51. *OR*, 24(3):53–54; *OR*, 24(1):350; Simon and Marszalek, eds., *PUSG*, 7:357–358; John Merrilies Diary, March 21, 1863, CHM; John McClernand to David Porter, January 25, 1863, David Dixon Porter Papers, MHS.

52. *OR*, 24(3):349–355, 651; Clarke, *Reminiscence and Anecdotes*, 91; W. L. Ritter, "An Incident of the Deer Creek Expedition of 1863," *Southern Historical Society Papers* 9, no. 6 (June 1881): 280–281; Scott, *The History of the 67th Regiment Indiana Infantry Volunteers*, 24; Marshall, *History of the Eighty-third Ohio Volunteer Infantry*, 62–63; John Jones to parents, February 27 and March 1, 1863, John G. Jones Papers, LC; William Christie to brother, February 5, 1863, James C. Christie and Family Papers, MNHS; John N. Bell Diary, April 6, 1863, OHS; Henry Franks to sister, March 22, 1863, Henry W. Franks Letters, OHS; Samuel W. Ferguson Memoirs, undated, VICK, 31–33, copy in Samuel W. Ferguson Papers, LSU.

53. *OR*, 24(3):631.

54. *OR*, 24(1):18; *OR*, 24(3):61–62, 636, 642; "The Mystery of the Indianola," Port Royal, South Carolina *The New South*, March 28, 1863; H. B. Payton to sister, March 8, 1863, H. B. Payton Letters, OCM.

55. *OR*, 24(1):18–19; *OR*, 24(3):70–71, 642–643; Seth Phelps to David Porter, February 5, 1863, and David Porter to Seth Phelps, February 14, 1863, Seth Ledyard Phelps Letterbook, MHS.

56. *OR*, 24(1):361–370; *ORN*, 24:377–381; *SOR*, 3:347–350; Joiner, *Mr. Lincoln's Brown Water Navy*, 115–116; Samuel Bartlett to brother, March 16, 1863, Bartlett Family Papers, TU; William T. Mumford Diary, March 3, 1863, OCM; Carter Stevenson to John Pemberton, February 27, 1863, John C. Pemberton Papers, RG 109, E 131, NARA.

57. *OR*, 24(1):361–370; *ORN*, 24:377–381; *SOR*, 3:347–350; Joiner, *Mr. Lincoln's Brown Water Navy*, 115–116; William T. Mumford Diary, March 3, 1863, OCM; Carter Stevenson to John Pemberton, February 27, 1863, John C. Pemberton Papers, RG 109, E 131, NARA; Samuel Bartlett to brother, March 16, 1863, Bartlett Family Papers, TU.

58. *OR*, 24(3):67, 97–98, 646; *ORN*, 24:381, 397; Bearss, *The Vicksburg Campaign*, 1:674; Porter, *Incidents and Anecdotes*, 134; E. Cort Williams, "The Cruise of 'The Black Terror.' (Porter's Dummy at Vicksburg)," in *Sketches of War History 1861–1865: Papers Read Before the Ohio Commandery of the Military Order of the Loyal Legion of the United States*, 9 vols. (Cincinnati: Robert Clarke Company, 1890), 3:144–165; "Destruction of the Indianola," Vicksburg *Whig*, March 5, 1863; Curtis P. Lacey Diary, March 11, 1863, NL; Hearn, *Admiral David Dixon Porter*, 201; Winchester Hall, *The Story of the 26th Louisiana Infantry, In the Service of the Confederate States* (N.p.: n.p., 1890), 56; William L. Shea and Terrence J. Winschel, *Vicksburg Is the Key: The Struggle for the*

Mississippi River (Lincoln: University of Nebraska Press, 2003), 68; R. R. Hall Diary, "Diary of Pioneer Wichitan Reveals Horrors of War," February 25, 1863, OCM; Samuel Gordon to wife, March 1, 1863, Samuel Gordon Papers, ALPL; William Kennedy to wife, March 13, William J. Kennedy Papers, ALPL; Samuel Lougheed to Jennie, March 8, 1863, Samuel D. Lougheed Papers, ALPL; Israel P. Rumsey Diary, February 26, 1863, NL; William F. Willey Diary, February 25, 1863, OHS.

59. *OR*, 24(3):69–70.
60. Simon and Marszalek, eds., *PUSG*, 7:355.

Chapter 7. "The Yankee Boats Are Here"

1. Rowland, *Mississippi*, 2:72–74; Rowland, *Mississippi*, 1:803; Ownby and Wilson, eds., *The Mississippi Encyclopedia*, 727–728; "Memory of Historic Malmaison Lingers," Carrollton *Conservative*, March 21, 1968. For more on Leflore, see James Taylor Carson, "Greenwood LeFlore: Southern Creole, Choctaw Chief," *Journal of Mississippi History* 65, no. 4 (Winter 2003): 355–373.

2. Rowland, *Mississippi*, 2:72–74; Ownby and Wilson, eds., *The Mississippi Encyclopedia*, 727–728.

3. Ownby and Wilson, eds., *The Mississippi Encyclopedia*, 727–728; Rowland, *Mississippi*, 2:72–74; Rowland, *Mississippi*, 1:803.

4. *OR*, 24(3):652, 657; William Lowery Diary, March 4, 1863, ADAH; L. D. Bradley to wife, March 1, 1863, L. D. Bradley Letter, UNT.

5. *OR*, 24(3):648, 650–654, 663–664, 669, 683; James McCulloch Diary, March 5, 1863, UGA; Henry Reese to Mrs. Tuomey, February 26, 1863, Henry W. Reese Jr. Papers, UA; William Lowery Diary, February 24, 1863, ADAH.

6. *OR*, 24(3):648, 650–654, 663–664, 669, 683; Henry Reese to Mrs. Tuomey, February 26, 1863, Henry W. Reese Jr. Papers, UA.

7. *OR*, 24(3):650, 653–654, 659, 662–663; *OR*, 52(2):420; Hall, *The Story of the 26th Louisiana Infantry*, 55; Steven E. Woodworth, *Jefferson Davis and His Generals: The Failure of Confederate Command in the West* (Lawrence: University Press of Kansas, 1990), 201; E. W. Mitchell to wife, March 3, 1863, E. W. Mitchell Letter, VICK.

8. *OR*, 24(3):657–658, 662, 668, 670; *OR*, 24(1):250, 255; Anderson, *Memoirs*, 271; Bevier, *History of the First and Second Missouri Confederate Brigades*, 109; William A. Ruyle Memoir, undated, HCWRTC, USAHEC, 13.

9. *OR*, 24(3):668–669; John Moss to wife, March 9, 1863, John R. Moss Letters, TSLA; William T. Mumford Diary, March 18, 1863, OCM; Charles J. Sauter Diary, March 1, 1863, VICK; Unknown to F. E. Bissel, April 19, 1863, Carolyn Jones Letter, VICK.

10. *OR*, 24(3):649, 654, 665, 670.

11. *OR*, 24(3):657, 659–661, 663, 668–670; Samuel G. French, *Two Wars: An Autobiography of Gen. Samuel G. French* (Nashville: Confederate Veteran, 1901), 180.

12. Jones, *A Rebel War Clerk's Diary*, 1:237; Jason Niles Diary, March 24, 1863, UNC.

13. *OR*, 24(3):648, 658–659, 664, 667; Adoniram Withrow to wife, March 10, 1863, Adoniram Judson Withrow Papers, UNC; George Chatfield to mother, March 20, 1863, George H. Chatfield Letters, CWD, USAHEC.

14. *OR*, 24(3):649–650.

15. *OR*, 24(3):656–657, 659, 662–663, 665, 667, 669; *OR*, 24(1):412, 421; R. A. Lambert, "In the Mississippi Campaigns," *Confederate Veteran* 37, no. 8 (August 1929): 292–294; Smith, *James Z. George*, 63; J. Z. George to John J. Pettus, March 4, 1863, Governor John J. Pettus Correspondence and Papers, 1859–1863, MDAH; James W. Raab, *W. W. Loring: Florida's Forgotten General* (Manhattan, KS: Sunflower University Press, 1996), 94; Maury, *Recollections of a Virginian*, 177; Alice Hirsch, "Company G, 22nd Mississippi Infantry," Isaac E. Hirsh Papers, MSU, 26.

16. *OR*, 24(3):656–657, 659, 662–663, 665, 667, 669; *OR*, 24(1):389, 412, 421; Hirsch, "Company G, 22nd Mississippi Infantry," Isaac E. Hirsch Papers, MSU, 27; Bearss, *The Vicksburg Campaign*, 1:506; "List of Negroes working on the Fortifications at Fort Pemberton," May 6, 1863, John G. Devereux Papers, UNC; 20th Mississippi Events, March–April 1863, J. S. Wheeler File, OCM; John Wilson to Lizzie, April 2, 1863, John A. Wilson Letters, MDAH; Edward J. Dunn Memoir, undated, OCM, 5.

17. *OR*, 24(1):45, 380, 385, 399; *ORN*, 24:283–284; John W. Griffith Diary, February 22, 1863, OHS; Russ Jr., ed., "The Vicksburg Campaign as Viewed by an Indiana Soldier," 265; Joseph C. Gordon Diary, March 12, 1863, OCM; James F. Mallinckrodt Diary, March 1 and 3, 1863, OCM; Cyrus Cochran to companion, March 21, 1863, Cyrus T. Cochran Papers, ALPL.

18. *OR*, 24(1):393, 410; *ORN*, 24:267; William Vermilion Diary, March 2, 1863, UCSD.

19. *OR*, 24(1):410; *ORN*, 24:262; William Vermilion Diary, March 3 and 4, 1863, UCSD; Leonard Ross to Watson Smith, March 4 and 8, 1863, Watson Smith Papers, USNA.

20. *OR*, 24(1):388, 393, 399, 409–410; *ORN*, 24:260, 263; William Vermilion Diary, March 8, 1863, UCSD; Minos Miller to Martha Hornaday, February 2, 1863, Minos Miller Letters, UAR; Lloyd Tilghman to J. R. Waddy, March 8, 1863, John C. Pemberton Papers, RG 109, E 131, NARA.

21. *OR*, 24(1):394; William Vermilion to wife, March 4, 1863, William F. Vermilion Papers, UCSD.

22. *OR*, 24(1):394, 399, 410.

23. *OR*, 24(1):394–395, 410–411; *ORN*, 24:267; Joseph Ledergerber Diary, March 28, 1863, ALPL; Alexander Ewing to parents, March 25, 1863, Alexander K. Ewing Papers, ALPL; Ira Payne to parents, March 28, 1863, Ira A. Payne Papers, ALPL; Thomas Watson to family, March 18, 1863, Thomas Watson Papers, ALPL.

24. *OR*, 24(1):388, 397, 399, 410–411, 421; Owens, *Steamboats and the Cotton Economy*, 56; William Vermilion Diary, March 10, 1863, UCSD.

25. *OR*, 24(1):388, 397, 399, 410–411, 421; William Vermilion Diary, March 10, 1863, UCSD; Owens, *Steamboats and the Cotton Economy*, 56.

26. *OR*, 24(3):87.

27. *OR*, 24(1):378, 391, 394, 409–411; Report of Ammunition aboard *Baron De Kalb*, March 12, 1863, Watson Smith Papers, USNA.

28. *OR*, 24(1):390, 395, 411; *ORN*, 24:246, 268; S. B. Evans, "Seeking a Back Door to Vicksburg," *The Midland Monthly* 5, no. 4 (April 1896): 374; Ballard, *Vicksburg*, 181; James Slack to wife, March 15 and 26, 1863, James R. Slack Letters, ISL; Frederick Davis to father, March 12, 1863, Frederick E. Davis Papers, EU.

29. *OR*, 24(1): 379, 395, 415, 421.

30. *OR*, 24(1):415; C. B. Haddon Memoir, 1921–1922, OCM, 10; Smith, "The Futile Star of the West," 65; Glenn, "A Vanderbilt at Greenwood," 366–367; "Star of the West," undated, Star of the West File, OCM.

31. *OR*, 24(3):721.

32. *OR*, 24(1):379, 388, 395, 412, 415–416; Herman Hattaway and Archer Jones, *How the North Won: A Military History of the Civil War* (Urbana: University of Illinois Press, 1983), 343; Lockett, "The Defense of Vicksburg," 485; Albert Hiffman Memoirs, undated, Hiffman Family Papers, MHS; William Vermilion to wife, March 17, 1863, William F. Vermilion Papers, UCSD.

33. *OR*, 24(1):379, 395, 416; *History of the Forty-sixth Regiment Indiana Volunteer Infantry*, 48–50; William Vermilion to wife, March 17, 1863, William F. Vermilion Papers, UCSD; Augustus Sinks Journal, undated, ISL, 28; James Jermyn Diary, March 2 and 12, 1863, OCM; Frederick E. Davis Diary, January 13, 1863, Frederick E. Davis Papers, EU.

34. *OR*, 24(1):379–380, 389.

35. *OR*, 24(1):379, 395, 416; *OR*, 24(3):666; *ORN*, 24:246, 269; Alexander Ewing to parents, March 6, 1863, Alexander K. Ewing Papers, ALPL; Paul Dorweiler Diary, March 11, 1863, CWTI, USAHEC.

36. *OR*, 24(1):379–380, 388, 395, 397, 412, 416; *ORN*, 24:247; "The Yazoo Pass Expedition," July 25, 1907, *National Tribune*; William Vermilion to wife, March 17, 1863, William F. Vermilion Papers, UCSD.

37. *OR*, 24(1):379, 395; Joiner, *Mr. Lincoln's Brown Water Navy*, 126; Allen W. Miller Diary, March 11 and 12, 1863, LC.

38. *OR*, 24(1):395, 412, 667; *ORN*, 24:247, 273–275; Jason Niles Diary, March 13, 1863, UNC; Raab, *W. W. Loring*, 96; Augustus Sinks Journal, undated, ISL, 29; Karl Kneitel to wife, March 21, 1863, Karl Kneitel Letter, VICK; Joseph Ledergerber Diary, March 13, 1863, ALPL.

39. *OR*, 24(1):395, 412, 667; *ORN*, 24:247, 273–275; Joseph Ledergerber Diary, March 13, 1863, ALPL; Augustus Sinks Journal, undated, ISL, 29; Karl Kneitel to wife, March 21, 1863, Karl Kneitel Letter, VICK.

40. *OR*, 24(1):412, 416; Karl Kneitel to wife, March 21, 1863, Karl Kneitel Letter, VICK.

41. *OR*, 24(1):379–381, 397, 412–413, 416; James Slack to wife, March 15, 1863, James R. Slack Letters, ISL.

42. *OR*, 24(1):379, 667.

43. *OR*, 24(1):380, 413, 416; John Meriwether to wife, March 15, 1863, Meriwether Family Papers, UA; William Vermilion to wife, March 20, 1863, William F. Vermilion Papers, UCSD; Allen W. Miller Diary, March 13 and 15, 1863, LC.

44. *OR*, 24(1):379, 380–381, 400; William Vermilion to wife, March 17 and 20, 1863, William F. Vermilion Papers, UCSD.

45. *OR*, 24(1):380, 400.

46. *OR*, 24(1):380.

47. *OR*, 24(3):669–670.

48. *OR*, 24(3):75; Simon and Marszalek, eds., *PUSG*, 7:323, 409; Simon and Marszalek, eds., *PUSG*, 8:24; Marszalek, Nolen, and Gallo, eds., *Personal Memoirs of Ulysses S. Grant*, 309.

49. *OR*, 24(3):75; Marszalek, Nolen, and Gallo, eds., *Personal Memoirs of Ulysses S. Grant*, 309; Simon and Marszalek, eds., *PUSG*, 7:323, 409; Simon and Marszalek, eds., *PUSG*, 8:24; Craig L. Symonds, *Lincoln and His Admirals: Abraham Lincoln, The U.S. Navy, and the Civil War* (New York: Oxford University Press, 2008), 199.

50. *OR*, 23(2):111; William M. Lamers, *The Edge of Glory: A Biography of General William S. Rosecrans* (Boston: Harcourt, Brace & World, 1961), 254–255.

51. Simon and Marszalek, eds., *PUSG*, 7:396, 491; James C. Mahan, *Memoirs of James Curtis Mahan* (Lincoln, NE: The Franklin Press, 1919), 112; Simon and Marszalek, eds., *PUSG*, 8:9; Fred Grant Memoir, undated, USGPL, 1–2. For a condensed published version of Fred's memoir, see Frederick D. Grant, "A Boy's Experience at Vicksburg," in *Personal Recollections of the War of the Rebellion: Addresses Delivered before the Commandery of the State of New York, Military Order of the Loyal Legion of the United States*, A. Noel Blakeman, ed. (New York: G. P. Putnam's Sons, 1907): 86–100.

52. *OR*, 24(3):80, 82–84, 88, 91, 108, 123; *OR*, 24(1):19; Edward Hartley to Emy, March 26, 1863, Papers of Em, Civil War Collection, MHS; Samuel D. Pryce, *Vanishing Footprints: The Twenty-Second Iowa Volunteer Infantry in the Civil War*, Jeffry C. Burden, ed. (Iowa City: Camp Pope Bookshop, 2008), 87; Luther Cowan Diary, February 23, 1863, and Luther Cowan to Mollie, March 6, 1863, and Luther Cowan to Harriet, March 17, 1863, Luther H. Cowan Papers, TSLA; Hovey Manuscript, undated, IU, 45; William Steel to sister, February 22, 1863, Hugh Gaston Letters, IHS; Wilfred B. McDonald Diary, March 6 and April 16, 1863, Bennett Grigsby Papers, IHS; Elliot Morrow to sister, March 13, 1863, Elliot Morrow Papers, OHS; John Boucher to wife, March 1, 1863, Boucher Family Papers, CWD, USAHEC; Samuel P. Harrington Diary, March 16, 1863, Rudolph Haerle Collection, USAHEC.

53. *OR*, 24(3):80, 82–84, 88, 91, 108, 123; *OR*, 24(1):19; Edward Hartley to Emy, March 26, 1863, Papers of Em, Civil War Collection, MHS; Pryce, *Vanishing Footprints*, 87; Luther Cowan Diary, February 23, 1863, and Luther Cowan to Mollie, March 6, 1863, and Luther Cowan to Harriet, March 17, 1863, Luther H. Cowan Papers, TSLA; John E. Smith to Aimee, March 12, 1863, Kirby Smith Collection; Samuel P. Harrington Diary, March 16, 1863, Rudolph Haerle Collection, USAHEC; William Rigby to brother, March 10, 1863, William T. Rigby Papers, UIA; William Steel to sister, February 22, 1863, Hugh Gaston Letters, IHS; Wilfred B. McDonald Diary, March 6 and April 16, 1863, Bennett Grigsby Papers, IHS; Elliot Morrow to sister, March 13, 1863, Elliot Morrow Papers, OHS; John Boucher to wife, March 1, 1863, Boucher Family Papers, CWD, USAHEC.

54. *OR*, 24(3):76, 80, 82–84, 88, 91–92; Leo M. Kaiser, ed., "'In Sight of Vicksburg': Private Diary of a Northern War Correspondent," *Historical Bulletin* 24, no. 4

(May 1956): 204, 206; Stephen Hurlbut to John E. Smith, March 15, 1863, Kirby Smith Collection; Payson Shumway to wife, April 6, 1863, Payson Z. Shumway Papers, ALPL.

55. *OR*, 24(3):95, 104, 106.

56. *OR*, 24(3):85, 89–90; Kaiser, ed., "The Civil War Diary of Florison D. Pitts," 33, 35–36, 209; James C. Sinclair Diary, March 10, 1863, CHM; Albert C. Boals Diary, March 21, 1863, ALPL; John Bennett to father, January 2, 1863, John Bennett Letter, Civil War Collection, MHS; George D. Carrington Diary, February 16, 1863, CHM; David Grier to Anna, March 1, 1863, Grier Family Papers, MHS; J. H. Hammond to David Porter, March 10, 1863, David Dixon Porter Papers, MHS; Job H. Yaggy Diary, April 1, 1863, ALPL; George B. Marshall Reminiscences, 1912, ISL, 37–38; Lewis Trefftys to W. F. Trefftys, March 14, 1863, Lewis Trefftys Papers, ALPL; M. A. DeWolfe Howe, ed., *Home Letters of General Sherman* (New York: Charles Scribner's Sons, 1909), 242, originals in William T. Sherman Papers, LC; Samuel Gordon to wife, March 1, 1863, Samuel Gordon Papers, ALPL; William Kennedy to wife, March 11, 1863, William J. Kennedy Papers, ALPL; Abram J. Vanauken Diary, February 13, 1863, ALPL; John Jones to parents, April 11, 1863, John G. Jones Papers, LC; Israel P. Rumsey Diary, April 9, 1863, NL.

57. *OR*, 24(1):19–20, 44, 122, 125; *OR*, 24(3):85, 102–103; Simon and Marszalek, eds., *PUSG*, 7:383–384, 402; Marszalek, Nolen, and Gallo, eds., *Personal Memoirs of Ulysses S. Grant*, 309; Van Dorn and Masters, eds., *The 57th Ohio Veteran Volunteer Infantry*, 144; Curtis P. Lacey Diary, March 5, 1863, NL; Kaiser, ed., "'In Sight of Vicksburg,'" 208; James Giauque to family, March 15, 1863, Giauque Family Papers, UIA; Herman Salomon, "Civil War Diary of Herman Salomon," *Wisconsin Magazine of History* 10, no. 2 (December 1926): 207, original in WHS; George White to parents, March 8, 1863, White Family Papers, UIA; Edward E. Schweitzer Diary, March 2, 1863, CWTI, USAHEC; Charles to friend, March 15, 1863, Letter from Charles, VICK; Cyrus Rayhill to unknown, March 10, 1863, Cyrus Rayhill Correspondence, IHS; Israel P. Rumsey Diary, March 12–13, 1863, NL; Reuben H. Falconer Diary, March 8, 1863, OHS.

58. *OR*, 24(1):19–20, 44, 122, 125; *OR*, 24(3):85, 102–103; Simon and Marszalek, eds., *PUSG*, 7:383–384, 402; Marszalek, Nolen, and Gallo, eds., *Personal Memoirs of Ulysses S. Grant*, 309; Edward E. Schweitzer Diary, March 2, 1863, CWTI, USAHEC; Van Dorn and Masters, eds., *The 57th Ohio Veteran Volunteer Infantry*, 144; Curtis P. Lacey Diary, March 5, 1863, NL; Reuben H. Falconer Diary, March 8, 1863, OHS; Kaiser, ed., "'In Sight of Vicksburg,'" 208; James Giauque to family, March 15, 1863, Giauque Family Papers, UIA; Salomon, "Civil War Diary of Herman Salomon," 207; Israel P. Rumsey Diary, March 12–13, 1863, NL; George White to parents, March 8, 1863, White Family Papers, UIA; Charles to friend, March 15, 1863, Letter from Charles, VICK; Cyrus Rayhill to unknown, March 10, 1863, Cyrus Rayhill Correspondence, IHS.

59. *OR*, 24(3):85, 89–90; Kaiser, ed., "The Civil War Diary of Florison D. Pitts," 33, 35–36; James C. Sinclair Diary, March 10, 1863, CHM; Kaiser, ed., "'In Sight of Vicksburg,'" 209; Albert C. Boals Diary, March 21, 1863, ALPL; George D. Carrington Diary, February 16, 1863, CHM; David Grier to Anna, March 1, 1863, Grier Family Papers, MHS; Job H. Yaggy Diary, April 1, 1863, ALPL; Lewis Trefftys to W. F. Trefftys, March 14, 1863, Lewis Trefftys Papers, ALPL; Howe, ed., *Home Letters of General Sherman*,

242; Samuel Gordon to wife, March 1, 1863, Samuel Gordon Papers, ALPL; William Kennedy to wife, March 11, 1863, William J. Kennedy Papers, ALPL; Abram J. Vanauken Diary, February 13, 1863, ALPL; Israel P. Rumsey Diary, April 9, 1863, NL.

60. *OR*, 24(3):79, 81–82; James Owen to father, March 14, 1863, James B. Owen Letters, TSLA; Kaiser, ed., "'In Sight of Vicksburg,'" 207; Mildred Throne, ed., *The Civil War Diary of Cyrus F. Boyd, Fifteenth Iowa Infantry, 1861–1863* (Baton Rouge: Louisiana State University Press, 1998), 125, manuscript in Kansas City Public Library; Luther Cowan Diary, February 23, 1863, Luther H. Cowan Papers, TSLA; Marcus Brucker to wife, February 28, 1863, Magnus Brucker Letters, IHS; James Vanderbilt to mother, February 26 and March 12, 1863, James C. Vanderbilt Papers, ISL; James D. Heath Diary, February 28, 1863, OCM; Joseph Stockton Diary, March 14, 1863, VICK, original in ALPL; John Sheriff to parents, March 15, 1863, John Sherriff Family Papers, ALPL.

61. *OR*, 24(3):76, 86; Woodworth, *Nothing but Victory*, 300; Frank Tupper to mother, March 24, 1863, Frank W. Tupper Papers, ALPL; Simon and Marszalek, eds., *PUSG*, 8:38; Kaiser, ed., "'In Sight of Vicksburg,'" 209, 218; Whaley, *Forgotten Hero*, 127–128; Luther Cowan Diary, February 26, 1863, Luther H. Cowan Papers, TSLA; Ira Blanchard, *I Marched with Sherman: Civil War Memoirs of the 20th Illinois Volunteer Infantry*, Nancy Ann Mattingly, ed. (New York: toExcel, 1992), 81; John Wickiser to judge, March 8, 1863, John H. Wickiser Papers, ALPL; John W. Griffith Diary, March 4, 1863, OHS.

62. *OR*, 24(3):76, 79, 86; Tamara A. Smith, "A Matter of Trust: Grant and James B. McPherson," in *Grant's Lieutenants: From Cairo to Vicksburg*, Steven E. Woodworth, ed. (Lawrence: University Press of Kansas, 2001), 156; Marcus Brucker to wife, March 8, 1863, Magnus Brucker Letters, IHS; James Vanderbilt to mother, March 6, 1863, James C. Vanderbilt Papers, ISL.

63. *OR*, 24(3):98; *OR*, 24(1):20; Simon and Marszalek, eds., *PUSG*, 7:411, 489; John Sheriff to father, March 15, 1863, John Sherriff Family Papers, ALPL.

64. *OR*, 24(3):77, 89, 104–105; William T. Sherman to David Porter, March 3, 1863, David Dixon Porter Papers, MHS.

65. *OR*, 24(3):86; *OR*, 24(1):20; *ORN*, 24:261.

66. *OR*, 24(3):86–87, 93; *OR*, 24(1):20; Carlos Forbes to Mary, March 4, 1863, Carlos Forbes Correspondence, OHS; Alexander McConaughey to sister, February 19, 1863, Alexander McConaughey Collection, OHS.

67. *OR*, 24(3):86–87; James to Sue, March 18, 1863, John L. Harris Papers, ALPL; Frank Tupper to father, March 19, 1863, Frank W. Tupper Papers, ALPL.

68. *OR*, 24(3):90, 96.

69. *OR*, 24(3):90–91.

70. *OR*, 24(3):96, 105.

71. *OR*, 24(3):94; *OR*, 24(1):403.

72. *OR*, 24(3):98–99, 103; *OR*, 24(1):19, 404–405.

73. *OR*, 24(1):405–406; Alonzo L. Brown, *History of the Fourth Regiment of Minnesota Infantry Volunteers During the Great Rebellion, 1861–1865* (St. Paul, MN: The Pioneer Press Company, 1892), 170; *Sanborn Family in the United States and Brief Sketch of Life of John B. Sanborn* (St. Paul, MN: H. M. Smyth Printing Co., 1887), 55–56; Stone,

Memoir of George Boardman Boomer, 245; Joseph Stockton Diary, March 23, 1863, VICK.

74. *OR*, 24(3):105; Israel Rumsey to brother, March 8, 1863, Israel P. Rumsey Letters, NL.

75. *OR*, 24(3):110–111.

76. Adoniram Withrow to wife, March 10, 1863, Adoniram Judson Withrow Papers, UNC; Solomon Barnes to wife, February 4, 1863, Solomon M. Barnes Letters, IHS; William F. Willey Diary, March 10, 1863, OHS; Elliot Morrow to sister, March 13, 1863, Elliot Morrow Papers, OHS.

Chapter 8. "The Enemy Press Me on All Sides"

1. *OR*, 5:41.

2. *OR*, 7:477; *ORN*, 1, 22:331, 365, 384, 387, 438.

3. *ORN*, 22:314, 495; Joiner, *Mr. Lincoln's Brown Water Navy*, 26–29; Edwin C. Bearss, *Hardluck Ironclad: The Sinking and Salvage of the Cairo*, rev. ed. (Baton Rouge: Louisiana State University Press, 1980), 190–191.

4. Bearss, *Hardluck Ironclad*, 88–188.

5. *OR*, 24(3):134.

6. *OR*, 24(3):114–115; Alexander Ewing to parents, March 18, 1863, Alexander K. Ewing Papers, ALPL.

7. *OR*, 24(1):413, 416–417.

8. *OR*, 24(1):380, 382, 398.

9. *OR*, 24(1):382–383, 417; *ORN*, 24:247–248, 276; Alexander Ewing to parents, March 18, 1863, Alexander K. Ewing Papers, ALPL.

10. *OR*, 24(1):383, 396; *ORN*, 24:248, 272–273, 283; Karl Kneitel to wife, March 21, 1863, Karl Kneitel Letter, VICK; W. A. Rorer to Susan, April 2, 1863, W. A. Rorer Letters, DU.

11. *OR*, 24(1):413–414.

12. *OR*, 24(1):382–384, 390, 393, 396; *OR*, 24(3):120, 127; Marszalek, Nolen, and Gallo, eds., *Personal Memoirs of Ulysses S. Grant*, 313; John Myers to wife, March 29, 1863, John Myers Letters, BCAS.

13. *OR*, 24(1):413–414; *OR*, 24(3):677.

14. Allen W. Miller Diary, March 17–18, 1863, LC.

15. *OR*, 24(1):385–386, 416; *ORN*, 24:253, 277–278, 281, 284, 286; George R. Yost Diary, March 18, 1863, ALPL; Benjamin Underwood to brother, March 21, 1863, Benjamin W. Underwood Letters, OCM; Augustus Sinks Journal, undated, ISL, 30; Allen W. Miller Diary, March 17, 1863, LC.

16. *OR*, 24(1):385–386, 398, 416; James Slack to wife, March 21, 1863, James R. Slack Letters, ISL.

17. *OR*, 24(1):414–415; *OR*, 24(3):683, 685–688; Edward J. Dunn Memoir, undated, OCM, 5–6; Sam Martin to James Chalmers, March 30, 1863, John C. Pemberton Papers, RG 109, E 131, NARA.

18. *OR*, 24(3):124; *OR*, 24(1):385, 398, 406–407; Jenkins Lloyd Jones, *An Artilleryman's Diary* (Madison: Wisconsin History Commission, 1914), 40, original in WHS; Joel Strong Reminiscences, 1910, MHS, 10, copy in OCM; William Vermilion to wife, March 20, 1863, William F. Vermilion Papers, UCSD; John B. Elliott Diary, March 15, 1863, ISL; Anson Hemingway Diary, March 16–17, 1863, VICK; Thomas Watson to family, March 18, 1863, Thomas Watson Papers, ALPL; John F. Lester Diary, March 14, 17, and 21, 1863, IHS; John S. Jackman Diary, March 24–27, 1863, LC; James Alcorn to wife, March 16, 1863, James L. Alcorn and Family Papers, MDAH; Joseph Ledgerber Diary, April 1, 1863, ALPL; James B. Logan Diary, March 30, 1863, ALPL; Lyman M. Baker Memoir, undated, ALPL, 4–5; John Boucher to wife, April 12, 1863, Boucher Family Papers, CWD, USAHEC; George Ditto Diary, March 17, 1863, ALPL; Isaac Vanderwarker Diary, March 15–16, 1863, CWD, USAHEC.

19. *OR*, 24(3):124; *OR*, 24(1):385, 398, 406–407.

20. *OR*, 24(3):118, 127, 132; Map of Steele Bayou, undated, Steele's Bayou File, MDAH.

21. *OR*, 24(1):28, *OR*, 24(3):112, 119, 134–135; Jenney, "With Sherman and Grant," 200.

22. *OR*, 24(3):112; *ORN*, 24:474; Bearss, *The Vicksburg Campaign*, 1:550; Porter, *Incidents and Anecdotes*, 145.

23. *OR*, 24(3):112, 119; *OR*, 24(1):21; *ORN*, 24:474, 493; Bearss, *The Vicksburg Campaign*, 1:551; Skaptason, "The Chicago Light Artillery at Vicksburg," 436; Cadwallader, *Three Years with Grant*, 51; Charles J. Sauter Diary, March 16–25, 1863, VICK.

24. *OR*, 24(3):112–113; *OR*, 24(1):21, 437–438, 453; *ORN*, 24:474, 493; Gibson and Gibson, *Assault and Logistics*, 277; Simon and Marszalek, eds., *PUSG*, 7:423; James Boyd Diary, March 17, 1863; Israel P. Rumsey Diary, March 16, 1863, NL; Saunier, *A History of the Forty-seventh Regiment Ohio Veteran Volunteer Infantry*, 125; James Boyd Diary, March 20, 1863, ALPL; Edward E. Schweitzer Diary, March 22–23, 1863, CWTI, USAHEC; R. R. Hall Diary, "Diary of Pioneer Wichitan Reveals Horrors of War," March 15–16, 1863, OCM; Special Orders 42, March 20, 1863, Hugh Ewing Papers, OHS, ALPL.

25. *OR*, 24(3):113–114.

26. Porter, *Incidents and Anecdotes*, 147, 149, 157–159; W. A. C. Michael, "How the Mississippi Was Opened," in *Civil War Sketches and Incidents: Papers Read by Companions of the Commandery of the State of Nebraska, Military Order of the Loyal Legion of the United States* (Omaha: The Commandery, 1902), 45–46; W. H. Michael, "Mississippi Flotilla," June 28, 1888, *National Tribune*.

27. *OR*, 24(3):112–113; *OR*, 24(1):21, 437–438, 453; *ORN*, 24:474, 493; Simon and Marszalek, eds., *PUSG*, 7:423; Israel P. Rumsey Diary, March 16, 1863, NL; Saunier, *A History of the Forty-seventh Regiment Ohio Veteran Volunteer Infantry*, 125; R. R. Hall Diary, "Diary of Pioneer Wichitan Reveals Horrors of War," March 15–16, 1863, OCM; Special Orders 42, March 20, 1863, Hugh Ewing Papers, OHS; James Boyd Diary, March 17 and 20, 1863, ALPL; Edward E. Schweitzer Diary, March 22–23, 1863, CWTI, USAHEC.

28. *OR*, 24(1):455–456, 466; Maury, *Recollections of a Virginian*, 176–177; Samuel

W. Ferguson Memoirs, undated, VICK, 37; George Barnes to Samuel Ferguson, March 19, 1863, John C. Pemberton Papers, RG 109, E 131, NARA.

29. *OR*, 24(1):455–456, 465–466; *OR*, 24(3):674; Carter Stevenson to John Pemberton, March 21, 1863, John C. Pemberton Papers, RG 109, E 131, NARA.

30. *OR*, 24(1):456, 459; *OR*, 24(3):682; Martin Van Kees Diary, March 20, 1863, OCM; "History of the 33rd Mississippi Infantry, Part V," 2001, Steele's Bayou Expedition, File, MDAH; William Barksdale to Ferrell, March 12, 1863, William R. Barksdale Papers, MDAH.

31. *OR*, 24(1):461–465; *OR*, 24(3):684; Herman Hattaway, *General Stephen D. Lee* (Jackson: University Press of Mississippi, 1988), 80–82; Maury, *Recollections of a Virginian*, 176–177; "The Steele's Bayou Expedition of the Civil War," undated, Steele Bayou File, MDAH, 4; Abner J. Wilkes Memoir, undated, OCM, 5; Chambers, "My Journal," 259.

32. *OR*, 24(1):431–433; *ORN*, 24:687; Bearss, *The Vicksburg Campaign*, 1:553; Sherman, *Memoirs*, 1:307; R. R. Hall Diary, "Diary of Pioneer Wichitan Reveals Horrors of War," March 16, 1863, OCM; Edward E. Schweitzer Diary, March 23, 1863, CWTI, USAHEC.

33. *OR*, 24(1):431–432; Sherman, *Memoirs*, 1:308.

34. *OR*, 24(1):431, 439; *ORN*, 24:475; R. R. Hall Diary, "Diary of Pioneer Wichitan Reveals Horrors of War," March 16, 1863, OCM.

35. *OR*, 24(1):431–432; *OR*, 24(3):123.

36. *ORN*, 24:475, 477–478, 493–495; Van Dorn and Masters, eds., *The 57th Ohio Veteran Volunteer Infantry*, 148–149.

37. *ORN*, 24:475; Bearss, *The Vicksburg Campaign*, 1:556; Tomblin, *The Civil War on the Mississippi*, 218.

38. *OR*, 24(1):21; *OR*, 24(3):687, 692–693; William Morton to wife, March 7, 1863, William Morton Letters, OCM; E. T. Rhea to siblings, March 21, 1863, E. T. Rhea Letter, VICK.

39. *OR*, 24(3):685, 687; Lockett, "The Defense of Vicksburg," 485.

40. *OR*, 24(3):678, 691, 693.

41. *OR*, 24(3):676–678; James Owen to father, March 14, 1863, James B. Owen Letters, TSLA; John Meriwether to wife, March 6, 1863, Meriwether Family Papers, UA; Samuel Fowler Diary, April 30, 1863, SU; Map of Grand Gulf, undated, John C. Pemberton Papers, RG 109, E 131, NARA.

42. *OR*, 24(3):672–673, 676, 680, 686, 689, 694, 697–698; George Johnson to wife, March 24, 1863, George B. Johnson Letters, OCM; James Woodward to father, March 19, 1863, James W. Woodard Correspondence, SHSM; Phillip Thomas Tucker, *The Forgotten "Stonewall of the West": Major General John Stevens Bowen* (Macon, GA: Mercer University Press, 1997), 179; Zeno Elwell to friend, 1863, Zeno P. Elwell Letter, OCM; John Pemberton to Jefferson Davis, March 15, 1863, John C. Pemberton Papers, RG 109, E 131, NARA; John Bowen to J. J. Reeve, March 15, 1863, John Bowen to R. W. Memminger, March 20, 1863, John Bowen to John Pemberton, March 20, 1863, and R. R. Hutchinson to Captain Landis, March 18, 1863, all in John Bowen Letter Book, RG 109, Chapter II, Vol. 274, NARA.

43. *OR*, 24(3):166, 672–673, 675–678, 680, 682, 684.

44. *OR*, 24(3):673, 676–677, 688; W. R. Eddington Memoir, undated, ALPL, 6; Simon and Marszalek, eds., *PUSG*, 7:372; Oake, *On the Skirmish Line*, 94; Samuel Fowler Diary, March 20, 1863, SU.

45. *OR*, 24(3):694.

46. *OR*, 24(3):679, 681, 684–685–687, 689, 691, 695. For Pettus, see Robert W. Dubay, *John Jones Pettus, Mississippi Fire-eater: His Life and Times, 1813–1867* (Jackson: University Press of Mississippi, 1975).

47. *OR*, 24(3):675, 689.

48. John Meriwether to wife, March 21, 1863, Meriwether Family Papers, UA.

Chapter 9. "We Intend to Take the Boats"

1. Smith, *Early Struggles for Vicksburg*, 425, 428.

2. *OR*, 24(1):22, 24; Luther Cowan to wife, March 17, 1863, Luther H. Cowan Papers, TSLA.

3. David Grier to Anna, March 20, 1863, Grier Family Papers, MHS.

4. John Q. Anderson, ed., *Brokenburn: The Journal of Kate Stone, 1861–1868* (Baton Rouge: Louisiana State University Press, 1955), 184; Luther Cowan to wife, March 17, 1863, Luther H. Cowan Papers, TSLA.

5. Kenneth P. Williams, *Grant Rises in the West: From Iuka to Vicksburg, 1862–1863* (Lincoln: University of Nebraska Press, 1997), 290; James Slack to wife, March 26, 1863, James R. Slack Letters, ISL; James L. Alcorn Diary, March 15, 1863, MDAH.

6. *OR*, 24(3):124; *OR*, 24(1):385, 398, 406–407; Jones, *An Artilleryman's Diary*, 40; Joel Strong Reminiscences, 1910, MHS, 10; William Vermilion to wife, March 20, 1863, William F. Vermilion Papers, UCSD; John B. Elliott Diary, March 15, 1863, ISL; Anson Hemingway Diary, March 16–17, 1863, VICK; Thomas Watson to family, March 18, 1863, Thomas Watson Papers, ALPL; John F. Lester Diary, March 14, 17, and 21, 1863, IHS; John S. Jackman Diary, March 24–27, 1863, LC; James Alcorn to wife, March 16, 1863, James L. Alcorn and Family Papers, MDAH; Joseph Ledergerber Diary, April 1, 1863, ALPL; James B. Logan Diary, March 30, 1863, ALPL; Lyman M. Baker Memoir, undated, ALPL, 4–5; John Boucher to wife, April 12, 1863, Boucher Family Papers, CWD, USAHEC; George Ditto Diary, March 17, 1863, ALPL; Isaac Vanderwarker Diary, March 15–16, 1863, CWD, USAHEC.

7. *OR*, 24(3):124; *OR*, 24(1):385, 398, 407; *ORN*, 24:287; John S. Jackman Diary, March 28, 1863, LC; John F. Lester Diary, March 21, 1863, IHS; Alexander Ewing to parents, March 18, 1863, Alexander K. Ewing Papers, ALPL; James D. Heath Diary, March 15 and 17, 1863, OCM; Isaac Vanderwarker Diary, March 21, 1863, CWD, USAHEC; George Ditto Diary, March 21, 1863, ALPL. See also the Quinby orders to Ross in Army of the Tennessee Papers, LSU.

8. *OR*, 24(1):407–408; William Vermilion to wife, March 23, 1863, William F. Vermilion Papers, UCSD; John F. Lester Diary, March 23, 1863, IHS; Augustus Sinks Journal, undated, ISL, 30; William Rorer to Susan, April 2, 1863, W. A. Rorer Letters, DU; Karl Kneitel to wife, March 21, 1863, Karl Kneitel Letter, VICK.

9. *OR*, 24(1):417; *OR*, 24(3):686–688; Owens, *Steamboats and the Cotton Economy*, 57; John B. Elliott Diary, March 24, 1863, ISL; George Ditto Diary, March 23, 1863, ALPL.

10. William Rorer to Susan, April 2, 1863, W. A. Rorer Letters, DU; Joseph Stockton Diary, March 29, 1863, VICK; George Ditto Diary, March 25 and 31, 1863, ALPL; John Wilson to Lizzie, March 31, 1863, John A. Wilson Letters, MDAH; Ira Payne to parents, April 4, 1863, Ira A. Payne Papers, ALPL.

11. *OR*, 24(1): 407–408; *ORN*, 24:288; William Vermilion to wife, March 29, 1863, William F. Vermilion Papers, UCSD.

12. *OR*, 24(1):409; Russ Jr., ed., "The Vicksburg Campaign as Viewed by an Indiana Soldier," 265; William Vermilion to wife, March 29, 1863, William F. Vermilion Papers, UCSD; L. D. Bradley to wife, March 31, 1863, L. D. Bradley Letter, UNT; George Ditto Diary, March 27, 1863, ALPL.

13. *OR*, 24(3):134; *ORN*, 24:291; John Merrilies Diary, March 21, 1863, CHM; William Britton to editors, March 22 and April 1, 1863, William B. Britton Letters, OCM.

14. *OR*, 24(3):114–115, 120, 129.

15. *OR*, 24(3):116, 121.

16. *OR*, 24(3):144–145; James Slack to wife, March 28, 1863, James R. Slack Letters, ISL.

17. *OR*, 24(3):112, 118–119, 121, 124.

18. *OR*, 24(3):148–149; *OR*, 24(1):409; *History of the Forty-sixth Regiment Indiana Volunteer Infantry*, 48; Stone, *Memoir of George Boardman Boomer*, 246; Alexander Ewing to parents, March 25 and 29, 1863, Alexander K. Ewing Papers, ALPL.

19. *OR*, 24(3):689–691, 693, 701; Ballard, *Vicksburg*, 178–179; Ballard, *Pemberton*, 133; J. Z. George to Bettie, April 10, 1863, James Z. George Papers, MDAH; Ballard, "Misused Merit," in *Civil War Generals in Defeat*, 156; William A. Drennan to his Wife, May 30, 1863, William A. Drennan Papers, MDAH; J. A. Wilson to "Lizzie," March 31, 1863, John A. Wilson Letters, MDAH.

20. *OR*, 24(3):118, 127, 132.

21. *OR*, 24(3):132, 151; Joseph Ledergerber Diary, March 28, 1863, ALPL.

22. *ORN*, 24:494; William Jolly to sister, undated 1863, William H. Jolly Letters, SHSIIC.

23. *OR*, 24(1):456–458, 466–467; *OR*, 52(2):435; *ORN*, 24:476; Samuel W. Ferguson Memoirs, undated, VICK, 37–39; Porter, *Incidents and Anecdotes*, 160; Bearss, *The Vicksburg Campaign*, 1:557, 563; M. D. L. Stephens Recollections, undated, MDAH, 14; *Vicksburg Campaign: Driving Tour Guide* (N.p.: Friends of the Vicksburg Campaign and Historic Trail, 2008), 44.

24. *OR*, 24(1):456–458, 466–467; *OR*, 52(2):435; *ORN*, 24:476; Porter, *Incidents and Anecdotes*, 160; Bearss, *The Vicksburg Campaign*, 1:557, 563; W. L. Ritter, "Sketch of the Third Battery of Maryland Artillery," *Southern Historical Society Papers* 10, nos. 8–9 (August–September 1882): 396; M. D. L. Stephens Recollections, undated, MDAH, 14; Samuel W. Ferguson Memoirs, undated, VICK, 37–39.

25. *OR*, 24(1):72, 433; *OR*, 24(3):683; *ORN*, 24:476, 698; Edmund Pettus to wife,

March 21, 1863, Edmund W. Pettus Papers, ADAH; James H. St. John Diary, March 21, 1863, ISL.

26. *OR*, 24(1):459–460, 467; M. D. L. Stephens Recollections, undated, MDAH, 14; Samuel W. Ferguson Memoirs, undated, VICK, 37, 41.

27. *OR*, 24(1):431–434, 436.

28. *OR*, 24(1):450–451, 455–457, 463–464; *OR*, 24(3):691; *History of the 37th Regiment, O.V.V.I., Furnished by Comrades at the Ninth Reunion Held at St. Mary's, Ohio, Tuesday and Wednesday, September 10 and 11, 1889* (Toledo, OH: Montgomery and Vrooman, 1890), 19–20; Hall, *The Story of the 26th Louisiana Infantry*, 58; Henry R. Brinkerhoff, *History of the Thirtieth Regiment Ohio Volunteer Infantry, From Its Organization, To the Fall of Vicksburg, Miss.* (Columbus, OH: James W. Osgood, Printer, 1863), 55–57; Tunnard, *A Southern Record*, 220; Chambers, "My Journal," 259; Claudius W. Sears Diary, April 28, 1863, MDAH.

29. *OR*, 24(1):431–433, 436–437, 467; Sherman, *Memoirs*, 1:308; M. D. L. Stephens Recollections, undated, MDAH, 14.

30. *OR*, 24(1):433–434, 457, 460; Sherman, *Memoirs*, 1:308; Samuel W. Ferguson Memoirs, undated, VICK, 40; James Boyd Diary, March 21, 1863, ALPL.

31. *ORN*, 24:476–477, 488–489; Porter, *Incidents and Anecdotes*, 163; "Military History of Captain Thomas Sewell," 1889, DU.

32. Porter, *Incidents and Anecdotes*, 163.

33. *OR*, 24(1):433, 439; James Boyd Diary, March 21, 1863, ALPL.

34. *OR*, 24(1):433, 439, 467; *ORN*, 24:477, 698; Bearss, *The Vicksburg Campaign*, 1:571; James Boyd Diary, March 21, 1863, ALPL; Michael, "How the Mississippi Was Opened," 48.

35. *OR*, 24(1):435, 442, 457; Sherman, *Memoirs*, 1:308–309; James Boyd Diary, March 22, 1863, ALPL; Andrew McCornack to parents, March 28, 1863, Andrew McCornack Letters, Wiley Sword Collection, USAHEC.

36. *OR*, 24(1):440, 458, 466.

37. *OR*, 24(1):435, 440, 443, 447–448; Sherman, *Memoirs*, 1:309–310; Porter, *Incidents and Anecdotes*, 168; James Boyd Diary, March 22, 1863, ALPL.

38. *OR*, 24(1):435, 438, 443–444, 450, 459, 466–467; *ORN*, 24:477, 495, 688; M. D. L. Stephens Recollections, undated, MDAH, 15; Elbert D. Willett Diary, March 21, 1863, ADAH; *History of Company B (Originally Pickens Planters) 40th Alabama Regiment Confederate States Army 1862–1865* (Anniston, AL: Norwood, 1902), 29.

39. *OR*, 24(1):444, 448, 457–458, 460; *ORN*, 24:477, 495, 688; Van Dorn and Masters, eds., *The 57th Ohio Veteran Volunteer Infantry*, 148; J. A. Orr Reminiscences, undated, MDAH.

40. *OR*, 24(1):444, 448, 457–458, 460; *ORN*, 24:477, 495, 688; J. A. Orr Reminiscences, undated, MDAH.

41. *OR*, 24(1):435–436, 442, 451–452, 454, 461; *ORN*, 24:496; Bearss, *The Vicksburg Campaign*, 1:562; Grecian, *History of the Eighty-third Regiment, Indiana Volunteer Infantry*, 27–28; James Boyd Diary, March 26, 1863, ALPL; Van Dorn and Masters, eds., *The 57th Ohio Veteran Volunteer Infantry*, 148; *History of Company B*, 29; Edward E. Schweitzer Diary, March 26, 1863, CWTI, USAHEC.

42. *OR*, 24(1):461, 467.

43. *OR*, 24(1):23; *OR*, 24(3):127–128, 135, 145; Ebenezer Werkheiser to sister, March 30, 1863, Ebenezer Werkheiser Letters, VICK; Joseph C. Gordon Diary, March 25, 1863, OCM; Gus to Kate, March 27, 1863, James A. B. Butterfield Correspondence, ALPL; John W. Griffith Diary, March 26, 1863, OHS; Isaac Home to parents, March 25, 1863, Isaac M. Home Papers, KHS.

44. *OR*, 24(1):23, 434; *OR*, 24(3):127–128; *ORN*, 24:477–479; Van Dorn and Masters, eds., *The 57th Ohio Veteran Volunteer Infantry*, 151; James Leeper to Mary, March 28, 1863, James Leeper Correspondence, IHS.

45. Cadwallader, *Three Years with Grant*, 52.

46. *OR*, 24(1):415, 456; *ORN*, 24:479; J. C. M. to editor, April 23, 1863, E. Merton Coulter Collection, UGA.

47. Jenney, "Personal Recollections of Vicksburg," 256; Samuel W. Ferguson Memoirs, undated, VICK, 41.

48. *OR*, 24(1):455; Ballard, "Misused Merit," in *Civil War Generals in Defeat*, 156; Douglas Maynard, ed., "Vicksburg Diary: The Journal of Gabriel M. Killgore," *Civil War History* 10, no. 1 (March 1964): 38.

49. *OR*, 24(3):149, 152–153, 157; Lewis Van Tuyl to cousin, March 11, 1863, Lewis Van Tuyl Papers, UMC.

50. *OR*, 24(3):136–140, 151; *OR*, 24(1):28; *OR*, 52(1):345; Earl J. Hess, "Grant's Ethnic General: Peter J. Osterhaus," in *Grant's Lieutenants: From Cairo to Vicksburg*, Steven E. Woodworth, ed. (Lawrence: University Press of Kansas, 2001), 206; Simon and Marszalek, eds., *PUSG*, 7:452; Lash, *A Politician Turned General*, 118–119; Charles Hamilton to Stephen Hurlbut, March 11, 1863, Charles S. Hamilton Papers, RG 94, E 159, NARA.

51. *OR*, 24(3):159; *OR*, 10(1):174–190.

52. Frank Tupper to father, March 29, 1863, Frank W. Tupper Papers, ALPL. For more on women posing as men, see Shelby Harriel, *Behind the Rifle: Women Soldiers in Civil War Mississippi* (Jackson: University Press of Mississippi, 2019).

53. *OR*, 24(1):20, 23; *OR*, 24(3):126; Van Dorn and Masters, eds., *The 57th Ohio Veteran Volunteer Infantry*, 142–144; James C. Sinclair Diary, March 3, 1863, CHM; Edward J. Dunn Memoir, undated, OCM, 5; Ebenezer Werkheiser to sister, March 30, 1863, Ebenezer Werkheiser Letters, VICK.

54. *OR*, 24(3):112, 120, 131–132, 135, 159; *OR*, 24(1):403; Kaiser, ed., "'In Sight of Vicksburg,'" 215, 219; John Merrilies Diary, March 30, 1863, CHM; John B. Fletcher Diary, March 17, 1863, ALPL; Luther Cowan Diary, March 16, 1863, and Luther Cowan to wife, March 17, 1863, Luther H. Cowan Papers, TSLA; John W. Chambers Diary, March 16, 1863, ISU; R. S. Finley to friends, March 20, 1863, Robert S. Finley Papers, UNC; John Hardin to father, March 20, 1863, Sesquicentennial Manuscript Project, IHS.

55. *OR*, 24(3):123, 125–126, 698; *OR*, 24(1):21, 469, 474, 486; Isaac O. Shelby Diary, March 23, 1863, UNC; Samuel Fowler Diary, April 30, 1863, SU.

56. *OR*, 24(3):131, 133; *OR*, 24(1):474–475.

57. *OR*, 24(3):132, 136–137, 143; *OR*, 24(1):23, 473, 475–481; "Running the

Vicksburg Batteries," *Harper's Weekly*, April 18, 1863; Richard and Richard, *The Defense of Vicksburg*, 125–126; John Linfor to friend, April 10, 1863, Civil War Collection, UMEM; John Barnes to uncle, March 29, 1863, John W. Barnes Letters, DU.

58. *OR*, 24(3):132, 136–137, 143; *OR*, 24(1):23, 473, 475–477; Raleigh to Rosa, March 30, 1863, Civil War Officer Letter, LSU.

59. *OR*, 24(1):23.

60. *OR*, 24(3):126; "Some Things Our Boy Saw in the War," 1911, Lewis F. Phillips Papers, CWTI, USAHEC, 32.

61. *OR*, 24(3):148, 151–152; *OR*, 24(1):23.

62. *OR*, 24(3):152; *ORN*, 24:479.

63. *OR*, 24(3):126.

64. *OR*, 24(3):127, 134, 159–160; *OR*, 52(1):346; Simon and Marszalek, eds., *PUSG*, 7:475; Timothy C. Young Diary, April 2, 1863, VICK; Cloyd Bryner, *Bugle Echoes: The Story of the Illinois 47th* (Springfield, IL: Phillips Bros. Printers, 1905), 77; Masters, ed., *Sherman's Praetorian Guard*, 108–109; George M. Lucas Diary, April 5, 1863, ALPL; John Merrilies Diary, March 28, 1863, CHM.

65. *OR*, 24(3):147.

CHAPTER 10. "THIS IS THE ONLY MOVE I NOW SEE AS PRACTICABLE"

1. Simon and Marszalek, eds., *PUSG*, 7:479–480; Badeau, *Military History of Ulysses S. Grant,* 1:180–181; Allen J. Ottens, *General John A. Rawlins: No Ordinary Man* (Bloomington: Indiana University Press, 2021), 258; Richardson, *A Personal History of Ulysses S. Grant*, 292; John Davis to wife, March 20, 1863, John F. Davis Letters, OCM; Van Dorn and Masters, eds., *The 57th Ohio Veteran Volunteer Infantry*, 151; Kaiser, ed., "'In Sight of Vicksburg,'" 210; John Merrilies Diary, March 31, 1863, CHM; Luther Cowan to Kingsley Olds, February 25, 1863, Luther H. Cowan Papers, TSLA; Murat Halstead to Salmon Chase, April 1, 1863, and John A. McClernand to Abraham Lincion, March 15, 1863, Abraham Lincoln Papers, LC.

2. Jomini, *The Art of War*, 50–53, 298–313.

3. Clausewitz, *On War*, 115–131.

4. "Ulysses S. Grant," April 9, 1885, *National Tribune;* Young, *Around the World with General Grant*, 2:616.

5. *OR*, 24(1):25; Howe, ed., *Home Letters*, 252, 254; Simon and Marszalek, eds., *PUSG*, 8:9; Thomas R. Latimer to parents, April 20, 1863, Latimer Family Collection, USAHEC.

6. Marszalek, Nolen, and Gallo, eds., *Personal Memoirs of Ulysses S. Grant*, 319; *OR,* 24(1): 44; Ottens, *General John A. Rawlins*, 254; Terrence J. Winschel, "The Vicksburg Campaign," in *The Cambridge History of the American Civil War*, 3 vols., Aaron Sheehad-Dean, ed. (Cambridge, UK: Cambridge University Press, 2019), 1:254.

7. *OR*, 24(1):25–26, 29, 73; Chernow, *Grant*, 249; Simpson, *Ulysses S. Grant*, 177; Marszalek, *Commander of All Lincoln's Armies*, 176–177; Jane Turner Censer, ed., *The*

Papers of Frederick Law Olmsted, 12 vols. (Baltimore: Johns Hopkins University Press, 1977–present), 4:581; R. T. St. John to Abraham Lincoln, February 2, 1863, David Shunk Papers, VICK.

8. Mary A. Livermore, *My Story of the War: A Woman's Narrative of Four Years' Personal Experience as Nurse in The Union Army, and in Relief Work at Home, in Hospitals, Camps, and at the Front During the War of the Rebellion. With Anecdotes, Pathetic Incidents, and Thrilling Reminiscences Portraying the Lights and Shadows of Hospital Life and the Sanitary Service of the War* (Hartford, CT: A. D. Worthington and Company, 1890), 308–317; R. R. Hazard to A. W. Plammenburg, February 11, 1863, Couzins Family Papers, MHS; Kaiser, ed., "'In Sight of Vicksburg,'" 205, 210; List of Medicines, February 21 and 22, 1863, Howard A. Cooper Papers, Civil War Collection, MHS; George Chittenden to wife, March 15, 1863, Chittenden Family Papers, ISL; J. J. Moulton to sister, January 13, 1863, Martin Family Letters, Civil War Collection, MHS; Cyrus Rayhill to unknown, March 10, 1863, Cyrus Rayhill Correspondence, IHS; Peter Myers to friend, January 31, 1863, Peter Myers Letters, IHS.

9. *OR*, 24(1):25, 28; Young, *Around the World with General Grant*, 2:616; Richardson, *A Personal History of Ulysses S. Grant*, 290.

10. James Leeper to Mary, March 28, 1863, James Leeper Correspondence, IHS; Edward Wood to wife, April 25, 1863, Edward J. Wood Letters, IHS; Clarkson Fogg to father, May 3, 1863, Clarkson Fogg Letters, VICK; George W. Gordon Diary, April 24, 1863, USAHEC.

11. *OR*, 24(1):26; Simon and Marszalek, eds., *PUSG*, 7:463; U. S. Grant to David Porter, April 4, 1863, David Dixon Porter Papers, MHS.

12. *OR*, 24(1):71; Hearn, *Admiral David Dixon Porter*, 225–226; Simon and Marszalek, eds., *PUSG*, 7:196, 409; Cadwallader, *Three Years with Grant*, 61; Dana, *Recollections of the Civil War*, 30; James Vanderbilt to mother, April 12, 1863, James C. Vanderbilt Papers, ISL; Charles Lutz to brother, April 11, 1863, Charles Lutz Letters, CWD, USAHEC; Donald L. Miller, *Vicksburg: Grant's Campaign That Broke the Confederacy* (New York: Simon and Shuster, 2019), 324; Simpson, *Ulysses S. Grant*, 178; George O. Smith, "Brief History of the 17th Regiment of the Illinois Volunteer Infantry, U.S.A.," undated, George O. Smith Papers, ALPL, 5; Job H. Yaggy Diary, April 8, 1863, ALPL; Williams, *Lincoln and His Generals*, 225, 227; Philip Bonney to wife, April 10, 1863, Philip C. Bonney Papers, ALPL; John Sheriff to father, April 9, 1863, John Sherriff Family Papers, ALPL; Edmund Newsome Diary, April 8, 1863, OCM, copy in MDAH; Charles Beal to brother, April 14, 1863, Charles W. Beal Papers, ALPL; George W. Modil Diary, April 8, 1863, MDAH.

13. Simon and Marszalek, eds., *PUSG*, 8:30; Bruce Catton, *U. S. Grant and the American Military Tradition* (Boston: Little, Brown and Co., 1954), 98; Samuel Gordon to wife, April 8, 1863, Samuel Gordon Papers, ALPL; Frederick A. Henry, *Captain Henry of Geauga: A Family Chronicle* (Cleveland: Gates Press, 1942), 152.

14. *OR*, 24(1):24, 26, 44; *OR*, 24(3):166, 168, 710; Simon and Marszalek, eds., *PUSG*, 7:268; Marszalek, Nolen, and Gallo, eds., *Personal Memoirs of Ulysses S. Grant*, 319; Kaiser, ed., "'In Sight of Vicksburg,'" 221; Simon and Marszalek, eds., *PUSG*, 8:9,

110; Chambers, "My Journal," 261; Clarke, *Reminiscence and Anecdotes*, 87; Fred Grant Memoir, undated, USGPL, 3–4; Henry J. Seaman Diary, April 1, 1863, CWTI, USAHEC, copy in VICK.

15. *OR*, 24(1):24, 26, 44; *OR*, 24(3):166, 168, 710; Clarke, *Reminiscence and Anecdotes*, 87; Fred Grant Memoir, undated, USGPL, 3–4; Simon and Marszalek, eds., *PUSG*, 7:268; Marszalek, Nolen, and Gallo, eds., *Personal Memoirs of Ulysses S. Grant*, 319; Kaiser, ed., "'In Sight of Vicksburg,'" 221; Henry J. Seaman Diary, April 1, 1863, CWTI, USAHEC; Simon and Marszalek, eds., *PUSG*, 8:9, 110; Chambers, "My Journal," 261.

16. Fred Grant Memoir, undated, USGPL, 4–5.

17. *OR*, 24(3):179–182; *OR*, 24(1):72, 74; *ORN*, 24:479; Simon and Marszalek, eds., *PUSG*, 7:414–415; Marszalek, Nolen, and Gallo, eds., *Personal Memoirs of Ulysses S. Grant*, 374; James Lee McDonough, *William Tecumseh Sherman: In the Service of My Country: A Life* (New York: W. W. Norton & Company, 2016), 397; Simon and Marszalek, eds., *PUSG*, 8:25; Archer Jones, *Civil War Command and Strategy: The Process of Victory and Defeat* (New York: The Free Press, 1992), 159; Sherman, *Memoirs*, 1:315, 317; Wilson, *Under the Old Flag*, 159; Smith, *Life and Letters of Thomas Kilby Smith*, 289; Howe, ed., *Home Letters*, 252, 254; William T. Sherman to Willard Warner, April 19, 1863, Willard Warner Papers, TSLA; S. H. M. Byers, *With Fire and Sword* (New York: The Neale Publishing Company, 1911), 54; Henry Newhall to sister, February 25, 1863, Henry M. Newhall Papers, ALPL.

18. *OR*, 24(3):179–182; *OR*, 24(1):72, 74; *ORN*, 24:479; Simon and Marszalek, eds., *PUSG*, 7:414–415; Marszalek, Nolen, and Gallo, eds., *Personal Memoirs of Ulysses S. Grant*, 374; James Lee McDonough, *William Tecumseh Sherman: In the Service of My Country: A Life* (New York: W. W. Norton & Company, 2016), 397; Simon and Marszalek, eds., *PUSG*, 8:25; Archer Jones, *Civil War Command and Strategy: The Process of Victory and Defeat* (New York: The Free Press, 1992), 159; Sherman, *Memoirs*, 1:315, 317; Wilson, *Under the Old Flag*, 159; Smith, *Life and Letters of Thomas Kilby Smith*, 289; Howe, ed., *Home Letters*, 252, 254; William T. Sherman to Willard Warner, April 19, 1863, Willard Warner Papers, TSLA; S. H. M. Byers, *With Fire and Sword* (New York: The Neale Publishing Company, 1911), 54; Henry Newhall to sister, February 25, 1863, Henry M. Newhall Papers, ALPL.

19. *OR*, 24(3):164, 182–183; *OR*, 24(1):28, 74–75; Kiper, *Major General John A. McClernand*, 211; Stoker, *The Grand Design*, 262; Dana, *Recollections of the Civil War*, 32; William Smith to wife, May 8, 1863, William A. Smith Letters, TU; Peter Osterhaus to John McClernand, April 14, 1863, Letters Sent, RG 393, E 3221, NARA.

20. *OR*, 24(3):164, 182–183; *OR*, 24(1):28, 74–75; Terrence J. Winschel, *Triumph and Defeat: The Vicksburg Campaign, Vol. 2* (New York: Savas Beatie, 2006), 52; Kiper, *Major General John A. McClernand*, 211; Terrence J. Winschel, "Fighting Politician: John A. McClernand," in *Grant's Lieutenants: From Cairo to Vicksburg*, Steven E. Woodworth, ed. (Lawrence: University Press of Kansas, 2001), 131; Michael B. Ballard, "Grant, McClernand, and Vicksburg: A Clash of Personalities and Backgrounds," *The Vicksburg Campaign: March 29–May 18, 1863*, Steven E. Woodworth and Charles D. Grear, eds. (Carbondale: Southern Illinois University Press, 2013), 145; Stoker, *The*

Grand Design, 262; Dana, *Recollections of the Civil War*, 32; William Smith to wife, May 8, 1863, William A. Smith Letters, TU; Peter Osterhaus to John McClernand, April 14, 1863, Letters Sent, RG 393, E 3221, NARA.

21. *OR*, 24(1):26, 29, 495; *OR*, 24(3):164, 168, 174; 35th Iowa Infantry Memoir, undated, OCM, 3; Seth Hall to wife, April 22, 1863, Seth Hall Letters, OCM; John Merrilies Diary, March 31, 1863, CHM; Robert S. Martin Diary, April 4–30, 1863, SIU; Samuel Gordon to wife, April 8, 1863, Samuel Gordon Papers, ALPL; Curtis P. Lacey Diary, April 2–3, 1863, NL.

22. Jenney, "Personal Recollections of Vicksburg," 256–257; Buckles, *Not Afraid to Go Any Whare*, 27.

23. *OR*, 24(1):26, 29, 495; *OR*, 24(3):164, 168, 174; 35th Iowa Infantry Memoir, undated, OCM, 3; Seth Hall to wife, April 22, 1863, Seth Hall Letters, OCM; John Merrilies Diary, March 31, 1863, CHM; Robert S. Martin Diary, April 4–30, 1863, SIU; Samuel Gordon to wife, April 8, 1863, Samuel Gordon Papers, ALPL; Curtis P. Lacey Diary, April 2–3, 1863, NL.

24. *OR*, 24(1):139, 490–491, 495; *OR*, 24(3):164, 713; *Vicksburg Campaign: Driving Tour Guide*, 64; Bearss, *The Vicksburg Campaign*, 2:27; Bridge, ed., *These Men Were Heroes Once*, 112; *SOR*, 3:353–355; Townsend, *Yankee Warhorse*, 80; Terrence J. Winschel, *Triumph and Defeat: The Vicksburg Campaign* (Mason City, IA: Savas Publishing Company, 1999), 19–20; Soman and Byrne, eds., *A Jewish Colonel in the Civil War*, 267; William A. Sypher Diary, April 5, 1863, CHM; Alexander Shall Diary, April 2, 1863, VICK; Reuben H. Falconer Diary, April 7, 1863, OHS.

25. *OR*, 24(1):139–140, 491–492, 496; Bearss, *The Vicksburg Campaign*, 2:31; Winschel, ed., *The Civil War Diary of a Common Soldier*, 43; Simon and Marszalek, eds., *PUSG*, 8:26; Peter Osterhaus to John McClernand, April 8, 1863, Letters Sent, RG 393, E 3221, NARA; General Orders 31, April 2, 1863, General and Special Orders, RG 393, E 3230, NARA.

26. *OR*, 24(1):47, 492; William Rand to father and brother, April 12 and 16, 1863, Rand Family Papers, ALPL.

27. Peter Osterhaus to John McClernand, April 12, 1863, Letters Sent, RG 393, E 3221, NARA.

28. Paul H. Hass, ed., "The Vicksburg Diary of Henry Clay Warmoth: Part I (April 2, 1863–April 27, 1863)," *Journal of Mississippi History* 31, no. 4 (November 1969): 336–338.

29. *OR*, 24(1):124, 492; *OR*, 24(3):170.

30. *OR*, 24(1):490, 492–493; *OR*, 24(3):174; Grabau, *Ninety-Eight Days*, 65; Townsend, *Yankee Warhorse*, 82; Bridge, ed., *These Men Were Heroes Once*, 113–117; George Roberts to wife, April 17, 1863, George W. Roberts Collection, ISL.

31. *OR*, 24(1):490; Grabau, *Ninety-Eight Days*, 65; Oran Perry, "The Entering Wedge," in *War Papers Read Before the Indiana Commandery Military Order of the Loyal Legion of the United States* (Indianapolis: The Commandery, 1898), 366–376; Samuel Gordon to wife, April 19, 1863, Samuel Gordon Papers, ALPL.

32. *OR*, 24(1):493; *OR*, 24(3):175; Bearss, *The Vicksburg Campaign*, 2:31; John F. Marszalek, *Sherman: A Soldier's Passion for Order* (New York: The Free Press, 1993), 216; Maynard, ed., "Vicksburg Diary," 41; Charles Enslow to wife, April 6, 1863, Charles Calvin Enslow Papers, LC; George R. Lee Diary, April 6, 1863, ALPL; General Orders, April 7, 1863, General and Special Orders, RG 393, E 3230, NARA.

33. *OR*, 24(1):493–494; *OR*, 24(3):171, 186, 188; Soman and Byrne, eds., *A Jewish Colonel in the Civil War*, 267; Simon and Marszalek, eds., *PUSG*, 8:28, 38–39; Pryce, *Vanishing Footprints*, 91; James C. Sinclair Diary, April 6 and 9, 1863, CHM; Kaiser, ed., "The Civil War Diary of Florison D. Pitts," 35; Florison Pitts to father, April 14, 1863, Florison D. Pitts Papers, CHM.

34. *OR*, 24(3):188, 190; Simon and Marszalek, eds., *PUSG*, 8:19.

35. *OR*, 24(1):73; *OR*, 24(3):231; Simon and Marszalek, eds., *PUSG*, 7:391–392, 410, 413; Simon and Marszalek, eds., *PUSG*, 8:35; Kaiser, ed., "The Civil War Diary of Florison D. Pitts," 35; Soman and Byrne, eds., *A Jewish Colonel in the Civil War*, 248; R. S. Finley to friends, March 20, 1863, Robert S. Finley Papers, UNC; Henry Field to Mary Ann Given, June 13, 1863, John G. Given Letters, ALPL; Samuel Gordon to wife, May 6, 1863, Samuel Gordon Papers, ALPL; Special Orders 96, April 14, 1863, General and Special Orders, RG 393, E 3230, NARA.

36. *OR*, 24(1):73; *OR*, 24(3):231; Clausewitz, *On War*, 403; Simon and Marszalek, eds., *PUSG*, 7:391–392, 410, 413; Simon and Marszalek, eds., *PUSG*, 8:35; Kaiser, ed., "The Civil War Diary of Florison D. Pitts," 35; Soman and Byrne, eds., *A Jewish Colonel in the Civil War*, 248; R. S. Finley to friends, March 20, 1863, Robert S. Finley Papers, UNC; Henry Field to Mary Ann Given, June 13, 1863, John G. Given Letters, ALPL; Samuel Gordon to wife, May 6, 1863, Samuel Gordon Papers, ALPL; Special Orders 96, April 14, 1863, General and Special Orders, RG 393, E 3230, NARA.

37. *OR*, 24(3):187, 187; *OR*, 24(1):74; Simon, ed., *The Personal Memoirs of Julia Dent Grant*, 111; Cadwallader, *Three Years with Grant*, 60.

38. *OR*, 24(3):171–172; *OR*, 52(1):346; Simon and Marszalek, eds., *PUSG*, 7:301; Sherman, *Memoirs*, 1:313; David Stuart to soldiers, April 3, 1863, and William Kennedy to wife, April 8, 1863, William J. Kennedy Papers, ALPL; James Boyd Diary, April 7, 1863, ALPL; S. M. Dayton to David Stuart, April 3, 1863, and General Orders 19, April 4, 1863, David Stuart Papers, RG 94, E 159, NARA.

39. Simon and Marszalek, eds., *PUSG*, 8:164; Parrish, *Frank Blair*, 162, 164; Marszalek, Nolen, and Gallo, eds., *Personal Memoirs of Ulysses S. Grant*, 396; William Kennedy to wife, April 8, 1863, William J. Kennedy Papers, ALPL.

40. *OR*, 24(1):418; *ORN*, 24:479; W. A. Rorer to his cousin, April 2, 1863, W. A. Rorer Letters, MDAH; M. D. L. Stephens Recollections, undated, MDAH, 16; William Vermilion to wife, April 6, 1863, William F. Vermilion Papers, UCSD.

41. *OR*, 24(1):419–420; *OR*, 24(3):696; *OR*, 52(2):446; Maury, *Recollections of a Virginian*, 177; Martin Van Kees Diary, March 28, 1863, OCM; Winfield Featherston to R. W. Memminger, March 30, 1863, John C. Pemberton Papers, RG 109, E 131, NARA.

42. *OR*, 24(1):418–420; *OR*, 52(2):451–452; Bryan S. Bush, *Lloyd Tilghman:*

Confederate General in the Western Theater (Morley, MO: Acclaim Press, 2006), 171; Maury, *Recollections of a Virginian*, 178; Alexander Ewing to parents, April 2, 1863, Alexander K. Ewing Papers, ALPL.

43. Bearss, *The Vicksburg Campaign*, 1:545–546; Stone, *Memoir of George Boardman Boomer*, 248; Brown, *History of the Fourth Regiment of Minnesota Infantry Volunteers*, 171; Mark Grimsley and Todd D. Miller, eds., *The Union Must Stand: The Civil War Diary of John Quincy Adams Campbell, Fifth Iowa Volunteer Infantry* (Knoxville: University of Tennessee Press, 2000), 85, originals in John Quincy Adams Campbell Diaries, WRHS; Henry Cole Quinby, *Genealogical History of the Quinby (Quimby) Family in England and America* (Rutland, VT: The Tuttle Company, 1915), 429.

44. *OR*, 24(1):401, 418–419; James D. Heath Diary, April 2, 1863, OCM; William Vermilion to wife, April 6, 1863, William F. Vermilion Papers, UCSD; J. Z. George to Bettie, April 10, 1863, James Z. George Papers, MDAH; George R. Lee Diary, March 23, 1863, ALPL; George M. Shearer Diary, April 5, 1863, UIA; L. D. Bradley to wife, April 11, 1863, L. D. Bradley Letter, UNT; John F. Lester Diary, April 5, 1863, IHS; Daniel Hughes Diary, April 5, 1863, IHS, copy in ISL; John Wilson to Lizzie, April 6, 1863, John A. Wilson Letters, MDAH; John Boucher to wife, April 12, 1863, Boucher Family Papers, CWD, USAHEC; Isaac Vanderwarker Diary, April 2–3, 1863, CWD, USAHEC.

45. *ORN*, 24:283, 694; Jeffrey L. Patrick, ed., *Three Years with Wallace's Zouaves: The Civil War Memoirs of Thomas Wise Durham* (Macon, GA: Mercer University Press, 2003); 106; John F. Lester Diary, April 10, 1863, IHS; John B. Elliott Diary, April 10, 1863, ISL; Aaron Dunbar and Harvey M. Trimble, *History of the Ninety-third Regiment Volunteer Infantry From Organization to Muster Out* (Chicago: The Blakely Printing Co., 1898), 21; John S. Jackman Diary, April 6–7, 1863, LC; Isaac Vanderwarker Diary, April 5 and 9, 1863, CWD, USAHEC; George Ditto Diary, April 8–10, 1863, ALPL; Unknown to Sam Henderson, April 10, 1863, John C. Pemberton Papers, RG 109, E 131, NARA; Joseph Ledergerber Diary, April 7 and 9, 1863, ALPL.

46. *OR*, 24(1):420–421; *OR*, 52(2):454; Daniel Ramsey to his mother, April 28, 1863, Andrew W. Ramsey and Family Papers, MDAH; H. N. Faulkinbury Diary, April 20, 1863, MDAH.

47. *OR*, 24(1):26, 417; *OR*, 24(3):189.

48. James Z. George to his wife, April 10, 1863, James Z. George Papers, MDAH; John Boucher to wife, April 12, 1863, Boucher Family Papers, CWD, USAHEC.

49. *OR*, 24(1):502; *OR*, 24(3):158; John Merrilies Diary, April 2, 1863, CHM; C. A. Reynolds to Ralph Voorhies, April 2, 1863, Ralph P. Voorhies Letters, OCM; Calvin Ainsworth Diary, April 29, 1863, UMB.

50. Simon and Marszalek, eds., *PUSG*, 7:332–333; *Military History and Reminiscences of the Thirteenth Regiment of Illinois Volunteer Infantry*, 301; Henry J. Seaman Diary, April 4, 1863, CWTI, USAHEC.

51. *OR*, 24(3):158; Adoniram Withrow to wife, April 1, 1863, Adoniram Judson Withrow Papers, UNC.

52. *OR*, 24(1):502, 507, 509; *OR*, 24(3):173; Bek, ed., "The Civil War Diary of John T. Buegel, Union Soldier, Part II," 506; John N. Bell Diary, April 4, 1863, OHS; Henry J.

Seaman Diary, April 4, 1863, CWTI, USAHEC; Noble W. Wood Diary, April 3–4, 1863, UCB.

53. *OR*, 24(1):502–504, 507–508; Owens, *Steamboats and the Cotton Economy*, 59; Maynard, ed., "Vicksburg Diary," 40; Elbert D. Willett Diary, April 6, 1863, ADAH; *History of Company B*, 30; Carter Stevenson to Robert Memminger, April 5, 1863, and Carter Stevenson to John Pemberton, April 6, 1863, John C. Pemberton Papers, RG 109, E 131, NARA.

54. *OR*, 24(1):509; Samuel W. Ferguson Memoirs, undated, VICK, 42.

55. *OR*, 24(1):502–505, 508; Noble W. Wood Diary, April 6–7, 1863, UCB; J. J. Moulton to brother, April 21, 1863, Martin Family Letters, Civil War Collection, MHS; William Dupray to sister, April 15, 1863, Morgan Family Papers, UW; *Military History and Reminiscences of the Thirteenth Regiment of Illinois Volunteer Infantry*, 303; Charles Foster Diary, March 8, 1863, VICK; Calvin Ainsworth Diary, April 6, 1863, UMB; Samuel W. Ferguson Memoirs, undated, VICK, 42–43; Charles Miller Memoir, undated, VICK, 40–41; John N. Bell Diary, April 6–7 and 24, 1863, OHS; Henry J. Seaman Diary, April 7, 1863, CWTI, USAHEC.

56. *OR*, 24(1):502–504, 509–510; Edwin Obriham to brother, April 15, 1863, Edward C. Obriham Letters, VICK; Clarke, *Reminiscence and Anecdotes*, 90–91; Henry J. Seaman Diary, April 8, 1863, CWTI, USAHEC.

57. *OR*, 24(1):502; Oake, *On the Skirmish Line*, 101; William Dupray to sister, April 15, 1863, Morgan Family Papers, UW; Adoniram Withrow to wife, April 17, 1863, Adoniram Judson Withrow Papers, UNC; John N. Bell Diary, April 7–8, 1863, OHS; Henry J. Seaman Diary, April 8, 1863, CWTI, USAHEC.

58. *OR*, 24(1):502, 504–507, 511; Hattaway, *General Stephen D. Lee*, 83; William Dupray to sister, April 15, 1863, Morgan Family Papers, UW; Henry J. Seaman Diary, April 9, 1863, CWTI, USAHEC.

59. *OR*, 24(1):504–507, 509; Hattaway, *General Stephen D. Lee*, 83; Rebecca Blackwell Drake and Margie Riddle Bearss, eds., *My Dear Wife: Letters to Matilda: The Civil War Letters of Sid and Matilda Champion of Champion Hill* (N.p.: n.p., 2005), 73, 79.

60. *OR*, 24(1):501–502, 510–511; *OR*, 24(3):186; Bek, ed., "The Civil War Diary of John T. Buegel, Union Soldier, Part II," 507; Adoniram Withrow to wife, April 24, 1863, Adoniram Judson Withrow Papers, UNC; Noble W. Wood Diary, April 10–11 and 18, 1863, UCB; William Rigby to brother, April 13, 1863, William T. Rigby Papers, UIA; William Dupray to sister, April 15, 1863, Morgan Family Papers, UW; John N. Bell Diary, April 16, 1863, OHS; Henry J. Seaman Diary, April 10, 1863, CWTI, USAHEC; Thomas Larkin to wife, April 9, 1863, Thomas G. Larkin Papers, KHS.

61. *OR*, 24(1):509–510; John N. Bell Diary, April 22, 1863, OHS.

62. *OR*, 24(1):505, 510; A. Achen to "Headquarter Ohio Union," undated, A. Achen Papers, CHM; Jacob Flory to parents, April 28, 1863, Jacob Flory Letters, OCM; Calvin Ainsworth Diary, April 7, 1863, UMB; Henry J. Seaman Diary, April 10, 1863, CWTI, USAHEC; John W. Chambers Diary, April 8, 1863, ISU.

63. Williams, "The Cruise of 'The Black Terror,'" 3:165.

64. *OR*, 24(3):709, 715, 730, 732; W. H. Claiborne Diary, April 11, 1863, J. F. H.

Claiborne Papers, UNC; J. B. Sanders to family, April 22, 1863, J. B. Sanders Papers, MDAH; M. R. Banner to wife, April 12, 1863, Banner Family Letters, OCM; James Ferguson to wife, April 21, 1863, James Ferguson Letters, OCM; Joseph Pendleton to sister, March 28, 1863, Joseph W. Pendleton Letters, OCM; Henry Morgan to Ellen, April 4, 1863, Henry T. Morgan Letters, CWD, USAHEC.

65. *OR*, 24(3):714, 717, 724, 732; W. Lipscomb to father, April 27, 1863, W. H. Lipscomb Letters, TSLA; William Thurman to family, April 12, 1863, William Thurman Letters, TSLA; J. Wood Coleman Journal, April–May 1883, TSLA.

66. *OR*, 24(3):709, 712–714, 719, 724–725, 729, 731; *OR*, 52(2):422, 457; Tunnard, *A Southern Record*, 218, 225.

67. *OR*, 24(3):708, 710, 716, 725–728.

68. *OR*, 24(3):709–710, 715, 717; Wiley Bartlett to wife, March 31, 1863, Wiley Bartlett Letters, TSLA.

69. *OR*, 24(3):713–714, 720, 724–725, 730–732, 735, 737; Grabau, *Ninety-Eight Days*, 69; Woodworth, *Nothing but Victory*, 321; Isaac H. Elliott, *History of the Thirty-third Regiment Illinois Veteran Volunteer Infantry in the Civil War, 22nd August 1861, to 7th December, 1865* (Gibson City, IL: The Association, 1902), 37; Tucker, *The Forgotten "Stonewall of the West,"* 197; George Bradley Memoir, undated, OCM, 5; "Personal Memoirs of I. V. Smith," 1902, SHSMC, 26; John Reeve to Carter Stevenson, April 4, 1863, John C. Pemberton Papers, RG 109, E 131, NARA; John Bowen to Carter Stevenson, April 4 and 7, 1863, John Bowen Letter Book, RG 109, Chapter II, Vol. 274, NARA.

70. *OR*, 24(3):709, 711–712, 714, 719, 724, 730–731, 734, 738–739; Bearss, *The Vicksburg Campaign*, 2:125–126; M. M. Owen to father, April 7, 1863, Owen Family Papers, TSLA; T. C. Ryan, "Experiences of a Soldier in the Civil War," undated, OCM, 2.

71. *OR*, 24(3):708–709, 713, 731, 733, 737; *Harper's Weekly* front page, April 4 and 11, 1863; Thomas Smith Manuscript, undated, MDAH, 5, copy in Columbus Sykes Papers, CWD, USAHEC.

72. *OR*, 24(3):735.

Chapter 11. "They Are About to Execute Some Plan"

1. Theodore St. John to Janie, January 27, 1863, Theodore E. St. John Papers, LC; Richard and Richard, *The Defense of Vicksburg*, 126; Peter Osterhaus to John McClernand, April 20, 1863, Letters Sent, RG 393, E 3221, NARA.

2. John Barnes to uncle, March 29, 1863, John W. Barnes Letters, DU.

3. *OR*, 24(2):337; Grabau, *Ninety-Eight Days*, 39–44; Daniel, *Engineering in the Confederate Heartland*, 74; Bearss, *The Vicksburg Campaign*, 2:60–61, 63; J. T. Hogane, "Reminiscences of the Siege of Vicksburg," *Southern Historical Society Papers* 11, nos. 4–5 (April–May 1883): 224 (223–227).

4. *OR*, 24(2):337; Bearss, *The Vicksburg Campaign*, 1:459–460; Bearss, *The Vicksburg Campaign*, 2:61, 63.

5. *OR*, 24(2):337; Bearss, *The Vicksburg Campaign*, 1:459–460; Bearss, *The Vicksburg*

Campaign, 2:61, 63–64; I. A. King to brother, March 21, 1862, I. A. King Letter, UA; A. L. Slack Diary, April 1, 1863, VICK, 4.

    6. *OR*, 24(2):337; Bearss, *The Vicksburg Campaign*, 1:459–460; Bearss, *The Vicksburg Campaign*, 2:64.

    7. *OR*, 24(3):222; *OR*, 24(1):133; Richard and Richard, *The Defense of Vicksburg*, 133; John Merrilies Diary, April 20, 1863, CHM; Edward E. Schweitzer Diary, April 20, 1863, CWTI, USAHEC.

    8. *OR*, 24(3):186, *ORN*, 24:565; Grabau, *Ninety-Eight Days*, 74; R. Blake Dunnavent, "'We Had Lively Times Up The Yazoo': Admiral David Dixon Porter," in *Grant's Lieutenants: From Cairo to Vicksburg*, Steven E. Woodworth, ed. (Lawrence: University Press of Kansas, 2001), 178; L. P. Brockett, *The Camp, The Battle Field, and the Hospital; Or, Lights and Shadows of the Great Rebellion* (Philadelphia: National Publishing Company, 1866), 235–241; Richard and Richard, *The Defense of Vicksburg*, 126; James Leeper to Mary, March 28, 1863, James Leeper Correspondence, IHS; USS *Pittsburg* Logbook, April 15–16, 1863, RG 24, E 118, NARA.

    9. *OR*, 24(1):517; *ORN*, 24:553–555; Joiner, *Mr. Lincoln's Brown Water Navy*, 130; Gary D. Joiner, "Running the Gauntlet: The Effectiveness of Combined Forces in the Vicksburg Campaign," in *The Vicksburg Campaign: March 29–May 18, 1863*, Steven E. Woodworth and Charles D. Grear, eds. (Carbondale: Southern Illinois University Press, 2013), 8–23; Charles E. Affeld Diary, April 16, 1863, VICK; James Owen to father, April 21, 1863, James B. Owen Letters, TSLA; Cyrus Delany to brothers, April 19, 1863, Cyrus M. Delany Letters, TSLA; Leonard Loomis to wife, February 11, 1863, Leonard Loomis Letters, Douwe B. Yntema Collection, AM.

    10. *OR*, 24(1):517; Simon and Marszalek, eds., *PUSG*, 8:52; Marszalek, Nolen, and Gallo, eds., *Personal Memoirs of Ulysses S. Grant*, 321; Silas T. Trowbridge, *Autobiography of Silas Thompson Trowbridge, M.D.* (Carbondale: Southern Illinois University Press, 2004), 114–115; Wilson, *Under the Old Flag*, 164; Simon, ed., *The Personal Memoirs of Julia Dent Grant*, 111–112; Fred Grant Memoir, undated, USGPL, 6; Special Orders 139, January 23, 1863, Orders and Letters, RG 393, E 3227, NARA.

    11. *ORN*, 24:553, 555, 559; Lewis A. McBroom, "Running the Blockade," April 16, 1863, American Song Sheets Collection, DU; USS *Pittsburg* Logbook, April 16, 1863, RG 24, E 118, NARA.

    12. *OR*, 24(1):517; *ORN*, 24:554, 559; *OR*, 52(2):416; Bearss, *The Vicksburg Campaign*, 2:65–66; Miller, *Vicksburg*, 347; Lockett, "The Defense of Vicksburg," 485; Ballard, *Vicksburg*, 198; Robert L. Bachman Memoir, undated, OCM, 18; A. L. Slack Diary, April 1, 1863, VICK, 5; Maury, *Recollections of a Virginian*, 188; Chambers, "My Journal," 261; W. H. Claiborne Diary, April 17, 1863, J. F. H. Claiborne Papers, UNC; David Porter to John Dorman, January 27, 1888, John H. Dorman Papers, OHS; William T. Mumford Diary, April 16, 1863, OCM.

    13. *ORN*, 24:552–553, 555–556, 682; Porter, *Incidents and Anecdotes*, 176; James Kays to brother, April 17, 1863, Kays Family Papers, ALPL.

    14. *ORN*, 24:553, 557, 559.

    15. *ORN*, 24:553, 558–559.

16. *ORN*, 24:553, 559–560.

17. *ORN*, 24:561–562, 690; Henry Walke to John Dorman, February 9, 1888, John H. Dorman Papers, OHS.

18. *OR*, 24(1):30, 517; *ORN*, 24:553, 557, 563; *OR*, 24(3):201, 207–208; Sherman, *Memoirs*, 1:317–318; Charles Dana Gibson and E. Kay Gibson, *Dictionary of Transports and Combatant Vessels Steam and Sail Employed by the Union Army, 1861–1868* (Camden, ME: Ensign Press, 1995), 148; Special Orders 58, April 16, 1863, Hugh Ewing Papers, OHS; Hugh Ewing Diary, April 17, 1863, OHS; James Worthington to Lizzie, April 23, 1863, James K. Worthington Letters, CWTI, USAHEC.

19. *ORN*, 24:563, 704; Asa Bean to unknown, April 10, 1863, Bean Family Papers, UIA.

20. Chambers, "My Journal," 261–262; W. H. Claiborne Diary, April 17 and 20, 1863, J. F. H. Claiborne Papers, UNC; Ben Bounds Memoir, undated, OCM, 13, copy in MDAH; Mary Ann Loughborough, *My Cave Life in Vicksburg: With Letters of Trial and Travel* (New York: D. Appleton and Company, 1864), 14; Unknown to mother, April 19, 1863, Adoniram J. Sanders Correspondence, IHS; William T. Mumford Diary, April 16, 1863, OCM.

21. *OR*, 24(1):517; *ORN*, 24:551–552, 554, 556–557, 559, 564–565, 682; Walke, *Naval Scenes and Reminiscences*, 353; John Rice to brother, April 19, 1863, John B. Rice Letters, RBHPC; Sherod Horton to wife, April 18, 1863, Sherod Horton Letters, VICK; James Vanderbilt to mother, April 17, 1863, James C. Vanderbilt Papers, ISL.

22. *OR*, 24(3):200; Townsend, *Yankee Warhorse*, 84; George B. Marshall Reminiscences, 1912, ISL, 40; Hass, ed., "The Vicksburg Diary of Henry Clay Warmoth: Part I," 343.

23. *OR*, 24(1):76; Simon and Marszalek, eds., *PUSG*, 8:30; Fred Grant Memoir, undated, USGPL, 7–8.

24. *OR*, 24(1):518; *ORN*, 24:566, 568; *OR*, 24(3):753, 756; *OR*, 52(2):458–459; Bearss, *The Vicksburg Campaign*, 2:74; L. J. Sanders Diary, April 16, 1863, WKU; Richard and Richard, *The Defense of Vicksburg*, 131–132; R. W. Memminger, "The Surrender of Vicksburg—A Defense of General Pemberton," *Southern Historical Society Papers* 12, nos. 7–9 (July–September 1884): 354; John Merrilies Diary, April 17, 1863, CHM; George D. Carrington Diary, April 16, 1863, CHM; W. H. Claiborne Diary, April 17, 1863, J. F. H. Claiborne Papers, UNC; James Slack to wife, April 18, 1863, James R. Slack Letters, ISL; Joseph Alexander to friend, April 17, 1863, Joseph S. Alexander Letters, OCM.

25. "Personal Memoirs of I. V. Smith," 1902, SHSMC, 26; George Bradley Memoir, undated, OCM, 5; Curtis P. Lacey Diary, April 17, 1863, NL.

26. *OR*, 24(3):185, 191, 193, 196, 202, 773; *OR*, 24(1):520; John Pemberton to Franklin Gardner, April 17, 1863, Letters and Telegrams Sent, RG 109, Chapter 2, Vol. 60, NARA; Edwin Levings to parents, April 25, 1863, Edwin D. Levings Papers, University of Wisconsin-River Falls; Joseph Young to wife, April 22, 1863, Joseph W. Young Letters, IHS; DeBenneville Randolph Keim Diary, April 22, 1863, Civil War Collection, UMEM; William Sooy Smith, "The Mississippi Raid," *Military Essays and Recollections*.

Essays and Papers Read Before the Illinois Commandery, 4 vols. (Chicago: Order of the Commandery, 1907), 4:380. For Streight's Raid, see Bearss, *The Vicksburg Campaign*, 2:129–177, and Edwin C. Bearss, "Colonel Streight Drives for the Western and Atlantic Railroad," *Alabama Historical Quarterly* 26 (Summer 1964): 133–186; Charles S. Patchen Diary, April 10, 1863, ALPL. For Bryant and Sooy Smith, see H. H. Bennett Diary, April 17, 1863, WHS and Van Bennett Diary, April 17, 1863, WHS; Charles Brush to father, April 20, 1863, Brush Family Papers, ALPL; Thomas R. Hodgson Diary, April 18, 1863, OCM. For the raid itself, see Smith, *The Real Horse Soldiers*; S. L. Woodward, "Grierson's Raid, April 17th to May 2d, 1863," *Journal of the United States Cavalry Association* 14, no. 52 (April 1904): 685–710; S. L. Woodward, "Grierson's Raid, April 17th to May 2d, 1863," *Journal of the United States Cavalry Association* 15, no. 53 (July 1904): 94–123; Dave Roth, "Grierson's Raid, April 17–May 2, 1863: A Cavalry Raid at Its Best," *Blue & Gray Magazine* 10, no. 5 (June 1993): 12–24, 48–65.

    27. B. H. Grierson to T. W. Lippincott, March 13, 1886, Benjamin H. Grierson Papers, ALPL; "Army Correspondence," May 4, 1863, Canton (Illinois) *Weekly Register*; S. A. Forbes to sister, April 13, 1863, Stephen A. Forbes Papers, UI.

    28. *OR*, 24(3):197; *OR*, 24(1):522; Benjamin H. Grierson, *A Just and Righteous Cause: Benjamin H. Grierson's Civil War Memoir*, Bruce J. Dinges and Shirley A. Leckie, eds. (Carbondale: Southern Illinois University Press, 2008), 144–146; S. A. Hurlbut to B. H. Grierson, April 13, 1863, Benjamin H. Grierson Papers, ALPL; James Cole to cousin, April 7, 1863, James M. Cole Papers, ALPL; Jasper F. Smith Obituary, February 14, 1930, Verdan, Oklahoma, *News*. For soldiers left behind, see Collier Family Papers, CWD, USAMHI and Obadiah Ethelbert Baker Diary, April 20, 1863, Obadiah Ethelbert Baker Papers, HL. For the battery's armament, see Battery K, 1st Illinois Artillery Muster Roll, RG 94, E 57, NARA.

    29. *OR*, 24(1):521–523, 529; Grierson, *A Just and Righteous Cause*, 148–150; Raid Instructions, undated, William T. Sherman Letters, MDAH; "Ex-Slave Autobiography," Joe Rollins, West Point, Mississippi, Miscellaneous Papers, MSU. For Grierson's compositions, see his papers in ALPL and Benjamin Henry Grierson Vertical File, Gettysburg College.

    30. *OR*, 24(1):523, 530, 534; S. A. Forbes, "Grierson's Cavalry Raid," *Transactions of the Illinois State Historical Society* (Springfield, IL: Phillips Bros. State Printers, 1908), 102.

    31. *OR*, 24(1):530–531, 534; Grierson, *A Just and Righteous Cause*, 152; "Skirmish in Chickasaw County," April 23, 1863, Jackson *Daily Mississippian*.

    32. *OR*, 24(1):252, 543–544, 551–553; *OR*, 24(3):770; Grabau, *Ninety-Eight Days*, 119; John to Jennie, April 28, 1863, John Letter, FHS; James Burton to Daniel Ruggles, April 19, 1863, Civil War Collection, LMU; James H. Rives to John J. Pettus, May 2, 1863, John J. Pettus Correspondence, MDAH.

    33. *OR*, 24(1):523–524; Grierson, *A Just and Righteous Cause*, 153–154, 156; "The Enemy in Starkville," April 21, 1863, Jackson *Daily Mississippian*; B. H. Grierson to Alice, April 21, 1863, Benjamin H. Grierson Papers, ALPL. For Surby's activities, see R. W. Surby, *Grierson Raids, and Hatch's Sixty-four Days March, with Biographical Sketches*,

also, the Life and Adventures of Chickasaw, the Scout (Chicago: Rounds and James, 1865), and R. W. Surby, *Two Great Raids. Col. Grierson's Successful Swoop Through Mississippi. Morgan's Disastrous Raid Through Indiana and Ohio. Vivid Narratives of Both These Great Operations, with Extracts From Official Records. John Morgan's Escape, Last Raid, and Death* (Washington, DC: National Tribune, 1897).

34. *OR*, 24(1):524.

35. *OR*, 24(1):528; Henry C. Forbes, "Grierson's Raid," Henry C. Forbes Papers, CHM, 14–15, copy in Henry C. Forbes Papers, UI.

36. *OR*, 24(1):524.

37. *OR*, 24(1):567; *OR*, 24(3):204, 207, 212.

38. *OR*, 24(1):30, 565–569; *OR*, 24(3):215; Marszalek, Nolen, and Gallo, eds., *Personal Memoirs of Ulysses S. Grant*, 327; George D. Carrington Diary, April 22, 1863, CHM; Wilbur F. Crummer, *With Grant at Fort Donelson, Shiloh and Vicksburg, and An Appreciation of General U.S. Grant* (Oak Park, IL: E. C. Crummer and Co., 1915), 93–96; John M. Adair, *Historical Sketch of the Forty-fifth Illinois Regiment, With a Complete List of the Officers and Privates and an Individual Record of Each Man in the Regiment* (Lanark, IL: Carroll County Gazette Print, 1869), 9; E. Z. Hays, *History of the Thirty-second Regiment Ohio Veteran Volunteer Infantry* (Columbus, OH: Cott & Evans Printers, 1896), 39; Luther Cowan Diary, April 21, 1863, Luther H. Cowan Papers, TSLA; John Hardin to father, April 24, 1863, Sesquicentennial Manuscript Project, IHS; S. C. Beck, "A True Sketch of His Army Life" (N.p.: n.p., n.d.), 6, copy in OCM and VICK; Job H. Yaggy Diary, April 21, 1863, ALPL; James McLaughlin to father, May 11, 1863, James McLaughlin Papers, ISL.

39. *OR*, 24(1):564, 567; *OR*, 24(3):212, 217; Andrew Sproul to wife, April 22, 1863, Andrew J. Sproul Papers, UNC.

40. *OR*, 24(1):78, 564–565, 569–570; *OR*, 24(3):215–216; John Hardin to father, April 24, 1863, Sesquicentennial Manuscript Project, IHS; "Running the Batteries," undated, William E. Strong Papers, ALPL, 4, printed as William E. Strong, "The Campaign Against Vicksburg," in *Military Essays and Recollections: Papers Read Before the Commandery of the State of Illinois, Military Order of the Loyal Legion of the United States*, 4 vols. (Chicago: A. C. McClurg and Company, 1894), 2:313–354; Special Orders 60, April 20, 1863, Hugh Ewing Papers, OHS.

41. *OR*, 24(3):756, 759–760, 762, 773; *OR*, 52(2):416; Bearss, *The Vicksburg Campaign*, 2:80; Richard and Richard, *The Defense of Vicksburg*, 133; John Pemberton to Jefferson Davis, April 18, 1863, John C. Pemberton Papers, RG 109, E 131, NARA.

42. *OR*, 24(1):564–566; James Worthington to Lizzie, April 23, 1863, James K. Worthington Letters, CWTI, USAHEC.

43. *OR*, 24(1):564–566; *OR*, 24(3):231; Gibson and Gibson, *Dictionary of Transports*, 316; James A. Fowler and Miles M. Miller, *History of the Thirtieth Iowa Infantry Volunteers. Giving a Complete Record of the Movements of the Regiment from Its Organization Until Muster Out* (Mediapolis, IA: T. A. Merrill, Printer, 1908), 10; Joseph Skipworth to wife, April 23, 1863, Joseph Skipworth Papers, SIU.

44. *OR*, 24(1):570; *OR*, 24(3):778; Richard and Richard, *The Defense of Vicksburg*, 133; Joseph Skipworth to wife, April 23, 1863, Joseph Skipworth Papers, SIU.

45. *OR*, 24(1):565–566, 569; Hovey Manuscript, undated, IU, 47; James McLaughlin to father, May 11, 1863, James McLaughlin Papers, ISL.

46. *OR*, 24(1):565–566.

47. *OR*, 24(1):565, 567–568, 570.

48. *OR*, 24(1):565, 568–569.

49. *OR*, 24(1):565, 570; *ORN*, 24:704; Robert Hamilton to wife, April 23, 1863, Robert Hamilton Letters, VICK.

50. *OR*, 24(1):31, 565; Sherman, *Memoirs*, 1:318; Augustus Sinks Journal, undated, ISL, 32.

51. *OR*, 24(1):570; Stephen Croom Diary, April 22, 1863, VICK.

52. Richard and Richard, *The Defense of Vicksburg*, 134; John Merrilies Diary, April 26, 1863, CHM.

53. *OR*, 24(3):740–741, 744–746, 758.

54. *OR*, 24(3):747–748, 751–753, 756–757, 760–761, 765–766; *OR*, 24(1):252; James Willis, *Arkansas Confederates in the Western Theater* (Dayton, OH: Morningside, 1998), 345; Henry George, *History of the 3d, 7th, 8th and 12th Kentucky C.S.A.* (Louisville, KY: C. T. Dearing Printing Co., 1911), 55–56; G. H. Burns to wife, April 17, 1863, G. H. Burns Letters, VICK; James R. Binford, "Recollections of the Fifteenth Regiment of Mississippi Infantry, C.S.A.," undated, Patrick Henry Papers, MDAH, 41; John Wilson to Lizzie, April 14 and 17, 1863, John A. Wilson Letters, MDAH.

55. *OR*, 24(3):746, 748–749, 753, 755–756, 758, 761, 770, 776; Grabau, *Ninety-Eight Days*, 91; Maurice K. Simons Diary, April 17, 1863, OCM; Kaiser, ed., "'In Sight of Vicksburg,'" 209; Stephen Croom Diary, April 3, 17, and 22, 1863, VICK; John L. Power Diary, April 21, 1863, MDAH.

56. *OR*, 24(3):744, 753–755, 770; "Personal Memoirs of I.V. Smith," 1902, SHSMC, 26; James Woodard to Casey, April 26, 1863, James W. Woodard Letters, OCM; Anderson, *Memoirs*, 281; John Bowen to Carter Stevenson, April 19 and 20, 1863, John Bowen Letter Book, RG 109, Chapter II, Vol. 274, NARA.

57. *OR*, 24(3):756, 761, 770, 774–776; Ballard, *Vicksburg*, 205; M. D. L. Stephens Recollections, undated, MDAH, 16; W. Goodman to Lloyd Tilghman, April 22, 1863, and Thomas Waul to John Pemberton, April 27, 1863, John C. Pemberton Papers, RG 109, E 131, NARA.

58. *OR*, 24(3):753, 769, 773, 775, 776.

59. *OR*, 24(3):774, 778–779; William George Pirtle Memoirs, 1907, FHS, 135; William Loring to John Pemberton, April 23, 1863, John C. Pemberton Papers, RG 109, E 131, NARA.

60. *OR*, 24(3):191–192, 195, 201, 208–209, 212–213, 221, 224–225; *OR*, 24(1):75–76; Benjamin Underwood to siblings, April 19, 1863, Benjamin W. Underwood Letters, OCM; John Wallace to father, April 14, 1863, John M. Wallace Papers, CHM; Luther Cowan Diary, April 19, 1863, Luther H. Cowan Papers, TSLA; John Carr Diary, April 18,

1863, HCWRTC, USAHEC; Harry Watts Reminiscence, 1915, ISL, 64; Augustus Sinks Journal, undated, ISL, 31; James Slack to wife, April 14, 1863, James R. Slack Letters, ISL.

61. David W. Reed, *Campaigns and Battles of the Twelfth Regiment Iowa Veteran Volunteer Infantry. From Its Organization, September, 1861, to Muster Out, January 20, 1866* (N.p.: n.p., 1903), 113–114; Florison Pitts to father, April 14, 1863, Florison D. Pitts Papers, CHM.

62. *ORN*, 24:552, 567, 701; *OR*, 24(1):494, 496–497; *OR*, 24(3):197, 201; Hass, ed., "The Vicksburg Diary of Henry Clay Warmoth: Part I," 341, 343.

63. *OR*, 24(3):197–198, 201, 205, 210–215, 220, 227; *OR*, 24(1):31, 47, 78, 601; *OR*, 52(1):352; Luther Cowan to N. P. Rindlaub, April 21, 1863, Luther H. Cowan Papers, TSLA; Hass, ed., "The Vicksburg Diary of Henry Clay Warmoth: Part I," 347; Masters, ed., *Sherman's Praetorian Guard*, 112; Kaiser, ed., "The Civil War Diary of Florison D. Pitts," 36; Edward E. Schweitzer Diary, April 21, 1863, CWTI, USAHEC; Jones, *An Artilleryman's Diary*, 47; George D. Carrington Diary, April 8 and 11, 1863, CHM; Hovey Manuscript, undated, IU, 46; William Rigby to brother, April 17, 1863, William T. Rigby Papers, UIA; James Slack to wife, April 16, 17, and 20, 1863, James R. Slack Letters, ISL; James McPherson to colonel, April 25, 1863, James B. McPherson Papers, ALPL; Elliot Morrow to sister, May 4, 1863, Elliot Morrow Papers, OHS; William Britton to editors, April 21, 1863, William B. Britton Letters, OCM; Oscar E. Stewart Memoir, undated, OCM, 17; Charles E. Affeld Diary, April 21, 1863, VICK.

64. *OR*, 24(3):197–198, 201, 205, 210–215, 220, 227; *OR*, 24(1):31, 47, 78, 601; *OR*, 52(1):352; *Vicksburg Campaign: Driving Tour Guide*, 70; Edward E. Schweitzer Diary, April 21, 1863, CWTI, USAHEC; Luther Cowan to N. P. Rindlaub, April 21, 1863, Luther H. Cowan Papers, TSLA; Hass, ed., "The Vicksburg Diary of Henry Clay Warmoth: Part I," 347; Masters, ed., *Sherman's Praetorian Guard*, 112; Kaiser, ed., "The Civil War Diary of Florison D. Pitts," 36; Jones, *An Artilleryman's Diary*, 47; George D. Carrington Diary, April 8 and 11, 1863, CHM; Hovey Manuscript, undated, IU, 46; William Rigby to brother, April 17, 1863, William T. Rigby Papers, UIA; James Slack to wife, April 16, 17, and 20, 1863, James R. Slack Letters, ISL; Oscar E. Stewart Memoir, undated, OCM, 17; Charles E. Affeld Diary, April 21, 1863, VICK; James McPherson to colonel, April 25, 1863, James B. McPherson Papers, ALPL; Elliot Morrow to sister, May 4, 1863, Elliot Morrow Papers, OHS; William Britton to editors, April 21, 1863, William B. Britton Letters, OCM.

65. *OR*, 24(3):231–234, 236, 238–239, 241–242, 245; *OR*, 24(1):75, 78, 126–127, 141, 159, 601, 634, 725–726, 778; *OR*, 24(2):59, 203, 296; Marszalek, Nolen, and Gallo, eds., *Personal Memoirs of Ulysses S. Grant*, 324; Masters, ed., *Sherman's Praetorian Guard*, 113; James C. Sinclair Diary, April 24, 1863, CHM; Luther Cowan Diary, April 25–26, 1863, and Luther Cowan to Mollie, May 5, 1863, Luther H. Cowan Papers, TSLA; John Merrilies Diary, April 28, 1863, CHM; Hovey Manuscript, undated, IU, 47; Harry Watts Reminiscence, 1915, ISL, 65; Beck, "A True Sketch of His Army Life," 6; John E. Smith to Aimee, May 5, 1863, Kirby Smith Collection; Joseph Stockton Diary, April 23, 1863, VICK; Charles E. Affeld Diary, April 22, 1863, VICK; John W. Chambers Diary,

April 21 and 27, 1863, ISU; Manning F. Force, "Personal Recollections of the Vicksburg Campaign," in *Sketches of War History 1861–1865 Papers Read Before the Ohio Commandery of the Military Order of the Loyal Legion of the United States 1883–1886*, 9 vols. (Cincinnati: Robert Clarke Company, 1888), 1:295; Jones, *An Artilleryman's Diary*, 47, 49; George M. Lucas Diary, April 24, 1863, ALPL; Olynthus B. Clark, ed., *Downing's Civil War Diary* (Des Moines: The Historical Department of Iowa, 1916), 109, 111; Israel M. Piper Diary, March 21 and 24, 1863, OCM, copy in VICK; Edwin Loosley to wife, May 6, 1863, Edwin A. Loosley Papers, SIU; William Rigby to brother, April 20, 1863, William T. Rigby Papers, UIA; John W. Griffith Diary, April 26, 1863, OHS; Isaac Vanderwarker Diary, April 23, 1863, CWD, USAHEC; Grimsley and Miller, eds., *The Union Must Stand*, 91; Francis A. Dawes Diary, April 27, 1863, CWTI, USAHEC; John Carr Diary, April 22, 1863, HCWRTC, USAHEC.

66. *OR*, 24(3):197–198, 201, 205, 210–215, 220, 227; *OR*, 24(1):31, 47, 78, 601; *OR*, 52(1):352; Oscar E. Stewart Memoir, undated, OCM, 17; Charles E. Affeld Diary, April 21, 1863, VICK; Luther Cowan to N. P. Rindlaub, April 21, 1863, Luther H. Cowan Papers, TSLA; Hass, ed., "The Vicksburg Diary of Henry Clay Warmoth: Part I," 347; Masters, ed., *Sherman's Praetorian Guard*, 112; Kaiser, ed., "The Civil War Diary of Florison D. Pitts," 36; Edward E. Schweitzer Diary, April 21, 1863, CWTI, USAHEC; F. A. F., *Old Abe, The Eighth Wisconsin War Eagle. A Full Account of His Capture and Enlistment, Exploits in War and Honorable as Well as Useful Career in Peace* (Madison, WI: Curran and Bowen, 1885), 37–38; John Melvin Williams, *"The Eagle Regiment," 8th Wis. Inf'ty Vols.: A Sketch of Its Marches, Battles and Campaigns from 1861–1865 with Complete Regimental and Company Roster, and a Few Portraits and Sketches of Its Officers and Commanders* (Belleville, WI: Recorder Print, 1890), 16; Jones, *An Artilleryman's Diary*, 47; George D. Carrington Diary, April 8 and 11, 1863, CHM; Hovey Manuscript, undated, IU, 46; William Rigby to brother, April 17, 1863, William T. Rigby Papers, UIA; James Slack to wife, April 16, 17, and 20, 1863, James R. Slack Letters, ISL; Elliot Morrow to sister, May 4, 1863, Elliot Morrow Papers, OHS; William Britton to editors, April 21, 1863, William B. Britton Letters, OCM.

67. *ORN*, 24:565; *OR*, 24(3):194, 205, 212, 215, 227; *OR*, 24(1):30–31; Simon and Marszalek, eds., *PUSG*, 8:87; Wilson, *Under the Old Flag*, 167; George M. Lucas Diary, April 13, 1863, ALPL; James Giauque to sister, April 19, 1863, Giauque Family Papers, UIA.

68. *OR*, 24(3):211, 221–222, 228.

69. *OR*, 24(3):225–227, 773.

Chapter 12. "Attracting Attention from Grant"

1. Marszalek, *Commander of All Lincoln's Armies*, 43–46.
2. Jomini, *The Art of War*, 198–205, 305.
3. Clausewitz, *On War*, 238–239, 680–682.
4. *Field Manual 3–0: Operations* (Washington, DC: Department of the Army, 2008), A1–A2.

5. *OR*, 24(1):524–524; Operator Jones to John Pemberton, April 24, 1863, John C. Pemberton Papers, RG 109, E 131, NARA.

6. Smith, *The Real Horse Soldiers*, 194–199.

7. *OR*, 24(1):253, 255; Bearss, *The Vicksburg Campaign*, 2:236; Maurice K. Simons Diary, April 25 and 28, 1863, OCM; Luther S. Baechtel Diary, May 7, 1863, MDAH; M. R. Banner to wife, April 26, 1863, Banner Family Letters, OCM. For more on the Southern Railroad and its rebuilding after the war, see Southern Railroad Records, AU.

8. *OR*, 24(1):524–526, 544; Grierson, *A Just and Righteous Cause*, 161; William W. Loring to John C. Pemberton, April 23, 1863, John J. Pettus Correspondence, MDAH.

9. *OR*, 24(1):526; Grierson, *A Just and Righteous Cause*, 162.

10. *OR*, 24(1):526; Grierson, *A Just and Righteous Cause*, 165–166; "The Raid at Hazlehurst—From Ours Jackson Boys," April 30, 1863, Jackson *Daily Mississippian*.

11. *OR*, 24(1):526–527, 533, 540; Grierson, *A Just and Righteous Cause*, 172–173; R. R. Hutchinson to Wirt Adams, April 17 and 27, 1863, Wirt Adams Collection, UM; "Skirmish at Union Church in Jefferson County," April 29, 1863, Jackson *Daily Mississippian*; W. A. Rorer to Susan, June 13, 1863, W. A. Rorer Letters, DU; William Dunaway to wife, May 8, 1863, William E. Dunaway Papers, UI.

12. *OR*, 24(1):527–528, 543; Grierson, *A Just and Righteous Cause*, 174, 177; W. A. Rorer to cousin, June 13, 1863, W. A. Rorer Letters, DU, copy Lionel Baxter Collection, CWTI, USAHEC.

13. Grierson, *A Just and Righteous Cause*, 176–177.

14. Jason Niles Diary, January 11, 1864, UNC; E. T. Eggleston Diary, April 25, 1863, VICK; Horace P. Milton to John, May 8, 1863, Horace P. Milton Letters, LSU; Edwin R. Havens to parents, May 13, 1863, Havens Family Papers, Michigan State University; "Brief Record of General Grierson's Services During and Since the War, With Special Testimonials and Recommendations from General Officers, Senators, Representatives, and Other Officials, 1861–1882," 1882, Benjamin Henry Grierson Papers, NL; Henry Elsey, "The Grierson Raid," undated, Stephen A. Forbes Papers, UI. For newspaper accounts, see "Colonel Grierson's Brilliant Raid in Mississippi," May 13, 1863, Urbana (Ohio) *Union*; "Details of Grierson's Great Raid," June 10, 1863, Sacramento *Daily Union*; "The Great Cavalry Exploit of the Times," May 5, 1863, New Orleans *Era*; "The Grierson Raid," September 7, 1863, Canton (Illinois) *Weekly Register*; "The Great Federal Raid," May 5, 1863, Natchez *Daily Courier*; "Grierson's Big Raid," undated, Thomas W. Lippincott Papers, ALPL; "The Yankee Raid in Mississippi," undated, Mobile *Advertiser and Register*, copy in Stephen A. Forbes Papers, UI; "Incidents of the Raid," May 23, 1863, Memphis *Daily Bulletin*; "Camp Correspondence," May 26, 1863, Canton (Illinois) *Fulton City Register*; "Colonel Grierson's Cavalry Raid," May 10, 1863, New York *Times*; "The Great Raid of the War," May 20, 1863, Chicago *Tribune*; "Colonel Grierson at New Orleans—What He Learned by His Raid," May 20, 1863, Cleveland *Morning Leader*; "The Great Raid of the War," May 28, 1863, Goshen (Indiana) *Times*; "The Rebellion to be Crushed with Cavalry," June 10, 1863, Edgefield (South Carolina) *Advertiser*; "Col. Grierson," June 6, 1863, *Frank Leslie's Illustrated Newspaper*; "From One of Grierson's

Cavalry," June 5, 1863, Litchfield (Illinois) *Union Monitor*. For Grierson on front cover of *Harper's Weekly*, see June 6, 1863, edition.

15. *OR*, 24(3):784–785, 787, 791, 805; *OR*, 24(1):253; Smith, *The Real Horse Soldiers*, 300–301; Bearss, *The Vicksburg Campaign*, 2:236; Ballard, *Pemberton*, 139; Maurice K. Simons Diary, April 23, 1863, OCM.

16. *OR*, 24(3):788–789.

17. *OR*, 24(3):782, 786, 788–789, 793–794, 804; G. H. Burns to wife, April 29, 1863, G. H. Burns Letters, VICK; Lemuel Cline to Lizzie, May 2, 1863, Lemuel Cline Letters, VICK; John Douthit to companion, May 2, 1863, John M. Douthit Letters, VICK; Maynard, ed., "Vicksburg Diary," 44; Stephen Croom Diary, April 25, 1863, VICK; Ned to Alice, April 25, 1863, E. H. and D. G. Ingraham Letters, ALPL.

18. *OR*, 24(3):781–800; Smith, *The Real Horse Soldiers*, 300–301.

19. *OR*, 24(3):781, 785–787, 798.

20. *OR*, 24(3):781–783, 785–787, 789, 793–794, 798–800, 803.

21. *OR*, 24(3):782–784, 790; Bearss, *The Vicksburg Campaign*, 2:258; Carter Stevenson to John Pemberton, April 27, 1863, John C. Pemberton Papers, RG 109, E 131, NARA; Northern, ed., *All Right Let Them Come*, 85; Richard and Richard, *The Defense of Vicksburg*, 134; Chambers, "My Journal," 262; William L. Roberts Diary, April 22, 1863, ADAH; W. H. Claiborne Diary, April 18, 1863, J. F. H. Claiborne Papers, UNC.

22. *OR*, 24(3):792–793.

23. *OR*, 24(3):788, 792, 797; Smith, *The Real Horse Soldiers*, 300–301; A. S. Abrams, "The Siege of Vicksburg," undated, VICK.

24. *OR*, 24(3):788, 792, 797; A. S. Abrams, "The Siege of Vicksburg," undated, VICK; Smith, *The Real Horse Soldiers*, 300–301.

25. *OR*, 24(3):797, 800; *OR*, 24(1):257; Woodworth, *Jefferson Davis and His Generals*, 205.

26. *OR*, 24(3):785, 788–789, 791, 803, 805.

27. William Jolly to family, April 24, 1863, William H. Jolly Letters, SHSIIC; Payson Shumway to cousin, June 13, 1863, Z. Payson Shumway Letters, NL.

28. *OR*, 24(3):229–230; *OR*, 24(1):47–48, 81, 127–128, 142; Grabau, *Ninety-Eight Days*, 88–89; Simon and Marszalek, eds., *PUSG*, 8:63, 119; John Bowen to John Pemberton, April 25, 1863, John C. Pemberton Papers, RG 109, E 131, NARA.

29. *OR*, 24(3):186, 231; *OR*, 24(1):79, 126, 593, 642, 780; *OR*, 24(2):197, 314; Kaiser, ed., "The Civil War Diary of Florison D. Pitts," 37; Merrick J. Wald Diary, April 28, 1863, OCM; Robert Hamilton to wife, April 23, 1863, Robert Hamilton Letters, VICK; Edmund Newsome Diary, April 27, 1863, OCM; Isaac Vanderwarker Diary, April 28–29, 1863, CWD, USAHEC.

30. *OR*, 24(1):80–81; William A. Sypher Diary, April 21, 25, and 26, 1863, CHM; Luther Cowan Diary, April 28, 1863, Luther H. Cowan Papers, TSLA; Thomas N. McCluer Diary, April 22, 1863, OCM; Robert Hamilton to wife, April 23, 1863, Robert Hamilton Letters, VICK; James Boyd Diary, March 31, 1863, ALPL; William Murray Diary, April 26, 1863, VICK; John B. Fletcher Diary, April 18, 1863, ALPL.

31. *OR*, 24(1):80–81; Hass, ed., "The Vicksburg Diary of Henry Clay Warmoth: Part I," 340; Simon and Marszalek, eds., *PUSG*, 8:122, 132; Commager, ed., *The Blue and the Gray*, 2:63; Robert Hamilton to wife, April 23, 1863, Robert Hamilton Letters, VICK; Kaiser, ed., "The Civil War Diary of Florison D. Pitts," 35; Hass, ed., "The Vicksburg Diary of Henry Clay Warmoth: Part I," 344, 346.

32. *ORN*, 24:627–628; *OR*, 24(1):668; Bearss, *The Vicksburg Campaign*, 2:307–309; Tucker, *Westerners in Gray*, 122–123; Bevier, *History of the First and Second Missouri Confederate Brigades*, 172–176; Anderson, *Memoirs*, 289–296; James Woodard to wife, May 8, 1863, James W. Woodard Letters, OCM; Stephens Croom Diary, April 17, 1863, VICK; John Bowen to R. W. Memminger, March 28, 1863, John Bowen Letter Book, RG 109, Chapter II, Vol. 274, NARA.

33. *OR*, 24(1):31, 81; Andrew Sproul to wife, April 27, 1863, Andrew J. Sproul Papers, UNC; George B. Marshall Reminiscences, 1912, ISL, 41; William Murray Diary, April 28, 1863, VICK; W. R. Eddington Memoir, undated, ALPL, 7; Joseph R. Winslow Diary, April 27, 1863, VICK; Samuel P. Harrington Diary, April 21, 1863, Rudolph Haerle Collection, USAHEC.

34. *OR*, 24(1):31, 81; Samuel P. Harrington Diary, April 21, 1863, Rudolph Haerle Collection, USAHEC; Andrew Sproul to wife, April 27, 1863, Andrew J. Sproul Papers, UNC; George B. Marshall Reminiscences, 1912, ISL, 41; William Murray Diary, April 28, 1863, VICK; Joseph R. Winslow Diary, April 27, 1863, VICK; W. R. Eddington Memoir, undated, ALPL, 7.

35. *OR*, 24(1):187, 571; *OR*, 24(3):229–230, 234–236; Edwin Loosley to wife, May 6, 1863, Edwin A. Loosley Papers, SIU; James Fogle to family, undated, James S. Fogle Papers, ISL; D. W. Wood, *History of the 20th O.V.V.I. Regiment, and Proceedings of the First Reunion at Mt. Vernon, Ohio, April 6, 1876* (Columbus, OH: Paul and Thrall, Book and Job Printers, 1876), 20; James Slack to wife, April 18, 1863, James R. Slack Letters, ISL; John Jones to parents, April 16, 1863, John G. Jones Papers, LC; Francis R. Baker Memoir, undated, ALPL, 9–10; George R. Lee Diary, April 19, 1863, ALPL; Peter Osterhaus to James Keigwin, April 27, 1863, Letters Sent, RG 393, E 3221, NARA.

36. *OR*, 24(1):48, 571–573.

37. *OR*, 24(3):231–234, 236, 238–239, 241–242, 245; *OR*, 24(1):75, 78, 126–127, 141, 159, 601, 634, 725–726, 778; *OR*, 24(2):59, 203, 296; Masters, ed., *Sherman's Praetorian Guard*, 113; James C. Sinclair Diary, April 24, 1863, CHM; Luther Cowan Diary, April 25–26, 1863, and Luther Cowan to Mollie, May 5, 1863, Luther H. Cowan Papers, TSLA; John Merrilies Diary, April 28, 1863, CHM; Harry Watts Reminiscence, 1915, ISL, 65; Beck, "A True Sketch of His Army Life," 6; Joseph Stockton Diary, April 23, 1863, VICK; Charles E. Affeld Diary, April 22, 1863, VICK; John W. Chambers Diary, April 21 and 27, 1863, ISU; Force, "Personal Recollections of the Vicksburg Campaign," 1:295; Jones, *An Artilleryman's Diary*, 47, 49; George M. Lucas Diary, April 24, 1863, ALPL; Israel M. Piper Diary, March 21 and 24, 1863, OCM; Edwin Loosley to wife, May 6, 1863, Edwin A. Loosley Papers, SIU; William Rigby to brother, April 20, 1863, William T. Rigby Papers, UIA; John W. Griffith Diary, April 26, 1863, OHS; Isaac Vanderwarker Diary, April 23, 1863, CWD, USAHEC; Grimsley and Miller, eds., *The*

Union Must Stand, 91; Francis A. Dawes Diary, April 27, 1863, CWTI, USAHEC; John Carr Diary, April 22, 1863, HCWRTC, USAHEC.

38. *OR*, 24(3):231–234, 236, 238–239, 241–242, 245; *OR*, 24(1):75, 78, 126–127, 141, 159, 601, 634, 725–726, 778; *OR*, 24(2):59, 203, 296; Marszalek, Nolen, and Gallo, eds., *Personal Memoirs of Ulysses S. Grant*, 324; Masters, ed., *Sherman's Praetorian Guard*, 113; James C. Sinclair Diary, April 24, 1863, CHM; Luther Cowan Diary, April 25–26, 1863, and Luther Cowan to Mollie, May 5, 1863, Luther H. Cowan Papers, TSLA; John Merrilies Diary, April 28, 1863, CHM; Hovey Manuscript, undated, IU, 47; Harry Watts Reminiscence, 1915, ISL, 65; Beck, "A True Sketch of His Army Life," 6; John E. Smith to Aimee, May 5, 1863, Kirby Smith Collection; Joseph Stockton Diary, April 23, 1863, VICK; Charles E. Affeld Diary, April 22, 1863, VICK; John W. Chambers Diary, April 21 and 27, 1863, ISU; Jones, *An Artilleryman's Diary*, 47, 49; George M. Lucas Diary, April 24, 1863, ALPL; Clark, ed., *Downing's Civil War Diary*, 109, 111; Israel M. Piper Diary, March 21 and 24, 1863, OCM; Edwin Loosley to wife, May 6, 1863, Edwin A. Loosley Papers, SIU; William Rigby to brother, April 20, 1863, William T. Rigby Papers, UIA; John W. Griffith Diary, April 26, 1863, OHS; Isaac Vanderwarker Diary, April 23, 1863, CWD, USAHEC; Grimsley and Miller, eds., *The Union Must Stand*, 91; Francis A. Dawes Diary, April 27, 1863, CWTI, USAHEC; John Carr Diary, April 22, 1863, HCWRTC, USAHEC.

39. *OR*, 24(3):231–234, 236, 238–239, 241–242, 245; *OR*, 24(1):75, 78, 126–127, 141, 159, 601, 634, 725–726, 778; *OR*, 24(2):59, 203, 296; Marszalek, Nolen, and Gallo, eds., *Personal Memoirs of Ulysses S. Grant*, 324; Masters, ed., *Sherman's Praetorian Guard*, 113; James C. Sinclair Diary, April 24, 1863, CHM; Luther Cowan Diary, April 25–26, 1863, and Luther Cowan to Mollie, May 5, 1863, Luther H. Cowan Papers, TSLA; John Merrilies Diary, April 28, 1863, CHM; Hovey Manuscript, undated, IU, 47; Harry Watts Reminiscence, 1915, ISL, 65; Beck, "A True Sketch of His Army Life," 6; Joseph Stockton Diary, April 23, 1863, VICK; Charles E. Affeld Diary, April 22, 1863, VICK; John W. Chambers Diary, April 21 and 27, 1863, ISU; Jones, *An Artilleryman's Diary*, 47, 49; George M. Lucas Diary, April 24, 1863, ALPL; Israel M. Piper Diary, March 21 and 24, 1863, OCM; Edwin Loosley to wife, May 6, 1863, Edwin A. Loosley Papers, SIU; William Rigby to brother, April 20, 1863, William T. Rigby Papers, UIA; John W. Griffith Diary, April 26, 1863, OHS; Isaac Vanderwarker Diary, April 23, 1863, CWD, USAHEC; Grimsley and Miller, eds., *The Union Must Stand*, 91; Francis A. Dawes Diary, April 27, 1863, CWTI, USAHEC; John Carr Diary, April 22, 1863, HCWRTC, USAHEC.

40. *OR*, 24(1):47, 82; Commager, ed., *The Blue and the Gray*, 2:63, 65; Peter Osterhaus to Colonel, April 27, 1863, and unknown to W. B. Scates, April 28, 1863, Letters Sent, RG 393, E 3221, NARA; Peter Osterhaus to soldiers, April 27, 1863, General and Special Orders, RG 393, E 3230, NARA.

41. *OR*, 24(1):47, 82; Commager, ed., *The Blue and the Gray*, 2:63, 65.

42. General Orders 29, April 28, 1863, Benjamin Spooner Letters, ISL.

43. *ORN*, 24:606–607, 609–610.

44. *ORN*, 24:607, 611, 613, 621; *OR*, 24(1):32, 48; *OR*, 24(3):237, 240; Grabau, *Ninety-Eight Days*, 137; Commager, ed., *The Blue and the Gray*, 2:66; "Personal Memoirs

of I.V. Smith," 1902, SHSMC, 26; Judson Gill to Sophia, May 6, 1863, C. Judson Gill Letters, VICK.

45. "Personal Memoirs of I.V. Smith," 1902, SHSMC, 27.

46. *ORN*, 24:618–619, 625; Hovey Manuscript, undated, IU, 47–48; A. L. Slack Diary, April 1, 1863, VICK, 7; USS *Pittsburg* Logbook, April 29, 1863, RG 24, E 118, NARA.

47. *ORN*, 24:608, 611, 613–618, 620–623; Dana, *Recollections of the Civil War*, 42.

48. *ORN*, 24:608, 611, 613–618, 620–623.

49. *ORN*, 24:608, 611, 613–618, 702.

50. *OR*, 24(1):574; *ORN*, 24:613, 628–629, 633; Bobby Roberts and Carl Moneyhon, *Portraits of Conflict: A Photographic History of Mississippi in the Civil War* (Fayetteville: University of Arkansas Press, 1993), 225; M. R. Banner to wife, April 29, 1863, Banner Family Letters, OCM; James Kidd Memoir, undated, OCM, 9–10.

51. *ORN*, 24:608, 610–611, 613, 614, 616, 626, 683; *OR*, 24(3):229; Marszalek, Nolen, and Gallo, eds., *Personal Memoirs of Ulysses S. Grant*, 332; Fred Grant Memoir, undated, USGPL, 9–10.

52. *ORN*, 24:608, 610–611; *OR*, 24(1):48, 82; "Personal Memoirs of I.V. Smith," 1902, SHSMC, 27; William Rigby Journal, April 29, 1863, William T. Rigby Papers, UIA.

53. *ORN*, 24:608, 610; Marszalek, Nolen, and Gallo, eds., *Personal Memoirs of Ulysses S. Grant*, 332; "Personal Memoirs of I.V. Smith," 1902, SHSMC, 27; William Rigby Journal, April 29, 1863, William T. Rigby Papers, UIA.

54. *ORN*, 24:608, 610, 615–616, 618, 623–624; *OR*, 24(1):82.

55. *ORN*, 24:618, 624–625; Myron Knight Diary, April 29, 1863, OCM.

56. *OR*, 24(1):574; *ORN*, 24:6293; Tucker, *The Forgotten "Stonewall of the West*," 218–221; John Bowen to John Pemberton, April 29, 1863, John C. Pemberton Papers, RG 109, E 131, NARA.

Chapter 13. "We Land the Army in the Morning"

1. Bearss, *The Vicksburg Campaign*, 2:346; Ronald C. White, *American Ulysses: A Life of Ulysses S. Grant* (New York: Random House, 2016), 265; Miller, *Vicksburg*, 365; Martin N. Bertera, *De Golyer's 8th Michigan Black Horse Light Battery* (Wyandotte, MI: TillieAnn Press, 2015), 96; Jim Miles, *A River Unvexed: A History and Tour Guide of the Campaign for the Mississippi River* (Nashville: Rutledge Hill Press, 1994), 374.

2. John Whiteclay Chambers II, *The Oxford Companion to American Military History* (New York: Oxford University Press, 1999), 31–32.

3. Russell F. Weigly, *The American Way of War: A History of United States Military Strategy and*

Policy (Bloomington: Indiana University Press, 1973), 254–262; Millett, Maslowski, and Feis. *For the Common Defense*, 353–355.

4. Ian W. Toll, *The Conquering Tide: War in the Pacific Islands, 1942–1944* (New

York: Norton, 2015), 17–18; Ian W. Toll, *Twilight of the Gods: War in the Western Pacific, 1944–1945* (New York: Norton, 2020), 572–573.

5. Jomini, *The Art of War*, 158–159, 205–210, 226–230.

6. *OR*, 24(3):234.

7. *ORN*, 24:598; C. S. O. Rice Memoir, 1967, TSLA, 21, copy in UTK; Henry A. Robinson to wife, June 18, 1863, Henry A. Robinson Papers, IHS; Eli W. Thornhill Memoir, undated, OCM, 9; Carter Stevenson to John Pemberton, April 17, 1863, John C. Pemberton Papers, RG 109, E 131, NARA.

8. *OR*, 24(3):240, 245; *ORN*, 24:591; Thorndike, ed., *The Sherman Letters*, 201, 203; John F. Marszalek, "'A Full Share of All the Credit': Sherman and Grant to the Fall of Vicksburg," in *Grant's Lieutenants: From Cairo to Vicksburg*, Steven E. Woodworth, ed. (Lawrence: University Press of Kansas, 2001), 18.

9. *OR*, 24(3):242–244; *ORN*, 24:587, 596; *OR*, 24(1):752; Howe, ed., *Home Letters*, 257.

10. *OR*, 24(1):576–578; *ORN*, 24:589, 594; Grabau, *Ninety-Eight Days*, 131–132; Parrish, *Frank Blair*, 166; Saunier, *A History of the Forty-seventh Regiment Ohio Veteran Volunteer Infantry*, 133–134; James H. St. John Diary, April 29–30 and May 1, 1863, ISL; Charles E. Affeld Diary, April 29–May 1, 1863, VICK.

11. *OR*, 24(1):576–578; *ORN*, 24:587, 589–593, 595; *OR*, 52(2):464; Louis Hébert Autobiography, 1894, UNC, 12, copy in LSU; Charles E. Affeld Diary, May 1, 1863, VICK; James N. Carlisle Diary, May 1, 1863, VICK.

12. *OR*, 24(1):576–578; *ORN*, 24:587, 589–593, 595; *OR*, 52(2):464; James N. Carlisle Diary, May 1, 1863, VICK; Charles E. Affeld Diary, May 1, 1863, VICK; Louis Hébert Autobiography, 1894, UNC, 12.

13. *OR*, 24(1):576–578; *ORN*, 24:590; Brinkerhoff, *History of the Thirtieth Regiment Ohio Volunteer Infantry*, 60–63; Clarke, *Reminiscence and Anecdotes*, 94; Curtis P. Lacey Diary, April 30–May 1, 1863, NL; Israel P. Rumsey Diary, April 30, 1863, NL.

14. Charles E. Affeld Diary, April 30, 1863, VICK; Edward E. Schweitzer Diary, April 29–May 1, 1863, CWTI, USAHEC; George M. Rogers Diary, May 1, 1863, ISL.

15. *OR*, 24(1):577–578; *ORN*, 24:590; Charles E. Affeld Diary, April 30, 1863, VICK; Clarke, *Reminiscence and Anecdotes*, 94; George M. Rogers Diary, May 1, 1863, ISL; Edward E. Schweitzer Diary, April 29–May 1, 1863, CWTI, USAHEC.

16. *ORN*, 24:596; Thomas White to mother, May 11, 1863, Thomas K. White Papers, OHS; Seth Wells Diary, April 30, 1863, OCM; Tunnard, *A Southern Record*, 230; John Wilson to Lizzie, March 2, 1863, John A. Wilson Letters, MDAH; James Boyd Diary, May 1, 1863, ALPL; Clarkson Fogg to father, May 3, 1863, Clarkson Fogg Letters, VICK; Edward E. Schweitzer Diary, May 1, 1863, CWTI, USAHEC.

17. *OR*, 24(1):578; *ORN*, 24:590–591, 594, 598; *OR*, 24(1):575, 752; Jenney, "With Sherman and Grant," 202; *SOR*, 3:366; Sherman, *Memoirs*, 1:319; Northern, ed., *All Right Let Them Come*, 88; John L. Power Diary, April 29–May 1, 1863, MDAH; Tunnard, *A Southern Record*, 227–229; M. R. Banner to wife, April 29, 1863, Banner Family Letters, OCM; James Ferguson to wife, May 2, 1863, James Ferguson Letters, OCM; Maurice K. Simons Diary, April 29–30, 1863, OCM; Stephens Croom Diary, April 29, 1863, VICK.

18. *OR*, 24(3):229, 237; *OR*, 24(1):726; Poem, undated, Nathan A. Corbin Papers, ALPL; Wilson, *Under the Old Flag*, 171.

19. *OR*, 24(3):229–230; *OR*, 24(1):47–48, 81, 127–128, 142; Grabau, *Ninety-Eight Days*, 88–89; Simon and Marszalek, eds., *PUSG*, 8:63, 119; John Bowen to John Pemberton, April 25, 1863, John C. Pemberton Papers, RG 109, E 131, NARA.

20. *OR*, 24(1):48; Elliott, *History of the Thirty-Third Regiment Illinois Veteran Volunteer Infantry*, 236–237; Simon and Marszalek, eds., *PUSG*, 8:113–114; Marszalek, Nolen, and Gallo, eds., *Personal Memoirs of Ulysses S. Grant*, 332–333; Beck, "A True Sketch of His Army Life," 6; M. A. Sweetman, "From Milliken's Bend to Vicksburg," August 22, 1895, *National Tribune*.

21. *OR*, 24(1):48; Remini, *Andrew Jackson and the Course of American Empire*, 55, 62; Milton Lomask, *Aaron Burr: The Conspiracy and Years of Exile, 1805–1836* (New York: Farrar, Straus and Giroux, 1982), 208–216; "Vinegar Bend," Natchez *Times*, September 30, 1953, copy in Bruinsburg Subject File, MDAH; "Beginning of the End," Jackson *Daily News*, December 21, 1979, copy in Bruinsburg Subject File, MDAH; "So Much History Unfolded at Bruinsburg, So Little Remains," Vicksburg *Evening Post*, March 23, 1986, copy in Bruinsburg Subject File, MDAH; Marszalek, Nolen, and Gallo, eds., *Personal Memoirs of Ulysses S. Grant*, 332–333; Elliott, *History of the Thirty-Third Regiment Illinois Veteran Volunteer Infantry*, 236–237; Simon and Marszalek, eds., *PUSG*, 8:113–114; Sweetman, "From Milliken's Bend to Vicksburg," August 22, 1895, *National Tribune*; Beck, "A True Sketch of His Army Life," 6.

22. *ORN*, 24:610–611; Young, *Around the World with General Grant*, 2:619.

23. *OR*, 24(3):246, 248; *OR*, 24(1):32; Peter J. Perrine Diary, April 30, 1863, OHS; Field Orders 1, April 29, 1863, General and Special Orders, RG 393, E 3230, NARA; James McPherson to mother, May 4, 1863, Wilfred S. Foerster Collection, Rutherford B. Hayes Presidential Center.

24. *OR*, 24(1):32, 642; Commager, ed., *The Blue and the Gray*, 2:66; Special Order 449, April 29, 1863, Walter Scates to captain, April 29, 1863, John A. McClernand Papers, ALPL.

25. Dana, *Recollections of the Civil War*, 43–44.

26. *OR*, 24(1):48, 83, 142, 159; Albert C. Boals Diary, April 30, 1863, ALPL; James C. Sinclair Diary, April 30, 1863, CHM; W. R. Eddington Memoir, undated, ALPL, 7; John Sheriff Diary, April 30, 1863, John Sherriff Family Papers, ALPL; USS *Pittsburg* Logbook, April 30, 1863, RG 24, E 118, NARA; Carlos Colby Memoir, undated, Bilby Collection, USAHEC, 4.

27. Larry J. Daniel, "Bruinsburg: Missed Opportunity or Postwar Rhetoric?," *Civil War History* 32, no. 3 (September 1986): 259; Special Order 120, April 30, 1863, John A. McClernand Papers, ALPL.

28. Daniel, "Bruinsburg," 266.

29. White, *American Ulysses*, 267; Abraham Lincoln, "Proclamation 97—Appointing a Day of National Humiliation, Fasting, and Prayer," March 30, 1863. Online by Gerhard Peters and John T. Woolley, *The American Presidency Project*, www.presidency

.ucsb.edu/ws/?pid=69891; Unnamed Soldier's Diary, April 30, 1863, Civil War Collection, UMEM; Reuben H. Falconer Diary, April 30, 1863, OHS.

30. *OR*, 24(1):48, 83, 142, 159; Andrew Flick Diary, April 30, 1863, ALPL; Harry Watts Reminiscence, 1915, ISL, 67; USS *Pittsburg* Logbook, April 30, 1863, RG 24, E 118, NARA.

31. *ORN*, 24:684, 691, 699, 702, 706; *OR*, 24(1):593; *OR*, 24(2):314; *History of the Forty-sixth Regiment Indiana Volunteer Infantry*, 56; Hovey Manuscript, undated, IU, 48; Howard, *History of the 124th Regiment Illinois Infantry Volunteers*, 25; William Rigby Journal, April 30, 1863, William T. Rigby Papers, UIA; Augustus Sinks Journal, undated, ISL, 33; John Hancox to brother, May 5, 1863, John B. Hancox Letter, VICK.

32. Shea and Winschel, *Vicksburg Is the Key*, 106; Grabau, *Ninety-Eight Days*, 146; *History of the Forty-sixth Regiment Indiana Volunteer Infantry*, 56; Fulfer, *A History of the Trials and Hardships of the Twenty-Fourth Indiana Volunteer Infantry*, 55.

33. Howard, *History of the 124th Regiment Illinois Infantry Volunteers*, 75; Augustus Sinks Journal, undated, ISL, 33; W. R. Eddington Memoir, undated, ALPL, 7; William H. Kinkade Diary, April 30, 1863, ALPL; Robert Ridge Diary, April 30, 1863, ALPL.

34. Shea and Winschel, *Vicksburg Is the Key*, 104–105; Grabau, *Ninety-Eight Days*, 139; Richardson, *A Personal History of Ulysses S. Grant*, 304.

35. Elliott, *History of the Thirty-Third Regiment Illinois Veteran Volunteer Infantry*, 237; Woodworth, *Nothing but Victory*, 339; Pryce, *Vanishing Footprints*, 92; John H. Burnham, *The Thirty-third Regiment Illinois Infantry in the Civil War, 1861–1865; Prepared by Capt. J.H. Burnham at the Request of the Directors of the Illinois Historical Society for the 1912 Annual Meeting of that Society* (N.p.: n.p., 1912); Joseph Myers, "The First to Land at Bruinsburg," May 20, 1886, *National Tribune*; "Condensed Letters," December 4, 1884, *National Tribune*.

36. Fred Grant Memoir, undated, USGPL, 11.

37. *ORN*, 24:684, 691, 699, 702, 706; Isaac Myler to Libbie, May 7, 1863, Isaac S. Myler Papers, ALPL; Kaiser, ed., "The Civil War Diary of Florison D. Pitts," 37; Job H. Yaggy Diary, April 30, 1863, ALPL; USS *Pittsburg* Logbook, April 29–30, 1863, RG 24, E 118, NARA; Tomblin, *The Civil War on the Mississippi*, 252; Samuel Gordon to wife, May 6, 1863, Samuel Gordon Papers, ALPL; Ira Payne to parents, May 4, 1863, Ira A. Payne Papers, ALPL; Bering and Montgomery, *History of the Forty-Eighth Ohio Vet. Vol. Inf.*, 79; William Rand to parents, May 6, 1863, Rand Family Papers, ALPL; Isaac Jackson to Sallie, May 27, 1863, Isaac Jackson Papers, UMC; Samuel P. Harrington Diary, April 29, 1863, Rudolph Haerle Collection, USAHEC.

38. *OR*, 24(1):634, 643; *OR*, 24(2):204; John S. Kountz, *Record of the Organizations Engaged in the Campaign, Siege, and Defense of Vicksburg* (Knoxville: University of Tennessee Press, 2011), 12; Winschel, *Triumph and Defeat*, 31; "History of the Corps," May 18, 1893, *National Tribune*; Gibson and Gibson, *Dictionary of Transports*, 152; Luther Cowan Diary, May 1, 1863, Luther H. Cowan Papers, TSLA; Gould D. Molineaux Diary, April 30, 1863, Augustana College; Edwin Loosley to wife, May 6, 1863, Edwin A. Loosley Papers, SIU; Samuel Joseph Churchill Memoir, undated, OCM, 2–3.

39. *OR*, 24(1):601, 726, 774; *OR*, 24(2):61; Simon and Marszalek, eds., *PUSG*, 8:122; Paul H. Hass, ed., "The Vicksburg Diary of Henry Clay Warmoth: Part II (April 28, 1863–May 26, 1863)," *Journal of Mississippi History* 32, no. 1 (February 1970): 63; Wilson, *Under the Old Flag*, 172; Patrick, ed., *Three Years with Wallace's Zouaves*, 115.

40. *OR*, 24(1):48, 142–143, 615; *OR*, 24(2):31; *SOR*, 3:369; Woodworth, *Nothing but Victory*, 338; Francis A. Dawes Diary, April 30, 1863, CWTI, USAHEC; Samuel P. Harrington Diary, April 29, 1863, Rudolph Haerle Collection, USAHEC; James K. Bigelow, *Abridged History of the Eighth Indiana Volunteer Infantry, from Its Organization, April 21st, 1861, to the Date of Re-enlistment as Veterans, January 1, 1864* (Indianapolis: Ellis Barnes Book and Job Printer, 1864), 18; Alexander Shall Diary, April 30, 1863, VICK; Field Orders 2, April 30, 1863, General and Special Orders, RG 393, E 3230, NARA.

41. *OR*, 24(1):48.

42. *OR*, 24(1):627; Edwin C. Bearss with J. Parker Hills, *Receding Tide: Vicksburg and Gettysburg: The Campaigns That Changed the Civil War* (Washington, DC: National Geographic, 2010), 105; Henry G. Hicks, "The Campaign and Capture of Vicksburg," in *Glimpses of the Nation's Struggle: Military Order of the Loyal Legion*, 6 vols. (St. Paul, MN: Davis, 1909), 6:96; S. C. Jones, *Reminiscences of the Twenty-second Iowa Volunteer Infantry, Giving Its Organization, Marches, Skirmishes, Battles, and Sieges, as Taken from the Diary of Lieutenant S. C. Jones of Company A* (Iowa City: n.p., 1907), 29–30; Daniel Roberts to family, May 6, 1863, Daniel Roberts Correspondence, ISL; Ira Payne to parents, May 4, 1863, Ira A. Payne Papers, ALPL; "Hovey's Division at Port Gibson," January 8, 1885, *National Tribune*; Elliot Morrow to sister, May 4, 1863, Elliot Morrow Papers, OHS.

43. *SOR*, 3:369; Bearss, *The Vicksburg Campaign*, 2:345; Shea and Winschel, *Vicksburg Is the Key*, 108; Howard, *History of the 124th Regiment Illinois Infantry Volunteers*, 76; Carlos Colby Memoir, undated, Bilby Collection, USAHEC, 1–2; William Murray Diary, April 30, 1863, VICK; John Sheriff Diary, April 30, 1863, John Sherriff Family Papers, ALPL; Mason, *The Forty-second Ohio Infantry*, 190; James Harrison Wilson, "A Staff Officer's Journal of the Vicksburg Campaign, April 30 to July 4, 1863," *Journal of the Military Service Institution of the United States* 43, no. 154 (July–August 1908): 93–109, 93; William A. Shunk, "The Vicksburg Campaign," in *War Papers Read Before the Commandery of the State of Wisconsin, Military Order of the Loyal Legion of the United States*, 4 vols. (Milwaukee: Burdick & Allen, 1914), 4:151; Force, "Personal Recollections of the Vicksburg Campaign," 1:296.

44. *SOR*, 3:369; Bearss, *The Vicksburg Campaign*, 2:345; Shea and Winschel, *Vicksburg Is the Key*, 108; Howard, *History of the 124th Regiment Illinois Infantry Volunteers*, 76; Hass, ed., "The Vicksburg Diary of Henry Clay Warmoth: Part II," 64; Carlos Colby Memoir, undated, Bilby Collection, USAHEC, 1–2; William Murray Diary, April 30, 1863, VICK; John Sheriff Diary, April 30, 1863, John Sherriff Family Papers, ALPL; Mason, *The Forty-second Ohio Infantry*, 190; Shunk, "The Vicksburg Campaign," 4:151; Force, "Personal Recollections of the Vicksburg Campaign," 1:296. Windsor burned in 1890. See "Burning of the Daniell Residence," Port Gibson *Southern Reveille*, February 21, 1890, copy in Windsor Subject File, MDAH; "Windsor's Grandeur Lives on in

Ruins," Jackson *Clarion Ledger*, July 18, 1965, copy in Windsor Subject File, MDAH. For the only known rendering of Windsor, see the Henry Otis Dwight Papers, OHS.

45. *OR*, 24(1): 143, 186, 593, 601, 643; *OR*, 24(2):235; Ballard, *Vicksburg*, 223; Grabau, *Ninety-Eight Days*, 147; George Crooke, *The Twenty-first Regiment of Iowa Volunteer Infantry: A Narrative of Its Experience in Active Service, Including a Military Record of Each Officer, Non-Commissioned Officer, and Private Soldier of the Organization* (Milwaukee: King, Fowle & Co., 1891), 54; Shea and Winschel, *Vicksburg Is the Key*, 102, 109; Osborn H. Oldroyd, *A Soldier's Story of the Siege of Vicksburg. From the Diary of Osborn H. Oldroyd* (Springfield, IL: self-published, 1885), 3; Luther Cowan Diary, April 30, 1863, Luther H. Cowan Papers, TSLA; W. S. Morris, *History, 31st Regiment Illinois Volunteers: Organized by John A. Logan* (Herrin, IL: Crossfire Press, 1991), 56–57; John A. Leavy Diary, 1863, VICK, 9; George Chittenden to wife, May 4, 1863, Chittenden Family Papers, ISL; James Slack to wife, May 5, 1863, James R. Slack Letters, ISL; John W. Griffith Diary, April 30, 1863, OHS.

46. Scott, *The History of the 67th Regiment Indiana Infantry Volunteers*, 28.

47. Bearss, *The Vicksburg Campaign*, 2:345; Woodworth, *Nothing but Victory*, 340; William F. Hollingsworth Diary, April 30, 1863, OCM; Pryce, *Vanishing Footprints*, 93–94; J. H. Rowell Diary, May 1, 1863, Eureka College; Cyrus Willford Reminiscences, 1899, OHS, 239.

48. Samuel P. Harrington Diary, April 29, 1863, Rudolph Haerle Collection, USAHEC.

49. *OR*, 24(3):248; *OR*, 24(1):601, 614–615; Stephen D. Lee, "The Campaign of Vicksburg, Mississippi, in 1863—From April 15 to and Including the Battle of Champion Hills, or Baker's Creek, May 16, 1863," in *Publications of the Mississippi Historical Society*, 13 vols. (Oxford: Mississippi Historical Society, 1900), 3:24; James S. McHenry Diary, May 1, 1863, ALPL; James B. Logan Diary, May 1, 1863, ALPL; James Woodson Diary, May 1, 1863, ALPL.

50. *OR*, 24(3):801–804; *OR*, 24(1):575.

51. *OR*, 24(1):575–576, 657; John Bowen to John Pemberton, April 30, 1863, John C. Pemberton Papers, RG 109, E 131, NARA.

52. *OR*, 24(1):658, 675, 678; Edward Tracy to James Seddon, February 29, 1863, Henry De Lamar Clayton Sr. Papers, UA; William Lowery Diary, April 18 and 30, 1863, ADAH; John Bowen to John Pemberton, April 30, 1863, John C. Pemberton Papers, RG 109, E 131, NARA.

53. *OR*, 24(3):803–806; *OR*, 24(1):576.

54. *OR*, 24(3):803–806; *OR*, 24(1):256, 576; John Bowen to John Pemberton, April 30, 1863, John C. Pemberton Papers, RG 109, E 131, NARA.

55. *OR*, 24(1):257, 296–318; Carter Stevenson to John Pemberton, April 29, 1863, and Jefferson Davis to John Pemberton, May 1, 1863, John C. Pemberton Papers, RG 109, E 131, NARA.

56. *OR*, 24(1):257, 296–318, 328–329, 660; Chambers, "My Journal," 262; Claudius W. Sears Diary, April 30, 1863, MDAH; John Bowen to John Pemberton, May 1, 1863, John C. Pemberton Papers, RG 109, E 131, NARA.

57. *OR*, 24(2):663; Ben Bounds Memoir, undated, OCM, 14.

58. *OR*, 24(2):663–664; William L. Roberts Diary, April 29, 1863, ADAH; James Kidd Memoir, undated, OCM, 9.

59. *OR*, 24(2):672, 675; H. Grady Howell, Jr., *Going to Meet the Yankees: A History of the "Bloody Sixth" Mississippi Infantry, C.S.A.* (Jackson: Chickasaw Bayou Press, 1981), 151; John C. Rietti, *Military Annals of Mississippi: Military Organizations Which Entered the Service of the Confederate States of America from the State of Mississippi* (N.p.: n.p., 1895), 49; Chambers, "My Journal," 262–263; Francis Baxter Memoir, undated, Francis M. Baxter Papers, MDAH; Joseph W. Westbrook Memoir, 1903, CWD, USAHEC, 4.

60. *OR*, 24(2):664.

Epilogue: "But I Was on Dry Ground"

1. Lemuel Cline to Lizzie, May 2, 1863, Lemuel Cline Letters, VICK; Luke Roberts to unknown, January 24, 1863, Luke R. Roberts Letters, HCWRTC, USAHEC; Marszalek, Nolen, and Gallo, eds., *Personal Memoirs of Ulysses S. Grant*, 334.

2. Lemuel Cline to Lizzie, May 2, 1863, Lemuel Cline Letters, VICK; Stephens Croom Diary, April 19, 1863, VICK.

3. Clarke, *Reminiscence and Anecdotes*, 94.

4. *OR*, 24(1):31; William Kennedy to wife, April 26, 1863, William J. Kennedy Papers, ALPL; Simon and Marszalek, eds., *PUSG*, 7:480, 491; Simon and Marszalek, eds., *PUSG*, 8:132.

5. Milt Shaw to Alf, January 31, 1863, Milton W. Shaw Papers, FHS; Masters, ed., *Sherman's Praetorian Guard*, 113; David Grier to Anna, April 22, 1863, Grier Family Papers, MHS; Henry Oman to unknown, March 10, 1863, Henry Oman Papers, UNC.

6. John Hardin to father, March 20, 1863, Sesquicentennial Manuscript Project, IHS; A. Achen to "Headquarter Ohio Union," undated, A. Achen Papers, CHM; William Dupray to sister, April 15, 1863, Morgan Family Papers, UW; Charles Enslow to wife, April 17, 1863, Charles Calvin Enslow Papers, LC; March 21 notation, Cyrus D. McElroy Letter, MDAH; J. J. Moulton to sister, April 28, 1863, Martin Family Letters, Civil War Collection, MHS.

7. Jenney, "Personal Recollections of Vicksburg," 256; "The Defenders of Vicksburg," *Southern Historical Society Papers* 21 (1893): 195; *OR*, 24(1):46.

8. E. B. Reese Memoir, 1930s, Mayfield and Sanders Family Materials, IHS, 9–10; Stoker, *The Grand Design*, 262; Badeau, *Military History of Ulysses S. Grant*, 168.

9. Wilson, *Under the Old Flag*, 160; Young, *Around the World with General Grant*, 615; Hattaway and Jones, *How the North Won*, 342.

10. Lee, "The Campaign of Vicksburg, Mississippi, in 1863," 23.

11. Ballard, "Misused Merit," in *Civil War Generals in Defeat*, 155; Clausewitz, *On War*, 443, 453, 633, 639, 684–693.

12. Badeau, *Military History of Ulysses S. Grant*, 177; John C. Pemberton, *Pemberton: Defender of Vicksburg* (Chapel Hill: University of North Carolina Press, 1942), 84.

13. G. P. Clarke to comrade, July 22, 1899, William M. Cleaveland Letters, CWD, USAHEC.

14. F. T. Demingway to S. A. Forbes, May 7, 1910, Stephen A. Forbes Papers, UI; David Porter to John Dorman, January 27, 1888, John H. Dorman Papers, OHS.

15. David Porter to John Dorman, January 27, 1888, John H. Dorman Papers, OHS.

16. David Porter to John Dorman, January 27, 1888, John H. Dorman Papers, OHS.

BIBLIOGRAPHY

Manuscripts

Abraham Lincoln Presidential Library, Springfield, Illinois
    Francis R. Baker Memoir
    Lyman M. Baker Memoir
    Charles W. Beal Papers
    Albert C. Boals Diary
    Philip C. Bonney Papers
    James Boyd Diary
    Bruce Family Papers
    Brush Family Papers
    James A. B. Butterfield Correspondence
    Civil War Diary
    Cyrus T. Cochran Papers
    James M. Cole Papers
    Nathan A. Corbin Papers
    George Ditto Diary
    W. R. Eddington Memoir
    Alexander K. Ewing Papers
    John B. Fletcher Diary
    Andrew Flick Diary
    John G. Given Papers
    Samuel Gordon Papers
    Benjamin H. Grierson Papers
    John and Alexander Harper Papers
    John L. Harris Papers
    John A. Higgins Papers
    E. H. and D. G. Ingraham Letters
    Francis M. Johnson Diary
    Kays Family Papers
    Price K. Kellogg Diary

William J. Kennedy Papers
William H. Kinkade Diary
Joseph Ledergerber Diary
George R. Lee Diary
Thomas W. Lippincott Papers
James B. Logan Diary
Samuel D. Lougheed Papers
George M. Lucas Diary
John A. McClernand Papers
James S. McHenry Diary
James B. McPherson Papers
Isaac S. Myler Papers
Henry M. Newhall Papers
Charles S. Patchen Diary
Ira A. Payne Papers
William L. Rand Letters
Rand Family Papers
Cyrus W. Randall Papers
Robert Ridge Diary
Jonas H. Roe Papers
George W. Russell Papers
John Sherriff Family Papers
Payson Shumway Papers
George O. Smith Papers
William E. Strong Papers
Lewis Trefftys Papers
Frank W. Tupper Papers
Abram J. Vanauken Diary
William F. Warren Papers
Thomas Watson Papers
John H. Wickiser Papers
James A. Woodson Diary
Job H. Yaggy Diary
George R. Yost Diary

Alabama Department of Archives and History, Montgomery, Alabama
    Isaac B. Coleman Letter
    William Lowery Diary
    Edmund W. Pettus Papers
    William L. Roberts Diary
    Elbert D. Willett Diary

Archives of Michigan, Lansing, Michigan
    Frank E. Gunn Collection
    Douwe B. Yntema Collection
        Leonard G. Loomis Letters

Atlanta History Center, Atlanta, Georgia
    Antebellum and Civil War Collection
        William Rogers Letter
    George H. Daniel Correspondence
Auburn University, Auburn, Alabama
    Southern Railroad Records
Augustana College, Rock Island, Illinois
    Gould D. Molineaux Diary
Boston Antheum, Boston, Massachusetts
    Confederate Collection
        "The Siege of Vicksburg, Its Approaches by Yazoo Pass and Other Routes"
Butler Center for Arkansas Studies, Little Rock, Arkansas
    John Myers Letters
    Dick Ransom Collection
    Oliver H. P. Scott Letter
Chapman University, Orange, California
    Thomas H. Johnson Letter
Chicago History Museum, Chicago, Illinois
    A. Achen Papers
    Albert H. Bodman Papers
    William L. Brown Papers
    George D. Carrington Diary
    Henry C. Forbes Papers
    John Merrilees Diary
    Florison D. Pitts Papers
    Richard R. Puffer Papers
    Arnold Rickard Diary
    James C. Sinclair Diary
    William A. Sypher Diary
    John M. Wallace Papers
De Kalb County Historical and Genealogical Society, Sycamore, Illinois
    Wilson E. Chapel Diary
Duke University, Durham, North Carolina
    American Song Sheets Collection
        Lewis A. McBroom, "Running the Blockade"
    John W. Barnes Papers
    A. J. McConnico Papers
    "Military History of Captain Thomas Sewell"
    W. A. Rorer Letters
    B. L. C. Wailes Diary
Emory University, Atlanta, Georgia
    Civil War Collection
        Phillip Fall Letter
    Frederick E. Davis Papers

Eureka College, Eureka, Illinois
    J. H. Rowell Diary
Filson Historical Society, Louisville, Kentucky
    John Letter
    William George Pirtle Memoirs
    Milton W. Shaw Papers
Gettysburg College, Gettysburg, Pennsylvania
    Benjamin Henry Grierson Vertical File
Gilder Lehrman Institute, New York, New York
    Mansfield Lovell Letter
    Dabney H. Maury Letter
Grenada Public Library, Grenada, Mississippi
    Joel C. Watson Diary
Harvard University, Cambridge, Massachusetts
    Houghton Library
        Frederick M. Dearborn Collection
            Dabney Maury Letter
            Earl Van Dorn Letter
Huntington Library, San Marino, California
    Obadiah E. Baker Diary
    Mansfield Lovell Papers
    Lionel A. Sheldon Memoir
Indiana Historical Society, Indianapolis, Indiana
    Solomon M. Barnes Letters
    Hugh Bay Letters
    Magnus Brucker Letters
    Hugh Gaston Letters
    Bennett Grigsby Papers
    Joseph Hotz Papers
    Daniel Hughes Diary
    Jolly Family Papers
    James Leeper Correspondence
    John F. Lester Diary
    Mayfield and Sanders Family Papers
    Peter Myers Collection
    Cyrus Rayhill Correspondence
    Henry A. Robinson Papers
    Rowland-Shilladay Papers
    Asa Sample Diary
    Adoniram J. Sanders Correspondence
    Sesquicentennial Manuscript Project
    Vincent Wicker Papers
    Edward J. Wood Papers
    Joseph W. Young Letters

Indiana State Library, Indianapolis, Indiana
    Jack K. Carmichael Papers
    Chittenden Family Papers
    John B. Elliott Diary
    James S. Fogle Papers
    George B. Marshall Reminiscences
    James McLaughlin Papers
    Daniel Roberts Correspondence
    George W. Roberts Papers
    George M. Rogers Diary
    Augustus G. Sinks Papers
    James R. Slack Letters
    Benjamin Spooner Letters
    James H. St. John Diary
    James C. Vanderbilt Papers
    Harry Watts Reminiscences
Indiana University, Bloomington, Indiana
    Hovey Manuscript
Iowa State University, Ames, Iowa
    John W. Chambers Diary
Kansas City Public Library, Kansas City, Missouri
    Cyrus Boyd Diary
Kansas Historical Society, Topeka, Kansas
    Isaac M. Home Papers
    Lyman U. Humphrey Correspondence
    Thomas G. Larkin Papers
Library of Congress, Washington, DC
    Blair Family Papers
    Mrs. Douglas W. Clark Collection
        R. B. Beck Diary
    Charles Calvin Enslow Papers
    John S. Jackman Diary
    John G. Jones Papers
    Abraham Lincoln Papers
    Thomas Lyons Diary
    Allen W. Miller Diary
    George W. Morgan Papers
    Edward Paul Reichhelm Papers
    William T. Sherman Papers
    "The Siege of Vicksburg, Its Approaches by Yazoo Pass and Other Routes"
    Bela T. St. John Papers
    Theodore E. St. John Papers
    James H. Wilson Papers

Louisiana State University, Baton Rouge, Louisiana
   Army of the Tennessee Papers
   Autobiography of Louis Hébert
   Rowland Chambers Diary
   Civil War Officer Letter
   Samuel W. Ferguson Papers
   Sidney O. Little Letters
   Horace P. Milton Letters
   "The Siege of Vicksburg, Its Approaches by Yazoo Pass and Other Routes"
Loyola Marymount University, Los Angeles, California
   Civil War Collection
      James Burton Letter
Michigan State University, East Lansing, Michigan
   Havens Family Papers
Minnesota Historical Society, St. Paul, Minnesota
   James C. Christie and Family Papers
Mississippi Department of Archives and History, Jackson, Mississippi
   James L. Alcorn Diary
   James L. Alcorn and Family Papers
   Joseph D. Alison Diary
   Luther S. Baechtel Diary
   William R. Barksdale Papers
   Francis M. Baxter Papers
   Ben Bounds Memoir
   Broadsides
      "Official Report," June 21, 1828
   Louisa Russell Conner Memoir
   William A. Drennan Papers
   H. N. Faulkinbury Diary
   Fontaine Family Papers
   James Z. George Papers
   Abraham Hagaman Memoir
   Patrick Henry Papers
      James R. Binford, "Recollections of the Fifteenth Regiment of Mississippi Infantry, C.S.A."
   William H. McCardle Papers
   Cyrus D. McElroy Letter
   Samuel M. Meek Papers
   Mississippi Governor, John J. Pettus, Correspondence and Papers, 1859–1863, Series 757
   Edmund Newsome Diary
   Andrew W. Ramsey and Family Papers
   J. A. Orr Reminiscences

John C. Pemberton Papers
J. L. Power Diary and Letters
W. A. Rorer Letters
J. B. Sanders Papers
Claudius W. Sears Diary
Secretary of State Records, RG 28
    Election Returns, 1817–2007
William T. Sherman Letters
M. D. L. Stephens Recollections
Subject Files
    Bruinsburg
    Malmaison
    Mississippi Central and Tennessee Railroad
    Steele's Bayou
    Steele's Bayou Expedition
    Windsor
    Yazoo Pass
Thomas T. Smith Manuscript
John A. Wilson Letters
Mississippi State University, Starkville, Mississippi
    Isaac E. Hirsh Papers
    Miscellaneous Papers
        Joe Rollins, "Ex-Slave Autobiography"
Missouri Historical Society, St. Louis, Missouri
    Alphabetical Files
        Joel Strong Reminiscences
    Frank and Montgomery Blair Papers
    Civil War Collection
        John Bennett Letter
        Howard A. Cooper Papers
        Joseph A. Fardell Papers
        Martin Family Letters
        David T. Massey Letters
        Missouri Legislature Petition
        Papers of Em
        Tallman Family Letters
    Couzins Family Papers
    Hamilton R. Gamble Papers
    Grier Family Papers
    Thomas Butler Gunn Diary
    Hiffman Family Papers
    Harry W. Pflager Letters
    Seth Ledyard Phelps Letterbook
    David Dixon Porter Papers

National Archives and Records Administration, Washington, DC
   RG 24—Records of the Bureau of Naval Personnel
      E 118—Logbooks of U.S. Navy Ships
         USS *Pittsburgh* Logbook
   RG 94—Records of the Adjutant General's Office, 1762–1984
      E 57—Muster Rolls of Volunteer Organizations
         Battery K, 1st Illinois Artillery Muster Roll
      E 159—Generals' Papers
         Hugh Ewing Papers
         Ulysses S. Grant Papers
         Charles S. Hamilton Papers
         James B. McPherson Papers
         David Stuart Papers
   RG 109—War Department Collection of Confederate Records, 1825–1900
      E 94—Department of Mississippi and East Louisiana, Orders and Circulars, 1862–1865
      E 97—Army of the Mississippi, Orders and Circulars, 1861–1865
      E 131—John C. Pemberton Papers
      Chapter 2, Vol. 60—Letters and Telegrams Sent, Department of Mississippi and East Louisiana, 1863
      Chapter 2, Volume 274—Letter Book, Brig. Gen. J. S. Bowen's Command, August 1862–November 1863
   RG 393—Records of the United States Army Continental Commands
      E 3221—9th Division, XIII Corps, Letters Sent, 1861–1863
      E 3227—9th Division, XIII Corps, Orders and Letters Forwarded, 1863
      E 3230—9th Division, XIII Corps, General and Special Orders Issued, 1863
      E 5541—XIII Corps, General Orders Issued, 1863–1864
      E 5545—XIII Corps, Special Orders Issued, 1863
      E 6305—XVII Corps, General Orders Issued, 1862–1865
Navarro College, Corsicana, Texas
   Edward E. Potter Papers
Newberry Library, Chicago, Illinois
   Chase H. Dickinson Correspondence
   Benjamin Henry Grierson Papers
   Curtis P. Lacey Diary
   Israel P. Rumsey Papers
   Z. Payson Shumway Letters
Ohio Historical Society, Columbus, Ohio
   Jonathan H. Beach Letters
   John N. Bell Diary
   John H. Dorman Papers
   Henry Otis Dwight Papers
   Dykes Family Papers

Hugh Ewing Papers
Rueben H. Falconer Diary
Henry W. Franks Letters
Carlos Forbes Correspondence
John W. Griffith Diary
William B. Hays Letter
Townsend P. Heaton Papers
George H. Hildt Letters
Ohio Knox Papers
Alexander McConaughey Collection
Samuel S. Miner Papers
Elliot Morrow Papers
Peter J. Perrine Diary
John M. Sullivan Papers
Flavius J. Thackara Diary
Ernest A. Warden Diary
Thomas K. White Papers
William F. Willey Diary
Cyrus Willford Reminiscences
Lucius B. Wing Correspondence

Old Courthouse Museum, Vicksburg, Mississippi
    35th Iowa Infantry Memoir
    Matthew R. Adams Letters
    Joseph S. Alexander Letters
    Joseph D. Alison Diary
    Robert L. Bachman Memoir
    Banner Family Letters
    S. C. Beck, "A True Sketch of His Army Life"
    John Bond Diary
    Ben Bounds Memoir
    John A. Bowman Letters
    George Bradley Memoir
    William B. Britton Letters
    Andrew Bush Letters
    Samuel Churchill Memoir
    Isaac B. Coleman Letter
    John F. Davis Letters
    Eugene Duncan Memoir
    Edward J. Dunn Memoir
    Zeno P. Elwell Letter
    James Ferguson Letters
    Jacob Flory Letters
    Ben Giddens Letters

Joseph C. Gordon Diary
C. B. Haddon Memoir
R. R. Hall Diary
Seth Hall Letters
D. D. Hammack Letters
James D. Heath Diary
Isaac E. Herring Letters
John Hipple Letter
Thomas R. Hodgson Diary
William F. Hollingsworth Diary
James Jermyn Diary
George B. Johnson Letters
James T. Kidd Memoir
Myron Knight Diary
Parker Leeper Letter
James F. Mallinckrodt Diary
Thomas N. McCluer Diary
Alexander F. McGahey Letters
Thomas K. Mitchell Diary
George W. Modil Diary
William Morton Letters
William T. Mumford Diary
Matthias Murphy Letter
Edmund Newsome Diary
H. B. Payton Letters
Joseph W. Pendleton Letters
Israel M. Piper Diary
T. C. Ryan Memoir
Jared Sanders Letter
Maurice K. Simons Diary
Star of the West File
Oscar E. Stewart Memoir
Joel Strong Reminiscences
Archie Thompson Diary
Eli W. Thornhill Memoir
Raymond Trahan Papers
Benjamin W. Underwood Letters
Martin Van Kees Diary
Ralph P. Voorhies Letters
Merrick J. Wald Diary
Seth Wells Diary
Abner J. Wilkes Memoir
J. S. Wheeler File

BIBLIOGRAPHY

    R. A. Wilson Letter
    James W. Woodard Letters
Rutherford B. Hayes Presidential Center, Fremont, Ohio
    Wilfred S. Foerster Collection
    John B. Rice Letters
Kirby Smith Collection, Barrington, Illinois
    John E. Smith Letters
Southern Illinois University, Carbondale, Illinois
    Edwin A. Loosley Papers
    Robert S. Martin Diary
    Joseph Skipworth Papers
Stanford University, Stanford, California
    Samuel Fowler Diary
    Frederick Steele Papers
State Historical Society of Iowa, Des Moines, Iowa
    Elisha Coon Letters
State Historical Society of Iowa, Iowa City, Iowa City, Iowa
    Keen Family Papers
        William H. Jolly Letters
    Seneca B. Thrall Papers
State Historical Society of Missouri, Columbia, Missouri
    John T. Buegel Diary
    William E. Lewis Letters
    George E. Townsend Letters
    James W. Woodard Correspondence
Tennessee State Library and Archives, Nashville, Tennessee
    Wiley Bartlett Letters
    Samuel D. Bayless Letters
    James R. Burton Letters
    Mary Ellet Cabell Letter
    J. Wood Coleman Journal
    Luther H. Cowan Papers
    Cyrus M. Delany Letters
    Elijah Hall Letters
    George Jones Letters
    Lillard Family Papers
    W. H. Lipscomb Letters
    William H. Merriman Letters
    John R. Moss Letters
    James B. Owen Letters
    C. S. O. Rice Memoir
    James C. Snell Letters
    Spencer B. Talley Memoir

William Thurman Letters
Willard Warner Papers
Tulane University, New Orleans, Louisiana
    Bartlett Family Papers
    Don A. Pardee Papers
    William A. Smith Letters
Ulysses S. Grant Presidential Library, Starkville, Mississippi
    Fred Grant Memoir
    Vicksburg File
        James H. Wilson Papers
United States Army History and Education Center, Carlisle, Pennsylvania
    Anders Collection
        John D. Brownley Memoir
        Hezekiah C. Clock Letters
    Bilby Collection
        Carlos Colby Memoir
    Civil War Documents Collection
        Boucher Family Papers
        Thomas Buchanan Letter
        Charles Bullard Memoir
        George H. Chatfield Letters
        William M. Cleaveland Letters
        Collier Family Papers
        Charles Lutz Letters
        Henry T. Morgan Letters
        John M. Smith Letters
        Ann Sturdivant Collection
            William A. Montgomery Letters
        Columbus Sykes Papers
            T. T. Smith Reminiscences
        Isaac Vanderwarker Diary
        Joseph W. Westbrook Memoir
    Civil War Times Illustrated Collection
        Lionel Baxter Collection
            Mansfield Lovell Letter
            W. A. Rorer Letters
        Francis A. Dawes Diary
        Paul Dorweiler Diary
        Lewis F. Phillips Papers
        Henry J. Reynolds Memoir
        Henry J. Seaman Diary
        Edward E. Schweitzer Diary
        James K. Worthington Letters

Harrisburg Civil War Roundtable Collection
   John Carr Diary
   Coco Collection
      Joseph Stockton Diary
   Luke R. Roberts Letters
   William A. Ruyle Memoir
   George W. Gordon Diary
  Rudolph Haerle Collection
   Samuel P. Harrington Diary
  Richard M. Hunt Collection
   Latimer Family Collection
  Wiley Sword Collection
   Andrew McCornack Letters
United States Naval Academy, Annapolis, Maryland
  Watson Smith Papers
University of Alabama, Tuscaloosa, Alabama
  Henry De Lamar Clayton Sr. Papers
  Robert Jemison Jr. Papers
  I. A. King Letter
  Meriwether Family Papers
  Henry W. Reese Jr. Papers
  Sheldon C. Treat Correspondence
University of Arkansas, Fayetteville, Arkansas
  Core Family Papers
  Minos Miller Letters
University of California—San Diego, San Diego, California
  William F. Vermilion Papers
University of Colorado Boulder, Boulder, Colorado
  Noble W. Wood Diary
University of Georgia, Athens, Georgia
  E. Merton Coulter Collection
  James McCulloch Diary
University of Illinois, Urbana, Illinois
  William E. Dunaway Papers
  Henry C. Forbes Papers
  Stephen A. Forbes Papers
University of Iowa, Iowa City, Iowa
  Bean Family Papers
  Joseph Child Diary
  Giauque Family Papers
  Robert J. Moyle Letters
  David J. Palmer Papers
  William T. Rigby Papers

George M. Shearer Diary
White Family Papers
University of Memphis, Memphis, Tennessee
   Civil War Collection
      DeBenneville Randolph Keim Notebook
      John Linfor Letters
      Unnamed Soldier's Diary
University of Michigan, Ann Arbor, Michigan
   Bentley Library
     Calvin Ainsworth Diary
   Clements Library
     Schoff Civil War Collection
       Isaac Jackson Papers
       Sidney Little Papers
       Virgil H. Moats Papers
       Lewis Van Tuyl Papers
University of Mississippi, Oxford, Mississippi
   Wirt Adams Collection
   Lionel Baxter Collection
      Mansfield Lovell Letter
University of Missouri, Columbia, Missouri
   I. V. Smith Memoirs
University of North Carolina, Chapel Hill, North Carolina
   Joseph D. Alison Diary
   Autobiography of Louis Hébert
   J. F. H. Claiborne Papers
   John G. Devereux Papers
   Robert S. Finley Papers
   Jason Niles Diary
   Henry Oman Papers
   John C. Pemberton Papers
   Isaac O. Shelby Diary
   Andrew J. Sproul Papers
   Samuel Addison Whyte Diary
   Adoniram Judson Withrow Papers
University of North Texas, Denton, Texas
   L. D. Bradley Letter
University of South Carolina, Columbia, South Carolina
   John Crenshaw Letter
   Paul Hamilton Papers
University of Southern Mississippi, Hattiesburg, Mississippi
   Thomas Gore Memoir
   Milton W. Shaw Letter
   Southern Railroad Company Letter

University of Tennessee, Knoxville, Tennessee
    David G. Farragut Papers
    C. S. O. Rice Memoir
University of Virginia, Charlottsville, Virginia
    William S. Hillyer Papers
University of Washington, Seattle, Washington
    Samuel D. Lougheed Papers
    Morgan Family Papers
University of Wisconsin-River Falls, River Falls, Wisconsin
    Edwin D. Levings Papers
Vicksburg National Military Park, Vicksburg, Mississippi
    Letters/Diaries/Journals
        A. S. Abrams, "The Siege of Vicksburg"
        Charles E. Affeld Diary
        Calvin Ainsworth Diary
        Dempsey J. Ashford Diary
        S. C. Beck, "A True Sketch of His Army Life"
        George H. Burns Letters
        James N. Carlisle Diary
        Lemuel Cline Letters
        Stephen Croom Diary
        John M. Douthit Letters
        E. T. Eggleston Diary
        Samuel W. Ferguson Memoir
        Clarkson Fogg Letters
        Charles Foster Diary
        C. Judson Gill Letters
        Robert Hamilton Letters
        John B. Hancox Letter
        Simon Helmick Diary
        Anson Hemingway Diary
        Sherod Horton Letters
        Will H. Jolly Letters
        Carolyn Jones Letter
        Karl Knietel Letters
        John A. Leavy Diary
        Joseph Lesslie Letters
        Letter from Charles
        Charles Dana Miller Memoir
        Cyrus K. Miller Letter
        E. W. Mitchell Letter
        William Murray Diary
        E. T. Rhea Letter
        John Ruckman Letters

  Obriham Family Letters
  Nicholas Ollemar Letter
  John C. Pemberton Papers
  Israel M. Piper Diary
  David Dixon Porter Correspondence
  Jared Sanders Letters
  Charles J. Sauter Diary
  Henry J. Seaman Diary
  Alexander Shall Diary
  Henry A. Shubert Letter
  David Shunk Papers
  A. L. Slack Diary
  David Spigener Letter
  Joseph Stockton Diary
  Ebenezer Werkheiser Letters
  Joseph R. Winslow Diary
  Timothy C. Young Diary
Western Kentucky University, Bowling Green, Kentucky
  L. J. Sanders Diary
Western Reserve Historical Society, Cleveland, Ohio
  John Quincy Adams Diaries
Wisconsin Historical Society, Madison, Wisconsin
  H. H. Bennett Diary
  Van Bennett Diary
  Jenkins Lloyd Jones Diary
  Herman Salomon Diary

Newspapers

Canton (Illinois) Fulton City *Register*
Canton (Illinois) *Weekly Register*
Carrollton *Conservative*
Chicago Tribune
Cleveland *Morning Leader*
Edgefield (South Carolina) *Advertiser*
Frank Leslie's Illustrated Newspaper
Goshen (Indiana) *Times*
Harper's Weekly
Hinds County *Gazette*
Holly Springs *South Reporter*
Jackson *Clarion Ledger*

Jackson *Daily Mississippian*
Jackson *Daily News*
Jackson *Mississippian and State Gazette*
Jackson *Weekly Mississippian*
Knoxville *Daily Register*
Litchfield (Illinois) *Union Monitor*
Memphis *Daily Bulletin*
Mobile *Advertiser and Register*
Natchez *Daily Courier*
Natchez *Times*
New Orleans *Era*
New York *Times*
Port Gibson *Southern Reveille*
Port Royal (South Carolina) *The New South*
Sacramento *Daily Union*
Urbana (Ohio) *Union*
Verdan (Oklahoma) *News*
Vicksburg *Whig*
Vicksburg *Evening Citizen*
Vicksburg *Evening Post*

Published Primary and Secondary Sources

Abrams, A. S. *A Full and Detailed History of the Siege of Vicksburg*. Atlanta: Intelligencer Steam Power Presses, 1863.
Adair, John M. *Historical Sketch of the Forty-fifth Illinois Regiment, With a Complete List of the Officers and Privates and an Individual Record of Each Man in the Regiment*. Lanark, IL: Carroll County Gazette Print, 1869.
"Again in Vicksburg." June 7, 1894, *National Tribune*.
Allardice, Bruce S. *Confederate Colonels: A Biographical Register*. Columbia: University of Missouri Press, 2008.
Ambrose, Stephen E., and Douglas Brinkley. *The Mississippi and the Making of a Nation: From the Louisiana Purchase to Today*. Washington, DC: National Geographic, 2002.
Anderson, Ephraim McD. *Memoirs: Historical and Personal Including the Campaigns of the First Missouri Confederate Brigade*. St. Louis: Times Publishing Co., 1868.
Anderson, John Q., ed. *Brokenburn: The Journal of Kate Stone, 1861–1868*. Baton Rouge: Louisiana State University Press, 1955.
"Arkansas Post." *Southern Historical Society Papers* 22 (1894): 10–13.
Badeau, Adam. *Military History of Ulysses S. Grant, From April, 1861, to April, 1865*, 2 vols. New York: D. Appleton & Co., 1881.
Ballard, Michael B. "Grant, McClernand, and Vicksburg: A Clash of Personalities and

Backgrounds." In *The Vicksburg Campaign: March 29–May 18, 1863*, Steven E. Woodworth and Charles D. Grear, eds. Carbondale: Southern Illinois University Press, 2013, 129–152.

———. "Misused Merit: The Tragedy of John C. Pemberton." In *Civil War Generals in Defeat*, Steven E. Woodworth, ed. Lawrence: University Press of Kansas, 1999, 141–160.

———. "Misused Merit: The Tragedy of John C. Pemberton." In *Confederate Generals in the Western Theater*, 4 vols., Lawrence Lee Hewitt and Arthur W. Bergeron Jr., eds. Knoxville: University of Tennessee Press, 2010, 1:103–121.

———. *Pemberton: The General Who Lost Vicksburg*. Jackson: University Press of Mississippi, 1991.

———. *Vicksburg: The Campaign That Opened the Mississippi*. Chapel Hill: University of North Carolina Press, 2004.

Barton, Thomas H. *Autobiography of Dr. Thomas H. Barton, The Self-made Physician of Syracuse, Ohio*. Charleston: West Virginia Printing Co., 1890.

Bearss, Edwin C. "Colonel Streight Drives for the Western and Atlantic Railroad." *Alabama Historical Quarterly* 26 (Summer 1964): 133–186.

———. *Hardluck Ironclad: The Sinking and Salvage of the Cairo*, rev. ed. Baton Rouge: Louisiana State University Press, 1980.

———. *Rebel Victory at Vicksburg*. Vicksburg: Vicksburg Centennial Commission, 1963.

———. *The Vicksburg Campaign*, 3 vols. Dayton, OH: Morningside, 1985.

Bearss, Edwin C., with J. Parker Hills. *Receding Tide: Vicksburg and Gettysburg: The Campaigns That Changed the Civil War*. Washington, DC: National Geographic, 2010.

Beck, S. C. "A True Sketch of His Army Life." N.p.: n.p., n.d.

Bek, William G., ed. "The Civil War Diary of John T. Buegel, Union Soldier." *Missouri Historical Review* 40, no. 4 (July 1946): 503–530.

Bennett, Stewart, and Barbara Tillery, eds. *The Struggle for the Life of the Republic: A Civil War Narrative by Brevet Major Charles Dana Miller, 76th Ohio Volunteer Infantry*. Kent, OH: Kent State University Press, 2004.

Bentley, W. H. *History of the 77th Illinois Volunteer Infantry, Sept. 2, 1862–July 10, 1865*. Peoria, IL: Edward Hine, Printer, 1883.

Bergeron, Arthur W., Jr. "Martin Luther Smith and the Defense of the Lower Mississippi River Valley, 1861–1863." In *Confederate Generals in the Western Theater: Essays on America's Civil War*, 4 vols., Lawrence Lee Hewitt and Arthur W. Bergeron Jr., eds. Knoxville: University of Tennessee Press, 2011, 3:61–85.

Belknap, William W. *History of the Fifteenth Regiment, Iowa Veteran Volunteer Infantry, from October, 1861, to August, 1865, When Disbanded at the End of the War*. Keokuk: R. B. Ogden and Son, Print., 1887.

Bering, John A., and Thomas Montgomery. *History of the Forty-Eighth Ohio Vet. Vol. Inf.* Hillsboro, OH: Highland News Office, 1880.

Bertera, Martin N. *De Golyer's 8th Michigan Black Horse Light Battery*. Wyandotte, MI: TillieAnn Press, 2015.

Bevier, R. S. *History of the First and Second Missouri Confederate Brigades 1861–1865 and From Wakaruse to Appomattox, A Military Anagraph.* St. Louis: Bryan, Brand and Company, 1879.

Bigelow, James K. *Abridged History of the Eighth Indiana Volunteer Infantry, from Its Organization, April 21st, 1861, to the Date of Re-enlistment as Veterans, January 1, 1864.* Indianapolis: Ellis Barnes Book and Job Printer, 1864.

Bishop, S. W. "The Battle of Arkansas Post." *Confederate Veteran* 5, no. 4 (April 1897): 151–153.

Black, III, Robert C. *The Railroads of the Confederacy.* Chapel Hill: University of North Carolina Press, 1952.

Blanchard, Ira. *I Marched with Sherman: Civil War Memoirs of the 20th Illinois Volunteer Infantry*, Nancy Ann Mattingly, ed. New York: toExcel, 1992.

Bodman, Albert H. "'In Sight of Vicksburg': Private Diary of a Northern War Correspondent," Leo M. Kaiser, ed. *Historical Bulletin* 24, no. 4 (May 1956): 202–221.

Brady, Lisa M. *War Upon the Land: Military Strategy and the Transformation of Southern Landscapes during the American Civil War.* Athens: University of Georgia Press, 2012.

Bridge, Carolyn S., ed. *These Men Were Heroes Once: The Sixty-ninth Indiana Volunteer Infantry.* West Lafayette, IN: Twin Publications, 2005.

Brinkerhoff, Henry R. *History of the Thirtieth Regiment Ohio Volunteer Infantry, From Its Organization, To the Fall of Vicksburg, Miss.* Columbus, OH: James W. Osgood, Printer, 1863.

Brinton, John H. *Personal Memoirs of John H. Brinton, Major and Surgeon U.S.V., 1861–1865.* New York: Neale Publishing Company, 1914.

Brockett, L. P. *The Camp, The Battle Field, and the Hospital; Or, Lights and Shadows of the Great Rebellion.* Philadelphia: National Publishing Company, 1866.

Brown, A. F. "Van Dorn's Operations in Northern Mississippi—Recollections of a Cavalryman." *Southern Historical Society Papers* 5, no. 4 (October 1878): 151–161.

Brown, Alonzo L. *History of the Fourth Regiment of Minnesota Infantry Volunteers During the Great Rebellion, 1861–1865.* St. Paul, MN: The Pioneer Press Company, 1892.

Brown, George W. "Service in the Mississippi Squadron, and Its Connection with the Siege and Capture of Vicksburg." In *Personal Recollections of the War of the Rebellion: Addresses Delivered before the Commandery of the State of New York, Military Order of the Loyal Legion of the United States, 1883–1891,* 4 vols. New York: The Commandery, 1891, 1:303–313.

Browning, Judkin, and Timothy Silver. *An Environmental History of the Civil War.* Chapel Hill: University of North Carolina Press, 2020.

Bryner, Cloyd. *Bugle Echoes: The Story of the Illinois 47th.* Springfield, IL: Phillips Bros. Printers, 1905.

Buckles, Stanley D. *Not Afraid to Go Any Whare: A History of the 114th Regiment Illinois Volunteer Infantry.* Bend, OR: Maverick Publications, 2019.

Burdette, Robert J. *The Drums of the 47th.* Indianapolis: The Bobbs-Merrill Company, 1914.

Burke, Eric Michael. *Soldiers from Experience: The Forging of Sherman's Fifteenth Army Corps, 1862–1863*. Baton Rouge: Louisiana State University Press, 2023.
Burnham, John H. *The Thirty-third Regiment Illinois Infantry in the Civil War, 1861–1865; Prepared by Capt. J.H. Burnham at the Request of the Directors of the Illinois Historical Society for the 1912 Annual Meeting of that Society*. Np: n.p., 1912.
Bush, Bryan S. *Lloyd Tilghman: Confederate General in the Western Theater*. Morley, MO: Acclaim Press, 2006.
Byers, S. H. M. *With Fire and Sword*. New York: The Neale Publishing Company, 1911.
Cadwallader, Sylvanus. *Three Years with Grant*, Benjamin P. Thomas, ed. Lincoln: University of Nebraska Press, 1996.
"Capt. John W. Dunnington." *Confederate Veteran* 4, no. 3 (March 1896): 84.
Caraway, L. V. "The Battle of Arkansas Post." *Confederate Veteran* 14, no. 3 (March 1906): 127–128.
———. "The Battle of Arkansas Post." *Confederate Veteran* 36, no. 5 (May 1928): 171–173.
Carson, James Taylor "Greenwood LeFlore: Southern Creole, Choctaw Chief." *Journal of Mississippi History* 65, no. 4 (Winter 2003): 355–373.
Carter, Arthur B. *The Tarnished Cavalier: Major General Earl Can Dorn, C.S.A.* Knoxville: University of Tennessee Press, 1999.
Castel, Albert. *General Sterling Price and the Civil War in the West*. Baton Rouge: Louisiana State University Press, 1968.
Catton, Bruce. *Grant Moves South*. Boston: Little, Brown, and Company, 1960.
———. *U. S. Grant and the American Military Tradition*. Boston: Little, Brown and Co., 1954.
Censer, Jane Turner, ed. *The Papers of Frederick Law Olmsted*, 12 vols. Baltimore: Johns Hopkins University Press, 1977–present.
Chambers, John Whiteclay II. *The Oxford Companion to American Military History*. New York: Oxford University Press, 1999.
Chambers, William P. "My Journal." *Publications of the Mississippi Historical Society, Centenary Series*, 5 vols. Jackson: Mississippi Historical Society, 1925, 5: 221–386.
Chatelain, Neil P. *Defending the Arteries of Rebellion: Confederate Naval Operations in the Mississippi River Valley, 1861–1865*. El Dorado Hills, CA: Savas Beatie, 2020.
Chernow, Ron. *Grant*. New York: Penguin Press, 2017.
Clark, Olynthus B., ed. *Downing's Civil War Diary*. Des Moines: The Historical Department of Iowa, 1916.
Clarke, George Powell *Reminiscence and Anecdotes of the War for Southern Independence*. Np: n.p., n.d.
Clausewitz, Carl von. *On War*. London: N. Trubner and Co., 1873.
Cobb, James C. *The Most Southern Place on Earth: The Mississippi Delta and the Roots of Regional Identity*. New York: Oxford University Press, 1992.
Coleman, Roger E. *The Arkansas Post Story: Arkansas Post National Monument*. Santa Fe: Southwest Cultural Resources Center, 1987.
Commager, Henry Steele, ed. *The Blue and the Gray*, 2 vols. New York: Meridian, 1994.

"Condensed Letters." December 4, 1884, *National Tribune*.

Crooke, George. *The Twenty-first Regiment of Iowa Volunteer Infantry: A Narrative of Its Experience in Active Service, Including a Military Record of Each Officer, Non-Commissioned Officer, and Private Soldier of the Organization*. Milwaukee: King, Fowle & Co., 1891.

Crummer, Wilbur F. *With Grant at Fort Donelson, Shiloh and Vicksburg, and An Appreciation of General U.S. Grant*. Oak Park, IL: E. C. Crummer and Co., 1915.

Dana, Charles A. *Recollections of the Civil War*. New York: D. Appleton and Co., 1898.

Daniel, Larry J. "Bruinsburg: Missed Opportunity or Postwar Rhetoric?" *Civil War History* 32, no. 3 (September 1986): 256–267.

———. *Engineering in the Confederate Heartland*. Baton Rouge: Louisiana State University Press, 2022.

Davis, George B., Leslie J. Perry, and Joseph W. Kirkley. *Atlas to Accompany the Official Records of the Union and Confederate Armies*. Washington, DC: Government Printing Office, 1891–1895.

Davis, William C. *Jefferson Davis: The Man and His Hour: A Biography*. New York: Harper Collins, 1991.

"The Defenders of Vicksburg." *Southern Historical Society Papers* 21 (1893): 183–206.

Drake, Rebecca Blackwell, and Margie Riddle Bearss, eds. *My Dear Wife: Letters to Matilda: The Civil War Letters of Sid and Matilda Champion of Champion Hill*. N.p.: n.p., 2005.

Dubay, Robert W. *John Jones Pettus, Mississippi Fire-eater: His Life and Times, 1813–1867*. Jackson: University Press of Mississippi, 1975.

Dunbar, Aaron, and Harvey M. Trimble. *History of the Ninety-third Regiment Volunteer Infantry From Organization to Muster Out*. Chicago: The Blakely Printing Co., 1898.

Dunnavent, R. Blake. "'We Had Lively Times Up the Yazoo': Admiral David Dixon Porter." In *Grant's Lieutenants: From Cairo to Vicksburg*, Steven E. Woodworth, ed. Lawrence: University Press of Kansas, 2001, 169–181.

Elliott, Isaac H. *History of the Thirty-third Regiment Illinois Veteran Volunteer Infantry in the Civil War, 22nd August 1861, to 7th December, 1865*. Gibson City, IL: The Association, 1902.

Evans, S. B. "Seeking a Back Door to Vicksburg." *The Midland Monthly* 5, no. 4 (April 1896): 372–379.

F. A. F. *Old Abe, The Eighth Wisconsin War Eagle. A Full Account of His Capture and Enlistment, Exploits in War and Honorable as Well as Useful Career in Peace*. Madison, WI: Curran and Bowen, 1885.

Field Manual 3–0: Operations. Washington, DC: Department of the Army, 2008.

Fitzpatrick, L. A. "Obstructing Grant's Advance." *Confederate Veteran* 25, no. 1 (January 1917): 25.

Flood, Charles Bracelen. *Grant and Sherman: The Friendship That Won the Civil War*. New York: Farrar, Straus and Giroux, 2005.

Forbes, S. A. "Grierson's Cavalry Raid." *Transactions of the Illinois State Historical Society*. Springfield, IL: Phillips Bros. State Printers, 1908, 99–130.

Force, Manning F. "Personal Recollections of the Vicksburg Campaign." In *Sketches of War History 1861–1865 Papers Read Before the Ohio Commandery of the Military Order of the Loyal Legion of the United States 1883–1886, Volume 1*. 9 vols. Cincinnati: Robert Clarke Company, 1888, 293–309.

Ford, C. Y. "Pot Shot." *Confederate Veteran* 24, no. 4 (April 1916): 167–168.

Fowler, James A., and Miles M. Miller. *History of the Thirtieth Iowa Infantry Volunteers. Giving a Complete Record of the Movements of the Regiment from Its Organization Until Muster Out*. Mediapolis, IA: T. A. Merrill, Printer, 1908.

"Frank M. Bell." *Confederate Veteran* 11, no. 1 (January 1903): 32.

Franke, Brandon. "Waul's Texas Legion: Towards Vicksburg." *East Texas Historical Journal* 53, no. 1 (2015): 1–17.

French, Samuel G. *Two Wars: An Autobiography of Gen. Samuel G. French*. Nashville: Confederate Veteran, 1901.

Fulfer, Richard J. *A History of the Trials and Hardships of the Twenty-Fourth Indiana Volunteer Infantry*. Indianapolis: Indianapolis Printing Company, 1913.

Fuller, J. F. C. *The Generalship of Ulysses S. Grant*. Bloomington: Indiana University Press, 1958.

"Gen. Thomas J. Churchill." *Confederate Veteran* 15, no. 3 (March 1907): 122–123.

George, Henry. *History of the 3d, 7th, 8th and 12th Kentucky C.S.A.* Louisville, KY: C. T. Dearing Printing Co., 1911.

Gibson, Charles Dana, and E. Kay Gibson. *Assault and Logistics: Union Army Coastal and River Operations, 1861–1866*. Camden, ME: Ensign Press, 1995.

———. *Dictionary of Transports and Combatant Vessels Steam and Sail Employed by the Union Army, 1861–1868*. Camden, ME: Ensign Press, 1995.

Glenn, Audrey. "A Vanderbilt at Greenwood: The Star of the West." *Journal of Mississippi History* 16, no. 4 (October 1954): 258–267.

Grabau, Warren E. *Ninety-Eight Days: A Geographer's View of the Vicksburg Campaign*. Knoxville: University of Tennessee Press, 2000.

Grant, Frederick D. "A Boy's Experience at Vicksburg." In *Personal Recollections of the War of the Rebellion: Addresses Delivered before the Commandery of the State of New York, Military Order of the Loyal Legion of the United States*, A. Noel Blakeman, ed. New York: G. P. Putnam's Sons, 1907, 86–100.

"Grant's Failure at Lake Providence." *Confederate Veteran* 22, no. 10 (October 1914): 459–460.

Grecian, J. *History of the Eighty-third Regiment, Indiana Volunteer Infantry. For Three Years with Sherman*. Cincinnati: John F. Uhlhorn, Printer, 1865.

Grierson, Benjamin H. *A Just and Righteous Cause: Benjamin H. Grierson's Civil War Memoir*, Bruce J. Dinges and Shirley A. Leckie, eds. Carbondale: Southern Illinois University Press, 2008.

Grimsley, Mark, and Todd D. Miller, eds. *The Union Must Stand: The Civil War Diary of John Quincy Adams Campbell, Fifth Iowa Volunteer Infantry*. Knoxville: University of Tennessee Press, 2000.

Gudmestad, Robert. "Elusive Victory: The Union Navy's War along the Western Waters." *Civil War History* 67, no. 2 (June 2021): 79–109.
Hall, Winchester. *The Story of the 26th Louisiana Infantry, In the Service of the Confederate States*. Np: n.p., 1890.
Harriel, Shelby. *Behind the Rifle: Women Soldiers in Civil War Mississippi*. Jackson: University Press of Mississippi, 2019.
Harrison, Robert W. "Early State Flood-Control Legislation in the Mississippi Alluvial Valley." *Journal of Mississippi History* 23, no. 2 (April 1961): 104–126.
———. "Levee Building in Mississippi Before the Civil War." *Journal of Mississippi History* 12, no. 2 (April 1950): 63–97
Hartje, Robert G. *Van Dorn: The Life and Times of a Confederate General*. Nashville: Vanderbilt University Press, 1967.
Hass, Paul H., ed. "The Vicksburg Diary of Henry Clay Warmoth: Part I (April 2, 1863–April 27, 1863)." *Journal of Mississippi History* 31, no. 4 (November 1969): 334–347.
———. "The Vicksburg Diary of Henry Clay Warmoth: Part II (April 28, 1863–May 26, 1863)." *Journal of Mississippi History* 32, no. 1 (February 1970): 60–74.
Hattaway, Herman. *General Stephen D. Lee*. Jackson: University Press of Mississippi, 1988.
Hattaway, Herman, and Archer Jones. *How the North Won: A Military History of the Civil War*. Urbana: University of Illinois Press, 1983.
Hays, E. Z. *History of the Thirty-second Regiment Ohio Veteran Volunteer Infantry*. Columbus, OH: Cott & Evans Printers, 1896.
Hearn, Chester G. *Admiral David Dixon Porter: The Civil War Years*. Annapolis, MD: Naval Institute Press, 1996.
Heinman, Kenneth J. *Civil War Dynasty: The Ewing Family of Ohio*. New York: New York University Press, 2012.
Henry, Frederick A. *Captain Henry of Geauga: A Family Chronicle*. Cleveland: Gates Press, 1942.
Hess, Earl J. "Grant's Ethnic General: Peter J. Osterhaus." In *Grant's Lieutenants: From Cairo to Vicksburg*, Steven E. Woodworth, ed. Lawrence: University Press of Kansas, 2001, 199–216.
Hicks, Henry G. "The Campaign and Capture of Vicksburg." In *Glimpses of the Nation's Struggle: Military Order of the Loyal Legion*, 6 vols. St. Paul, MN: Davis, 1909, 6: 82–107.
History of Company B (Originally Pickens Planters) 40th Alabama Regiment Confederate States Army 1862–1865. Anniston, AL: Norwood, 1902.
History of the 37th Regiment, O.V.V.I., Furnished by Comrades at the Ninth Reunion Held at St. Mary's, Ohio, Tuesday and Wednesday, September 10 and 11, 1889. Toledo, OH: Montgomery and Vrooman, 1890.
"History of the Corps." May 18, 1893, *National Tribune*.
History of the Forty-sixth Regiment Indiana Volunteer Infantry, September, 1861–September, 1865. Logansport, IN: Press of Wilson, Humphreys and Co., 1888.

Hogane, J. T. "Reminiscences of the Siege of Vicksburg." *Southern Historical Society Papers* 11, nos. 4–5 (April-May 1883): 223–227.

"Hovey's Division at Port Gibson." January 8, 1885, *National Tribune*.

Howard, R. L. *History of the 124th Regiment Illinois Infantry Volunteers, Otherwise Known as the "Hundred and Two Dozen," From August, 1862, to August, 1865*. Springfield, IL: H. W. Rokker, 1880.

Howard, Richard L. "The Vicksburg Campaign." In *War Papers Read Before the Commandery of the State of Maine, Military Order of the Loyal Legion of the United States, Volume 2*. Portland, ME: Lefavor-Tower Company, 1902, 2:28–40.

Howe, M. A. DeWolfe, ed. *Home Letters of General Sherman*. New York: Charles Scribner's Sons, 1909.

Howell, Grady, Jr. *Going to Meet the Yankees: A History of the "Bloody Sixth" Mississippi Infantry, C.S.A*. Jackson: Chickasaw Bayou Press, 1981.

In Memoriam: Charles Ewing. Philadelphia: J. B. Lippincott, 1888.

Jenney, William L. B. "Personal Recollections of Vicksburg." In *Military Essays and Recollections: Papers Read before the Commandery of the State of Illinois, Military Order of the Loyal Legion of the United States*, 5 vols. Chicago: The Dial Press, 1899, 3:247–265.

———. "With Sherman and Grant from Memphis to Chattanooga: A Reminisce." In *Military Essays and Recollections: Papers Read Before the Commandery of the State of Illinois, Military Order of the Loyal Legion of the United States*, 5 vols. Chicago: Cozzens and Beaton Company, 1907, 4:193–214.

Johnston, William P. *The Life of Gen. Albert Sidney Johnston, Embracing His Services in the Armies of the United States, the Republic of Texas, and the Confederate States*. New York: D. Appleton and Co., 1878.

Joiner, Gary D. *Mr. Lincoln's Brown Water Navy: The Mississippi Squadron*. New York: Rowman & Littlefield, 2007.

———. "Running the Gauntlet: The Effectiveness of Combined Forces in the Vicksburg Campaign." In *The Vicksburg Campaign: March 29–May 18, 1863*, Steven E. Woodworth and Charles D. Grear, eds. Carbondale: Southern Illinois University Press, 2013, 8–23.

Jomini, Henri de. *The Art of War*. Philadelphia: J. B. Lippincott & Co., 1862.

———. *Summary of the Art of War, or, A New Analytical Compend of the Principal Combinations of Strategy, of Grand Tactics and of Military Policy*. New York: G. P. Putnam & Co., 1854.

Jones, Archer. *Civil War Command and Strategy: The Process of Victory and Defeat*. New York: The Free Press, 1992.

Jones, J. B. *A Rebel War Clerk's Diary: At the Confederate States Capital, Volume 1: April 1861-July 1863*, 2 vols., James I. Robertson, Jr., ed. Lawrence: University Press of Kansas, 2015.

Jones, James Pickett. *Black Jack: John A. Logan and Southern Illinois in the Civil War Era*. Carbondale: Southern Illinois University Press, 1967.

Jones, Jenkins Lloyd. *An Artilleryman's Diary*. Madison: Wisconsin History Commission, 1914.
Jones, S. C. *Reminiscences of the Twenty-second Iowa Volunteer Infantry, Giving Its Organization, Marches, Skirmishes, Battles, and Sieges, as Taken from the Diary of Lieutenant S. C. Jones of Company A*. Iowa City: n.p., 1907.
Jordan, Thomas, and J. P. Pryor. *The Campaigns of Lieut.-Gen. N. B. Forrest, and of Forrest's Cavalry, with Portraits, Maps, and Illustrations*. New Orleans: Blelock & Company, 1868.
Journal of the Senate of the State of Mississippi at their Twelfth Session. Jackson: Peter Isler, 1829.
Kaiser, Leo M., ed. "The Civil War Diary of Florison D. Pitts." *Mid-America: An Historical Review* 40, no. 1 (January 1958): 22–63.
Kelley, Arthell. "The Geography." In *A History of Mississippi*, 2 vols., Richard A. McLemore, ed. Hattiesburg: University & College Press of Mississippi, 1973, 1:3–23.
Kennedy, Joseph C. G. *Population of the United States in 1860: Compiled from the Original Returns of the Eighth Census Under the Direction of the Secretary of the Interior*. Washington, DC: Government Printing Office, 1864.
Kiper, Richard L. *Major General John A. McClernand: Politician in Uniform*. Kent, OH: Kent State University Press, 1999.
Krick, Robert K. "'Snarl and Sneer and Quarrel': General Joseph E. Johnston and an Obsession with Rank." In *Leaders of the Lost Cause: New Perspectives on the Confederate High Command*, Gary W. Gallagher and Joseph T. Glatthaar, eds. Mechanicsburg, PA: Stackpole Books, 2004, 165–203.
Kountz, John S. *Record of the Organizations Engaged in the Campaign, Siege, and Defense of Vicksburg*. Knoxville: University of Tennessee Press, 2011.
Lambert, R. A. "In the Mississippi Campaigns." *Confederate Veteran* 37, no. 8 (August 1929): 292–294.
Lamers, William M. *The Edge of Glory: A Biography of General William S. Rosecrans, U.S.A.* New York: Harcourt, Brace, and World, 1961.
Lash, Jeffrey N. *A Politician Turned General: The Civil War Career of Stephen Augustus Hurlbut*. Kent, OH: Kent State University Press, 2003.
Lee, Stephen D. "The Campaign of Vicksburg, Mississippi, in 1863—From April 15 to and Including the Battle of Champion Hills, or Baker's Creek, May 16, 1863." In *Publications of the Mississippi Historical Society*, 13 vols. Oxford: Mississippi Historical Society, 1900, 3:21–53.
———. "Details of Important Work by Two Confederates Telegraph Operators, Christmas Eve, 1862 Which Prevented the Almost Complete Surprise of the Confederate Army at Vicksburg." *Publications of the Mississippi Historical Society*, 13 vols. Oxford: Mississippi Historical Society, 1904, 8:51–55.
Livermore, Mary A. *My Story of the War: A Woman's Narrative of Four Years' Personal Experience as Nurse in The Union Army, and in Relief Work at Home, in Hospitals, Camps, and at the Front During the War of the Rebellion. With Anecdotes, Pathetic*

Incidents, and Thrilling Reminiscences Portraying the Lights and Shadows of Hospital Life and the Sanitary Service of the War. Hartford, CT: A. D. Worthington and Company, 1890.

Lockett, S. H. "The Defense of Vicksburg." In *Battles and Leaders of the Civil War*, 4 vols. New York: Century Company, 1884–1887), 3:482–492.

Lomask, Milton. *Aaron Burr: The Conspiracy and Years of Exile, 1805–1836.* New York: Farrar, Straus and Giroux, 1982.

Long, E. B. *The Civil War Day by Day: An Almanac, 1861–1865.* New York: Doubleday, 1971.

Loughborough, Mary Ann. *My Cave Life in Vicksburg: With Letters of Trial and Travel.* New York: D. Appleton and Company, 1864.

Mahan, James C. *Memoirs of James Curtis Mahan.* Lincoln, NE: The Franklin Press, 1919.

Marshall, T. B. *History of the Eighty-third Ohio Volunteer Infantry, The Greyhound Regiment.* Cincinnati: n.p., 1912.

Marszalek, John F. *Commander of All Lincoln's Armies: A Life of General Henry W. Halleck.* Cambridge, MA: Harvard University Press, 2004.

———. "'A Full Share of All the Credit': Sherman and Grant to the Fall of Vicksburg." In *Grant's Lieutenants: From Cairo to Vicksburg*, Steven E. Woodworth, ed. Lawrence: University Press of Kansas, 2001, 5–20.

———. *Sherman: A Soldier's Passion for Order.* New York: The Free Press, 1993.

———. *Sherman's Other War: The General and the Civil War Press.* Kent, OH: Kent State University Press, 1999.

Marszalek, John F., David F. Nolen, and Louie P. Gallo, eds. *The Personal Memoirs of Ulysses S. Grant: The Complete Annotated Edition.* Cambridge, MA: Harvard University Press, 2017.

Mason, F. H. "Arkansas Post." August 28, 1884, *National Tribune*.

———. *The Forty-second Ohio Infantry: A History of the Organization and Services of That Regiment in the War of the Rebellion; With Biographical Sketches of Its Field Officers and a Full Roster of the Regiment.* Cleveland, OH: Cobb, Andrews and Co., Publishers, 1876.

Masters, Daniel A., ed. *Sherman's Praetorian Guard: Civil War Letters of John McIntyre Lemmon, 72nd Ohio Volunteer Infantry.* Perrysburg, OH: Columbian Arsenal Press, 2017.

Maury, Dabney H. *Recollections of a Virginian in the Mexican, Indian, and Civil Wars.* New York: Charles Scribner's Sons, 1894.

Maynard, Douglas, ed. "Vicksburg Diary: The Journal of Gabriel M. Killgore." *Civil War History* 10, no. 1 (March 1964): 33–53.

McAlexander, U. G. *History of the Thirteenth Regiment United States Infantry, Compiled from Regimental Records and Other Sources.* Np: Regimental Press, Thirteenth Infantry, 1905.

McCluney, Larry A. *The Yazoo Pass Expedition: A Union Thrust into the Delta.* Charleston: History Press, 2017.

McDonough, James Lee. *William Tecumseh Sherman: In the Service of My Country: A Life.* New York: Norton, 2016.

McPherson, James B. *Battle Cry of Freedom: The Civil War Era.* New York: Oxford University Press, 1988.

Memminger, R. W. "The Surrender of Vicksburg—A Defense of General Pemberton." *Southern Historical Society Papers* 12, nos. 7–9 (July–September 1884): 352–360.

Merrius, F. W. "The 'Bones' of the Star of the West." *Confederate Veteran* 7, no. 10 (October 1899): 457–458.

Michael, W. A. C. "How the Mississippi Was Opened." In *Civil War Sketches and Incidents: Papers Read by Companions of the Commandery of the State of Nebraska, Military Order of the Loyal Legion of the United States.* Omaha: The Commandery, 1902, 34–58.

———. "Mississippi Flotilla." June 28, 1888, *National Tribune.*

Miles, Jim. *A River Unvexed: A History and Tour Guide of the Campaign for the Mississippi River.* Nashville: Rutledge Hill Press, 1994.

Military History and Reminiscences of the Thirteenth Regiment of Illinois Volunteer Infantry in the Civil War in the United States 1861–1865. Chicago: Women's Temperance Publishing Association, 1892.

Miller, Donald L. *Vicksburg: Grant's Campaign That Broke the Confederacy.* New York: Simon and Shuster, 2019.

Millett, Allan R., Peter Maslowski, and William B. Feis. *For the Common Defense: A Military History of the United States from 1607 to 2012.* New York: Free Press, 2012.

Monroe, W. H. H. "A Battle in the Bayous." *National Tribune*, October 5, 1899.

Morgan, George W. "The Assault on Chickasaw Bluffs." In *Battles and Leaders of the Civil War*, 4 vols. New York: Century Company, 1884–1887, 3:462–470.

Morris, W. S. *History, 31st Regiment Illinois Volunteers: Organized by John A. Logan.* Herrin, IL: Crossfire Press, 1991.

Myers, Joseph. "The First to Land at Bruinsburg." May 20, 1886, *National Tribune.*

Noe, Kenneth W. *Through the Howling Storm: Weather, Climate, and the American Civil War.* Baton Rouge: Louisiana State University Press, 2020.

Northern, Charles Swift, III, ed. *All Right Let Them Come: The Civil War Diary of an East Tennessee Confederate.* Knoxville: University of Tennessee Press, 2003.

Oake, William Royal. *On the Skirmish Line Behind a Friendly Tree: The Civil War Memoirs of William Royal Oake, 26th Iowa Volunteers*, Stacy D. Allen, ed. Helena, MT: Farcountry Press, 2006.

The Official Records of the Union and Confederate Navies in the War of the Rebellion, 30 vols. Washington, DC: Government Printing Office, 1894–1922.

Oldroyd, Osborn H. *A Soldier's Story of the Siege of Vicksburg. From the Diary of Osborn H. Oldroyd.* Springfield, IL: self-published, 1885.

Ottens, Allen J. *General John A. Rawlins: No Ordinary Man.* Bloomington: Indiana University Press, 2021.

Owens, Harry P. *Steamboats and the Cotton Economy: River Trade in the Yazoo-Mississippi Delta.* Jackson: University Press of Mississippi, 1990.

Ownby, Ted, and Charles Reagan Wilson, eds. *The Mississippi Encyclopedia*. Jackson: University Press of Mississippi, 2017.

Parrish, William E. *Frank Blair: Lincoln's Conservative*. Columbia: University of Missouri Press, 1998.

Patrick, Jeffrey L., ed. *Three Years with Wallace's Zouaves: The Civil War Memoirs of Thomas Wise Durham*. Macon, GA: Mercer University Press, 2003.

Pemberton, John C. *Pemberton: Defender of Vicksburg*. Chapel Hill: University of North Carolina Press, 1942.

Pereyra, Lillian. "James Lusk Alcorn and a Unified Levee System." *Journal of Mississippi History* 27, no. 1 (February 1965): 18–41.

Perry, Oran. "The Entering Wedge." In *War Papers Read Before the Indiana Commandery Military Order of the Loyal Legion of the United States*. Indianapolis: The Commandery, 1898, 366–376.

Peterson, Merrill D. *Thomas Jefferson & the New Nation: A Biography*. New York: Oxford University Press, 1970.

Pierson, Enos. *Proceedings of Eleven Reunions Held by the 16th Regiment, O. V. I., Including Roll of Honor, Roster of the Survivors of the Regiment, Statistics, &c., &c.* Millersburg, OH: Republican Steam Press, 1887.

Porter, David Dixon. *Incidents and Anecdotes of the Civil War*. New York: D. Appleton and Company, 1885.

Pryce, Samuel D. *Vanishing Footprints: The Twenty-Second Iowa Volunteer Infantry in the Civil War*, Jeffry C. Burden, ed. Iowa City: Camp Pope Bookshop, 2008.

Quinby, Henry Cole. *Genealogical History of the Quinby (Quimby) Family in England and America*. Rutland, VT: The Tuttle Company, 1915.

Raab, James W. *W. W. Loring: Florida's Forgotten General*. Manhattan, KS: Sunflower University Press, 1996.

Raum, Green B. "With the Western Army." December 12, 1901, *National Tribune*.

Reardon, Carol. *With a Sword in One Hand & Jomini in the Other: The Problem of Military Thought in the Civil War North*. Chapel Hill: University of North Carolina Press, 2012.

Reed, David W. *Campaigns and Battles of the Twelfth Regiment Iowa Veteran Volunteer Infantry. From Its Organization, September, 1861, to Muster Out, January 20, 1866*. Np: n.p., 1903.

Remini, Robert V. *Andrew Jackson and the Course of American Empire, 1767–1821*. New York: Harper & Row, 1977.

———. *Andrew Jackson and the Course of American Freedom, 1822–1832*. New York: Harper & Row, 1981.

Richard, Allen C., Jr., and Mary Margaret Higginbotham Richard. *The Defense of Vicksburg: A Louisiana Chronicle*. College Station: Texas A&M University Press, 2004.

Richardson, Albert D. *A Personal History of Ulysses S. Grant*. Hartford, CT: American Publishing Company, 1868.

Rietti, John C. *Military Annals of Mississippi: Military Organizations Which Entered the Service of the Confederate States of America from the State of Mississippi*. Np: n.p., 1895.

Ritter, W. L. "An Incident of the Deer Creek Expedition of 1863." *Southern Historical Society Papers* 9, no. 6 (June 1881): 280–281.

———. "Sketch of the Third Battery of Maryland Artillery." *Southern Historical Society Papers* 10, nos. 8–9 (August–September 1882): 392–401.

Roberts, Bobby, and Carl Moneyhon. *Portraits of Conflict: A Photographic History of Mississippi in the Civil War*. Fayetteville: University of Arkansas Press, 1993.

Roland, Charles P. *Albert Sidney Johnston: Soldier of Three Republics*. Austin: University of Texas Press, 1964.

Roth, Dave. "Grierson's Raid, April 17–May 2, 1863: A Cavalry Raid at Its Best." *Blue & Gray Magazine* 10, no. 5 (June 1993): 12–24, 48–65.

Rowland, Dunbar. *Mississippi; Comprising Sketches of Counties, Towns, Events, Institutions and Persons, Arranged in Cyclopedic Form*, 3 vols. Atlanta: Southern Historical Printing Association, 1907.

Rowland, Dunbar, and H. Grady Howell, Jr. *Military History of Mississippi: 1803–1898, Including a Listing of All Known Mississippi Confederate Military Units*. Madison, MS: Chickasaw Bayou Press, 2003.

Russ, William A., Jr., ed. "The Vicksburg Campaign as Viewed by an Indiana Soldier." *Journal of Mississippi History* 19, no. 4 (October 1957): 263–269.

Salomon, Herman. "Civil War Diary of Herman Salomon." *Wisconsin Magazine of History* 10, no. 2 (December 1926): 205–210.

Sanborn, John B. "The Campaign Against Vicksburg." In *Glimpses of the Nation's Struggle, Second Series: A Series of Papers Read Before the Minnesota Commandery of the Military Order of the Loyal Legion of the United States, 1887–1899*, 6 vols. St. Paul, MN: St. Paul Book and Stationary Company, 1890, 2:114–145.

Sanborn Family in the United States and Brief Sketch of Life of John B. Sanborn. St. Paul, MN: H. M. Smyth Printing Co., 1887.

Saunier, Joseph A. *A History of the Forty-seventh Regiment Ohio Veteran Volunteer Infantry, Second Brigade, Second Division, Fifteenth Army Corps, Army of the Tennessee*. Hillsboro, OH: The Lyle Printing Company, 1903.

Schmelzer, Paul L. "Politics, Policy, and General Grant: Clausewitz on the Operational Art as Practiced in the Vicksburg Campaign." In *The Vicksburg Campaign: March 29–May 18, 1863*, Steven E. Woodworth and Charles D. Grear, eds. Carbondale: Southern Illinois University Press, 2013, 214–228.

———. "A Strong Mind: A Clausewitzian Biography of U. S. Grant." PhD diss., Texas Christian University, 2010.

Scott, R. B. *The History of the 67th Regiment Indiana Infantry Volunteers, War of the Rebellion*. Bedford, IN: Herald Book and Job Print, 1892.

Shea, William L. *Union General: Samuel Ryan Curtis and Victory in the West*. Lincoln, NE: Potomac Books, 2023.

Shea, William L., and Terrence J. Winschel. *Vicksburg Is the Key: The Struggle for the Mississippi River*. Lincoln: University of Nebraska Press, 2003.

Sherman, William T. *Memoirs of General William T. Sherman: Written by Himself*, 2 vols. New York: D. Appleton and Co., 1875.

Shunk, William A. "The Vicksburg Campaign." In *War Papers Read Before the Commandery of the State of Wisconsin, Military Order of the Loyal Legion of the United States*, 4 vols. Milwaukee: Burdick & Allen, 1914, 4:141–159.

Simon, John Y., ed. *The Personal Memoirs of Julia Dent Grant [Mrs. Ulysses S. Grant]*. New York: G. P. Putnam's Sons, 1975.

Simon, John Y., and John F. Marszalek, eds. *The Papers of Ulysses S. Grant*. 32 vols. Carbondale: Southern Illinois University Press, 1967–2014.

Simpson, Brooks D. *Ulysses S. Grant: Triumph Over Adversity, 1822–1865*. Boston: Houghton Mifflin Company, 2000.

Skaptason, Bjorn. "The Chicago Light Artillery at Vicksburg." *Journal of the Illinois State Historical Society* 106, nos. 3–4 (Fall/Winter 2013): 422–462.

Smith, Hannis S. "The Futile Star of the West." *Journal of Mississippi History* 14, no. 1 (January 1952): 63–66.

Smith, Tamara A. "A Matter of Trust: Grant and James B. McPherson." In *Grant's Lieutenants: From Cairo to Vicksburg*, Steven E. Woodworth, ed. Lawrence: University Press of Kansas, 2001, 151–167.

Smith, Timothy B. *Champion Hill: Decisive Battle for Vicksburg*. New York: Savas Beatie, 2004.

———. *Corinth 1862: Siege, Battle, Occupation*. Lawrence: University Press of Kansas, 2012.

———. *The Decision Was Always My Own: Ulysses S. Grant and the Vicksburg Campaign*. Carbondale: Southern Illinois University Press, 2018.

———. *Early Struggles for Vicksburg: The Mississippi Central Campaign and Chickasaw Bayou, October 25–December 31, 1862*. Lawrence: University Press of Kansas, 2022.

———. *Grant Invades Tennessee: The 1862 Battles for Forts Henry and Donelson*. Lawrence: University Press of Kansas, 2016.

———. *James Z. George: Mississippi's Great Commoner*. Jackson: University Press of Mississippi, 2012.

———. *Mississippi in the Civil War: The Home Front*. Jackson: University Press of Mississippi, 2010.

———. *The Mississippi Secession Convention: Delegates and Deliberations in Politics and War, 1861–1865*. Jackson: University Press of Mississippi, 2014.

———. *The Real Horse Soldiers: Benjamin Grierson's Epic 1863 Civil War Raid Through Mississippi*. El Dorado Hills, CA: Savas Beatie, 2018.

———. *Shiloh: Conquer or Perish*. Lawrence: University Press of Kansas, 2014.

———. *The Siege of Vicksburg: The Climax of the Campaign to Open the Mississippi River, May 23–July 4, 1863*. Lawrence: University Press of Kansas, 2021.

———. *The Union Assaults at Vicksburg: Grant Attacks Pemberton, May 17–22, 1863*. Lawrence: University Press of Kansas, 2020.

———. "Victory at Any Cost: The Yazoo Pass Expedition." *Journal of Mississippi History* 67, no. 2 (Summer 2007): 147–166.

Smith, Walter George. *Life and Letters of Thomas Kilby Smith, Brevet Major-General United States Volunteers, 1820–1877*. New York: G. P. Putnam's Sons, 1898.

Smith, William Sooy. "The Mississippi Raid." *Military Essays and Recollections. Essays and Papers Read Before the Illinois Commandery*, 4 vols. Chicago: Order of the Commandery, 1907, 4:379–391.
Soman, Jean Powers, and Byrne, eds. *A Jewish Colonel in the Civil War: Marcus M. Spiegel of the Ohio Volunteers*. Kent, OH: Kent State University Press, 1985.
Stoker, Donald. *The Grand Design: Strategy and the U.S. Civil War*. New York: Oxford University Press, 2010.
Stone, Mary Amelia (Boomer). *Memoir of George Boardman Boomer*. Boston: Press of Geo. C. Rand & Avery, 1864.
The Story of the Fifty-fifth Regiment Illinois Volunteer Infantry in the Civil War, 1861–1865. Clinton, MA: W. J. Coulter, 1887.
Strong, William E. "The Campaign Against Vicksburg." In *Military Essays and Recollections: Papers Read Before the Commandery of the State of Illinois, Military Order of the Loyal Legion of the United States*, 4 vols. Chicago: A. C. McClurg and Company, 1894, 2:313–354.
Supplement to the Official Records of the Union and Confederate Armies, 100 vols. Wilmington, NC: Broadfoot Publishing Company, 1994.
Surby, R. W. *Grierson Raids, and Hatch's Sixty-four Days March, with Biographical Sketches, also, the Life and Adventures of Chickasaw, the Scout*. Chicago: Rounds and James, 1865.
———. *Two Great Raids. Col. Grierson's Successful Swoop Through Mississippi. Morgan's Disastrous Raid Through Indiana and Ohio. Vivid Narratives of Both These Great Operations, with Extracts from Official Records. John Morgan's Escape, Last Raid, and Death*. Washington, DC: National Tribune, 1897.
Sweetman, M. A. "From Milliken's Bend to Vicksburg." August 22, 1895, *National Tribune*.
Symonds, Craig L. *Joseph E. Johnston: A Civil War Biography*. New York: Norton, 1992.
———. *Lincoln and His Admirals: Abraham Lincoln, The U.S. Navy, and the Civil War*. New York: Oxford University Press, 2008.
Thorndike, Rachel Sherman, ed. *The Sherman Letters: Correspondence Between General and Senator Sherman from 1837 to 1891*. New York: Charles Scribner's Sons, 1894.
Throne, Mildred, ed. *The Civil War Diary of Cyrus F. Boyd, Fifteenth Iowa Infantry, 1861–1863*. Baton Rouge: Louisiana State University Press, 1998.
Toll, Ian W. *The Conquering Tide: War in the Pacific Islands, 1942–1944*. New York: Norton, 2015.
———. *Twilight of the Gods: War in the Western Pacific, 1944–1945*. New York: Norton, 2020.
Tomblin, Barbara Brooks. *The Civil War on the Mississippi: Union Sailors, Gunboat Captains, and the Campaign to Control the River*. Lexington: University Press of Kentucky, 2016.
Townsend, Mary Bobbitt. *Yankee Warhorse: A Biography of Major General Peter Osterhaus*. Columbia: University of Missouri Press, 2010.
Trowbridge, Silas T. *Autobiography of S. T. Trowbridge, M.D.* Np: n.p., 1872.

———. *Autobiography of Silas Thompson Trowbridge, M.D.* Carbondale: Southern Illinois University Press, 2004.

Tucker, Phillip Thomas. *The Forgotten "Stonewall of the West": Major General John Stevens Bowen.* Macon, GA: Mercer University Press, 1997.

———. *Westerners in Gray: The Men of and Missions of the Elite Fifth Missouri Infantry Regiment.* Jefferson, NC: McFarland & Company, 1995.

Tunnard, W. H. *A Southern Record: The History of the Third Regiment Louisiana Infantry.* Baton Rouge: n.p., 1866.

"Ulysses S. Grant." April 9, 1885, *National Tribune.*

Van Dorn, Robert J., and Daniel A. Masters, eds. *The 57th Ohio Veteran Volunteer Infantry.* Perrysburg, OH: Columbian Arsenal Press, 2021.

Vicksburg Campaign: Driving Tour Guide. Np: Friends of the Vicksburg Campaign and Historic Trail, 2008.

Wailes, L. A. "A War Mystery." *Confederate Veteran* 29, no. 2 (February 1921): 65.

Walke, Henry. *Naval Scenes and Reminiscences of the Civil War in the United States, on the Southern and Western Waters During the Years 1861, 1862 and 1863.* New York: F. R. Reed, 1877.

War of the Rebellion: A Compilation of the Official Records of the Union and Confederate Armies. Washington, DC: U.S. Government Printing Office, 1880–1901.

Warner, Ezra J. *Generals in Blue: Lives of the Union Commanders.* Baton Rouge: Louisiana State University Press, 1964.

———. *Generals in Gray: The Lives of the Confederate Commanders.* Baton Rouge: Louisiana State University Press, 1959.

Weigley, Russell F. *The American Way of War: A History of United States Military Strategy and Policy.* Bloomington: Indiana University Press, 1973.

Whaley, Elizabeth J. *Forgotten Hero: General James B. McPherson.* New York: Exposition Press, 1955.

White, Ronald C. *American Ulysses: A Life of Ulysses S. Grant.* New York: Random House, 2016.

Williams, E. Cort. "The Cruise of 'The Black Terror.' (Porter's Dummy at Vicksburg)." In *Sketches of War History 1861–1865: Papers Read Before the Ohio Commandery of the Military Order of the Loyal Legion of the United States,* 9 vols. Cincinnati: Robert Clarke Company, 1890, 3:144–165.

Williams, Kenneth P. *Grant Rises in the West: From Iuka to Vicksburg, 1862–1863.* Lincoln: University of Nebraska Press, 1997.

Williams, John Melvin. *"The Eagle Regiment," 8th Wis. Inf'ty Vols.: A Sketch of Its Marches, Battles and Campaigns From 1861–1865 with Complete Regimental and Company Roster, and a Few Portraits and Sketches of Its Officers and Commanders.* Belleville, WI: Recorder Print, 1890.

Williams, T. Harry. *Lincoln and His Generals.* New York: Alfred A. Knopf, 1952.

Willis, James. *Arkansas Confederates in the Western Theater.* Dayton, OH: Morningside, 1998.

Willison, Charles A. *Reminiscences of a Boy's Service with the 76th Ohio, In the Fifteenth Army Corps, Under General Sherman, During the Civil War, By That "Boy" at Three Score*. Menasha, WI: The George Banta Publishing Company, 1908.

Wilson, James Harrison. "A Staff Officer's Journal of the Vicksburg Campaign, April 30 to July 4, 1863." *Journal of the Military Service Institution of the United States* 43, no. 154 (July–August 1908): 93–109.

———. *Under the Old Flag: Recollections of Military Operations in the War for the Union, the Spanish War The Boxer Rebellion, Etc.*, 2 vols. New York: D. Appleton and Co., 1912.

Winschel, Terrence J. "The Absence of Will: Joseph E. Johnston and the Fall of Vicksburg." In *Confederate Generals in the Western Theater: Essays on America's Civil War*, 4 vols. Lawrence Lee Hewitt and Arthur W. Bergeron Jr., eds. Knoxville: University of Tennessee Press, 2010, 2:75–92.

———. "Fighting Politician: John A. McClernand." In *Grant's Lieutenants: From Cairo to Vicksburg*, Steven E. Woodworth, ed. Lawrence: University Press of Kansas, 2001, 129–150.

———. *Triumph and Defeat: The Vicksburg Campaign*. Mason City, IA: Savas Publishing Company, 1999.

———. *Triumph and Defeat: The Vicksburg Campaign, Vol. 2*. New York: Savas Beatie, 2006.

———. "The Vicksburg Campaign." In *The Cambridge History of the American Civil War*. 3 vols. Aaron Sheehan-Dean, ed. Cambridge, UK: Cambridge University Press, 2019, 1:246–268.

———, ed. *The Civil War Diary of a Common Soldier: William Wiley of the 77th Illinois Infantry*. Baton Rouge: Louisiana State University Press, 2001.

Wood, D. W. *History of the 20th O. V. V. I. Regiment, and Proceedings of the First Reunion at Mt. Vernon, Ohio, April 6, 1876*. Columbus, OH: Paul and Thrall, Book and Job Printers, 1876.

Wood, Wales W. *A History of the Ninety-fifth Regiment Illinois Infantry Volunteers, From its Organization in the Fall of 1862, Until Its Final Discharge from the United States Service, in 1865*. Chicago: Tribune Company's Book and Job Printing Office, 1865.

Woodward, S. L. "Grierson's Raid, April 17th to May 2d, 1863." *Journal of the United States Cavalry Association* 14, no. 52 (April 1904): 685–710.

———. "Grierson's Raid, April 17th to May 2d, 1863." *Journal of the United States Cavalry Association* 15, no. 53 (July 1904): 94–123.

Woodworth, Steven E. *Jefferson Davis and His Generals: The Failure of Confederate Command in the West*. Lawrence: University Press of Kansas, 1990.

———. *Nothing but Victory: The Army of the Tennessee, 1861–1865*. New York: Knopf, 2005.

Woodworth, Steven E., and Charles D. Grear, eds., *The Vicksburg Campaign: March 29–May 18, 1863*. Carbondale: Southern Illinois University Press, 2013.

"The Yazoo Pass Expedition." July 25, 1907, *National Tribune*.

Young, John Russell. *Around the World with General Grant: A Narrative of the Visit of General U.S. Grant, Ex-President of the United States, to Various Countries in Europe, Asia, and Africa, in 1877, 1878, 1879. To which are Added Certain Conversations with General Grant on Questions Connected with American Politics and History.* New York: American News Company, 1879.

INDEX

A. W. Baker (ship), 136
Abbeville, Mississippi, 35
Adams, John (general), 102, 345
Adams, John (president), 1
Adams, Wirt, 99, 113, 341, 347, 378
Alabama, 11, 31–32, 97–98, 134, 235, 314, 321, 327–329, 385
Alabama Troops: 40th Infantry, 253, 290, 294
Alamo, Battle of, 53
Alcorn, James L., 129, 150–151, 163, 202, 211, 221
Alexandria, Louisiana, 137, 299
Amite River, 342
Anaconda Plan, 3
Anderson, Thomas S., 71, 73
Anglo Saxon (steamer), 320, 324–325, 355
Antietam, Battle of, 13, 26
Appalachian Mountains, 116
Arcadia (steamer), 255, 293
Arkansas, 5, 7, 17, 20, 32, 37–38, 43–44, 51, 77–78, 83, 86, 93, 123, 127, 134, 150
Arkansas, CSS, 12
Arkansas Troops
   19th Infantry, 52–54, 56, 62, 71, 399
   24th Infantry, 399
   Crawford's Infantry Battalion, 52, 399
   Hart's Battery, 52–54, 56, 64–65, 68, 399
Arkansas County, 50
Arkansas Post, Arkansas, 42–43, 46–54, 56, 66, 69, 76–78, 80–81, 87–91, 97, 103–104, 111, 114, 138, 152, 160, 166, 203, 212, 236, 273
Arkansas Post, Battle of, 49–82, 395–399
Arkansas River, 42–44, 46–54, 78, 80, 88, 166

Army of the Mississippi, 40, 87, 95, 395–398; First Corps, 40–41, 87, 395–396; Second Corps, 40–41, 87, 396–398
Army of the Potomac, 364, 376
Army of the Tennessee, xiii, 41, 89, 93, 95, 134, 143, 204, 329, 365, 371, 391; XIII Corps, 41, 87, 93, 95, 163, 192, 213, 274, 382–384; XV Corps, 41, 87, 135, 193, 225, 254, 264, 275; XVI Corps, 86, 133, 259; XVII Corps, 37, 87, 106, 123, 125, 135, 193, 259, 383
Asboth, Alexander, 86
Ashton, Louisiana, 197–198
Associated Press, 158
Attala County, Mississippi, 175
Austerlitz, Battle of, 25, 113

Bache, George M., 57
Baldwin, William E., 385–386, 388
Baldwin, William H., 67
Baldwin's Ferry, Mississippi, 141
Balfour Mansion, 21
Ballard, Michael, 244, 274, 392
Ballinger, Richard H., 372
Bankston, Mississippi, 343
Baron de Kalb, USS, 46–47, 57–59, 76, 160, 162, 178, 182–183, 185–187, 190, 215, 217, 219, 223, 320, 368
Barrett, Samuel, 61
Barteau, Clark R., 315, 317
Batesville, Mississippi, 134
Baton Rouge, Louisiana, 4, 85, 199, 296, 340–342, 345, 378
Bayou Baxter, 124–125, 197–198

Bayou Macon, 123–124, 197
Bayou Pierre, 174, 233, 328, 348–349, 353, 371–373, 382–388
Bayou Vidal, 278–280, 331–332, 353–354
Beauregard, P. G. T., 11, 13
Beck's Ferry, Mississippi, 154
Bellagio Plantation, 124
Belle Creole (steamer), 285
Belmont, Battle of, 390
Beltzhoover, Daniel, 301
Bender, Griffin, 340
Bennett Thomas W., 276
Benton, USS, 304–305, 307, 311–312, 350, 358, 360–362, 377, 379, 394
Berwick Bay (steamer), 136
Bethel Church, 383, 386
Big Bayou, 121
Big Black River, 19, 33, 101, 134, 136, 141, 143, 173–174, 233, 271, 278, 281, 328–329, 344–346, 348–350, 356–357, 371–372, 386–387
Bissell, Josiah, 104, 197–198, 281
Black Bayou (Steele's Bayou operation), 223, 225–230, 248, 252–253, 257
Black Bayou (Steele's Greenville operation), 290–291, 293
Blackburn, William D., 337, 341
Black Hawk, USS, 46, 57–58, 72, 229, 368
Black River, 123, 125
Blair, Francis P. Jr., 60, 62, 66–67, 90–91, 108–109, 205, 283–284, 288, 333, 367, 369, 397
Blake, Benson, 22, 367–369, 386
Blake Plantation, 22, 367–369, 386
Blount, Ambrose A., 67–68
Blucher, Leberacht von, 22
Blue Wing (steamer), 42, 51, 77, 91
Blythe, Green L., 134, 144
Bodman, Albert, 136, 193, 197
Bogue Phaliah, 292, 296
Bolivar, Tennessee, 16
Bolivar County, Mississippi, 150
Bonaparte, Napoleon, xix, 22, 50
Boomer, George, 111, 119, 202, 243, 285
Bosworth, Felix, 197
Bowen, John S., 102, 153, 174, 211, 232–233, 261, 297, 313, 327–328, 335, 345–351, 363, 372, 378, 384–388
Bowers, Theodore, 192
Bradford, J. D., 387
Bragg, Braxton, 8, 13, 21, 37, 98, 235, 298
Brand, Frederick, 169
Breese, Kidder R., 368, 370–371
Brent, Joseph L., 168–169
Brierfield, 83
British, 2–3, 50, 292, 364, 366
Brooke Battery, 303
Brown, George (lieutenant commander), 137, 168–169
Brown, George W. (acting master), 127–131
Brown, Isaac N., 142, 151, 154–155, 176–177, 181, 183, 234, 291
Brownsville, Arkansas, 43
Bruinsburg, Mississippi, 212–213, 372–373, 375, 377–380, 385–387
Bruinsburg Road, 372, 382, 388
Bryant, George E., 314
Buckson's Plantation, 121
Buehler, Theodore E., 349, 377
Buford, Abraham, 296, 298, 327–328, 344
Buford, Napoleon B., 284
Bunch's Bend, Louisiana, 125
Burbridge, Stephen G. 67–70, 72, 75, 167, 227, 290–291, 356, 395
Burlington, Iowa, 105
Burnside, Ambrose, xiii, 191
Butler, Benjamin, 12, 84–86

Cadwallader, Sylvanus, 115, 225, 257
Cairo, USS, 21, 168, 214–215, 219, 223, 368
Caldwell, Samuel, 72
Camp McClernand, 276
Canal (Vicksburg) operations, xiv, 12, 84–86, 104–112, 116, 118–121, 123, 125–126, 135–140, 151–152, 164–166, 168–170, 172–175, 191–192, 195–196, 203–204, 212, 231, 233–234, 242, 260–261, 263, 275, 295, 297, 299–300, 330
Canton, Mississippi, 16
Cape Girardeau, Missouri, 5
Carl (steamer), 131, 222
Carondelet, Missouri, 214

Carondelet, USS, 214, 223, 227, 255, 304, 306, 308–309, 311, 358, 377, 379, 394
Carr, Eugene A., 192, 281, 332, 351, 354, 357, 381, 383, 388
Carrington, George, 116
Carroll County, Mississippi, 171
Carrollton, Mississippi, 216
Carthage, Mississippi, 343
Catahoola Parish, Louisiana, 278
Catton, Bruce, xxi, 271
Chalmers, James R., 173, 220, 345
Chambers, William Pitt, 32, 152, 228
Champion, Sidney S., 293
Champion Hill, Battle of, xvi
Chancellorsville, Battle of, 191, 364
Chaney, W. J., 245
Charm (steamer), 386
Chattanooga, Tennessee, 13, 97–98, 327
Chesterville, Mississippi, 315
Chicago, Illinois, 61–62, 264
Chicago *Times*, 119, 257
Chicago *Tribune*, 136, 193
Chickamauga, Battle of, 26
Chickasaw Bayou, Battle of., xiii–xiv, xvi, xix–xx, 22–23, 25–26, 30–32, 38–39, 41–43, 60, 67, 69, 90, 96, 100, 102, 111, 118, 138, 143, 152, 205, 215, 228, 236, 290, 304, 366, 368, 375–376, 381, 393
Chickasaw Bluffs, 4, 7, 150
Chickasaw Indians, 50, 127
Chillicothe, USS, 160, 163, 178, 182, 184–188, 190, 215, 217–219, 286
Choctaw, USS, 320, 368
Choctaw County, Mississippi, 149
Choctaw Indians, 171
Christian Commission, United States, 269
Christmas, 21, 238
Chunky, Mississippi, 315, 338
Churchill, Thomas J., 51–54, 56, 59, 61, 65, 69, 71–77, 80, 399
Cincinnati, Ohio, 242, 393
Cincinnati, USS, 46–47, 57–59, 214–215, 225–226, 245, 253, 320
City Class Gunboats, 160, 212, 214, 223, 304, 320, 357–358, 360

City of Vicksburg (steamer), 103, 136
Civil Rights Movement, 145
Civil War, xix–xx, 9, 25, 83, 145, 150–151, 171, 214, 267, 271; Eastern Theater, 15
Clark, Charles, 151
Clark Bayou, 353
Clarke, George, 100
Clarke's Plantation, 186
Clausewitz, Carl von, xv, xx–xxiii, 81, 89, 118, 145, 238, 266–268, 274, 282–283, 336–337, 391–392
Clayton Bayou, 185
Coahoma County, Mississippi, 150
Cockrell, Francis M., 297, 313, 328, 331, 351, 388
Coldwater River, 16–17, 19, 36, 129, 132–133, 143–144, 146, 148, 153–159, 161–163, 177–180, 182, 190, 199–200, 202, 221–222
Coleman, David C., 226
Cole Plantation, 158
Columbus, Kentucky, 4, 7–9, 11, 19, 56, 86
Columbus, Mississippi, 99, 328–329, 347
Columbus, Ohio, 76
Conestoga, USS, 46, 141
Confederate States of America, 183; Congress, 124, 297; Secretary of War, 33, 80, 175; Senate, 28; War Department, 25, 28, 152, 175
Confederate Troops: 1st Infantry Battalion, 327
Cooley, Charles G., 70
Copperheads, 26, 266
Corinth, Mississippi, xix, 11, 13–16, 28–29, 36, 39, 99, 133–134, 177, 314, 328, 350, 360
Cornyn, John, 121
Cowan, Luther, 164, 238, 383
Crawford, William, 52, 399
Crocker, Marcellus M., 354
Cumberland Gap, 11
Cumberland River, 9, 11, 15
Curtis, Samuel R., 43, 93
Curtiss' Plantation, 182
Cypress Bend, Mississippi, 167

Dahlia (tug), 255
Dana, Charles A., 271, 273–274, 283, 320, 329, 349–350, 358, 373, 375–376
Dancing Rabbit Creek, Treaty of, 171
Daniell, Smith Coffee, II, 213, 382
Davies, Thomas A., 86
Davis, Charles, 13
Davis, Frederick, 58, 76, 162
Davis, Jefferson, 9, 13, 25, 28–30, 32–33, 51, 80, 83, 98, 127, 137, 151, 169, 175, 221, 235, 239, 280, 298, 312, 321, 347, 386
Davis, Joseph, 83, 137, 169
Davis Bend, Mississippi, 83
Davis' Mill, Mississippi, 17
Dawson, Charles L., 54
De Baun, James, 341
Decatur, Mississippi, 319
De Courcy, John F., 67, 69, 90, 396
Deer Creek, 100, 114, 148, 167, 173, 175, 205, 209, 223, 227–229, 231–232, 234, 245, 247–250, 252, 254–257, 263, 288, 290–291, 293, 295–296, 330
Deimling, Francis C., 349
Deitzler, George W., 123–124
Delaware River, 364
Delta, xiii, 5, 7–9, 11–12, 14–17, 20, 22–23, 31, 51, 95, 98, 103, 113, 127–129, 134, 139, 142–146, 148–151, 153, 156, 161, 163, 172, 175–177, 181–182, 200–202, 209, 215, 218–223, 231–233, 238, 242–245, 256, 268, 285, 287, 293, 296, 298–299, 327
Denver, Colorado, 49
Denver, James, 165
Department of Mississippi and East Louisiana, 27, 98, 138, 172, 236
Department of the Mississippi, 12
Department of the Tennessee, 14
Depot Battery, 301
Deshler, James, 52, 54, 56, 61–66, 69, 71, 73–76, 79–80, 399
DeSoto (tug), 103, 137–138
De Soto Point, Louisiana, 83, 306, 308
Devil's Backbone, 301
Dew Drop (steamer), 293

Diana (steamer), 178, 180
Dickens, E. V., 176
Dick Fulton (steamer), 160
Diligent (steamer), 225–226, 230
Disharoon's Plantation, 362, 372–373, 376, 379–380, 383
Dodge, Grenville, 314
Donelson, Andrew Jackson, 196
Douglas, Stephen A., 124
Dowd's Plantation, 158
Dr. Beaty (steamer), 168–169
Drumgould's Bluff, 103, 370
Duck Hill, Mississippi, 328
Duckport Canal, 275, 297, 327, 334, 355
Duff, William L., 123–125
Dunaway, William, 341
Dunbar, R., 278–279, 331
Dunbar's Plantation, 278–279, 331
Dunnington, John W., 50–53, 59, 65, 70–71, 75, 399
Du Rossett Bayou, 353
Dwight, Henry Otis, 213

Eads, James B., 214–215
Eagle Bend, Mississippi, 225, 229–230, 247, 252, 256–257
Eagle Lake, 83
Eclipse (steamer), 351
Edward J. Gay (steamer), 139
Edwards Station, Mississippi, 100, 139
Egypt, 115, 150
Elkhorn Tavern, Battle of, 360
Ellet, Alfred, 261–262
Ellet, Charles R., 58, 135–138, 169, 199, 262
Ellis' Cliff, Mississippi, 175
Elzy, James, 312
Emancipation Proclamation, 25
Emerson, Frank, 68
Emma (steamer), 161, 178
Emma Bett (steamer), 293
Empire City (steamer), 320–321, 323–325
England, 49
Ennis, J. J., 75
Enterprise, Mississippi, 328, 344
Era No. 5 (steamer), 137–138, 141
Europe, xix, 1, 16, 49–50, 365
Ewing, Hugh, 37–38, 87, 109, 249, 254, 309

INDEX

Farragut, David G., 12–13, 84–86, 199, 233–234, 261–263, 300–301, 304
Farrell, Michael, 97
Fayette, Mississippi, 341
Featherston, Winfield S., 228, 232–233, 247–249, 252–253, 255, 257, 284–285, 290–291, 328, 345
Ferguson, Samuel W., 167, 227–228, 232, 245–248, 253–254, 256–257, 288, 290–294
Fern (tug), 229
Fisher, Cyrus W., 254
Fish Lake, 167
Fisk, Clinton B., 135, 160, 181, 219, 242
Fisk, Leander B., 324
Fitzhugh, Robert H., 51
Fletcher's Landing, Arkansas, 46, 71
Florence, Alabama, 134
Foote, Andrew H., 11, 56–57
Forbes, Henry C., 318–319, 337, 344
Force, Manning F., 354
Fore Plantation, 228–229, 253–255
Forest Queen (steamer), 304, 309–310, 313
Forest Rose, USS, 46, 127, 129, 160
Forney, John H., 210, 327, 346, 368, 370, 386
Forrest, Aaron H., 129, 144, 156
Forrest, Nathan Bedford, xx, 21, 26, 30, 34, 36, 86, 98, 193
Fort Cobun, 351, 357–358, 360–361
Fort Donelson, Battle of, 9, 11–12, 14, 56–58, 215, 390
Fort Henry, Battle of, 5, 9, 11–12, 14, 56–57, 160, 215
Fort Hindman, Arkansas, 49, 52, 61, 71, 75, 79
Fort Jackson, Louisiana, 12, 84
Fort Pemberton, Mississippi, 155, 170, 172, 175–177, 182–183, 185–186, 189, 207, 209, 215–218, 222–223, 233–234, 239–245, 257, 284–287, 290–291, 293–294, 296, 312, 321, 328
Fort Pillow, Tennessee, 56
Fort Randolph, Tennessee, 56
Fortress Monroe, Virginia, 364–365
Fort St. Philip, Louisiana, 12
Fort Sumter, South Carolina, 154
Fort Taylor, Louisiana, 137
Fort Wade, Mississippi, 351, 357–358, 360–361

Foster, Claiborne J., 321
Foster, Jacob, 70–71
Foster, James P., 178, 185–186, 190, 217, 219–220, 238–241
France, xix–xx, 22, 49–50, 171
Fredericksburg, Virginia, 26, 32, 364
French, Daniel, 70
French, Samuel G., 151, 175, 290, 293
French and Indian War, 50
Friar's Point, Mississippi, 148, 175
Fuller, J. F. C., xiii–xiv

Gaines' Landing, Arkansas, 42
Gallatin, Mississippi, 351
Gardner, Franklin, 102, 109, 136, 174, 296, 342, 345
Garland, Robert R., 52–54, 56, 64–65, 68–69, 71, 73–76, 80, 399
Garlandville, Mississippi, 340, 342
Garrard, Theophilus T., 276, 280
Garrott, Isham G., 385
Garvey, Mr., 137–138
General Price, USS, 223, 304–305, 307–308, 334, 355, 362, 394
George, James Z., 144, 176–177, 190, 220, 244, 287
Georgetown, Mississippi, 340
Georgia, 86, 167, 257, 314
Georgia Troops: 40th Infantry, 257
Gettysburg, Battle of, 26
Gholson, Samuel, 317
Gillespie, Clayton C., 73
Glass Bayou, 301
Golden Age (steamer), 293
Good Intent Plantation, 249
Gorman, Willis A., 35, 42–43, 88, 93, 106, 128, 131–134, 157, 159
Graham, George W., 320
Grand Gulf, Mississippi, xvi, 4, 120, 169, 174, 209, 211–212, 233, 261, 263–264, 272, 274, 281–282, 297, 313, 321, 327–331, 334, 341, 345–351, 353, 356, 361–363, 365–366, 370–373, 375, 378–380, 382, 384–387, 390; Battle of, 356–361
Grand Junction, Tennessee, 16, 134
Grant, Fred, 191–192, 271–272, 312, 361, 379

Grant, Julia, 93, 112, 116, 126, 133, 191, 266–267, 271, 305, 312, 350, 390
Grant, Ulysses S., xii–xvi, xix–xxiii, 3, 8, 11–12, 14–17, 19–24, 26–27, 30–44, 48, 50, 78–82, 87–96, 103, 113–118, 139, 141, 145, 167, 203–204, 206–208, 212, 235–238, 259–260, 266–274, 297–300, 336–337, 349–351, 364–365, 387, 389–392; and Bruinsburg crossing, 372–373, 375–382, 384; and Canal operations, 86, 104–112, 119–120, 163–164, 195–196, 260; and Duckport Canal operation, 275; and Grand Gulf attack, 346–348, 357, 361–363; and Grierson's Raid, 134, 166, 194, 314, 338, 340–343, 345; and Lake Providence operations, 121, 123–126, 164–165, 197–198, 260–261; and Louisiana march, 278–279, 281–282, 329–335, 353–356; and naval operations, 135, 137, 168, 199, 261–264, 393–394; and Sherman's Chickasaw Bayou feint, 366–368, 370–371; and Steele's Bayou Expedition, 223, 225, 229–231, 247, 250, 255–258; and Steele's Greenville operation, 292, 294–295; and Vicksburg batteries passage, 301, 303–305, 309, 311–313, 319–322, 325–326; and Willow Bayou operation, 121; and Yazoo Pass Expedition, 126–133, 142–143, 154, 157, 159–161, 177, 179, 182, 188, 200–202, 215–216, 218, 220, 222, 234, 241–244, 283–288
Green, Martin E., 102, 327, 387–388
Greensburg, Louisiana, 341
Greenville, Mississippi, 5, 145, 148, 167, 205, 227, 283, 288, 290–294, 296–298, 327, 330, 336, 366
Greenwood, Mississippi, 131, 142, 145–146, 153–156, 170–172, 176, 179–180, 186, 199–201, 215–216, 218, 221, 223, 232–233, 239, 244, 263, 287, 296
Greer, James A., 307, 394
Gregg, John, 32
Grenada, Mississippi, xx, 16–17, 21–23, 25, 28, 31, 33–36, 40, 97, 99, 102, 107, 109, 132, 142–143, 146, 153–154, 156, 176, 179, 273
Grier, David, 69, 116–117, 194, 390
Grierson, Alice, 314, 318
Grierson, Benjamin H., 134, 165, 194, 207–209, 313–319, 328, 337–348, 351, 363, 378, 382
Grierson's Raid, xvi, 313–319, 326, 328, 337–348, 354, 366, 384, 386–387, 393
Griffith, Henry H., 61
Grove, Mrs., 112, 116
Gulf of Mexico, 5, 96, 116, 154
Gwin, William M., 225

Hagaman, Abraham, 112
Halleck, Henry W., xv, xxi, 11–14, 16, 20, 27, 37–39, 81, 85–86, 89, 92–96, 109–110, 112, 120–121, 164–165, 168, 192, 195–196, 198–199, 231, 237, 242, 258–259, 261–263, 265, 267–270, 272, 274, 309, 319, 325, 336–337, 351, 367, 373, 390–392
Hall's Ferry, Mississippi, 141, 346
Hamilton, Charles S., 16, 34–35, 86, 119, 134–135, 165–166, 194, 258–259
Hampton, Wade, 151
Hankinson's Ferry, Mississippi, 141, 386
Hardee's Plantation, 249
Hard Scrabble Farm, 373
Hard Times, Louisiana, 233, 328, 349, 351, 353–354, 356–357, 363, 373
Harper's Weekly, 87, 262, 299, 342
Harris, Charles L., 383–384
Harrison, Isaac F., 276, 297, 353
Hart, Levi W., 61
Hart, William, 52–54, 56, 64–65, 68, 399
Hartford, USS, 199, 233
Harvey, Joel, 175
Harvey, Louis P., 269
Hatch, Edward, 134, 165, 314–315, 317
Hatchie Bridge, Battle of, 360
Hatchie River, 36
Hawkins, John P., 333
Haynes' Bluff, Mississippi, 22, 95–96, 101, 103, 127, 132, 139, 143, 146, 148, 177, 179, 199, 222–223, 227–228, 230, 232–233, 248, 256–257, 264, 271–272, 296, 327, 346, 367

Hazlehurst, Mississippi, 340–341, 347
Hebert, Louis, 101, 103, 368–370
Helena, Arkansas, 7, 17, 20, 35, 38, 42–43, 77, 93, 106, 127–129, 131, 133–135, 142, 157, 161, 179–181, 192, 199–201, 216, 221–222, 241–244, 264, 286, 288, 294, 330, 332, 354
Henderson, Sam, 159; Henderson's Scouts, 142
Henderson (steamer), 131, 158
Henry Clay (steamer), 304, 309–311, 322, 394
Henry von Phul (steamer), 305
Hercules (dredge), 195
Hickenlooper, Andrew, 202
Higgins, Edward, 141, 169, 301
Hill, A. P., 229
Hill, J. C., 229
Hillis, David B., 355
Hill Plantation, 228–229, 247, 249–250, 252–254
Hoel, William R., 308, 311, 394
Hoffman, Louis, 61
Holly Springs, Mississippi, xx, 16–17, 19, 21, 24, 28, 34–38, 146, 165, 318
Holmes, T. C., 276, 278, 281, 332
Holmes, Theophilus, 50, 53, 80, 97, 276
Holt's Bayou, 353
Hooker, Joseph, 191, 267, 376
Hope (steamer), 155, 293
Horizon (steamer), 320, 324–325, 380
Hovey, Alvin P., 17, 135, 179, 192, 199, 242, 244, 330, 332, 354, 356, 380, 383
Hovey, Charles E., 60–63, 72, 79, 108–109, 397
Hudson River, xix
Humphrey, Lyman, 58, 63
Humphreys, Andrew A., 119
Humphreys, Benjamin G., 151
Hunt's Mill, Mississippi, 131, 158–159
Hurlbut, Stephen A., 36, 86, 119, 133–135, 164–166, 193–194, 243, 258–259, 265, 273, 313–314, 336
Hurst, D. W., 228, 255
Hushpuckanaw River, 296
Hutchinson, Augustus S., 62

Illinois, 5, 7–8, 17, 20–21, 34–35, 42–43, 61, 65, 70–71, 74, 76, 78, 88, 91–92, 105–106, 116, 123–124, 126, 128, 161, 163, 169, 195–196, 202, 214, 221–222, 225–226, 240, 250–251, 266, 275–276, 286, 288, 292, 309, 313–314, 320, 324–325, 330, 332–333, 337, 342–344, 350, 353, 355–357, 373, 375, 377–378, 380, 382, 393
Illinois Troops
  8th Infantry, 380
  11th Infantry, 320
  13th Infantry, 63, 103, 288, 290, 397
  18th Infantry, 258
  20th Infantry, 320, 324
  29th Infantry, 357
  31st Infantry, 259, 320
  33rd Infantry, 350
  45th Infantry, 238, 320, 324, 383
  55th Infantry, 60, 64, 398
  56th Infantry, 163
  72nd Infantry, 393
  77th Infantry, 69, 76, 116, 390, 395
  97th Infantry, 69, 78, 395
  108th Infantry, 69, 395
  113th Infantry, 64, 252, 397
  116th Infantry, 64, 230, 250, 252, 397
  118th Infantry, 70, 396
  124th Infantry, 115, 195, 320, 379–380
  127th Infantry, 60, 64, 398
  131st Infantry, 69, 395
  2nd Cavalry, 167, 276, 278, 353
  3rd Cavalry, 278–279, 372, 397
  6th Cavalry, 315, 317
  7th Cavalry, 315, 317–318, 337, 341
  15th Cavalry, 106
  Battery A, 1st Light Artillery, 61–62, 398
  Battery B, 1st Light Artillery, 61–62, 398
  Battery H, 1st Light Artillery, 61, 398
  Battery K, 1st Light Artillery, 315
  Battery G, 2nd Light Artillery, 380
  Chicago Mercantile Battery, 70–71, 396
  Kane County Cavalry, 397
  Thielemann's Cavalry Battalion, 398
Indiana, 17, 19, 70, 78, 82, 109, 118, 126, 148, 152, 157, 159–160, 163, 182, 185, 187, 194, 196, 198, 221, 241–242, 269, 276, 280, 286, 304, 311, 321, 323, 325, 330, 332–333, 358, 378, 381, 383–384, 390

Indiana Troops
  16th Infantry, 67–68, 395
  23rd Infantry, 320, 380
  24th Infantry, 377–378
  43rd Infantry, 160
  46th Infantry, 160, 377–378
  47th Infantry, 160, 185, 188, 380
  49th Infantry, 71, 278, 280, 353, 396
  54th Infantry, 396
  60th Infantry, 47, 66–68, 395
  67th Infantry, 68, 349, 377, 395
  69th Infantry, 70, 276, 278, 280, 396
  83rd Infantry, 64, 252, 255, 398
  1st Cavalry, 158–159
  2nd Cavalry, 320
  4th Cavalry, 395
Indianola, USS, 137–138, 141, 168–170, 198–199, 280, 331
Indian Territory, 171
Industrial Revolution, 50
Ione Plantation, 280, 311
Iowa, 8, 16, 23, 43, 48, 56, 62, 76, 86, 93, 105, 113, 119, 128, 148, 158–159, 161–163, 179, 189, 192–193, 197, 219, 281, 286, 288, 291–292, 294, 317–318, 330–331, 333–334, 377–378, 383
Iowa Troops
  4th Infantry, 397
  9th Infantry, 63, 397
  12th Infantry, 330
  17th Infantry, 355
  21st Infantry, 383
  22nd Infantry, 378, 384
  25th Infantry, 63, 397
  26th Infantry, 63, 397
  28th Infantry, 384
  29th Infantry, 160, 179, 242
  30th Infantry, 63, 322, 397
  31st Infantry, 62–63, 397
  33rd Infantry, 160
  34th Infantry, 63, 397
  36th Infantry, 160, 187
  1st Battery, 61, 397
  3rd Battery, 160
  2nd Cavalry, 134, 314–315, 317
Island No. 10, Tennessee, 56, 305
Issaquena County, Mississippi, 149–150
Itawamba County, Mississippi, 149
Ivanhoe, Mississippi, 141
Ivy (tug), 305, 357
Iwo Jima, Battle of, 365

J. A. Rawlins (steamer), 197
Jackson, Andrew, 2, 372
Jackson, Andrew Jr., 301, 321–325
Jackson, Mississippi, xxi, 12, 15, 19, 25, 28–29, 32, 40, 84, 97–99, 102, 106, 109, 134, 139–140, 142, 152, 171–173, 208–209, 231, 233, 271, 297, 313, 317, 328, 338, 340, 344–345, 347, 370, 386, 393
Jackson, William H., 31
Jacksonville, Illinois, 313–314
James, Joshua, 280, 311, 331
James Plantation, 280–281, 328, 331
James River, 364
Japan, 365
Jarlow Creek, 342
Jefferson, Thomas, 1–2
Jenney, William, 104, 119, 257, 275, 391
Jenny Lind (steamer), 180
Jessie Benton (tug), 223
Jews, 35, 264
John Bell (steamer), 180
Johnson, Abda, 257
Johnson, Walter H., 226
Johnson Plantation, 22
Johnston, Albert Sidney, 8–9, 11, 51
Johnston, Joseph E., 29–32, 80, 97–99, 102–103, 107, 138, 141, 172, 174–175, 232, 234–235, 298, 326–327, 329, 347–348, 384
Johnston, Theodore, 100–101, 139
Joliet, Luis, 49
Jomini, Henri, xv, xix–xxiii, 13, 15–17, 20–24, 31, 40, 81, 118, 143, 145, 236–238, 266–267, 282–283, 291, 336–337, 365–366, 391–392
Jones, John B., 25, 28, 175
J. S. Pringle (steamer), 221
Juliet, USS, 46
J. W. Cheeseman (steamer), 320, 323–324

Kansas Troops: 7th Cavalry, 166
Keigwin, James, 353–354, 383

INDEX

Kennard, George W., 324
Kennon, Beverly, 111
Kentucky, 4, 7–9, 11, 13, 16, 19, 28, 56, 75, 77, 86, 276
Kentucky Campaign, 13, 51
Kentucky Troops (US):
   3rd Infantry, 396
   7th Infantry, 71
   19th Infantry, 69, 396
   22nd Infantry, 396
Key West (steamer), 161–162
Key West No. 2 (steamer), 180
Kilgore, Benjamin, 317
Knox, Thomas, 90–91
Kosciusko, Mississippi, 187, 343
Kossak, William, 225

Lady Lobdell, 177
Lady Richardson, 177
Lafayette, USS, 304–305, 307–308, 358, 361, 394
La Grange, Tennessee, 16, 34, 313–314, 317, 338, 345
Lagow, Clark B., 320, 325
Lake Bruin, 354
Lake Plantation, 22–23
Lake Providence, Louisiana, xiv, 109, 123–127, 135, 140, 164–165, 192–197, 199–200, 202, 206, 231, 256, 260, 263, 265, 270, 274, 300, 310, 313, 330, 350, 355
Lake Saint Joseph, 353–354
Lake Village, Arkansas, 123
Lancaster, USS, 262, 270
Landgraeber, Clemens, 62
Landram, William J., 69–70, 76, 117, 395
La Salle, Robert Cavalier Sieur de, 49
Lauman, Jacob G., 193
Lavinia Logan (steamer), 162
Lee, Albert, 166, 194
Lee, Robert E., xiii, 13, 32
Lee, Stephen D., 22–23, 30–31, 228, 233, 249, 257, 290, 292–294, 325, 328, 391–392
LeFleur, Louis, 171
LeFleur's Bluff, Mississippi, 171
Leflore, Greenwood, 171–172
Leflore County, Mississippi, 171
Leggett, Mortimer D., 35, 198, 256

Lewers, James, 167
Lewis, James M., 216
Lexington USS, 46, 77
Liberty, Mississippi, 341
Lincoln, Abraham, 14, 20, 25, 27, 38, 41, 79–81, 88–90, 104, 172, 175, 195, 212, 214, 265, 268–269, 283–284, 288, 376
Linden (steamer), 368
Lindsey, Daniel W., 59, 67, 71, 74, 80, 395
Lioness (steamer), 160
Little Rock, Arkansas, 38, 43–44, 50–51, 53, 78, 87–88
Little Rock Road, 60, 67
Little Sunflower River, 148
Lockett, Samuel, 141, 327, 387
Logan, John A., 87, 106, 116, 125–126, 135, 164–165, 193, 196, 199–200, 202, 242, 256, 260, 283, 320, 332, 354–355, 373, 383
Loring, William W., 31, 33–34, 99, 102, 107, 109, 142, 144, 151, 153–156, 172, 175–177, 183–189, 209, 216–221, 228, 232–234, 239–240, 243–244, 257, 284–287, 295–297, 328–329, 340–345, 387
Louis XIV, 49
Louisiana, xiii, 1–2, 4–5, 8, 13, 21, 26, 40, 44, 49–50, 83–84, 96–97, 100, 102, 111, 114, 121, 136–137, 140, 144, 151–152, 165, 168, 173–174, 231, 238, 260, 262, 274, 282, 296, 299–300, 303, 306, 310, 313, 321–324, 336, 338, 344–347, 354, 369, 380, 383, 385
Louisiana Purchase, 1
Louisiana Troops
   3rd Infantry, 149, 369
   17th Infantry, 290
   21st Infantry, 369
   22nd Infantry, 303
   26th Infantry, 249
   27th Infantry, 312, 321
   9th Cavalry Partisan Rangers, 341
   15th Cavalry Battalion, 276
   Denson's Cavalry Company, 399
   Nutt's Cavalry Company, 399
   1st Heavy Artillery, 301
   8th Heavy Artillery, 301
   Pointe Coupee Artillery, 183

Louisville, Kentucky, 120, 195
Louisville, Mississippi, 318
Louisville, USS, 46–47, 57, 212, 214, 223, 229, 247, 251, 253–254, 304, 306–308, 358, 362, 379, 394
Louisville and Nashville Railroad, 11
Lovell, Mansfield, 29
Lucas, Thomas J., 68
Luella (steamer), 131, 180, 242
Lynch, John P., 323

Macon, Mississippi, 318–319, 329
Magenta (cottonclad), 234
Magnolia (steamer), 116, 119, 225
Mahan, Dennis Hart, xix–xx, 291, 391
Malmaison, 171
Malmborg, Oscar, 60, 67
Marine Hospital Battery, 303
Marmora, USS, 46, 160, 179, 217
Marquette, Jacques, 49
Marshall County, Mississippi, 149
Mary Keene (steamer), 154
Maryland, 13, 167, 247
Mattie Cook (steamer), 131, 158
Maury, Dabney H., 102, 174, 209–210, 227–228, 232, 247, 285, 287, 296, 327
Maxwell, W. C., 144, 156
McArthur, John, 19, 87, 110, 112, 123, 125, 135, 165, 202, 256, 260, 354–355
McClellan, George B., 267
McClernand, John A., x, xii, 20, 27, 37–44, 46–48, 51–52, 56–57, 60, 66, 72, 75, 77–82, 87–95, 102, 114–115, 134, 166–167, 192, 203–204, 213, 236, 259, 266, 273–274, 297, 328, 349–351, 366, 395; and Bruinsburg crossing, 371–373, 375–376, 380–384; and Canal operations, 86, 104–108, 110–111, 120, 163, 175, 196; and Duckport Canal operation, 275; and Grand Gulf attack, 357, 361; and Lake Providence operation, 123; and Louisiana march, 276, 278–282, 331–334, 353–355; and Steele's Bayou Expedition, 258; and Vicksburg batteries passage, 301, 305, 311–312, 319, 326; and Yazoo Pass Expedition, 132, 218, 244

McCullough, Robert, 144, 156, 190, 220
McGinnis, George, 379
McIntosh, G. W., 68
McLaughlin, James, 323
McNutt, Mississippi, 243
McPherson, James B., 16, 35, 37, 86–87, 106, 114, 117, 135, 148, 193, 195, 206, 237, 259, 264, 273–274, 350; and Bruinsburg crossing, 373, 383; and Lake Providence operation, 123, 125–126, 164–165, 197–198, 260–261; and Louisiana march, 332, 354–355; and Steele's Bayou Expedition, 256; and Yazoo Pass Expedition, 199–202, 243–244
McRae, George, 176
Mediterranean Sea, 365
Memphis, Tennessee, xx–xxii, 4–5, 7–8, 11–12, 14–17, 20, 27, 36–38, 40, 42, 50, 77, 89, 92–93, 95, 102–103, 106, 110, 125–127, 129, 133–135, 145–146, 149–150, 164–166, 193, 196, 199, 242, 257, 261, 265, 273, 295, 298, 305, 314, 328, 368, 392
Memphis and Charleston Railroad, 33–34, 133, 328
Meridian, Mississippi, 12, 98, 173, 315, 328–329, 338, 340, 344–345
Meriwether, Minor, 154–156
Merrilies, John, 241
Methodists, 135, 181
Mexico, 364
Mexican War, 51, 364
Michigan Troops: 7th Light Artillery, 276, 353, 396
Millar's Bend, Mississippi, 291
Milliken's Bend, Louisiana, 134, 140, 142, 175, 193, 196, 271, 276, 280–281, 294, 330, 332, 354–355
Minnehaha (steamer), 93
Minnesota, 2, 242
Minnesota Troops: 4th Infantry, 381
Mint Spring Bayou, 301
Mississippi, xiii, xvi, xx, xxii, 2–5, 7–9, 11–15, 20–21, 26–31, 33–35, 40, 80, 83–84, 86, 90, 97–103, 113, 127, 133–134, 141, 143–146, 149–151, 163,

165, 167–168, 171–173, 175, 177, 194, 196, 202, 207, 215, 218, 220–221, 234–235, 237–238, 240, 245, 249, 252, 254, 268–269, 278, 284, 287, 293–295, 298, 310, 313, 315, 318–319, 326–327, 329, 337–338, 342, 344–345, 347, 357, 368–369, 375–376, 378–379, 386–387, 389; Legislature, 25, 172; Secession Convention, 150, 163, 211

Mississippi Troops
  1st Infantry Battalion, 249
  4th Infantry, 388
  6th Infantry, 327, 388
  15th Infantry, 97
  20th Infantry, 216, 388
  22nd Infantry, 228, 247
  26th Infantry, 216, 285, 328
  31st Infantry, 254–255
  33rd Infantry, 228, 247, 287
  35th Infantry, 240
  36th Infantry, 100
  46th Infantry, 32, 228, 306
  1st Cavalry Battalion, 144
  Adams Cavalry, 99, 341
  1st Light Artillery, 303
  14th Light Artillery, 303
  Pettus Flying Artillery, 327
Mississippi and Tennessee Railroad, 16, 40
Mississippi Central Campaign, xiii–xiv, xix, 34, 86, 118, 127, 143, 236, 273, 393
Mississippi Central Railroad, xiii–xiv, xx, 15–16, 34, 153, 155, 315, 328, 344–345
Mississippi Marine Brigade, 298
Mississippi River, xiv, 2–5, 7, 9, 11–13, 20–22, 32–33, 37, 39–40, 42–44, 46, 49–51, 78, 80, 83, 88, 91, 93–96, 99–100, 103, 113–115, 117, 134, 139–140, 145–146, 148–150, 166, 194, 203, 207–208, 212, 237, 266, 268–269, 274, 298–299, 327, 338, 340, 343, 350, 364–365, 389–390; and Bruinsburg crossing, 372, 384; and Canal operations, 84, 104, 106–107, 110, 119–120, 171, 175, 195, 260; and Duckport Canal operation, 275; and Grand Gulf attack, 345–348; and Lake Providence operations, 121, 123–126;

and Louisiana march, 276, 279–281, 330–331; and naval operations, 136–138, 168, 263; and Sherman's Chickasaw Bayou feint, 370–371; and Steele's Bayou Expedition, 225, 229; and Steele's Greenville operation, 291, 294; and Vicksburg batteries passage, 300, 311, 319, 323, 326; and Willow Bayou operation, 121; and Yazoo Pass Expedition, 127–128, 142, 151, 154, 159, 179, 182, 215, 219, 222, 232, 242, 283, 285–287
Mississippi Squadron, xvi, 393
Mississippi Valley, 1, 4, 27, 49, 80–81, 125, 175, 237, 271, 294
Missouri Territory, 50
Missouri, 5, 7–8, 28–29, 60–62, 96, 102, 127, 159, 167, 192–193, 214, 221, 226, 253, 269, 286, 290, 294, 313, 328, 351, 357–358, 361
Missouri Troops (US)
  3rd Infantry, 62–63, 397
  6th Infantry, 64–65, 230, 250, 255, 397
  7th Infantry, 320, 322
  8th Infantry, 64–65, 121, 169, 225–226, 229–230, 250–251, 253, 398
  10th Infantry, 349
  12th Infantry, 62, 397
  17th Infantry, 62–63, 397
  29th Infantry, 397
  30th Infantry, 397
  31st Infantry, 397
  32nd Infantry, 397
  33rd Infantry, 160, 188
  6th Cavalry, 167, 278, 396
  10th Cavalry, 398
  Company A, 1st Light Artillery, 160
  Company F, 2nd Light Artillery, 62, 397
Missouri Troops (CS)
  1st Infantry, 297, 331
  Bledsoe's Battery, 167
Missouri River, 49
Mitchell's Crossroads, Mississippi, 179
Mizner, John K., 194
Mobile, Alabama, 8, 32, 98, 142, 175, 235, 296, 327, 345
Mobile (cottonclad), 234

Mobile and Ohio Railroad, 16, 21, 35, 99, 193, 315, 317–318, 329, 344
Moderator (steamer), 320, 323–325, 377, 380
Monarch, USS, 58, 78, 167
Montgomery, Alabama, 97–98, 107, 327
Montgomery's Plantation, 278
Moon Lake, 31, 83, 128–129, 133, 142, 148, 156, 158, 160–161, 176, 199–201, 243
Moore, John C., 176, 219, 291
Moore, Thomas O., 111
Morgan, George W., 41, 43, 46–47, 60, 64, 66–67, 69, 74–75, 80, 87, 90, 104, 107, 395
Morgan, John H., 227
Moro (steamer), 136
Morton, Oliver P., 196
Mound City, Illinois, 214
Mound City, USS, 214–215, 255, 304, 306, 308, 311, 331, 358, 360, 362, 379, 394
Mound Place, 163
Muddy Bayou, 225
Mule March, 314, 328
Murphy, John M., 223, 231, 245, 308–309, 394
Myers, Joseph, 378
Myrick, John D., 379

Napoleon, Arkansas, 37, 86, 88, 92, 96, 107
Natchez, Mississippi, 4–5, 136, 171, 175, 233, 297, 341
Nelson, Horatio, 190
New Albany, Mississippi, 315
New Carthage, Louisiana, 108, 263, 272, 276, 278–282, 297, 300, 308, 311–312, 324, 329, 331–334, 346, 349
New Era (steamer), 170, 198
New Orleans, Battle of, 2, 44
New Orleans, Jackson, and Great Northern Railroad, 16, 341, 343–344
New Orleans, Louisiana, 1–3, 8, 12–13, 16, 29, 150
Newton Station, Mississippi, 319, 337–338, 345, 347
New York, 394; 5th Avenue, 281
New York *Herald*, 90
Niagara Falls, New York, 129, 195
North Africa, 365
North America, 49–50

North Carolina, 364
Notrebe, Frederick, 44, 52
Noxubee River, 318

Oak Hill, Battle of, 360
Obion River, 21
Official Records, 344
Ogden, Fred N., 301, 323
Oglesby, Richard J., 350
Ohio, 17, 23, 26, 38, 62–63, 70–71, 76–77, 96, 107–108, 110–111, 113–115, 123, 128, 163, 167, 170, 195, 197, 202, 254, 256, 260, 264, 266, 276, 281–282, 333, 351, 353, 370, 376, 382
Ohio River, 49, 87, 201, 215
Ohio Troops
  16th Infantry, 396
  20th Infantry, 213
  30th Infantry, 249
  42nd Infantry, 396
  47th Infantry, 117, 225
  48th Infantry, 69, 396
  54th Infantry, 64, 152, 252, 254, 398
  56th Infantry, 379
  57th Infantry, 64–65, 252, 398
  58th Infantry, 357–358, 397
  72nd Infantry, 355
  76th Infantry, 62–63, 170, 397
  83rd Infantry, 67, 395
  96th Infantry, 68, 395
  114th Infantry, 71, 353, 396
  120th Infantry, 70, 281, 305, 378, 396
  4th Light Artillery, 61, 397
  8th Light Artillery, 398
  17th Light Artillery, 67, 396
Okinawa, 365
Oklahoma, 171
Old Abe (eagle), 333
Oliver, William S., 322, 324
Olmstead, Frederick L., 268
Omega Plantation, 121, 249
Opossum, 280
Orr, John A., 255
Orr, John M., 68
Osterhaus, Peter J., 41, 47, 67, 69–71, 87, 104, 112, 115, 164, 204, 274, 276, 278–281, 300, 312, 331–332, 334–335,

351, 353–355, 357, 371–372, 381–383, 396
Ouachita River, 7, 123, 125
Owen, Elias K., 57, 253, 308, 358
Owen, Richard, 66, 68
Oxford, Mississippi, 17, 19, 28, 146

Pacific Ocean, 365
Palo Alto, Battle of, 317
Panola, Mississippi, 134, 142, 220
Parish, John, 162
Parker, Job, 69
Parker's Crossroads, Battle of, 21
Parsons, Lewis B., 167, 242
Patterson, William F., 77, 276, 279–280, 334
Paulding, Mississippi, 343
Pearl River, 171, 318, 340, 344
Pemberton, John C., xx, xxiii, 17, 19, 22–23, 26–34, 80, 97–103, 118, 139–141, 207–209, 211, 236, 238, 296–299, 327–328, 351, 385–387, 392; and Bruinsburg crossing, 378, 382, 384; and Canal operations, 106–107, 109, 111–112, 173–175; and Grand Gulf attack, 346–348, 363; and Grierson's Raid, 317, 338, 340, 343–345; and Louisiana march, 329; and naval operations, 138, 168, 170, 39; and Sherman's Chickasaw Bayou feint, 370–3713; and Steele's Bayou Expedition, 228, 231, 257; and Steele's Greenville operation, 291–292, 295; and Vicksburg batteries passage, 313, 321, 326; and Yazoo Pass Expedition, 127, 142–144, 151–156, 159, 176–177, 183, 187, 190, 216, 218–219, 221, 232–234, 239, 243–244, 284, 286, 288
Peninsula Campaign, xix, 364
Pennsylvania, 27
Perkins, John, 280, 297
Perkins' Landing, Mississippi, 167
Perkins' Plantation, 280, 297, 311, 332–333, 354, 356
Perryville, Battle of, 13
Peters, George B., 99
Peters, Jessie, 99
Petral, USS, 160, 180, 222, 368

Pettus, John J., 235, 317, 326–327, 345
Phelps Bayou, 353
Philadelphia, Mississippi, 318–319
Pine Bluff, Arkansas, 88, 166
Pitts, Florison D., 113
Pittsburg Landing, Tennessee, 93
Pittsburg, USS, 214, 304–306, 308, 311, 358, 360–361, 380, 394
Pointe Clear Plantation, 278
Point of Rock, 351, 357
Polk, Leonidas, 9
Polkville, Mississippi, 146
Ponchatoula, Louisiana, 231
Pontchartrain, CSS, 52
Pontotoc, Mississippi, 36, 315, 317
Pontotoc County, Mississippi, 149
Pontotoc Ridge, 318
Pook, Samuel, 160, 214
Pope, John, 242
Porter, David D., xxii, 23, 38–39, 42–44, 46, 52–53, 56–59, 66, 75–76, 78–79, 87–88, 90–91, 95–96, 166–167, 192, 206, 213, 268, 270–274, 336, 349–351; and Bruinsburg crossing, 372–373, 377; and Canal operations, 84, 104, 120, 260; and Grand Gulf attack, 348, 357–358, 360–362; and Lake Providence operation, 123, 198, 261; and Louisiana march, 281–282, 331, 333–335, 356; and naval operations, 135–138, 168–170, 199, 262–264, 393–394; and Sherman's Chickasaw Bayou feint, 367–368, 370; and Steele's Bayou Expedition, 223, 225–231, 247–257; and Steele's Greenville operation, 290, 293; and Vicksburg batteries passage, 301, 303–307, 309, 311–312, 319, 326; and Yazoo Pass Expedition, 132, 160–161, 179, 182, 191, 200, 232, 234, 240, 244–245, 283–285
Port Gibson, Mississippi, 341, 346, 372, 382–388
Port Hudson, Louisiana, 4, 13, 32–33, 40, 99, 102, 108–109, 136–138, 141, 152, 168, 170, 172, 174, 199, 231, 233, 260–263, 274, 282, 295–296, 299, 312, 321, 330, 342, 390

Porter, J. A., 142–144, 156
Portlock, E. E., 56, 77
Post Bayou, 51, 54, 60, 62, 80
Prentiss, Benjamin M., 134, 158–160, 166, 178–179, 181–182, 192, 201, 216–218, 242–243
Price, Sterling, 28–29, 98, 102, 107, 140, 152–153
Pride, George G., 121, 195, 260
Prima Donna (steamer), 221
Prime, Frederick E., 110, 117, 120–121, 279
Prince, Edward, 315, 340
Putnam County, Ohio, 260

Quapaw Indians, 49
Queen of the West, 135–138, 141, 168–170, 198, 262, 280
Quinby, Isaac F., 36, 87, 106, 125, 135, 164–165, 193, 196–197, 199–202, 221–223, 238–245, 264, 284–286, 296, 330, 354

Railroad Battery, 301
Raleigh, Mississippi, 340
Ramsay, Frank M., 368
Ransom, Thomas E. G., 355
Rapidan River, 364
Rappahannock River, 26, 376
Rattler, USS, 46–47, 58–59, 160, 219
Raum, Green B., 163
Rawlins, John A., 195, 259, 268, 312
Reality Plantation, 249
Red River, 44, 49, 85, 123–125, 136–138, 153, 197, 233, 261, 330
Red Rover, USS, 46
Reddit, David, 109
Redfield, James H., 68
Reed, T. B., 139
Reeder, Josiah, 135
Regan's, 141
Revolutionary War, 50, 364
Reynolds, Arthur E., 285, 328
Rice, Americus V., 252–254
Richmond, Louisiana, 275–276, 278–281, 297–298, 355, 373
Richmond, Virginia, 17, 19, 25, 28, 30, 32, 37, 98, 102, 107, 138–139, 170, 174–175, 231, 235, 237, 295–298, 313, 326, 329, 332, 347, 363, 384
Ripley, Mississippi, 315
Robinson, Powhatton, 151, 154, 156
Rocky Mountains, 1, 49, 116
Roddey, Phillip D., 98
Rodney, Mississippi, 4, 100, 120, 346, 371, 373, 385
Rodney Road, 383, 388
Rolling Fork, 114, 224, 227–229, 231, 233, 245, 248, 254, 256, 284, 290–294
Romeo, USS, 46, 160, 368
Rosecrans, William S., 134, 190–191, 201, 242, 298, 326
Ross, Leonard F., 133, 159–162, 177–183, 185–190, 192, 199–202, 215–217, 220, 222–223, 238–240, 242–244, 286, 353
Roundaway Bayou, 121, 275–276, 278, 281, 297, 333–334
Ruggles, Daniel, 101, 298, 317, 328, 345
Rumsey (tug), 326
Russell, Daniel R., 216
Russell, James, 109
Rust, Albert, 102, 296, 298

Saint Charles, Arkansas, 56
Saint Joseph, Louisiana, 346
Saint Mary (steamer), 181
Salomon, Frederick, 160, 162
Sampson (dredge), 195
Sanborn, John B., xxiii, 201, 354, 371
Sanitary Commission, United States, 269
Satartia, Mississippi, 146, 148
S. Bayard (steamer), 160, 178, 180
Scott, Winfield, 3, 9
Seaman, Henry, 290
Sears, Claudius W., 386
Seddon, James A., 33, 80, 175
Sellers Plantation, 197
Shaifer, Abram K., 388
Sheldon, Lionel A., 67, 70, 281, 396
Shell Mound, 182
Shepperd, F. E., 153
Sherman, John, 41, 90, 96, 119
Sherman, William T., xx–xxii, 2, 7, 15, 17, 20–23, 25–27, 31–35, 37–43, 47–48, 60–62, 64–68, 76, 82, 87–88, 90–92,

94–96, 103, 113–114, 116, 118, 193, 204–205, 268, 271, 273–274, 290, 349–350, 386–387, 392, 396; and Bruinsburg crossing, 373, 378; and Canal operations, -104, 106–109, 111, 119–120, 196; and Chickasaw Bayou feint, 366–371; and Lake Providence operation, 124, 165; and Duckport Canal operation, 275; and Louisiana march, 280, 330, 332–334, 354–355; and naval operations, 135–138, 170, 264; and Steele's Bayou Expedition, 223, 225–227, 229–231, 247–256; and Steele's Greenville operation, 288; and Vicksburg batteries passage, 304–305, 309–311, 325; and Yazoo Pass Expedition, 245, 282–285
Shiloh, Battle of,11, 26, 38–39, 46, 65, 133–134, 259, 269, 280, 320, 330, 390; Hornet's Nest, 330
Shirk, James, 309–310, 360, 394
Shotwell (steamer), 351
Signal, USS, 46, 78, 160, 368
Silversparre, Axel, 291
Silver Wave (steamer), 225–226, 230, 304, 309, 324, 378
Skunk River, 179
Slack, James, 161, 163, 238, 313
Sloan, Thomas J., 115
Sloan, William D., 315
Smith (scout), 142, 144
Smith, Andrew J., 41, 47, 67, 69, 75, 87, 104, 167, 195, 333, 354, 383, 395
Smith, E. Kirby, 140, 234, 329
Smith, Giles A., 60–61, 63–64, 229, 250–254, 397
Smith, I. V., 313
Smith, John E., 193–194, 241–242, 264, 355
Smith, Martin L., 22, 102, 210, 232, 324, 346, 386
Smith, Milo, 63
Smith, Morgan L., 41, 43
Smith, Pliney, 278
Smith, Thomas Kilby, 60, 64, 82, 105, 109, 114, 252, 273, 370, 398
Smith, William F., 294
Smith, William Sooy, 313–314

Smith's (James) Plantation, 71
Smith's Landing, Arkansas, 46
Snyder's Bluff, Mississippi, 5, 22, 31, 100, 102–103, 117, 127, 143–144, 146, 155, 172, 232–233, 271–272, 291, 295–297, 321, 327, 345–346, 366, 368, 370–371, 386
Somerset Plantation, 280
Somerville, Tennessee, 35
South Carolina, 27
South Fort, 303
Southern Railroad of Mississippi, 15, 84, 134, 165, 172, 314, 317, 319, 343–344, 386
Spain, 49–50
Sparrow, Edward, 124
Spiegel, Marcus, 39, 70, 77, 281
Stanbrough Plantation, 276
Stanton, Edwin M., 12, 27, 39–40, 80, 86, 89, 268, 274
Starkville, Mississippi, 218, 329, 338
Star Spangled Banner, 290
Steele, Frederick, 41, 47, 52, 60–62, 64, 66, 75–76, 87, 104, 108–109, 111, 119, 137, 196, 205, 288–298, 327, 330, 332, 333, 336, 366, 396
Steele's Bayou, xiv, xvi, 148, 204, 206, 209, 212, 222–223, 225–226, 229, 231–234, 240, 243, 245, 247, 255–257, 261–263, 268–269, 274, 283, 287, 295–296, 304, 309, 393
Stephens, M. D. L., 254
Stevenson, Carter L., 31–32, 101–103, 106–107, 140, 166, 173–175, 208, 227–228, 232–235, 257, 290–291, 296–299, 312–313, 326–329, 345–347, 370–371, 378, 384, 386
Stewart, Warren, 106–107
St. Francis River, 7
St. John, A. P., 247
St. Louis, Missouri, 93, 126, 168, 330
St. Louis, USS, 214–215
Stone, George A., 63
Stone, Kate, 238
Stone, William M., 384
Stones River, Battle of, 26
Streight, Abel D., 314, 317, 328–329

Strong, Joel, 221
Strong, Joseph G., 384
Stuart, David, 41, 47, 60–61, 63–64, 66–67, 79, 87, 104, 106–107, 109, 119, 137, 196, 223, 225, 247, 254–256, 283, 397
Sullivan, Jeremiah C., 354
Summary of the Art of War, xix
Sunflower River, 132, 148, 167, 173, 223, 228–229, 257, 291–293, 296
Surby, Richard, 318, 341
Switzerland, 16
Switzerland, USS, 199, 262

Tallahatchie River, 17, 19, 21, 23, 26, 31, 35–36, 99–100, 133, 142, 146, 148, 153–154, 160, 165, 171–172, 175–176, 178–180, 182–183, 190, 218, 220–222, 231, 233, 238, 240, 284, 287, 314–315, 318
Tensas Parish, 278
Tensas River, 123, 125
Tarawa, 365
Taylor, James E., 213, 394
Taylor, Richard, 153, 165, 168, 173, 234
Taylor, Thomas H., 106
Templeton, William J., 68
Tennessee, 7, 11, 13–14, 16, 21, 26, 28–30, 35–36, 48, 56, 82, 86–87, 89, 97–99, 119, 133–134, 138, 141, 146, 152, 165, 175, 191, 193–194, 210, 232, 234–235, 237, 242, 267, 296, 298, 313, 317, 319, 326–329, 336, 342, 384
Tennessee River, xix, 4, 9, 11–12, 15, 21, 26, 36–37, 134, 298
Tennessee Troops
   1st Heavy Artillery, 301, 321
   2nd Cavalry, 315
Tensas Parrish, Louisiana, 278
Tentative Manual for Landing Operations, 365
Texas, 31, 68, 77, 80, 100
Texas Troops
   2nd Infantry, 216
   6th Infantry, 52–54, 65, 69, 71, 73, 399
   10th Infantry, 52, 54, 63–64, 399
   15th Cavalry (dismounted), 52, 54, 74, 399
   17th Cavalry (dismounted), 52, 54, 399
   18th Cavalry (dismounted), 52, 54, 399
   24th Cavalry (dismounted), 52–53, 72–73, 399
   25th Cavalry (dismounted), 52–53, 399
   Johnson's Cavalry Company, 399
   Richardson's Cavalry Company, 399
   Waul's Legion, 99, 107, 153, 155, 185, 188, 216
Thayer, John M., 60–63, 72, 108–109, 397
Thayer, Sylvanus, xix
Thirty-fifth Parallel (steamer), 181
Thistle (tug), 57, 231
Thomas, Lorenzo, 270, 283, 294, 305–306, 322–323, 327, 333, 350, 379
Thomas Plantation, 291, 293
Tigress (steamer), 38, 40, 42, 78, 320–325
Tilghman, Lloyd, 100, 102, 156, 176–177, 188, 244, 285, 298, 328, 345
Tippah County, Mississippi, 149
Tishomingo County, Mississippi, 150
Tonti, Henri de, 49
Torrence, USS, 46
Tourtellotte, John E., 381
Tracy, Edward, 385–388
Trinidad Plantation, 276
Tullahoma, Tennessee, 141, 235, 329, 347
Tunica, Mississippi, 145
Tunica County, Mississippi, 149–150
Tuscumbia, USS, 304, 306, 309–310, 312, 325, 334, 358, 360–361, 363, 377, 379, 394
Tuttle, James, 135, 264, 355
Tyler, USS, 367, 369

Union Church, Battle of, 341, 347
Union Church, Mississippi, 341
United States, xvi, xix, 2, 8, 12, 50, 75–76, 90, 171, 193, 255, 294, 331, 337, 342, 365; Army, 3, 294; Congress, 35, 50, 90, 131, 158, 160, 191, 258, 270–271, 284, 288, 350; Constitution, 41; Corps of Engineers, 84; Marine Corps, 365; Navy, 51, 75, 215; Navy Department, 59, 132, 191, 214, 365; President, 41, 166, 356; Secretary of War, 12, 39, 88, 94, 274; Senate, 90, 283, 288; Treasury Department, 193; War Department, 85, 93, 95, 259, 270–271

INDEX

United States Troops
  13th Infantry, 1st Battalion, 252–253, 398
  Engineer Regiment of the West, 104, 197
Universe (steamer), 114

Vaiden, Mississippi, 244
Valley Hill, 145
Van Dorn, Earl, xx, 13, 21, 28–32, 34, 36–37, 98–99, 134, 153, 165, 235, 298
Vaughan's Station, Mississippi, 153
Vaughn, John C., 326
Vera Cruz, Battle of, 197, 364
Vicksburg, Mississippi, xiii–xvi, xix–xxiii, 2, 4–5, 7–9, 12–16, 19–23, 25–33, 35, 37–44, 48, 69, 77, 78, 81–83, 87, 89–92, 94–103, 105–107, 109–111, 113–114, 116–118, 133, 139, 141, 145–146, 148–150, 171, 192–193, 203–206, 208–210, 212–213, 223, 227–228, 235–236, 238, 259, 265–274, 296–299, 327–328, 349–351, 386–392; and Bruinsburg crossing, 372–373, 378, 384; and Canal operations, 84–86, 104, 112, 119–120, 164, 173–175, 196, 260; and Duckport Canal operation, 275; and Grand Gulf attack, 346–348, 361–363; and Grierson's Raid, 134, 166, 194, 338, 342–345; and Lake Providence operation, 121, 124–126, 164–165, 261; and Louisiana march, 280–281, 329–330, 355; and naval operations, 135–138, 168–170, 199, 262–264, 393–394; and Steele's Bayou Expedition, 222–231, 247, 256–258; and Sherman's Chickasaw Bayou feint, 366–367, 370–371; and Steele's Greenville operation, 290, 292–295; and Vicksburg batteries passage, 301, 304–313, 319, 321, 322, 324–326; and Willow Bayou operation, 121; and Yazoo Pass Expedition, 127–128, 142–143, 151–153, 155, 157–159, 172, 177, 180, 186, 189–191, 215, 221–222, 232–234, 242, 245, 283, 287–288
Vicksburg, Shreveport, and Texas Railroad, 84
Vicksburg National Military Park, 215

Vicksburg *Whig*, 170
Virginia, xiii, 13–14, 26–27, 175, 191, 376
Virginia (West) Troops: 4th Infantry, 254–255

Wade, William, 261, 357, 360, 385, 387
Walke, Henry, 261, 307, 394
Walker, John G., 58, 178, 187, 190
Wall, J. Q., 188
Wallace, Lew, 259
Wall's Bridge, Battle of, 341
Walnut Bayou, 275, 355
Walnut Hills, 4, 7–8, 20, 22–23, 35, 145, 232, 381
Warmoth, Henry C., 279, 311, 380, 382
War of 1812, 3
Warrenton, Mississippi, 106, 120, 136, 168, 173–174, 232–233, 261, 263, 272, 303, 311, 323–325, 345–346, 348
Warrenton Road, 386
Washburn, Cadwallader, xx, 17, 131, 157–158, 160, 179
Washburne, Elihu, 131, 270–271, 288, 350, 382
Washington, DC, xxi, 12, 14, 16, 25, 40, 43, 79, 81, 89, 94, 119–120, 133–135, 191, 214, 222, 242, 265–266, 268, 270–271, 283, 304, 311, 349, 356, 362, 376, 392; Executive Mansion, 25
Washington, Edward, 253
Washington, George, 1, 163, 364
Water Battery, 301
Watson Plantation, 245
Waul, Thomas N., 99, 155–156, 176, 329
Webb, CSS, 111, 138, 168–169, 280
Webster, Daniel, 70
Weldon, Thomas, 156
Welles, Gideon, 104, 137, 264, 273, 311, 356–357, 361
Wellington, Duke of, 22
Western Hemisphere, 2
West Point, New York, xix, 52, 88, 238, 288, 293, 327
Westville, Mississippi, 340, 344
Whig Office Battery, 301
Whistling Dick, 303
Whistling Mary, 177

White River, 7, 34, 42, 44, 46, 52, 78, 81, 88, 93
Wicks, Franklin C., 53
Widow Blakely, 303
Wilderness, Battle of, 364
Wilkes, Franklin C., 73, 80
Williams, A. M., 51
Williams, T. Harry, 20
Williams, Thomas, 12, 84–86, 110
Williams' Bridge, Louisiana, 341–342
Willow Bayou, 121
Wilson, Byron, 306, 308, 360, 362, 394
Wilson, Frank, 71, 74
Wilson, James H., 110, 127–133, 156–159, 177–180, 182–183, 186–190, 200, 207, 216–218, 220, 239–240, 244, 268, 285, 305, 332, 371–372, 381, 392
Wilson Plantation, 249
Wilson's Creek, Battle of, 51
Windsor Mansion, xvi, 382
Winona, Mississippi, 244
Winschel, Terrence J., xvi, 268, 274
Wisconsin, 269, 355
Wisconsin Troops
    8th Infantry, 333
    11th Infantry, 381
    23rd Infantry, 68, 395
    28th Infantry, 160, 216
    1st Light Artillery, 70–71, 396
Wood, Peter, 61
Wood, R. L., 167, 245
Woods, Charles R., 154, 170
Woodworth, Selim E., 307, 362

World War I, 365
World War II, 365
Wyatt's Ferry, Mississippi, 17
Wyman's Hill Battery, 301, 324

Yaggy, Job, 195
Yalobusha River, xxii, 19, 22, 142, 146, 153–154, 160, 171, 179, 240, 273
Yankee Doodle, 76
Yates, Richard, 350, 382
Yazoo City, Mississippi, 142, 144, 146, 151, 153, 155, 160, 176, 179, 183, 199–200, 215–216, 218, 223, 243, 257, 329
Yazoo Pass, xiv, xvi, 98, 126, 129–130, 133, 142–143, 150–153, 156, 158, 163, 165, 170, 172, 174–175, 180, 190, 192, 194, 199–200, 202, 206–207, 209, 211, 215, 220, 222–223, 225, 231–232, 238–239, 243–244, 256, 258, 260, 262–265, 274, 283, 286, 295, 298, 320, 393
Yazoo River, 7, 15, 19–22, 31, 34, 39, 95–96, 103, 114, 117, 127, 131–133, 142–144, 146, 148, 151–154, 171–173, 175–177, 179–180, 182–183, 191, 199, 201, 209–210, 215–216, 218–219, 222–223, 225–233, 237, 240, 249, 255–257, 260, 271, 287, 295, 305, 320, 345–346, 355, 366, 368, 370–371, 386–387
Yocona River, 17, 19, 146, 315
Yost, George, 219
Young's Point, Louisiana, 93, 96, 104–106, 116, 134, 142, 202, 242, 257, 264, 294, 312, 320, 378